THE AUBRYS

-

FREE PEOPLE OF COLOR
IN
EARLY
NEW ORLEANS

AND OTHER ALLIED FAMILIES
INCLUDING
ALLAIN, BONNEVAL, BRINGIER,
CHIAPELLA, COUDRAIN,
DALCOUR, DELACHAISE, DOMINGON, DUPUY,
EDMUNDS, FLOT, FOY, GRANDMAISON,
LASSIZE, LATROBE, LEMELLE,
LORREINS, OZENNE, PINTA,
RABY, RIGAUD, ST. HUBERT,
WATKINSON, & WHITTAKER,

By

CAROL MILLS-NICHOL

Janaway Publishing Inc.
Santa Maria, California

Published by:

Janaway Publishing, Inc.
732 Kelsey Ct.
Santa Maria, California 93454
(805) 925-1952
www.janawaygenealogy.com

2021

Library of Congress Control Number: 2021930475
ISBN: 978-1-59641-459-4

Front Cover - Photo of Félicité Flot courtesy of Father Philip Flott.

Back Cover - Author's photo of rear of Eglée Aubry's property

on Bayou de Zaire, Madisonville, St. Tammany Parish, LA.

Made in the United States of America

This book is dedicated to the late Jim Skidmore,

my friend and publisher for over a decade. Although we never met in person,

Jim spent hours encouraging and mentoring my literary projects.

I know that he was beloved by all the authors in the Janaway stable whom he helped along the way.

I, for one, will always miss his critical eye, his patience and kindness to me, no matter how many last-minute

revisions I sent his way. Those of us who have dedicated ourselves to genealogical and historical research

have lost a great friend. May Jim rest in peace knowing that his work will be carried on

by his devoted and loving family at Janaway.

....

I would also be remiss during these difficult times if I did not give a shout-out to my husband Jack

and the doggy editing team, Rocky Red, Winston and Lily Belle,

for having the patience to see this latest book through with me.

TABLE OF CONTENTS

LIST OF ILLUSTRATIONS

INTRODUCTION

While researching my third book, *A Guide to the French and American Claims Commission 1880-1885*, I investigated the lives of 727 French citizens who had lived in the United States during the Civil War. I was struck by the presence of eleven claimants who had connections to or who were free people of color. One in particular, Eglée Aubry, stood out to me because, although she usually lived in New Orleans, she claimed to have lost property to the Union Army from her farm at Madisonville, St. Tammany Parish, LA. I started some research at the St. Tammany Parish Courthouse to see what I could find out about her life on the other side of Lake Pontchartrain She turned out to be an extraordinary woman, with three equally interesting sisters, a brother, and a mother who had been born when France was still in possession of the Louisiana territory. I was forced to set her aside to finish the work at hand, but I knew that my next book would be about her life and her genealogical affiliation with a large number of other Louisiana families.

The purpose of the French and American Claims Commission, which had been formed jointly by the United States and France on 25 June 1880, had been to investigate claims filed by French citizens against the United States for acts committed against them and/or their property by United States troops between 13 April 1861 and 20 August 1866. All claimants were required to submit a prescribed "memorial" outlining what was destroyed or taken from them by U.S. troops, along with any supporting documentation which could provide proof of their losses. Investigators were sent out by the United States to search for witnesses who could be used to deny the claim or refute the veracity of the claimant. Hearings were then held and oral testimony taken from both the claimant, if still living, and all available witnesses. The most difficult hurdle for the claimant was the question of citizenship. Those claimants alleging harm done to them during the Civil War in America not only had to have been French citizens at the time of the claim, they had to still be French citizens on 15 January 1880 an arbitrary date set by the Commission. Since many formerly French citizens had become naturalized Americans after the Civil War, they were precluded from claiming any monetary relief. Moreover, had they joined the Confederate armed forces, supplied the rebel army with goods or services during the conflict, held political office or voted, they were usually ineligible for any reparations. Claims against the United States from the French memorialists totaled $17,386,151.27. The average interest for twenty years at 5% almost doubled that initial amount. However, only 216 claims were paid in whole or in part. French citizens recovered $319,595.02 plus $305,971.33 in interest for a total of $625,566.35. There were only eight free people of color claimants out of the total 727 people who filed for themselves and/or their children. Before we explore the lives of Eglée Aubry, her sisters, Félicité, Azélie, and Mercelite, her brother Martin, her mother, Marguerite Cécile, as well as their connections to many other Louisiana families, it may be worthwhile to set forth the circumstances of the other families who were also claimants.

Louise Sudour, was born ca. 1824 in in the French Antilles. She was first enumerated in the 1840 United States Federal Census for New Orleans as an unmarried free woman of color. She was the mother of four children with Robert Gibbs Hobbs, a well-to-do merchant, born on 17 June 1811, at Weston, Middlesex Co., MA. Hobbs had been a shoe merchant in New Orleans but died on a trip back to visit his brother on 16 September 1850 at Bangor, Penobscot Co., ME. He had recognized his natural children with Louise and left each of them $10,000 in his will. Louise gave birth to another child, Thomas Homer Ansley on 18 December 1851, her son with Thomas Ansley, a cotton broker, who worked at #16 St. Charles Street. In 1857 Louise bought from the succession of Judah Touro, a property at #114 Rampart Street between St. Louis and Toulouse which included a two-story brick house and another frame building used as a stable. Federal troops occupied her stables for almost a year during the Civil War, but she was paid no rent. She sued for $6,500 plus interest and was awarded $250 at 5% interest from 1 September 1863 on 29 March 1882 for a total of $507.25. Because, as a free woman of color, she could never have been legally married either to Hobbs or Ansley, her French citizenship remained intact. Had she been legally married to either man, both U.S. citizens, according to both French and American law in the 19th century, she and her children would have automatically become American citizens, and thus, ineligible to claim under the terms of the Commission.

Rose Félicie Landry, the widow of Auguste Joseph Parfait Nepveux, sued as tutrix of her children, for $1,250 plus $1,290.16 in interest for a steamboat and horse taken by General William B. Franklin in May 1863 at St. Martinville, LA. Rose Félicie Landry was born ca. 1832 in St. Martin Parish, LA, to Darcourt Landry, a plantation owner, and his wife Marie Louise Eucharistie Lenormand. Auguste Nepveux was a schoolmaster employed on the Darcourt Landry plantation He was born Auguste Parfait Joseph Nepveux on 22 March 1824 at Noeux-les-Mines, Pas-de-Calais, France, to twenty-eight-year-old Augustin Barthélémy Joseph Nepveux and his wife, Emilie Joseph Fontaine. Rose Félicie and Auguste were married on 29 January 1851 at Mobile, Mobile Co., AL. The Darcourt

Landry family, including eighteen-year-old Félicie, had been enumerated in the 1850 federal census as "mulatto," which would explain the trip out of state to have the marriage performed. Félicie Nepveux, a free woman of color married to a Frenchman, did not, unfortunately, pursue her claim.

Pierre Bax's heirs, sued through the administrator of his estate, for $30,932 plus 6% interest for sugar and molasses taken by General Nathaniel P. Banks in April 1864 at Alexandria, LA. Bax was born Jean Pierre Bax on 5 February 1802 at Pieusse, Aude, France, to Jean Bax, a farmer and his second wife, Marguerite Bénajean. He was enumerated in the 1850 United States Federal Census as forty-eight-year-old "T. Back," a merchant with $500 in assets, living in Natchitoches, Natchitoches Parish, LA, with thirty-two-year-old Louise, a person of color, and three children all said to be "mulatto." Shortly thereafter he and his eldest son, André, set out for Mexico, then travelled to California where they eventually boarded a ship for Peru. After a stay in Lima, they made their way to Chagres, Panama, where they boarded the schooner *Alderman* which arrived in New Orleans on 3 May 1852. They were listed on the manifest as fifty-one-year-old "B. Bax" and sixteen-year-old "A. Bax," both merchants from "Nackatush." Pierre's twenty-two-year-old son, André Bax's 1858 New Orleans death certificate gave his place of birth as Baton Rouge. Fifty-eight-year-old Pierre was enumerated in the 1860 federal census for Alexandria, Rapides Parish, LA, with Louisiana Bax, a person of color, and two children: fourteen-year-old Gustavus and twelve-year-old Pierre. According to testimony in the Bax case file, he died in Alexandria in 1868. Pierre's companion, Louisa Bax, died at Alexandria in December 1869 from consumption. Peter Bax, Jr. moved to New Orleans and appeared in an 1871 *New Orleans City Directory* as "Peter Bax," a "colored" grocer who lived and worked on Gravier Street. Augustus Frank Bax, died in New Orleans on 16 May 1894. James Madison Wells, Jr. was the public administrator for the 12th Judicial District, Rapides Parish, after the Civil War. He applied for administration of Pierre Bax's estate in March 1875, on behalf of Peter Bax, deceased in 1868. The claim was denied in 1884 because the United States did not recognize Bax's surviving sons as his legal heirs, nor were they mentioned by the administrator of his estate because Bax and Louisa could not have been legally married in Louisiana.

Adèle Ozenne, the widow of Charles Ovide Decuir, both free people of color, sued for $11,949 plus 6% interest for cotton, cattle, etc., taken by Major Lewis in May 1863. Charles Ovide Decuir was said to have been born in 1797 in Saint Martin Parish to Godefroy Decuir and Emerantine Lavillebeuve Carrière (aka Emeranthe Charles). Ovide Decuir married Adèle Ozenne born to Edouard Ozenne, a Caucasian, and Chalinette DeBlanc, a "free mulatress" on 27 June 1837 at Saint Martin of Tours Church in Saint Martinville LA. The parents of ten children, the Decuirs owned a large plantation which they cultivated with the help of five slaves. The Union soldiers who came through the territory in 1863 did not discriminate when it came to the destruction of property, or the confiscation of cotton, cattle, horses, and food in order to supply their troops. As slave owners, the Decuir family was thought to be Confederate sympathizers. The family remained on their farm after the war where Ovide died on 26 February 1880. Adèle Ozenne filed her claim, alleging that her husband, Charles Ovide Decuir had been born a citizen of France before the Louisiana Purchase in 1803 and that, as his wife, she had become a French citizen as well, thereby having the right to sue for damages to their property during its occupation by Union forces in May 1863. Because her husband was a free man of color he had not, under the terms of the U.S. Constitution, become a citizen of the United States in 1803. The counsel for the United States filed an opinion, similar to the one filed in the case of Eglée Aubry, stating that the treaty of cession of the Louisiana territory to the United States contained no provision by which the French colonists could have retained their French citizenship. It had been ordered that all inhabitants be admitted as soon as possible as citizens of the United States in accordance with the Federal Constitution. However, since Ovide Decuir was a person of color, his citizenship was not recognized until the ratification of the fourteenth amendment to the Constitution in 1868. Once a citizen in 1868, he began to exercise his rights. Evidence had been found that he was a qualified voter in Iberia Parish. It followed therefore that Adèle, as his wife, was a citizen of the United States when she filed the claim, which was dismissed for want of jurisdiction.

Adèle Luppé sued for $1,200 plus $1,464 in interest for warehouse, etc., destroyed by U.S. authorities on 10 August 1862 at Baton Rouge, LA. Adèle, a Louisiana native, was the widow of Adolphe Édouard Bory, born on 5 November 1812 at Morannes, Maine-et-Loire, France, to Jean Édouard Bory and his wife, Anne Marie Jary. According to her own testimony before the Commission, Adèle Luppé was born on 8 February 1826 at Baton Rouge. Adolphe and Adèle were married on 8 November 1847 at Cincinnati, Hamilton Co., OH, by Bishop John Baptist Purcell. A copy of the original marriage record was furnished at the hearing in 1881. Adèle testified that she was living on her own in Baton Rouge during the Civil War, while her husband, a physician, resided at Saint-Laurent, Maine-et-Loire, France. Adele claimed that she had lost a frame warehouse measuring 30X50 feet, worth $800, as well as a small frame building used as a bakery, measuring 15X20 feet, located near the corner of Main and Church Streets, across from St. Joseph's Catholic Church. She affirmed that the buildings were burned during the battle of Baton Rouge in August 1862, leaving only her brick store known as the Grange. Her claim was disallowed because the U.S. investigators found several witnesses who swore that the fire which cost Mrs. Bory her buildings actually took place in 1864, caused accidentally by sparks from the kitchen of a building directly behind the Bory place. In an amended memorial, Adèle Bory also claimed that Union soldiers occupied her buildings between December 1862 and February 1863, a good while after those same buildings were said to have been destroyed. She asked for an additional $90 in rent. Her claims were declared contradictory, absurd and fraudulent.

Marie Pradier, a free woman of color, sued for $1,725 plus interest for horses, cows taken, and person imprisoned by U.S. authorities in November 1863 at New Iberia, LA, as the widow of Auguste Ollé, who was born, "Bertrand Ollé, at Ardiège, Haute Garonne, France, on 13 May 1832 to Michel Ollé and Jeanne Fuzéré. "Auguste" Ollé, an eighteen-year-old baker from Ardiège, Haute-Garonne France, received a passport at Bordeaux on 21 April 1852 to come to Louisiana to join his elder brother. Auguste began a relationship with Marie Pradier, who according to a witness in this case was a "griffonne," that is, a woman of African American and Native American or "mulatto" ancestry. Auguste and Marie were the parents of three children. Auguste Ollé was interred on 4 April 1868, having died the previous day. During his lifetime, Auguste, who had a small farm at Abbeville in Vermilion Parish, but also worked as a baker, made many trips into New Iberia, one of which in April 1863 was the cause of this claim. He described in an 1864 deposition made in French that he was seized by Union soldiers on the road from Côte Gelée (now Broussard, Lafayette Parish) to New Iberia, and imprisoned there by Colonel Smith of the 114th New York Volunteers for two days. His horse, saddle and bridle were taken from him and not returned upon his release. In November 1863 his farm was raided in his absence and seven cows, six calves and one mule were taken away. The Ollé claims were disallowed based on the Civil Code of Louisiana, Article 204, revised in 1870, which stated that the acknowledgement of an illegitimate child could not be made in favor of children whose parents were incapable of contracting a marriage at the time of conception. Therefore, neither Marie Pradier nor her children were legitimate heirs of Auguste Ollé. Marie Pradier's son, Adolphe Ollé, filed a similar claim which was rejected for the same reason as his widowed mother's, for $1225 plus interest for cows, etc. taken by General William B. Franklin on 12 November 1863 at Abbeville, LA.

Louise Antonine Müh, a woman of color and the widow of Paul Robert Vidal, sued for $14,232 plus 6% interest for cotton taken by Colonel Coates in August 1863 at Kingston, MS. She filed, although failed to prosecute it, on behalf of herself and her daughter Marie Gabrielle Vidal. Louise was born on 17 January 1840 at New Orleans to Louis Müh, a jeweler and watch maker, born on 21 March 1801 at Wissembourg, Bas-Rhin, France, to Frédéric Müh and his wife Madeleine Schindler. Louise's mother was Delphine Barbet, who was identified in the 1830 federal census for New Orleans as a free woman of color living with her female slave. Delphine, and her three daughters by Louis Müh, were sent to live in Paris, France, as early as 1855, according to a friend who testified in a legal proceeding subsequent to Müh's death on 13 November 1882. Louise Antonine Müh was married at Paris, France, on 13 December 1866 to forty-five-year-old Paul Vidal, born on 2 December 1821 at "Porto Ricco" (Antilles) to Paul Vidal and Louise Adèle Combes. In her memorial, as well as in records filed by Paul Vidal at New Orleans with the French Consul, Louis Müh was present at the marriage of his daughter, who was illegitimate, but recognized by him. Vidal, who had come to Louisiana in 1830, was a cotton merchant and factor working on his own behalf during the Civil War. In November 1862, George C. Payne, on a trip to Natchez, Adams Co., MS, bought 100 bales of cotton for Vidal. To protect his purchase from vandals, Vidal had fifty bales stored at Kingston, Adams Co., MS, and the other fifty were left on the Aventine Plantation of George B. Shields. In August 1863, after Vidal took the oath as prescribed by foreign neutrals not to aid in the war as long as France remained at peace with the United States, he tried but failed to get a pass to go to Mississippi from General Nathaniel Banks to look after his purchase. That same month, the fifty bales stored at Kingston were seized under the orders of General Ransom, commanding the post at Natchez. No receipts were given. Paul Vidal returned to Paris in 1866 where he was married to Louise Müh, and where their daughter, Marie Gabrielle, was born on 20 September 1872. Vidal died on 13 September 1873. Louise Müh Vidal's first memorial was not signed by her or notarized and was rejected on 24 October 1881. Her attorney applied to refile but his request was denied.

Eglée Aubry's claim for $5,200 plus 6% interest for damages from the United States for the occupation of buildings by General Cuvier Grover in the parish of St. Tammany, Louisiana, in February, 1864, was dismissed for want of jurisdiction on 28 June 1881. Just as the widow Ovide Decuir's claim had been dismissed because, as a free person of color, her husband had become a citizen of the United States in 1868 with the ratification of the 14th Amendment to the U.S. Constitution, Aubry's claim was similarly dismissed because she had automatically become an American citizen in 1868. There is, however, much more to say about her, and about her ancestors, siblings, and descendants, which is the subject of this book.

Many experts have discussed the sociological and historical underpinnings of the free people of color using a select number of them as examples to illustrate one observation or another, such as the statistical comparison of the numbers of free people of color versus slaves or the comparison of the frequency of self-purchase versus manumission by a third party. One of the more popular examples chosen has been Jacqueline Lemelle. The manumission of Jacqueline and her three daughters, by her companion, Jacques Lemelle, has been central to many studies. Jacqueline and her children, however, also play a big part in this book, as important members of the extended Aubry family. What we cannot glean from the many statistics concerning the numbers of free people of color in New Orleans is their many connections to one another both by blood and by marriages, legal or otherwise, as well as their relationships with the white population.

Before 1769 there were but a few free people of color because the manumission of slaves had been very difficult under French rule, and could only be accomplished with permission from the Superior Council. When Spain finally took over the Louisiana colony in 1769, seven years after it had been ceded to them in 1762 by the French King, there were probably between 100 and 400 free colored citizens. The Spanish instituted self-purchase, which opened the door for many slaves to buy freedom for themselves. The practice of manumission on the whole became a simple trip by the interested parties to the local notary to secure freedom either gratuitously or for an agreed upon price. From that time on, the numbers of free persons of color expanded exponentially. Their numbers were also increased by the thousands of free people of color that fled Saint Domingue/Haiti beginning in 1792 and ending with Haitian independence in 1805. Many of those fleeing Saint-Domingue had chosen to settle in Cuba. However, after having started to rebuild their lives, all the French, free people of color and whites alike, were expelled from that island in 1809 after the start of the Peninsular War between France and Spain. As a result, a new wave of immigrants came to New Orleans including 3,300 free people of color. So, by 1810 there were almost 5,000 free colored inhabitants of Louisiana. At statehood in 1812, Louisiana counted 7,585 free people of color. By 1830 there were 11,906 free colored people in New Orleans, which grew to 19,266 ten years later, but shrank to 9,905 in 1850 due to governmental restrictions in the face of the fears of slave revolts as well as the growing abolitionist movement in the broader United States. Many free people of color in the 1850s in New Orleans weighed their options in the face of continuing legislative repression. Some chose to return to Haiti, others chose Mexico, or France and some went out west to California, or north to New England. While many in the Aubry family circle, who survived the Civil War and the countless epidemics which ran rampant in the city, stayed in New Orleans, others made their way to France, the Pacific Coast, or up north to the Atlantic Seaboard. Away from Louisiana, many Aubry descendants melted seamlessly into the greater Caucasian population. However, amongst even those who stayed in New Orleans, many simply eventually blended in with the white population.

While Martin Aubry, who chose to live away from New Orleans, married a free woman of color and raised a large family, his four sisters remained in the city. Because there were many more eligible white males than white females in New Orleans, especially in the early nineteenth century, many men chose to start a family with a woman of racially-mixed ancestry. Similarly, free women of color found that there were many fewer free men of color from whom to choose because many more enslaved women had been freed by their masters than men. The result was that free women of color accepted the companionship of white men more frequently than the smaller pool of men from their own racial background. As the century wore on, however, this dynamic would slowly change. Many free women of color found their lives upended when their white companion chose to contract a marriage with a white woman. Amongst the four Aubry sisters, this happened to Eglée Aubry. She had lost her first companion to death, however, after bearing three sons to her second companion, he went on to marry a white woman and have a legitimate family. Mercelite, as well, lost her first companion and father of her two children to yellow fever. However, after bearing a child for another white man, she was abandoned so that he might marry a more "suitable" companion. Félicité Aubry, on the other hand, ended one relationship with an older white man to find a stable relationship with one of his younger white friends. The fourth sister, Zélie, had a long relationship with a white immigrant from France, who never abandoned her for a legitimate marriage.

We will spend the next few hundred pages exploring these varied relationships between four free women of color and their companions, their children, grandchildren and beyond, in relationship to the changing times, first in the French and later Spanish colony of Louisiana, then in the state of Louisiana, both before and after the Civil War, during and after Reconstruction, and into the twentieth century. We will never discover all of the Aubry sisters' secrets because they left no diaries, and few, if any, letters. Their lives were marked by revelations in ecclesiastical and civil vital records, notarial entries, wills and successions, and in an occasional newspaper article. From these findings we have attempted to reconstruct their lives. Their stories, however, are never over, their existence never definitively categorized, because any day, someone else will find a new clue to their lives hidden away in some dusty corner. Their descendants will carry on their stories and create stories of their own to tell. They will, at the very least, know how far back in the history of Louisiana, and of the larger Gulf South, their roots were planted, and from where their immigrant ancestors came. But this book is only the beginning, and is for someone else to expand, to correct and to verify.

ACKNOWLEDGEMENTS

The internet has made research much easier than it used to be. The bare bones of the lives of one's ancestors are now generally shared freely on many of the genealogy websites. But vital records, alone, do not tell the story of those who came before us. They are only a jumping-off point, although invaluable nonetheless. Amongst my go-to resources has always been the Church of Jesus Christ of Latter-Day Saints which has been in the forefront of genealogical research now for decades with their free website *Familysearch.org*, and its companion *Findagrave.com*. Their followers have microfilmed millions of records from all over the world, which, in many cases, have preserved them from destruction.

Ancestry.com, and its newspaper site, *Newspapers.com*, although pricey, are invaluable as well. *Genealogybank.com*, also a site devoted mainly to the digitization of newspapers from all over America, is easy and economical to use, while *Fold3.com* specializes in military records. Since I am a Louisiana researcher, I also rely heavily on digitized records available from France and its overseas possessions. Most every French "département" has its own website, and most have both church and civil records available from the late sixteenth century, through World War I. Some even have census records taken every five years from the mid-1820s through the early twentieth century. The Gironde archives (archives.gironde.fr) has copies of passports issued from the early 1800s until 1889 which include the records of 44,000 persons who sailed from Bordeaux to various parts of Europe, North and South America, including their signatures, their physical descriptions, their ages, and places of birth.

The French also have a treasure trove of records from their former overseas possessions located at the "Archives nationales d'outre-mer," including vital records from the Caribbean (Guadeloupe, Saint-Domingue, etc.), Africa (Algeria, Morocco, the Congo, etc.), Southeast Asia (Cambodia, Laos, Vietnam), and North America including Canada, Louisiana, Illinois, etc. accessible at: http://anom.archivesnationales.culture.gouv.fr/caomec2/.

There have also been many people who have gone above and beyond what was required of their jobs to facilitate the flow of information from their various archives into my hands. I cannot say enough about the staff of the Research Center at the Civil District Court for the Parish of Orleans headed by Chelsey Richard Napoleon, Clerk of Court and Ex-Officio Recorder. I must have requested and received hundreds of documents from the Notarial Archives Research Center. Sally Sinor, Siva Blake, and Janine Smith, all intrepid archivists, were always able to locate these hand-written treasures that I needed, many written in French and Spanish, out of the 40,000,000 signed acts that New Orleans notaries produced over the course of three centuries all of which have been carefully preserved. The pages from these records which I requested were copied, and sent out electronically often appearing in my in-box the same day. Siva, Sally and Janine never ceased to amaze me with their kindness, their expertise, and their obvious love for research.

On the other side of the lake, Robin L. Perkins, Director of Records Management at the St. Tammany Parish Courthouse, St. Tammany Parish, LA, was the first to put me on the track of some fascinating documents concerning the life and exploits of Eglée Aubry, who was a property owner in Saint Tammany before the Civil War. What was most amazing to me was that she recognized Aubry's name and in only a few minutes had located several court filings that Eglée had initiated against a troublesome neighbor. She was also instrumental in helping to find documents on the Lorreins and Flot families that played an important part in this story. I also wish to thank Stephanie Ballard, the Archives clerk, Robin's able assistant, who is an historian in training with one of the best. I might add that Ms. Perkins has dossiers on many of the important Saint Tammany Parish families which she has compiled, and which she generously shares with those who are interested.

I also received many baptismal, marriage and burial documents from the Archdiocese of New Orleans and wish to thank Emilie Leumas, the Archivist, and her able staff, Katie Vest, and Kimberly Johnson, research archivists, for locating the records I needed, and for patiently answering my telephone queries when I found another subject to investigate.

Joe Smith from the Notre Dame University Archives, which is home to reams of correspondence between the Roman Catholic Church and its clergy worldwide, but especially in Louisiana, helped me to locate an important document concerning the Grass family of Baton Rouge. The website, with summaries of thousands of these communications is available here: http://archives.nd.edu/search/calendar-search.htm

Karen Horton, the Archivist at the Archdiocese of Mobile, Alabama, Archives, also went above and beyond to find valuable documents concerning the Lorreins, Leflot (Flot) and Pinta families who had settled in Mobile in the first half of the eighteenth century, before moving on to New Orleans.

Early on in this project, I took a chance and contacted a church by email in Nervi, Italy, where I believed Geromo/Geronimo Chiapella had been baptized in the mid-1700s. There was no guarantee that the records still existed, or that this was even the church where Chiapella had received the sacrament. Several weeks went by, and I received an email from Giovanni Lorenzo Poggi, the archivist for the parrocchia plebana di. S. Siro di Nervi, with not only the baptismal record for Geromo Chiapella, but also for several of his siblings, as well as the marriage record of his parents. Genealogy miracles do happen.

Lori Schexnayder, the research services library associate at Tulane University Special Collections (Howard-Tilton Memorial Library, 6801 Freret Street, New Orleans, LA 70118) was very helpful to me during my quest for information on and copies of documents from the Prosper Foy collection. Scans of several of these precious documents have made their way into the book to help explain the complicated relationship between a white father and his own children of color.

Jordan Rushing, historian with the Vicksburg and Warren County Historical Society, Vicksburg, MS, facilitated my use of the lovely vintage photo of the monument to the Louisiana soldiers who lost their lives at the Battle of Vicksburg, carved by Florville Foy in 1887. He also provided historical insight into the photographer, J. Mack Moore who recorded life in Vicksburg from the late 1800s until the 1940s.

Anyone who researches New Orleans and its history eventually winds up at the Historic New Orleans Collection (HNOC). I wish to thank Rebecca Smith, Head of Reader Services at the Williams Research Center, HNOC, for providing me with the wonderful reproduction of the Joseph Pilié map dated 18 August 1808 showing a plan of New Orleans with the names of all the property owners. This is a snapshot in time which is essential to the understanding of how the city grew. The *Collins C. Diboll Vieux Carré Digital Survey* (www.hnoc.org/vcs/) , an electronic version of the Vieux Carré Survey housed at HNOC is also an invaluable guide which traces the chains of title of French Quarter properties from the beginnings of the city in the 1720s through the twentieth century. She also provided a copy of Plate #5, a map of the path of the British invasion of Louisiana in 1815, drawn by Arsène Lacarrière Latour for his 1816 book intitled *Historical Memoir of The War in West Florida and Louisiana in 1814-15, With an Atlas.*

As luck would have it, I managed to contact the great-granddaughter of Marie Emma Chiapella and Ernest Joseph Edmunds, Kate Scow, a professor of soil science at the University of California, Davis, who was kind enough to give me some insight into the lives of Marie Emma Chiapella and her husband Ernest Joseph Edmunds, and their descendants.

I must also thank three fellow researchers, who contributed information to this book. Father Phil Flott, the keeper of the flame for all things Flot, Flott, LeFlot, shared important information, as well as photographs of Chiapella and Flot family members for this book. Jack Belsom, a longtime New Orleans resident, is the local expert on the Duvernay family, and author of the book *Opera in New Orleans*. He guided me through the ins and outs of the Duvernay family and their connections with the Coudrains, two of whom would become Chiapellas by adoption. Sian Zelbo became my research partner as we explored the relationship between Prosper Foy and Zélie Aubry. A PhD. candidate at Columbia University, and a mathematician, Ms. Zelbo's dissertation was on Edgar Joseph Edmunds, grandson of Prosper Foy and Zélie Aubry. She has focused her research on his professional life as a mathematician and the struggles he had as a free man of color navigating the New Orleans secondary education system as Reconstruction gave way to the rise of Jim Crow segregation laws in the state in the last quarter of the nineteenth century. To one and all, my grateful thanks.

Carol Mills-Nichol

24 August 2020

ABBREVIATIONS AND SPELLING

Throughout this book we have quoted liberally from the baptism, marriage and funeral records, published between 1987 and 2004, in nineteen volumes covering the years from 1718 through 1831, by the Roman Catholic Church of the Archdiocese of New Orleans. Those references appear in parentheses after each citation. Baptisms recorded at St. Louis Cathedral appear with this type of reference:

St. Louis Cathedral baptisms appear as:
(SLC, B2, 171) for St. Louis Cathedral, Baptism Book 2, page 171.

St. Louis Cathedral marriages appear as:
(SLC M1, 222) for St. Louis Cathedral Marriage Book 1, page 222.

Funeral records for St. Louis Cathedral appear as:
(SLC, B1, 77) for St. Louis Cathedral Burial Book 1, page 77 (Later volumes switched from using "B" for burial to "F" for Funeral)

Some early ecclesiastical records from the Cathedral were sent to France and retrieved for the publication of their books and are marked with the abbreviation "AN" for Archives Nationales de Paris instead of SLC and appear this way:

(AN, F 1725, 43) for Archives Nationales, Funeral + year + page.

As more churches opened, some records appear with the following abbreviations:

SCB – St. Charles Borromeo Church, Destrehan
SMNO – St. Mary, New Orleans (Chartres Street).

Note: The following are abbreviations used in the above documents from the Archdiocese's publications:

b = baptized; bn = born; s. = godparents, sponsors; i. = buried, interred; m = married; mgp = maternal grandparents; pgp = paternal grandparents.

We have also quoted, though less extensively, from the Diocese of Baton Rouge, Catholic Church Records, Volume 1B, Pointe Coupée Records, 1722-1769, Volume 2, 1770-1803, and Volume 3, 1804-1819, the last two being St. Joseph of Baton Rouge records, published by the Department of Archives, Diocese of Baton Rouge. Records from the church will appear in parentheses followed by the volume number and page after each citation as:

SJO (St. Joseph Catholic Church of Baton Rouge)
PCP (Pointe Coupée Parish Church of St. Francis)

NARC – Notarial Archives Research Center

SSDI - The Social Security Death Index, available at *Ancestry.com,* is abbreviated as "SSDI" and appears in parenthesis next to the applicable record.

NARA – National Archives and Records Administration, Washington D.C.

FHL – Family History Library (Familysearch.org)

The given names in baptismal, marriage and death records appeared in any one of three languages: French, Spanish, or English in Louisiana records. Within each language, the problem of literacy complicates, what was recorded on paper as to both given and surnames. For example, the Italian surname "Chiapella" was, converted to "La Chiapella," and became so common that Jérome Chiapella, ordinarily signed as "La Chiapella" The name also appears misspelled as "La Chapelle," "Lachiapella," and Lachiappella."

The surname "Coudrain" very often appeared as "Coudrin." The Spanish, however, used "Coudren" When quoting from documents we have attempted to use the spelling given in the document, otherwise we have chosen to use "Coudrain". Shortly before Pierre Coudrain died in New Orleans in 1779, he had written out a will on 28

March 1779, which he revoked two months later on 1 June 1779, stating that he had had it written when very ill and in great danger for his life ("como estaba muy enfermo, y en gran peligro de la vida"). He signed this document as seen below using "Coudrain.":

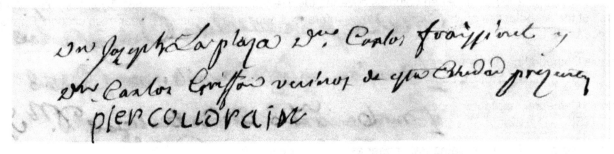

Notarial Archives Research Center, hereinafter NARC, Untitled entry, dated 1 June 1779, passed by Notary Juan Bautista Garic, Volume 11, p. 297 recto. Courtesy Hon. Chelsey Richard Napoleon, Clerk of Civil District Court, Parish of Orleans.

Some Frequently Used Given Names and Surnames

Celestin (Fr. & En.) appears also as Celestino (Sp.) and occasionally Zelestino (Sp.)

Charles (Fr. & En.) appears as Carlo (It.) or Carlos (Sp.)

Étienne (Fr.) appears as Estevan (Sp.) or Stephen (En.)

Eloisa (Sp.) appears as Héloïse (Fr.), and Louise (En.), Zélie (Fr.), and Azélie (Fr.)

Amada (Sp.) appears as Aimée (Fr.)

Agathe (Fr.) also appears as Agatha (En.)

Félicité (Fr.) appears as Felicitas (Sp.) or Félicie (Fr.)

Philippe (Fr.), appears as Felipe (Sp.) or Philip (En.)

Juana (Sp.) appears as Jeanne (Fr.) or Jane (En.)

Mercelite (Fr.) appears as Marcelitta (Sp.), but also is used interchangeably with "Marguerite."

Margarita (Sp.) also appears as Marguerite (Fr. and En.)

Jean-Baptiste (Fr.) appears as Juan Bautista (Sp.)

Jacques (Fr.) appears as Santiago (Sp.) or James (En.)

Jérome (Fr. & En.) appears as Geromo or Gerolamo (It.), Hieronymus (Latin), or Geronimo (Sp. & En.)

Louis (Fr. & En.) appears as Luis (Sp.)

Guillaume (Fr.) appears as Guillermo (Sp.) or William (En.)

Pierre (Fr.) appears as Pedro (Sp.) and Peter (En.)

Zabela (Sp.), appears as Isabella (Sp.), Isabelle (Fr.), and Elizabeth (En.)

The surname Aubry appears as "Aubrie," "Obry," "Oubry" and "Obrie"

The surname, Lorreins, is often spelled "Lorance," "Laurance," "Laureins," or "Lorence"

The surname, Flot, also appears as Flott, Flou, Le Flou, Le Flot, Leflau, Le Flour, and Le Flaut

The surname "Duvernay" which appears to be the preferred spelling in many documents, is also spelled "Duvernet" or "Duverne." In French "ay", "et" and "é" (the accent is routinely left off) are all pronounced as the English letter "a" in "aim." Eventually the family settled on "Duvernay," which we have chosen to use in most cases.

CHAPTER 1

MARGUERITE CÉCILE AUBRY

According to her baptismal record, Marie Eglée Aubry was born Maria Aubry, a free quadroon, on 3 January 1805 to Margarita Aubry, a free "mulata" and an unknown father. She was baptized by Fr. Antonio de Sedella on 17 May 1806 who duly recorded it in Spanish in Book #19, p. 65 of *Baptisms of Slaves and Free People of Color*. Her godparents were Celestino Vizot/Bizot and the child's sister, Éloisa Aubry.

Archdiocese of New Orleans, *St. Louis Cathedral, New Orleans Baptism of Slaves and Free People of Color 1805-1806*, Digital Collections-#303 Image 125/200 at https://archives.arch-no.org/sacramental_records. Baptism of Maria Aubry, free Quadroon.

The document is in very poor condition, as are many of the records from this era. Besides the obvious tears in it, information from the subsequent page has bled through. An abstract of this document, however was recorded in Volume 8 of the *Sacramental Records of the Roman Catholic Church of the Archdiocese of New Orleans 1804-1806*, published in 1993, which listed the mother's and child's names, the date of birth and baptism of the child, as well as her godparents.

Marguerite Aubry was said to have been 103 years old when she died in New Orleans in 1861. While a birth date of 1758 seems a bit early considering that her last child was born in January 1805, we believe that she was probably born at the very end of French rule in the Louisiana Territory, between 1760 and 1769. Emily Epstein Landau captured the flavor of the city better than most when she wrote "New Orleans was a European colonial city, a 'Latin American' colony, a West Indian enclave, an American frontier town, and a port city – all within the Deep South."[1] Marguerite Aubry was one of those rare individuals whose lifespan mirrored its history as a French, then Spanish, briefly again French, and finally an American city. As a free person of color in the eighteenth century, she would have been one of a very few. In a 1732 census taken in New Orleans, there were only six free people of color, all said to be mulatto. According to the 1769 census there were 99 free people of color, with 68 of them being mulatto out of a total population of 3,190. The free colored population had grown in 1778 to 353, with 248 designated

---

[1] Emily Epstein Landau, *Spectacular Wickedness: Sex, Race and memory in Storyville, New Orleans* (Baton Rouge, LA: Louisiana State University Press, 2013), 34.

as mulatto out of a total population of 3,659. In 1803, after the Louisiana Purchase a full 23.8% or 1,335 residents of New Orleans were free people of color. By then, the total population had grown to 8,056.[2]

It is clear from those statistics that Marguerite Aubry was born at a time when there were less than 100 free colored persons living in the city. Some family members have claimed that she was a child born to Charles Philippe-Aubry, a French soldier who was the Colonial Administrator and last French Governor of the colony after it had been ceded to Spain by France in 1762 at the Treaty of Fontainebleau. Aubry had been a soldier for over twenty years in 1762. Born on 27 July 1722 at Paris, France, the son of Jean Jacques Charles Aubry, a lawyer, and his wife Catherine Jeanne de Boissy, he had already served in the French and Indian War (Seven Years War), having been captured and tortured by the Iroquois who were fighting alongside the British to protect Fort Niagara in 1759. He was rescued by the British and returned to New York where he was released. Returning to France in 1760, he was awarded the Cross of the Order of St. Louis for his services, and was reassigned to Louisiana to command the garrison at New Orleans. He served there from 1762 under the Colonial Governor, Jean-Jacques Blaise D'Abbadie, and succeeded him as governor after the latter's death in 1765. Aubry welcomed Antonio de Ulloa, the new Spanish Governor, who, when the Spanish Crown failed to send necessary troops to take over the colony in 1766, relinquished his authority back to Aubry, who remained Governor of the Louisiana Territory until 1769, with the arrival of Alejandro O'Reilly. The latter had been sent from Havana to quell the rebellion of some French citizens, who had sent emissaries to France to plead with the King for the colony's return to France, and, failing that, had subsequently banished Ulloa and his wife from the colony in 1768. Captain-General Alejandro O'Reilly arrived the following year to restore order and establish Spanish domination over the wayward colony. He and his 2000 Spanish troops entered New Orleans on 18 August 1769. The following day he started an investigation into the coup d'état and demanded that Aubry turn over the names of the leaders of the conspiracy. Aubry's complicity with this investigation earned him the enmity of the French population of New Orleans. Six of the conspirators were given lengthy prison sentences. However, four prominent New Orleans citizens were executed for treason including the Colony's Attorney General, Nicolas Chauvin de Lafrenière. Denis-Nicolas Foucault, the Commissaire-Ordonnateur (Comptroller) of the colony was sent back for trial to France, accused by Aubry of aiding and abetting the uprising. His actions against Foucault had been fueled by a long-simmering hatred for the man, who had refused to raise Aubry's salary above 6,000 livres, while Foucault himself, had lived in luxury with many servants. Aubry, it was said, had always been looked down upon by French society in New Orleans because of his meager assets, his plain living accommodations, and his one and only servant. In an article intitled "Two Original and Newly Found Documents of the Departure, Shipwreck, and Death of Mr. Aubry, the Last French Governor in Louisiana," written in 1897 for the Louisiana Historical Society, Dr. Gustavus Devron, uncovered more details about the last moments of Charles-Philippe Aubry's life, who, after leaving New Orleans on the *Père de Famille* on 23 November 1769, along with 58 French troops, a small number of civilians, six double-barrel caste iron canons, as well as a cargo of indigo and furs, was shipwrecked on 17 February 1770 at the mouth of the Garonne River, near Bordeaux. Only four men survived, including the Captain, Jacques Jacquelin. All later testified to Aubry's death. There was also evidence given by Captain Cabarn de Trépis that Aubry had left New Orleans with a fortune in silver and gold.

Seven years later, Colonel Chevalier Jean de Champigny published the *État présent de la Louisiane toutes les particularités de cette Province d'Amérique: Pour servir de suite â l'Histoire des Européens dans les Deux Indes* (Present State of Louisiana, All the Particulars of this American Province. To serve as a sequel to the History of the Europeans in the Two Indies) which included a description of the last governor of the Louisiana Territory:

> Mr. Aubry was a little, dry, lean, ugly man, without nobility, dignity or carriage. His face would seem to announce a hypocrite, but in him this vice sprang from excessive goodness, which granted all, rather than displease; always trembling for the consequences of the most indifferent actions, a natural effect of a mind without resource, light; always allowing itself to be guided, and thus from rectitude in conduct; religious through weakness than from principle; incapable of wishing evil but doing through a charitable human weakness; destitute of magnanimity or reflection; a good soldier; but a bad leader; ambitious of honors and dignity, but possessing neither nor capacity to bear the weight.

Dr. Devron concluded that "Aubry, through his servile obedience to the orders of his master Louis XV, became the

---

[2] Virginia Dominguez, *White by Definition – Social Classification in Creole Louisiana* (New Brunswick, NJ: Rutgers University Press, 1986), 24, 25, 116.

lacquey of Ulloa and his detective and later became the cowardly informer upon his countrymen on the arrival of the Spanish Governor O Reilly. For this last act he is despised by all sons of Louisiana as this action is by them considered disgraceful and infamous."[3] There is no doubt that the simmering hatred for Aubry colored the description of this man who had engineered the death by firing squad of Lafrenière, Jean-Baptiste de Noyan, Pierre Caresse, Pierre Marquis, Joseph Milhet, and lengthy prison sentences for Joseph Petit, Balthazar de Mazan, Julien-Jérome Doucet, Jean Milhet, Pierre Poupet and Pierre Hardy de Boisblanc. What had become more of a scandal to the French colonists was the death of Joseph Philippe Roy Villeré, husband of Louise Marguerite Delachaise, who was the granddaughter of Jacques Auguste Delachaise, identified at his death in 1730 as a Royal Commissioner and First Councilor of the Superior Council of Louisiana. Roy Villeré had been complicit in the conspiracy, but was convinced by Aubry to abandon his plan to flee to British protection at Manchac. He was told that if he surrendered to O'Reilly he would be pardoned. He was, instead, arrested and confined to a frigate in the Mississippi River. According to Louisiana historian Charles Gayarré, Roy Villeré died the day of his arrest "raving mad." It was said that his wife had arrived to see him but was refused entry onto the ship due to the absence of the ship's captain. Upon hearing her voice, Roy Villeré struggled with his guards and was stabbed to death in the ensuing melee.[4]

The fact remains that we do not know the connection between Marguerite Aubry, a free mulatto, and Charles-Philippe Aubry, the much-reviled last Governor of French Louisiana. Was the only servant in Aubry's household during his stay in New Orleans between 1762 and 1769, Marguerite's mother? Had this servant borne a child with Aubry, who was living unmarried in New Orleans? Or did Marguerite use the Aubry name simply because her mother had been Aubry's slave. One thing is certain is that Marguerite would not have consistently been referred to in records as a "mulata," if her father had not been a white man.

Were there, however, any other likely male Aubrys in the colony at that time who could have fathered Marguerite? Jean-Pierre François Bruno Aubry, born at Rouen, France in 1753, son of Pierre François Aubry and Marie Geneviève Lorat/L'Erat, married Elizabeth Roche, the widow of Jean Lafitte, on 28 October 1784. They were the parents of two legitimate children: Charles born in 1785 and Léocadie, born in 1789.[5] Bruno Aubry made a will in New Orleans in 1786 after the birth of his first child. In it he did not recognize any natural children. The family returned to Angers, Maine-et-Loire, France, ca. 1805, where his wife, Elizabeth died in October 1806, and he followed in April 1818.[6] Had Marguerite been part of this family, either by kinship or had her mother simply served in this Aubry household? Just as with Charles-Philippe Aubry, there are no records yet discovered to prove or disprove any of these possibilities.

In his 1794 will, Pedro (Pierre) Aubry, a New Orleans silver and goldsmith, stated that he was unmarried, but that he had fathered two children, Pedro Estevan (Pierre Étienne) and Maria Genoveva (Marie Geneviève) Aubry by the free black woman, Maria Emilia Aubry, all former slaves of his. As his only heirs he left the children a farm seven leagues from the city, two slaves, some livestock, furniture and household goods.[7] Had Marguerite been his child, would he have not mentioned her in the will? Perhaps not, since she was already an adult and the mother of several children. However, there is no concrete proof that Marguerite Aubry was allied with this male Aubry either.

Still other researchers have identified her as Marguerite Cécile, the daughter of Étienne Villeré (b. abt. 1747), a freed West African slave, and Régine Born, and the mother of Martin Aubry, a resident of St. Martin Parish.

---

[3] Gustavus Devron, M.D. "Two Original and Newly Founded Documents of the Departure, Shipwreck and Death of Mr. Aubry, the last French Governor in Louisiana," *Louisiana Historical Society*, Vol.2, Part 1, (1897): 33,34.

[4] Charles Gayarré, *History of Louisiana The French Domination*, Vols. 1,2. (New York, NY: Redfield, 1854); republished by Book Renaissance at www.ren-books.com, Vol. 2, 303-305.

[5] Rev. Earl C. Woods and Dr. Charles E. Nolan, eds. *Sacramental Records of the Roman Catholic Church of the Archdiocese of New Orleans, Volume 4, 1784-1790* (New Orleans, LA: Archdiocese of New Orleans, 1989), 13, 267.

[6] *The Augustan Society Omnibus*, v. 12,(1990) at Family Search Digital Library, (http://www.familysearch.org/library/books/, Identifier 2388312) Image 124/164, Items 151-153.

[7] Kimberly S. Hanger, "Patronage, Property and Persistence: The Emergence of a Free Black Élite in Spanish New Orleans," in Jane G. Landers, ed., *Against the Odds: Free Blacks in the Slave Societies of the Americas* (London & Portland, OR: Frank Cass & Co., Ltd., 1996), 44-64.

Etienne, also referred to as "Sambo," bought his own freedom on 19 November 1781 for 400 piastres[8] from Louise Marguerite Delachaise, widow of Joseph Philippe Roy Villere, the conspirator previously described who had met his end on a frigate in the Mississippi River on 29 August 1769 thanks to the machinations of Charles-Philippe Aubry. According to these researchers, Marguerite Cécile Villere was born ca. 1766 in St. Charles Parish. Original records we have found do not indicate that Marguerite Cécile ever used the name "Villeré." Moreover, as a "mulatress" one of her parents would have had to be white and Étienne Villeré was West African by birth, although we do not know the ethnicity of "Régine Born," due to a lack of any other records where she was named.

The earliest legal record that we have found which bears Marguerite Cécile's signature was from a sale made by Constance Simon, a free "mulata," to Marguerite Cécile dated 9 June 1804 which was passed in the office of notary Pierre Pedesclaux. Constance stated in the document that on 20 October 1793 she, along with her sister, Geneviève, since deceased, had bought a piece of property measuring 30 feet facing on St. Ann Street by 75 feet deep for 225 "piastres gourdes"[9] from Hilaire Boutet. However, the true owner and occupant of the property since October 1793 had been the free mulata, Marguérite Cécile, who had paid for the land herself, and had had the buildings constructed on the property at her own expense. It was not until 1804 that Constance Simon and Marguerite Cécile signed the document where the former legally signed over the property to Marguerite. A copy of the women's signatures along with those of the notary, Pierre Pedesclaux and two witnesses, Jean-Baptiste Ramires and Joachim Lozano may be seen below:

NARC, "Cession et Transport," dated 9 June 1804, passed by Notary Pierre Pedesclaux, Volume 46, folio 622 verso. Courtesy Hon. Chelsey Richard Napoleon, Clerk of Civil District Court, Parish of Orleans.

While Marguerite Cécile regularly used the surname Aubry, when giving information concerning herself for census records and the like, it appears that she considered her legal name to be Marguerite Cécile, the name she used on all the notarized documents we could find. Could "Marguerite Cécile" have been the name which appeared on her freedom papers, if she had originally been enslaved? If this were so, she would have had to show the paper when she transacted business before a notary. We have concluded that the woman, Marguerite Cécile, who appeared as the mother of Martin Aubry, a free quadroon, in his 19 November 1811 St. Martin Parish marriage

---

[8] "Piastre" is the French word for peso. There are 8 escalins in one piastre (French) and eight reales to one peso (Spanish). The peso and the piastre which were equivalent to one another were roughly equivalent to one American dollar.

[9] 1 piastre gourde sonnant de Mexique (Fr.) or 1 peso fuerte (Spanish) is the equivalent of 1.75 pesos (Sp.), 1.75 piastres (Fr.) or 1.75 (USD). Source: Gwendolyn Midlo Hall, *Slavery and African Ethnicities in the Americas: Restoring the Links* (Chapel Hill, NC: University of North Carolina Press, 2005), Appendix, p. 175.

record to Lucille, a "mulatresse, daughter of Marie griffe" freed by Mr. Ozenne, fils (Jr.)," was also the mother of Félicité, Zélie, Mercelite, and Marie Eglée Aubry. Martin's mother, Marguerite Cécile was identified as a "free mulatress." Martin's father was not named in the document, but Martin's birth was said to have taken place in New Orleans, not in St. Martin Parish where he was married. The French, faded and barely legible, reads in our translation: "Martin Aubry, a free quadroon from this Parish, native of New Orleans, illegitimate and minor son of Marguerite Cécile, a free mulatress:"

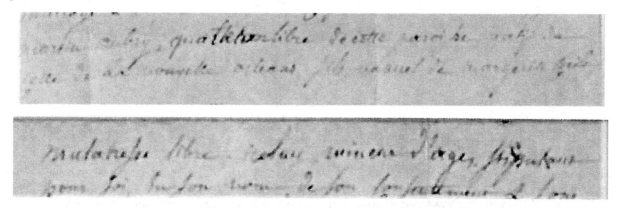

"Martin Aubry, quarteron libre de cette paroisse natif de la Nouvelle Orleans, fils naturel de Marguerite Cécile mulatresse libre, lui mineur d'âge" (Original record courtesy of Candy Brunet, Associate Archivist, Diocese of Lafayette, Lafayette Parish, LA.

We could not identify a birth record for Martin amongst those housed at St. Louis Cathedral. We did find, however, several original records which connected Martin to his mother, Marguerite Cécile, and to one of his siblings. On 18 June 1814, Marguerite Cécile bought a thirty-five-year-old slave named Guy, at a succession sale and auction from the estate of the deceased Joseph Pavie, through his administrator, Antoine Fromentin, for 550 piastres. The note that she signed for the purchase was endorsed and guaranteed by Prosper Foy, the father of Marguerite Cécile's daughter Zélie/Azélie Aubry's two children. On 10 December 1816, Marguerite Cécile, through Philippe Pedesclaux, a New Orleans notary, signed a legal document giving Martin Aubry power of attorney to sell the slave Guy for her. This power of attorney was attached to an act of sale for Guy dated 21 May 1817, filed at the St. Martin Parish Courthouse, by Martin Aubry who had sold Guy to Edmond and Ursin Ozenne for 900 piastres, with a 500 piastre cash down payment and an additional 400 piastres due a year from the date of sale. It is clear from the typescript documents from the St. Martin Parish courthouse that the originals had been signed by both Martin Aubry and Marguerite Cécile at a time when many free people of color, as well as many whites, especially women, were unable to write. Below is a copy of Marguerite Cécile's signature on her 1814 purchase of Guy from the estate of Joseph Pavie:

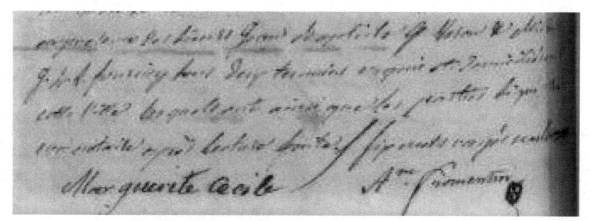

NARC, "Vente d'esclave – Antoine Fromentin à Marguerite Cécile," dated 18 June 1814, passed by Notary Marc Lafitte, Volume 4, p. 203. Courtesy Hon. Chelsey Richard Napoleon, Clerk of Civil District Court, Parish of Orleans.

Fourteen years later, Marguerite Cécile signed a document which made her curatrix ad bona to her granddaughter "Marguerite Aubry (sic – Foy) f.w.c., a minor above the age of puberty" in an action brought by her daughter, Zélie Aubry, to get permission from the court to sell the slave Philotine, a gift to Marguerite Félicité and Eliza Pauline from Prosper Foy, their father:

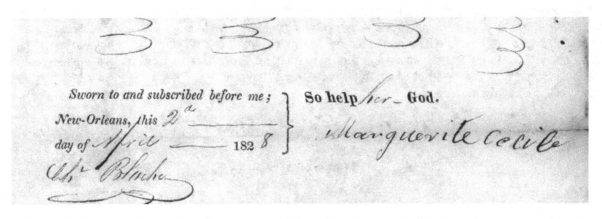

"Louisiana, Orleans Parish Estate Files, 1804-1846," database with images, *FamilySearch* (https://familysearch.org accessed 20 May 2019), Aubry, Zelie (1828), image 1 of 24, citing information from the New Orleans City Archives.

As can be seen, the signatures are identical and compare favorably with the 1804 signature taken from the sale of the St. Ann Street property by Constance Simon to Marguerite Cécile. Another document, contemporaneous with Martin Aubry's 1811 marriage, shows that when Marguerite temporarily ceded the St. Ann Street property to Manuel Laura on 7 May of that year in consideration of his having lent her 750 piastres for six months that she also signed "Marguerite Cécile:" She repaid Laura and the sale was annulled on 10 October 1811, a fact written in the margin of the original document:

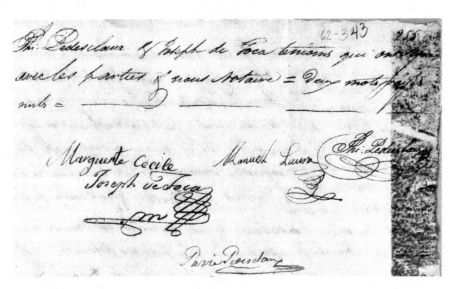

NARC, "Marguerite Cécile to Manuel Laura," dated 7 May 1811, passed by Notary Pierre Pedesclaux, Volume 62, folio 254 recto. Courtesy Hon. Chelsey Richard Napoleon, Clerk of Civil District Court, Parish of Orleans.

We know that in his 1811 marriage to Lucille Ozenne, Martin Aubry had required the permission of his mother to wed, since he was under the age of 21 years. This would put his birth no earlier than 19 November 1790. Martin continued to live with his family at Bayou Tortue in St. Martin Parish, where he was a farmer and property owner. Aubry, whose name appears as "Martin Aubrie," served between 16 December 1814 and 25 March 1815 during the Battle of New Orleans in Captain Alexandre Lemelle's Company of Free Men of Color as a First Lieutenant.[10]

Martin Aubry and his wife were the parents of at least eleven children: Martin (b. 11 October 1814), Charles (b. abt. 1817, d. 1822), Martin Louis (b. 18 February 1818), Maximilien Martin (b. 12 March 1820), Marie Clémence

---

[10] Thomas Harrison, compiler, National Park Service, *Troop Roster, Tennessee Volunteers & Militia, Kentucky Volunteers & Militia, Battalion of Free Men of Color, Louisiana Volunteers & Militia.* (https://www.nps.gov/jela/learn/history culture/upload/CHALTroop Roster.pdf), dated 28 May 1954, 116.

(b. 4 Nov 1821), Alexandre (b. 17 September 1823), Lucien (b. 17 April 1825), Charles (b. 27 October 1827), Octave (b. 7 November 1830), Joseph (b. 6 June 1832), and Louise (b. 20 August 1833). Another child, Marguerite, for whom there is no birth record, had died before 1851 when her father's succession was finally settled.[11] In the St. Martin Parish baptism record for their third and fourth children, Martin Louis Aubry, and Maximilien Martin Aubry, Fr. Marcel Borella who officiated at the ceremonies, recorded the paternal grandparents as "Martin Aubris and Marguerite Cécile." This information has led some researchers to conclude that Marguerite Cécile's partner was a certain Martin Aubry. We were unable to find any person called Martin Aubry/Aubris who could have been the father of these children either in St. Martin or in Orleans Parish. In the only baptism record we have found for another one of Marguerite Cécile's children, Marie (Eglée) Aubry, born in 1805, no father was listed. We can only hope that other records may turn up some day to solve this problem.

Marguerite's daughter, Marie Eglée was her youngest, born in the first decade of the nineteenth century. She did, however, have three daughters all born before 1800. We believe that Félicité Aubry was probably born ca. 1788. After searching the baptismal records for slaves and free people of color which are available online from the Archdiocese of New Orleans, we found one possibility. This identification is based solely on the fact that this is the only "Felicie" baptized between 1788-1792, who was a free "quadroon," born to a free "mulata" named Margarita. (Line 6 "hija de Margte, mulata libre). Nowhere is the surname Aubry mentioned in this entry, as far as it can be read. The date of baptism was 16 July 1788, and the date of birth 15 June 1788. Since Felicité's first child, Edmond Dupuy, was born in 1806, we know that a 1788 birth date is a reasonable possibility, and anything later than 1791-1792 would be highly unlikely.

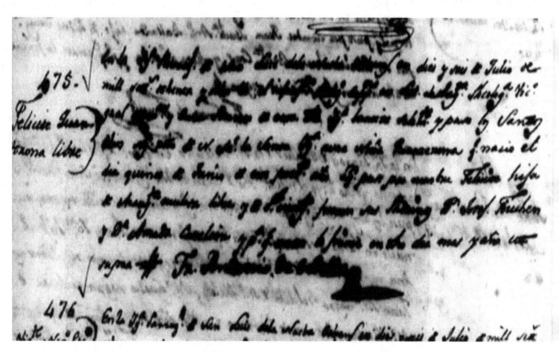

Archdiocese of New Orleans, *St. Louis Cathedral, New Orleans Baptism of Slaves and Free People of Color 1786-1792*, Digital Collections-#475 Image 66/358 at https://archives.arch-no.org/sacramental_records.

---

[11] Martin Aubry died in St. Martin Parish on 10 August 1844. His wife, Lucille Ozenne had died on 31 August 1834. The part of his succession that belonged to his daughter Marie Clémence, later the wife of Jacques Delille, and a resident of New Orleans, was handled on 27 April 1851 by the notary Achille Chiapella, father of her aunt, Eglée Aubry's mixed-race sons. Note: Two other minor children, Émile and Tréville, for which we have no records, were mentioned in the 1844 succession. (*Louisiana, Wills and Probate Records, 1756-1984,*" digital images, *Ancestry.com (*https://www. ancestry.com: accessed 3/20/2019), citing "Estate Files From Attakapas County and Parish, LA and St. Martin Parish, LA," Louisiana. Parish Court (St. Martin Parish); Probate Place: St. Martin, Louisiana,*" Case #1020, Succession of Martin Aubry, Image 275/627.

Unfortunately, we have been unable to find a probable baptismal certificate for Marguerite's child, Zélie Aubry. Her 1870 death record indicated that she was 78 years old when she passed. The United States Federal Census record for that year gave her age as 70 years old. Since her first child, Elena Foy, was born in 1810, her likely date of birth was ca. 1793-1795.

Similarly, we found no credible baptismal record for Mercelite Aubry. We believe she was born ca. 1797 and may have been baptized as Marguerite, as she occasionally appears with that name in church records. Her 1852 death record indicated that she was about fifty-five years old at death. It is, of course, possible that both Zélie and Mercelite were baptized simply as "Marie," or "Maria" and that other names were given to them later as children, as was the case with Marie Eglée.

Another indication we have of the presence of Marguerite Aubry, in New Orleans was a census taken in 1797 in order to collect a tax of 12 reales per chimney on the residents in order to maintain the town's "lighting department." Margarita Aubry, living at house #9 in the Third Ward of the city was taxed three pesos for having two chimneys. (Note: There were 8 reales to one peso which was the equivalent of about one dollar at the time.)[12]

Since Louisiana was not a state in 1800, there was no federal census in that year to record Marguerite's family. There was however, a census prepared by Matthew Flannery for the New Orleans City Council, submitted on 5 August 1805 where there was only one "Margarette," enumerated. She was a free woman of color living in house #32 on Dauphine Street, north side. No surname was given. There were two free children of color under sixteen years of age and two free adults of color over sixteen years of age as well as two slaves living in the household.[13]

There was, however, an 1810 federal census for the Territory of Orleans, which was formed in 1804 and existed until Louisiana statehood in 1812. This area was comprised of what is today the state of Louisiana, with the exception of West Florida which was annexed from the Spanish in 1812, and the Sabine Free Territory which served as a buffer zone between Louisiana and Spanish Texas until the Adams-Onis Treaty of 1819. In that census, both "Margte. Aubrie," and her daughter "Félicité Aubrie" were enumerated as residents of Bourbon Street, the former with four household members (probably herself, Zélie, Mercelite and Eglée) and one slave, and the latter with four household members, probably herself and children Edmond, Léon, and Alexandre Édouard Dupuy. No other details were forthcoming except that both women as well as others in their household were designated as free people of color.[14] It is noteworthy that the same census shows that "L.A. Dupuy," the father of Félicité's children lived next door to her. Félicité's first child with Louis Alexandre Dupuy, "Edemundo, free quadroon," had been born on 29 August 1806 and baptized by Father Jean-Pierre Koüne on 8 April 1809 at St. Louis Cathedral:

---

[12] See the original document at the New Orleans Public Library Special collections website: http://nutrias.org/exhibits/purchase/page7.htm.

[13] See: http://louisianadigitallibrary.org/islandora/ object/fpoc-p16313coll51%3A35436 . Image 27/46.

[14] Another free woman of color, Félicité Lorreins, was also living on Bourbon Street in 1810. We will explain the Lorreins-Aubry connection in the next chapter.

Archdiocese of New Orleans, *St. Louis Cathedral, New Orleans Baptism of Slaves and Free People of Color 1809-1809*, Digital Collections-#866 Image 36/134 at https://archives.arch-no.org/sacramental_records.

The child's surname does not appear in the margin, but his given name, Edemundo, and his status as a free quadroon, does. He was baptized the "natural" son of Alexandre Dupuis, whose own native country was omitted (line 5 above), and "Felicitas Obry," a native of New Orleans (line 6 above). "Obry" is often seen in place of "Aubry" and is simply the phonetic spelling of the French pronunciation of the surname. The child's godparents were Émile Senet and Marcilitta (Mercelite) Obry, his aunt. The couple had a second child, Léon Dupuy, whose missing baptismal certificate eventually enabled us to ascertain that Félicité, Eglée, and Zélie were indeed sisters, and the latter two both aunts of Léon Dupuy. On 9 December 1864, a number of years after their sister Félicité's death, the two women went to St. Louis Cathedral with Léon Dupuy to get his baptismal certificate. Because he could not produce this record, Léon had thought it safer to register as a free person of color at the office of the Mayor of New Orleans in 1861. A transcription of that record reads: "DUPUY, Leon, quadroon, 51, plasterer, born New Orleans, LA, recorded upon certificate of Messrs. Achille CHIAPELLA and Louis RIGAUD dated New Orleans, 18 May, 1861, on file. 5 ft. 8 1/2 inches, registered 18 May 1861."[15]

Why were these actions necessary? They were brought about by events which had occurred in the Caribbean Islands between 1790 and 1810. In the earliest part of the century, between 1805 and 1810, there had been an influx of whites, free people of color, and slaves, who had initially fled the island of Saint-Domingue at the turn of the century, due to the slave uprisings and the establishment of the Republic of Haiti. Some refugees had settled immediately in New Orleans, and along the Eastern Seaboard. Others had gone to Cuba. After Napoleon's invasion of Spain, all foreigners were expelled by the Cuban government in March 1809. For several months after that, at least thirty-four vessels loaded with almost 6,000 whites, free people of color, and slaves, landed in New Orleans. While the total population of New Orleans in 1805 had been 8,475 including 1,566 free people of color and 3,105 slaves, five years later the total population was 17,242 including 4,950 free people of color and 5,961 slaves.[16] With the influx of so many people of color who made up just over 63% of the total population in 1810, there grew a fear of slave insurrections. There had been several small slave revolts in the Louisiana Territory before Louisiana statehood, but the specter of a full-scale revolt of people of color had become a stark reality to the white population. The fact that free people of color had always enjoyed more privileges in Louisiana than in any other of the United States, including the right to own property including slaves, to sue for their rights in court, even to sue whites, did not reassure the white population that if a slave revolt came about, that free people of color would not join enslaved

---

[15] Judy Riffel, compiler and editor, *New Orleans Register of Free People of Color 1840-1864* (Baton Rouge, LA: Le Comité des Archives de la Louisiane, Inc., 2008), 148. Note regarding these two witnesses: Achille Chiapella, a New Orleans notary fathered three of Eglée Aubry's children. Louis Rigaud fathered three children with Marie Joseph Sophie Foy, the daughter of Prosper Foy and Zélie Aubry.

[16] Dominguez, *White by Definition*, 116.

blacks in an attempt to take over the territory and proclaim a black republic. Another factor which stoked the fear of whites was the drum beat of abolition that was resounding throughout the northern United States. As a consequence, the Louisiana legislature, began passing laws to restrict the entrance of free blacks into the state.[17] An 1830 act of the legislature required that all free negroes, griffes (black and native American mixture), and mulattos who had entered Louisiana after its statehood in 1812, and before January 1, 1825, had to enroll themselves with the office of the Mayor of New Orleans. An additional law was passed in 1843 requiring all free persons of color who came to the state prior to 1838 and who had consistently lived there, to register their names, ages, places of birth, occupation, and previous place of residence with the Parish Judge. These registers were kept between 1840 and 1864, although not everyone complied. Another 1843 law allowed New Orleans police to arrest free blacks not born in Louisiana and to hold them in jail until it could be proven that they were not a threat to peace. For that reason, many free blacks found it necessary to carry proof of their birth in the state. Since the majority of New Orleans free blacks were Roman Catholic, the existence of their baptismal record would assure that they would not be molested. Léon's baptismal record, however, could not be found. In lieu of an original, he was able to obtain, with the help of his two aunts, a document, written in French, which attested to his birth and baptism. The document, which can be seen below was signed by Eglée Aubry, her sister Zélie, their nephew Léon Dupuy, the Curé of St. Louis Cathedral, Fr. Celestin Mainhaut, and the Diocesan Archivist, Hippolyte Tacon. It was dated 9 December 1864 and stated that after a search of the church archives the original act of baptism could not be located. Léon's maternal aunts affirmed that he had been born the natural child of Alexandre Dupuy and of Félicité Aubry in January 1808 and baptized by a priest at St. Louis Cathedral in 1809. His godparents were Jacques Joly and Aimée Sarpy. The declaration was inserted into the church registers, where it was preserved using the number 848:

Bureau des Archives de l'Eglise métropolitaine et paroissiale de St. Louis

No. 848. Léon Dupuy

Ce neuvième jour de décembre de l'an Mil huit cent soixante quatre,

Devant moi, Cln Mainhaut, Curé de cette Eglise St. Louis de la Nlle Orléans, ont comparu:

D'une part, Sr. Hippolyte Tacon, archiviste de cette Eglise, lequel déclare n'avoir pu trouver dans les registres tenus à sa garde, l'acte de baptême du nommé Léon Dupuy,

D'autre part, Dames Zélie et Eglé Aubry, tantes maternelles du dit Léon Dupuy, résidant en cette ville, lesquelles déclarent que leur neveu Léon Dupuy fils naturel de Alexandre Dupuy et de Félicité Aubry, né en janvier 1808 a été baptisé par un prêtre de cette Paroisse dans le courant de l'année 1809, et qu'il a eu pour Parrain: Sr. Jacques Joly, et pour Marraine: Dlle. Aimée Sarpy.

Et j'ai ordonné que cette déclaration fut insérée dans les registres de cette église, signée, avec moi, par les réclamants et par l'Archiviste, témoin.

H. Tacon Léon Dupuy Eglé Aubry
témoin. C. Mainhaut, Curé Zélie Aubry

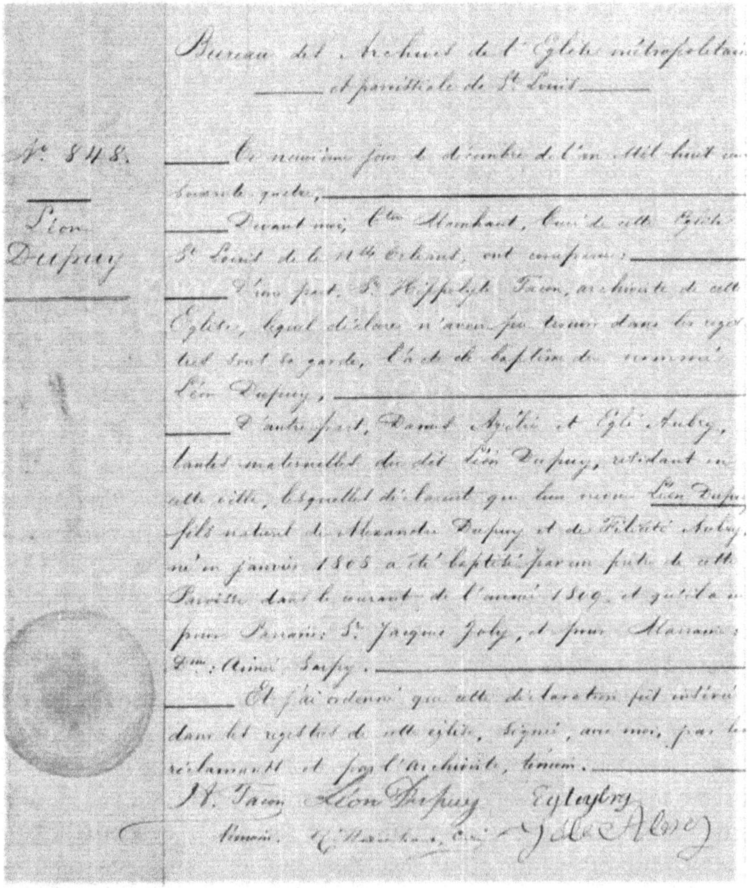

Archdiocese of New Orleans, *St. Louis Cathedral, New Orleans Baptism of Slaves and Free People of Color 1811-1811*, Digital Collections-#848, Image 1/200 at https://archives.arch-no.org/sacramental_records.

[17] For other information see: Loren Schweninger, "Antebellum Free Persons of Color in Postbellum Louisiana," in *Louisiana History: The Journal of the Louisiana Historical Association,* Vol. 30, No. 4 (Autumn, 1989), 345-364.

Marguerite Cécile Aubry did not appear in another federal census record until 1830. According to that year's United States Federal Census for New Orleans, "Margueritte Obry" was living between Bayou Road and Lake Pontchartrain, with three slaves, and six other free people of color of various ages, excluding herself. No specifics were given in census records until 1850, when names for all the persons living in the household were recorded. We suspect that her daughter, Eglée was probably living with her in 1830, along with the latter's first child, Marguerite Lorreins, born on 1 November 1822. By 1830, Marguerite's older daughters, Zélie, Félicité and Mercelite were living in their own households. In 1840, Marguerite "Aubri", a free woman of color was living in Ward 3, with thirteen other free people of color, including three children under ten years of age, and one woman, presumably herself, over the age of fifty-five. Thereafter she was absent from any census record. We know, however that she died in 1861 because her death was reported by her twenty-year-old grandson, Stephen Octave Chiapella, son of Marguerite's youngest daughter, Eglée:

Courtesy of State of Louisiana, Secretary of State, Division of Archives, Records Management, and History. *Vital Records Indices*. Baton Rouge, LA, USA citing *Orleans Death Indices 1804-1876*; Vol. 22, p. 84.

The original record reads:

> Be it remembered that on this day to wit: Fourteenth of March in the year of our Lord one thousand eight hundred and sixty-one, and the eighty-fifth of the Independence of the United States of America, before me, PIERRE LACOSTE, duly commissioned and sworn RECORDER OF BIRTHS and DEATHS in and for the Parish and City of Orleans personally appeared Mr. Octave Chiapella, native of New Orleans, aged twenty years, residing on Maine [Dumaine] Street between Robertson and Claiborne Streets hereby declares that Mrs. Marguerite Aubry, a native of New Orleans, aged one hundred and three years (103 years), died in this city on the seventh of March eighteen hundred and sixty-one (7th March 1861). Deceased leaving two children.

Zélie and Eglée Aubry were still living at the time, while Martin, Félicité, and Mercelite had predeceased their mother.

The document was signed by Octave Chiapella and two witnesses: Eugene Jorda and Louis Garic. To add some historical context, less than two months earlier, on 26 January 1861, Louisiana had seceded from the Union. New Orleans, however, would fall back under the control of United States General Benjamin Franklin Butler's five-thousand-man invasion force on 1 May 1862.

Marguerite Cécile Aubry's four daughters had a total of thirty-one children amongst them, at least twenty-one of whom lived to be adults. They watched as Louisiana seceded from the Union and was defeated in the Civil War. Many of them lived through Reconstruction and its aftermath. Free people of color saw many hard-fought freedoms that they had had, both before and after the Civil War dwindle away as Democrats retook the reins of local government. Marguerite and her children had grown up and lived most of their lives in a three-tier society. Planted squarely in the middle, between the white citizens and slaves, Louisiana's free people of color had been a force unto themselves during the early nineteenth century. They were mostly literate, French speaking, and Catholic. The men dominated the New Orleans landscape as tradesmen: tailors, cigar makers, plasterers, carpenters, shoemakers, blacksmiths, masons, coopers, barbers, painters, and upholsterers. There were even a number of merchants and grocers. The women worked as seamstresses, hairdressers, dressmakers and rooming house owners. Robert C. Reinders in his article intitled "The Free Negro in the New Orleans Economy, 1850-1860," has provided us with some important information. Two free men of color were working in New Orleans in the mid-nineteenth century: as physicians: Alexandre Chaumette and Louis Charles Roudanez. Both had been educated in France. There were two architects: Joseph Abeillard and Nelson Fouché. Norbert Rillieux, was an engineer and inventor who left New Orleans for Paris before the Civil War. Thomy Lafon and Honoré Pottier were commission brokers. Lucien Mansion and George Alcès had cigar factories. After restrictive laws were passed by the Louisiana Legislature in 1855, Lucien Mansion provided funds for free people of color to immigrate to Haïti or Mexico. CeCe Macarty (aka Eulalie de Mandeville Macarty) was the best-known female free colored entrepreneur. She had an importing business that she started from a bequest from her Macarty relatives, and turned it into an enterprise worth $155,000 at her death in 1845.

Free people of color, both men and women, invested their earnings in real estate. Reinders indicates that free people of color owned $2,462,470 in real estate in 1836. Downward political pressure on the group caused this figure to plummet to around $755,765 in 1850 and $739,890 in 1860. Ironically, free women of color owned more real estate outright than did their white sisters.[18] Many free colored women who had relationships with white men that they could not, by law, marry, remained free to manage their own affairs, buy and sell property, sue in court, if necessary, without having to obtain permission from a spouse. Marguerite's daughters each maintained one or more relationships with white men, bore their children, and shared financial responsibilities with them. Each of her daughters owned and managed her own real estate. They also owned slaves. Some may be startled at this statistic, but Reinders discovered by studying the 1830 federal census for Orleans Parish that "2351 slaves were owned by 735 New Orleans "free negro masters." 153 owned five or more slaves; 23 owned between ten and twenty. Cecee Macarty owned thirty-six."[19]

While statistics can be enlightening, and most of the sociological treatises on free people of color are replete with them, they are usually thin on concrete examples, and rarely, if ever, discuss the familial relationships which bound them together. Until the great influx of free people of color from Saint-Domingue and Cuba between 1805 and 1810 in Louisiana, the free colored population was very small and opportunities for relationships within this group were limited. Moreover, free women of color historically had outnumbered their male counterparts. On the other hand, white males had always outnumbered available white females in New Orleans. This imbalance led to the many instances of cross-racial mixing in the city. One of the more popular examples used by sociologists and historians of this phenomenon is the family of Jacqueline Lemelle (aka Jacqueline Dupard or Jacqueline Dusuau). Although almost a generation older than Marguerite Aubry, Jacqueline's relationship with three different white men created a link which bound the Girardy, Coudrain, Chiapella, Delachaise, Dusuau De La Croix, and Pinta families across racial lines throughout the nineteenth century. The life of Eglée Aubry, Marguerite's youngest daughter, claimant #25 at the French and American Claims Commission, one of the first to petition it for redress for damages to her St. Tammany Parish, LA, farm, and the pivotal person in this extended Louisiana Creole family, will be explored in the subsequent chapters of this book, along with the lives of her siblings and her many relatives by marriage.

---

[18] Robert C. Reinders, "The Free Negro in the New Orleans Economy, 1850-1860," *Louisiana History: The Journal of the Louisiana Historical Association,* Vol. 6, no.3 (Summer 1965), 275, 277, 278, 280, 281, 284.

[19] Reinders, "The Free Negro in the New Orleans Economy, 1850-1860," 282.

CHAPTER 2

EGLÉE AUBRY AND THE LORREINS CONNECTION

NARC, Signature of Louis Hilaire Lorreins, father of Marguerite Odalie Lorreins dated 24 January 1820 (Estate of) Jacques (Baptiste) Lorreins to Louis H. Lorreins – Sale of land and slave, Michel de Armas, Volume 19, Act #23. Courtesy Hon. Chelsey Richard Napoleon, Clerk of Civil District Court, Parish of Orleans.

The first independent record we found for Marie Eglée Aubry appeared in the baptismal record for her first child, Marguerite "Lorrence," born to Louis "Lorrence" and "Egle Oubry" on 1 November 1822 and baptized on 21 February 1824 at St. Louis Cathedral. Marguerite "Lorrence" was more often called "Odalie" or "Odile" "Lorrence/Lorrains/Lorance and was enumerated in her mother's household in the United States Federal Census records for 1850, 1860, 1870 and 1880. Below is a copy of the baptismal record written in French for Marguerite "Lorrence" which reads: "In the year 1824 on 21 February was baptized Marguerite born in New Orleans on 1 November 1822, natural daughter of Mr. Louis Lorrence and of Miss Eglé Oubry natives and residents of this parish. The godfather is Mr. J.B. Colsson, the godmother Miss Marguerite Doubraire."

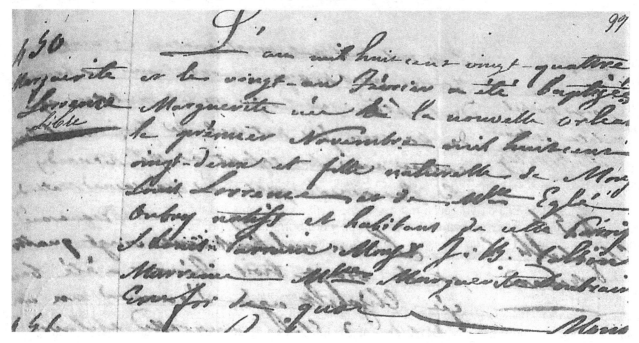

Baptismal record for Marguerite Lorrence, libre (free). Archives of the Archdiocese of New Orleans, Saint Louis Cathedral Records Vol. 18 S/FPC, p. 97, #450. (Courtesy of Emilie Leumas, Archivist – Kimberly Johnson and Katie Vest – Researching Archivists.)

It took a lot of time to finally uncover the identity of Louis "Lorrence," Marguerite's father, due to the misspelling of his surname. Its discovery hinged on the identification of Marguerite Odalie's godfather, J. B. Colsson, which also explained Marie Eglée Aubry's connection to St. Tammany Parish, located on the other side of Lake Pontchartrain, opposite the city of New Orleans. We unearthed a record which indicated that J.B. Colsson, had been the captain of the schooner *Céléste*, owned by James/Jacques Lorreins:

138. CELESTE, schooner, of Bayou St. John. Built at Tchefuncta (now Madisonville), 1811. 30 4/85 tons; 50 ft. 8 in. x 14 ft. 8 in. x 4 ft.8 in. One deck, two masts, square stern. Previously enrolled, No. 5, May 15, 1812, at New Orleans (document missing). Registered, No. 52, Dec. 1, 1813. Owner: James Lorreins, Tchefuncta (now Madisonville). Master: Daniel Edwards, Tchefuncta (now Madisonville). Registered, No. 7, May 25, 1814. Owners: James Dreux, James Lorreins, merchants, Tchefuncta (now Madisonville). Master: John Albarago. Registered, No. 24, Sept. 10, 1814. Owners: Francois Dreux, New Orleans; James Lorreins, Tchefuncta (now Madisonville). Master: John B. Colsson.[20]

Members of the Lorreins family were early immigrants to Mobile, Louisiana Territory, and were often listed with the "dit" name Tarascon. The owner of the *Celeste* James/Jacques Lorreins's grandfather, also Jacques Lorreins, was probably born on 12 December 1700 at Tarascon, Parish Sainte Marthe, Bouches-du-Rhône, France to Abauly (?) Lourrains, a shoemaker and his wife, Jeanne Roman. French baptismal records are notoriously difficult to read. We looked at almost one thousand records at Tarascon, and the nearby towns of Avignon and St. Didier, and found very few records for "Lorreins" or a variant thereof, and only one for Jacques Lorreins which read: "L'an que dessus [1700] 12 décembre a été baptisé Jacques Lourrains, fils de Abauly Lourains, cordonnier et Jeanne Roman mariés, étant nay [né] dejourd'hui, son parrain Jacques Ayminy/Aiminy, menager, sa marraine Claire Roman sa tante fait par moy soussigné avec le pere et parrain." (In the above year 12 December was baptized Jacques Lourrains son of Abauly Lourains, shoemaker and Jeanne Roman married being born today his godfather Jacques Ayminy home owner his godmother, Claire Roman his aunt done by me the undersigned with the father and godfather)

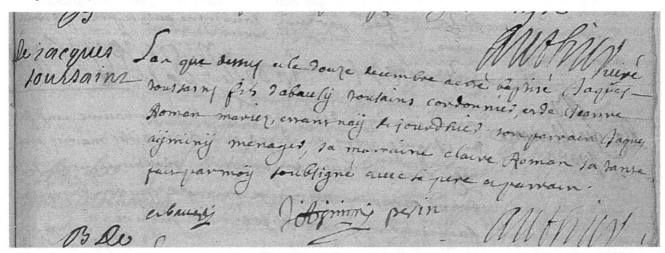

Tarascon, Bouches-du-Rhône France, Registres paroissiaux et d'état civil [Civil and Parish Registrations], Baptême [Baptisms] 1700, Sainte Marthe, not numbered for Jacques Lourrains, digital image, *Archives départementales des Bouches-du-Rhône*, "État Civil en ligne, "http://www.archives 13.fr/archives13/CG13/ : accessed 7/30/2019), Image 51/ 54.

Jacques Lorreins dit Tarascon married Marie Avril de Tourigny and they immigrated to Fort Condé de la Mobile, Louisiana Territory, where their four children were born, the earliest probably being Charles Lorreins dit Tarascon on 29 June 1727. His baptismal record translated from the French reads:

---

[20] Survey of Federal Archives, *Ships Registers and Enrollments of New Orleans, Louisiana/ prepared by the Survey of Federal Archives in Louisiana, Division of community services programs, Work projects administration,* Volume 1, 1804-1820, Baton Rouge, LA: Louisiana State University, 1941, 21. Available at https://catalog.hathitrust.org/Record/000968981, Image 81/398.

#492 - Pierre Charles Lorins -On Thursday 3 July 1727, I, Missionary Priest of the Company of Jesus in my function as Curé at Fort Condé of Mobile in the absence of the Rev. Father Mathias, have baptized with the ordinary ceremonies of the Church Pierre Charles Lorins, son of Jacques Lorins and Marie Avril, born on 29 June 1727 of legitimate marriage. Godparents were Charles Bouguiet, soldier in Mr. Marchand's Company and Marie Le Mire, who gave him the name of Pierre Charles. In faith of which I have signed on the same day and year as above. S. Fontanille, Vautier, Bruguiet, Lorreins, Marie Le Mire, Father Le Petit, S.J. Curé.[21]

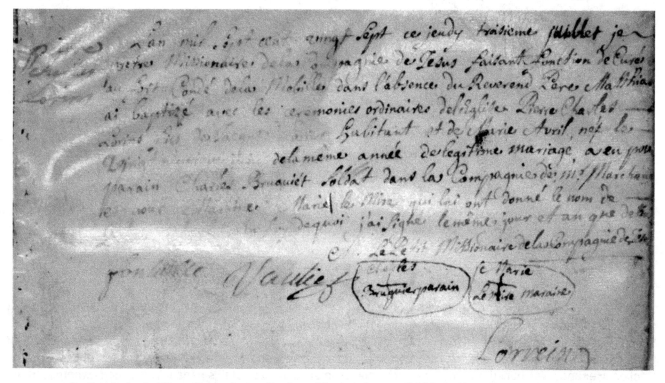

Baptismal record of Pierre Charles Lorins. Courtesy of the Archdiocese of Mobile Archives, Karen Horton, Archivist.

Although the priest spelled the name "Lorins," it is clear from this record that the father signed "Lorreins." Neither godparent, however was literate, as both signed with an "x."

Charles Lorreins's sister, Marie Pelagie Lorreins, later the wife of Jean-Baptiste Brazilier was born on 13 April 1729 and her baptismal record translated from the French reads:

#574 – Marie Pelagie Lorinze – On 24 April 1729, I, a Capuchin Apostolic Missionary Priest, in my function as Curé to Fort Condé of Mobile, baptized a girl born on 13 April 1729 of legitimate marriage between Jacques Lorinze, resident, and Marie Avril, her parents. Godparents were Joseph Boisier de Tremoulet, Jr., in Mr. Marchand's Company, and Andrée Guillette, wife of Mr. Bourbon, who gave her the name of Marie Pelagie. They signed with me on the day and year as before. S[ponsors]. Joseph Boissy de Tremoulet, Andrée Guillette, Father Mathias, Curé.[22]

A copy of the original baptism record may be seen on the next page:

---

[21] Ann Calagaz, Ed., *Sacramental Records of the Roman Catholic Church of the Archdiocese of Mobile, Vol. 1, Section 1, 1704-1739* (Mobile, AL: Archdiocese of Mobile, 2001), 185.
[22] Calagaz, ed., Sacramental records, 228.

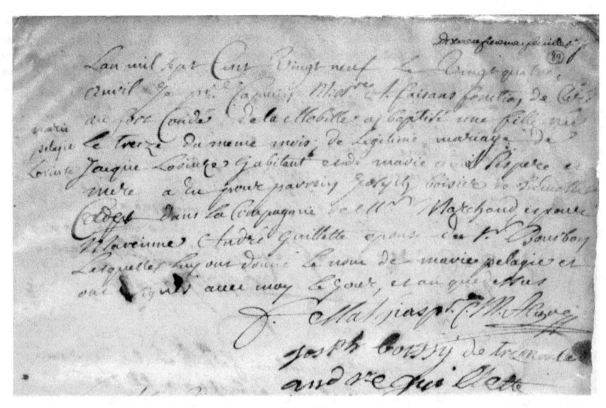

Baptismal record of Marie Pelagie Lorinze. Courtesy of the Archdiocese of Mobile Archives, Karen Horton, Archivist.

Two more children, Elizabeth (b. ca. 1723), later the wife of Jean-Baptiste Gauthreau and Jacques in ca.1734,[23] had been born to the couple before the death of Marie Avril de Tourigny, their mother, on 23 June 1738: "Deceased in this parish of St. Pierre of Mobile, Diocese of Quebec, Marie Avril de Tourigny, of the Diocese of Sens?, wife of Jacques Laurens dit Tarascon, after having confessed and receiving the Sacrament of Extreme Unction. Her body was buried with the usual ceremonies in the cemetery of this parish, in testimony wherein I have signed. Frère Agnan of Chaumont in Bassigny, Apostolic and Royal missionary pastor of Mobile."[24] Members of the Lorreins family began their move from Mobile ca. 1750 when Charles Lorreins dit Tarascon married Marie Louise Girardy, daughter of Joseph Girardy, one of the first residents of Bayou St. John, and his wife Marie Jeanne Henry. Before Mobile had been ceded to the British in 1763, after the signing of the Treaty of Paris which ended the French and Indian War, the entire Lorreins family had resettled either at Bayou St. John, New Orleans, or across Lake Pontchartrain in St. Tammany Parish.

Jacques Lorreins dit Tarascon (b. 1732-34?) married Marie Louise Baudin/Bodin dit Miragouin, ca. 1755 in Louisiana. Marie Louise was born in Mobile ca. 1734 to Nicolas Baudin dit Miragouin, a native of Tours, Indre-et-Loire, France, and his wife, Françoise Paillet, born at Lorient, Morbihan, France. Jacques and Marie Louise Baudin's son, Jacques Baptiste Lorreins dit Tarascon, was born on 23 January 1774. His baptismal certificate recorded at St. Louis Cathedral reads: "Laurreins, Jacques Baptiste (Jacques, surnamed Tarascon, and Marie Louise Baudin) b. April 23, 1774, bn. January 23, 1774, s. Jean Baptiste Brasilliez (@Brasillier) and Madeleine Brasilier (@ Brasillier) sp. Depre (SLC B7, 38)." On 15 November 1771, four years before Jacques Baptiste's birth, his father called "Santiago Lorreins" in Spanish Louisiana, had bought a tract of land on Bayou St. John from the de Kernion

---

[23] There is an entry in Calagaz, ed. *Sacramental Records*, p. 297, which gives the birth of a "girl" (une fille, née) born on 27 August 1734 and baptized on 12 November 1734 to Jacques Laurenson [*sic*] and Marie Avril, "his" parents, who was named "François." Godparents: François Renaud and Françoise Huet. Is this the child later called "Jacques?". There are signatures for Elizabeth Lorreins his elder sister, Françoise Huet, Lorrein, Petit and Father Victorin Dupui, Curé. The original record is much too faint to be reproduced here. Because of the document's condition, the possible confusion about the sex of the child being baptized, and to make matters worse, the godparents first names being "François" and "Françoise," we cannot be sure which godparent gave the child its name. There is no baptismal record for Elizabeth, probably their first-born child.

[24] Jacqueline Olivier Vidrine, *Love's Legacy: The Mobile Marriages Recorded in French, Transcribed with Annotated Abstracts in English, 1724-1786* (Lafayette, LA: University of Southwestern Louisiana, 1985), 166,167.

family, which extended 22 arpents[25] along the bayou by a depth of 40 arpents. At his death on 29 June 1784 he had two large tracts of land which were divided amongst his children: Françoise Lorreins, the wife of Jean Louis Allard; Pelagie Lorreins (b. 1762) later the wife of Pierre de Juzan, and Jacques Baptiste Lorreins. The elder Lorreins's land on Bayou St. John was described by Samuel Wilson in his book *The Pitot House on Bayou St. John.* The first section had a frontage on the bayou of 20 arpents which contained a four-room house with a gallery, a separate kitchen, a store room, six slave cabins, and an additional house nearby in bad condition. Wilson concluded that the new house was the one built by Lorreins, and the old house was the original de Kernion dwelling. Lorreins owned another farm which extended eight arpents on Bayou St. John, with a large house and a new storeroom. Both properties were planted with fruit trees.[26]

Jacques Baptiste Lorreins, took his almost four-thousand-peso inheritance from his father and eventually settled across Lake Pontchartrain at present-day Madisonville, St. Tammany Parish. During his life J.B. Lorreins acquired two large plots of land: a 2657 arpent tract on the east side of the Tchefuncte River in Madisonville (formerly called Houltonville) where he settled in 1804, and whose claim was upheld in his favor by the United States Land Office in 1814 by right of possession, to the detriment of Charles Parent, Sr., another claimant. Lorreins owned a large brickyard on his property. The Lorreins's plantation encompassed what is today the Fairview-Riverside State Park and part of the Deloaks and Beau Chêne subdivisions.[27] Lorreins also owned 640 acres on the Bogue Falaya River in Covington, St. Tammany Parish.[28] The 1812 Saint Tammany Parish Tax Roll, made by Benjamin A. Hickborn, listed 355 tax payers, with 322 men, 239 women and 835 children as well as 301 slaves in the parish. Amongst the most influential citizens was "John Lorance" (aka Jacques Baptiste Lorreins) who owned 16 slaves, a schooner, and 1000 head of cattle.[29]

Jacques Baptiste Lorreins married Marguerite Louise Urseaux de Livois (b. 1764 at Mobile, Louisiana Territory) ca. 1796. Their children, however, were all born in New Orleans and baptized at St. Louis Cathedral. His eldest, Louis Hilaire, father of Marguerite Odalie Lorreins, was born on 16 July 1797: "Laurrains [@Laurreins] Luis Hilario (Santiago Bautista and Margarita Luisa Urseaux De Livois, natives of this parish), b. Jan. 6, 1798, bn. Jul. 16,1798 [*sic* -1797], pgp. Santiago Laurrains and Maria Luisa Baudin, mgp. Guillermo Santiago Urseaux De Livois and Henriqueta De St. Agnette De Livois, s. Luis Hilario Boutte and Felicitas Allard (SLC, B14, 53)." Four other children followed: Pierre Albert on 9 September 1798 (SLC, B14, 112), Susana Delfina on 24 April 1800 (SLC, B24, 127), Vincent Théodule on 20 August 1801 (SLC, B17, 30), and Henriette Coralie born ca. 1803 and baptized on 30 January 1804 (SLC, B17, 42).

Jacques Baptiste Lorreins's wife died in New Orleans and was interred in the St. Louis Parish Cemetery on 25 October 1804. (SLC, F6, 43) After her demise, Jacques Baptiste moved permanently to his land in St. Tammany Parish, where he was a merchant, owner of the schooner *Céleste*, a large brick yard and a farm. In 1816 he contracted a marriage with Marguerite Edwards, daughter of Morgan Edwards, the first sheriff of St. Tammany Parish, and his wife, Marguerite Smith. Marguerite had been married to Samuel Simms in 1805, but was separated from him. Marguerite Edwards Lorreins's birth record is worth a look because of the difficulty the Spanish priest had with Anglo-Saxon names. It appears that Morgan Edwards may have been "Morgan Edward Hewett" or some variant thereof: "Heruet Smitte [@Heruet Smitt] Margarita (Morgon Eduardo, native of Ireland, Protestant, and Margarita Smitte, native of Nueva Llorca [New York], Protestant), b. Apr. 5, 1793, bn. Jul. 30, 1789, pgp. David Heruet and Margarita Bradle, natives of Dublin in Ireland, mgp. Mauricio Smitte and Maria Smitte, natives of Nueva Llorca, s. Andrés Almonester Y Roxas, absent, p. Joseph Capitillo, and Maria Irene Luisa Goffigon (SLC, B 11, 254)." Lorreins and Marguerite Edwards had one child, Marguerite Delphine, born on 9 July 1809 and baptized at St. Louis Cathedral on 7 February 1818. Some say Jacques Baptiste Lorreins died on 25 November 1819. Other genealogists state that he died in 1818. We know with certainty, however, that he was present at the baptism of his daughter, Marguerite Delphine Lorreins at St. Mary's Church on Chartres Street, New Orleans, on 7 February 1818. Delphine, however, died the same year. After the death of Jacques Baptiste Lorreins, Louis Hilaire was named

---

[25] An arpent is equal to about 0.84628 acres.
[26] Samuel Wilson, Jr., *The Pitot House on Bayou St. John* (Gretna, LA: Pelican Publishing Co., 1992), 6,7.
[27] Ethel Haas Boagni, *Madisonville, Louisiana* (Mandeville LA: St. Tammany Parish Historical Society, 1980), 14, 88 (Note: In this book J.B. Lorreins's name is spelled "Jacque Lorance."
[28] Robin L. Perkins, Director of Records Management – St. Tammany Parish Courthouse, St. Tammany Parish, LA, "Flou (Flot), Lorreins, Marchand connection in St Tammany" Typescript available at St. Tammany Parish Courthouse.
[29] Frederick S. Ellis, *St. Tammany Parish L'Autre Côté du Lac* (Gretna, LA: Pelican Publishing Co, 1981), 86-87.

curator for his younger siblings, Albert, Théodule and Coralie Lorreins with his paternal aunt, Pelagie Lorreins Juzan, acting as surety for him in 1819. He was released from his obligation in 1825, when all his siblings reached their majority. Louis partnered with his brother, Théodule, in the ownership of the schooner *Calypso* in 1825, with Jean Baptiste Frédéric Colsson's half-brother Pierre Rodolphe as its skipper:

> 156. CALYPSO, schooner, of Covington. Built on Tchefuncta River, St. Tammany Parish, 1825. 20 42/95 tons; 46 ft. 7 in. x'14 ft. 1O in. x 3 ft. 8 in. One deck, two masts, square stern, plain head. Previously Enrolled, No. 76, Aug. 10, 1833, having been altered in dimensions. Owners: Louis Lorreins, Theodore [*sic*] Lorreins, St. Tammany Parish. Master Peter R. Colsson."[30]

It is necessary to examine the relationships within the Colsson family and their similarities to the Lorreins, father and sons, to understand the family dynamics at play. Jean-Baptiste Frédéric Colsson, master of Jacques Baptiste Lorreins's schooner the *Céleste*, was born in the French West Indies and baptized later at St. Louis Cathedral: "Colsson, Jean-Baptiste Frederick, son of Pierre and Marie Dubourg) b. 1 Oct 1790, bn. Sept 25, 1788, s. Juan Bautista Labatut and Maria St. Martin (SLC, B11, 109)." The printed copy does not reveal all that was actually written in the original record. Colsson was baptized as the "hijo natural" or "illegitimate son" of Pierre Colsson and Marie Dubourg. In discussing the early arrival of some emigrants from Saint-Domingue, Gabriel Debien and René LeGardeur's article "The Saint-Domingue refugees in Louisiana, 1792-1804," published in the Brasseaux and Conrad anthology, *The Road to Louisiana: The Saint-Domingue Refugees, 1792-1809*, wrote: "Nor was Jean-Baptiste-Frédéric Colson, son of Pierre and of Marie Dubourg, born at Port-au-Prince on September 25, 1788, and baptized in New Orleans on October 1, 1790, a part of this group. He was not able to come with his parents before early 1790."[31] We wonder if he did come with both parents, as we were unable to find a death record for his mother in the St. Louis Cathedral records. Did Pierre Colsson leave Marie Dubourg behind to emigrate with his son? It is clear from the baptismal record that his parents were not legally married. Was Marie Dubourg perhaps, a free woman of color who died in Saint-Domingue? It remains, however, that Pierre Colsson's son was always classified as "white." By examining the original record, it can be seen that the baptism was added out of order at the very bottom of the page in minuscule handwriting, the record of Fr. Luis Guigues, inserted amongst others written by Fr. Ignacio de Olot. There are, in addition, two marginal notes, one indicating that the baptism was "found in loose papers" belonging to Fr. Guigues, the other stating that Colsson died on 17 April 1835.

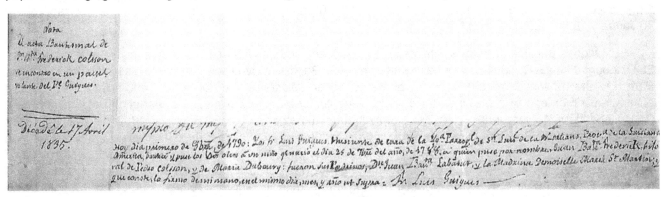

Baptismal record for Jean-Baptiste Frederick Colsson. Archives of the Archdiocese of New Orleans, Saint Louis Cathedral Records Vol. 2 , p. 109 No number (Courtesy of Emilie Leumas, Archivist – Kimberly Johnson and Katie Vest – Researching Archivists.) Note: the word "natural" started on line 2, and continued as "ral", on line 3 but was cut off due to the length of the line.

Jean-Baptiste Frédéric Colsson's father, Pierre married at New Orleans on 7 January 1797: "Colsson, Pedro (Juan and Ana De Marionis), native city of Bordeaux in France m. Genoveba Chouriac, Jan. 7, 1797, w. Juan Bautista Labattut, Juan Bautista Delonde, Juan Bautista Serpy (SLC, M5, 111)." It is implied that this was the first marriage for both the bride and groom in the absence of the designation of "widow" or "widower" for either of them

---

[30] Survey of Federal Archives, *Ships Registers and Enrollments of New Orleans, Louisiana/ prepared by the Survey of Federal Archives in Louisiana, Division of community services programs, Work projects administration,* Volume 3, 1831-1840, Baton Rouge, LA: Louisiana State University, 1941, 32. Available at https://catalog.hathitrust.org/Record/000968981, Image 74/346.

[31] Carl A. Brasseaux and Glenn R. Conrad, eds., *The Road to Louisiana: The Saint-Domingue Refugees, 1792-1809* (Lafayette, LA: University of Louisiana at Lafayette Press, 1992), 141.

in the original record written by Fr. Antonio de Sedella. They were the parents of five children: Marie Thérèse Minette (born as "Genoveba" on 11 October 1798 (SLC, B14, 84), and referred to in Pierre Colsson's last will and testament as his eldest daughter, Marie), Pedro Rodulpho (b. 5 July 1801, SLC, B14, 172), Henrrique Pedro (b. 21 May 1807, SLC, B20, 183), Juan Bautista Zenon (b. 3 August 1809, SLC, B22, 65), and Genoveba Hanrrietta (b. 4 April 1812, SLC, B25, 27). Jean-Baptiste Frédéric's five half-siblings would later play an interesting role in his succession record after his death.

Both Louis Hilaire Lorreins and Jean-Baptiste Frédéric Colsson would father children with free women of color before their early deaths. Both men, as had their fathers, been residents of St. Tammany Parish as well as New Orleans. Jean-Baptiste Frédéric's father Pierre Colsson died on 22 November 1814 "on the other side of Lake Pontchartrain, his corpse was embalmed and brought to this capital and buried in the parish cemetery on Nov. 26 (SLC F 7, 280)." Earlier in that year, on 8 July 1814, he had prepared his will wherein he left his estate to his wife, Geneviève Chouriac and his five legitimate children. He also left to "Frederick Colsson" the sum of 500 piastres, without mentioning any relationship to him.[32] The elder Colsson had died on the eve of the Battle of New Orleans which began on 8 January 1815. The entire city had been in turmoil, and was preparing for a British invasion from the Gulf of Mexico. It is not surprising to find that his son, Jean-Baptiste Frédéric Colsson, at the behest of Governor William C.C. Claiborne, helped to form a battalion of marines composed of three companies of French sailors consisting of 210 men. The third company of fifty men was commanded by Captain J.B. Colsson. They were stationed at Plaquemine from 17 December 1814 until 13 March 1815 at the conclusion of the fighting. We can assume that Colsson was in command of Jacques-Baptiste Lorreins's schooner, *Céleste* which had been registered at New Orleans on 10 September 1814.[33]

Jean-Baptiste Frédéric Colsson had been living with Marguerite Doubrère, a free woman of color, in New Orleans, when they both stood as godparents for Louis Hilaire Lorreins and Eglée Aubry's first child: "Lorrence, Marguerite (Louis and Egle Oubry, both natives and residents of this city), b. Feb. 21, 1824, bn. Nov. 1, 1822, in New Orleans sponsors: J.B. Colson and Marguerite Doubraire (SLC, B34, 97, See photo p. 13)." Marguerite Odalie Lorreins/Lorrains/Lorrence would be the only surviving child of Louis Hilaire Lorreins and Eglé Aubry. The couple would have a son, Gustave Joseph Lorrins [sic] born on 10 June 1833 who died on 4 June 1834.

Gustave Joseph Lorrins, baptized on 18 September 1833, natural son of Mr. Louis Lorrins of St. Tammany Parish and Marie Eglé Aubry of this parish, born on 10 June 1833. Godfather: Joseph St. Hubert. Godmother: Julie Latrobe. (Eglé Aubry's niece), Archives of the Archdiocese of New Orleans, Saint Louis Cathedral Records Vol. 23 S/FPC, p. 314, #2075 (Courtesy of Emilie Leumas, Archivist – Kimberly Johnson and Katie Vest – Researching Archivists.) Note: Godparents Joseph St. Hubert and Anne Julia Latrobe were married in 1833 -See Chapter 19.

---

[32] "Louisiana, Orleans Parish Will Books, 1805-1920," [database with]images, *FamilySearch.org* (https://familysearch.org/ark:/61903/3:1:3QS7-89MY-581?cc=2019728&wc=SJ76 -W36%3A341294101 : accessed 11/4/2019), Will book 1815-1817, Vol 2, image 172 of 271 – Pierre Colsson; City Archives & Special Collections, New Orleans Public Library, New Orleans.

[33] "Un Foreign Frenchmen, "A l'éditeur du Courrier (Letter to the Editor)", *Courrier de la Louisiane*, Friday August 16, 1822, digital image, *Genealogybank.com* (https:www.genealogybank.com: accessed 3 August 2019), p. 1, col. 5.

Death of Gustave Lorreins, free colored child born in this parish, age one year, natural son of the late Mr. Lorreins and of Eglée Aubry, free woman of color, buried in the cemetery of the Parochial Cathedral of New Orleans, on 4 June 1834, having died the day before at 4:00 P.M. Archives of the Archdiocese of New Orleans, Saint Louis Cathedral Records Vol. 10,S/FPC, p. 315, #2125. (Courtesy of Emilie Leumas, Archivist – Kimberly Johnson and Katie Vest – Researching Archivists.)

Jean-Baptiste Frédéric Colsson and Marguerite Doubraire/Doubrere were already the parents of a daughter, Marie Emma: "Colsson, Marie Emma (Jean-Baptiste and Marguerite Doubrere, both natives of Santo Domingo, residents of this parish), b. June 25, 1825, bn. May 27, 1825 in New Orleans, s. Jean Baptiste Felix Doubrere, child's maternal grandfather and Marie Joseph Foigon [sic Foison], child's maternal grandmother (SLC, B35, 86)." Another child, Edward Volmar Colsson had been born on 28 December 1826 to the couple but died before 1831. Ever wary of Louisiana inheritance laws, the couple went before notary Theodore Seghers on 28 December 1831 to recognize Marie Emma as their child and to allow her to use the father's surname. Jean-Baptiste Frédéric Colsson, through Marguerite and their daughter Emma, was linked to the family of Jean Baptiste Félix Doubrere, a white immigrant to New Orleans from Saint-Domingue, and to his wife Marie Joseph Foison, a free woman of color, throughout life and into death. J.B. F. Doubrere died in 1828. His death record states that his father, Felix Doubrere, was a deceased ship's surgeon, and his mother was Marie Rousin, both from Nantes, Loire-Atlantique, France, where their son had been born on 29 August 1770. Jean-Baptiste Félix Doubrère was interred on 11 February 1828, having died, a bachelor, the previous day. (SLC, F 14, 249). In his will dated 10 February 1828, Doubrere indicated that had never been married, but had lived with Marie Joseph Foison, a free woman of color, with whom he had six children: Pierre Félix, Marguerite, Elizabeth, Mathilde, Françoise Eléonore, and Marie Françoise (alias Aurore). He appointed Jean-Baptiste Frédéric Colsson, companion of his daughter, Marguerite, as his testamentary executor to look after his estate which consisted only of his inheritance in France from his late father, as well as any monies to which he might be entitled from the indemnities accorded the French colonists for properties belonging to him seized during the Haitian Revolution. He wrote: "Je donne et lègue tout ce que je possède à ladite Marie Joseph Foison et à ma petite famille. (I give and bequeath all that I possess to Marie Joseph Foison and to my little family)"[34]

Seven years later, on 17 April 1835, Jean-Baptiste Frédéric Colsson followed him to the grave, dying on Rue Orléans between Burgundy and Rampart Streets, leaving his estate to his daughter Marie Emma Colsson. There are over fifty pages in his succession. At the beginning, his half-siblings, Minette, Charles Zenon, Pierre Rudolphe, Henry and Geneviève Henriette Colsson asked to be put into possession of his estate so that they might give it to his ten-year-old daughter, Marie Emma Colsson, as had been his wish. Further along in the process they signed a statement indicating that they were not entitled to his estate because Jean-Baptiste Frédéric was the natural son of their father and another woman. Pierre Claude Samory, Marguerite Doubrere's sister Françoise Eléonore's husband, was designated as tutor to Marie Emma, a position relinquished to him by the child's mother, Marguerite Doubrère. Colsson's estate included 18 plots of ground in Faubourg Washington, seven slaves, five of

[34]"Louisiana, Orleans Parish Will Books, 1805-1920," digital images, FamilySearch.org (https://familysearch.org/ark:/61903/3:1:3QSQ-G9MY-PYMX?cc=2019728&wc=SJ76-W3D%3A341294301 : accessed 11/4/2019), Will book 1824-1833, Vol 4, Image 190 of 511; City Archives & Special Collections, New Orleans Public Library, New Orleans.

whom had already been donated to Marie Emma by her mother, and a house in the faubourg Marigny fronting sixty feet on Grandshommes (Greatmen St.), with 100 foot of frontage on Français (Frenchmen St.). After all debts were paid, the child inherited almost 3000 piastres which was paid out over the years to her tutors for her education and upkeep. Members of the Jean-Baptiste Frédéric Colsson family were interred in St. Louis Cemetery #2, the resting place of many free people of color in a large free-standing tomb: J.B. Colsson (no date), J.B.F. Doubrere (Marguerite's father), M. Joseph Doubrere (aka Marie Joseph Foison, Marguerite's mother who died 9 September 1854), Marie L. Leblanc (aged 18 months, a child of Marie Emma and her husband Alfred Leblanc), Marguerite Doubrere,(Marie Emma's mother), and M. Emma Leblanc, née Colsson, (Marie Emma, wife of Alfred Leblanc with who she had three other children: Aimée born 1857, Eugene, born 1859 and Frederick, born 1861). Marie Emma died on 6 September 1863. Lise (Elizabeth) Doubrere (Marguerite's sister, aged 80 years, born about 1803, who died on 6 February 1883) was also interred there. Below is a photo of the Colsson-Doubrere family tomb in St. Louis Cemetery #2. At the top of the monument is a characteristic flower carving from the chisel of Prosper Florville Foy, master marble carver, and son of René Prosper Foy and Zélie Aubry, Eglée Aubry's sister.

Louis Hilaire Lorreins's only surviving child with Marie Eglée Aubry, Marguerite Odalie Lorreins could not, however, benefit from a generous father because he died intestate, and apparently suddenly, on 26 November 1833, shortly after having been registered as the owner of the schooner *Calypso*, with his brother Victor Théodule, and just two months after his son, Gustave Joseph had been born in New Orleans to him and to Marie Eglée Aubry.

However, after his father, Jacques Baptiste's death in 1818, and up until his final illness and death, Louis had made his home almost exclusively in St. Tammany Parish. On 10 September 1818 he registered the family's cattle brands at the St. Tammany Parish Courthouse:

"This 10th day of September 1818, Lewis Lorrance deposits the following brands of the family of James Lorrance," in Mark and Brand Book A, pages 7,8, housed at the St. Tammany Parish Justice Center, 701 N. Columbia Street, Covington, LA 70433, courtesy of Robin L. Perkins, Director of Records Management – St. Tammany Parish Courthouse, St. Tammany Parish, LA. Note: A brand had evidently been registered for Susana Delphine, Lorreins, Louis Hilaire Lorreins's half-sister, daughter of his father and Marguerite Edwards. Delphine may have died only months or even days later.

On 24 January 1820, Louis had purchased 640 acres on the Bogue Falaya River in Covington from his father's estate where he raised cattle and farmed. He also engaged in a mercantile business using the schooner *Calypso* by means of which he delivered meat and other produce to the city of New Orleans. Below is a section of the document which memorialized the sale of the 640 arpents of land on the Bogue Falaya, which his father had owned for about ten years and a half, and had operated as a cattle ranch (vacherie), as well as the sale of the slave, Baptiste, aged about thirty years, a fine domestic as well as ploughman for 1300 piastres. The land was his for 400 piastres, for a total of 1700 piastres which he pledged to pay as soon as his father's estate was liquidated.

NARC, Estate of Jacques Lorreins to Louis H. Lorreins, Sale of land and slave, Michel de Armas dated 24 January 1820, Volume 19, Act #23. Courtesy Hon. Chelsey Richard Napoleon, Clerk of Civil District Court, Parish of Orleans. (See his signature, p. 13)

Louis Hilaire Lorreins remained in business in St. Tammany Parish until his premature death, however he was not always successful. On 29 May 1828 Louis was sued by John Powell for allegedly having failed to pay

$11.25 for the killing of forty-five "beeves at 25 cents per beef" at the former's butcher stall and block in Covington. A trial was held at which time it was discovered that no more than 20 cattle had been dispatched, and further that Louis Lorreins had offered to pay for their slaughter, which was rejected by the plaintiff. The Justice of the Peace, H. T. Tyson, ruled that Lorreins owed Powell five dollars, but that Powell would pay the cost of the suit. Powell appealed the verdict, which was overturned in the Parish Court with regards to the costs. Lorreins was ordered to pay Powell the $5.00 along with costs in both courts.[35]

Lorreins, age 33 years, was enumerated in the 1830 federal census for St. Tammany Parish living with one other white male aged 20-29, one white female aged 60-69 (perhaps his aunt, Pelagie Lorreins Juzan); three free colored females, one 24-35, and two aged 36-54, as well as a free colored man aged 55-100. Fifteen slaves were also counted in this census including eleven males and four females.[36] On 3 September 1833 Louis, facing considerable debt, was forced to mortgage the 640 acres to the Union Bank of Louisiana. The land was the same as had been described in his purchase of it on 24 January 1820, to wit: bounded on the west by the Bogue Falia, on the north by John Nelder, and on the south and west by Penns and Parent. Also included in the mortgage were the following slaves: Frank, aged about 45, Eulalie, about age 45, Charlotte a griffe about 11 years old, Marcel, a mulatto boy, age 9, Baptiste aged about 40, and Pierre aged about 20. He received $5,000 and was to pay 10% interest on the loan which was due on 3 September 1834. It was left to Louis Lorreins' heirs to sort out the financial difficulties after his death only a few months later in New Orleans.

"Mr. Louis Lorreins died on 26 November 1833 in the city of New Orleans at Dr. Chauveau's residence at 2:00 P.M. He was about 36 years old, a native of this parish, a bachelor and legitimate son of the late Mr. Jacques Lorreins and the late Mrs. Marguerite [Urseau de Livois]. His body was buried near Covingtown (sic), Parish of St. Tammany in the state of Louisiana." Archives of the Archdiocese of New Orleans, Saint Louis Cathedral Records Vol. 1833-1836, p. 48, #375. (Courtesy of Emilie Leumas, Archivist – Kimberly Johnson and Katie Vest – Researching Archivists.)

Louis Lorreins had apparently, unlike his friend Jean-Baptiste Frédéric Colsson, never attempted to take any legal steps to protect his eleven-year-old daughter, Marguerite Odalie, or his baby son, Gustave Joseph. In a document dated 5 September 1834, Albert Lorreins, Theodule Lorreins, and Coralie Lorreins, wife of Omer Gusman affirmed that Louis had died leaving no ascendants or descendants, and that they were his only heirs. After initially asking for time to try to pay down the debt, they acquiesced a month later to the seizure and sale of the land and slaves, after having paid the bank only $600. The land was then sold on 31 October 1834 to Louis Lorreins's aunt, Pelagie Lorreins, the widow of Pierre Juzan for $4,375.

---

[35] Justice Court #13, John Powell vs. Louis Lorreins dated 29 May 1828 and Appeal Case #275: John Powel, Appellant vs. Louis Lorreins, Appellee, transcript filed 7 July 1828. St. Tammany Parish Justice Center, Covington, LA.

[36] 1830 United States Federal Census, St Tammany Parish, Louisiana, Louis Lorreins household, digital image, *Ancestry.com* (https://www.ancestry.com: accessed 3/20/2019), Series: *M19*; Roll: *43*; Page: *71*, citing Family History Library Film: *0009686*, No date of enumeration, Image 11/22.

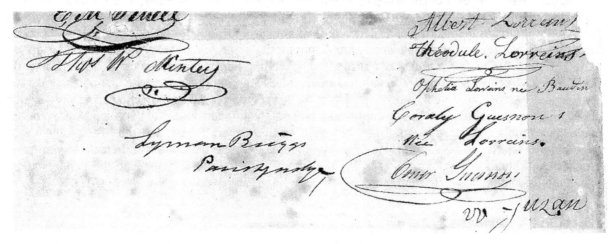

Excerpt from "Sale of property, Heirs of Louis Lorreins to Pelagie Lorreins Juzan," dated 31 October 1834 in *Lyman Briggs Papers #2517*, St. Tammany Parish Justice Center, Covington, LA. Documents courtesy of Robin L.. Perkins, Director of Records Management.

Signatures from document above: Albert Lorreins, Théodule Lorreins, his wife Ophelia Baudin, Coraly Lorreins, and her husband, Omer Guesnon, and the Widow (Vv.) Juzan.

Before Louis Lorreins death, Eglée Aubry had had another child, Françoise Obry, born on 23 March 1829 in New Orleans and baptized on 15 August of the same year. The father was listed as "unknown." Had this been

Louis Lorreins's child, we believe that he probably would have recognized her as he had done with Marguerite Odalie and Gustave Joseph.

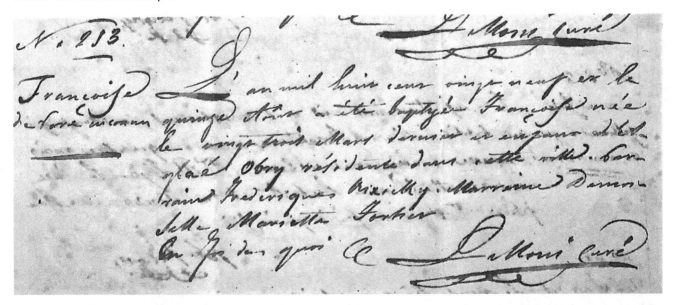

On 15 August 1829 the Rev. L. Moni baptized Françoise born on 23 March 1829 to Aglaé (one of the few times we see this spelling) Obry a native of this city. The godfather is Frédérique Rixicky and the godmother Miss. Marietta Fortier. In the margin was written "Françoise de père inconnu" (Françoise from an unknown father). Archives of the Archdiocese of New Orleans, Saint Louis Cathedral Records Vol. 22 S/FPC, p. 39, #213. (Courtesy of Emilie Leumas, Archivist – Kimberly Johnson and Katie Vest – Researching Archivists.)

We could find no more information on Françoise, and believe that she probably died when quite young.

One would have thought that Eglée Aubry's association with the Lorreins family would have ended with Louis Hilaire's death, but perhaps it did not. Just as the Lorreins family had been early settlers in the Madisonville area of St. Tammany Parish, Aubry and her children would live for extended periods on a small farm in the little town of Madisonville on the Tchefuncte River. While we know that Eglée Aubry, according to her own written testimony, owned property in Madisonville, we also found a puzzling conveyance record, while searching in the St. Tammany Parish Courthouse Archives, dated 22 November 1850, intitled "Mrs. M. Thompson to Mrs. Aglaë Lorreins. Sale of Town Lot." This date was less than two months before Eglée would purchase her farm in Madisonville. The document memorialized the sale by Mrs. Matilda Thompson, wife of Samuel C. Thompson, to "Madame Aglaë Lorreins, a free woman of color, residing in the Parish of St. Tammany," of a town lot (#4 in Square #12) in the Division of St. John, in the town of Covington.[37] The purchaser paid Mrs. Thompson $125 cash for the property. Was the purchaser really Aglaë/Eglée Aubry whom we had never seen referred to as Mrs. Lorreins. Although Aubry always signed for herself when she bought property, the purchaser's signature is nowhere on the document. The signature underneath that of Matilda Thompson and her husband Samuel C. Thompson is that of "Adelaide Fortier." We could find no person in the Lorreins family who had ever used the first name Aglaé, but do know that "Eglée" was probably Aubry's own spelling of the French name "Aglaë," which spelling was used in the above baptismal record for her child Françoise. At least one notary had substituted the spelling "Aglaë" for "Eglée," in an additional document we have found. Eglée, however, always signed "Eglée" or "Eglé." The problem with this document, parts of which can be seen on the following page, is that she did not sign it herself. Moreover, if any money did change hands it was, according to the document, "paid by the purchaser to the vendor out of the presence of the Recorder and witnesses:"

---

[37] See p. 156 for a map of the Division of St. John in Covington where Charles Watkinson and Félicité Flot also had property beginning in 1842. Their daughter, Orelia married Eglée Aubry's son, Rene Achille Chiapella in 1859.

UNITED STATES OF AMERICA.

STATE OF LOUISIANA,
Parish of St. Tammany,

BE IT KNOWN AND REMEMBERED, That on this *Twenty Second* day of *November* in the year of our Lord, one thousand eight hundred and fifty and in the year of the Independence of the United States of America the seventy-*fifth* —

BEFORE ME, *John Say Monteu*. Recorder of the Parish of St. Tammany, State of Louisiana, duly authorised by law to exercise the powers of NOTARY PUBLIC therein; personally came and appeared *Mrs Matilda Thompson. wife of Samuel C. Thompson of this Parish and State, Separate of property and herein authorised and assisted by her said husband in the execution of these presents*

who did declare and say, that for the consideration hereinafter expressed, *She does* by these presents grant, bargain, sell, convey, transfer, assign and set over, with a full guarantee against all troubles, debts, mortgages, claims, evictions, donations, alienations or other incumbrances whatsover, unto *Madame Aglae Lorreins. a free woman of Color, residing in the Parish of St Tammany State aforesaid*

here present accepting and purchasing for *herself her* heirs and assigns, and acknowledging delivery and possession thereof *A certain Lot or parcel of Ground lying & being Situate in the Town of Covington. Parish of St Tammany State of Louisiana with all the Buildings & improvements thereon. and more Particularly described as Lot number "Four", in Square number "Twelve," in the Division of St John of said Town of Covington. being the Same property which this vendor acquired by purchase from Thomas S. Page by act passed before E M Towel late Recorder of this Parish on the twenty Second day of April 1847.*

A. McN. Bain
Joseph Evans

Matildee Thompson
Sam C. Thompson
Adelaide Foster

John S. Montee
Recorder

St. Tammany Parish Courthouse Records (Covington, St. Tammany Parish, LA), *Conveyance Office Book* B-2, p. 452-454, Act. # 156, "Mrs. M. Thompson to Mrs. Aglae Lorreins, Sale of Town Lot," first page, and signatures.

Adelaïde Fortier was the lawful wife of Pierre Albert Lorreins, the younger brother of the late Louis Hilaire Lorreins who was the father of Eglé Aubry's first two children. Did she sign in place of "Aglaë Lorreins," because the Lorreins family had actually paid for the property, or had Adelaïde simply acted as an agent in the deal? Robin L. Perkins, Director of Records Management at the St. Tammany Parish Courthouse was kind enough to try to trace the ownership of Lot #4 in Square 12 from Aglaë Lorreins on down. She found that William C. Morgan sold the lot to William H. Morgan on 8 August 1889 (COB "N," p. 222) and stated that he had acquired the lot at a sale held at the courthouse in Covington by Constable S.B. Staples on 27 October 1877, in the suit of "Town of Covington vs. Heirs of Aglaë Lorreins." A check of Conveyance Office Book "I," pp. 232-233 from 27 October 1877 showed that Morgan had indeed purchased the lot from Staples on a writ of fieri facias, processed through the Justice Court. This document did not name anyone as owner of the lot, in fact it read "unknown owners." [38] Since Eglée Aubry died in 1882, not in 1877, why would the Town of Covington have sued her "heirs?" The identity of "Aglaë Lorreins, a free woman of color," therefore, remains an open question.

Louis Hilaire Lorreins's only surviving child, Marguerite Odalie Lorreins, never had children of her own. She was married late in life to José/Joseph Vila, a native of Catalonia, Spain, who worked in New Orleans as a "caulker" and ships' carpenter. According to his 5 June 1858 naturalization petition, Vila arrived in New Orleans in January 1837 when under the age of 18 years, and lived in both New Orleans and Madisonville, St. Tammany Parish, LA. [39] Joseph Vila was enumerated in the United States Federal Census for 1840 living in Ward 1, with another male slightly older than himself. [40] He soon began a relationship with a free African American woman, Jeanne Rose, with whom he had at least six children within ten years: Joseph, born 5 December 1841; Louise, born 19 September 1843; Marie Joseph, born 5 March 1846; Zulma, born 10 December 1847; Clemence, born 23 November 1849; and Ernest, born 22 December 1851. [41] He was enumerated with Jeanne Rose in the 1850 federal census as a white male "caulker" from Spain, with Jeanne, the latter's mother, Henriette Rose, a blind, forty-five-year-old African American, and their first five children, who were designated as "mulatto." [42]

He met Odalie Lorreins in the early 1850s and moved in with her, her mother, Eglée Aubry, and Eglée's three sons with the New Orleans notary, Achille Chiapella. Not only do they appear all together in the 1860 United States Federal Census for New Orleans, but we also know that Joseph Vila claimed in his 1858 petition for naturalization that he also lived in Madisonville, St. Tammany Parish, LA, most likely at Eglée Aubry's Madisonville farm where she and her family spent a good deal of time. It is probable that he worked at one of the shipyards along the Tchefuncte River in Madisonville to make money for the family. Jeanne Rose, on the other hand, was enumerated in the 1860 federal census in the Seventh Ward, New Orleans, where her six children by Joseph Vila were recorded with the surname "Bellard." They were living together with Jean Mesnard, a tailor, and his mixed-race wife, Andries. [43]

Joseph Vila, aged 53, "the son of Joseph Vila and Catherine Angeli, a native of Spain" married "Marguerite O. Lorrains, aged 43, the daughter of ___ Lorrains and Aglae Aubrie" in New Orleans on 27 October 1870, at a time

[38] Robin L. Perkins, Director of Records Management, St. Tammany Parish Courthouse, Covington, St. Tammany Parish, LA, to the author in email dated 30 December 2019. This lot is the site of the Mattina Bella restaurant located on 421 East Gibson Street in Covington.

[39] "Louisiana Naturalization Records, 1836-1998," digital image, *Ancestry.com* (https://www.ancestry.com: accessed 6/18/2019), citing NARA - Southeast Region, Atlanta, GA; *Orders Admitting Aliens to Citizenship, compiled 03/1836 - 03/1903*; Series Number: *4499444*; Record Group Title: *Records of District Courts of the United States*; Record Group Number: *21,* Petition #262 dated 5 June 1858, Image 298/530.

[40] 1840 United States Federal Census, Orleans Parish, LA, Ward 1, Joseph Vila household, digital image, *Ancestry.com* (https://www.ancestry.com: accessed 8/15/2017), citing NARA microfilm publication M704, Roll 132, p 84, FHL microfilm 9,691. No date of enumeration, Image 179/452.

[41] All the children have New Orleans Birth certificates. Vila and Jeanne Rose lived on Frenchmen St. between Love and Goodchildren.

[42] 1850 United States Federal Census, Orleans Parish, LA, Ward 1, Dwelling #1766, Family #1991, Henriette Rose household, *Ancestry.com* (https://ancestry.com: accessed 4/12/2018), citing NARA microfilm publication M432, Roll 238, p. 100B, Date of enumeration: 27 August 1850, Image 200/204.

[43] 1860 United States Federal Census, Orleans Parish, LA, Ward 7, Dwelling #2135, Family #2696, Jean Mesnard household, *Ancestry.com* (https://ancestry.com: accessed 4/12/2018), citing NARA microfilm publication M653, FHL Film 803419, p. 549, Date of enumeration: 7 July 1860, Image 309/332.

when interracial marriages were lawful. One of the witnesses was Odalie's half-brother, R.A. Chiapella, the other, Eugene Meilleur, a family friend.

Courtesy of State of Louisiana, Secretary of State, Division of Archives, Records Management and History. *Vital Records Indices*. Baton Rouge, LA, USA citing *Orleans Parish Marriage Records, 1831-1968*, Baton Rouge, LA, 70804. Marriage of José Vila and Marguerite O. Lorrains, Vol. 1, p. 563.

The couple never had any children together. The 1880 United States Federal Census for Orleans Parish, LA, had been taken in June 1880, just weeks after sixty-four-year-old Joseph Vila died on 24 April 1880. His New Orleans death record gave his place of death as #229 Common Street in New Orleans, the address where "Mary" (Marie Eglée) Aubry, a seventy-five-year-old widow and her daughter, the widow "O Vilas," were living in 1880. Vila's information also appeared in the 1880 federal census for Laharpe Street, in New Orleans, where he was recorded as a "sixty-four-year-old divorced ship carpenter," with his son Joseph, a "mulatto shoemaker" born to him and to Jeanne Rose in 1841. This entry, however, was crossed out. Vila died of "phthisis pulmonalis" (tuberculosis). Odalie Lorreins Vila's half-brother, Stephen Octave Chiapella, reported the death and signed the death certificate:

Courtesy of State of Louisiana, Secretary of State, Division of Archives, Records Management and History. *Vital Records Indices*. Baton Rouge, LA, USA citing *Orleans Death Indices 1877-1895*; Vol. 76, p. 594.

"Odile," the widow of "Joseph Villa," appeared for the last time in the *1890 New Orleans City Directory* living at # 53 Barracks Street.[44] Marguerite Odalie Lorrains, the widow Joseph Vila (colored), aged 71 years, died in New Orleans at #55 Hospital Street on 10 March 1894. The cause of death was paralysis. The certificate was signed by

---

[44] "New Orleans, Louisiana Directories, 1890-1891," digital image, *Ancestry.com* (https://www.ancestry.com: accessed 4/20/2019). citing the *New Orleans City Directory, 1890*. New Orleans, LA: L. Soards, 1890.

Dr. Felix Formento, husband of Henriette Louise Chiapella, one of Achille Chiapella's legitimate children with Marie Louise Pollock.

Courtesy of State of Louisiana, Secretary of State, Division of Archives, Records Management, and History. *Vital Records Indices*. Baton Rouge, LA, USA citing *Orleans Death Indices 1804-1876*; Vol. 105 p. 1107.

CHAPTER 3

EGLÉE AUBRY AND THE CHIAPELLA-LEMELLE CONNECTION

After the death of Louis Hilaire Lorreins, Eglée Aubry had three children with Michel Étienne (Achille) Chiapella, a New Orleans notary, and later on, the President of the Union Insurance Company in that city. Their first child, Michel René Achille Chiapella was born on 23 April 1837. No baptismal record could be found for Joseph Émile Chiapella, born ca. 1839, or Stephen Octave Chiapella, whose death record gave a birth date of 15 September 1840. Eglée Aubry was enumerated with her four living children in the 1850 United States Federal Census for Municipality #1, Ward 1, New Orleans, including her daughter, Odile "Lorance," aged 27, and her sons, Achille, aged 13, Émile, aged 11, and Octave, aged 10. The entire family was said to be "mulatto."[45] The sons' individual stories will be told in Chapters 11-17 of this book. It is, however, necessary to explore the history of the Chiapella family which is complicated and goes back to the eighteenth century when Jérome Chiapella, and later his brother, Charles Chiapella immigrated from Italy to Spanish New Orleans.

Jérome Chiapella[46] was a merchant, a captain of his own ocean-going vessels, and an active slave trader in New Orleans, where he lived until about 1810 when he returned to Europe to finish his days in Bordeaux, Gironde, France. After the United States purchased Louisiana in 1803, Americans were deeply suspicious of the loyalty of the "foreigners" who lived in Louisiana, who for over one hundred years had had close ties to France and then to Spain. In an effort to discover which residents of New Orleans might be eligible to participate in a new democratic form of government, President Thomas Jefferson tasked General James Wilkinson to "investigate" some of the better-known citizens living in the city. Wilkinson chose Evan Jones, a longtime resident of New Orleans, and "Labigarre" (aka Peter De Labigarre), who had been in New Orleans only a short time and who was described as "a Frenchman by birth, but American in his partialities, he is a man of understanding, but of so-so reputation, he married a Livingston and sells antiseptic gas." [47] Jefferson received a written report from Wilkinson on 1 July 1804, which he used to select candidates for various positions in the government and in the military in Louisiana, which was a territory from 1803 until statehood in 1812. These recommendations from Delabigarre and Jones appear as "Characterization of New Orleans Residents," dated 1 July 1804, a confidential report which was later published in *The Territorial Papers of the United States, Volume, IX, The Territory of Orleans, 1803-1812.*[48] The evaluations of these individuals were numbered 1-119, with some of the numbers written in the hand of Jefferson, himself. The subjects of these portraits included Frenchmen such as de Boré, Pitot, Allard, and Livaudais as well as Anglo-Saxons such as George Pollock, Beverly Chew, Daniel Clark, and Dr. Robert Dow. Chiapella appeared as numbers 17 and 57. It's unclear whether Jones or Delabigarre had offered the comments. In #17 we find: "Mr. Chiappella – A beast in grain; without the smallest education, talents or Respectability tho one of the Richest men in the Country."[49] In #57 we read "Jerome Chiapella: Merchant – Born in Genoa, rich but deeply ignorant, much devoted to the Spanish govt. from which he received many favours; however incapable of holding any office – dubious morals." [50] He was neither recommended for a position on the Supreme Court of the territory or for military service. Chiapella's lack of favorability in the eyes of the American government was apparently twofold. He had, for years, lived openly with a free woman of color. More damning, however, was the fact that he was so rich that he had often lent money to the Spanish government in New Orleans to cover its bills. A.P. Nasatir reported in his "Government Employees and Salaries in Spanish Louisiana" the following: "In addition there is credited to us four hundred and eighty reales de plata which we pay to Don Geronimo LaChiapella for the salary which Miguel Maria, sacristan of the parish of Galvestown earned in the first third of the year 1800 at the rate of 15 pesos per month, which sum was accredited by him to Don Francisco Ramon Canes, assignee of the cited sacristan, on account of lack of funds in

---

[45] 1850 United States Federal Census, Orleans Parish, LA, Ward 1,Dwelling #219, Family #220, Eglée Aubry household, *Ancestry.com* (https://www.ancestry.com: accessed 4/9/2018), citing NARA microfilm publication M432, Roll 235, p. 12B, Date of enumeration: 20 July 1850, Image24/90.

[46] Jérome Chiapella appears under many different names in civil and ecclesiastical records. His given name is variously Geromo, Geronimo, and Jérome. His surname is variously Chiapella, Lachiapella, La Chiapella and even Chapella or Lachapelle. Similarly, Charles Chiapella appears as Carlo or Carlos Chiapella, Lachiapella, or Lachapelle. Late 18th and early 19th century Louisiana notarial and other records seemed to favor "Lachiapella," as did Chiapella himself.

[47] Delabigarre had been married to Margaret Beekman in New York on 27 June 1795 and died in New Orleans on May 30, 1807. His wife was a member of the Beekman-Livingston allied families.

[48] Clarence Edwin Carter, ed., *The Territorial Papers of the United States, vol. IX, The Territory of Orleans 1803-1812.* (Washington D.C., United States Government Printing Office, 1940), 248-258.

[49] Ibid., 250.

[50] Ibid., 253.

this royal treasury on June 11, 1800."[51] It is no wonder that Don Geronimo Lachiapella, after forty years in Louisiana, saw no future in staying in the city. His adopted son, Celestin, would also leave Louisiana for France in due course, while his other adopted son, Étienne (Stephen) Chiapella, grandfather of Eglée Aubry's children with Étienne's son "Achille" Chiapella, would finish his days in New Orleans. But who was Jérome Chiapella and from where did he come?

He was born Geromo Chiapella on 12 March 1742/43[52] at Nervi, about four miles from the center of Genoa, Italy, to Ciro/Siro Chiapella and his wife, Angela Maria Chiappe. Since the baptismal record is in Latin, his given name appeared as "Hieronymus." Below is a copy of one of his ordinary signatures:

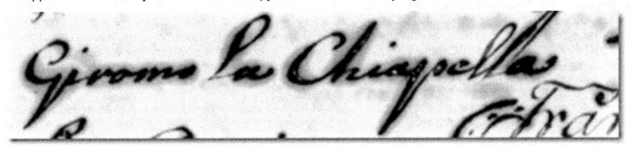

Lachiapella's signature as witness to the marriage contract of Pierre Coudrin and Pelagia Duvernay dated 22 November 1770, Louisiana Colonial Document Collection, Louisiana Historical Center. Available at: http://lacolonialdocs.org/document/13965, p. 4 of 5.

Because, in Chiapella's last will and testament dated 2 July 1806, done at New Orleans in Spanish, he indicated that he was born at Nervi, Italy, we wrote to the archives of the Parish Church of San Siro di Nervi in hopes that they might still have his baptismal record, or perhaps those of his siblings whom he had named in his will. We were gratified to receive six baptismal records, including that of "Gerolamo" Chiapella, as well as the marriage record for his parents seen below from Giovanni Lorenzo Poggi, the Church archivist:

16 Febbraio 1730 matrimonio di Siro Chiappella e Angela Chiappe
Archivio Chiesa Plebana di S. Siro in Genova Nervi

16 February 1730, marriage of Siro Chiappella son of Giovanni Battista Chiappella and Angela Maria Chiappe daughter of Hieronymus Chiappe, the parents of Jérome and Charles Chiapella.[53]

The baptism of Gerolamo/Hieronymus Chiapella, son of Siro (son of Giovanni Bautista) and Angela Chiappe (daughter of Gerolamo) done on 17 March 1743 may be seen on the following page.

---

[51] A. P. Nasatir, ed. "Government Employees and Salaries in Spanish Louisiana," *The Louisiana Historical Quarterly*, Volume 29 #4 (October 1946), 1025.

[52] Note some of these 18th century birth dates are double dated due to the transition from the Julian to the Gregorian calendar in 1752.

[53] Original marriage record of Siro Chiappella and Angela Maria Chiappe dated 16 February in marriages for 1730, courtesy of the Archivio Chiesa Plebana di S. Siro in Genova Nervi, Giovanni Lorenzo Poggi, archivist.

17 Marzo 1743 Battesimo di Gerolamo Chiappella di Siro q. G.B. e Angela Chiappe q. Gerolamo
Archivio Chiesa Plebana S. Siro di Genova Nervi

March 17, 1743, baptism of Gerolamo/Hieronymus Chiappella, son of Syro (son of Giovanni Bautista Chiapella) and Angela Maria Chiappe (daughter of Hieronymus Chiappe).[54]

We were also provided with baptismal records for Maria Teresa (4 March 1731), Pietro Paolo (9 June 1731), Cathalina (9 September 1737), Maria Nicoletta (6 August 1738), and Giovanni Battista (8 March 1739). Other siblings that inherited from "Geromo" Chiapella, according to his last will and testament, included his sisters Benita, Geronima, Magdelena, and his brother Carlo/Charles Chiapella, It is probable that due to the lack of baptismal records for these last four children at Nervi, that they had received the sacrament elsewhere.

It should not be forgotten that New Orleans was a very small town in 1769, a town that had been thrown into chaos when it had been learned that France had ceded the colony to Spain in 1762. After seven years of uncertainty and political upheaval, some misguided subjects of the Crown had led an insurrection which culminated in the arrival of 3000 Spanish troops commanded by General Alejandro O'Reilly to secure the colony for the Spanish Crown. O'Reilly's investigation and execution or imprisonment of 12 of the leading citizens of New Orleans was fresh in the minds of the population. (See pp. 2,3) We believe that it is during this period of upheaval between 1762 and 1769 that Geronimo LaChiapella appeared on the scene in New Orleans. As a young man he always was captain of his own sailing vessels, an occupation to which the Genovese were especially suited. He probably spent some time trading for goods and slaves in the French and Spanish islands of the Caribbean including, Saint-Domingue, Martinique, and Cuba, before putting down roots in New Orleans. His first recorded slave sale was on 18 September 1769 to Manuel Roch, who purchased a three-year-old creole boy named Joseph from him for $200 before the Notary Joseph Fernandez.[55] On 21 August 1870 he bought a female creole[56] slave called Mary Anne for 438 piastres from Joseph Roth. On 18 September 1770, before Notary Andrés Almonester, he traded the Louisiana creole Mariana, age 20, to Juana Dauville Chauvin for Luisa, a 24-year-old black creole, and on 9 October he sold the same Luisa to his friend Joseph Roth for 200 piastres.

The next record we found for Chiapella in New Orleans was his signature as a witness to the marriage contract between Pierre Coudrain and Marie Pelagie Duvernay, reproduced on p. 34, which was signed on 22 November 1770 in New Orleans before Jean-Baptiste Garic and written in Spanish. Pedro Coudrin, a native of the city, and a master silversmith, the son of Pedro Coudrin and Margarita Papin, natives of the bishopric of La Rochelle in Poitou, France, in the company of Joseph Roth and Geronimo Lachiapella, his friends, contracted to marry Pelagia Duverne, a native of this parish, legitimate daughter of Louis Joseph Duvernay and his wife, Maria Rosa Girardy whose family were early residents of Bayou St. John. Girardy's first wife, Françoise, referred to as

---

[54] Original baptismal record of Hieronymus Chiappella dated 17 March 1743, courtesy of the Archivio Chiesa Plebana di S. Siro in Genova Nervi, Giovanni Lorenzo Poggi, archivist.

[55] Unless otherwise noted all slave transactions by LaChiapella were taken from: Gwendolyn Midlo Hall, compiler, "Louisiana, Slave Records, 1719-1820" [database on-line], *Ancestry.com* (https://www.ancestry.com: accessed 2/2/2019) citing Midlo Hall's database intitled *Afro-Louisiana History and Genealogy 1719-1820, which* may also be downloaded from: http://www.ibiblio.org/laslave/.

[56] Note, when "creole" is used in this context it means the enslaved person was a native of the Louisiana territory. The word "bruto" was used to describe a slave born in Africa.

"Françoise Indienne," was a Native American woman with whom he had a daughter, Angélique Girardy.[57] Marie Rose, Pelagia's mother, was Louis Duvernay's daughter by his second wife, Marie Jeanne Henry. Witnesses for the bride were Louis Duvernay, her father, and neighbors Martin Braquier, Philip Lavigne, and Carlos Tarascon.[58] Carlos Lorreins dit Tarascon also lived at Bayou St. John with his wife, Marie Louise Girardy, Pelagia's maternal aunt. Carlos/Charles Lorreins dit Tarascon, was the paternal granduncle of Louis Hilaire Lorreins, father of Eglée Aubry's daughter, Marguerite Odalie Lorreins (See pp.16-18).

Pelagie and Pierre Coudrain were the parents of five children: Pierre, born on 5 October 1771 (SLC B6, 121), buried 1 December 1772 (SLC,F1, 10); Anselm, born on 22 April 1773 (SLC B7, 27); Celestino (b. 2 April 1775 (SLC B7, 59); Elizabeth, born 18 February 1776 (SLC B7, 65), and Éstevan, born on 12 November 1777 (SLC B9, 24). Two of those children, Celestino/Celestin[59] and Estevan/Etienne were raised by Jérome Chiapella after their father Pierre Coudrain died. Having probably fallen ill sometime in March of 1779, Coudrain wrote out a will where he named his wife, Pelagie Duvernay, saying they had been married for about ten years, and gave the names and ages of his children, only to revoke his will in writing on 1 June 1779:

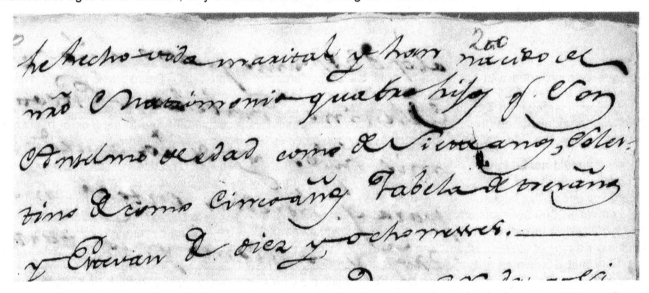

NARC, "Testamento," dated 28 March 1779, passed by Notary Juan Bautista Garic, Volume 11, p. 200 recto. Courtesy Hon. Chelsey Richard Napoleon, Clerk of Civil District Court, Parish of Orleans. Note: It reads "from this marriage was born four children: Anselmo, age about 6 years, Celestino, age about 5 years, Zabela, about 3 years and Estevan age 18 months.

Pierre Coudrain probably died soon after revoking his will. Pelagie Duvernay Coudrin was married on 23 November 1779 (SLC M4, 60) to Jean-Baptiste Bagneris, a French immigrant from Toulouse, Haute-Garonne, France, and went on to have five more children. It was said that Bagneris did not get along with his stepsons, Estevan and Celestino, so their mother gave them over to Chiapella, who had been a friend to her late husband, to raise.

While Estevan Coudrain's birth record is virtually illegible, Celestino's is quite clear, even with the Reverend Father Cyrillo de Barcelona's difficulty with French surnames. He baptized Celestino Cudren y Berne, the legitimate son of Pedro Cudren and Pelagia Berne, born on 2 April 1776, and baptized on 11 April 1776. His godparents were Vincente Rieu(x) and Anna Juana Emilia Renod, all living in this parish:

---

[57] Angélique was married to Pierre Alain Dugue, who was massacred at Fort Rosalie, Natchez Post, LA, in November 1729. She later married Jean-Baptiste Rejas dit Laprade, with whom she had two daughters, one of whom, Marie Louise Laprade (b. 1733), married Antoine Duvernay. Antoine was Marie Pelagie Duvernay's paternal uncle.

[58] *The Louisiana Historical Quarterly*, Vol 6 #3, (July 1923), "Index to Spanish Judicial records -Notarial Acts 1770." (Baton Rouge, LA: Ramires-Jones Printing Co., 1923), 535. Original record at: http://lacolonialdocs.org/document/13965 document/13965.

[59] Because Louisiana had belonged to France, then to Spain, given names appear either in French or Spanish. Even after Louisiana was bought by the United States, church documents and notarial records continued to be written in whatever language was spoken by the contracting parties.

Baptismal record for Celestino Coudren. Archives of the Archdiocese of New Orleans, Saint Louis Cathedral Records, Vol. VII, p. 59, Not numbered. (Courtesy of Emilie Leumas, Archivist – Kimberly Johnson and Katie Vest – Researching Archivists.)

During the Spanish period many New Orleanians were slave owners because the trade was not strictly regulated during the time Spain controlled Louisiana between 1763 and 1803. Several rulings, however either encouraged, or, at times, stopped slave importation altogether, although slave smuggling continued more or less unabated. In 1777 slave trade was reopened with the French colonies and by 1782 slaves could be imported duty-free. Slave trade was banned in 1797 by the Spanish Crown, however petitions by local Louisiana merchants and planters forced the Crown to reopen the trade on 29 November 1800. Jérome Chiapella and his brother, Charles, were active participants in the importation and selling of slaves during the last thirty years of the eighteenth century. They brought slaves over from the Caribbean islands, not only for their own use but to sell. Amongst the twenty-five merchant-traders in New Orleans who dealt in slaves, Chiapella was the fourth most active, importing 99 slaves between 1783 and 1796. Only Daniel Clark with 289 slaves, Jean-Baptiste Labatut with 130 slaves, Jean Dupuy with 124 slaves and Oliver Pollock with 107 slaves were more active according to Douglas B. Chambers who extracted these figures from Gwendolyn Midlo Hall's *Databases for the Study of Afro-Louisiana History and Genealogy*.[60]

Chiapella owned the frigate *Misisipiano/Misisipy*, which he sold to Jean Dupuy in December 1791, as well as the *Nuestra Senora del Carmen* and the *Mariana,* which plied the waters of the Caribbean bringing cargo and slaves back from Dominica, Jamaica, Saint-Domingue, and Martinique. As a younger man Chiapella was the captain of his own vessels, a job he later relinquished to Antoine Delague. There are countless records of Chiapella's activities catalogued in Gwendolyn Midlo Hall's previously cited databases where he is listed as either Geronimo or Geromo La Chiapella. For example, on 23 August 1785, before Notary Raphael Perdomo, Geromo LaChiapella, of New Orleans, sold to Antonio Fanburini, four adult slaves named Gota, Lazaro, Coral and Dizy from the ship *Nuesta Senora del Carmen*, a slave ship out of Jamaica with Captain LaChiapella. On 18 June 1787 before the Notary Raphael Perdomo, Geronimo La Chiapella sold to Lorenzo B. Guevara, two slaves for 1050 piastres apiece from the slave ship *Misisipy* which landed from Jamaica on 14 June 1787 with "Captain LaChiapella." Subsequent to that landing Captain Delague had taken over the *Misisipy* and then the *Mariana*, with Geronimo LaChiapella listed as the seller of certain slaves and the owner of the vessel. For example, on 5 October 1790 before the notary Pierre Pedesclaux, Chiapella sold to Catiche Destrehan, a free mulata, a thirty-year-old female black for 240 piastres. A notation indicated that the seller brought the slave over on his own ship with Captain Delague at the helm. On 14 March 1791 before the notary Pierre Pedesclaux, Geronimo LaChiapella of New Orleans, sold to Pierre Sainpe (Sarpy?) two male black adults for 660 piastres apiece, brought over by Captain Delague on the *Mariana*, a ship owned by the seller. On 23 February 1791, again before Pierre Pedesclaux, LaChiapella sold to Alejandro and Pedro Lavigne four black male "brut" slaves for 1000 piastres in indigo each, which had been brought over on his own ship, the *Mariana* by Captain Dudon. The last entry concerning LaChiapella's slave dealings in Midlo Hall's database was dated 12 July 1800 when before the Notary Pedesclaux, Geromo LaChiapella sold to Francisca La Claire, a free mulata, the black female slave Margarita, age 30, and her three-year-old child for 800 piastres.

[60] Douglas B. Chambers, "Slave trade merchants of Spanish New Orleans, 1763-1803: Clarifying the colonial slave trade to Louisiana in Atlantic perspective," in *New Orleans in the Atlantic World: Between Land and Sea*, ed. William Boelhower, (New York and Oxford: Routledge, 2010), 183.

Chiapella also freed a number of slaves from time to time that he had kept for his own use. Under Spanish law it was much easier to free slaves than it had been under French rule. The latter required permission of the Superior Council to allow freedom be given to a slave. Many times, freedom was granted only for heroic action on the part of the slave to save his master, or for service to the Crown by fighting in a war, or for hunting down escaped slaves. Frenchmen, of course, found ways to manumit their enslaved mistresses as well as their children. The Spanish allowed "coartacion," or self-purchase, wherein a price was fixed between master and slave for their freedom. If a price could not be settled upon, an arbitrator was brought in to make that decision. Chiapella's manumissions, however, were mostly "gratuitous." The first record which appeared in Midlo Hall's database of freed slaves was "Luisa" a twenty-one-year-old black female who was given a conditional release requiring no money change hands, but that she would continue to work for Chiapella for four years as if she were still his slave. He cancelled this requirement a year later. In 1781 the free woman Carlota bought her son Gabriel for 700 piastres from Chiapella. In 1799, Chiapella freed the mother, Adelaida and her son José, again gratuitously. On 2 January 1784. Chiapella freed the forty-year-old black female, Saneta for her services rendered and after she had paid 200 piastres towards her freedom. In 1803 he freed a twenty-six-year-old male mulatto slave he had bought from Nicolas Forstall in 1800, whose name was not given, also without exacting any price. After Chiapella's decision to leave Louisiana, Angelica, aged 50, was freed on 22 July 1806 via a power of attorney wielded by Modeste Lefebvre and Domingo Langourand, upon Chiapella's authorization. A year later, on 23 March 1807, the same two freed by power of attorney, the forty-year-old black male Cezar in Chiapella's name.[61]

Chiapella's main source of income was not only the importation of slaves. As the owner of the brigantine *Nuesta Senora del Carmen*, he was a merchant who took Louisiana's exports to places as far away as Great Britain, as well as to Bordeaux, France. He also sailed to and from Cuba and Saint-Domingue. It is inevitable that Chiapella was also associated with Oliver Pollock, one of the better-known members of that Irish-Scottish immigrant family, who had come to Philadelphia before the American Revolution. An oft-overlooked aspect of the war between Great Britain and the thirteen colonies was the part that played out in the Louisiana Territory, which had recently become a Spanish Colony. Eight years previously, a young Oliver Pollock, also a merchant shipowner, had arrived in the Spanish colony in 1769, from Baltimore with a brig loaded with flour for the town which had just seen an influx of several thousand Spanish soldiers who had accompanied General Alejandro O'Reilly to pacify the colony which was in revolt against its new owners. This influx of people had seen prices for food staples skyrocket, and the townspeople were on the brink of starvation. Pollock offered the flour to O'Reilly for $15 per barrel, about 2/3 the current asking price. O'Reilly, because of Pollock's act of generosity, granted him a free-trade to Louisiana during his lifetime.[62] From that time on Pollock and his wife, Margaret O'Brien called New Orleans their home. It is where their seven children were all born. Pollock, though born at Coleraine, Londonderry, Ireland, ca. 1737, was a staunch American patriot. He partnered with the Spanish Governor Bernardo Galvez, during the subsequent American Revolution, who appointed him "Commissioner of the estados solidos" in 1779 a title which appeared in the baptism of his daughter Maria Antonia Cyrilla Pollock on 28 August 1779 at St. Louis Cathedral (SLC, B9,72) as well as "Commissioner for the United States Provinces," a title which appeared in English in the baptismal record for his son, Diego Pollock, which took place at St. Louis Cathedral on 3 October 1780. (SLC, B9, 106). Pollock along with several other American merchants in New Orleans, with the approbation of Galvez, had begun to supply arms and ammunition to the American colonists in Pennsylvania during the years 1776-1778. The arms which came through the port of New Orleans were transported by ships owned by French and Spanish merchant seamen out of Cuba and the French West Indies. This commerce had caused Great Britain to take out letters of marque against Spanish ships. One of those ship owners who participated in this "illicit trade" was "Geronimo LaChiapella". In the summer of 1779, Spain finally declared war on Great Britain. That summer Pollock had signed an agreement with "Geronimo La Chapelle" involving the exchange of pelts from Louisiana for unspecified goods from Bordeaux. In a letter from the Honorable Francis Lewis writing on 21 July 1779 on behalf of the Committee of Commerce to Benjamin Franklin, Minister Plenipotentiary from the United States of America to the Court of France, Lewis expressed concern that he had "drawn on Messrs. Samuel and J.H. Delap, sundry bills amounting to $10,897 at 90 days sight, but it is uncertain whether Mr. Geronimo La Chapelle will be there when they arrive, or that Messrs. Delaps may have funds of mine in their hands to do honor to those bills, I have taken the liberty of writing the Honorable. Benjamin Franklin Esqr. Your Ambassador at Paris very minutely on this subject in order he may see those bills paid for the credit of the

---

[61] Gwendolyn Midlo Hall, comp. *Louisiana, Freed Slave Records, 1719-1820* – Freedom of Cezar dated 23 March 1807.

[62] George Washington Cable, *The Creoles of Louisiana*, (Gretna, LA: Pelican Publishing Co. 2000) 86,87. First published in 1884 by Charles Scribner's Sons.

States:"[63] Once Spain had declared war on Great Britain, Galvez's hands were no longer tied and he aroused the men of Louisiana to join his Spanish troops, including men from the German and Acadian coast, a large contingent of Native Americans, as well as nine American volunteers including Oliver Pollock to seize British possessions including Bayou Manchac, and Fort Panmure outside of Baton Rouge, both of which had been in British hands. Following those victories, with the aid of some Cuban troops, they took Fort Charlotte on the Mobile River in March of 1780, and Pensacola in 1781. These naval victories were made possible, in no small part, by Oliver Pollock who had outfitted a small armed Spanish schooner furnished by Galvez called the *West Florida,* first in 1778 to "clean out" Lake Pontchartrain of British vessels. A year later after those victories, he used the same vessel, under the command of Captain William Pickles, under American colors, to join Galvez's fleet at Mobile in order to seize it from the British. Pollock's order to Pickles was dated 20 January 1780 which read in part:

> [...] give all the assistance in your power to Governor Galvez, the commander-in-chief of the Spanish fleet, for the reducing of those places, for the space of twenty days, or longer, if necessary, as requested by the commander-in-chief of the Spanish fleet; after which should you be in want of provisions, you will deliver my letter to Don Bazilio Xemenez, or the commissary general of the Spanish fleet, or any who will furnish you with what you may think necessary for your voyage, then you will proceed to Havana, & there deliver my letter to Monsieur Geronimo Zacheapella who I expect will ship a cargo of tafia [rum made from sugar cane] & sugar on board your vessel, to the amount of two or three thousand dollars, for the account of the United States, which you will receive on board & proceed immediately for the port of Philadelphia, or any other port on the continent you may think most safe from the enemy. For your government on that point you must procure the best intelligence possible at Havana, & proceed accordingly.
> And should it so happen that Mr. Geronimo is not there, or cannot supply you with the above cargo and the necessaries for your vessel, in that case you must apply to His Excellency Governor Navarro, or any other person you can procure it from, for which you will draw on the Honorable the Congress, and if that should not take, you may draw on me, at as long a sight as you can, and I will do honour to your drafts: [...][64]

The "tafia and sugar" on board was most likely a cover for the importation of fire arms from the islands by Chiapella who was supporting the Spanish government's war with the British during the American Revolution. Chiapella was still, apparently in Havana later on that year and had met Oliver Pollock who had brought with him a bill of exchange from Thomas Salas del Manzano requesting that the latter be paid 250 pesos as 25% interest for money he had lent Chiapella. Back in New Orleans, in late November 1780 Chiapella sought to defend himself. Pollock testified that he had brought the bill of exchange to Chiapella in Havana. The latter demanded that the case go to arbitration to settle the suit. As a result, Chiapella was ordered to pay 8% interest for the money, or 80 pesos to del Manzano.[65]

In the midst of his dealings with Pollock, on 25 March 1780, the cash-strapped Chiapella sold his brigantine *Nuestra Senora del Carmen,* which he had previously bought at Bordeaux, Gironde , France, from James Rouselle, along with all its chains, anchors, sails and rigging, to Patrick Morgan and James Mather for 6,000 piastres, of which 3,000 had already been paid. The company of Morgan and Mather agreed to pay the remaining 3,000 piastres in four months. The signatures on the six-page document, written in Spanish, agreed to by Chiapella and the company of Morgan and Mather before the notary Leonardo Mazange may be seen on the following page:

[63] "To Benjamin Franklin from the Committee of Commerce, 21 July 1779," *Founders Online,* National Archives, accessed April 11, 2019, https://founders. archives.gov/documents/Franklin/01-30-02-0081. Source: *The Papers of Benjamin Franklin,* vol. 30, *July 1 through October 31, 1779,* ed. Barbara B. Oberg. New Haven and London: Yale University Press, 1993, pp. 124–125.

[64] Rev. Horace Edwin Hayden, "The Pollock Family of Pennsylvania," in *Historical Register: Notes and Queries, Historical and Genealogical, Relating to Interior Pennsylvania for the Year 1883,* Vol. 1, No. 1, ed. Dr. William Henry Egle (Harrisburg, PA: Lane S. Hart, Printer and Binder, 1883), 56.

[65] "Suit for payment of Debt of 250 pesos. Thomas Salas del Manzano vs. Geromo (Geronimo) La Chiapella," Spanish file #3570 (v. 13, 1780) on line at: https://www. crt.state.la.us/dataprojects/museum/spanishcolonial/07_Jan_19_1779_to-Dec_9 _1780.pdf.

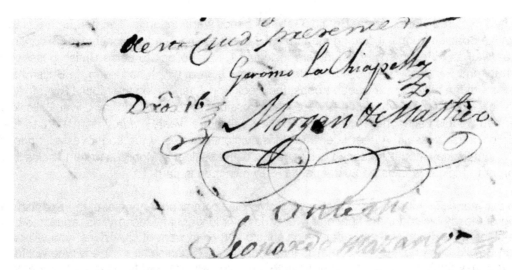

NARC, Sale of Brigantine *Nuestra Senora del Carmen* by Geromo Lachiapella to Patricio Morgan and Santiago Mather dated 25 March 1780, passed by Notary Leonardo Mazange, Volume 1, folios 228-231. Courtesy Hon. Chelsey Richard Napoleon, Clerk of Civil District Court, Parish of Orleans.

On 9 February 1782, Chiapella had acquired one-half interest in the 150-ton brigantine *Maria,* which he had bought from Thomas Wilkins before the notary Andrés Almonester y Roxas. Francisco Riana was Chiapella's partner in this endeavor. A month later, the pair sold their one-half interest in the brigantine to Juan Argote, a native of Cadiz, Spain, and resident of New Orleans, for 3250 pesos cash. Argote renamed the vessel the *San Antonio.*[66]

On 19 June 1782 Chiapella's new brigantine, also named the *Nuestra Senora del Carmen*, sank two leagues from La Balize opposite the Pass à Lutra [*sic*, Loutre] after having run up on the mast of a sunken ship. On 2 July 1782 there was a lengthy legal proceeding brought by the Captain, Antonio Lague (*sic* Delague) to prove the shipwreck. The latter stated that, as Captain of the brigantine owned by Geronimo LaChiapella, he had been granted a passport to sail to London carrying goods belonging to the merchants Benjamin Gouber, Santiago Mather, Santiago Farley and Juan Tait, residents of Pensacola. He began the voyage from London back to New Orleans on April 15th, and reached La Balize on June 18th. After taking the proper soundings, the ship proceeded the next day for New Orleans, but sank. Chiapella testified on 10 July 1782 that he was the owner and had insured the brigantine in the city of London according to the customs of the trade on the chance that it might not arrive back in New Orleans safely. He renounced, therefore, all claim to the ship, and its cargo, and gave to the underwriters anything that could be salvaged, claiming only the insurance money. The return cargo, listed on pages 47-149 of the original manuscript, contained:

332 hogsheads of china = 240 pesos; the ship with 2 large anchors one small one, a bell, two pumps, a mainmast and bowsprit = 3000 pesos; 41 barrels of nails = 1405 pesos; 31 barrels of beer = 500 pesos. Other cargo: whetstones, stone coal, a trunk, 200 lbs. pepper at 170 pesos, dry goods such as Limbourg, woolen stuffs, blue and various colors; 16 ells of purple cloth, hats, tin plate, jars, silk material, cotton handkerchiefs plain and colored, white flannel, boots, bunting, muslin, blue stripes stuff, Irish Linen, Bretagnes, a sort of fine linen; Sirscaca linen?; thread, handkerchiefs, velvet, cotton goods, camlet, pieces of chintz, silk stockings, taffeta silk, feathers (plumes), nankeen cotton, ribbon, point and silk lace, 150 lbs. crude thread, calico, white linen, nankeen cotton coverlets, bed ticking, cables and rigging for mainmast, sails, a stream cable 3 inches thick, cordage, main sails, one inch cords, sounding lines, lamps, candlesticks, coffee pot, bridles, saddles, saddle girths, fishing net, canvas, white cordage, 2 barrels of meat, one barrel of red ochre, marmalade, 4 large saws for sawmills, a clock, medicine chest, fruit of mustard no value, because useless, one barrel smoked fish, 10 barrels paint, 1 barrel of sulfur, 18 bottles linseed oil, 3 barrels butter, iron flower pots, 3 pianofortes, etc.

The amount received for the sale of the ship and cargo was 38,768 pesos 4.5 reales. Paid out of this was 22,607 pesos 6 reales for the salaries of the Captain and crew for the round trip, provisions for the laborers who were sent

[66] Laura L. Porteous, ed. "Index to the Spanish Judicial records of Louisiana, LXXI," *The Louisiana Historical Quarterly, Vol 19 #4* (October 1936), 1123,1124.

to the Balize to repair the ship and recover the cargo, and money to hire slaves to do the work. The underwriters received 12,121 pesos 1.5 reales. At the auction for the recovered cargo, Chiapella purchased 200 pounds of pepper for 153 pesos.[67]

The year 1782 was significant in the life of Geronimo Chiapella for another reason. A twenty-two-year-old free woman of color, Agathe Lemelle gave birth to a daughter, Jeanne Aimée (Juana Amada) La Chaise, the future wife of Celestin Chiapella. Although no birth record has so far been located, we found in the succession papers of Agathe's father, Jacques Lemelle, in a catalog of outstanding debts, a list of treatments provided to the Lemelle household during the course of Jacques' nearly two-year illness. Dated 18 July 1782, there is a notation that Dr. Robert Dow treated "l'enfant d'Agate" (Agata's child) with a vial of an absorbent mixture of magnesium and rhubarb:

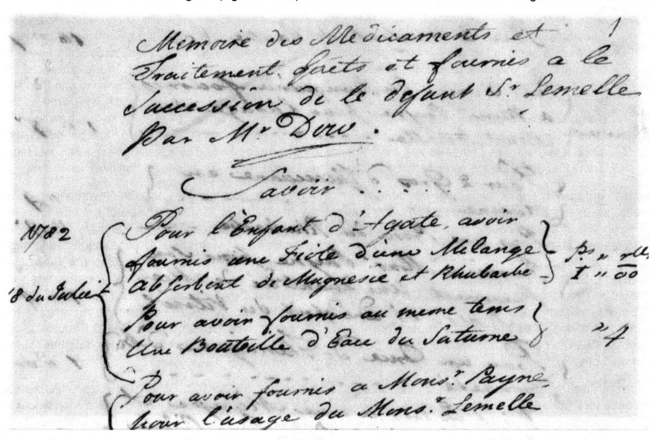

Medicines (lines 6-8 above) provided to the Lemelle household on 18 July 1782 by Dr. Robert Dow from 1784 lawsuit by Dow requesting payment for his services (See note #67).

That treatment for the baby Amada/Aimée, along with her 1864 death record giving her age as 82 years provided us with her likely birth year - 1782. It can only be hoped that the "Saturn water," a mixture of lead acetate, lead oxide, water and brandy was not for the child.[68] Amada's father was Louis August Delachaise, grandson of Jacques Auguste Delachaise, the Comptroller and First Councilor of the Superior Council of Louisiana, sent there in 1722 by the French king to audit the Company of the Indies records. Intensely unpopular with New Orleans residents, he reported negatively back to the King about the corruption in the city which he blamed on Jean Baptiste le Moyne de Bienville, four times the Governor of French Louisiana. Delachaise had been accompanied to the colony by his wife Marguerite Lecailly (1675-1741) and five children. He died unexpectedly on 6 February 1729/1730, which gave rise to the suspicion that he had been poisoned by one of his many enemies. His only son, Jacques Delachaise married Marguerite Marie Darensbourg, a native of St. Charles Parish ca. 1740. The bride was the daughter of the Swedish immigrant Charles Frederick D'Arensbourg and his German wife, Marguerite Metzerine who had settled in St.

[67] Laura L. Porteous, ed. "Index to the Spanish Judicial records of Louisiana, XLVIII," *The Louisiana Historical Quarterly, Vol 19 #1* (January 1936): 242-251.

[68] Louisiana Historical Center, *Louisiana Colonial Document Collection,* "Don Roberto Dow vs. Succession of Santiago Lemelle ," dated 31 March 1784, page 48/75: Available on line at: http://lacolonialdocs.org/document/ 16220.

Charles Parish, called the "German Coast" because of the many Teutonic immigrants in the area. They were the parents of nine children, the last of which, Louis Auguste Delachaise, born on 16 March 1756 at Providence Plantation in St. Charles Parish, and baptized at St. Louis Cathedral on 4 May 1756 (SLC B3, 57) led a life of adventure and intrigue. It is doubtful that his little daughter, Amada Lachaise, knew much of him in her life. As a baby she was raised in the household of her grandfather, Jacques Lemelle. Chiapella and Lemelle had much in common. They were both ships' captains engaged in the Caribbean mercantile and slave trade and they both lived with free women of color.

Jacques Lemelle was the eldest son of François Lemelle dit Bellegarde and Marie Louise Mariette, both immigrants to Louisiana. Mariette's immigrant story was told by Marcel Giraud in Volume 5 of his history of French Louisiana:

> Sometimes a woman would come to the office of the Company's representative in La Rochelle and express the wish to settle in the colony. The agent would agree at once, giving her the 200 livres she needed to assemble her trousseau, along with 15 sols per day to meet her living expenses before she embarked; he would also promise, in a deed, authenticated by a notary, to maintain her during the voyage and until she was settled. This happened, for example to Marie-Louise Mariette, aged nearly 16 from Treves, the daughter of a surgeon and medical officer in Saillant's regiment. She applied to go to 'the new town of Orleans' in Louisiana in order to 'work to the best of her ability and settle down there.' She set out in April 1728, along with three other women (one of them a widow accompanied by her daughter) for whom Henry Edme had promised the same conditions; she married in the colony about six months later.

Indeed, the marriage took place after her June arrival in the colony, five months later. On November 7, 1728, François Lemesle called Bellegarde, a native of Paris, from the Parish of St. Sulpice, son of the late François Lemesle and of Marie Coquelin and Marie Louise Mariette, native of Treves (now Trier) in Germany, daughter of the late Louis Mariette, Surgeon Major of the Regiment of the Swiss, and of Marguerite Zeresse, signed a marriage contract at New Orleans in front of Sieur Jean Baptiste de Chavannes, secretary of the Superior Council of Louisiana, Sieur Jacques Delachaise, Jr, the Kings Commissioner for the colony, and others. The marriage was solemnized the following day at St. Louis Cathedral by the Vicar General, Fr. Raphael, a capuchin priest. (SLC, M1, 162). They were the parents of three children. Their eldest son, Jacques Lemelle's baptism was recorded at the Archives Nationales de France, and copied into the Archdiocese of New Orleans, Sacramental Records as 14 August 1729. Their second son, Jean François Denis Lemelle was born ca. 1738, and their only daughter, Marie Jeanne Lemelle, the future wife of Denis Braud, was born ca. 1740.

While Jean François Denis Lemelle, established himself as a planter in St. Landry Parish, his brother Jacques took to the sea, becoming a ship's captain, sailing back and forth to Saint-Domingue and Martinique, to bring back rum and other island staples which he sold from his store on #45 Royal Street in New Orleans. Jean François Denis Lemelle maintained two families near Opelousas, St. Landry Parish, LA, one with his legitimate spouse, Charlotte Labbé, and the other with Marie Jeanne, dit Davion (b. ca. 1750), the daughter of the "mulatress" slave Jacqueline (aka Jacqueline Dupard), whose origins are unknown. Jacques Lemelle remained in New Orleans and set up a household with the slave Jacqueline, the mother of Marie Jeanne Davion, his brother's mistress.

Jacques purchased Jacqueline as his slave ca. 1762 after she had delivered their first child, Agathe, born on 4 May 1760 and baptized the following day:

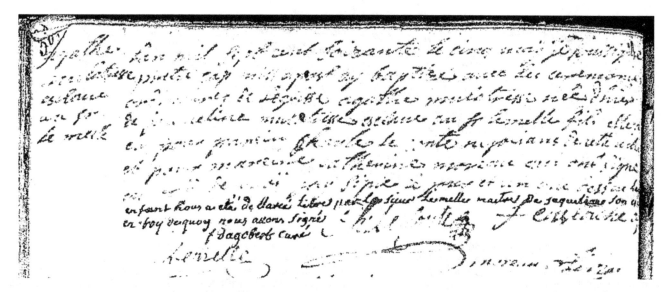

L'an mil sept cent soixante le cinq may je soussigne pretre capucin Missionaire apostolique ay baptisé avec les cérémonies ordinaires de l'église Agathe mulatresse née d'hier de Jacqueline mulatresse esclave au Sieur Lemelle Fils elle a eu pour parrain Charles LeConte negociant de cette ville, et pour marraine Catherine moreau qui ont signé en foy de quoi jay signe le jour et an que depuis .Laquelle enfant nous a été déclaré libre par le Sieur Lemelle maître de Jacqueline son esclave...... (On 5 May 1760, I the undersigned Apostolic Missionary Capucin, baptized Agathe, mulatress, born yesterday of Jacqueline mulatress slave of Sieur Lemelle, Jr. Her godfather is Charles Le Conte, a merchant of this city. Her godmother is Catherine Moreau, with everyone signing the register. The said child has been declared Free by Sieur Lemelle, master of Jacqueline, his slave. Signed by Fr. Dagobert and Lemelle). [69]

    According to information researched by Jennifer M. Spear in her book *Race Sex and Social Order in Early New Orleans*,[70] Jacques Lemelle left on a year-long trip back to France in late 1765, and upon his return found out that Jacqueline had given birth to another child, Louis Dusuau De La Croix. with Don Joseph Dusuau De La Croix, one of many children that the latter would father with various free women of color. Jacques had left Jacqueline in charge of his household, his slaves, and his store in his absence, and this new child caused a rupture between them. He forgave her, however, and agreed to manumit Louis. To that end he sold on 19 July 1767 a "five-month-old male quadroon, son of a mulatress Jacqueline owned by him" for the sum of 800 pesos to Gaspard Gardelle. The child was to remain with Jacqueline until he was eighteen months old, and if kept longer, a charge of 20 sols per day would be paid by Gardelle for his upkeep. The purchaser also agreed to give him his liberty.[71] It is not known how long Louis remained with his mother in the Lemelle household, or if he was eventually turned over to Gardelle. Louis, however, did not inherit from Lemelle, but instead from his birth father, Dusuau de la Croix, upon the latter's death in 1804.

    Jacques Lemelle and Jacqueline had two more daughters together. The first, Marie Jeanne Françoise, who was most always identified as "Tonton" in civil records, was born on 14 August 1769, and baptized on 7 September 1769:

---

[69] Archdiocese of New Orleans (Orleans Parish, LA), *St. Louis Cathedral, New Orleans, Baptism Marriage, Funeral*, *St. Louis Cathedral, New Orleans, Combination 1759-1762*, unnumbered, Baptism of Agata, mulatresse esclave de Lemelle, 5 May 1760; Digital Images. (https://archives.arch-no.org/sacramental _records: accessed 3/5/2028, Image 49/115. Note: Transcriptions of all three baptismal records of the Lemelle sisters done in 1787 by Fr. Antonio de Sedella may be found here: Louisiana Historical Center, *Louisiana Colonial Documents Digitization Project*, "Agata, Juana Francisca and Marie Adelaida Lemelle to administer own property," dated 29 July 1785: Available on line at: http://lacolonialdocs.org/document/ 14920.

[70] (Baltimore, MD: Johns Hopkins University Press, 2009) 151-152.

[71] Louisiana Historical Center, *Louisiana Colonial Documents Digitization Project,* "Jacques Lemelle to Gardelle," dated 19 July 1767: Available on line at http://lacolonialdocs.org/document/12249.

L'an mil sept cent soixante-neuf le sept de septembre je soussigne ay baptisé avec les ceremonies ordinaire de leglise jeanne françoise née le quatorze du mois d'aout de la presente annee de Jacqueline mulatresse esclave à M. Lemelles lequel maitre ma dclaré qu'il voulait que la dite jeanne Françoise soit baptisé libre : le parrain a été M. Jean Baptiste François de Macarty la marraine Mademoiselle jeanne Françoise de Macarty qui ont signes avec moi le jour et an que dessus Fr. Dagobert curé, Macarty, LeBreton, Lemelle. (On 7 September 1769, I the undersigned baptized Jeanne Francoise born on 14 August of the present year to Jacqueline, mulatress slave of Mr. Lemelle who declared to me that he wishes the child to be baptized as free. Godfather Jean Baptiste François de Macarty. Godmother, Jeanne Françoise de Macarty who signed with me on the day and year above.)[72]

Their third child, Marie Adelaïde, was born on 11 October 1771, and baptized on 7 November of the same year. Although Lemelle never formally recognized his children with Jacqueline, he took care to baptize all three of his daughters with Jacqueline as "mulatresses, free at birth." While the first two baptisms omitted mention of a father, the third, Adelaide's, indicated that the father was unknown:

L'an mil sept cent soixante onze le sept novembre je soussigné ay baptisé avec les ceremonies ordinaires de l'eglise Marie Adelaïde ne le onze octobre de la presente année de Jacqueline mulatresse esclave a M. Lemelle laquelle enfant a été déclaré libre par le Sieur Lemelle son maitre et d'un père inconnu, Le parraine a été M. Cazouche, negociant, la marraine Demoiselle Marie Braux lesquels ont signés avec moy le jour et an que dessus Fr. Dagobert, Marie Braud, Lemelle. (On November 7, 1771, I the undersigned baptized Marie Adelaide born on October 11 of the present year to Jacqueline a mulatress slave of Mr. Lemelle, which child was declared to be free by Mr. Lemelle, her master, and born of an unknown father. The godfather was Mr. Carmouche, a merchant. The godmother Miss. Marie Braud, all who signed with me on the day and year above. Fr. Dagobert, Lemelle, Marie Braud).[73]

---

[72] Archdiocese of New Orleans (Orleans Parish, LA), *St. Louis Cathedral, New Orleans, Baptism Marriage, Funeral*, *St. Louis Cathedral, New Orleans, Baptism, Marriage, Funeral 1764-1774*, unnumbered, Baptism of Jeanne Françoise, mulatresse esclave de Lemelle, 7 September 1769; Digital Images. (https://archives.arch-no.org/sacramental_records: accessed 2/3/2018), Image 67/209.

[73] Ibid., unnumbered, Baptism of Marie Adelaïde Lemelle free daughter of Jacqueline, 7 November 1771; Digital Images. (https://archives.arch-no.org/ sacramental_records: accessed 2/3/2018), Image 136/209.

On November 10, 1772, Santiago/Jacques Lemelle went before the notary Andrés Almonester Y Roxas, and formally manumitted his forty-two-year-old "mulatta" slave, Jacqueline (referred to in Spanish records as a "parda" libre, or free mulatta), and her three children: the "thirteen-year-old quadroon Agata," the "three-year-old quadroon, Tonton," and the "one-year-old quadroon Adelaida." The manumission was made without payment. In December of that same year, Jacqueline purchased the freedom of her first child, twenty-two-year-old Marie Jeanne dit Davion, as well as the latter's child, Julie, from Jacques' brother, Jean François Denis Lemelle, for 200 pesos.[74]Julie had been born ca. 1770 to Jean François Denis Lemelle and Marie Jeanne Davion. They continued to have children together including Louis (b. 1772), Catherine (b. 1774), Jacqueline (b. 1775), Adelaide (b. 1777), Hildebert (b. 1780) and François Donato (b. 1785). In 1784 and 1786, François Denis Lemelle had transferred a total of about 800 acres of land in St. Landry Parish to Marie Jeanne, which after his death in 1789, she and her three sons developed, with the help of fifteen slaves that Lemelle had also given her.[75]

Jacques Lemelle, a ship's captain, was according to a 1764 document, master of the brigantine *L'Espérance* (The *Hope*). Returning from a voyage to Cap Français, Saint-Domingue, with a mixed cargo of produce and slaves in July 1764, Captain Lemelle and two passengers identified only as J. Chalon and Leclair de Ferrier attested to the fact that a Congo slave, sold by Mr. Lary to Mr. Demain, died on board from a bloody flux and fever. Because of the deteriorated condition of the slave's clothes, they were thrown overboard:[76]

Signature of Jacques Lemelle in affidavit of death of slave on brigantine *Esperance* (3 July 1764), Louisiana Colonial Document Collection, Louisiana Historical Center, Available at http://lacolonialdocs.org/document/10462, p. 2 of 3.

---

[74] See acts of Don Garic, No. 3, Folio 366, 5 December 1772 and October 1775 for Marie Jeanne Davion's freedom papers.

[75] See Carl A. Brasseaux, Keith P. Fontenot, and Claude F. Oubre, *Creoles of Color in the Bayou Country*, Jackson, MS: University Press of Mississippi, 1994, for the complete story of the St. Landry Lemelles.

[76] Louisiana Historical Center, *Louisiana Colonial Documents Digitization Project,* "Affidavit," dated 3 July 1764: Available on line at: http://lacolonialdocs.org/document/10462.

By November 4, 1768, Lemelle, now the captain of the ship *La Liberté*, gave a power of attorney to Mr. Thibaut of Cap Français, Saint-Domingue, to collect monies due him for goods he sold to the merchant Mr. Daligand at the Cape.[77]

Jacques Lemelle and his family appeared in the 1778 census of New Orleans in household #421 on the left side of Ste. Ursulle Street (now Ursulines) as "Jacques Lemelle," a male white, between the ages of 13 and 39 years of age, with "Jacqueline," a free mulatress, between 13 and 39 years of age. His children included one male mixed-race child under the age of 13 (perhaps Louis Dusuau), two mixed-race females under 13 (Tonton and Adelaida), and one mixed-race child over 13 (Agata). He also kept one black female slave between 13 and 39 years of age under his roof.[78]

Jacques Lemelle had always relied upon Jacqueline, formerly his slave, but after 1772, a free woman, to manage his store on Royal Street when he was away at sea. Towards the end of his life, Lemelle must have relied more heavily upon his eldest daughter, Agata, to look after his affairs. He was successful in protecting his children's interests after his death on 21 March 1784. His succession record which was 165 pages long left very specific bequests. He stated that he was the son of Francisco Lemelle and Maria Luisa Maret [*sic*], both deceased, the former from Paris and the latter from Germany, and that he was a native of New Orleans. To his brother, François Denis Lemelle he left 3000 pesos, the contents of his bedroom, a writing desk, a large table, and one-half of his table cloths and napkins. To his nephew, Santiago Braud, the son of his sister, Marie Jeanne, he willed 200 pesos and all of his nautical instruments. He gave to his grand-nephews, sons of Santiago Braud, who live in France and whose names he did not know, 300 pesos each. Jacqueline and his children each received 200 pesos, and the girls were given the house on Royal Street, said to be worth about 2000 pesos. He stipulated that the house could not be sold or alienated until after Jacqueline's death. Jacqueline was given the slave Francisca, a thirty-five-year-old washerwoman worth 350 pesos, and the girls inherited the negress, Eulalia, about 25 years of age, also worth 350 pesos. Jacqueline and his daughters all received the other one-half of his table linens, the kitchen furniture, bed linen, bed, sofa, and his handkerchiefs. Jacques' other property on Royal Street was to be sold for the benefit of Jacqueline and his children. Lemelle named Francisco Blache his executor and recommended that he continue to advise Jacqueline and his daughters how to increase their property. On 30 April 1784 the inventory and appraisal of the estate was approved by the court, and on 3 June the estate was liquidated to pay off any creditors, after which Jacqueline and her daughters were left an additional 1368 pesos to be divided equally. On 29 July 1785, as the process of settling the estate drew to a close, his three daughters sought emancipation from the court in order to be put into possession of what they had inherited. Below are the signatures of Agathe, Marie Jeanne "Tonton", and Adelaïde on that document:

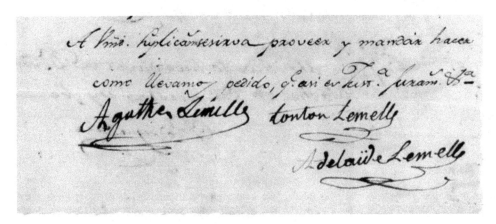

Succession of Jacques Lemelle, Louisiana Colonial Document Collection, Louisiana Historical Center–. Available at: http://www.lacolonialdocs.org/document/14832, p. 341 of 352.

---

[77] Louisiana Historical Center, *Louisiana Colonial Documents Digitization Project,* "Power of Attorney," dated 4 November 1768: Available on line at: http://lacolonialdocs.org/document/12846.

[78] Gwendolyn Midlo Hall, editor, *Databases for the Study of Afro-Louisiana History and Genealogy 1699-1860*. (Baton Rouge, LA: Louisiana State University Press, 2000). CD-ROM. 1778 Census, #418, Family #421 – Jacques Lemelle.

In a final petition, Agathe Lemelle demanded to have the records of the succession given to her in order that she be able to make an exact statement of what still may be due the estate, as well as any debts which were still left to be paid. On 28 July 1788 Judge Joseph Foucher ordered that she be given the records to review for a period of eight days.[79]

Four months before Agathe was put in possession of those papers, the city had been thrown into turmoil by a fire which consumed almost a third of what is now the French Quarter on 21 March 1788. It had started at the corner of Chartres and Toulouse and quickly spread north, sparing the buildings on the riverfront but consuming the structures between Conti and St. Ann to the east, and north to Dauphine, including the Church, the jail, and the army barracks. On 5 April 1782, Jérome Chiapella had bought a two-story house situated on two lots at the corner of Royal and Conti from Philibert Farges for 3900 pesos, which he had sold on 28 August 1787 to Pierre Jourdan for 5000 pesos with terms. The house was destroyed in the 1788 fire, along with Jourdan's kitchen, storerooms, and merchandise, for which he claimed 8,000 piastres in losses:

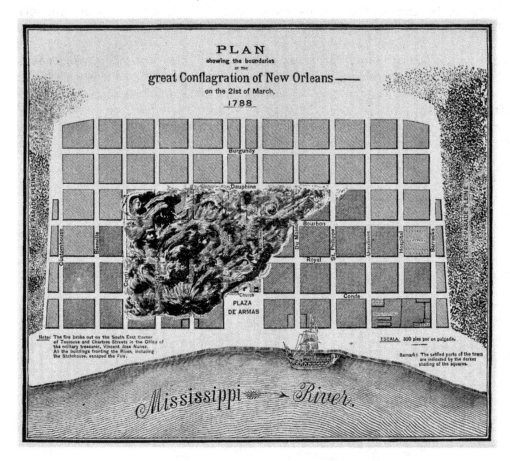

The Great New Orleans Fire of 1788 showing the area in flames behind the Plaza de Armas (Jackson Square), published in 1886. (Library of Congress: lcweb2.loc.gov-GreatConflagration).

On 14 July 1789 Jourdan retroceded the property back to Chiapella which now consisted of two lots of charred remains and brick rubble for 3500 pesos. On that same day Chiapella purchased an adjoining lot measuring 72 feet on Royal Street by 120 feet deep from Marie Couturier Degruis for 800 pesos. The address was 326-334 Royal (630-634 Conti). This location is where Chiapella would rebuild and where he and Agathe Lemelle, her daughter Amada Lachaise, and his two adopted sons, Celestino/Celestin and Estevan/Étienne Coudrain would eventually live with their large retinue of slaves until six or so years after the Louisiana Purchase. It was also the

---

[79] Louisiana Historical Center, *Louisiana Colonial Documents Digitization Project,* "Proceedings instituted in consequence of the death of Santiago Lemelle," dated 21 March 1784, Images. 1-352. Signatures above on image 341/352: Available on line at: http://lacolonialdocs.org/ document/ 14832.

location where Celestin would marry in 1803. The property was sold long after Chiapella and Agathe Lemelle had left for France on 17 May 1817 to Jean Noel Destrehan for 30,000 piastres.[80]

In the early 1780s, Chiapella had taken charge of Marie Pelagie Duvernay Coudrain Bagneris's two sons, Celestino and Estevan Coudrain to raise. As many well-to-do New Orleanians before and after him had done, he sent both boys to France to be educated. In 1791 he and Agathe were still, however, maintaining two separate residences. "Geromo Lachapelle" was enumerated on Conti Street, as a merchant living with 22 slaves, of which two were racially mixed, and one was a child. "Agata Lemelle" was enumerated living on Royal Street, in the house left to her by her father, with one female mulatto child under 17 years (her daughter Amada, no doubt), one female mulatto adult (perhaps her sister "Tonton," who never had children), one male mulatto adult, and four black female slaves.[81] Agathe sought to increase her holdings by buying and selling slaves, some of which she had purchased from Chiapella. For example, on 5 January 1795, she sold a twenty-year-old female black slave named Sofy for 500 piastres to Louis Fortin, a slave she had originally purchased from Chiapella. In 1803 she purchased a fifteen-year-old female named Benedic for 400 piastres and in 1805 she purchased a thirteen-year-old female named Finette for 400 piastres.

Two hurricanes in August 1794 which destroyed many of the ships at anchor in New Orleans and decimated crops throughout the area were followed by a second fire which destroyed 212 houses in the French Quarter on 8 December 1794. It had started in a hay storage facility in the French Quarter one block up from the river, on the left side of Jackson Square. In an 11 December 1794, map, its location is #19 (casa en que empezo el fuego = house where the fire started). LaChiapella lost his house on Royal at Conti, (#155) and another designated as #230 in the 18th block, which we could not identify. Agathe Lemelle was not listed amongst those who lost property in the fire:

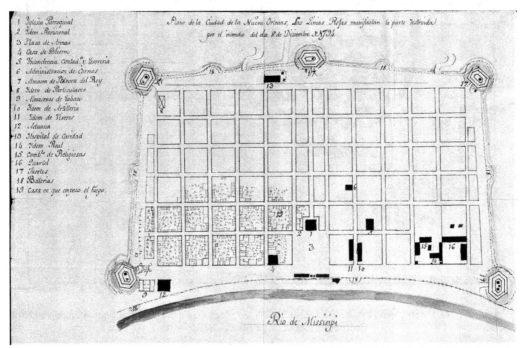

"Plano de la Ciudad de la Nueva Orleans, las Linias Rojas manifiestan la parte destruida por el incendio del dia 8 de Diziembre de 1794", i.e. Plan of the City of New Orleans, the lines indicate the part destroyed by the fire of 8 December 1794. By Anónimo, 1794 - Archivo General de Indias (Sevilla, España), Public Domain, https://commons.wikimedia.org/w/index.php?curid=74609131.[82]

---

[80] See chain of title for 326-334 Royal Street at Collins C. Diboll Vieux Carré Digital Survey (HNOC) (https://www.hnoc.org/vcs/property_info.php?lot=11263-01).

[81] Gwendolyn Midlo Hall, editor, *Databases for the Study of Afro-Louisiana History and Genealogy 1699-1860*. (Baton Rouge, LA: Louisiana State University Press, 2000). CD-ROM. Gould Household Censuses 1791 Census, #59 – "Geromo Lachapelle"; #593 – "Agata Lemelle".

[82] See it on line: https://commons.wikimedia.org/wiki/File:1794_mapa_incendio_ Nueva_Orleans_AGI.jpg.

CHAPTER 4

JÉROME CHIAPELLA AND AGATHE LEMELLE

It was in the mid-1790s that the bond between Agathe Lemelle and Jérome Chiapella, who was eighteen years her senior, became permanent. After her mother Jacqueline's death ca. 1790, she had been on her own, living independently with her daughter and her sisters. A few years after the death of their father, Jacques Lemelle, in 1784, Agathe's sister Marie Adelaide had settled down with Louis Bruno Giraudeau, a French immigrant from Bordeaux, Gironde France, with whom she would have eight children. Agathe's only child with Louis Auguste Delachaise was almost in her teens, and it was clear that the child's father was too embroiled in trying to bring down the Spanish regime and to restore the Louisiana colony to France to seek out a permanent relationship with her. Reports of his subversive activities had, since 1790, put his location in Saint-Domingue. The complicated, but enduring relationship between Agathe and Jérome Chiapella, her daughter Amada Lachaise ,and Jérome's adopted son Celestin Coudrain Chiapella was about to unfold.

Although only heads of household were enumerated in the 1795 New Orleans Census, we believe that Agathe Lemelle and her daughter were living with Jérome Chiapella, listed as the white male owner of dwelling #155 in quarter #2. In the first house listed in his name, he, as well as two racially mixed free female adults (Agathe and perhaps her sister, Tonton), along with 30 slaves (one mulatto child, one mulatto male, 20 male slaves and 8 female slaves) were recorded as residents in a house with four chimneys.[83] In the adjacent house with two chimneys, also listed as #155, Chiapella was renting to one white male adult, named Antoine deSagne identified as a ship's captain (capitaine de navire). Next to DeSagne, also renting from Chiapella, lived a merchant named "Laforasth" (Laforest?). This place had, according to the record, no chimneys! "Agatte" Lemelle was enumerated as the non-white owner of house #34, with three chimneys in an outlying neighborhood, which was rented out to Mr. Martin, a Caucasian dance instructor.[84]

Notwithstanding the two disastrous fires, and the seasonal hurricanes, the 1790s had also been a difficult time for the slave trade, especially from the French possessions in the Caribbean. While slavery was not abolished after the 1789 French Revolution and its founding document, the Declaration of the Rights of Man, it caused a wave of slave unrest in Saint-Domingue. For that reason, on 21 May 1790 the Spanish government in Louisiana prohibited slaves and free blacks or mulatto refugees from entering Louisiana. A major slave revolt in Saint-Domingue in 1791 exacerbated the anxiety that it would spread to the colony. Many of the local slave traders such as Chiapella, had been making their money by importing enslaved African Americans from Saint-Domingue and Martinique With that source of income drying up, Chiapella had turned to regular merchandising as well as to the buying and selling of real estate much of which he acquired at bargain prices after the two devastating fires of 1788 and 1794. On 26 October 1790 he had purchased a lot with a Fifty-foot frontage on Bourbon Street which was 120 feet deep with a four-bay frame shotgun cottage on it from José Maria de la Barra. He sold it to Pierre Guenon on 17 April 1801 for 1800 pesos. In that same year he had purchased a lot of ground with a sixty- foot frontage on Dauphine Street by 120 feet deep from Gilberto Leonard which he retroceded back to him on 7 February 1806. Chiapella also owned two lots next to the corner lot at Royal and Customhouse Streets with a 70-foot frontage on Royal by 118 feet deep which he bought from Antonio Ceulino on 12 December 1796. (See p. 57 for sale of this property)[85]

The new Spanish governor, Francisco Luis Hector, Baron de Carondelet, who took power in June of 1792 had been faced with the aftermath of a small slave conspiracy in Pointe Coupée Parish. In the summer of 1791, a group of Mina slaves plotted to kill the local merchant Jean-Baptiste Tournoir in order to steal guns from his warehouse, after which they would claim their freedom. They set the date for the insurrection for 7 July 1791 but bad weather and muddy roads forced them to postpone it for two days. In the meantime, however, an Ado slave

---

[83] The number of chimneys were used by the Spanish for purposes of taxation in order to evaluate the property's worth.

[84] Gwendolyn Midlo Hall, ed., *Databases for the Study of Afro-Louisiana History and Genealogy 1699-1860*. (Baton Rouge, LA: Louisiana State University Press, 2000). CD-ROM, Gould Household Censuses, 1795 Census for Jérome LaChiapella (#96,97,98) and Agatte Lemelle (#506).

[85] Collins C. Diboll Vieux Carré Digital Survey (https://www.hnoc.org/vcs/). Insert "Lachiapella" in search box.

named Venus, who belonged to George Olivo, Sr., got wind of the plot. She told her godmother Françoise and the latter's father, George Creole, as well as another slave, Pedro Chamba. The four slaves went straight to George Olivo's house to tell him of the plot. He, in turn, sent word to the Post Commander, Valentin LeBlanc, who authorized patrols of the post, especially the roads and the slave cabins. In all, sixteen Mina men were arrested, jailed in New Orleans, and tried before the Spanish Court. In disturbing testimony one of the alleged instigators, Pierre Bahy, stated that he had been awaiting orders from Cap Français, Saint-Domingue in order to start the coup. This sent a chill through the white population of Louisiana. However, many of the planters whose slaves had been jailed sought their immediate release, declaring that they would be bankrupt, if the slaves were not returned to them as they were not only losing their services, but they were obliged to pay for their upkeep while incarcerated.[86] Carondelet, who had just taken power, set up a fund to reimburse slave owners for runaway, killed or imprisoned and executed slaves. He ruled that all slaveowners would henceforth pay a tax of two reales for each slave they owned in order to establish the fund. He also decreed that free blacks would have to keep their freedom papers with them at all times or face arrest. As usual, these laws were only sporadically enforced, and tax on slave owners had been proposed as voluntary, so most refused to pay it. Because of the possible coordination of the slave uprising in Pointe Coupée with instigators in Saint-Domingue, Carondelet petitioned the Spanish Crown to halt the entry of slaves from the French and British colonies in the Caribbean in July of 1792, which was granted but then rescinded by the Crown on 24 January 1793.[87] The uprising of 1791 had taught the inhabitants of Louisiana that the rebellious spirit which had had its roots in the French Revolution, had travelled across the ocean to Saint-Domingue, and had already taken root in their colony.

After the French Revolution the mayors of Bordeaux, France, and New Orleans sent petitions to Paris to ask the new government to seek the return of Louisiana to France. This spirit of return had not died down since the first abortive attempt had been put down by General Alejandro O'Reilly in 1769. The father of Agathe Lemelle's daughter, Amada LaChaise, was central to the plot to return the colony to the French. Born in 1756 in St. Charles Parish, Louis Auguste Delachaise's godparents were his eldest brother Charles Auguste Delachaise and his sister, Louise Marguerite Delachaise. When he was thirteen years old, his godmother, the wife of Joseph Philippe Roy Villeré had become a widow as the result of the failed plot by her husband and other French colonists, who had sought the return of the colony to France. (See p. 3) It is clear that Louis Auguste Delachaise had grown up in a family whose simmering hatred for Spanish rule had fueled his revolutionary spirit. Although probably educated in France, he had returned to Louisiana in the late 1770s. The French Revolution and the plight of Louisiana's slaves and its colonists still under Spanish Rule had caused him to embrace Jacobinism with an enthusiasm which drove him to abandon his child, Amada Lachaise and her mother, Agathe Lemelle. He returned to France and joined the army. He was part of a contingent of French Jacobin troops sent by the French Revolutionary government to Saint-Domingue to maintain order. His first appearance there according to Gabriel Debien and René LeGardeur in an essay entitled "The Saint-Domingue Refugees in Louisiana, 1792-1804," was in 1790:

> We find him [Auguste Delachaise] on July 30, 1790, as one of the governor's commissioners for the Port-au-Prince volunteer corps. He was one of the co-founders of the Society of the Friends of the Revolution in Cap-Républicain where he supposedly established in October 1792, a "black list" of 143 people. He had demanded the immediate departure of all those who filled or who had filled public posts. [...] He "had fought with distinction against the insurgent negroes and during all the agitation he had demonstrated that he was one of the most ardent revolutionaries as long as it was only a matter of combatting the landed aristocracy and the government's party." [...] As Garran de Coulon put it "he conserved for France the tender attachment that this interesting colony [Louisiana] always showed him."[88]

---

[86] Frances Bailey Kolb, "Contesting Borderlands: Policy and Practice in Spanish Louisiana, 1765-1803," PhD diss. (Vanderbilt University, 2014), 424-427.

[87] Gilbert C. Din, *Spaniards, Planters, and Slaves The Spanish Regulation of Slavery in Louisiana*, 1763-1803, (College Station, TX: Texas A&M University Press, 1999), 140-143.

[88] This essay appeared in Carl A. Brasseaux and Glenn R. Conrad, eds., *The Road to Louisiana: The Saint-Domingue Refugees, 1792-1809*, (Lafayette, LA: The University of Louisiana at Lafayette Press, 1992), 181.

By the summer of 1793, Delachaise, who by then had become "Citizen Lachaise," having dropped the "de" from his name as a rejection of his French nobility and a sign of solidarity with the French revolutionary government, had arrived back in America as their agent to join a number of men including George Rogers Clark, and the French Ambassador to Washington, Edmond C. Genêt, in a plot to enlist men from Tennessee and Kentucky to join an invasion of the Spanish-held colony. The people of Tennessee and Kentucky had been petitioning the United States government, to no avail, to negotiate with Spain in order to get free navigation of the Mississippi River. Citizen Lachaise's first task was to bring the newly formed Democratic Society of Lexington into the fold by convincing them that the only way forward was to back a French-led invasion of the Spanish Colony with the guarantee that a French Louisiana would grant them free access to the Mississippi River. These men referred to as the "kaintocks," were to join forces with freedom fighters from Saint-Domingue as well as with rebellious slaves, to take over Louisiana in the name of the new French Republic. In October 1793 the Society enthusiastically backed this invasion which was to be led by George Rogers Clark who styled himself as "Major General in the Armies of France and Commander-in-chief of the French Revolutionary Legions on the Mississippi River." He sent out an appeal in January 1794 via a Cincinnati, Ohio, newspaper, the *Centinel of the Northwest Territory*, to raise volunteers for the project.[89]

In the meantime, the Governor of Spanish Louisiana, the Baron de Carondelet took measures to see that any Jacobin rebels in New Orleans were rounded up and jailed or exiled. He had at least sixty of the group, who were attempting to convince the local population to cooperate with a French takeover, deported. President George Washington, for his part, sent troops to quell the rebellion and demanded that the French recall Genêt. Thwarted in their plan to invade Spanish Louisiana, Auguste Lachaise addressed the Democratic Society of Lexington on 29 May 1794, a transcript of which was included in Charles Gayarré's *History of Louisiana. The Spanish Domination, Vol. III.* Gayarré concluded that Genêt had chosen Delachaise because of his military training to lead the Kentucky volunteers down the Ohio and Mississippi Rivers into Spanish Louisiana which had been his home, as well as for his oratorical skills which are in full view in this farewell speech:

Citizens, Unforeseen events, the effects of causes which it is unnecessary here to develop, have stopped the march of two thousand brave Kentuckians, who, strong, in their courage, in the justice of their rights, in the purity of their cause, and in the general assent of their fellow citizens, and convinced of the brotherly dispositions of the Louisianians, waited only for their orders to go and take away, by the irresistible power of their arms, from those despotic usurpers the Spaniards, the possession of the Mississippi, secure for their country the navigation of it, break the chains of the Americans and of their French brethren in the province of Louisiana, hoist up the flag of liberty in the name of the French Republic, and lay the foundation of the prosperity and happiness of two nations destined by nature to be but one, and so situated as to be the most happy in the universe.

Citizens: The greater the attempts you have made towards the success of that expedition, the more sensible you must be of the impediments which delay its execution, and the more energetic should your efforts be towards procuring new means of success. There is one from which I expect the greatest advantages and which may be decisive – that is, an address to the National Convention, or to the Executive Council of France. In the name of my countrymen of Louisiana, in the name of your own interest, I dare once more to ask you this new proof of patriotism.

Being deprived of my dearest hopes, and of the pleasure, after an absence of fourteen years and a proscription of three, of returning to the bosom of my family, my friends, and my countrymen, I have only one course to follow -- that of going to France and expressing to the representatives of the French people the cry, the general wish of the Louisianians to become part of the French Republic. – informing them, at the same time, of the most ardent desire which the Kentuckians have had, and will continue to have for ever, to take the most active part in my undertaking tending to open to them the free navigation of the Mississippi.

The French republicans, in their sublime constitutional act, have proffered their protection to all those nations who may have the courage to shake off the yoke of tyranny. The Louisianians have the most sacred right to it. They are French, but have been sacrificed to despotism by arbitrary power. The honor, the glory, the duty of the National Convention is to grant them their powerful support.

---

[89] Thomas Perkins Abernathy, The South in the New Nation, 1789-1819: A History of the South, (Baton Rouge, LA: Louisiana State University Press, 1961), 123.

Every petition or plan relative to that important object would meet with the highest consideration. An address from the Democratic Society of Lexington would give it a greater weight.

Accept Citizens, the farewell, not the last, of a brother who is determined to sacrifice everything in his power for the liberty of his country, and the prosperity of the generous inhabitants of Kentucky. Salut en la patrie.

Auguste La Chaise[90]

But it was not quite farewell for La Chaise, who spent several more months in the United States. According to Grace King in *Creole Families of New Orleans*, LaChaise was spotted in Philadelphia in 1794 as a member of the Jacobin Society.[91] Moreover, it was he, who was blamed at the time for the 1795 Pointe Coupée slave uprising which occurred between 12 April 1795 and 15 May of the same year. News of the planned uprising was, however, reported to Captain Guillaume Duparc at the Pointe Coupée Post by two slaves, Juan Bautista Herrera and Maria Luisa on 10 April 1795. Arrests were soon made, including the leader, Antoine Sarrazin, a mulatto owned by Julien Poydras, as well as slaves belonging to Colin Lacour, Charles Dufour and Simon Croizet. By 15 May 1795, there were sixty prisoners incarcerated in the local jail. In order to maintain peace at Pointe Coupée, Carondelet sent Captain Carlos de Grand-Pré, the acting commandant of the Natchez Post to the area with the galley *Luisiana* to act as a floating prison. Trials were held between 8 and 19 May 1795, which revealed that the plot had been a real one and that Natchez was supposed to revolt the same day. Two white men, a German tailor named Rockemborgh and a man identified as "Bouyaval," were said to be involved. Those not executed were brought to New Orleans aboard the frigate *Misisipi* (perhaps the frigate *Misisipiano* originally owned by Geronimo LaChiapella which he had sold to Jean Dupuy in 1791), and then sent to Havana to serve out their sentences. On 22 June 1795 Carondelet closed Louisiana to all slave imports and on 19 February 1796 banned the entry of all blacks into Louisiana.[92]

Carondelet and the colonists believed that the slaves had been incited by agents of the French government, in particular by LaChaise, who became *persona non grata* in Louisiana. On 13 September 1796, the Baron de Pontalba wrote to his wife: "Mme. Marré of Charleston declared that LaChaise had told her that he was the instigator of the troubles in Pointe Coupée; that he had missed his chance this time, but that he would try again to do better the next time."[93] Writing of Auguste LaChaise to President Thomas Jefferson in his *Réflexions historiques et politiques sur la Louysiane*, Saint-Domingue refugee Dr. Paul Alliot repeated the rumors of the day:

An inhabitant of New Orleans well known in Jérémie, Island of St. Domingue, because of his murders, thefts [and] devastations, has gone to the United States, to the Ohio River, and [via] the Mississippi to Pointe Coupée, the area more heavily populated in slaves than anywhere else. Hoping to disrupt everything to profit from the colonists' misery, he made the acquaintance of several black men and convinced them to revolt by showing them how happy those [blacks] in St. Domingue were. If the Spanish government, which had been warned of these stormy developments in time [to take action], had not reestablished order by dispatching troops and by having about sixty of the renegades hanged, the colonists would have found themselves without means of support. Seeing his attempt fail, the head of the insurrection fled to the United States, and the Negroes left behind by this villain returned to their farms.[94]

Louis Auguste LaChaise ultimately returned to Saint-Domingue, leaving Agathe and his daughter behind in New Orleans, where he rejoined the French Army under General Leclerc, who had been tasked by the Emperor Napoleon to restore order on the island. He was killed in 1803, some say simply in an ambuscade, others claim that it was in a naval battle and that his body was buried with honors in the Gulf of Mexico.[95]

---

[90] Charles Gayarré, *History of Louisiana. The Spanish Domination*, Vol. 3. (Gretna, LA: Pelican Publishing Co., 1974), 341-344.

[91] Grace King, *Creole Families of New Orleans*, (New Orleans, LA: Cornerstone Book Publishers, 2010), 165.

[92] Jack D.L. Holmes, "The Abortive Slave Revolt at Pointe Coupée, Louisiana 1795," in *Louisiana History: The Journal of the Louisiana Historical Association*, Vol. 11, No. 4 (Autumn 1970): 341-362.

[93] Debien and LeGardeur, "The Saint-Domingue Refugees in Louisiana," in Brasseaux & Conrad, *The Road to Louisiana,* 183.

[94] Ibid., 183.

[95] The idea that he was buried at sea appears in *Old Families of Louisiana* by Stanley C. Arthur and George Campbell Huchet de Kernion. These authors also claim that he was married to the daughter of Pierre Foucher, who was the granddaughter of Étienne de Boré. This is completely false. Marie Antoinette Foucher, daughter of Pierre and Françoise Elizabeth Boré, married

After the 1795 aborted slave revolt, Carondelet attempted to secure better conditions for the slave population, including the guarantee of proper food and clothing, a fair work schedule, time off for their own planting and leisure, redress before the court if injured by one's owner, and burial in the Catholic cemetery instead of on the owner's plantation. In an effort to placate the owners whose slaves had participated in the uprising, Carondelet attempted to exact a payment of six reales per slave owned by all those in New Orleans and all the outlying districts in Lower Louisiana in order to reimburse those who had lost their slaves due to execution or imprisonment. Jérome Chiapella's brother Carlo/Charles, a resident of Pointe Coupée during the time of the slave uprisings, paid 16 pesos 4 reales (about $16.50 USD) for the 22 slaves he owned.[96] His brother, Jérome Chiapella, a resident of the second quarter of New Orleans, paid 120 escalins (about $15 USD) for having twenty slaves.[97] Of course, not everyone paid this voluntary taxation, and those whose slaves had been exiled or executed, lost their investments.

Given the events that had unfolded around Amada Lachaise's father,[98] Louis Auguste, Citizen Lachaise, notorious in the United States as well as in Spanish Louisiana for having fomented the 1795 Pointe Coupée slave revolt, it is understandable that Agathe Lemelle and her daughter, Amada, would seek refuge in Chiapella's household during the volatile years between 1795 and 1803 before the Louisiana territory was sold to the United States. It was also during these last few years of the eighteenth century that young Amada Lachaise and Celestin Coudrain Chiapella would become reacquainted.

Philippe Auguste Delachaise, a lawyer and native of Opelousas, St. Landry Parish, who was the son of Honoré Delachaise and Céleste Chrétien, on 14 April 1822. (SLC M7, 14)

[96] Winston DeVille, "Slave Owners of Pointe Coupée and False River in 1795," in *Mississippi Mélange*, Volume 1. (Baton Rouge, LA: Provincial Press, 1995), 53.

[97] Judy Riffel, "Colonial Period - 1795 Tax on Slaveowners," *Le Comité des Archives de la Louisiane,* (http://www.lecomite.org/members/raconteur.html).#archive) Originally published in *Le Raconteur* : vol. XII, nos.2, 3, 4; vol. XIII, nos. 1,2; vol. 13, no. 1.

[98] Although Louis Auguste Delachaise had dropped the "de" from his name for political reasons, the "de" absent from Amada's surname was a result of her being the illegitimate daughter of a titled landowner. It would be the same for all illegitimate children of nobility. The "natural" offspring of the Delachaise family used the name "Lachaise," not Delachaise. Similarly, the "natural" offspring of the Delassize family used the name Lassize, In France, however, several records show Amada Lachaise, wife of Celestin Chiapella as "Jeanne Aimée Delachaise."

CHAPTER 5

CELESTIN COUDRAIN CHIAPELLA AND AMADA LACHAISE

After one of Jérome Chiapella's two adopted sons, Celestin Coudrain, arrived back from France ca. 1797 where he had been studying, he moved back into the Chiapella household and formed a relationship with Agathe Lemelle's daughter, Amada LaChaise. Within the year, they had started a family together. Their first child, Amada Maria, but always called Marie Camille, was born ca. July 1798. There is, however, no existing baptismal record for her. A boy, Geronimo Bautista, was born ca. 1800 but died at about three years of age and was interred on 27 January 1803 (SLC, F4, 123). Geronimo was identified as the "natural child of Don Zelestino LaChapella and Amada Lemell [...] baptized with Holy Water by Father Cappelan of the infantry regiment 'fias de Mexico.'"

Archdiocese of New Orleans (Orleans Parish, LA), *St. Louis Cathedral, New Orleans, Funerals 1793-1803*, Digital Images, Funeral #1115, p. 123, Geronimo Lachapella, illegitimate son of Don Celestino LaChapella and Amada Lemell, dated 27 January 1803, Image 126/141. (https://archives.arch-no.org/sacramental_records: accessed 2/3/2018).

The child's death had occurred just six months after Celestin Coudrain Chiapella lost his birth mother to yellow fever. Although he had been back in New Orleans for five years, he had not returned to his mother's house, but had remained with his beloved step-father, as his mother's second husband was still living. Marie Pelagie Duvernay Coudrain Bagneris was buried on 19 June 1802, after confessing and receiving extreme unction. She could not receive the Eucharist because of her death by yellow fever with "Bomitos" (vomiting) She was interred in the Parish Churchyard at age forty-six, a native of the city, born to "Luis Duverne" and "Rosa Josefa Gibar" [*sic* Girardy,] and the wife of "Juan-Baptisto Baneris" [*sic*, Bagneris] (d. 1812). The Spanish priest who wrote the record, Father Domingo Joachim Solano had the usual problem trying to spell the French surnames. He also, as were many in Spanish New Orleans at that time, in a habit of substituting a "b" for a "v" when expressing themselves in writing (e.g. "bomitos" for "vomitos.")

Courtesy of the Archives of the Archdiocese of New Orleans, Saint Louis Cathedral Records, Sacramental Register of St. Louis Cathedral Funerals – Vol. 1799-1803, p. 114, #994, Funeral of Maria Pelagia Duverne, wife of Juan Bautista Baneris, (Courtesy of Emilie Leumas, Archivist – Kimberly Johnson and Katie Vest – Researching Archivists.)

Celestin and Amada's next five children were all baptized on 18 May 1813: Ana born on 22 June 1802 (SLC B25, 75); Juana Celestina born on 28 November 1803 (SLC B25, 75); Augusto born on 1 November 1806 (SLC, B25, 76); Catharina born on 4 July 1808 (SLC, B 25, 76). Angelica/Angèle/Angélique Chiapella, whose nickname was Étrenne,[99] was born on 1 January 1812, and was baptized on 18 May 1813 (SLC B-25, 76). Once again, as with their previous four children baptized on that date, her paternal grandparents were listed as Geromo Chiapella and Pelagia Duverne. At the same time in May 1813, Celestin and Amada's marriage was recorded as having taken place on 30 October 1803. The most legible of the five baptisms, that of Juana Celestina, is seen on the following page written in Spanish by Father Antonio de Sedella. In this entry the "La" is crossed out everywhere indicating that the family was returning to the original Italian spelling of the name. Fr. de Sedella also chose to use the ordinary Spanish naming pattern with both the father's and mother's surname for the child. Note as well that Amada's surname "Lachaise," was used and not her mother's surname "Lemelle." Finally, the child's paternal grandfather was said to have been "Geromo Chiapella," although her paternal grandfather had actually been Pierre Coudrain. The document reads in part: "Baptism of Juana Celestina Chiapella y LaChaise. On May 18, 1813, I Father Antonio de Sedella, Capucin, priest of the parish church of St. Louis, New Orleans, baptized with holy oil a girl born on 28 November 1803, legitimate daughter of Celestino Chiapella and Amada La Chaise, natives and residents of this city: Paternal grandparents Geromo Chiapella and Pelagia Duverne: Maternal grandparents: Augusto LaChaise and Agatha Lemel, the child has been given the name Juana Celestina. Her godparents: Esteban [Étienne Coudrain] Chiapella and Maria Chiapella, uncle and sister of the child. Representing the godmother is Victoria Maroteau.[100] [...]. It important to note that the five baptisms were recorded in the Saint Louis Cathedral Baptism Book for Whites 1811-1815, Part II. Nowhere was there mention that the children's mother, Amada Lachaise was illegitimate, or that she was a person of color:

---

[99] An "étrenne" is a gift given in France on New Year's Day.
[100] Victoria Maroteau was the wife of Modesto Lefebvre, longtime confidant and business manager of Jérome Chiapella.

Celestin Coudrain Chiapella had returned to Louisiana earlier than his younger brother, Estevan/Étienne Coudrain and was clearly his adopted father's favorite son. Moreover, as the spouse of Jérome's companion Agathe Lemelle's only daughter, he was the recipient of much largesse from the couple. There is no doubt that they gave him the money to start his own plantation in St. Bernard Parish which grew in size and was described in later years in an 1831 petition to the United States House of Representatives which was used to verify his claim as: "a plantation on the Mississippi about nine miles below the city of New Orleans [...] that [...] contains according to a survey made by a deputy surveyor of the United States to whom the original titles were exhibited the quantity of three thousand and eighty seven acres [...]".[101]

Jérome Chiapella, who had been treated so favorably by the Spanish Government, but snubbed by the new American regime as an immoral and possibly dangerous inhabitant of the newly acquired Louisiana Territory, started making his plans to leave for Europe in the first decade of the nineteenth century. He did however make one very large land purchase before he left. On 5 October 1803, "Geronimo LaChiapella," assisted by his son "Celestino," petitioned the Spanish Intendant Don Juan Ventura Morales asking to purchase 120,000 arpents of land in West Florida. Morales ordered the Surveyor General of the province of West Florida to survey the land, a task which was completed in January 1804. In the meantime, Chiapella sold his 124-132 Royal St property which he had bought from Antonio Ceulino on 12 December 1796 to Joseph McNeil on 24 November 1803 for 75,000 "pesos fuertes" before notary Adolph Mazureau.[102] On 28 March 1804, LaChiapella was given a title to the West Florida property by Morales. The majority of the 120,000 arpents (101,375 acres) was situated between the Amite

---

[101] Walter Lowrey, ed., *American State Papers : Documents, legislative and Executive of the Congress of the United States in relation to the Public Lands from the First Session of the First Congress to the First Session of the Twenty-Third Congress: March 1, 1789 to June 15, 1834*, Vol 5, (Washington, DC: Duff and Green, 1834) 534,535. This information available at: https://books.google.com/books?id=5xFFAQAAMAAJ&pg=PA535&dq=Chiapella+%2B+St.+Bernard+Parish&hl=en&sa=X&ved=2ahUKEwiJw7us1pHkAhUF2qwKHezSBQMQ6wEwCHoECAkQAQ#v=onepage&q=Chiapella%20%2B%20St.%20Bernard%20Parish&f=false.

[102] The Collins C. Diboll Vieux Carré Digital Survey, Historic New Orleans Collection, https://www.hnoc.org/vcs/property_info.php?lot=1120. Note: This became the site of the Merchant's Exchange building in 1835, whose frontage was on Exchange Place, a "new" street directly behind Royal Street.

and Tickfaw Rivers and ended in the cypress swamps at Lake Maurepas. Below is a map of approximately 94,000 arpents situated between the Amite and Tickfaw Rivers (No. 1706) belonging to "Don Geronimo Lachapella (*sic*)":

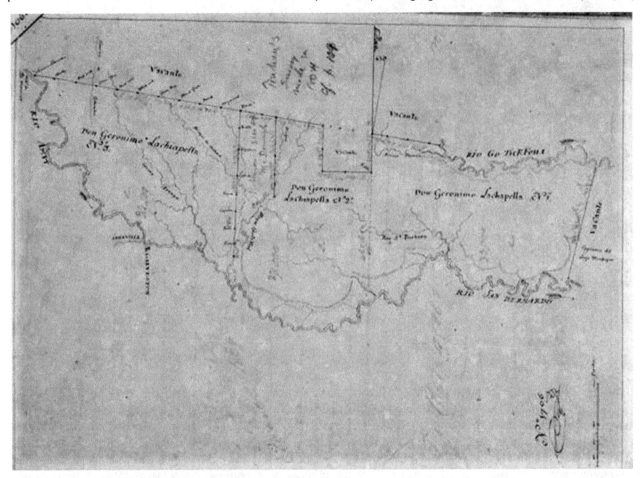

Pintado Papers, Mss. 890, 1223, Louisiana and Lower Mississippi Valley Collections, LSU Libraries, Baton Rouge, LA. Note the spelling: Rio Amit (Amite River) to the left; Upper right: Rio Go Tickfoua (Tickfaw River); Middle right just below "vacante" "Cypriera del Lago Monrepas" or "Cypress swamp of Lake Maurepas." [103]

Was it luck or wisdom that guided Chiapella when he turned around and on 7 May 1804 sold 60,000 arpents of his purchase to John McDonogh and Shepherd Brown? On 11 December 1805, Chiapella sold the remaining 60,000 arpents to William Donaldson, who on the same day bought the other 60,000 arpents from McDonogh and Brown. However, on 20 January 1806, Donaldson sold the entire 120,000 acres back to McDonogh and Brown for 35,000 piastres gourdes. This land speculation led to almost seventy-five years of litigation because the 120,000 arpents of land, almost 100,000 of which lay in St. Helena Parish, LA, was in the disputed territory of West Florida. The United States government claimed that it had bought this area when it made the Louisiana purchase from France which was finalized on 20 December 1803. The Spanish government disagreed and between 1803 and 1810 the Spanish remained in the area. The people of West Florida declared themselves an independent republic in September 1810, but United States forces took over the area that same December. That part of West Florida which lay between the Mississippi and Pearl Rivers was incorporated with Louisiana when it became the eighteenth state in the union on 30 April 1812. The boundary disputes between the United States and France were not officially settled until 22 February 1819 with the Adams-Onis treaty. However, ownership of the McDonogh lands would be disputed in Congress well into the third quarter of the nineteenth century.

---

[103] Additional acreage of 12,900 arpents on the Tickfaw, bought by Chiapella can be found on plan #1707. There are also 8,840 additional arpents shown on plan # 1708 and 3,770 arpents on Plan # 1709, both of which are on the Pearl River, all which were part of the 1806 sale. To see the other maps go to https://louisianadigitallibrary.org/ and put the name "LaChapella" in the search box.

On 15 March 1804 "Jérome La Chiappella" was appointed one of the original superintendents to establish a Bank of Discount, Deposit and Exchange with a capital of $600,000 divided in to shares of $100 each authorized by Territorial Governor William C.C. Claiborne. The subscriptions were under the direction of Chiapella, Evan Jones, J. F. Merieult, Paul Lanusse, William Garland, Edward Livingston, Pierre Sauvé, Joseph Tricou, John Lanthois, William Donaldson, Nicolas P. Girod, John McDonogh, Benjamin Morgan, H.B. Trist, Michel Fortier and Beverly Chew, a veritable who's who of mercantile New Orleans.[104]

"Gerome La Chiapella" filed an oath of allegiance to the United States on 16 April 1804 at the United States Customhouse at New Orleans, wherein he abjured his allegiance "to every foreign Prince, Potentate, State or Sovereignty whatever, and particularly to the King of Spain and the Emperor of France signing in his usual way:[105] His adopted son, Étienne Coudrain, also signed an affidavit as "Stephen La Chiapella" six months later in order to secure his Seaman's Certificate.

Signature of Gerome La Chiapella for his Oath of Allegiance dated 16 April 1804.

On 16 May 1804 Chiapella sold his ship the *Aimable Céleste*, which he had originally purchased from an agent acting on behalf of Allen Shepherd, a resident of New York, on 1 April 1802, to Armand Duplantier for $10,500 piastres. Chiapella sold the ship with all its sails, rigging, masts, cables, anchors and anything else belonging to it to Duplantier in exchange for one lot of ground on Rue Conti measuring 62.5 feet of frontage on that street, which Duplantier had bought from Valentin Robert Avart as attorney, to Pierre Favrot, a Lieutenant Colonel in the Spanish Army, on 6 January 1801 for $6,000. Duplantier signed a promissory note to Chiapella for the additional $4,500 payable in full by 31 December 1804. It is noteworthy that Pierre Pedesclaux, who usually penned his documents in Spanish or French, recorded this sale in English. It was clear that Chiapella, advanced in age was consolidating his assets in order to move back to Europe. That he chose Bordeaux and not Genoa, Italy, was no surprise because his as well as his adopted sons' merchandising and shipping businesses were carried on between New Orleans and the French port.[106]

On 15 November 1804 Chiapella became a member of the first Territorial Grand Jury which met on that date. He, along with Jacques Pitot, then Mayor of New Orleans, George Pollock, Michel Fortier, Arthur and Benjamin Morgan, and other mostly English-speaking residents of the city, were sworn in by J.B. Prévost, one of the judges of the Superior Court of the Territory of Orleans.[107]

On 11 May 1805 the Mayor of New Orleans, Jacques/James Pitot and the City Council agreed to pay Matthew Flannery to do a census of the city and its suburbs. The task was completed on 5 August 1805. "Geromes La Chiapella" was living in house #19 on Rue St. Louis with his family. Unfortunately, no names, other than the head of the household, were given. The rest of the household was listed by sex, race and age. In the Chiapella household there were two white males over sixteen years (we suppose Chiapella and his adopted son Celestino); one white male under sixteen years (?); two white females above sixteen years (Agathe Lemelle and Amada La

[104] [By Authority], "Louisiana Bank," *The Union*, March 15, 1804, digital image, *Genealogybank.com* (https://www.genealogybank.com:accessed 8/20/2019), p. 1, col. 4.

[105] "Citizenship Affidavits of US-born Seamen at Select Ports, 1792-1869,"digital image, *Ancestry.com* (https://www.ancestry.com: accessed 2/2/19) citing *Proofs of Citizenship Used To Apply For Seamen's Protection Certificates for the Port of New Orleans, Louisiana, 1800, 1802, 1804–1812, 1814–1816, 1818–1819, 1821, 1850–1851, 1855–1857,* NARA Microfilm publication M1826, Roll 1, Record Group 36, Image 3/503.

[106]NARC, Pierre Pedesclaux, Notary, Volume 47 – folios 516 & 517 both sides. "Sale and Exchange, Gerome Lachiapella to Armand Duplantier," Courtesy Hon. Chelsey Richard Napoleon, Clerk of Civil District Court, Parish of Orleans.

[107] "New Orleans, November 28," (New York) *Morning Chronicle*, January 5, 1805, digital image, *Genealogybank.com* (https://www.genealogybank.com: accessed 20 August 2019), p. 2, col. 5.

Chaise); three white females under sixteen years (Celestin's daughters Amada Maria, Ana, and Juana Celestina); one mulatto male below sixteen years (possibly José, a male mulatto Chiapella manumitted along with his mother Adelaïda in 1799). There were also thirteen slaves in the household: two males above age sixteen, one below sixteen, six females above age sixteen and four females below age sixteen.

Marie Jeanne Françoise (Tonton) Lemelle was another person of interest in this census. She was listed as "Tonton Lemelle" living at #5 Rue d'Orleans, a free person of color over the age of sixteen years, with four slaves including two males under age sixteen and two females under age sixteen. It is noteworthy that Chiapella did not tell the census taker that either Agata or Amada were free women of color, nor were Celestin's children identified as such, yet Tonton Lemelle must have informed the census taker or perhaps he already knew that she was a free woman of color. Even in early census records, but right through the twentieth century, statistics separating people of color from the white population were very inaccurate, resulting in the undercounting of the free colored residents of the state. For what it is worth, Flannery counted 3551 whites, 1566 free people of color, 3105 slaves and 253 "all other persons" for a total of 8475 residents of New Orleans and the suburbs.[108]

On 2 July 1806, in preparation for his departure, Chiapella filed his last will and testament in New Orleans. It was written in Spanish, but when it was filed at Bordeaux, Gironde, France, on 27 August 1822, it was translated into French. We have taken the information from the French copy which appeared in *Histoire et Généalogie de la Famille Cotton de Bennetot Normandie* by Arlette Cotton de Bennetot in which we found the following information:[109]

Chiapella identified himself as "Don Gérome Chiapella," unmarried,[110] a native of Nervi, in the states of Genoa, legitimate son of Don Ciro Chiapella and Dona Angela Maria Chiappe, both from the same town and both deceased. He gave to his brother, Jean-Baptiste Chiapella, and his sisters Dona Maria, Dona Magdelena, and Dona Benita Chiapella the sum of 200,000 or more silver Genovese pounds in coin (espèces sonantes) which were stored in Genoa, and directed that his brother would divide it equally amongst them. He also left them to divide the net amount after the sale of some merchandise also stored in Genoa. He left his brother and partner in New Orleans, Don Carlos Chiapella, 16,000 piastres.[111] He left his sisters Dona Geronima and Dona Cathalina each 10,000 piastres. He left to his adopted son Don Estevan/Étienne Coudrin (Stephen Chiapella) 12,000 piastres. He gave to Agathe Lemelle a piece of property situated in New Orleans, Rue Royale, measuring 60 feet in front by 120 feet deep, on one side bordering land belonging to him, on the other, belonging to the free negress Genevieve. He also willed Agathe 6,000 piastres and the two slaves Cathalina and Marante. To Agathe's daughter, Aimée/Amada La Chaise, without identifying her as the wife of Celestin Coudrain Chiapella, and to Amada's three daughters Camille (Amada Maria), Anne (Ana), and Celestine (Juana Celestina) each 4,000 piastres. In addition, he gave Camille, a griffe woman named Sally with her offspring. To Anne he gave the negress Marie, and to Celestine, the negress named Sophie. He gave to Zenon, a free quadroon, who had been the slave of Nicolas Forstall, Sr., the sum of 4,000 piastres.[112] These bequests, excluding the Genovese silver, amounted to 70,000 piastres or about $1,489,361 in today's dollars. He signed the document as "Geromo Chiapella."

He also stated that the following items should be included in his assets: 100,000 piastres held by Don Eugene Langlois, a merchant in Bordeaux; 12,000 or so piastres held by Don Joseph Thibaud in New York in debts to be recovered; 30,000 or so piastres held by his brother Jean-Baptiste Chiapella, a merchant in Genoa; three additional pieces of property in New Orleans and twenty-one slaves. He left to Camille, Anne and Celestine, the daughters of Aimée/Amada LaChaise, the land and house where he was living in New Orleans with all the furniture and silver on the condition that they remain there until their majority, after which the property could be sold and the

---

[108] Rosemonde E. and Emile Kuntz Collection, Manuscripts Number 600, Louisiana Research Collection, Howard-Tilton Memorial Library, Tulane University, New Orleans, LA, Census for Geromes La Chiapella (image 8/46) and for Tonton Lemelle (Image 3/46). To see the entire census go to: https://louisianadigitallibrary.org/islandora/ object/fpoc-p16313coll51%3A35429.

[109] Arlette Cotton de Bennetot, *Histoire et généalogie de la Famille Cotton de Bennetot – Normandie*, (Bordeaux, France : Arlette Cotton de Bennetot, 1981), 140-144.

[110] When he wrote out this will in New Orleans, he was not lawfully wed to Agathe.

[111] One piastre or one peso in 1822 was roughly equivalent to one American dollar. One American dollar in 1822 is the equivalent of $21.28 today, therefore, Don Carlos Chiapella received the equivalent of $340,425 in 2019 dollars.

[112] We believe that Zenon is the slave whom Chiapella manumitted on 30 March 1803, although no name was given. He was described as a male mulatto, age 26 which Chiapella had bought from Nicolas Forstall in 1800.

proceeds divided amongst them. He also cancelled any debts belonging to his brother, Don Carlos/Charles Chiapella, and freed four slaves because of their good service: the negress Angélique, the mulatto Charles, as well as Cambridge, and Marsella. Finally, he nominated his one and only universal beneficiary to be Celestin Coudrain, because of the great love and tenderness he had for him. He left to him the residue of his estate both in New Orleans, and outside of the city and country. He indicated finally that if Celestin so wished he could adopt the surname "Chiapella." Jérome Chiapella nominated Dominique Langourand and Modeste Lefebvre to be his executors, as well as to see to his burial in a modest grave, the location of which they would choose. Geronimo Chiapella's vast estate was worth in today's dollars well over $4,510,638, not including the Genovese silver, slaves and New Orleans real estate..

His slave, Angélique, however, did not have to wait until his death to be manumitted. On 22 July 1806, Modeste Lefebvre and Dominique Langourand, with Chiapella's power of attorney, appeared before the notary Estevan Quinones to free the fifty-year-old slave Angelica/Angélique gratuitously for her good service.[113]

All property owners were shown on an 1808 map of the French Quarter which was made by the cartographer, Gilbert Joseph Pilié. According to this map, Chiapella, listed in error as "LaChapelle," owned four properties. He had three pieces of property at the corner of Royal and Conti, one building faced Royal, the other faced Conti. The third stood at the corner of the two streets. The fourth property, where Chiapella was enumerated with his family in 1805, faced St. Louis Street and was one house from the corner of St. Louis and Royal, in the square bounded by St. Louis, Chartres, Toulouse and Royal Streets. A copy of a six-block portion of the Pilié map is seen below. Counting from the top left, the Chiapella properties are in blocks 4 and 6 and are labeled "La Chapelle."

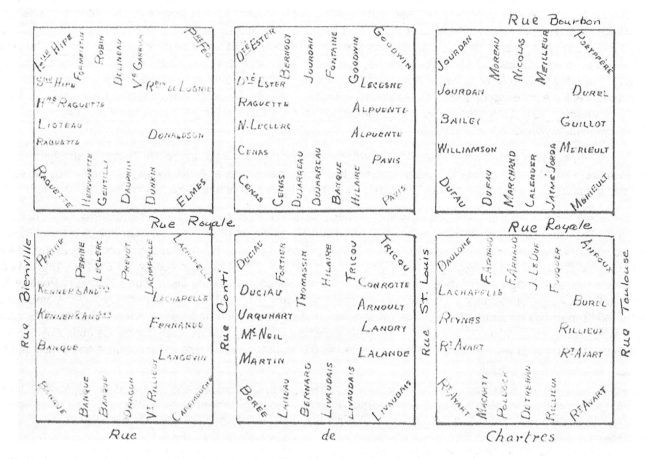

Six block area taken from Plan de la Ville de la Nouvelle Orléans (Map of New Orleans), done in 1808 by Gilbert Joseph Pilié. (The Historic New Orleans Collection, 2008.0003.3)

---

[113] "Louisiana, Freed Slave Records, 1719-1820," [database on-line], Ancestry.com (https://www.ancestry.com: accessed 3/4/2019) citing Gwendolyn Midlo Hall, compiler, Afro-Louisiana History and Genealogy, 1719-1820. This database is also available at http://www.ibiblio.org/laslave/.

By the time the above map was made, we believe that Jérome Chiapella and Agathe Lemelle had already left for Bordeaux, Gironde France. The couple wed at Bordeaux on 1 December 1810. They both gave their address as Fossés de l'Intendance #46. They were married at that address because, Jérome Chiapella, as he was known in France, had presented a physician's note dated 17 November 1810 affirming that he was too ill to make the trip to the Town Hall. The two parties to the marriage were described as: "Mr. Jerome Chiappella, aged of about 70 years, native of Nervi, near Genoa in Italy, land owner, formerly a resident of New Orleans, and for two years now a resident of Bordeaux at Fossés de l'Intendance #46, son of the late Cyr... Chiappella and Angella Maria Chiappé, both deceased in Genoa. And Miss Agathe Lemelle, aged about 38 years, a native of New Orleans, daughter of the late Jacques Lemelle and of Jacqueline Dupard, both deceased at New Orleans." Further below in the marriage document it was stated that they had no living ancestors (n'ayant aucuns ascendants vivants). The witnesses were Pierre Maillères, a royal notary, Eugène Langlois, and Pierre Commagère, both merchants and Jean Henry Coupry, a neighbor. Everyone signed the document except for Chiapella who stated that he could not because of a weakness he had in his right hand.[114]

While Chiapella and his wife Agathe Lemelle lived out the rest of their lives quietly at Bordeaux, Celestin and his wife Amada/Jeanne Aimée LaChaise remained on their plantation in St. Bernard Parish about nine miles below the city of New Orleans. He and his brother Étienne/Estevan Chiapella, who had followed in his adopted father's footsteps to become captain of his own vessel the *Aimable Matilda*, made numerous trips back and forth to Bordeaux over the course of the next twenty years.

Celestin and Amada were the parents of four more children, three of whom were born in New Orleans and baptized at St. Louis Cathedral Church: Marie Petrone (b. abt. 1813), who died "as a very young child" on 31 August 1815 (SLC F, 11). Celestin Chiapella, Jr., also known as Auguste Celestin Chiapella was born a few months before the Battle of New Orleans on 1 September 1814, and baptized after the end of the War of 1812 on 29 July 1816 (SLC B-28, 63). Jeronimo Modesto Chiapella was born on 28 October 1816 and baptized on 28 June 1817. (SLC B-28, 117) He was named for Modesto Lefebvre, Geronimo LaChiapella's right-hand-man in Louisiana, and an executor of his will, who held power of attorney to see to his affairs in Louisiana. Modesto and his wife, Victoria Maroteau were the child's godparents. Celestin and Amada's last child, Marie Thérèse Camille Chiapella was born on 16 September 1819 at Bordeaux, Section II, Gironde, France. Celestin Chiapella registered his last child at the Town Hall two days later on 18 September 1819."[115]

Chiapella was enumerated in the 1810 territorial census for Louisiana, in the 7th District, Left Shore (now St. Bernard Parish) on the plantation. Included were two white males over age twenty-six, five other free persons (except Indians), and eighty-four slaves.[116] Celestin may have been present but Amada and the children were not.

Celestin and Amada's wedding date had always presented difficulty for them during their residence in New Orleans. They had asked the Abbé Koüne who had ostensibly officiated at the original marriage to insert it in the record, out of order, on 18 May 1813 when five of their children had also been baptized. According to their own testimony at the time, and according to Abbé Koüne's recollection, it had taken place on 30 October 1803. As a consequence, a marriage record dated 30 October 1803 was inserted by Abbé Jean-Pierre Koüne in Volume 3, page 125, Act #374, for marriages which had taken place between 1811 and 1816, in order to rectify the omission. In the 1813 marriage document the parents recognized Amada Maria, who had been born on 15 July 1798, and Ana, who had been born on 22 June 1802 as their legitimate offspring. While Ana, Juana Celestina, Augusto, Catherina and Angelica were baptized on the same day as the marriage record was redone, that is on 18 May 1813,

[114]Bordeaux, Gironde, France, Registres des actes de mariage de Bordeaux, Section 1, [Section 1, Bordeaux Marriage Registrations], 1810, Marriage #270, Jérome Chiappella to Agathe Lemelle, digital image, *Archives départementales de la Gironde*, "État Civil en ligne," (https://archives.gironde.fr/: acc. 23 August 2019), Cote 4E 926, Image 210/231. Note: Fossés de l'Intendance is now called the Cours du 12 Mars.

[115] Bordeaux, Gironde, France, Registres des actes de naissance de Bordeaux, Section 2, [Section 2, Bordeaux Birth Registrations], 1819, Birth #1377, Marie Thérèze Camille Chiappella, digital image, *Archives municipales de Bordeaux*, "État Civil en ligne," (https://archives.bordeaux-metropole.fr/: acc. 23 August 2019), Cote 1E 99, Image 135,136/191. Note: In this case Amada Lachaise was recorded as Jeanne Aimée Delachaise.

[116] 1810 United States Federal Census, New Orleans, Orleans Parish, LA, 7th District, Left Shore, Line 9 (right column) Celestin Lachiapella household, digital image, *Ancestry.com* (https://www.ancestry.com accessed 10/1/2019), citing NARA microfilm publication M252, Roll 10. Date of enumeration not given. Image 59/65.

Amada Maria (aka Camille) did not receive the sacrament. Almost twenty years later the reason behind all this confusion with the marriage date would be laid bare in a court case which ended by the couple leaving Louisiana to permanently relocate in France. (See next chapter for details)

The War of 1812 was another watershed moment in the lives of Celestin, Amada and their children, whose vast plantation was on the edge of the Battle of New Orleans. On 20 January 1806 Celestin Chiapella had been appointed a Second Lieutenant in the First regiment of the Militia of the Territory of Orleans. He probably would not have considered that in the early part of the next decade that the Americans would be, once again at war with Great Britain, and that their entry into Louisiana would be only miles from his plantation.

While searching for the exact location of the Chiapella Plantation in St. Bernard Parish, we discovered the maps of Arsène Lacarrière Latour, born on 13 October 1778 at Aurillac, Cantal, France, to Guillaume de Lacarrière de Latour and his wife Louise Marguerite Daudin. Latour studied architecture and art at the École de Beaux Arts in Paris. He became a military engineer and architect, who after the defeat of the Napoleonic Army in Saint-Domingue in 1804, came to America. Latour partnered with Hyacinthe Laclotte ca. 1806 in New Orleans, opening an office there at the corner of Royal and Orleans. At first successful, designing amongst other buildings, the first Orleans Street Theater and remodeling and adding a third story to the LeMonnier residence, their partnership was dissolved in 1813, possibly due to Latour's association with H. Bonneval Latrobe, whose father Benjamin had sent him down to oversee a project in New Orleans. The City Council had given M. Benjamin Latrobe and Associates a contract to deliver clean water to New Orleans out of the Mississippi River utilizing steam engine pumps. This project which saw the light in 1811 was interrupted by the turmoil caused by an impending second war with Great Britain. In the spring of 1812 Latour was granted citizenship by the Louisiana Supreme Court. He was also said to carry a United States passport, although we could find no record of it.[117]

Before and during the crucial Battle of New Orleans in 1814-1815. Latour and his former associates, Laclotte and Henry Sellon Boneval Latrobe, became indispensable to the war effort to attempt to ready the city of New Orleans for possible attack by the British. General Andrew Jackson gave Latour, who reported directly to him, the title of Major and Principal Engineer of the Seventh Military District, U.S. Army. Latour employed his engineering skills to design fortifications for the Americans to be used to protect from the advancing British troops along the Mississippi River. Because of those efforts in the field he was able to report several weeks before the decisive 8 January 1815 battle, that the British had penetrated Louisiana with the help of the Spanish and Portuguese fisherman who inhabited a village near where Bayou Mazant, the principal branch of Bayou Bienvenu, emptied into Lake Borgne.[118] Latour drew eight maps for an Atlas, published separately from the book he wrote, intitled *Historical Memoir of the War in West Florida and Louisiana in 1814-1815*, both of which were published in Philadelphia in 1816 by John Conrad & Co. The following are two partial scans of Plate #5 intitled "Map Shewing the Landing of the British Army, its several Encampments and Fortifications on the Mississippi and the Works they erected on their Retreat, also the different posts Encampments and Fortification made by the several Corps of the American Army during the whole Campaign." Celestin Chiapella's plantation, designated as belonging to "C. Lachapelle," is shown as it was in 1815 in both views of this map:

---

[117] Jean Garrigoux, trans. Gordon S. Brown, *A Visionary Adventurer: Arsène Lacarrière Latour 1778-1837 The Unusual Travels of a Frenchman in the Americas,* (Lafayette, LA: University of Louisiana at Lafayette Press, 2017), 80-84.

[118] Arsène Lacarrière Latour, *Historical Memoir of The War in West Florida and Louisiana in 1814-15, With an Atlas.* (Gainesville, FL: University of Florida Press, 1964, Facsimile reproduction of the 1816 Edition complete with maps), 79.

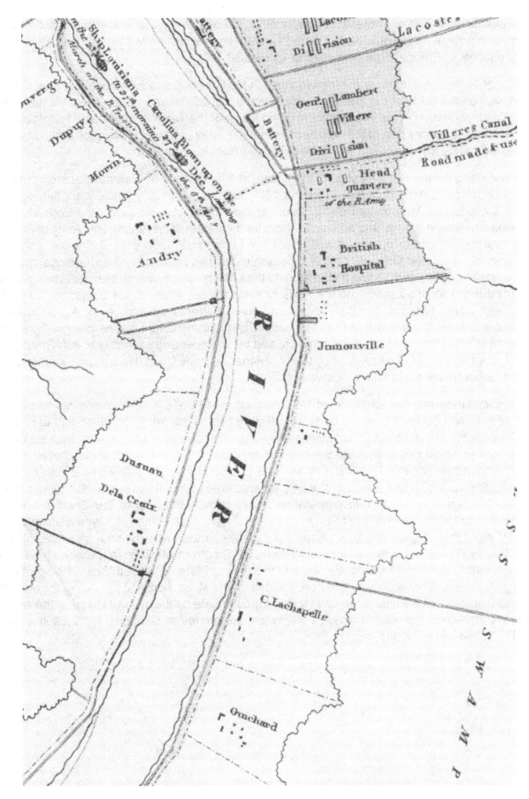

Partial scan of Plate #5 – From bottom East Bank of the Mississippi River: Plantations: Guichard, C. La Chapelle [*sic*, Celestin Lachiapella], Jumonville, and the shaded area which is the Villere Plantation, site of the British Encampment, Headquarters of General Pakenham and British Hospital. (The Historic New Orleans Collection 1979.238.7)

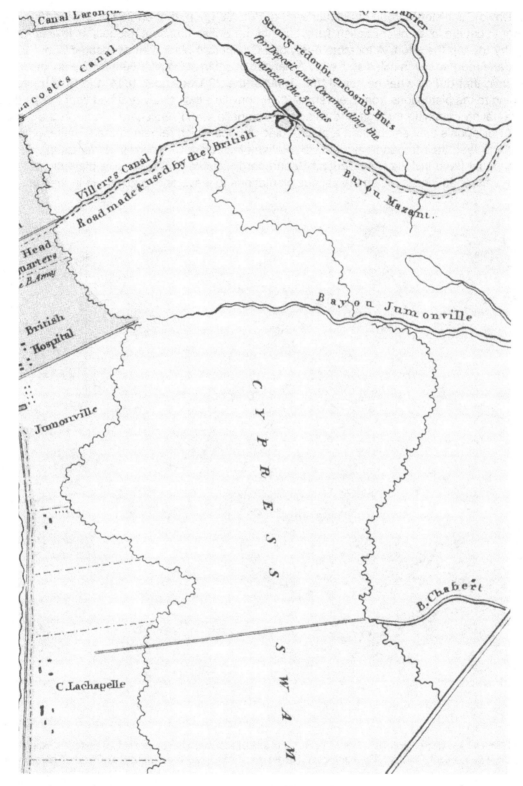

Partial scan of Plate #5 – C. Lachapelle (Celestin Lachiapella) plantation (botton left), in relation to path taken by the British down Bayou Mazant to the Villeré Canal (Shaded area and dotted line) and into the Villeré Plantation in what was called the "Affair of the 23rd December" [1814]. Part of Denis De La Ronde's 3rd Regiment Louisiana Militia was taken prisoner by the British along with Villeré's young son at 4:00 A.M. They all escaped the same day. (The Historic New Orleans Collection 1979.238.7)

Celestin Chiapella, recorded as "Celestin Lachiapella," had enlisted as a private in Colonel Pierre Denis de La Ronde's Third Regiment Louisiana Militia, although no dates of service were given. We do not know if he saw any action with the regiment. From information in *The Papers of Andrew Jackson*, Volume III, 1814-1815, we know from a letter from David Bannister Morgan, headquartered at Fort St. Leon, that on 26 December 1814, he was trying to fulfil an order to cut the levee near English Turn, but that the British had sent "piquets as low as Mr. [Celestin] La Chapelles" to try to stop the effort. A footnote described Chiapella's plantation as located about 2.5 miles below Villeré's Canal and roughly seven miles above the American position at English Turn.[119] We do know, from Latour's *Historical Memoir*, that during what he called "the Affair of the 28 December 1814" the British had taken all the horses belonging to the plantations from Bienvenu's to Jumonville's inclusively and had sent troops down as far as Philippon's Plantation marching through and pillaging Chiapella's and Guichard's land on the east bank of the Mississippi. At Philippon's they established a post of black troops which remained there until the final evacuation. They took cattle to feed their troops from all the plantations including, Chiapella's, as far as the end of Terre aux Boeufs, which would have included the Toutant Beauregard, Ducros and Delassize plantations. Moreover, the British troops encouraged the slaves on the various plantations to leave and to join them in the fight.[120]

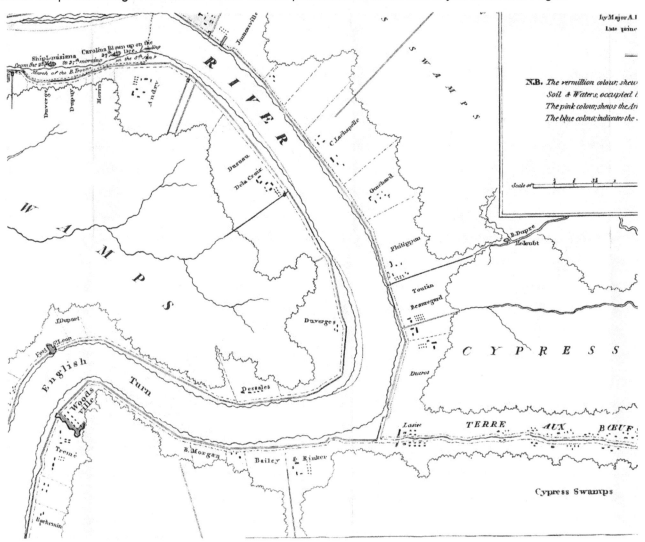

Partial scan of Plate #5 showing English Turn, Fort St. Léon, Terre aux Boeufs, and from bottom to top, east bank, plantations of Lassize, Ducros, Toutant Beauregard, Philippon, Guichard, C LaChapelle and Jumonville. (The Historic New Orleans Collection 1979.238.7)

Eleven days later, the Americans were victorious at the Battle of New Orleans, and on 9 January 1815 General Lambert sued for peace. When Jackson answered that he would only deal with the British Commander-in-Chief, Lambert indicated that he was the Commander, so it became known that General Edward Michael Pakenham

---

[119] Harold D. Moser, David R. Hoth, Sharon Macpherson, John H. Reinbold, eds. *The Papers of Andrew Jackson Volume III, 1814-1815.* (Knoxville, TN: The University of Tennessee Press, 1991), 223.

[120] Latour, *Historical Memoir*, 125.

had been killed and Generals Keane and Gibbs wounded. Louisiana troops spent the next few weeks flushing out British stragglers, and attempting to round up as many slaves who were still in the area. The British, during their retreat, had taken with them all the slaves willing to follow, and during their several weeks in the area had fed themselves at the expense of the plantation owners. At Villeré's, the owner's son, then about fourteen years of age, was offered about $500 for 80 head of cattle that had been slaughtered, but refused, knowing that they were worth at least, $3000.[121]

Celestin Chiapella was in the thick of it when it came time to try to recover his slaves. On 20 January 1815, British General John Lambert sent the following letter to Major General Andrew Jackson:

> Sir, Mr. Celestin Chiapella the bearer of this, is a Person whom previous to the British Force making a movement on the night of the 18th, I had from some particular circumstances thought right to detain for a few days. I shall send him back tomorrow and I have requested him to deliver this, the object of which is to acquaint you that to my great surprise, I found on reaching my Head Quarters, that a considerable number of Slaves had assembled there under the idea of embarking with the army. Every pains had been taken to persuade them to remain peaceably at home, Mr. Celestin has taken with him those that chose to return with him, & the remainder will be given to any proprietors that may claim them & sending a Person who may have influence with them as soon as possible, will be the readiest mode & I will add every facility to their being sent back. [...][122]

On 8 February 1815 General John Lambert sent the following letter to Major General Jackson, which read in part:

> What I said respecting the slaves regard those that I could not prevent coming to us when I was on shore. I am not at the anchorage where Mr. Livingston and Mr. White have been received; and indeed, I have nothing to say to it. I did all I could to persuade them to return at the time, but no one was willing, as will be testified by Mr. Celestin [Chiapella], a proprietor whom I had detained until the British forces had evacuated their last position: this gentleman saw the slaves that were present, and did all he could to urge them to go back.[123]

Celestin Chiapella and the other planters were determined to have their slaves returned. In one of the final appendices of Latour's book, a list of planters and the slaves they lost was published. Only the Villeré's had lost more: Jacques and Gabriel Villeré (52), Celestin Lachiapella (43), Messrs. Jumonville de Villiers (20), Lacoste (13), Bienvenu (10), Ducros (9), Léandre Lacoste (8), Delaronde (7), Delassize (6), Philippon (5), Mendez and Delino (4 each), Bronier and Reggio (3 each), Beauregard (2), Veillon and Solis (2), Mendez, Macarty, Delery, Harang (1 each).[124]

The slaves, however, who left on vessels with the British for their Caribbean possessions, were not returned to them. The owners brought their claims before the first session of the Nineteenth U.S. Congress on 6 December 1825 with proof of ownership. Chiapella offered the names of forty three slaves that had been taken away, or had gone voluntarily with the British when they evacuated St. Bernard Parish in 1815, to wit: Bill, Christopher, Ado, Charity, Samby, Peter, Michael, Isaac, Hector, Prince, Harris, Honoré, Soulas, Coissy, Friday, Coffy, James, Zephyr, Rabasse, Gallo, Jean-Baptiste, Joe, Lapaix, James Corego, William, Henry, Fine, Sophie, Denise, Rosalie, Azimia, Françoise, Félicité, Rosette, Babet, Josephine, Suzane, Jean, Vincent, Rougeau, Louis, Petit Charles and Charles Soussier. Awards were finally authorized on 2 March 1827 under the First Article of the Treaty of Ghent, which had stated in part that: "All territory, places, and possessions whatsoever taken by either party from the other during the war, or which may be taken after the signing of this Treaty, excepting only the Islands hereinafter mentioned, shall be restored without delay and without causing any destruction or carrying away any of the Artillery or other public property originally captured in the said forts or places, and which shall remain therein upon the

[121] Latour, *Historical Memoir*, 201.
[122] Moser, ed., *The Papers of Andrew Jackson, 1814-1815*, 253.
[123] Latour, *Historical Memoir*, Appendix, No. XXXVII, p. lxxxi.
[124] Latour, *Historical Memoir*, Appendix, No. LXVII, p. clxxxi.

Exchange of the Ratifications of this Treaty, or any Slaves or other private property." Celestin Chiapella was awarded $18,705 under Warrant #9476 on 23 July 1827 for the loss of forty-three slaves.[125]

On 4 February 1818, before the notary Philippe Pedesclaux, Celestin Chiapella, with a power of attorney from Gérome Chiapella, then living at Bordeaux, sold a plantation to Paul Lanusse. It was described as a "habitation établie en Sucrerie," a sugar plantation, three leagues below the city of New Orleans, situated between the properties of Messrs. Ducros, father and son, and Mr. Magloire Guichard with all of the implements, carts, cattle horses and other animals, and with seventy slaves. The plantation consisted of three sections: the first, belonging to Gerome Chiapella with 20 arpents 26 toises on the river, extending to Lake Borgne, bought from Jean François Siben and his wife Marguerite Chauvin Desilets on 3 July 1810; the second also belonging to Gerome Chiapella, consisting of 9.75 arpents on the river extending to Lake Borgne which he bought on 3 July 1810 from Jean François Merieult; the third belonging to Celestin Chiapella consisting of 10 arpents on the river by 38 arpents deep bought on 28 June 1811 from Barthelemy Lafon. The slaves were listed by name with their function and their age: Bazile, overseer (30), Augustin, worker (40), Laurent, worker (40), François, ploughman (65), Pierre, sugar maker (65), Figaro, field worker (65), Charlot, wagon driver (45), Malbrouck, wagon driver (30), Goufrau, wagon driver (45), Parfait, wagon driver (24) Jean Pierre, wagon driver and ploughman (24), and the following other field hands: Antoine, (20), Poulard, (45), Jean Louis, (35), Azick (40), Télémaque (50), Baptiste (50), Camarone (32), Sam (25), Braman (20), Cicéron (35), Gotty (20), Petit Capitaine (20), John (20), Gery (20), Couacou (16) Toussant (20),Bellard (20), Joe (35), Tom (30), Bill (20), Peter (20), Bill John (20), Étienne (50), Allick (50), Coffy (50), Martegas (50), Capitaine (35), Bob (30), Philippe (30), Isidore (20). Also sold were sixteen female slaves: Jeannette, dressmaker (40), Marie, field hand (30), Saly, field hand (30), Marie Louise (30), Fanchonette (30), Maritica (40), Yéyé, field hand (60) Vieille Marie (60), Julie (30), Sally (30), Mary (30), Suckey (30), Tumba (30), Maria (30), Rose, nurse (60) , Marianne (20) with her mulatto son Lindor (2); six male children: Janvier (12), Marcel (10) Rafael (10), Toussaint (8), Sonrose (12), July (12) and five female children: Charlotte (12), Julienne (1) Marie Louise's daughter, Charlotte (10), January (10), Nanette (1), daughter of Tumba.[126] The plantation, all of the buildings thereon, all the wagons, animals and slaves were sold to Paul Lanusse for 150,000 piastres. In order to complete the sale, the Notary had to seek permission from Celestin Chiapella's wife, because under Louisiana Civil Law, the wife had an implicit mortgage on all the husband's assets, even those owned jointly, in order to recover her dowry or any other assets she brought to the marriage. Although a free woman of color, the notary composing the document employed the honorific title "Dame," and recognized Amada as his legal wife.

At the same time, the Chiapellas gave power of attorney to "Gerome" Chiapella, living at Bordeaux, to consent to a marriage between their eldest daughter, Amada Maria to François Félix Audebert, and to oversee the marriage contract with a dowry of 10,000 piastres.[127] The wedding took place at Bordeaux, Section 2 on 22 October 1818. The twenty-year-old bride, Marie Camille Chiapella, born in New Orleans in July 1798, daughter of Mr. Celestin Chiapella and his wife, Mrs. Jeanne Aimée De La Chaise, married François Félix Audebert, a merchant, born at Bordeaux, Gironde, France on 14 February 1784, the son of Pierre Gilbert Audebert and his wife, Marguerite Dechante. Both Etienne Chiapella, uncle of the bride, a ship's captain, and her father, Celestin Chiapella were witnesses and signed the marriage document.[128] The couple never had any children.

[125] *An Account of the Receipts and Expenditures of the United States for the Year 1827* (Washington D.C.: H. de Krafft, Printer, 1828), 98.

[126] Some of the slaves had been bought from Durand on 23 October 1813 and Bailey and Rinker of Plaquemines Parish on 24 July 1815 per Midlo Hall, comp. *Louisiana, Slave Records, 1719-1820* – Entries 66648-66661 and 72283-72312.

[127] NARC, Philippe Pedesclaux, Notary, Volume 4 – January-May 1818, pp. 86-90 both sides. Courtesy Hon. Chelsey Richard Napoleon, Clerk of Civil District Court, Parish of Orleans.

[128] Bordeaux, Gironde, France, Registres des actes de mariage de Bordeaux, Section 2, [Section 2, Bordeaux Marriage Registrations], 1818, Marriage #240, François Félix Audebert to Marie Camille Chiapella, digital image, *Archives départementales de la Gironde*, "État Civil en ligne," (https://archives.gironde.fr/: accessed 5/6/2019), Cote 4E 975, Image 193/245.

CHAPTER 6

THE MARRIAGE CONTROVERSY AND THE CHIAPELLAS IN FRANCE

Celestin and Amada were spending more and more time at Bordeaux where they lived at Fossés de l'Hôtel de Ville, #10, in the second decade of the nineteenth century. Celestin, however, was in back New Orleans when on 8 December 1819, he sold to William Jerome Chiapella, a free man of color, a slave named Catherine, age 55 for $400 on the condition that the slave be freed.[129] William freed Catherine gratuitously before the Honorable James Pitot, Judge of the Parish Court, that same day.[130] Catherine, whose, full name was given as Catherine Gerome La Chiapella in her 1842 will, stated that she had been born in Guinea, Africa, and never knew her father and mother, having come to America as a small child. She had had children, although she had never been married, but none were still living. William and Catherine were both former slaves belonging to Jérome Chiapella, and probably took his name out of gratitude for their freedom. Catherine died on 14 January 1842. Her death was reported to the city by Rufino Thomas Fernandez, born at Galveztown,[131] LA, on 16 November 1799, who was the keeper of the records at St. Louis Cathedral. He stated that Catherine was about 100 years old and had been born in Tiamba, Africa.[132]

Celestin Chiapella and his family were absent from the 1820 federal census for Saint Bernard Parish, LA. With a married daughter living in Bordeaux and difficulties he saw ahead for himself and his racially-mixed wife and children if he continued to live in the United States, his solution was to slowly transfer all his assets abroad. On 5 October 1821 he paid 91,100 francs at auction for La Mission Haut-Brion, located outside of Pessac, near Bordeaux, including an impressive mansion, vats for fermentation, sheds, a stable, gardens and 37.5 acres of vineyards, which before the French Revolution had been cultivated by the Lazarist Fathers. Seized from the religious order after the Revolution the land was sold at auction in 1792 to Martial Victor Vaillant for 302,000 pounds. The land had languished from inattention until Chiapella purchased it from Vaillant's daughter almost thirty years later. Due to his connections in the United States, and also to the availability of his brother Étienne's brig, the *Aimable Matilda,* Chiapella turned his estate into a profitable business. His Cabernet Sauvignon, Merlot and Cabernet Franc wines became known and appreciated in the United States.

Jérome Chiapella died on 22 August 1822 at five o'clock A.M. at his home located at Fossés de l'Hôtel de Ville #10 at Bordeaux. He was identified as an eighty-year-old, native of "Nervy near Genoa," the son of "Sers Chiapella and Angella Marie Chiape" and the husband of Agathe Lemelle. Reporting the death was François Félix Audebert, a merchant, the husband of Celestin Chiapella's eldest daughter, Camille.[133]

Celestin Chiapella was enumerated in the 1830 federal census for St. Bernard Parish living on his plantation. Whether or not the Chiapellas were actually residing there at that time, or whether the place was being run by an agent and overseer, cannot be ascertained because no names were included with the exception of the head of household/owner. All that can be said was that three free white persons, two free persons of color and 122 slaves operating the over three-thousand-acre sugar cane plantation were enumerated in that census.[134]

Property owners in Louisiana whose land had been acquired through French or Spanish land grants had had to apply to the United States Congress to recognize their claims by presenting proof of ownership showing the

---

[129] NARC, "Sale of Slave, Celestin Chiapella to Wm. Jerome Chiapella," dated 8 December 1819, passed by Notary Philippe Pedesclaux, p. 1025. Courtesy Hon. Chelsey Richard Napoleon, Clerk of Civil District Court, Parish of Orleans.

[130] "Free People of Color in Louisiana/Emancipation petition of William Jerome Chiapella #74E, 1819," *The Louisiana Digital Library* https://louisianadigitallibrary.org/ :accessed 5/1/2019). See the document at https://louisianadigitallibrary.org/ islandora/object/fpoc-p16313coll51%3A56679.

[131] Galveztown was a Spanish settlement at the junction of the Amite River and Bayou Manchac in St. Helena Parish. It had been abandoned by 1810.

[132] Courtesy of State of Louisiana, Secretary of State, Division of Archives, Records Management, and History. *Vital Records Indices.* Baton Rouge, LA, USA, citing *Orleans Death Indices 1804-1876*; Vol. 10, p. 184.

[133] Bordeaux, Gironde, France, Registres des actes de décès de Bordeaux, Section 2, [Section 2, Death Registrations at Bordeaux], 1822, Death #735, Jérome Chiapella, digital image, *Archives départementales de la Gironde*, "État Civil en ligne," (https://archives.gironde.fr/: accessed 8/28/2019), Cote 3E 117, Image 75/117.

[134] 1830 United States Federal Census, St. Bernard Parish, LA, Celestin Chiapella household, digital image, *Ancestry.com* (https://www.ancestry.com accessed 10/1/2019), citing NARA microfilm publication M19 Roll 43, p. 325. Image 1/12.

chain of title back to the original grant. Celestin Chiapella's attorneys had made the necessary applications years before and a certain Deputy Surveyor for the United States named A. S. Phelps, had been shown the original grants, but had apparently never issued a certificate for the land. After reapplying to the Committee on Private Land Claims a confirmation of Chiapella's title was finally issued on 19 May 1832:

> Be it enacted by the Senate and House of Representatives of the United States of America in Congress assembled That Celestin Chiapella be, and he is hereby, confirmed in his title to a tract of land situated on the left bank of the Mississippi River about eight miles below the city of New Orleans containing the quantity of three thousand and eighty seven acres bounded above by lands of R. Ducros and below by lands of Magloire Guichard and which he holds by virtue of a French grant to Joseph Laloire dated July eighth seventeen hundred and twenty-three and another French grant to J. Laloire of January second seventeen hundred and sixty-seven and another French grant in favor of Mr. Chaperon dated January twenty-third seventeen hundred and fifty-nine and that a patent issue for the same according to a survey made by A.S. Phelps a deputy surveyor of the United States. Provided however That the proviso quantity of three hundred and ninety-three superficial arpens heretofore confirmed in the name of Mary de Monleon by the Board of Commissioners for the Eastern District of the Territory of Orleans, as evidenced by their certificate number one hundred and forty-six, shall be considered as forming part of the tract of land hereby confirmed. And provided further That this act shall be construed to operate merely as a relinquishment of title on the part of the United States and not to prejudice the rights of third persons.[135]

By this Act of Congress passed in May 1833, Chiapella was secure in his land, but he was still embroiled in a lawsuit with the Archdiocese of New Orleans concerning his 1803 marriage to Amada/Aimée LaChaise, which through his lawyers Moreau-Lislet and Soulé, he had commenced on 16 June 1831 in the District Court of the First Judicial District of the State of Louisiana. In his petition he stated that he and his wife had been married on 30 October 1803 by the Rev. P. Koüne, and witnessed by Dominique Langourand and Joachim Lozano, both deceased and Modeste Lefebvre, a merchant in the city, still living. In the year 1813, however, the Reverend P. Koüne perceived his omission and inscribed the act of marriage in the 1813 register, signed by Dominique Langourand and Modeste Lefebvre. The document, seen on the next page, written in Spanish reads in part that:

> On 30 October 1803, I, the undersigned curate of the parish church of St. Louis of New Orleans, having verbal permission from Don Thomas Hasset, vicar general of the Diocese of Louisiana, to dispense with the reading of three banns have wed Don Celestino la Chapella, a native of this city, adopted son of Don Geronimo la Chapella and of Maria Pelagia Duvernay and Dona Amada La Chaise, native and resident of this city, illegitimate daughter of Auguste La Chaise and of Agathe Le Mel, after which the parties wish to recognize two children born out of wedlock: the first, Amada Maria who was born on the 15th day of July 1798, and the other named Ana, who was born on the 22nd of June 1802. Having received their mutual consent in front of the witnesses Modesto Lefebvre, Domingo Langouran and Joachim Lozano who all signed with me on the day and year above. Signed: Mte. Lefebvre, Dominique Langourand, and P. Koüne

---

[135] "#784 – An Act for the Relief of Celestin Chiapella," *Index to the Executive Documents of the House of Representatives for the Third Session of the Forty-Sixth Congress, 1880-1881, Vol. 26 – No. 47, parts 2 and 3* (Washington: Government Printing Office, 1881), 350. Note: The tract was later acquired by Captain Henry Clement Story, and was known as the Story Plantation.

Archives of the Archdiocese of New Orleans, Saint Louis Cathedral Marriage Records Vol. 3, p. 125, #374. (Courtesy of Emilie Leumas, Archivist – Kimberly Johnson and Katie Vest – Researching Archivists.)

The given name "Geronimo" instead of "Celestin" precedes "La Chapella" in error in the margin. The groom was Don Celestino LaChapella, a native of the city, adopted son of Don Geronimo LaChapella and Dona Pelagia Duvernay. The bride was Dona Amada La Chaise, native and resident of the city, "natural" child of Augusto La Chaise and of Agathe "Le Mel." Although the date of marriage was given as 30 October 1803, it had been inserted into the marriage records for 1813 with no explanation.

The perceived problem, according to Celestin Chiapella was that there was no mention in the margin or elsewhere to explain the omission or explanation, which he alleged, might in the future be a cause of misunderstanding which would do injury to his children. Chiapella also stated that he had applied to the Reverend Louis Moni, Curate of the Parish of St. Louis of New Orleans, to have the omission rectified, by inscribing an explanation in the margin. Fr. Moni refused to do it. For that reason, Chiapella was suing the Archdiocese for $2,000 and asking that Fr. Moni be required to insert the judgment against the Church in the margin of the 1813 marriage document. He also asked that any relations who might be called to his inheritance in default of his children should be made parties to the suit including: Stephen Chiapella, Isabelle Coudrain, wife of the late Jean-Baptiste Saucier, Melanie Bagneris, widow of G. Desmillières , Alexis Bagneris, Seraphine Bagneris, wife of B. Phara, Louise Adèle Coudrain, wife of Louis Adolphe Bayon, Rosalie Luce Coudrain, widow of Victor Fromentin, Marie Celina Coudrain, Adèle Fromentin, widow of Anselm Coudrain, tutrix of Magdeleine, Pierre and Maria Zelia Coudrain, her minor children, and Zenon Bagneris, all residing in New Orleans, except Zenon Bagneris, who was a resident of Opelousas, St. Landry Parish, LA.

One might think that this suit was much ado about nothing. However, to Celestin's wife and children it was worth millions of dollars. The Territorial Louisiana Legislature enacted a new Civil Code in 1808, one part of which banned marriage between free white persons and free people of color and between free persons and slaves. At the same time the legislature declared exogamous marriages void, however, it failed to specify criminal or fiscal penalties. Non-marital sex went unmentioned. This is why Celestin was so moved to go to court to make sure that his 1803 marriage to Amada La Chaise was verified by the Church although it only appeared in the 1813 marriage book. If it had occurred in 1803 then the marriage was judicially legal, but if it had actually occurred in 1813, it would have been done illegally and Celestin's children would be illegitimate. As a consequence, their right to inherit would have been severely restricted. The 1808 law stated that participants in racially mixed relationships were respectively incapable of making to each other any donation of immovables (including slaves and property), and if they make a donation of movables, it could not exceed one tenth of part of the value of the whole estate.

The Reverend Louis Moni's explanation for his refusal to add an explanation of why an 1803 marriage record had appeared in an 1813 marriage register was that he thought it was a breach of duty to alter in any way public records entrusted to him and would not do so unless directed by the District Court. While most of the extended Coudrain and Bagneris family members answered that there was no reason for them to have been called into the suit which should be dismissed, Louise Adele Coudrain, Celestin Chiapella's niece (daughter of his brother Anselme Coudrain) assisted by her husband Louis Adolphe Bayon, appeared before the court on 11 July 1831. Louise Adèle testified that it was not true that Celestin and Amada had been married on 30 October 1803 and that the petition before the court was only begun "with the vow of eluding the dispositions of our laws which prohibit marriage between white people and persons of color, the above pretended wife of Celestin Chiapella being a free coloured woman, as will be shewn on the trial of this case."[136] She further alleged through her attorney that it was through fraud that the alleged celebration of marriage was inserted into the 1813 marriage book by the Rev. Koüne, who had no right to do so. On 15 July 1831 depositions were taken from two witnesses for the plaintiff, Celestin Chiapella. Modeste Lefebvre stated that he had known Chiapella and his wife since 1786 and that they had been married on 30 October 1803 in a little house situated on a lot where the Bank of Louisiana was since erected, belonging to Jérome Chiapella, by the Abbé Koüne. Lefebvre further stated that the late Dominique Langourand was also a witness to the marriage at which time Chiapella legitimized two children: Marie alias Camille and Annette. He added that Chiapella and his wife had had eight or ten other children, and when they decided to baptize some of them in 1813, it was then that they had discovered that the 1803 marriage had not been recorded. Chiapella complained to Fr. de Sedella, who called upon Abbé Koüne, who declared that he had lost the original record. A new record, authorized by Fr. Antonio de Sedella, was inserted in the book of marriages for 1813, signed by Lefebvre, the now late Dominique Langourand and Abbé Koüne. The question of Celestin's own parentage was also discussed. Levebve explained that Celestin, who was born "of the marriage of one Coudrain with the lady who afterwards married Mr. Bagneris," was taken to the home of Gerome Chiapella when a boy and then sent by Mr. Chiapella to France for his education. Upon returning Celestin had always used the name "Chiapella" in all of his legal documents. On cross examination, Lefebvre was asked if he knew that Jeanne Aimée LaChaise's mother, Agathe, was generally known to be a free woman of color, but he replied that while he knew that Mr. Gerome called her Agathe, he did not know anything about her being a person of color. He offered further, that since Louisiana was under the Spanish regime at that time, he never cared about it.

Celestin's brother, Étienne Chiapella, was also called to testify. He indicated that he was at the 1803 marriage which took place at the little house on which the Bank of Louisiana has since been built. He remembered that Lefebvre, Langourand, and others had witnessed the marriage conducted by Abbé Koüne. Etienne Chiapella was asked if he knew if banns had been posted for the 1803 marriage, but he said he did not, and did not know what the formalities in Louisiana might be, because he had been married in France. Isabelle Coudrain Saucier testified that she had never thought that Celestin and Jeanne Aimée had been married because such marriage would be a violation of the Civil Code of Louisiana enacted in 1808. Alexis and Zenon Bagneris claimed that they knew nothing about Celestin's marriage or anything else surrounding the circumstances. The case dragged on until 4 February 1832 when Chiapella's lawyers asked that Fernandez Ruffino, keeper of the registers of birth and marriages for the church of St. Louis of New Orleans be called to bring forth the register where the Chiapella-LaChaise marriage had been recorded.

On 1 June 1832 a judgment was rendered by Justice Joshua Lewis dismissing the petition with costs on the grounds that it was useless for Chiapella to have made his relations a part of the suit because they could not challenge the validity of his marriage until after his death. Moreover, it was not in the court's purview to direct in

---

[136] Supreme Court of Louisiana Digital Case Files – University of New Orleans, Earl K. Long Library, Chiapella et. ux. v. Moni et. al. at: http://dspace.uno.edu:8080/ xmlui/handle/123456789/17475 (Image 14 of 58).

what book the registry of the marriage should have been made. The only question was if the act was valid or not, a question which the court could not take up in the present form of action. On 11 June 1832, Chiapella's attorneys appealed the ruling. On 8 April 1833 the Louisiana Supreme Court ruled that Louisiana Civil Law was based almost word for word on the Napoleonic Code which did have a chapter on the "rectification des actes de l'état civil" (the correction of acts in the Civil Registry (for births, marriages and deaths), but that this paragraph was not copied into Louisiana Law, and that the failure to do so could not be attributed to a failure to notice it but to a different view being entertained of its utility. The appeal was, therefore, denied.

The question remains whether or not Celestin and Amada were actually married on 30 October 1803, or whether it was a convenient fiction to try to circumvent Louisiana law. When Jérome Chiapella filed his will in New Orleans in 1806, he did not identify Aimée/Amada La Chaise as Celestin's wife, or her three daughters as Celestin's children, although he left them large sums of money. Moreover, there are no existing baptismal records for either Amada Maria (Camille) or Ana (Annette) that were filed by Abbé Koüne in 1803. Could he have lost those as well? Ana was finally baptized in 1813, but there was no attempt to baptize Camille at that time. Abbé Koüne did tell his superior, Fr. Antonio de Sedella, in 1813 that he had lost the original 1803 marriage record and agreed to add it out of order ten years later. Was de Sedella complicit in this fiction? For almost one hundred years, both French and Spanish clerics had skirted the ever-changing, and sometimes conspicuously absent, civil law concerning interracial unions, preferring to protect the souls of their congregants rather than the letter of the law. Furthermore, both Jean-Pierre Koüne and another cleric, Father Claude Thoma, were refugees from Saint-Domingue, via Cuba. In 1812 Father John Olivier, wrote to Bishop John Carroll in Baltimore: "This city is inhabited by numerous strangers from every country without religion, without customs, and what has put the peak to scandal is the arrival of a great number of girls of color from Santo Domingo who spread corruption everywhere. If the conduct of Père Antoine and his two assistants Thoma and Kuan [Koüne] were above reproach I would have less to lament."[137] Olivier went on to complain to Bishop Carroll that both clerics had brought over their "mulatto" housekeepers with their children, that Père Antoine had made Thoma his assistant at the Cathedral, and that "Father Jean Koüne was no better. Koüne was also thought to be living with his mulatto housekeeper, His critics claimed that the children ate at the table with him and called him 'Papa.'" [138] Olivier had interdicted the two clerics from exercising their priestly duties, but de Sedella had ignored the interdiction and allowed them to continue in their mission. Was this just cruel gossip or was there some truth to the matter? When Koüne was on his deathbed on 17 August 1821, he sent for the Notary Marc Lafitte, who transcribed his last will and testament. Koüne lived in a house belonging to himself on one of the roads (later identified as Bayou Road) out of the city towards Bayou St. John. Koüne stated that he had been born in Faulquemont, Moselle, France, the legitimate son of Nicolas Koüne and his wife, Dorothée Claude, both deceased. He was about seventy years old, and a member of a religious order. He left to his sister Marie Koüne, the widow Girard, 1000 piastres, to his other sister, Madeleine Koüne, the widow Exard, 200 piastres, and to his brother Nicolas Koüne, 500 piastres. He willed his slave André to Simon Narcisse, the sixteen-year-old natural son of Marie, a free negress. To fourteen-year-old Marie Catherine Silvery, another child of the free negress, Marie, he left his slave Marguerite. To both of Marie's children he left the property on which he was living, which he bought at auction from Daniel Clark. Since the property was not completely paid for, he asked that it be paid off from proceeds in his succession and that they receive it free and clear. Koüne died on 20 August 1821.[139] Since the Abbé Koüne was comfortable with the three caste society of his former home, Saint-Domingue, and the freedom with which free people of color and whites mixed and intermarried, it is understandable that his officiating at the marriage of Celestin Chiapella and Amada La Chaise would not have presented a problem for him whether it happened legally in 1803 at Jérome Chiapella's house, or in contravention of Louisiana law in 1813. Needless to say, however, the die was cast for the couple who remained in France.

---

[137] Cited by Virginia Meacham Gould and Charles E. Nolan, editors in *No Cross, No Crown: Black Nuns in Nineteenth Century New Orleans* by Sister Mary Bernard Deggs (Bloomington and Indianapolis, IN: Indiana University Press, 2001), xxvii.

[138] Gould and Nolan, *No Cross, No Crown*, xxviii.

[139] "Louisiana, Wills and Probate Records, 1756-1984," digital images, *Ancestry.com* (https://www.ancestry.com: accessed 6/22/19), Will of Jean-Pierre Koüne, Will Book Vol. 3, 1817-1824, Image 236/475. In reading his inventory and succession papers, we discovered that Koüne had movables worth about $807 and an additional piece of property with 30 feet frontage on Royal St. between St. Philip and Ursulines which sold at auction in 1822 to Marie Elizabeth Delattre, f.w.c. for $4030. ("Louisiana, Wills and Probate Records 1756-1984," digital images, *Ancestry.com* (https://www.ancestry.com: accessed 6/22/19), Probate record for Jean Pierre Koüne dated 1 September 1821,Images 89-111.)

Since the death of Jérome Chiapella, his widow, Agathe Lemelle, managed their Louisiana holdings from Bordeaux via the family notary, M. Maillères. Amongst the papers of New Orleans notary Carlile Pollock, we found interesting correspondence from her concerning several of her properties in the city. In a letter dated 15 July 1830 she wrote to her property managers, Modeste Lefebvre and Jean Pierre Labattut, acknowledging $2477.41 credited to her account and talked about repairs to her property, indicating that while she had said previously only to do what was absolutely necessary, this must include repairs to the roofs. "Isn't it urgent," she queried, "that both Miss Guenigue who rents the house on Rue Dauphine and Mr. Jacob's son-in-law, or the new tenant in the St. Louis Street house, be sheltered from the rain?" Regarding the expense for tiling the floor in the store, she suggested that installing a wood floor would be more cost effective since the old one was completely rotted. She reiterated that she wanted to sell the St. Louis Street property and thought that 20,000 piastres was a moderate price. She closed that she was anxious to have an accounting of how much money the shipment of wine that she had sent via the *Mathilde*, had brought. She signed "Veuve Chiapella." (the widow Chiapella). After Celestin Chiapella had bought the Chateau la Mission Haut-Brion, he had spent money to modernize the operation and to strengthen the brand and began to ship large quantities of wine to New Orleans. It is evident from this letter that the wine business had been a family affair from the start, with Jérome Chiaplla, just before his death, involved in the enterprise, and later his widow, Agathe, also involved. Agathe Lemelle Chiapella did sell her St. Louis Street property on 19 September 1831 to Dominique Seghers for 20,000 piastres. Below is a copy of the last few lines of that 1831 letter which contains the signature of Agathe Lemelle.

NARC, Portion of a letter from the Widow Chiapella to Modeste Lefebvre and Jean-Pierre Labatut filed in the notarial archives of Carlile Pollock, along with papers for the sale of the St. Louis Street property to Dominique Seghers dated 19 September 1831, Volume 37, 9 pages Courtesy Hon. Chelsey Richard Napoleon, Clerk of Civil District Court, Parish of Orleans. Note: She signed Vve. (Widow) Chiapella.

Seventy-five-year-old Agathe Lemelle, a native of New Orleans, daughter of Jacques Lemelle and Jacqueline (omitted), widow of Jérome Chiapella died on 8 January 1833 at 11:30 P.M. at Bordeaux, Fossés du Chapeau Rouge #21. Her death was reported by Celestin Chiapella and François Félix Audebert, Celestin's son-in-law.[140] In the *Tables de décès et successions – 1er Bureau, Vol.6* (*Table of deaths and successions – 1st Office-Vol.6*), Agathe Lemelle, the widow Chiapella was listed, showing her last residence "Chapeau Rouge #21," her age (75), the presentation of a will turned over on 10 January 1833, and the date of settlement of the estate on 9 July 1833. Everything was left to her daughter "Anne Delachaise, the wife of Celestin Chiapella," which included 9,719 livres in furniture, cash and other income as well as 22,800 livres in immovables (real estate) at Bordeaux. Although Agathe had been born into slavery she died as a woman of status and means in her adopted home in France. It was a position, and a degree of wealth, that neither she nor her grandchildren would probably have been able to achieve in Louisiana.[141]

---

[140] Bordeaux, Gironde, France, Registres des actes de décès de Bordeaux, Section 1, [Section 1, Bordeaux Death Registrations], 1833, Death #45, Agathe Lemelle, digital image, *Archives départementales de la Gironde*, "État Civil en ligne," (https://archives.gironde.fr/: accessed 8/28/2019), Cote 4E 1092, Image 9/182.

[141] Bordeaux, Gironde, France, Tables de décès et successions – Tables des Successions et Absences : 1er Bureau, Volume 6 [Table of Deaths and Successions. Table of Successions and Absences, 1st Office, Volume 6], 1833, Line #3, Agathe Lemelle, digital image, *Archives départementales de la Gironde*, (https://archives.gironde.fr/: accessed 10/2/2019), Cote 3 Q 12, Image 109/211.

On the 1st and 8th of September 1833, banns were posted for the marriage of Celestin Chiapella and Jeanne Aimée de Lachaise at Bordeaux, Section 1, Gironde, France. The ceremony took place on 29 October 1833 between Celestin Coudrin, called Chiapella, age 57, a native of New Orleans born in 1776 to the late Pierre Coudrin and Pelagie Duvernet [sic] with Jeanne Anne Aimée de Lachaise, age 51, also born in New Orleans to the late Auguste de Lachaise and the late Agathe Lemelle, the widow of Jérome Chiapella. It was also recorded at Celestin's request that the couple had been married on 30 October 1803 in New Orleans by the Abbé Pierre-Jean Koüne, which had taken place under the existing laws of Louisiana, before two witnesses, Modeste Lefebvre and Dominique Langourand, their friends and merchants in New Orleans. From that union there were eight surviving children: Marie Camille born 15 July 1798, Anne born 22 June 1802; Jeanne Celestine born 28 November 1803, Catherine Aimée born 4 July 1808, Angélique Étrenne born 1 January 1812, Celestin born 1 September 1814, Jérome Modeste born 28 October 1816 and Marie, called Treizia born on 16 September 1819. All the children had been born in New Orleans, with the exception of Treizia who had been born at Bordeaux. The document also indicated that although their union as man and wife was longstanding, because of some "irregularities" attached to their original marriage, they were having this additional ceremony to ensure the right of inheritance of their children and to have the ceremony repeated according to the laws in France.[142]

In order to foil his rapacious Coudrain and Bagneris relatives, Celestin Chiapella further cemented his children's legacy by seeking permanent residence in France which was granted on 27 December 1833: "#4968 - Ordonnance du roi (Paris, 27 décembre 1833) portant que le Sieur Celestin Coudrin, né à la Louisiane (Nouvelle-Orléans), âgé d'environ 57 ans, propriétaire, demeurant à Bordeaux, département de la Gironde, est admis à établir son domicile en France, pour y jouir des droits civils tant qu'il continuera d'y résider." (#4968 – By order of the King (Paris, 27 December 1833), given that Mr. Celestin Coudrin, born in Louisiana (New Orleans). age of about 57 years, living at Bordeaux, department of the Gironde, is admitted to establish his domicile in France, and to be able to enjoy the civil rights as long as he continues to reside there.)[143]

Celestin, his wife, and children spent the rest of their lives at their lavish chateau outside of Bordeaux where Celestin became a celebrated vintner. Atop the chateau's tower was a weathervane in the shape of a sailing ship, a symbol of the link to his adopted father's past as a ship's captain, and to its continuation by his brother, Étienne, who had followed in Jérome Chiapella's footsteps. Ships owned by the Chiapellas would take Chateau La Mission Haut-Brion wines to New Orleans for many years where it would be marketed with his initials C.C. on the label. Chiapella, and later his son Jérome Modeste, also managed Châteaux Cos d'Estournel and Pomys at the nearby village of Saint-Estèphe. The family's Château La Mission Haut-Brion won the gold medal at the International Exhibition in London in 1862. Almost two hundred years after its founding the Chateau La Mission Haut-Brion brand is still one of the most highly prized French wines in production. A photograph of one of its 1955 labels may be seen on the next page. Below is a view of the weathervane atop the highest point of the Chateau.

[142] Bordeaux, Gironde, France, Registres des actes de mariage de Bordeaux, Section 1, [Section 1, Bordeaux Marriage Registrations], 1833, Marriage #409, Celestin Coudrin surnommé Chiapella to Jeanne de Lachaise, digital image, Archives départementales de la Gironde, "État Civil en ligne," (https://archives.gironde.fr/: accessed 8/31/2019), Cote 4E 1088, Image 197/206.
[143] Bulletin des Lois du Royaume de France, IX Série. Règne de Louis-Philippe 1er, Roi des Français, IIe Partie – Ordonnances, IIe Section – Tome Quatrième Contenant Les Ordonnances d'Intérêt local ou Particulier Rendues Pendant Le Deuxième Semestre de 1833. Nos 63 à 86 (Paris : L'Imprimerie Royale, février 1834), 967.

The Chateau, home of Celestin Chiapella and family has graced the label for over 150 years. The ship weathervane may be seen to the left on the tower. The Woltners sold the winery in 1935 to Domaine Clarence Dillon (Author's collection).

Amada La Chaise died at Bordeaux, Section 3, Gironde, France, on 1 November 1864. A brief civil record dated 2 November 1864, gave her name as Jeanne Aimée Delachaise, age 82, the wife of Celestin Chiapella. The names of her parents were left out of the record. She had died the evening before at one o'clock at Cour Napoléon #128.[144] Celestin Chiapella died, only a few years later on 10 January 1867. Said to be ninety-two years old, a native of New Orleans and a land owner, the widow of Anne de Lachaise, his death, which occurred that morning, was reported by two of his grandchildren, Marcel Chiapella, son of Celestin, Jr., and Joseph Labat, son of Ana/Annette Chiapella.[145] The Château La Mission Haut-Brion remained in the hands of the Chiapella heirs until 1884 when it was sold to the Établissements Duval de Paris. It fell back into American hands in 1935, when Clarence Dillon, father of the future United States Secretary of the Treasury, C. Douglas Dillon, bought the company. It is currently owned and managed by Prince Robert of Luxembourg, C. Douglas Dillon's daughter Joan's son by her second husband, Prince Charles of Luxembourg.

All of Celestin and Amada Lachaise Chiapella's children who reached adulthood married and remained in France, as did their descendants. Amada Marie Chiapella, who married François Félix Audebert on 22 October

---

[144] Bordeaux, Gironde, France, Registres des actes de décès de Bordeaux, Section 3, [Section 3, Bordeaux Death Registrations], 1864, Death #1284, Jeanne Aimée de Lachaise, digital image, *Archives départementales de la Gironde*, "État Civil en ligne," (https://archives.gironde.fr/: accessed 8/28/2019), Cote 4E 1417, Image 44/94.

[145] Bordeaux, Gironde, France, Registres des actes de décès de Bordeaux, Section 2, [Section 2, Bordeaux Death Registrations], 1867, Death #55, Celestin Chiapella, digital image, *Archives départementales de la Gironde*, "État Civil en ligne," (https://archives.gironde.fr/: accessed 8/28/2019), Cote 4E 1466, Image 11/274.

1818 at Bordeaux, Section 2, (Cote 2E 101 Image 94/123)[146] had no descendants. She died at Bordeaux on 4 July 1870 (Cote 3E 246, Image 172/304). Ana/Anette Chiapella married Joseph Labat at Bordeaux, Section 1, on 5 November 1825, (Cote 2E 128, Image 163/185). Although they had three sons (Casimir Évariste (b.1831, d. 1870), François Paul (b. 1833), and Joseph Aurélien (b. 1836) they had no grandchildren to carry forth the name. Ana Chiapella died on 28 April 1883 at Cénac-et-St.Julien, Dordogne, France.

Jeanne Celestine married Jean Hubert Raimond Cotton de Bennetot at Bordeaux, Section 1, on 16 August 1826, (Cote 2E 132, Image 126/195). The had three children all born at Bordeaux: Edmond (b. 13 July 1827), Ernestine (b. 3 November 1828) and Louisa Marie (b. 16 June 1830).[147] Celestine Chiapella died at Auterive, Haute Garonne, France on 13 August 1882.

Catherine Chiapella married Jean Marie Adolphe Darnaud at Bordeaux, Section 1, on 10 February 1836, (Cote 2E 163, Image 29/207). We believe that there were no children from this marriage. Catherine Chiapella Darnaud died at Bordeaux, Section 1, on 29 January 1859 (Cote 3E 209, Image 24/287).

Angélique "Étrenne" Chiapella married Pierre Augey, a medical doctor, on 5 February 1835 at Bordeaux, Section 1 (2E 160, Image 21/218). They had one child, Jeanne Marie Hermance Augey, born on 30 January 1836 (d. 1913). Angélique Chiapella died on 25 March 1867 at Bordeaux, Section 1, (Cote 3E 233, Image 39/172).

Celestin Chiapella, Jr., but who appears in French records as Auguste Celestin Chiapella was married to Marie Henriette Duchon-Doris at Bordeaux, Section 2, on 10 August 1844, (Cote 2E 180, Image 136/220). Their first child, Daniel Celestin, born in 1845 died without issue on 20 October 1874 at Paris, 12e, Ile-de-France, France. Their two other sons Jean Pierre Marcel (b. 1847) and Jérome Michel René (b. 1853) both lived to marry and have children.

Jeronimo Modesto Chiapella married Elizabeth Pauline Goudal on 3 October 1849 at Bordeaux, Section 2, (Cote 2E 190, Image 181/252). Their two children, Celestin Roger Chiapella (b. 1851) and Marthe Chiapella (b. 1854) both lived to marry and have children. Jérome Modesto Chiapella died at Bordeaux, Section 1, on 26 April 1890 (Cote 3E 307, Image 88/263).

Marie Thérèse Camille Chiapella, called Trézia married Anne-Pierre Garres at Bordeaux, Section 1, on 25 January 1840, (Cote 2E 171, Image 14/206). Their two sons, Jean Pierre Marie Camille and Celestin Volny Bernard were born on 13 October 1840 and 10 June 1842 respectively. Trézia Chiapella died on 27 June 1907 at Bordeaux, Section 3, (Cote 3E 360, Image 112/217).

Celestin Chiapella's son Auguste Celestin lived the rest of his life at the Chateau with his family. He died on 7 July 1890 at Bordeaux, Section 1 (Cote 3E 307, Image 129/263). The death was reported by his two surviving sons. He had led a life devoted to his father's viticulture, but he was also a celebrated naturalist. He converted several rooms of the chateau into aviaries, where he housed birds of all descriptions. He would often go to the docks to meet the ships and purchase exotic birds which he rescued from uncaring sailors. At one point he kept more than 250 species in his vast domain. He published his *Manuel de l'Oiseleur et de L'Oiselier*, [*The Bird Catcher and Bird Seller*] (Bordeaux: Féret et Fils and Paris: G. Masson, 1873-1874) in which he described how and what to feed hundreds of varieties of birds, how many and which species could live together in his enclosures, how to breed them and heal them. His love of birds came from his childhood in Louisiana at the plantation in St. Bernard Parish where he spent the first sixteen years of his life. He regretted that since his departure the "industrious and active Yankees" had replaced the rolling fields, primitive forests, and vast orchards with factories and railroads. (p. 132)[148]

---

[146] All the marriage records for Celestin Chiapella's children are available on the internet at https://archives.bordeaux-metropole.fr/archive/recherche/etatcivil2018/n:43 Insert Bordeaux, Section #, Type of act: Mariage, "type of document "registre d'état civil," and exact year in search box, then go to the image #, which we have provided in parenthesis. To search for deaths, remove "Mariage" and insert "décès." This site is free.

[147] For a genealogy of Celestine's children and grandchildren, see Arlette Cotton de Bennetot's *Histoire et Généalogie de la Famille Cotton de Bennetot*.

[148] All subsequent page numbers in parentheses refer to Chiapella's *Manuel de L'Oiseleur et de L'Oiselier*.

MANUEL

DE

L'OISELEUR ET DE L'OISELIER

CONTENANT :

La Manière de conserver et de faire produire tous les petits Oiseaux
de Cage et de Volière.

PAR

Célestin **CHIAPELLA**

———

Grand Dieu ! Que le Livre de la
Nature est séduisant, quelles mer-
veilles ne contient-il pas et à chaque
feuillet de ce magnifique Album,
avec quel charme apparaissent ta puis-
sance et ta sagesse ! Quel est l'homme
qui ne se sentirait saisi d'un senti-
ment religieux en le contemplant !

BORDEAUX	PARIS
FÉRET ET FILS	G. MASSON
Libraires-Éditeurs.	Libraire-Éditeur.
15, COURS DE L'INTENDANCE.	PL. DE L'ÉCOLE-DE-MEDECINE

1873 - 1874

Title Page of book written by Celestin Chiapella, Jr. (Author's collection).

He wrote "Quand j'étais enfant, je connaissais exactement le nombre de couples d'oiseaux établis dans le jardin et le verger qui entouraient la modeste habitation de mon père. – J'explorais tous les nids, et devenais un objet de terreur pour ces innocents volatiles. (p.43) (When I was a child, I knew exactly the number of bird couples living in the garden and the orchard which surrounded my father's modest house – I explored all the nests, and became an object of terror to those innocent creatures.) Further on, he added " Dans le temps que j'habitais la Louisiane, de 1814 à 1830, l'hiver amenait dans les champs cultivés du bords du Mississippi, une telle quantité d'oiseaux de différentes espèces que la lumière du soleil était parfois littéralement obscurcis par leurs vols innombrables" (p.131) (During the time I lived in Louisiana, from 1814 until 1830, winter brought into the cultivated fields on the banks of the Mississippi, such a quantity of birds of different species that the light from the sun was sometimes literally blocked out by their innumerable flights.) Many of the descriptions of the birds he had studied, were accompanied by reminiscences of the lush solitude of the St. Bernard Parish retreat where he was raised. Celestin, Jr.'s collection of birds earned him a silver medal from the Société linnéenne de Bordeaux (named for the famous Swedish naturalist Carl Linnaeus). Celestin, Jr.'s parent's decision to leave Louisiana, not only protected their family inheritance, but also assured their children a completely different future than they would have had, had they stayed in America.

CHAPTER 7

CHARLES CHIAPELLA and AMARANTHE LASSIZE

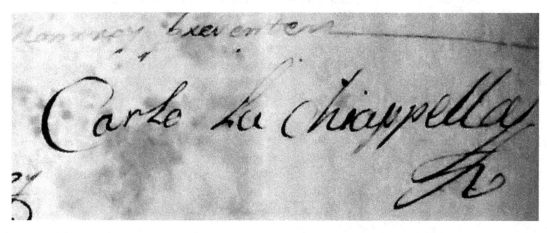

NARC. Signature of Carlo La Chiapella done on 3 March 1785 at New Orleans upon the sale of the slave Cofi to Jorge Renner for 775 piastres, before the notary Rafael Perdomo, Vol. 5, folio 175 recto. Courtesy Hon. Chelsey Richard Napoleon, Clerk of Civil District Court, Parish of Orleans.

Charles/Carlo Chiapella, whom we have mentioned before as having inherited from Jérome Chiapella, his brother, the sum of 16,000 piastres, came to Louisiana to join him ca. 1783. Carlo could not be found in the ecclesiastical records for S. Siro de Nervi, near Genoa, Italy where his three brothers, Pietro Paolo, Giovanni Battista and Geromo had been baptized. We believe that his family probably moved closer to Genoa, and that he was younger than Geromo. There were also no baptismal records at Nervi for his sisters, Benita, Geronima, or Magdelena, all of whom appeared as legatees in Jérome Chiapella's 1806 will.

Never the sailor like his brother who often took extended trips to the French islands in the Caribbean, and who planted his roots firmly in New Orleans, Charles preferred to remain a dealer in slaves at Pointe Coupée, and at other outlying parishes. Known variously as Carlo, Don Carlos, or Charles Lachiapella/Lachapell in Louisiana, he first appeared in records there on 12 June 1783 when Charles "Lachapell" sold to Madame André at Pointe Coupée three slaves for $800 each: a female age 30 and two boys, ages 12 and 14. He travelled to St. John the Baptist Parish to sell two slaves to Philip Conrad: Polidor and Jacques, for $675 apiece on 20 June 1783, Back at Pointe Coupée he sold on 2 August 1783 to Patin, the slave Cezar for $390. On 16 August 1783, he sold to the Widow Barra dit Leblond, Charles and François each for $750 at Pointe Coupée. On the same day, he sold to Porché (probably Simon) a slave named Gabriel for $350. On 25 August 1783 he sold to Guillaume André, the slave George for $100 and less than a month later two unnamed slaves each for $620.[149]

The only record for a 1784 slave sale found in the Midlo Hall records where Charles was the seller was dated 13 February 1784 in St. James Parish where he sold to Joseph Leblanc, fils, the slave Jacques for $300. In the year 1785 many of the Chiapella slave trades were carried out by the combined efforts of the company of Proffit, Ross and Lachiapella. George Proffit, David Ross and Jerome Lachapelle [*sic*] did a lively trade in Pointe Coupée Parish, selling forty slaves to Claude Trenouay on 17 October 1785 before the notary Rafael Perdomo each one for $310. Trenouay paid 8,000 piastres in cash and 1,933 pounds of indigo. The rest was due the following December.[150] Charles may not have been a party to this transaction, but Trenouay was, later on, one of Charles Lachiapella's best customers. In the over one thousand-page inventory of Trenouay's estate, probated after he was

---

[149] Gwendolyn Midlo Hall, editor, *Databases for the Study of Afro-Louisiana History and Genealogy 1699-1860*. (Baton Rouge, LA: Louisiana State University Press, 2000). CD-ROM. Note: All slave records have been taken from Midlo Hall's work, first published as a CD-Rom, later posted on-line, and also available at *Ancestry.com*.

[150] Gwendolyn Midlo Hall, *Africans in Colonial Louisiana: The Development of Afro-Creole Culture in the Eighteenth Century*, (Baton Rouge, LA and London: The Louisiana State University Press, 1995), 252.

shot and killed at his dining room table by one of his slaves on 9 July 1791, Charles' name appears a number of times, having, between July and September 1787, sold twenty slaves to the indigo planter.[151]

Records for Charles' transactions show that he was acting as a travelling representative for the Chiapella Brothers. On 3 March 1785 he was in New Orleans, where before Raphael Perdomo, he sold the 25-year-old male slave from the Carolinas, named Cofi, to Jorge Renner, living at the German Coast, for 775 piastres. On 18 March 1785, he was in St. John the Baptist Parish where he sold to Adam Weckner the slave Jacques, a creole from North Carolina for $270. On 1 October 1785 he sold five slaves, four females (Missi, Ama, Napoli and Coco), and one male named Bambara, to François Mayeux, all for 2000 piastres. On 8 November 1785 he was in the Attakapas Post at St. Martinville where he sold an unnamed slave to François Allain."

Housed at the Howard-Tilton Memorial Library at Tulane University, we found copies of two receipts issued by Charles Lachiapella for slave sales where he received indigo instead of cash. Both receipts were dated 8 December 1785. The first, seen below, is transcribed in French exactly as it was written and reads : "Je recu de Monsieur Vensant Porche la somme de cent cenquant nuffe livres de belle indigo a compte de un negrion que je lui ai vendu et livre Poiente Cuppe ce 8 xbre 1785 Charle La chiapelle."

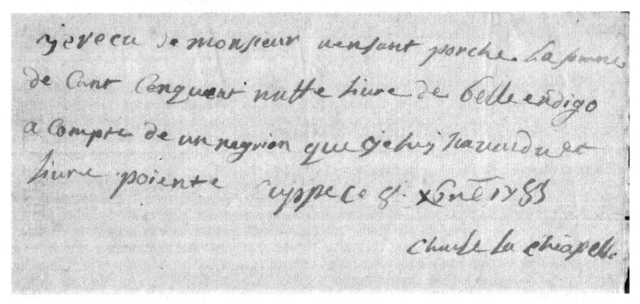

I received from Mr. Vincent Porché the sum of 159 pounds of fine indigo on account for a young negro boy that I sold to him and delivered at Pointe Coupée this 8 December 1785.[152]

The second receipt, issued the same day to Simon Porché reads: "Je recu de monsieur Simon Porche la somme de cant quatre vent dix livres de endigo a compte de un negrion que je lui ai vendu et livre poient cuppe ce 8 xbre 1785 Charle Lachiapelle." (I received from Mr. Simon Porché the sum of 190 pounds of indigo for a young negro boy that I sold and delivered to him Pointe Coupée this 8 December 1785):

---

[151] Louisiana Historical Center – Louisiana Colonial Digitization Project – Document #16761 – Intestate Succession of Claude Trenouay, planter at Pointe Coupée, murdered by runaway slave. Document dated 3 October 1792: http://www.lacolonialdocs.org/document/14278.

[152] Lachiapella indigo receipts 1781-1790, LaRC-M48, Tulane University Special Collections, Howard-Tilton Memorial Library, Tulane University, (Courtesy of Lori Schexnayder, Assistant University Archivist).

Charles La Chiapella's receipt to Simon Porché for sale of a young negro boy in exchange for 190 pounds of indigo.[153]

Charles Lachiapella invested some of his profits in land at Pointe Coupée Parish. He was included in a list of people who contributed to the fund to reimburse owners who had lost their slaves during the 1795 rebellion in Pointe Coupée. His plantation was located in the district of "Sieur Jean François Porché." LaChiapella lived near three Allain families, four Porché families, three Barra families, and one Patin family, all longtime residents of the area.[154] LaChiapella became a planter during the indigo boom, which lasted only a few years. Neither indigo nor tobacco, the first crops tried in the Louisiana Territory, were very successful. Neither was well suited to the climate, and furthermore, these same crops from the Caribbean islands were of better quality. We believe that he started this venture some time in 1787 when he bought fifteen slaves from his brother Jérome Chiapella, described as "brutos" from Africa of the Bambara, Chaba and Maninga nations, between twenty and twenty-two years old for 4,500 Mexican pesos that Carlo had paid his brother in cash.

[...]

---

[153] Lachiapella indigo receipts 1781-1790, LaRC-M48, Tulane University Special Collections, Howard-Tilton Memorial Library, Tulane University, (Courtesy of Lori Schexnayder, Assistant University Archivist).
[154] Winston Deville, *Mississippi Mélange, Vol. 1,* "Slave Owners of Pointe Coupée and False River in 1795," (Baton Rouge LA: Provincial Press, 1995), 53.

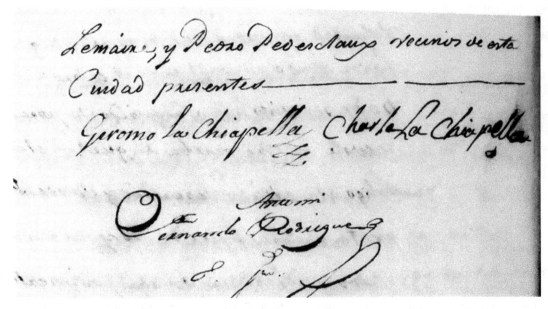

NARC, Sale of fifteen slaves by Geromo Lachiapella to his brother Charles la Chiapella before the notary Fernando Rodriguez, Volume 13, dated 3 October 1787, pp. 924, 925. Fragment of 924 verso and 925 verso, with signatures. Courtesy Hon. Chelsey Richard Napoleon, Clerk of Civil District Court, Parish of Orleans.

Charles Lachiapella bought a forty-five-year-old male slave named Agi from the Ledoux estate at Pointe Coupée for 465 piastres on 31 December 1788. Between 1789 and 1799 there were thirteen burials and nineteen baptisms of slaves living on Charles LaChiapella's indigo plantation which appear in the *Catholic Church Records of the Diocese of Baton Rouge for Pointe Coupée Parish: Individuals Without Surnames*. Of the thirteen burials nine of them were children."Negritte," "negrillon" and the misspelling, "negrion," were French words used to designate a small African American child, while "nègre" identified an adult male and "négresse" an adult female:

Negrillon slave of Charles LaChapelle bur. 3 Oct 1798 (PCP-6, 90).
Negrillon slave of Mr. Chiapela bur. 9 Dec 1789 (PCP 6, 438).
Negrillon slave of Mr. Chiapela bur. 9 Feb 1790 (PCP-6, 438).
Negrillon slave of C. Chiapella bur. 14 Oct 1790 (PCP-6, 439).
Negrite slave of Charles Chiapelle bur. 16 Sept 1794 (PCP-6, 446).
[omitted] Age 3 yrs. Infant slave of Charles Chiapelle bur. 10 Dec 1794 (PCP-6, 447).
[omitted] Negre slave of Charles LaChapelle bur. 2 Jan 1798 (PCP-6, 457).
[omitted] Negrillon slave of Charles Chiapelle bur. 16 Sept. 1798 (PCP-6, 473).
Charlotte, slave of Chiapelle bur. 28 Sept 1792 (PCP-6, 441).
Coffi, age 37 yrs., negre slave of Charles Chiapelle bur. 24 Feb 1799 (PCP-6, 459).
Jean Louis, negrion (Marguerite, slave of Charles Chaipelle) bur. 30 Dec 1795 (PCP-6, 450).
Noel, negrion slave of Charles Chapelle bur. 6 Oct 1794 (PCP-6, 446).
Pierre, negre slave of Charles Chiapelle bur. 26 July 1795 (PCP-6,449).

Nineteen baptisms(bt.) offered more information including first names, and the names of godparents (spo.):

Aveline, negresse (Margueritte, slave of Mr. Chapelle) bt. 25 Dec 1798 spo. Hubert, negrillon and Heleonore, negresse (PCP-6, 91).
Charlote, negresse slave of LaChapelle, bt. 19 June 1791, spo. Jean Louis, slave of Tournoir and Charlote (PCP-6, 29).
Charlote, negresse slave of LaChapelle, bt. 19 June 1791, spo. Jean Pierre and Marie, slave of LaChapelle (PCP-6, 29).
François, negre slave of Charles LaChapelle (Thérèse, slave of Charles LaChapelle) bt. 12 Aug. 1798 spo. (Omitted) PCP-6, 89).
Françoise, adult negresse slave of Mr. Chapelle, bt. 3 June 1797 spo. (omitted) (PCP-6, 76).
Genevieve (Beniba slave of Chapelle) bt. 30 Sept 1792 spo. Leveille and Marie Jeanne (PCP-6, 40).
Henriette, negritte (Fanchonete, negresse slave of Chiapelle) bt. 11 Oct. 1795 spo. Ludger and Sophie (PCP-6, 60).
Jean, slave of Chapelle bt. 19 June 1791 spo. Jeaning Dugai and Agathe Lejeune. (PCP-6, 29).

Jean Louis, negrion (Marguerite, negresse slave of Charles Chiapelle) bt. 11 Oct 1795 spo. Jean Louis and Pelagie (PCP-6, 60) [buried 30 Dec 1795].
Jean Pierre, age 3 wks., (Marguerite, negresse brute slave of Charles Chiapella) bt. 20 June 1790 spo. Jean Pierre rep. by Magloire and Marie Louise (PCP-6, 22).
Louis, negre slave of Mr. Chapelle, bt. 19 June 1791 spo. Jacque, slave of Guillaume and Charlotte, slave of Guillaume (PCP-6, 29).
Marguerite, negresse slave of Charles LaChapelle bt. 19 June 1791 spo. François Dugai and Clemence Aimont (PCP-6, 29).
Marguerite, negritte (Marguerite slave of Charles Chiapella) bt. 26 May 1793 spo. Jean, slave of Charles Chiapella and Antoinette, slave of Guillaume André (PCP-6, 44).
Marie Françoise, slave of Mr. Chapelle bt. 18 March 1798 [spo. omitted] (PCP-6, 86).
Marie Martha Belly, negresse slave of Chiapelle bt. 11 Oct. 1795 spo. François and Marie Martha (PCP-6, 60).
Nicolas, negre slave of Chapelle bt. 19 June 1791 spo. Nicolas and Marie (PCP-6, 30).
Noel, negrilon (Charlote, slave of Mr. Chapelle) bt. 16 Feb 1794 spo. Louis negre man and Helene (PCP-6, 49). [buried 6 Oct. 1794].
Pierre Valerien (Dorothée, free quadroon residing at Mr. Chapelle) bt. 18 April 1797, spo. Pierr Allin and Amélie Allin (PCP-6, 73).
Thérèse, negresse slave of Charles LaChapelle bt. 12 Aug. 1798 spo. (omitted) (PCP-6, 89).[155]

Charles Lachiapella was following the ecclesiastical rules set down by the Catholic Church in the Louisiana Territory concerning the baptism and burial of slaves. Some owners sought to avoid paying the burial fee for interment in consecrated ground by burying slaves on their own plantation. Moreover, religious instruction for slaves was usually not a priority for the white master. Lachiapella's slave Marguerite, who bore at least four children while owned by him, was identified as "brute" indicating that she was from Africa and not native born. She was, however, baptized according to the above record in 1791, and had had her son, Jean Pierre, baptized the year before.

One other baptismal record stands out, at least for the genealogist, the baptism of Pierre Valérien, on 18 April 1797, son of Dorothée, a free quadroon, who was residing with Charles at his Pointe Coupée plantation.[156] Dorothée's mother Amaranthe Lassize had come to live with Lachiapella after she was able to purchase herself from her former owner, Marie Perrine Piquery, the wife of Nicolas Laurent Delassize, former secretary to the Spanish General Alejandro O'Reilly, Captain in the Spanish Militia, and later, Adjutant Major and Commandant of the Pointe Coupée Post. Self-purchase was a legal way for a slave to secure his or her manumission that the Spanish, called coartacion, had introduced into Louisiana. While in French Louisiana manumission had been a difficult process, the Spanish government had introduced the laws of Castille and the Indies into the territory. According to Jennifer Spear in Race, Sex and Social Order in Early New Orleans, during the French era just sixty slave owners applied to manumit 146 slaves, and the number of racially mixed slaves was indeed very small:

The first census to identify mulattos was taken in 1763. There were 50 men and 58 women living in New Orleans. 27 men and 12 women lived in the city's environs. All were categorized as slaves. The free people of color were enumerated separately of which there were only nineteen: six negres, eight negresses, three négrillons and two negrittes. living in the city; 26 more lived upriver at Chapitoulas and down river at English Turn there was a settlement of 35 free negroes.[157]

Under Spanish law, slaves could be freed for service to the state, for being abused by their masters, or by invoking the right of self-purchase even if they did not have the owner's consent. Theoretically a price would be agreed upon between master and slave, and payments by the latter would be made until such time as the entire amount was given over. Then a simple trip to a notary to issue freedom papers would secure the slave's manumission. If no price could be agreed upon, then the dispute would be taken to court where a judge would settle

---

[155] Emilie G. Leumas & Roland Gravois, eds., Diocese of Baton Rouge Catholic Church Records Pointe Coupée Records 1770-1900: Individuals without Surnames (Baton Rouge, LA: Department of Archives, Catholic Diocese of Baton Rouge, 2007) 189-190.

[156] Emilie G. Leumas & Roland Gravois, eds., Diocese of Baton Rouge Catholic Church Records Pointe Coupée Records 1770-1900, 190.

[157] Jennifer M. Spear, Race Sex and Social Order in Early New Orleans, (Baltimore, MD: Johns Hopkins University Press, 2009), 85, 95.

on the price to be paid. Spear concluded that after four years under Spanish rule more slaves had been manumitted than all those freed under fifty years of French rule. Over 2000 slaves gained their freedom between 1769 and 1803 under the Spanish. About 40% were freed for no compensation, the other 60% paid a price.[158] Amaranthe Lassize paid 1000 pesos to Madame Delassize, née Piquéry, for her freedom on 9 September 1785. At that time, she was said to have been twenty years old, although we believe she was older, since her death record in 1815 gave her age as "about seventy." She left three children behind in slavery: Athanase, Dorothée, and Julia, the only child of hers for whom we have found a birth record: "Delasisse, Julie (Amarente mulatresse slave of Mr. Delasisse) bn. 3 April 1784, bt. 9 May 1784, spo. Paul Allain and Amélie Delasisse (PCP 2, 238a).[159]

Included in Amaranthe's manumission was the information that she had originally been owned by Marie Perrine Piquéry's mother, Jeanne Fadet, the wife of Pierre Piquéry. After Mme. Piquéry died on 6 July 1775 (SLC, F1, 37), her property was amicably divided amongst her heirs. On pages 5 and 6 of the 41-page document in French and Spanish, dated 8 November 1775, the fate of her fifty-two slaves was spelled out:

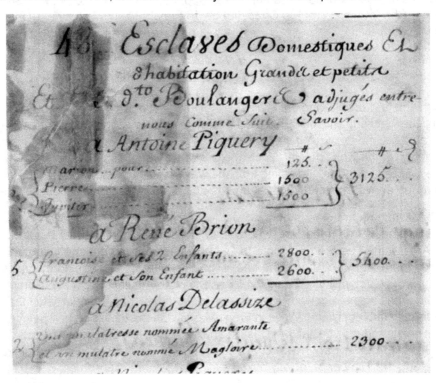

Succession of Veuve (Widow) Piquéry, Louisiana Colonial Document Collection, Louisiana Historical Center — Document #14278 –Available at: http://www.lacolonialdocs.org/document/14278, p. 5 of 41.

As shown above, Amaranthe, a "mulatresse," and Magloire, a "mulatre" male, worth together 2300 piastres, were willed to Nicolas Laurent Delassize in late 1775. Amaranthe had been raised in the household of Pierre Piquéry, an immigrant from Mons, Hainaut, Belgium, who came to Louisiana with his wife and two children in 1724 to work at the Sainte Reyne concession. However, after one year, he left to become a prosperous baker in New Orleans.[160] Amaranthe's first three children, all quadroons, were born into slavery in the Delassize household, beginning in

---

[158] Spear, *Race, Sex and Social Order in Early New Orleans*, 110.

[159] Emilie G. Leumas & Roland Gravois, eds., *Diocese of Baton Rouge Catholic Church Records Pointe Coupée Records 1770-1900*, 214.

[160] Piquery and wife were enumerated in a 1724 census at the St. Julien Place, about 8 leagues above New Orleans on the west side of the Mississippi River. That year, because blackbirds had destroyed his crop, he decided to take his family to New Orleans. In 1732 he was enumerated as "Piquery, baker," on Chartres Street with himself, his wife, three children, one orphan, two negro slaves and two slave children. Source: Charles R. Maduell, Jr., *The Census Tables for the French Colony of Louisiana from 1699 through 1732*, (Baltimore, MD: Genealogical Publishing Co., Inc., 1972), 46, 126. Note: We do not know when Pierre Piquéry died. He was alive for the baptism of his daughters Marianne on 6 March 1830 (AN, B. 1730, 111) and Louise on 17 March 1732(SLC, B1, 22). When Marianne married René Brion on 18 May 1761 (SLC, B4, 63) he was still living, but he was deceased by the time of his daughter, Marie Perrine's marriage to Nicolas Delassize on 7 June 1762. (SLC, B4, 70).

1777 with Athanase, then Dorothée, in 1779, and Julia in 1784. All used the Delassize/Lassize surname so it is possible that Nicolas Laurent Delassize, himself, was their father.

Nicolas Laurent Delassize, born on 23 February 1730 at Le Havre, Seine-Maritime, France, and Marie Perrine Piquéry had been married on 7 June 1762 in New Orleans. Their marriage contract, signed on the same day, indicated that he had been born at Havre de Grâce, Normandy, France, to Louis Jacques Delassize and Anne Catherine Garentier Marie Perrine brought to the marriage from the succession of her father, slaves, land, clothing and money valued at 18,000 livres of which one-third was community property and two-thirds was reserved for herself and the children.[161] The couple had ten children between 1763 and 1778: Marie Eulalie (23 March 1763, SLC, B5,12), Cézaire Hyacinthe (b. 25 June 1764, SLC B5, 55), Nicolas Alexandre (b. 28 May 1765, SLC, B5, 132), Vallery Jean (b. 9 March 1767, SLC B6, 63), Julie Cézaire (b. 20 Dec. 1768, SLC, B6,64), Marie (b. 12 October 1770, SLC, B6,93), Victor Évariste (b. 18 April 1773, SLC, B7, 24), Octave Louis (b.15 February 1775, SLC, B7, 47), Claude Augustine Eugénie (baptized 7 December 1776, SLC B7, 67), and Amélie (b. 13 June 1778, SLC, B9, 38).

Amaranthe was able to buy her freedom from the Delassize family during the time Nicolas Laurent was the Adjutant Major of the Spanish Militia at Pointe Coupée, and Post Commandant, a position he held until his death in November of 1788. In an abstract of the document recorded by Gwendolyn Midlo Hall, she wrote that the manumission was done account of the good services "Amarante" performed, and for 1000 piastres.[162] Once free, she moved to Charles Lachiapella's indigo plantation and lived there with him until she could negotiate the freedom of her children. On 18 September 1795 she was able to purchase Dorothée from her former owner, Marie Perrine Piquery Delassize, during the time when the latter sold off property and slaves she had inherited from her deceased husband's estate. Dorothée, inventoried as Dorotea, a quadroon, was sold back to her mother for 400 piastres.[163] She was probably about sixteen years of old at the time. It was only two years later that Dorothée gave birth to her first child, Pierre Valérien Allain, whose baptism record we have cited on p.83, probably a son of Pierre Valérien Allain (1775-1844) who lived in the same district as Charles Lachiapella in Pointe Coupée. Amaranthe had also given birth to one of the Allain children after her manumission. A son named Valefroy Allain was born ca. 1787, who was listed as one of her heirs in her 1815 last will and testament. Another child, Valery Blodins [sic, perhaps "Blondin"] was born ca. 1793 and also appeared in 1815 as one of her heirs. Both of these children were born free, after her manumission, and probably lived with her and Lachiapella at Pointe Coupée during the last decade of the eighteenth century. It may be worth noting that while Lachiapella was a slave trader and plantation owner who lived with a free colored family, he was also on 18 June 1794 and on 8 July 1794 accused by the slave Marie Louise, owned by Vincent Porché, of the crime of abusing her. Unfortunately, there was no resolution to this accusation that we could find.[164]

Amaranthe's eldest child, Athanase was manumitted gratis by Charles Lachiapella at the Pointe Coupée Post on 29 February 1796.[165] We have not been able to find when he purchased the child, who was said to be 15 years old at the time, although we believe that he was born about 1777 since he was identified as her thirty-eight-year-old son at her death in 1815. Although Gwendolyn Midlo Hall implied that because the manumission was gratis, that Charles Lachiapella was probably his father, we feel that he was freed by Lachiapella out of gratitude for Amaranthe having given birth that same year to Charles Lachiapella's only child, a son Jean-Baptiste, although we could find no record for it either. Before they left the district, Dorothée Lassize gave birth to Eulalie on 2 November 1798, whose father was also probably Pierre Valérien Allain. Eulalie was baptized on 28 August 1800 at St. Louis Cathedral by Fr. Flavius de Besançon after Dorothée's move from Pointe Coupée to New Orleans. No father was listed for Eulalie ("padre no conocido"), a free quadroon although she would use the surname Allain in

---

[161] Louisiana Office of the Lieut. Governor, Dept. of Culture, Recreation and Tourism, Information on line at: (https://www.crt.state.la.us/dataprojects/ museum/blackbook/Black_Book_81_1762_Jan-Jun.pdf) Image 173/191. Doc. # 8181.

[162] Gwendolyn Midlo Hall, comp. *Louisiana, Freed Slave Records, 1719-1820, Freedom of Amarante dated 9 September 1785*

[163] Ibid., Freedom of Dorotea by Marie P. Piquéry Delassize.

[164] Winston De Ville, *Slaves and Masters of Pointe Coupée. Louisiana: A Calendar of Civil records, 1762-1823,* (Ville Platte, LA: The Provincial Press, 1988), 22.

[165] Gwendolyn Midlo Hall, comp. *Louisiana, Freed Slave Records, 1719-1820,* Freedom of Athaneuse, mulatto by Lachapelle, dated 29 February 1796.

all subsequent records. Eulalie Allain would appear again in the interwoven Chiapella and Aubry genealogies upon her marriage in 1829 to Charles Beauvilaire Pinta.

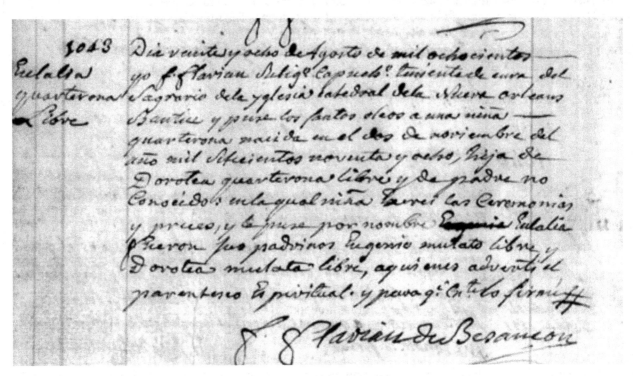

Archdiocese of New Orleans, *St. Louis Cathedral, New Orleans Baptism of Slaves and Free People of Color 1798-1801*, Digital Collections-#1043, Image 322/464 at https://archives.arch-no.org/sacramental_records.Baptism of Eulalie (Allain) on 28 August 1800

Amaranthe was finally able to obtain her daughter Julie's freedom, born in slavery on 3 April 1784, on 9 February 1801 from Jean François Robert Avart and his wife Amélie Delassize, for 800 piastres.[166] Amélie Delassize, as we have seen in Julie's birth record on p. 84, was her godmother. Amélie had inherited Julie from her mother's estate when fifty-six-year-old Marie Perrine Piquery Delassize died on 10 October 1797 (SLC, F4, 53). Amalie had married Avart, born on 7 February 1777 (SLC, B9, 14) to Valentin Robert Avart, Captain of the New Orleans Militia, and his wife Julie Allain (a member of the white Allain family), on 22 December 1800 (SLC, M5, 133).

Charles Lachiapella had been struggling for a long time with the indigo crops on his plantation. The quality of indigo in Louisiana had never been great, but the 1793 and 1794 season was a disaster because caterpillars had attacked the plants.[167] Another blight wiped out the 1796 harvest. He held on for a few more years, selling slaves with his brother, and trading slaves for indigo, which was as good as money at the time. After the slave revolt in Pointe Coupée in 1795, Governor Carondelet banned the importation of slaves the following year. Pressure, however, from Louisiana planters, forced him to open the trade again in November 1800, with the exception of the French Caribbean islands, which, it was feared, had become too infected with the French Revolutionary spirit.[168] Lachiapella made a decision to sell out in Pointe Coupée and on 4 December 1799 he sold his slaves and property to Sieur D. LeBlanc. On 28 December of the same year the sale was annulled, and on 12 February 1800 he sold 19 arpents of land to two neighbors, Vincent Porché and François Barra.[169]

From that time on, Lachiapella and Amaranthe Lassize's activities centered in New Orleans, where on 2 December 1800, Amaranthe bought a plot of ground with 60 foot of frontage on Dauphine Street by 120 feet deep

---

[166] Ibid., Freedom of Julia, quadroon by Avart and wife dated 9 February 1801.

[167] Charles Gayarré, *History of Louisiana. The Spanish Domination*, Vol. 3. (Gretna, LA: Pelican Publishing Co., 1974), 346.

[168] Midlo Hall, *Africans in Colonial Louisiana*, 278.

[169] Winston De Ville, *Pointe Coupée Documents 1762- 1803: A Calendar of Civil records for the Province of Louisiana* (Ville Platte, LA: Provincial Press, 1997), 87, 88.

from Daniel Clark for 600 pesos with a mortgage.[170] Working with the same notary, "Carlos" Lachiapella sold slaves: to Vicente Fernandez Tejeiro, on 4 August 1800, and to Louis Foucher, on 1 September 1800.[171] On 1 October 1800 he sold a thirty-year-old slave Carlota, with her one-year-old daughter for 675 pesos to Ignacio Delino, and finally on 11 October 1800, he sold a 22-year-old black female named Pegy to Anne Félicité Boutin, a free quadroon, for 400 piastres.[172]

On 25 April 1810, Charles Lachiapella, a resident of New Orleans sold five of his slaves to his adopted nephew, Celestin Chiapella, living on a plantation four leagues below the city. They were Lafortune – age 46, bought from Mme Bizotin? twenty years ago; Hector age 40, bought from his brother, Geronimo Lachiapella 20 years ago; Bazile about 40 years old bought at auction in Pointe Coupée 20 years ago; Jean Pierre, age 18, born on Charles's plantation; and William, age 27, bought from Francisco Gomes at Pensacola a year ago. He sold them for 1,850 piastres which Celestin had already given him.[173]

In 1803 Charles Lachiapella started another project, a farm on Pascagoula Bay in what was, at the time, Spanish West Florida. The area did not become part of the Mississippi Territory until 1812. On 26 April 1810 Charles gave to Amaranthe Lassize f.c.l., a resident of New Orleans, "because of his friendship for her," four arpents of ground with its depth (not stated), situated at Pascagoula Bay with all its buildings, as is, along with a pair of cattle, two calves and a horse. The property and buildings, which he had bought from Jean-Baptiste Nicolet in 1803 were not mortgaged.[174] After Pascagoula became part of the United States in 1812, Amaranthe registered her claim to the land, stating that the previous owner had been Charles Chappelle, and the land had been under cultivation from 1803 until the present.[175]

On the same day, Charles Lachiapella sold to Amaranthe Lassize, free of all debts and mortgages a negress named Benabale aged about 45 and her three children; Marie Marthe, negritte age 15; François, negritte age 12, and Félicité negritte age 9 years. He stated that he had bought the mother about twenty years ago from Jerome Lachiapella, his brother, and the children were born on his place. He sold them for 1500 piastres, of which Amaranthe had already paid him 500 piastres. As to the remaining 1000 piastres, Amaranthe agreed to pay him in four years until which time the 4 slaves were mortgaged to him.[176]

On 13 December 1813, as the result of an illness which confined her to bed, Amaranthe Lassize summoned the notary Michel de Armas to her rooms on Dauphine Street to make out her last will and testament. She stated her name, that she was free, about fifty-one years old, a native of Louisiana and the mother of six children: Athanaze, about thirty-eight years old, Dorothée, about thirty-six, Julie (Lassize), about thirty, Valefroy, about twenty-eight, Valery about twenty-two, and Jean-Baptiste about seventeen years old. All of her children were residents of New Orleans except for Jean-Baptiste who was in Lisbon. She left 100 piastres each to her daughter Dorothée's three daughters. She left her clothing and linens to Dorothée and Julie. The residue of her estate was to be divided equally amongst all her children. She appointed Samuel P. Moore, her executor.[177]

---

[170] NARC, Pedro Pedesclaux, Notary, Sale of land Clark to Lassize, Vo. 37, fol. 724, recto & verso. Courtesy Hon. Chelsey Richard Napoleon, Clerk of Civil District Court, Parish of Orleans.

[171] NARC, Pedro Pedesclaux, Notary, Sale of Slave to Tejeiro 4 August 1800, p. 483; Sale of slaves to Foucher, 1 September 1800, p. 523.

[172] Gwendolyn Midlo Hall, comp. *Louisiana, Slave Records, 1719-1820*, Sale of Carlota to Delino, and sale of Pegy to Boutin by Charles Lachiapella.

[173] NARC, Michel De Armas, Notary, Volume 10 –Sale of Slave – Chas. Lachiapella to Celestin Lachiapella, Act # 104, folio 103 verso and 104 recto. Courtesy Hon. Chelsey Richard Napoleon, Clerk of Civil District Court, Parish of Orleans.

[174] NARC, Michel De Armas, Notary, Volume 10 –Donation of land, Chas. Lachiapella to Amaranthe Lasise, Act # 105, folio 105 recto & verso. Courtesy Hon. Chelsey Richard Napoleon, Clerk of Civil District Court, Parish of Orleans.

[175] *American State Papers, Public Lands, Vol. III, March 4, 1789- June 15, 1834*, (Washington DC: Duff and Green, 1834), 30.

[176] NARC, Michel De Armas, Notary, Volume 10 –Sale of slaves with mortgage, Chas. Lachiapella to Amaranthe Lasize, Act # 106, folio 105 verso and 106 recto. Courtesy Hon. Chelsey Richard Napoleon, Clerk of Civil District Court, Parish of Orleans. Note: Charles Lachiapella signed a quittance on this mortgage on 16 December 1815 after Amaranthe's death.

[177] "Louisiana, Wills and Probate Records, 1756-1984," digital images, *Ancestry.com* (https://www.ancestry.com: accessed 5/29/19), citing *Record of Wills, 1807-1901; Louisiana Probate Court (Orleans Parish)*. Will of Amarante Lassize, f.c.l., dated 13 December 1813.

Amaranthe Lassize was interred in the parish cemetery on 18 April 1815 (SLC F10, 10). On 11 August 1815, her only minor child, nineteen-year-old Jean-Baptiste Chiapella petitioned the court to have his natural father, Charles Chiapella, be appointed as his curator ad bona, and the lawyer, Benjamin P. Porter as his curator ad litem. An inventory of the estate was held on 22 September 1815 at Amaranthe's late home on Dauphine Street between Bienville and Customhouse, said to be worth 1600 piastres. Her entire estate, including the plot of ground, the two houses, and back buildings, with two kitchens, as well as her personal effects, were appraised for 4,315 piastres (about 70,000 in 2019 dollars), including the following slaves together worth about 2,000 piastres: Benebale, aged about 50 years, cook and washerwoman; her daughter, Marie Marthe, a creole negress about 20 years old, a cook, and her infant George, a mulatto about 16 months old; her son, François, a creole negro, about 19 years old, a daily worker; and her daughter, Félicité, a creole negress aged about 15 years, a domestic servant. Signing this appraisal along with the executor Samuel P. Moore, and two witnesses were her children Valefroy Allain, Valery Blodins, Dorothée Lassize, and Charles Chiapella, curator ad bona for their son Jean-Baptiste Chiapella.[178] A copy of those signatures may be seen below:

douze piastres, tous lesquels objets ainsi que les papiers sus mentionnés sont demeurés à la disposition du sieur Samuel P. Moore, exécuteur testamentaire de la dite défunte, qui le reconnait s'en fait charge & a signé, ainsi que les parties et témoins sus mentionnés, les mêmes jour, mois & an que dessus & nous sommes retirés.

Dorothée Lassize Saml P. Moore

Valfroy allain vallery Blodins Charles Chiapella

Blondeau Brierre

Prosper Prieur

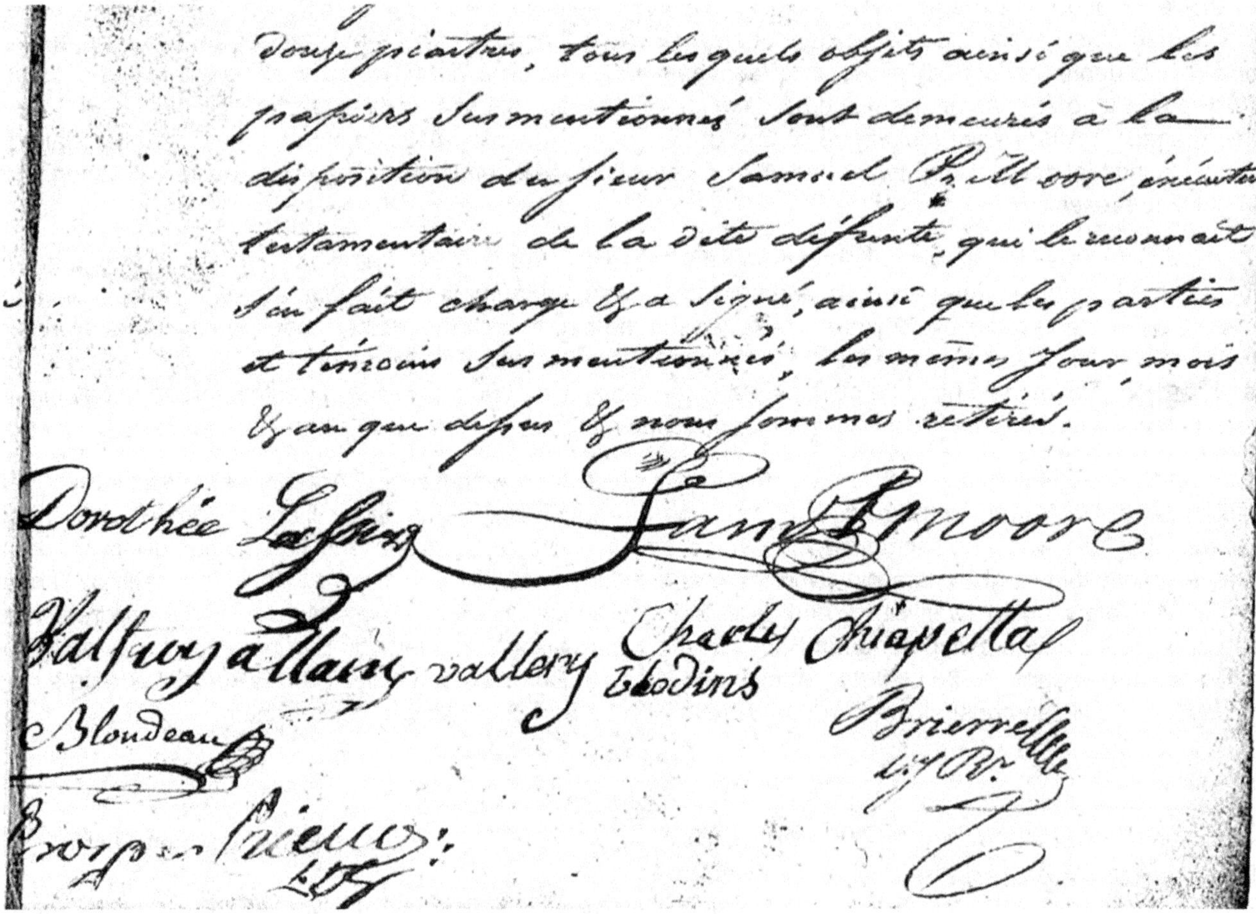

Signature page of 1815 inventory of the estate of Amaranthe Lassize,f.c.l. at "*Louisiana, Wills and Probate Records, 1756-1984,"* digital images, *Ancestry.com* (https://www.ancestry.com: accessed 5/292019) citing *Old Inventories L, 1809-1820*; *Orleans Parish (Louisiana). Clerk of Court,* Image 219/643. Full inventory – Images 216-222/643.

178 "Louisiana, Wills and Probate Records, 1756-1984,"digital images, *Ancestry.com* (https://www.ancestry.com: accessed 5/29/2019), citing *Successions, Probate L, 1805-1815*, Probate of Amthe. Lassese (*sic*) dated 14 June 1815, Images 1029-1044; Appointment of curators for Jean Baptiste Chiapella, Images 1040-1044.

One of the provisions of Amaranthe's will was that the slave Benabale could not be sold because of her good conduct and great loyalty to the family. To that end, Dorothée Lassize had each of her siblings sign a quittance (quit claim) for 50 piastres, or one-sixth of Benabale's worth had she been sold for her appraised value of 300 piastres. Moreover, at the auction sale for the property and slaves, Dorothée Lassize purchased Marie Marthe and her son George, Benabale's daughter and grandson, as well as Benabale's other daughter, fifteen-year-old Félicité, with her newborn child, for 1590 piastres. Benabale's nineteen-year-old son, François was sold out of the family to Jean Jacques Chessé. Athanase came to New Orleans from Rapides Parish where he was living to declare his quittance to his mother's estate after having received the 400 piastres (worth today about $6450) he was due as one-sixth of the remaining monies in the estate after all debts were paid, and after a 50 piastre reduction in favor of Benabale. The transaction was done before Michel de Armas on 24 January 1817. The absence of his signature on the above inventory of his mother's estate is explained by his declaration on the document that he did not know how to write. Valefroy Allain and Valery Blodins, two of Amaranthe's other sons signed their quittance on 7 May 1819 and accepted their inheritance:

NARC, Quittance of hereditary rights by Athanaze Lassize, h.d.c.l. to Samuel P. Moore, testamentary executor of Amaranthe Lassize, f.d.c.l. after payment of 400 piastres. Notary Michel de Armas, Volume 12, Act #30, dated 24 January 1817. Courtesy Hon. Chelsey Richard Napoleon, Clerk of Civil District Court, Parish of Orleans.

Amaranthe's son with Charles Lachiapella, Jean-Baptiste, who according to her 1813 will was in "Lisbon" at the time she wrote it, did not appear in 1817 to sign a quittance for the slave Benabale. Little is known of his life. However, we believe that he did serve in the War of 1812. A "Jean-Baptiste Chapelle" was enrolled as a private in Fortier's 1st Battalion of Free Men of Color also known as Fortier's Louisiana Militia. His length of service was from 16 December 1814 to 25 March 1815. Michel Fortier was the Lieutenant Colonel of the battalion. Pierre Lacoste was 1st Major, and Vincent Populus, a free man of color was the 2nd Major. Valery Blodins, another of Amaranthe's sons, served in the same battalion with Chiapella, also as a private.[179]

After the War of 1812, Chiapella worked as a house painter in New Orleans. He never married. He did, however, stand as the godfather to his half-brother Valefroy Allain's natural daughter with Isabel Agathe Harang on 25 April 1815. The child, Julia Allain was born on 19 November 1813 at New Orleans to Valefroy, a free quadroon and a native and resident of the city of New Orleans, and Agathe, also a free quadroon, born at Port-au-Prince Saint-Domingue. Although the godmother was said to have been Julia Allain, we believe that she might have been Julia Lassize, another of Valefroy Allain's half-siblings: The baptismal record, written in Spanish by Fr. Antonio de Sedella is unfortunately hard to read due to the bleeding through of the ink on the opposite page. In this document Jean Baptiste Chiapella appears as Juan Bautista Chapella on the next to last line of the record:

Baptismal record for Julia Allain. Archives of the Archdiocese of New Orleans, Saint Louis Cathedral Records Vol. 14- S/FPC, p. 109, #776. (Courtesy of Emilie Leumas, Archivist – Kimberly Johnson and Katie Vest – Researching Archivists.)

Jean-Baptiste Chiapella's death on 25 September 1833 was reported by Charles Fuselier almost four years after it happened, probably at the behest of John Winthrop, who in 1837 applied to become the curator of his vacant succession. The death record for Jean-Baptiste reads in part:

Be it remembered that on this day to wit the twenty-eighth of April in the year of our Lord one thousand eight hundred and thirty-seven [...] before me Vincent Ramos duly commissioned and sworn Recorder of Births and Deaths in and for the Parish of Orleans, personally appeared Charles Fuselier, a native of this city, aged twenty-nine years, a carpenter residing in this city Basin Street between Bienville and Customhouse Streets, who by these presents doth declare that Jean-Baptiste Chiapella, a native of this parish, aged about thirty-five years at the time of his Death, late a painter, residing in the city Died herein

---

[179] Thomas Harrison, compiler, National Park Service, *Troop Roster, Tennessee Volunteers & Militia, Kentucky Volunteers & Militia, Battalion of Free Men of Color, Louisiana Volunteers & Militia, 112.*

on the twenty-fifth of September in the year eighteen hundred and thirty-three at five o'clock P.M. in a house situated Remparts Streets, between St. Louis and Conty (*sic*) Streets. The said Chiapella was not married:

The interest in Jean-Baptiste Chiapella's vacant estate was heightened by a discovery Winthrop had made in 1837. Chiapella had $1,277.05 in cash which he had left in the hands of Laurent Williamson, Esq., that had been unclaimed. Had his father, Charles Lachiapella died or left the country by 1833? We could find no more information on Charles after he had signed the quittance in 1815 releasing Amaranthe Lassize's estate from the mortgage he had on the slave Benabale and her children whom he had sold to her on 26 April 1810. Moreover, there are no other records for the Jean-Baptiste Chiapella estate between 1833 and 1837, and no other indication that any other heirs, including his father, half-siblings or their children, had petitioned to get control of the succession.

However on 23 April 1838, Julie Allain, a resident of Jefferson Parish, the wife of Augustin Ovide Dauphin, and a daughter of Valefroy Allain, Chiapella's half-brother, along with her sister, Arseline Allain: "Allin, Arzelina daughter of Valefroy and Agata Harang [both]natives and residents of this parish b. Oct. 16, 1817, bn. Jan 15, 1816 s. Querubin Duconge and Victoria Soufrein (SLC, B29, 178)." They signed a document in the office of Amédée Ducatel relinquishing any claim to their deceased uncle, Jean-Baptiste Chiapella's estate to Chiapella's half-brother, Athanase Lassize, only under the condition that they be made save harmless from any debts which the estate might incur. A copy of the signature portion of the notarized act may be seen on the following page:

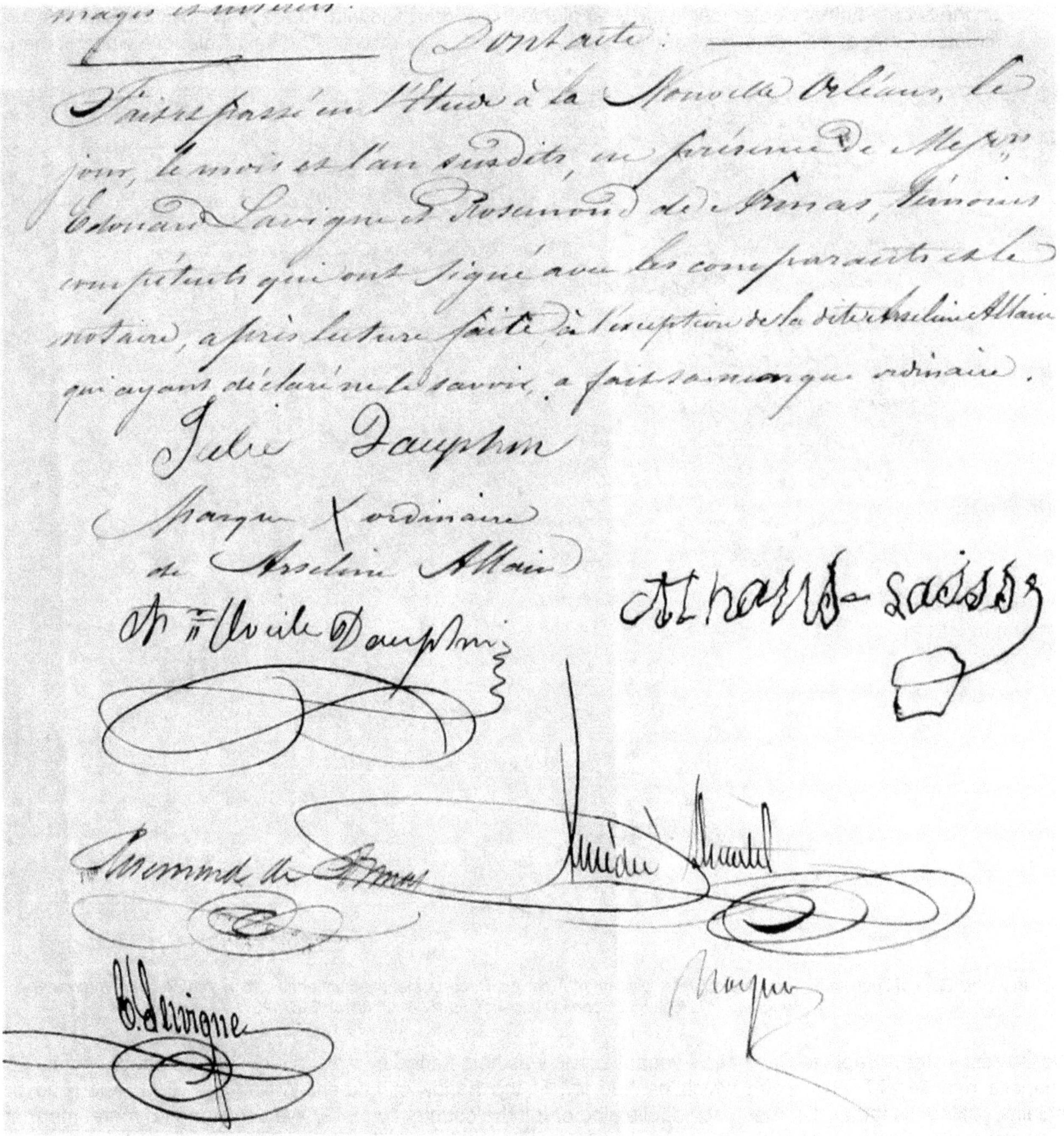

[Handwritten manuscript document in French cursive script, followed by several signatures and marks]

NARC, "Transport de droits de succession par Julie Allain, épouse d'A. Ovide Dauphin et Arceline Allain à Athanase Lassize" (Transfer of Succession rights from Julie Allain, wife of A. Ovide Dauphin and Arceline Allain to Athanase Lassize) dated 23 April 1838, passed by Notary Amédée Ducatel, Volume 7, Act #158. Courtesy Hon. Chelsey Richard Napoleon, Clerk of Civil District Court, Parish of Orleans. Note: Julie Allain, the wife of Ovide Dauphin, signed, but her sister Arceline Allain, signed with an "x." Athanase Lassize also signed.

CHAPTER 8

DOROTHÉE LASSIZE, PHILIP ZERBAN AND SAMUEL P. MOORE

NARC, Signatures of Samuel P. Moore and Dorothée Lassize – Sale of slaves from estate of Amaranthe Lassize to her daughter Dorothée, dated 4 October 1816 (Michel de Armas, Volume 11, Act 659.) Courtesy Hon. Chelsey Richard Napoleon, Clerk of Civil District Court, Parish of Orleans.

Spanish Louisiana like French Louisiana had always been a Catholic settlement. Towards the end of the eighteenth century, some American merchants, mainly of the Protestant faith had settled in the colony after the difficulties brought on by the Seven Years War and the American Revolution. Jews however, were a different story. The Spanish Black Code forbade the settlement of Hebrews in the territory. Isaac Monsanto, an immigrant from the Hague in Holland, where a large number of Sephardic Jews expelled from Spain had settled, had become one of French New Orleans' most successful merchants. He found himself expelled from the Spanish colony of Louisiana and his goods confiscated in 1769. He set up shop in British West Florida at Manchac, and was soon joined by his brothers, Emmanuel, Jacob and Benjamin. The four men worked as merchants, travelling up and down the Mississippi River, and occasionally into New Orleans to do business with men such as Oliver Pollock and Jérome Chiapella. After restoring order to the colony, Captain General Alejandro O'Reilly left New Orleans in 1770, and the Monsantos discovered that their being Jewish seemed no longer to be a problem. While they remained in Manchac for at least a decade, they began returning one by one to New Orleans and the surrounding area. By 1780 Benjamin Monsanto had established himself in Pointe Coupée. Another "foreigner" Charles Lachiapella arrived soon thereafter. The Monsanto brothers, as did many merchants, owned slaves and were active in the buying, selling, and trading of slaves on a small scale. Their sister Angelica was one of the first Monsantos to settle permanently in New Orleans when she married Dr. "Roberto Dow," a native of Scotland, and interim physician of the hospital," on 9 September 1781. Angelica was not identified as being Jewish, nor, was, for that matter, Robert Dow, identified as being a Scottish Presbyterian. Angelica's parents were written down in her marriage record as Pedro Davit Rodriguez Monsanto and Ester Levi. Angelica was a native of Amsterdam and the widow of George Urquhart. The marriage record was signed by Fr. Cyrillo de Barcelona. (SLC, M4, 114). One of the witnesses to their marriage was another Sephardic Jew living in New Orleans, Manuel Solis. Dr. Dow was the physician who on July 1782, had treated Agathe Lemelle's infant, Amada (Jeanne Aimée) Lachaise with a vial of an absorbent mixture of magnesium and rhubarb (See part of his bill, p. 41).

Benjamin Monsanto, believing that the pastures were greener in Natchez, where he and his brothers had visited and done business in the past, purchased land there in 1785. So did his brother Jacob, although their attempts as farming were a constant drain on their resources. Benjamin contracted to marry Clara Mota (aka Claire de La Motte) in February 1787. The daughter of Solomon la Mota and Rica Coen, she was a native of Curaçao, also Jewish by birth, who brought 2500 Mexican silver to the marriage as her dowry.[180] Benjamin died unexpectedly while he was in New Orleans with his wife, Clara, in order to settle some debts. His Saint Louis Cathedral death record reads in part: "Monsanto, Benjamin (David and Ester Levis), native of Haye, 40 yr., sp. Clara Motar, buried September 30, 1794." The original record indicates he was interred in the St. Louis Church Cemetery. (SLC, F4, 16).

---

[180] May Wilson McBee, compiler, *The Natchez Court Records 1767-1805: Abstracts of Early Records* (Baltimore, MD: Clearfield Co. Inc by Genealogical Publishing Co., Inc., 1994,2003), 117.

According to Bertrand Wallace Korn in his book, *The Early Jews of New Orleans*, the will of Emanauel/Manuel Monsanto was particularly revealing. He only survived Benjamin by two years and was buried in the Saint Louis Church Cemetery on 10 July 1796. Amongst other bequests, he left fifty pesos to the quadroon Sofia, daughter of the mulatress Mamy (aka Maimy William) who had been Jacob Monsanto's slave, whom the latter had freed on 4 August 1783 at age twenty-six for 300 pesos. Korn concluded, correctly or not, that Sofia had been Jacob's daughter. Both Sofia and Maimy had used the name Monsanto in civil records.[181]

Sofia Monsanto had two children with Frederick Zerban, a native of New York. The first, Carlos Phelipe Zerbonne y Monsanto, born free on 29 December 1784, was baptized on 14 November 1797. Only the mother's name was recorded on the baptism as Sofia Monsanto, a free mulatress." (SLC B13, 426). Federico Zerban and Sofia Monsanto had a second son, Federico, born on 10 December 1796 and baptized on 22 August 1798. The godfather was Samuel P. Moore, the executor of Amaranthe Lassize's estate, and later the father of Dorothée Lassize's eight children. The godmother was Clara Monsanto, the widow of Benjamin Monsanto. (SLC B15, 32).

The connections, however, do not end here. Frederick Zerban, the father of Sofia Monsanto's children, was briefly married to Isabel/Elizabeth Sara Moore, Samuel P. Moore's sister, "the widow of Robert Scott, and the daughter of the late Alexander Moore, Esq., merchant of Natchez in the Mississippi Territory."[182] In his last will and testament, written in 1802 Frederick Zerban identified his parents as John Wendell Zerban and Catherine Baker, both deceased. His wife was "Izavel Zara Moore, (daughter of Alexandro and Zara Moore), native of Natchez, widow of Roberto Scott, native of Ultonia in Ireland. Isabel Sara Moore died at the age of 24 years, [and] was buried 6 September 1801 in St. Louis Cathedral in the first section (SLC, F4, 101)." Frederick and Sara's only child, Sara Juana [Sarah Jane] "daughter of Frederico Zerban, native of Philadelphia in the United States of America and Zara Moor, native of Pensacola, both residents of this city, was born on 15 May 1801 and baptized on 11 November 1801. Her godparents were the child's uncle, Samuel Phelipe Moor, and Zara Hulings. (SLC, B14, 175)." Sara Juana died at age nine months and was interred on 2 February 1802 "in St. Louis Cathedral in the first section of the nave alongside the grave of her mother." (SLC, B14, 175).

In Frederick's 1802 will, he did not acknowledge or provide for his two children by Sofia Monsanto. He bequeathed $1000 to his sister Henrietta, who lived in Philadelphia, $3,000 to his sister Eleonore, along with all his household goods, and the one-half interest in the plantation known as Gentilly, situated three miles from New Orleans, which he owned jointly with Paul Darcantelle [*sic*, Darcantel], and $3000 to his brother Philip, a merchant living in New Orleans.

Philip, Frederick's brother, was a New Orleans pharmacist who sold patent medicines. He was also the father of Dorothée Lassize's child Zenon. In this barely legible document, the child indicated in the margin as "Zenin Zerbin, free quadroon" was baptized at age two years as Zenon Maria Zerbin by Fr. Sebastian Gili, on 10 April 1804, the son of Philip (Felipe) Zerbin and Dorothée Lassize. The godparents were Jean-Baptiste Cavelier and Maria Tomassin Andry:

[181] Bertrand Wallace Korn, *The Early Jews of New Orleans* (Waltham, MA: American Jewish Historical Society, 1969), 67,68.

[182] "Louisiana, Orleans Parish Will Books, 1805-1920," digital images, *FamilySearch.org* (https://familysearch.org/ark:/61903/3:1:3QS7-L9MY-PPTQ?cc=2019728&wc=SJ76-W38%3A341295101 : accessed 5/2/2019, Will book 1805-1815 vol 1, image 358-360/ 553; City Archives & Special Collections, New Orleans Public Library, New Orleans. Will of Frederick Zerban, undated but written in 1802.

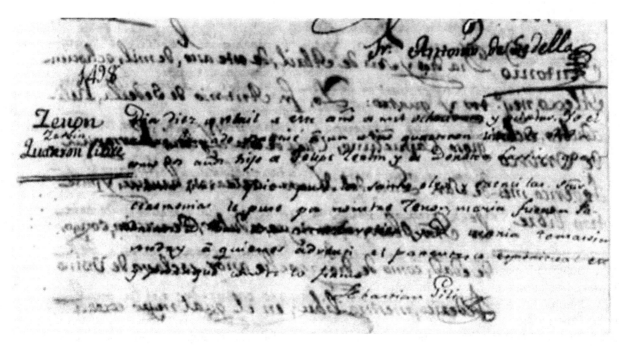

Archdiocese of New Orleans, *St. Louis Cathedral, New Orleans Baptism of Slaves and Free People of Color 1802-1804*, Digital Collections-#1498 Image 193/200 at https://archives.arch-no.org/sacramental_records. Baptism of Zenon Zerbin free quadroon.

Philip Zerban, however, had already contracted a marriage with Euphémie Fusellier. In that document Zerban, identified as the son of "Wendel and Catarina Baker, native of Philadelphia in the United States of America, sectarian (Protestant) who abjured his errors before the diocesan vicar general, married Euphémie Fusellier, daughter of Gabriel Fusellier and Helen Soileau, a native of this city, on 26 December 1800." The witnesses were Samuel P. Moore, Henry Stagg, husband of Euphémie's sister Josephine, and Besur [*sic* ?] Fusellier. (SLC, M5, 133). Their first child, Federico Juan (Frederick John) was born on 28 January 1802 (SLC, B17, 1), the same year as Dorothée's son Zenon Zerban. Philip Zerban's second child with his wife, a daughter Eugenia, was born on 18 January 1803 (SLC, B17, 25). After that birth, and the baptism of his child with Dorothée Lassize in 1804, the Saint Louis Cathedral records are silent on any further entries for Philip Zerban. He did continue to advertise as a druggist in the *Louisiana State Gazette*. In January 1806 his shop was located at #42 Royal Street, corner of Conti. A two-column advertisement in the 24 March 1807 *Louisiana State Gazette* identified Philip as selling the products of Richard Lee and Son (Baltimore, MD), at #41, the corner of Chartres and Conti opposite the Exchange. The remedies he sold included salves, powders and pills which would cure, venereal diseases, the itch, worms, "hooping (*sic)* cough," tooth aches, corns, asthma and the first stages of consumption.[183]

Dorothée Lassize was, however, seeking a more stable relationship. Both Philip and Frederick Zerban had had children with free woman of color, but both had contracted marriages with white women. Dorothée found her mate for life in Samuel Philip Moore, Frederick Zerban's brother-in-law. Perhaps the entangled relationships amongst the Zerban, Monsanto, and Moore white and free colored families can be partially explained because the Jewish Monsantos and the Protestant Zerbans and Moores were outsiders in a 98% Roman Catholic society. The free women of color, although Catholic, were outsiders as well by the tinge of color to their skin. Samuel was evidently not shaken by Dorothée having had a child with his brother-in-law. Perhaps he was only shocked that Philip Zerban had cheated on his legitimate spouse so soon after marriage.

---

[183] "Attention Just Received a General Assortment of Richard Lee & Son's, Patent and Family Medicines," *The Louisiana State Gazette,* 24 March 1807, digital image, *Genealogybank.com* (http://www.genealogybank.com: accessed 9/14/2019) p. 2, cols. 3, 4.

Emily Clark in her book, *The Strange History of the American Quadroon*, spent several pages on the relationship between Samuel Moore and Dorothée Lassize.[184] Moore was an American, born to an Irish Protestant immigrant, Alexander Moore, who settled initially in Virginia. After the end of the Seven Years' War in 1763, Moore moved to British West Florida where he was a merchant at Pensacola. Both Samuel and Sara Moore Scott Zerban had been born at Pensacola and baptized in the Anglican Church. As Great Britain made an effort to expand its territory on the eve of the American Revolution, the Moore family was granted land just north of Natchez, Adams Co., MS. In addition to his land holdings, Moore became an important merchant in the town of Natchez, exporting lumber and buying and selling slaves up and down the Mississippi River into New Orleans. Alexander Moore died in New Orleans in 1795. His death record reads in part "Alexander Moore, native of Ireland, 72 years (former) Protestant who abjured his errors during his sickness, widower of Juana Escriven (Jane Scott), was buried on June 2, 1795 (SLC, F4, 16). An inventory of Alexander Moore's property taken in November 1795, revealed that he owned just over 3000 arpents of land, in four parcels between 2.5 and 60 miles from Fort Panmure (formerly Fort Rosalie), 1000 arpents of land on Bayou Pierre, 30 miles from the Mississippi, slaves and indigo worth $15,163.[185]

Dorothée and Samuel's first child, Sara Virginia Moore, named for his deceased sister, was born on 10 August 1803 and baptized on 4 September 1804 by Fr. Antonio de Sedella. The marginal note indicates that the child was a free quadroon. Both parents were identified: Samuel as a native of Pensacola, and Dorothée as a native of New Orleans, however only the paternal grandparents, Alexander Moore and Juana Escriven were given, the parents of the mother being unknown. Both godparents were people of color. The godfather was Luis "Auory," an unidentified free "mulatto," but the godmother was Eulalie Allin [*sic*, Allain], Sara Virginia's half-sister, a free quadroon.

[...]

---

[184] Emily Clark, *The Strange History of the American Quadroon*, (Chapel Hill, NC: The University of North Carolina Press, 2013), 122-126.
[185] McBee, compiler, *The Natchez Court Records 1767-1805*, 119.

Archdiocese of New Orleans, *St. Louis Cathedral, New Orleans Baptism of Slaves and Free People of Color 1804-1804*, Digital Collections-#1486 Image 139/144 at https://archives.arch-no.org/sacramental_records. Baptism of Sara Virginia Moore, free Quadroon. (SLC, B16, 270.)

A second child, Samuel Philip Moore (Jr.) was born on 1 June 1804, but only baptized on 4 April 1812 (SLC, B25, 18). Little Sara Virginia died and was interred on 17 October 1804. (SLC, F5, 163)

Fortunately for Samuel P. Moore, the so-called "characterization of New Orleans Residents," offered to President Jefferson on 1 July 1804, was silent when it came to most of the English-speaking inhabitants of the city. The American government was more suspicious of the Continental European residents like Jérome Chiapella. Nor was an attempt made to characterize the Jewish Monsanto family, perhaps because they were considered to have been British subjects. Dr. Robert Dow, was clearly a favorite, but no mention was made of his wife, Angelica Monsanto. Moore was enumerated at # 51 Rue de Bourbon on the south side according to the 5 August 1805 Flannery Census of New Orleans. Only his name was given, but we can surmise that the male white over sixteen years of age was Samuel himself. He was living with two male mulatto children under sixteen years, probably Zenon Zerban, about age three, and his son with Dorothée, Sam, Jr. age 2. Also living in the household was a female mulatto over the age of sixteen, probably Dorothée, and one female mulatta under the age of sixteen, most likely

Eulalie Allain, Dorothée's daughter, who was about seven years old at the time. Two slaves, one male and one female, both adults, were also living there.[186]

Samuel was not, however, completely ignored by the new American Government. On 27 May 1808 he was appointed as the translator for the First Superior District Court.[187] Samuel Philip, Jr. and the couple's next two children Marie Antoinette/Antonia Euphémie, born on 23 October 1808 and Eulalie Uranie, born on 3 December 1810 were all registered in the baptism book for whites. In all three cases, Samuel Moore took the child to be baptized and Dorothée Lassize's name was omitted from the record. It was quite rare to see "madre no conocida,"(mother unknown). "Unknown" was usually a designation for an absent white father. In Maria Antonia's record, however, dated 12 July 1809, the day of her baptism, there is a marginal note which is just barely legible because of bleeding through of the previous page, but one can make out the last five words: "Lassize es mujer de color." (Lassize is a woman of color.) This notation may have been added at a later date.(SLC, B22, 7) The baptism came just one year after the Louisiana Territorial Legislature had outlawed marriages between whites and slaves or free people of color, so the couple, unable to marry, sought, as Emily Clark wisely surmises, to insure their children's futures by removing the stigma of an entry for them in the Baptism Book for Slaves and Free People of Color. It was a bold move for Samuel P. Moore to try to convince a priest to have his children recorded in the "book for whites." Samuel Moore, Jr. (SLC, B25, 18) and Eulalie Uranie Moore were only baptized as children on the same day 4 April 1812 and appear in the Book for Whites with the Spanish double surnames: Samuel Moor y Scott and Urania Moor y Scott, using the father's surname with the paternal grandmother's surname, Scott, instead of the mother's surname Lassize. It is possible also that de Sedella was complicit in this fiction.:

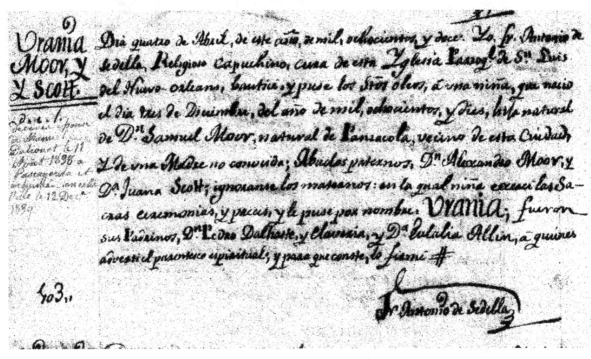

Archdiocese of New Orleans, *St. Louis Cathedral, New Orleans Baptism of Whites 1811-1815*, Digital Collections- #402 Image 44/110 at https://archives.arch-no.org/sacramental_records. Baptism of Urania Moor y Scott. (SLC, B25, 18).

Eulalie Allain appeared, once more as godmother to one of Moore's children, Eulalie Uranie, except there was no notation that she was a "free quadroon," as was the case when she stood for Sara Virginia Moore. Of the couple's four other children, only one, Maria Camille Moore, born on 18 May 1815 and baptized on 23 November 1817, appeared in the *St. Louis Cathedral Baptism of Slaves and Free People of Color*. Her godparents were her brother Samuel and her sister Euphémie. (SLC, B29, 186). The three other children: Marie Adelaide Eugénia, born on 14 April 1813 and baptized on 13 November 1821 (SLC, B31, 214), Antonio Roberto, born on 25 February 1814 and baptized on 12 November 1821 (SLC, B31, 214), and Alexandro Santiago, born on 17 July 1821, and baptized on

---

[186] Access the Matthew Flannery 1805 New Orleans census here: http://louisianadigitallibrary.org/islandora/ object/fpoc-p16313coll51%3A35436 . Image #25 of 46.

[187] Carter, ed., *The Territorial Papers of the United States, vol. IX, The Territory of Orleans 1803-1812*, 797.

13 November 1821 (SLC, B31, 214), all appear in the *St. Louis Cathedral Baptism Book for Whites*. In all three of the latter baptisms, both Samuel and Dorothée were identified as the parents.

It should not be forgotten that both Eulalie Allain and Zenon Zerban lived as young children with Samuel P. Moore and Dorothée Lassize although they were not always enumerated in the household. In the 1810 Federal Census, for example, Samuel Moore was enumerated living by himself with two slaves on Bienville Street, whereas, five years before, the whole family had all been living together per the Flannery Census of New Orleans. On 5 September 1810, Samuel Moore, Dorothée Lassize and Valerien Allain appeared before the notary Michel de Armas to enact a slave sale and donation in favor of Eulalie Allain, Valerien Allain's natural daughter. The document signed by all three provided for the sale of an eleven-year-old female slave named Mary by Moore to Valerien Allain for 350 piastres on the condition that the slave be donated back to eleven-year-old Eulalie Allain, It was made clear in the document that the transaction would not take place otherwise. It was stated in the document that Valerien, because of his fond attachment for his natural daughter Eulalie, that he relinquished all ownership of the slave Mary who was accepted by Dorothée Lassize the girl's mother and natural tutor on the child's behalf. Because Eulalie's father had not been included in the 1800 baptism record (See p. 85) this was Dorothée's way of getting her daughter legally recognized by her birth father.

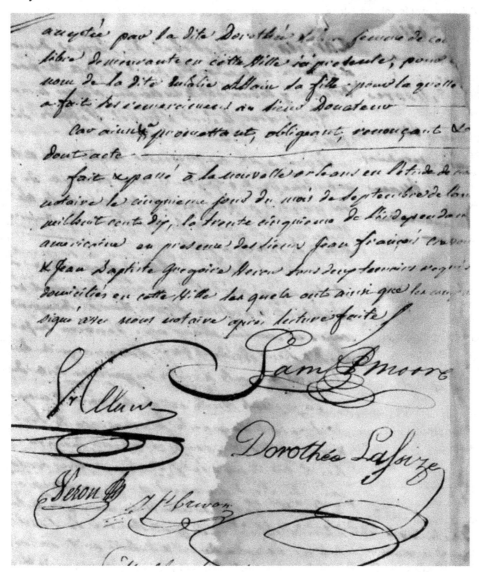

NARC, Signature page – Sale of slave from Samuel P. Moore to Valerien Allain. Donation of slave from Valerien Allain to Eulalie Allain, Michel De Armas, Notary, Volume 4, folio 318 verso. Courtesy Hon. Chelsey Richard Napoleon, Clerk of Civil District Court, Parish of Orleans.

Samuel and Dorothée bought and sold real estate in the French Quarter throughout their association. Samuel did a number of land transactions especially between1797 and 1801, bought and sold timbers, as well as slaves and worked at property development and construction on the eve of the American takeover of the Louisiana Territory. Because they were never legally wed, Dorothée, unlike her white married counterparts, was free to buy and sell and to make contracts, wills, even manumissions, on her own. Married women always needed the authorization of a spouse to engage in these pursuits. As a consequence, her name appears alone on a number of real estate transactions.

On 10 February 1825 the Louisiana Legislature passed an act allowing Dorothée Lassize to dispose of two of her properties situated at #110 and #112 Dauphine Street by means of a lottery. The houses first had to be appraised by two estimators, one appointed by her, the other appointed by the State Treasurer. If no agreement could be reached, a third member would be appointed to break the tie. The number of tickets sold could not exceed the estimated appraised value of the properties. Dorothée was obliged to advertise in French and in English in two New Orleans newspapers, the day, hour and location of the lottery drawing, which would take place before a Justice of the Peace, who would certify the winners in writing. For the privilege of holding the lottery Dorothée was indebted to the State for one percent of the appraised value of the property. On 1 January 1827, David Flower won the first property at #418 (current) Dauphine Street, at the lottery held at the Café de Hewlett at the corner of Chartres and St. Louis Streets in the presence of Judge Joachim de Bermudez and notary Felix de Armas.[188] On 10 April 1827 Jean Goulé. f.m.c and Elilien Larieux, f.m.c. who held ticket #50, won all the buildings and improvements at 420-422 (current) Dauphine Street in the lottery held at the Café de Hewlett in the presence of Judge Joachim Bermudez. Dorothée had previously bought both properties from Benoit Milbrouck on 19 May 1818.[189] From the proceeds of those two lotteries Dorothée was able to purchase a plot of ground located at #1016 (current) St. Louis Street from Marcelin Batique on 7 May 1825.[190]

She and Samuel Moore undertook to have a house constructed on the lot which was barely finished when Dorothée died on 19 April 1829. Dorothée Lassize's estate file showed that she had seven surviving children: Eulalie Allain, age 29, Zenon Zerban, age 27, Samuel Moore, Jr., age 25, Marie Antoinette Euphémie Moore, age 21 ½, Eulalie Uranie Moore, age 19, Charlotte (sic, Marie Adelaide) Eugénie Moore, age 17, and Alexander James Moore, under age 14. Antonio Roberto Moore and Marie Camille Moore, born respectively in 1814 and 1815 must have predeceased their mother, although we could find no burial records for them. The newly constructed house was put up for sale at Hewlett's Exchange on 18 June 1829, at the conclusion of a family meeting which had been held on 12 May of the same year to decide how the estate would be liquidated. It is interesting to note that one of the friends of the family at this meeting was Edmond Dupuy, the son of Félicité Aubry and his father, a white attorney, Louis Alexandre Dupuy.[191] Attached to the information about the #1016 St. Louis Street property at the Collins C. Diboll Vieux Carré Survey was an advertisement which ran in the 4 June 1829 edition of the *Louisiana Courier* submitted by the Register of Wills, Martin Blache, and approved by Samuel P. Moore, agent for the heirs of Dorothée Lassize. The property was described as having a frontage of 55 feet on St. Louis, between Burgundy and Rampart Streets, by 200 feet deep. The house was roofed with slates, consisting of five rooms and a closet, a staircase up to an attic with several rooms. There was also a two-story brick kitchen, roofed with slate, consisting of eight rooms, together with a garden. Also included in this advertisement was the following:

> The house in St. Louis Street, near Rampart, has been very lately built, and in the most solid and elegant manner, the steps to the entry in front are marble; and those in the yard are of stone; the entrance to the yard is paved with flagstones, also the kitchen and wine cellar, and a gallery and passage down to the garden, all the sleepers of the house and servants rooms are of cedar; the garden, flower plot and an alley

[188] The Collins C. Diboll Vieux Carré Digital Survey, Historic New Orleans Collection, (https://www.hnoc.org/vcs/property_info.php?lot=11431).

[189] The Collins C. Diboll Vieux Carré Digital Survey, Historic New Orleans Collection, (https://www.hnoc.org/vcs/property_info.php?lot=11430).

[190] The Collins C. Diboll Vieux Carré Digital Survey, Historic New Orleans Collection, https://www.hnoc.org/vcs/property_info.php?lot=11571.

[191] "Louisiana, Orleans Parish Estate Files, 1804-1846," database with images, *FamilySearch.org* (https://familysearch.org/ark:/61903/3:1:S3HT-63Y3-NVD?cc=1388197 &wc=MG4L-7MY%3A13750001%2C15627101 :accessed 5/22/2019), Lassize, Dorothée (1829) images 2 & 15 of 40; New Orleans City Archives. Note: Edmond Dupuy's father, Louis Alexandre Dupuy, died that same year on 14 October 1829.

from the carriage entry down to the garden are planted with the choicest of fruit trees, shrubbery and flowers... [192]

At her death Dorothée had land worth $8,600 including the property described above worth $7,000; a vacant lot adjoining with dimensions of 35 feet. by 200 feet worth $1200; and a lot of ground in Block #11, southwest of the city with 50 feet fronting on Jackson Street by 120 feet deep worth $400. Her total investment in slaves included: an unnamed enslaved girl age 13 worth $660; Henriette[193] enslaved creole mulatto girl of 13 years, a plaiter, ironer and house servant estimated at $600; George, age 16, Henriette's brother, a creole mulatto house servant worth $700; Charles, age 7, sold to Samuel Moore for $300; a creole griffe boy valued at $250; Benny, a creole black woman, age 60, sold to Samuel Moore for $370; Félicité, daughter of Benny, age 27 a plaiter, laundress and cook valued at $800; and Mary, age 48, an African woman in the country for a long time who was a laundress, cook and maid worth $300 and sold for same. Dorothée's entire estate including slaves, real estate, furniture and clothing was valued at $16,549.46 with debts of $12,986.46. This left $3,563 piastres to be divided amongst Dorothée's seven children. Each would receive 509 piastres, with a buying power of approximately $8,209. or more in today's money. This legacy would not have been as large had not Samuel P. Moore, who was owed $7,721 piastres for outstanding bills for the construction of the house on St. Louis Street, stated that he would take, $2,000 piastres instead in order not to cause a possible protracted litigation, and in order to benefit the heirs, five of whom were his own children:

NARC. Succession of Dorothée Lassize dated 23 December 1830, Théodore Seghers, Notary, Volume 3 Act 398, page 3. Courtesy Hon. Chelsey Richard Napoleon, Clerk of Civil District Court, Parish of Orleans.

---

[192] The Collins C. Diboll Vieux Carré Digital Survey, Historic New Orleans Collection, (https://www.hnoc.org/vcs/property_info.php?lot=11571).

[193] Henriette was emancipated in 1847 by Samuel Moore, Jr., per his late mother's wishes, as she had reached the age of thirty, a prerequisite for emancipation according to the Louisiana Civil Code.

The fifteen-page succession record laid out all of Dorothée's assets and debts including her funeral expenses, monies owed to physicians, the names of persons who owed her money, and the enormous expense of the St. Louis Street town house where she would never live. The couple had furnished the spacious and elegant home with mahogany furniture, marble-top tables, even a copper pump for the well. Several thousands of piastres had been spent on the brick for the house, the cedar posts for the frames, the hand-crafted doors, for which Dorothée's son, Zenon Zerban, had received 110 piastres, along with over 200 piastres for other carpentry work. The final page of the succession contained the signatures of all the parties, including husbands who had to sign authorizing their wives to act.

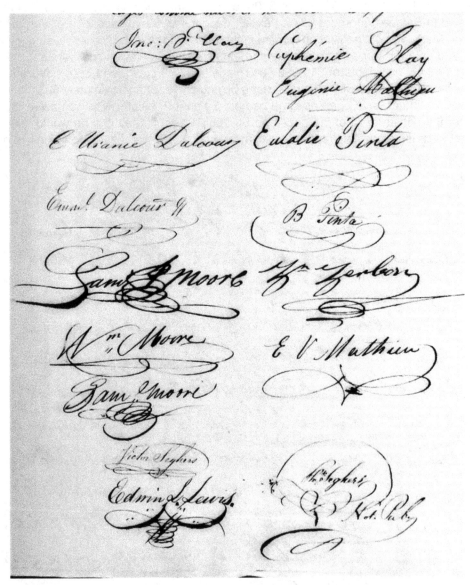

NARC. Succession of Dorothée Lassize dated 23 December 1830, Théodore Seghers, Notary, Volume 3 Act 398, page 3. Courtesy Hon. Chelsey Richard Napoleon, Clerk of Civil District Court, Parish of Orleans. Signatures: Jean Baptiste Clay, Euphémie (Moore) Clay, E. Uranie (Moore) Dalcour, Eugénie (Moore) Mathieu, Eulalie (Allain) Pinta, Emmanuel Dalcour, Beauvilaire Pinta, Samuel P. Moore, Zenon Zerban, William Moore, E. V. Mathieu, Sam Moore, Jr. Witnesses: Victor Seghers, Edwin Lewis, Theodore Seghers, Notary Public.

Samuel Philip Moore died in New Orleans on 13 June 1841, He had last appeared in civil records in the 1840 Federal Census for New Orleans where he was enumerated as an unmarried white male. His death record below summarizes his life as a seventy-one-year-old bachelor, a merchant and cotton broker, a native of "Penzacocola [*sic*] capital of the Occidental Florida," who died at #80 Dauphine Street in the First Municipality as reported by Rufino Thomas Fernandez, native of Galveztown in Louisiana, keeper of the records at St. Louis Cathedral:

762 Moore Samuel Philipp

BE it remembered that on this day to wit, the _fourteenth of June_ the year of our Lord one thousand eight hundred and _forty one_ and the sixty _fifth_ of the Independence of the United States of America, before me VINCENT RAMOS, duly commissioned and sworn Recorder of Births and Deaths in and for the Parish and City of Orleans, personally appeared, Mr Rufino Thomas Fernandez, born at Galveston in this State of Louisiana, on the sixteenth day of the month of November in the year Seventeen hundred and ninety nine, keeper of the Records of the Catholic and Cathedral Church of St Louis of this Parish of New Orleans, residing on St Ann Street between Conde and Royal Streets in this first Municipality, Who by these presents doth declare that Mr Samuel Philipp Moore, a native of Penzacocola, Capital of the Occidental Florida, aged about Seventy one years, formerly a merchant and lately a Cotton broker residing in this Parish for the fifty latt part years, Departed this life, yesterday the thirteenth instant at noon, at his domicil situate N° 80 on Dauphine Street in this first Municipality. He was the legitimate Son of the late Mr Alexander Moore and of the late Mrs Jeanne Scriven, and was a Bachelor

THUS done at New Orleans in the presence of the aforesaid Mr Rufino Thomas Fernandez as also in that of Messrs. Rudolph Kerndorfer and Emile Beauregard both of this city, witnesses by me requested so to be, who have hereunto set their hands together with me after due reading hereof, the day month and year first above written

Fred Kerndorffer   _E. Beauregard_   _Rue Fernandez_

Vincent Ramos
Recorder

His son and namesake, Samuel P. Moore, Jr., had married Maria Francesca Malvina Lowell, a free woman of color on 23 December 1826 (SLC, M7, 93). Malvina was the daughter of James Lowell, a white Protestant merchant from Massachusetts and Adelaide Raguet, a free woman of color and native New Orleanian. Sam and Malvina's first child, Eugenia Rose Moore, was born on 3 September 1828 (SLC. B41,43), and died on 5 February 1831 (SLC, F16, 102). Samuel Philippe Moore (III) was born on 17 April 1830. His baptismal record reads: "Moore, Samuel Philippe (Samuel and Marie Françoise Malvina Moore), b. July 28, 1830, bn. April 17, 1830, s. Samuel Philippe Moore and Eulalie Pinta. (SMNO, B2, 12). The child's godmother was Sam's half-sister Eulalie Allain, the wife of Charles Beauvilaire Pinta. Samuel Philip Moore III died on 14 July 1831. Samuel P. Moore, Jr., finally reported his death, as well as the previous death of his daughter, Eugénie Rose Moore, to the city on 19 September 1831. At that time, Sam, Jr., was employed as a cotton broker, probably working for his father, living in the Faubourg Ste. Marie, on Carondelet Street between Canal and Common Streets. A copy of the death record for his fourteen-month-old-son Samuel may be seen on the following page:

Moore Samuel
Philip.

Be it remembered that on this day to wit: the nineteenth of September in the year of our Lord one thousand eight hundred and thirty two, and the fifty Sixth of the Independence of the United States of America, Before me Vincent Ramos duly Commissioned and Sworn Recorder of Births and Deaths in and for the Parish of Orleans, Personally came and appeared Samuel Moore a native of this City and Parish, aged twenty Six years, Cotton Broker residing in this City Suburb St. Mary Carondelet Street between Canal and Common Streets, Who by these presents Doth Declare that his Son Samuel Philip Moore, aged forteen month, native of this City died there on the forteenth of July last pass at one o'clock A. M. in this Dwelling house of the Deponent, and that he was the lawful Son of Marie Francoise Malvina Samuel native of this City aged twenty years, and residing

this City.

This done at New Orleans in the presence of the aforesaid Samuel Moore as also in that of Messrs. Octave Leblanc and Amadeo Morel both of this City witnesses by me requested So to be who have hereunto Set their hands together with me after the reading hereof, the day month and year first above written.

Vincent Ramos
Recorder.

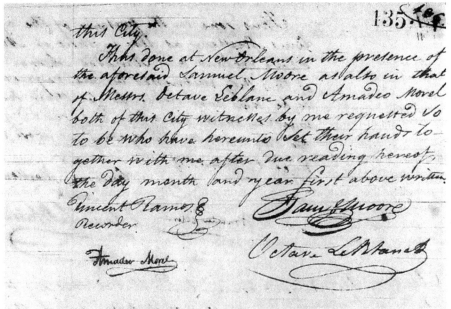

The couple's third and last child, Manuel Thomas Moore, was born on 3 November 1831 but died on 13 December of the same year. The child's birth record was one of a few which had also given the names of the grandparents, in this case Samuel Moore and Dorothée Lassize, deceased, and James Lowell, deceased, and Adelaide Rouquet [*sic*, Raguet] (SLC, B42, 37).

Samuel P. Moore, Jr.'s death record, with a racial designation, (Col.) added, which gave the date of his passing as 24 March 1886 at the age of eighty-two years and eight months, had several peculiar bits of information which were not true. First, it listed his place of birth as Richmond, VA, a fact which was not recorded on his St. Louis Cathedral baptismal record which appeared in the book for whites (Baptism of Whites 1811-1815, Part 1, Image 44/110, Baptism #401). It also indicated that he was a resident of New Orleans for fifty-four years which is also erroneous as he was a lifelong resident of the city:

Courtesy of State of Louisiana, Secretary of State, Division of Archives, Records Management, and History. *Vital Records Indices*. Baton Rouge, LA, USA citing *Orleans Death Indices 1804-1876*; Vol. 88, p. 1160.

Samuel, Jr.'s sister Marie Antoinette Euphémie Moore had married Jean-Baptiste François Clay, his wife Malvina Lowell's half-brother, on 17 November 1825. Jean-Baptiste François was the son of John Clay, a white Protestant Kentucky native and elder brother of Henry Clay who had an unsuccessful run for President of the United States in 1844, and Adelaide Raguet. (SLC, M7, 73). J.B. François Clay and Euphémie Moore had eleven children: "Juan Raguet Clay (Juan Francisco and Maria Antonia Euphemia Moore) both natives and residents of the city, b. 2 Dec 1828, bn 5 Nov 1826 s. Samuel Felipe Moore and Dorotee Lassize [their grandparents] (SLC B 39, 194)." Another child, Samuel Philippe Clay born to Jean François Clay and Marie Antoinette Euphémie Moore was baptized at 4½ months on 21 April 1829. His godparents were Samuel Moore and Louise Boisdoré (SLC B39, 247). The child died on 21 September 1830 (SLC, F16, 70). Eugénie Eulalie Clay was born on 4 August 1830 and baptized on 25 June 1831. Her godmother was Eulalie Allain Pinta (SLC, B41, 327). The couple's other eight children all had civil birth records which identified them as "colored:" Elizabeth Euphémie Clay born on 1 January 1832; Charlotte Emma Clay, born on 10 November 1833; Alfred Emmanuel Clay, born on 5 February 1836 (d. 17 September 1837); Edmond Eloi Clay, born on 19 November 1837; Marie Victoria Clay, born on 7 February 1840, Uranie Josephine Clay, born on 22 November 1842; Louise Amélie Clay, born on 12 March 1845; and Robert Michel Clay, born on 10 November 1848.[194]

Eulalie Uranie Moore married Emmanuel Dalcour[195], son of François Étienne Lalande-Dalcour and Angélique Aury, a free woman of color, on 1 December 1828 (SLC, M7, 131). They were the parents of four children: Lalande Étienne Emmanuel (b. 8 January 1831), Samuel Charles Florian (b. 19 March 1832), Marie Eulalie Emma (b. 12 November 1836), and Joseph Victor (b. 23 December 1837).[196] Eulalie Uranie Moore Dalcour died at Pascagoula, MS on 11 August 1838.[197] Emmanuel Dalcour immigrated to France, where he lived at Paris, Ile-de-France, France, at Rue Notre-Dame-de-Lorette, #39, in the 9th arrondissement. He died there at the age of sixty-five, on 18 April 1864, "the son of Estevan Lalande Dalcour and Angélique Aury, and the widower of Uranie Moore."[198] His daughter, Marie Eulalie Emma died a "religieuse célibataire" (a nun, probably a lay sister, as the death record does not identify her as living at a convent or cloister) on 1 October 1884 at Périgueux, Dordogne, France.[199] According to her succession record, she was the only surviving child of Emmanuel and Uranie Moore Dalcour. It is clear from that record that her three siblings, predeceased her and had no issue. She left a sizeable estate worth over $17,000 to the surviving children and grandchildren of her uncle, Pierre Dorestan Dalcour, and his wife Eulalie Allain, to be divided between Marie Angélique Dalcour, wife of Aristide Thibault, Marie Adelaide Dalcour, the wife of Charles Reggio, Eulalie Estelle Dalcour, wife of Emmanuel Daulnoy, the late Pierre Dalcour, whose children with Pilar Salgado resided in Mexico, and Lazare Dorestan Dalcour, widower of Eugénie Eulalie Clay (died 15 May 1869, daughter of Jean-Baptiste François Clay and Marie Antoinette Euphémie Moore), who lived both in Mexico and later back in New Orleans.[200]

Marie Adelaide Eugenia Moore (aka Charlotte Eugénie Moore) married Eloi Valmont Mathieu, a free "colored" Cuban refugee on 21 September 1829 (SLC, M3, 106). We do not believe that they had any children who reached adulthood as there were no children living with them according to the 1840 United States Federal Census.

None of the surviving Moore children married white partners, probably, in part because, they knew the difficulties that their parents had had legally and financially due to the laws against miscegenation, which would only be abolished for a time in Louisiana after the Civil War until the late 1880s. While Emmanuel Dalcour and his daughter Marie Eulalie Emma chose to immigrate to France before the Civil War, some of the descendants of his brother, Pierre Dorestan Dalcour, chose Mexico at around the same time.

---

[194] Courtesy of State of Louisiana, Secretary of State, Division of Archives, Records Management, and History. *Vital Records Indices*. Baton Rouge, LA, USA, from New Orleans, Louisiana Birth Records Index 1790-1899; Births of Elizabeth Euphémie Clay, Vol 2, p. 115; Charlotte Emma Clay, Vol. 4, p. 63; Alfred Emmanuel Clay, Vol. 4, p. 260; Edmond Eloi Clay, Vol. 4. P. 298; Marie Victoria Clay, Vol. 6, p. 107; Uranie Josephine Clay, Vol. 6, p. 189; Louise Amélie Clay, Vol. 6, p. 189; Robert Michel Clay, Vol. 10, p. 196.

[195] Emmanuel Dalcour was the brother of Eulalie Allain's first husband, Pierre Dorestan Dalcour (See Chapter 9).

[196] "Louisiana, Orleans Parish Estate Files, 1804-1846," database with images, *FamilySearch.org* (https://familysearch.org/ark:/61903/3:1:S3HT-DRKQ-Q24?cc=1388197&wc=MG4J-J4H%3A13750801%2C14024601 accessed 2 May 2019),Dalcour, Emanuel (1838), image 6 of 68; New Orleans City Archives.

[197] A notation on her St. Louis Cathedral baptismal record (SLC B25, 18) indicated that she died on 11 August 1838 in Pascagoula, MS, and was buried in this city [of New Orleans] on 12 December 1839. Spouse: Manuel Dalcourt (*sic*).

[198] Paris, Île-de-France, France, État-Civil 1860-1974 [Civil records 1860-1974], Décès 9e. (Deaths, Ninth district) Emmanuel Dalcour, digital image, *Archives.paris.fr*, (http://archives.paris.fr/s/4/etat-civil-actes/resultats/?: acc. 10 August 2020,) Cote V4E/1008, Act # 622, Image 18/31.

[199] Périgueux, Dordogne, France, Registres paroissiaux et d'état civil [Parish and Civil Registrations], Décès [Deaths], 1884, Death of Marie Eulalie Emma Dalcour, digital image, *Archives.dordogne.fr*, (https://archives.dordogne.fr/s/12/registres-paroissiaux-et-d-etat-civil/resultats/? : accessed 5/22/2020), Cote 5 E 317/236, Act 551, Image 144/200.

[200] "Louisiana, Wills and Probate Records, 1756-1984," digital images, *Ancestry.com* (https://www.ancestry.com: accessed 7/29/19), citing Louisiana District and Probate Courts, Civil District Court Case Papers, Case #13517 probated 20 February 1885, Marie Eulalie Emma Dalcour, Images 592-684. See also next chapter, p. 107 for births of the Allain-Dalcour children.

CHAPTER 9

EULALIE ALLAIN, PIERRE DALCOUR and CHARLES BEAUVILAIRE PINTA

Eulalie Allain, Dorothée Lassize's daughter with Pierre Valerien Allain married Pierre Dorestan Dalcour, the brother of her half-sister Eulalie Uranie Moore's husband Emmanuel Dalcour, on 24 November 1813 at St. Louis Cathedral. She had just turned fifteen years old. Only the names of the bride's and groom's mothers, Dorothea Lassize and Angelica Aury, were provided in the record, which was silent on the paternity of the newlyweds who were both free people of color (SLC, M3, 47). Pedro/Pierre Dalcour's father, however, was Pierre Étienne Lalande Dalcour, born on 2 May 1773 in New Orleans to Jean Étienne Lalande Dalcour and Vincente Adelaide Olivier de Vézin, both natives of New Orleans. (SLC B7, 25) Olivier de Vézin's father was a royal councilor, chief minister and surveyor general of the royal province of Louisiana. Angelique/Angelica Aury was a free woman of color born to Marie Adelaide Demouy according to Eulalie Allain's testimony recorded in the inventory papers for the estate of her late husband, Pierre Dorestan Dalcour who was buried in St. Louis Cemetery on 17 September 1722, at the age of twenty-eight. (SLC F12, 105). Eulalie added the following additional information about her late husband: "Pierre Dorestan Dalcour in his lifetime dwelt on a plantation belonging to his grandmother Marie Adelaïde Demouy, the widow of Pierre Langliche, alias Canouet, in the Metairie."[201]

Eulalie had five children with Dalcour during their marriage. Marie Angélique was born on 3 September 1814. She was baptized on 5 July 1815 with Angélique Aury, her grandmother, standing as her godmother, and Angélique's mother's husband, Pierre Langliche as her godfather (SLC B27,131). Marie Adelaïde Dalcour was born on 28 June 1816 and baptized on 26 July 1820 (SLC B30, 217). François Étienne Dalcour was her godfather, identified in error as the child's brother. He was, in fact, her uncle. Her godmother was said to be the child's sister, but was probably in fact her aunt, Marie Adelaide Dalcour, Pierre's sister. Pierre Dalcour was born on 16 August 1818 and baptized on 26 July 1820. The godparents were Emmanuel Dalcour, his uncle, and Dorothée Lassize, his grandmother. (SLC, B30, 217). Eulalie Estelle Dalcour was born on 20 November 1820 and baptized on 17 July 1821. Her godparents were Zenon Zerban and Marie Antoinette Euphémie Moore, the child's mother's half-siblings. (SLC B32, 75). The couple's last child, Lazare Dorestan Dalcour was born on 2 September 1822, just a few weeks before his father died. The child was baptized on 14 June 1824 with Samuel P. Moore acting as godfather and Judith Mandeville as godmother.[202] (SLC B33, 120).

The closeness of this blended family, whose white patriarch, Samuel P. Moore, was illustrated several times over in records we have seen. Not only did Samuel act as godfather to Dorothée's daughter's child, but he also acted as one of the appraisers for the estate of the late Pierre Dorestan Dalcour which finally was settled in 1830 in order to insure a fair allotment of monies for Eulalie Allain's children. Moreover, Eulalie chose her half-brother, Zenon Zerban as her minor children's under-tutor for the purposes of settling the estate of her late husband.

Eulalie was married again on 19 February 1829 to Charles Beauvilaire Pinta, whose white French-born father and free-colored mother had fled Saint Domingue during the Revolution The couple had settled for a time in Santiago de Cuba, having had at least four children there, before all the French immigrants were expelled from the island by its Spanish governor in 1809 due to Napoleon's having seized large portions of Spain in his quest to conquer the world. Just over 3,300 free people of color fled Cuba for New Orleans in 1809, along with 3000 slaves

---

[201] "Louisiana, Orleans Parish Estate Files," New Orleans City Archives, digital image, *Ancestry.com* (https://www.ancestry.com: accessed 5/6/2019) Inventory of the estate of Pierre Dorestan Dalcour dated 11 October 1831, Image 12/129.

[202] Lazare Dorestan Dalcour applied for a marriage license on 19 March 1851 to marry his half first cousin Eugénie Eulalie Clay, daughter of Jean-Baptiste François Clay and Marie Antoinette Euphémie Moore. They had four children. Marie was born in 1857 in Louisiana. The Dalcours moved to Mexico City, Mexico, in about 1858 where three more children were born: Leonardo Dorestan, on 6 December 1859, Maria Nathalia Dorestan, on 1 December 1864, and Maria Victoria, on 26 December 1866. They returned to Louisiana in about 1868 where Eugénie Eulalie died on 15 May 1869. Thereafter Lazare kept a grocery store in Plaquemines Parish, LA. Marie Nathalia eventually returned south of the border where she died on 22 September 1922 at Guadalajara, Jalisco, Mexico.

and 3000 whites, swelling the numbers of free people of color in the city to almost 5,000 by 1810. Free people of color made up almost one-third of the city's inhabitants and almost one-half of its free residents.[203]

Charles Beauvilaire Pinta's father was Jean-Baptiste Pinta, born about 1768 at Clamecy, diocese of Soissons, Aisne, France, to Louis Pinta and his wife Marie Jeanne Ferté. There are, unfortunately, no available original records from Clamecy to verify the actual date, the year being extrapolated from Pinta's declaration in his last will and testament written just before he died in 1820 that he was about fifty-two years old. Luce Henriette Grandmaison, his partner for life was born in Port-au-Prince, Saint-Domingue, ca. January 1787. A translation of her baptismal record which may be seen below reads: "On 20 March 1787 was baptized, Luce Henriette, terceroon, aged about 2.5 months, natural child of Modeste, called Rasteau, free quadroon, as is stated in her baptismal record from this parish dated 9 July 1764. Her godfather was Jacques Cameau, living at Boucassin, Her godmother, Luce, called Rasteau, her aunt, was living in this parish in faith of which I have signed along with the godfather, godmother and the infant's mother."[204]

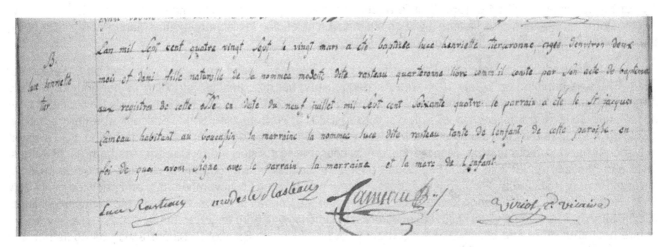

Source: France, Archives nationales d'outre-mer, état-civil numérisé, Port-au-Prince, Saint-Domingue, 1787, Image 15/129.

The term "tierceronne," which according to the dictionary definition is the child of a white person and a mulatto, was applied to Luce Henriette Grandmaison, whose mother was a quadroon. We have no hint as to her father, except that there were both white settlers named Rasteau as well as Grandmaison on the island.

It is fortunate that the date of her mother Modeste Rasteau's baptism was given in her daughter's record. Also available on line, it reads:

Today, July 9, 1764, I baptized Modeste, a free quadroon, born on May 13th of the present year, natural daughter of Louise Desbrosses, a free mulata, living in this town and an unknown father. The godfather was Mr. Ignace André Cadieu, a merchant residing in this town. The godmother was Agathe, a free mulata, residing at Croix-des-Bouquets, in faith of which I signed with the godfather, the godmother indicating that she could not write. (...)[205]

The original record may be found on the next page:

[203] Spear, *Race Sex and Social Order in Early New Orleans*, 179-185.

[204] Port-au-Prince, Saint-Domingue, Registres de l'état civil [Civil registrations], Tous actes [All records] 1787, not numbered, baptism of Luce Henriette, digital image, *Archives nationales d'outre-mer,* "État civil en ligne," (http://anom.archivesnationales.culture. gouv.fr/caomec2/: accessed. 9/24/2019), Image 15/ 135.

[205] Port-au-Prince, Saint-Domingue, Registres de l'état civil [Civil registrations], Tous actes [All records] 1764, not numbered, baptism of Modeste, Cart. libre., digital image, *Archives nationales d'outre-mer,* "État civil en ligne," (http://anom.archivesnationales.culture. gouv.fr/caomec2/: accessed 9/24/2019), Image 33/ 95.

Source: France, Archives nationales d'outre-mer, état-civil numérisé, Port-au-Prince, Saint-Domingue, 1764, Image 33/95.

We know that Jean-Baptiste Pinta had also lived at Port-au-Prince, Saint-Domingue, because he was working there as a jeweler as early as 1803, when he reported the birth of Anne Joseph, the natural daughter of Marguerite Brunet, unmarried, on 16 pluviose, an X (5 February 1802), which was registered on 22 fructidor, an XI (9 September 1803). He was thirty-five at that time, and was accompanied by twenty-two-year-old Léon Durège, both of whom signed the document.[206]

Jean-Baptiste Pinta and Luce Henriette Grandmaison's first three children were born in Cuba after they fled Saint-Domingue. Charles Beauvilaire Pinta was born ca. 1805 in Cuba. His sister, Silvanie Anne Pinta, was born there in about 1806. Louis Henri Pinta, born in Santiago de Cuba, was the first child for whom there was a baptismal certificate in New Orleans. He was said to have been born in Cuba on 1 August 1807 and was baptized at St. Louis Cathedral on 20 October 1810, with his sister Anne, as his godmother. (SLC, B22, 100) Another son, Jean/Juan Marcellin/Marcelino Pinta was baptized on the same day, having been born on 1 August 1809 in New Orleans. Both baptism records appear in the *Baptism of Whites for 1809-1811*, Part 1, with a caveat in the margin written much later in a different hand, indicating that the mother was a woman of color. If you search for these baptisms in the *Book for Slaves and Free People of Color 1810-1811*, Part 2, there is a notation in image 113/154 stating that the baptisms of Louis Henri and Jean Marcellin were entered into the Book of whites "par equivocation" – in an attempt to confuse. Their fourth child, Jean Claude Pholoé Pinta remains somewhat of a mystery. We believe he may have been born in Cuba before the French were exiled from that island. Other researchers indicated that he was born as late as 1811 in Louisiana, although we have found no baptismal record for him. Their next two children, Marie Josephine Pinta born on 31 August 1810 (SLC, B22, 120) and Jean Lucien Pinta, born on 24 July 1813 (SLC B25, 113), both died as children. Josephine was interred on 22 September 1815 (SLC F10,40), and Lucien was buried on 26 July 1815 (SLC, F7, 305). The couple's last child, Joseph Pinta was born on 22 June 1816 and baptized on 30 September of the same year. Both parents were identified along with their birth places. Although the paternal grandparents were noted in the record, the maternal grandparents were not (SLC B29, 71).

Jean-Baptiste Pinta was a gold and silversmith and jeweler in New Orleans, operating at 35 Bourbon Street. He and his family lived on nearby St. Ann Street. He also served as a Captain in the Second Regiment (Cavelier's) Louisiana Militia during the War of 1812.

---

[206] Port-au-Prince, Saint-Domingue, Registres de l'état civil [Civil registrations], Tous actes [All records] 1803, not numbered, baptism of Anne Joseph Brunet, digital image, *Archives nationales d'outre-mer,* "État civil en ligne," (http://anom.archivesnationales.culture. gouv.fr/caomec2/: accessed 9/24/2019), Image 98 & 99/104. Note: This is the last book of records kept before the French colony fell into chaos during the Revolution.

Jean-Baptiste Pinta would only survive his last child by four years. He was interred in the St. Louis Church Cemetery on 14 May 1820 (SLC F11,173). Although the Church record was silent on his actual date of death, the civil record, filled out by Joseph Gauthier, a fifty-two-year-old merchant on 24 July 1820, who was also one of his executors, declared that Pinta, from the Somme region of France, had died on 13 May 1820 at the age of forty-seven years. The decedent's parents were not given.

Courtesy of State of Louisiana, Secretary of State, Division of Archives, Records Management, and History. *Vital Records Indices*. Baton Rouge, LA, USA citing *Orleans Death Indices 1804-1876*; Vol. 1, p. 75. Death of Jean-Baptiste Pinta.

In his last will and testament, Jean-Baptiste Pinta stated that he had been born at Clamecy, Diocese of Soissons, Picardie, France, to Louis Pinta and his wife, Marie Jeanne Ferté, both deceased, that he was about fifty-two years old, and had never been married. He had, however, lived for many years with Luce Henriette Grandmaison, who has shared his life and work, and to whom there were born five surviving children: Charles Beauvilaire, age 16, Silvanie Anne, age 14; Henry, age 10, Claude Folsé [*sic*], age 9, and Joseph, age 4. He recognized them as his children and left them half of his estate. The other half went to his sisters and brothers in France. He left nothing specifically to Luce Henriette, but since she was the natural tutrix of her minor children, she was in charge of their portion of the estate until they reached maturity. Luce Henriette and her eldest son, Charles Beauvilaire Pinta continued in the gold, silver and jewelry business. She was listed in the U.S. Craftsperson's file as "Misse Grandmaison (jeweler, goldsmith), for the years 1822-1827, working at New Orleans.[207] The previous year, on 8 March 1821, she had apprenticed two of her younger sons: Louis Henri Pholoé, age 13 and Jean Claude Pholoé, age 12, to the furniture maker Jean Mercier in order to learn that trade. In that document she was referred to as "Miss Pinta f.d.c.l. (femme de couleur libre or free woman of color)." Mercier was to provide the boys with the skills to become joiners and cabinetmakers, and to send them to night school to learn to read and to write. He was also to feed and clothe them, all for a period of four years. Their mother was to continue to house them and to do their laundry. The two boys signed their first names, and their mother signed as "Misse Pinta," along with Jean Mercier, the children's new employer, and the Mayor of New Orleans, J. Ruffignac.[208]

---

[207] "U.S., Craftsperson Files, 1600-1995," digital images, *Ancestry.com*. (https://www.ancestry.com: accessed 9/26/2019, citing *Delaware, Craftsperson Files, 1600-1995*. File of Misse Grandmaison, Image 367/580.

[208] New Orleans (LA) Office of the Mayor. Indentures, 1809-1843. Louisiana Division/City Archives, New Orleans Public Library. Available for viewing at the Louisiana Digital Library: https://louisianadigitallibrary.org/islandora/object/fpoc-p16313coll51%3A43408.

Luce Henriette Grandmaison had two more children after the death of Jean-Baptiste Pinta. A son, Alexandre Grandmaison was born on 16 August 1824, and baptized on 2 April 1825 (SLC, B35, 14)[209] A child, Claire Philomène Augustine Grandmaison was born on 10 August 1837.

Luce Henriette Grandmaison died the following year on 16 November 1838. Her son, Charles Beauvilaire Pinta, a thirty-five-year-old silversmith living on Villeré Steet between Dumaine and St. Ann, reported the death on the 14th of December of that year. He indicated that his mother, "Luce Miss. Grandmaison," a native of Port-Au-Prince, Saint-Domingue, aged fifty-one years had died at a house on Union Street between Morales (now Marais) and Urquhart streets in the Marigny at the residence of her son, Joseph Pinta.

Courtesy of State of Louisiana, Secretary of State, Division of Archives, Records Management, and History. *Vital Records Indices*. Baton Rouge, LA, USA citing *Orleans Death Indices 1804-1876*; Vol. 6, p.232.

Only four of Jean-Baptiste Pinta's eight children outlived their mother, Luce Henriette Grandmaison. The couple's eldest child, Charles Beauvilaire Pinta, who continued his father's work as a silversmith and jeweler in New Orleans, and his wife, Eulalie Allain, daughter of Dorothée Lassize, had five children: Bovilar Eloi Pinta was born on 10 October 1829. Husband and wife Eloi Valmont Matthieu and Adelaide Eugenie Moore, Eulalie Allain's half-sister were the child's godparents (SLC B40, 138). Little Eloi died at five months of age and was interred on 20 March 1830 (SLC, F16, 21). Samuel Ernest Pinta was born on 5 May 1831. (SLC, B41, 327). Marie Adorea Pinta was born on 12 February 1833. Louis Adolph Pinta was born on 4 September 1836 and Beauvilaire Pinta was born on 5 November 1838. The last four children for whom there were civil birth registrations were categorized as "colored."[210]

---

[209] Luce Henriette's half-brother Jean-Baptiste Casimir Menial, another child of Modeste Rasteau, born ca. 1800 in Port-au-Prince, Saint-Domingue, also settled in Louisiana, in St. Martin Parish where he had a large family. He occasionally used the surname Pinta, as well as the surname Casimir. He was godfather to Luce Henriette's son Alexandre. Her daughter Silvanie was Alexandre's godmother.

[210] "New Orleans, Louisiana, Birth Records Index, 1790-1915," [database on-line], *Ancestry.com* (https:// www.ancestry.com: accessed 6/3/2019), citing *New Orleans, Louisiana Birth Records Index, 1790-1899*. Samuel Ernest, Vol. 2, p. 96; Marie Adorea, Vol 4, p. 64; Louis Adolphe Vol. 4, p. 257; Beauvilaire, vol. 6, p. 17.

Silvanie Anne Pinta, who died on 17 May 1847 in Mobile, Mobile Co., AL, had at least two children with François Prados: Charles ca. 1825 and Galathée Victorine in 1840.[211]

Jean Claude Pholoé Pinta, whose father indicated that he was nine years old at the time of the former's writing of his will in 1820, married Marie Victoria Raby on 15 November 1833 in Mobile, Mobile Co., AL.[212] There was also a license granted to him to marry Marguerite Collin on 28 October 1828, but we do not know if this marriage ever happened. In 1830, before he married Marie Victoria Raby, a woman named Marguerite Trouillet wrote out a will naming her friend Pholoé Pinta as the father of her two children, Emeline, about eight years old, and Louis Henry, about nine months. She left the proceeds of her late father, Alex Trouillet's estate, to Pinta and to her two children which consisted of two plots of land in Baldwin County, AL, as well as three lots of land situated in the town of Mobile, and one hundred head of horned cattle.[213] Jean Claude Pholoé Pinta and Marie Victoria Raby had five children together: Justine Josephine (b. 1834), Lucien (b. 1836), Nicolas (b. 1837), Ellen (b. 1839), and Elvina (b. 1843). Jean Claude died on 16 May 1853 in Mobile, and Marie Victoria Raby followed on 14 October 1860.

For the purposes of this study, we will only follow the life of Jean-Baptiste Pinta's last child, Joseph Pinta, and his wife, Julia Raby, because of their ultimate connection to the Chiapella family. Julia Raby was the younger sister of Marie Victoria Raby who had married Jean Claude Pholoé Pinta.

The Raby sisters' great-grandfather, Pierre Raby immigrated to New Orleans from Angoulême, Charente, France, in the 1750s. According to several of his children's baptismal records, he was a master cutler. It was impossible to trace Raby back to Angoulême because of the frequency of the Raby surname in the area. There was also no hint in Louisiana who his parents might have been. He married Marie Anne Gratien between 1754 and 1756, for which there is no record either. Marie Anne was a widow with five children from her previous marriage to Valentin Joseph Daublin, a master tool maker who had left Lorient, France, on the immigrant ship *La Loire* on 11 August 1720. Records show that he was born in Monbillart, Cambrai, Nord, France, around 1695. His brother, Pierre François, born three years later accompanied him to Louisiana to work on the Sainte Reyne Concession. Valentin-Joseph married Marie Marguerite Josephe DeCuire/Decuir on 20 November 1726 at St. Louis Church in New Orleans. (SLC M1, 118). Marie Marguerite had been born in Macon, diocese of Cambrai, Hainaut, Belgium. She immigrated to Pointe Coupée Parish with her parents Albert DeCuire and Marie Catherine Domer, who signed on as engagés to the Sainte Reyne Concession travelling with three other of their children on the same ship with Valentin-Joseph Daublin and his brother.[214] Marguerite DeCuire and Valentin Daublin had three children: Jean Pierre (b. abt. 1729), Nicolas (b. abt. 1731), and Marie Jeanne (b. abt. 1738). After Marguerite deCuire died, he married Marie Anne Gratien, with whom he had five children, before he died in 1752. François Joseph was baptized on 21 April 1743 (SBC, B1, 20). Marie Anne was born on 29 May 1744 (SCB B1, 28). Valentin Joseph followed on 25 February 1745. (SCB, B1, 39). Noel was born on 13 May 1747 (SCB B1, 44) and Antoine was baptized on 4 October 1750 (SCB, B1,61). All the baptisms of the Daublin children were recorded in the registers of St. Charles Borromeo Roman Catholic Church, at Destrehan, St. Charles Parish, LA. Marie Anne Gratien Daublin was left with three children from her husband's first wife and five of her own at the death of her first husband, only the eldest two of whom were adults. The estate was partitioned between the two sets of children, leaving Marie Anne as the tutrix of her five minor children, and a portion of her husband's estate to manage. She married Pierre Raby ca. 1754 and they had six children: Anne Marie, baptized on 30 May 1755 (SLC, B3, 43), Marie Magdaleine born on 19 September

[211] See more at: http://pintagenealogy.blogspot.com/search/label/Grandmaison.

[212] "Alabama, County Marriage Records, 1805-1967," digital image, *Ancestry.com* (https://www.ancestry.com: accessed 6/29/2019), citing *Marriage Records. Alabama Marriages.* County courthouses, Alabama. Film #001294412. Marriage license for Jean or Glode F. Pinta and Victoire Rabbie, Image 487/540. Collin marriage license image 79/540.

[213] "Alabama Wills and Probate Records, 1753-1999," digital images, *Ancestry.com* (https://www.ancestry.com: accessed 9/28/2019) citing Alabama Orphan's Court (Mobile County), Mobile, AL. Will of Margueritte Trouillet, Pigeon Hole #403, Files 2-168, Images 515-519.

[214] A thorough study of the Hainaut colonists to Louisiana has been made by Randy DeCuir, a direct descendant of Albert Decuire, and a noted genealogist specializing in Avoyelles Parish. Much of his work is on line at: http://web.archive.org/ web/20050306092837/http://www.geocities.com/ BourbonStreet/8230/. It is worth remembering that Pierre Piquery, a native of Taisnières-sur-Hon, Nord, France, father of Marie Perrine Piquery, the wife of Nicolas Laurent Delassize, was also on *La Loire*. Delassize may have been the father of several of Amaranthe Lassize's children.

1757 (SLC, B3, 83), Félicité, born on 12 April 1761 (SLC, B4, 51), Margueritte, born on 28 January 1763 (SLC, B5, 4), Antoine, born on 22 June 1764 (SLC, B5, 53), and Joseph Antoine, born on 10 November 1766 (SLC, B5, 151).

Joseph Antoine Raby, Marie Anne Gratiens' youngest child, had nine children with his wife Marie Thérèse DeFlandre. Their eldest child, also called Joseph Antoine Raby, was born on 10 September 1787: "Rabi, Josef (Josef and Maria Theresa De Flandes), b. Sep. 30, 1787, bn. Sep. 10, 1787, s Juan Bautista Flandes and Maria Juana [*] (SLC, B11, 37)." It was he who had a long-term relationship with a free woman of color which produced the two Raby sisters, Marie Victoria and Julia, who married the two Pinta brothers, Jean Claude Pholoé and Joseph Pinta.[215]

Joseph Antoine Raby, Jr.'s partner in life was Maria Louisa Croiset. There are as many variant spellings for "Croiset," including "Croizet," "Croisat," "Croisei" and "Croizei," as there are for "Raby," which can be found as "Rabi," "Rabby" "Rabbie," and even "Rabbi." Little is known about Maria Louisa Croiset. According to information available on *Findagrave.com* she was born circa 1776 at Pascagoula, Jackson Co., MS, and died on 10 March 1876 at the age of ninety-nine or one hundred years in Mobile Co., AL. She was interred at Magnolia Cemetery in Mobile (Square 6, Lot 26).[216] What we know verifiably about her from available documents begins with a baptismal record in the Archdiocese of New Orleans Sacramental Records for *Slaves and Free Persons of Color Baptismal Book* for 1812-1813. A daughter, Marcelina Croiset was born to Maria Luisa on 31 March 1812 and baptized on 16 March 1813 with Alexis Nicolas and Eulalia Laforet cited as the godparents (SLC, B26, 81). In the original record seen below, both mother and daughter were described as "free mulattas." The father's name was said to be "unknown." The godparents were also described as free "mulatos." Marcelina's godmother, Eulalia Laforet, would also be chosen as the godmother of Maria Louisa's first child with Joseph Antoine Raby, Jr., Marie Victoria Rabby.

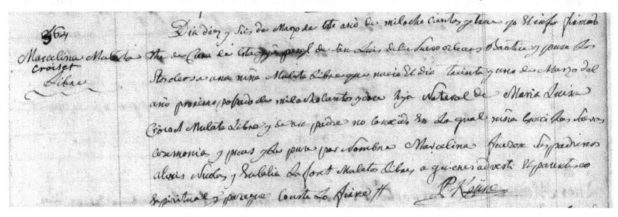

Archdiocese of New Orleans, *St. Louis Cathedral, New Orleans Baptism of Slaves and Free People of Color 1812-1813*, Digital Collections-#564 Image 161/200 at https://archives.arch-no.org/sacramental_records. Baptism of Marcelina Croiset, mulata libre. (SLC, B26, 81).

Maria Louisa Croiset had five children with Joseph Antoine Raby, Jr. Marie Victoria, a free quadroon was born on 16 November 1814 to "José Rabby, a resident of the city and Maria Louisa Croisé, a free mulata". She was baptized on 4 May 1815 at St. Louis Cathedral by the Rev. J.P. Koüne. No place of birth for her was indicated. Her

---

[215] We believe Joseph Antoine Raby's uncle, Antoine Raby (born 22 June 1764 to Pierre Raby and Marie Anne Gratien) may have been the father of at least three children of color: Antoine, Clarice and Marianne Raby. An unidentified white Antoine Raby fathered a child named Brigida Adelaida Raby, a free quadroon with a Juana Ducoder [*sic*?] in 1794. We have found no further baptism records for other children of his. Marianne Raby had a long-term relationship with Jean-Baptiste Baham, a white man whose family was very prominent in Madisonville, St. Tammany Parish, LA. Clarisse Raby had two children with Raymond Deveze, a native of France: Marcelite (b. 31 August 1805), and Raymond (b. abt. 1809, but no record). She had a son, Joseph Hopkins, son of James Hopkins from Ireland in 1811, and two children with Jean-Baptiste Dessus or Desonge or Desouge, a native of Paris: Jeanne Marie Josephine (born in 1816 and died in 1817), and Iréné Desonge born 3 December 1816. Antoine and Marianne were both alive when Clarice's estate was settled in 1827. (Clarice was buried on 7 August 1823 – SLC F12, 130).

[216] *Findagrave.com*, database with images, (www.findagrave.com; accessed 2/9/2019.), Memorial #194125337 - Marie Louise Croizei.

godparents were Nicolas Mafon (Mapon?), and Eulalia Laforet, a free mulata.(SLC B27, 111). A barely legible copy of the baptismal record, written in Spanish, is provided below:

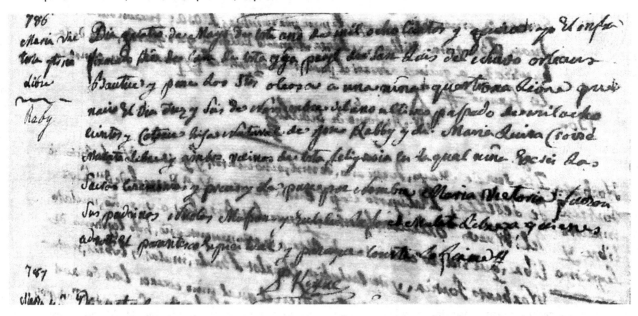

Archdiocese of New Orleans (Orleans Parish, LA), *St. Louis Cathedral Baptisms. Vol. 14 – S/FPC*, Act #786, p.111. (Courtesy of Emilie Leumas, Archivist – Kimberly Johnson and Katie Vest – Researching Archivists.)

Julia Raby was born about 1815 in Mississippi City, MS. By this time, her parents had decided to move out of Louisiana. In his last will and testament, Joseph Antoine Raby, Jr., stated that he had borrowed $2800 from Maria Louisa Croizai [sic] in December 1814. This was apparently in preparation for their becoming a family and starting over elsewhere. It appears also that Raby, Jr.'s father supported the move. Indeed Joseph, Sr.'s entire family would be instrumental in the relocation of the Rabys to Alabama. Joseph Antoine Raby and his son, Joseph Antoine, Jr. bought 640 acres of land at Bayou Coq d'Inde, commonly known as Bayou Coden on 10 October 1822, from Samuel Acre. Pierre, Anatole and Joseph Raby farmed the 640 acres of land, along with their father, Joseph Sr., who died on 6 April 1828 in Alabama and their mother, Marie Thérèse DeFlandre who died eleven years later. Upon his death Joseph Antoine Raby, Sr. left the 640 acres near Mobile, AL, to his heirs. In 1841 shortly before his son Joseph Jr.'s death, the remaining family members instituted court proceedings to partition the Raby property in Alabama. In 1841 these heirs included Joseph Raby, Jr., Ursin Raby, Pierre Raby, Anatole Raby and Basilise Raby Driscol, all of whom resided in the county of Mobile, State of Alabama, except Ursin and Basilise Driscol who live in Jackson Co., MS, both of whom who had sold their interest in their portion of the land to Pierre. Of the three plots of land, so divided, Joseph's heirs received lot #2 consisting of 309.455 acres.[217]

Joseph Jr. and Maria Louisa Croiset's other three children, Mary Anne, born about 1826, Josephine Delphine, born about 1830, and Joseph, born about 1833, were all born on Bayou Coden, an unincorporated fishing village in southern Mobile County, Alabama, located near Bayou Labatre on the western side of Mobile Bay. The partition of the Raby land had occurred just five months before the death of Joseph Antoine Raby, Jr. who expired on 12 October 1841. An inventory and auction of his estate was done shortly thereafter and included seven slaves: three men: William, Toney, and Isaac, Sally with her children Lucy, Eliza and Celeste, which netted about $3800. His personal items included a gold watch, a bureau, a sofa, one table, a clock, a looking glass all worth about $59. His farm animals and implements included two cows with calves, two ponies, and one jersey wagon and harness which were all sold for $50. His farm plus two smaller parcels were auctioned for $750. After a commission, the estate was worth about $4658. However, Raby, had stated in his will that he owed Maria Louisa "Croisai" $2800 plus interest for 28 years for a total of $4662, so the estate was technically insolvent. Joseph Antoine Raby, Jr. was

---

[217] " Alabama Wills and Probate Records 1753-1999," digital images, *Ancestry.com* (https://www.ancestry.com: accessed 10/2/2019), citing *Original Will Records*, Pigeon Hole # 303, Files 8-31, 1829-1837, Will of Joseph Raby (Jr.), Probate date: 28 October 1841 at Mobile AL, Images 49-69.

interred two days later at Magnolia Cemetery in Mobile, Mobile Co., AL.[218] Maria Louisa Croiset continued to live on the Raby[219] land at Bayou Coden On 1 September 1860 she was enumerated in that year's Federal Census living next to her son Joseph Rabby (b. 1833) and his wife, as a farmer with $2600 in personal property and $3,000 in real estate. At that time, she was said to be seventy-five-years-old, and a "mulatto" farmer. Her son Joseph, who was a twenty-nine-year-old male "mulatto," had $900 in personal property and the same $3000 in real estate as his mother.[220] While the *Findagrave.com* entry for Marie Louise Croizei, also interred at Magnolia Cemetery, indicated that she had been born in 1776, according to the 1860 census record her date of birth was probably nearer to 1786.[221]

. Julia Raby, daughter of Joseph Antoine Raby, Jr. and Maria Louisa Croiset, and Joseph Pinta, son of Jean-Baptiste Pinta and Luce Henriette Grandmaison were granted a license to marry on 5 January 1837 in Mobile, Mobile Co., AL, and were wed the same day:

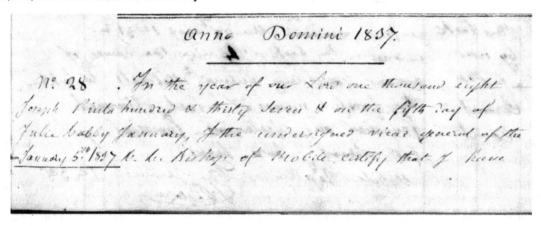

"In the year of our Lord one thousand eight hundred & thirty-seven & on the fifth day of January, I the undersigned vicar general of the C. C. Bishop, of Mobile certify that I have joined together in the holy bond of matrimony Joseph Pinta with Julie Rabby free colored persons native of this country. The dispensations for the publication of the three bans has been granted, the license had been obtained from the court & two witnesses were present. In faith whereof I have signed. M. Loras" Courtesy of the Archdiocese of Mobile Archives.

---

[218] Findagrave.com, database with images (www.findagrave.com; accessed 9/30/ 2019), *Memorial # 197422205 for Joseph Antoine Rabby.*

[219] Some of the Raby descendants adopted the spelling "Rabby" instead of the original French "Raby."

[220] 1860 United States Federal Census, Southern Division, Mobile AL, Dwelling #127, Family #105, Marie L. Croizait household, digital image, *Ancestry.com* (https://www.ancestry.com: accessed 2 October 2019), citing NARA microfilm publication M653. Date of enumeration: 9 July 1860, Image 18/131.

[221] Findagrave.com, database with images, (www.findagrave.com; accessed 9/30/ 2019), Memorial # 194125337. for Marie Louise Croizei.

They were the parents of nine children, all with the exception of the last, born in or near Mobile, Mobile Co., AL. For the purposes of this study, we will explore the life of their seventh child, Eulalie Pinta born on 13 February 1848 who is the connection between the Grandmaison, Pinta, Lassize, Allain and Raby families to the Aubry and Chiapella line. The baptism record of Eulalie Pinta, dated 20 February 1848, is below:

"In the year of our Lord 1848 on the 20th day of February I the undersigned Catholic priest of Mobile certify that I have baptized Eulalie born on the 13th day of February 1848 legitimate daughter of Joseph and Julie Pinta free people of color Sponsors Louis Ely and Marie Lafargue. In faith whereof I have signed. G. Chalon." Courtesy of the Archdiocese of Mobile Archives.

Briefly, however, the others born to the couple were Victoria, born on 3 December 1837, who married Joseph Luconey Montieu (f.m.c.) in 1857 in New Orleans. Joseph Pinta was born on 13 June 1840, who married Lavinia Wells on 13 June 1867, in New Orleans. Louisa Pinta was born on 20 June 1842 who married St. Meurice Nicolas Glaudin. Ernestine Pinta was born on 27 December 1845, who married Charles Gaignard in New Orleans on 2 August 1866. Nothing is known about William Pinta, who only appears in the 1860 Federal Census for New Orleans as an eleven-year-old boy born in Alabama. Jules and Richard Pinta, born in 1856 and 1858 respectively in Alabama, succumbed to a scarlet fever epidemic in New Orleans, the former dying on 24 March 1860, and the latter following on 27 March 1860. The couple's last child, Laura Luce Pinta was born on 20 December 1860 in New Orleans and married Richard Joseph Gardiol, a native of Chile, on 6 September 1883.[222] The Joseph Pinta family had moved back to New Orleans ca. 1859, where Pinta first tried the dry goods business, but eventually turned to cigar making and opened a cigar store on Canal Street, corner of Basin. The family lived at 164 Gasquet Street in the First District.

In the late 1860s, after the Civil War, the Pinta family was rocked with three deaths. Joseph Pinta, who had moved back to New Orleans with his family just eight years before, died on 13 February 1867. No cause of death was given on the certificate on the following page which indicated that he and the family were still living on Gasquet Street between Johnson and Galvez:

---

[222] Note: Laura Luce Gardiol followed Eulalie Pinta Chiapella Grass, her sister, to California after the death of her husband Richard Joseph Gardiol in Pulaski Co., AR, in1921. Five of her seven surviving children accompanied her out west. Walter Edward, born on 5 Mar 1887 in New Orleans, died in Sacramento, Sacramento Co, CA on 6 December 1982. Lawrence Stevens, born on 14 January 1893 in New Orleans, died in Los Angeles on 11 January 1988. Ernestine Viola, born on 28 March 1895 in New Orleans, died on 20 December 1991 in Ventura, Ventura Co., CA. Edwin Anthony, born in Welsh, Jefferson Davis Parish, LA on 18 October 1900, died in Coalinga, Fresno Co., CA on 15 February 1994. Loretta Gardiol, also born in Welsh, on 27 December 1903 died in Ventura, Ventura Co., CA on 9 April 1999. One child, Edna, born on 17 November 1888, died on 6 June 1889 in New Orleans. Her first-born, Luce Julia, born on 19 June 1884, married Jacob Denver Sargent and died in Lake Charles, Calcasieu Parish, LA, on 14 February 1957. Richard Joseph Gardiol, Jr., born on 19 November 1885, died in Front Royal, Warren Co., VA, on 3 August 1965.Laura Luce Pinta Gardiol died on 30 December 1918 in Coalinga, Fresno Co., CA. Source: *Findagrave.com* (https.www.findagrave.com: accessed 5/6/2019) Memorial # 23628783 for Laura L. Gardiol, buried at Calvary Cemetery, Fresno, Fresno Co., CA.

Be it Remembered, That on this day to wit: the *Thirteenth of February* in the year of our Lord one thousand eight hundred and sixty *seven* and the ninetyfirst of the Independence of the United States of America, before me, **F. M. CROZAT**, duly commissioned and sworn **Recorder of Births and Deaths,** in and for the Parish and City of Orleans personally appeared:

Madame Casanave a native of New Orleans residing in this city who by these presents declares that

Joseph Pinta a native of Louisiana aged about forty nine years Died on the Thirteenth instant (13 February 1867) in this city on Casquet street between Johnson and Galvez street

THUS DONE at New Orleans in the presence of the aforesaid *Madame Casanave* as also in that of Messrs. *Paul E Crozat & WH Crozat* both of this city, witnesses by me requested so to be, who have hereunto set their hands together with me after due reading hereof, the day, month and year first above written.

G Casanave

P E Crozat

F. M. Crozat
Recorder

Courtesy of State of Louisiana, Secretary of State, Division of Archives, Records Management, and History. *Vital Records Indices*. Baton Rouge, LA, USA citing *Orleans Death Indices 1804-1876*; Vol. 36, p. 200.

Eulalie Allain, widow by a first marriage to Pierre Dorestan Dalcour, and the wife in a second marriage to Charles Beauvilaire Pinta, died on 7 October 1869 in the parish of Plaquemines at the age of seventy years. The cause of death was said to be "dropsy." (excess fluid in the extremities, caused by heart failure or kidney disease). She was only identified as Mrs. B[auvilaire] Pinta:

Courtesy of State of Louisiana, Secretary of State, Division of Archives, Records Management, and History. *Vital Records Indices*. Baton Rouge, LA, USA citing *Orleans Death Indices 1804-1876*; Vol. 46, p. 71.

Eulalie Allain's husband, Charles Beauvilaire Pinta died in New Orleans on 18 March 1873. A native of Cuba, he was still living at 165 Gasquet Street. The cause of death was listed as "bronchitis" and was submitted by Dr. Roudanez. Louis Charles Roudanez was born free of a French merchant, Louis Roudanez and an African American mother, Aimée Potens, in St. James Parish, LA in 1823. He studied medicine in Paris, France, and arrived back in Louisiana in 1853. He took a second medical degree at Dartmouth in 1857 and returned to Louisiana where he remained as a physician. Roudanez founded the first bi-lingual African-American newspaper in the United States, *La Tribune*, successor to the French language *L'Union* both of which he started after the Civil War. He championed the right of free men of color who were property owners to be given the right to vote, a stand which caused friction between newly freed slaves and those people of color who had lived free for decades under French, Spanish, and then American domination. Ultimately his newspapers failed due to lack of support from the African American community, but he continued treating patients and died in New Orleans on 11 March 1890 Below is Charles Beauvilaire Pinta's death record:

Courtesy of State of Louisiana, Secretary of State, Division of Archives, Records Management, and History. *Vital Records Indices*. Baton Rouge, LA, USA citing *Orleans Death Indices 1804-1876*; Vol. 57, p. 469.

Julia Raby, Mrs. Joseph Pinta died on 5 September 1886. After the end of Reconstruction, Louisiana resumed the practice of indicating the race of decedents on their death certificates and used the designation "(Col.)" or "colored" on their forms. While neither, Julia's husband, Joseph Pinta, or her brother-in-law, Charles Beauvilaire Pinta or his wife, Eulalie Allain Pinta, had been designated as "colored" on forms issued in the 1860s and 1870s, it had become common practice by the late 1880s to include racial designations on vital records. At the time of her death "Julia Raby (Col.)," the widow of Joseph Pinta, aged about 71 years, was living at #508 Canal Street, and the cause of her death was listed as "scirrhus of pylorus," possibly stomach cancer:

Be it Remembered, That on this day, to-wit: the Sixth of September in the year of our Lord One Thousand Eight Hundred and eighty Six, and the One Hundred and Eleventh of the Independence of the United States of America, before me, JOSEPH HOLT, M. D., President Board of Health and Ex-Officio Recorder of Births, Deaths, and Marriages in and for the Parish of Orleans, personally appeared

Joseph Mansion, an Undertaker, a native of this city residing at No 88 Bourbon Street _____, who hereby declares, that Julia Raby, widow of Joseph Pinta (Col.) native of Mississippi City Miss, aged 71 years departed this life Yesterday, (5 Sept 1886) at No 508 Canal Street, in this city.

Cause of Death Scirrhus of Pylorus

Certificate of Dr. J. C. Castellanos

Joseph Mansion

Courtesy of State of Louisiana, Secretary of State, Division of Archives, Records Management, and History. Vital Records Indices. Baton Rouge, LA, USA citing Orleans Death Indices 1804-1876; Vol. 89, p. 1051.

Joseph and Julia Raby's daughter Eulalie Pinta married Stephen Octave Chiapella, son of Achille Chiapella and Eglée Aubry on 19 March 1873 in New Orleans. (See Chapter 15, p. 179)

CHAPTER 10

ÉTIENNE COUDRAIN CHIAPELLA

Étienne Coudrain Chiapella, Celestin Coudrain Chiapella's younger brother was only discussed briefly during our lengthy examination of the Jérome Chiapella family and its history in Louisiana. Étienne Coudrain, was adopted along with his elder brother, Celestin, by Jérome Chiapella, after the death of his father, Pierre Coudrain and the remarriage of his mother, Pelagie Duvernay. Although Étienne, also referred to in American documents as Stephen Chiapella and in Spanish documents as Estevan Chiapella, received a generous bequest of 12,000 piastres, which in today's buying power would represent almost $225,319, he was not specifically singled out by his adopted father in the same way as his brother was. Celestin, who inherited the bulk of his surrogate father's estate, was invited in the elder Chiapella's last will and testament to carry forth the Chiapella name by adopting it as his own. Although Etienne was not mentioned in this regard, he often used the Chiapella name exclusively, or used it in records as a "dit" name along with his birth name "Coudrain." Both boys were educated in France, but while Celestin came back to Louisiana towards the end of the eighteenth century, Étienne remained at Bordeaux and became a seafaring man like his adopted father, Jérome Chiapella. He was the owner and captain of ocean-going vessels that plied the Atlantic from Bordeaux to New Orleans, to New York, as well as to the British Isles. He spent much of his early years in Bordeaux where Jérome and the latter's wife, Agathe Lemelle, as well as his birth brother, Celestin, would eventually settle with his wife, Amada Lachaise, and their large brood of children.

We have proof that Étienne Coudrain Chiapella was in New Orleans in November of 1804 because on the 21st of that month he took an oath of allegiance stating that he was a native of "the Territory of Orleans and a citizen of the United States" before William C.C. Claiborne, the newly-appointed Governor of the territory. This document provided us with his description. "He was five feet four and one-half inches tall, with light brown hair and blue eyes. He had a dark complexion and had a scar on the left side of his upper lip and a scar on the front of his right thigh just by his hip bone." He signed as "Stephen La Chiapella." The document was countersigned by Henry Brown, a Notary Public[223]

At the time Chiapella signed this document, Louisiana was in a state of turmoil. Spanish troops had not left the territory. French residents were still in shock that, after having their hopes raised that Napoleon would retain control of Louisiana after taking it back from Spain, they found out that, in order to continue his wars in Europe he had needed money so badly that he had turned around and sold the territory to the United States. Moreover, the United States had appointed an American as Governor, who was making an effort to introduce English into the government and into the Judicial system. In March of 1804 the vast Louisiana Territory had been divided into the District of Louisiana and the Territory of Orleans which further alienated the populace. Landowners with French and Spanish land grants were afraid that they would lose their property because the Spanish had made certain grants on the eve of the cession of the territory back to the French, including large grants to Jérome Chiapella, which the United States claimed would be considered null and void. Neither the French nor the Spanish had any faith in the two men sent to govern the new territory. Charles Gayarré summarized local feelings about W.C.C. Claiborne and General James Wilkinson which had been expressed by Pierre Clement de Laussat, who had been sent by the French government to turn the colony over to the Americans: "the first [Claiborne] although has estimable qualities as a private man was a man of little intellect, extreme awkwardness and is beneath the position in which he is placed. The second, Wilkinson who has been long known here in the most unfavorable manner, is a rattle-headed fellow, full of odd fantasies. And frequently drunk. Neither men know a word of French or Spanish."[224]

Stephen Chiapella, in order to be able to obtain a certificate to work as a seaman, took the oath as soon as possible, as the new American government began to take hold. From that time on his life was devoted to his occupation which took him back and forth across the Atlantic Ocean. Little is known of his life between 1804 and 1810. However, an intriguing bit of information recently surfaced when the Bibliothèque Nationale de France (French

---

[223] "Citizenship Affidavits of U. S.-born Seamen at Select Ports, 1792-1869," digital image, *Ancestry.com* (https://www.ancestry.com: accessed 2/2/19) citing *Proofs of Citizenship Used To Apply For Seamen's Protection Certificates for the Port of New Orleans, Louisiana, 1800, 1802, 1804–1812, 1814–1816, 1818–1819, 1821, 1850–1851, 1855–1857,* NARA Microfilm publication M1826, Roll 1, Record Group 36, Oath of Stephen La Chiapella dated 21 November 1804, Image 3/503.

[224] Charles Gayarré, *History of Louisiana. The American Domination*, Vol. 4. (Gretna, LA: Pelican Publishing Co., 1974), 10.

National Library) made their Masonic database available on-line in February 2019. This database is called the "Fichier Bossu" after the man who created it, Jean Bossu, who during the 1960s and 1970s amassed a huge file of over 100,000 entries concerning celebrated and not-so-well-known Masons, mentions of which he found in books, newspapers and other printed matter. These entries can be maddeningly cryptic like the one below for Étienne Chiapella:

Fichier (File) entry of Jean Bossu concerning Étienne Chiapella (New Orleans, born about 1778) marin (sailor). Bibliothèque Nationale de France, on-line at BNF Gallica: https://gallica.bnf.fr/ark:/12148/btv1b10000064x/f36.image.

Etienne Chiapella, a sailor (marin) received on 19 August 1810 a certificate of "app. comp. et m.," perhaps a certificate of appreciation? of some sort from the Lodge called "Les Amis Réunis," who were prisoners of war at Plymouth, Mill Prison. But what does this mean? We discovered that "Les Amis Réunis" or "Reunited Friends" was a masonic lodge formed by prisoners of war at the Millbay Prison, Plymouth, Great Britain, in 1809. An interesting book intitled *French Prisoners' Lodges: A Brief Account of Twenty-Six Lodges and Chapters of Freemasons Established and Conducted by French Prisoners of War in England and Elsewhere between 1756 and 1814* written by John T. Thorp (Printed by Brother George Gibbons, King Street, London, 1900) offered some insight into "Les Amis Réunis:"

> Early in the present century a large number of French prisoners of war were confined in the Mill Prison Plymouth This prison was built especially for the purpose of accommodating the French, Spanish, and American prisoners upon land expressly given to the country for the purpose by the Prince of Wales afterwards George IV as the owner of the Duchy of Cornwall. The prison was very large for at times as many as 8,000 to 10,000 were located there. [...] The French prisoners confined in the prison in the year 1809 comprised a number of Freemasons who conducted a Lodge there under the name of Amis Réunis but beyond the bare fact of its existence nothing is known That such a Lodge was in active operation in 1809 is proved by an endorsement on a Certificate issued in 1797 by the Lodge Réunion Désirée (Desired Reunion) established by the Gd Orient of France at Port au Prince Island of St Domingo in the year 1783.[225]

The endorsement mentioned, which was the fourth in number, read, in a translation by Thorp: "Inspected at the Lodge of 'Reunited Friends' held at the Mill Prison, Plymouth, the 4th day of the 4th month of the Year of True Light 5809 – in open meeting."[226] It is very interesting that this lodge had a connection to Saint Domingue, as did Jérome Chiapella as well as his adopted son, Étienne. They had both sailed there many times, and did a regular business with the French islands, an activity which was made more difficult and even very risky during the revolt at Saint Domingue. The fact remains that we do not know why Etienne Chiapella received that certificate. Was he a prisoner of war of the British? Had his ship been captured during the Peninsular War (1807-1814), a military conflict between

[225] Thorp, *French Prisoners' Lodges*, 93.
[226] Thorp, *French Prisoners' Lodges*, 99. Note: The date is 4 April 1809. The Masonic year is the Gregorian year plus 4,000.

Napoleon's armies and Spain in which the British sided with Spain. British warships preyed on shipping in the Caribbean during that time? Or had he simply sailed to England in 1810 on business and visited the prison to bring aid to the men incarcerated there. Perhaps he had even helped some of them to escape. There were so many men incarcerated there during the first and second decade of the nineteenth century that military and naval officers were often let out on parole to live in towns in England designated as "parole towns." Many of those slipped away. Those kept in prison often had some liberties such as being allowed to organize a Masonic Lodge, under the watchful eyes of their captors, who may have themselves been Freemasons. Perhaps someday there will be a document found, or an article in an old newspaper which will shed some light on this mystery. For now, all we know is that Chiapella was at a meeting of Les Amis Réunis at Mill Prison on 19 August 1810, and was awarded a certificate.

Étienne Coudrain Chiapella was the father of two sons with Marie Thérèse Aimée Roman at Bordeaux, Gironde, France. The first was Jérome Émile Chiapella who was born to the couple on 18 May 1812 at Bordeaux, Section 1, Gironde France. The father was identified as Étienne Chiapella, age 33, an American householder living at #163 Allée des Noyers. The mother was identified as his wife, "Thérèze" Roman. Witnesses to the civil record were Jacques Bonnafous, a forty-year-old, dyer of cloth, and Jacques Mayal, a salesman.[227]

The couple's second child, also a son, was born on 20 June 1813, and registered two days later. This time the father, Étienne Chiapella, then thirty-four-years-old was identified as a sailor living at #72 Rue Judaique Saint Seurin with his wife, the child's mother, Thérèze Roman. The boy was given the name Michel Étienne Chiapella. Pierre Lachapelle, age 74, and Pierre Gambé, age 50, a tailor, were the witnesses.[228] The baby, Michel Étienne, however was generally known as "Achille" Chiapella, except on select civil records in Louisiana where his birth name was used. We do not know what happened to their first son, who lived at least until 1817. There are no records for him in Louisiana, and we have not yet found any death record for him in Bordeaux.

Although Thérèze Roman was identified as Étienne Chiapella's wife in the birth records of their two sons, the couple did not wed until four years later on 8 February 1817. He was married as Étienne "Coudrin, connu sous le nom de Chiapella" (Étienne Coudrin known under the name of Chiapella).According to the record filed at Bordeaux, he was thirty-nine years old, a native of New Orleans, born on 12 November 1777, a ship's captain, living at #72 Rue Judaique Saint Seurin, the son of the late Pierre Coudrin and the late Pelagie Duvernez, who both died in New Orleans. The bride was Thérèze Roman, twenty-five-years-old, a native of Bordeaux, born on 3 February 1792, daughter of Louis Roman, who had been missing for about twelve years, and his wife, Aimée Bertin, living also in Bordeaux. A missing person's report for the bride's father had been filed in Section II, Bordeaux on 9 December 1816, so that the marriage could go forward. The civil record concluded with the formal recognition of their two children born out of wedlock at Bordeaux as their own, thereby guaranteeing their rights in France under the law: "Jérome Émile Coudrin-Chiapella born on 18 May 1812 and Michel Étienne Coudrin-Chiapella born on 28 June 1813." [229]

Etienne Chiapella was at Bordeaux on 22 October 1818 when he was a witness to the marriage of his niece, Amada Maria (Marie Camille), Chiapella, his brother Celestin's daughter, to François Félix Audebert. (See p. 68). We also know that Étienne Chiapella, a forty-three-year-old planter from Louisiana arrived in New Orleans from Bordeaux with his fifty-five-year-old "mulatto slave Charles," along with two other passengers aboard the ship

[227] Bordeaux, Gironde, France, Registres des actes de naissance de Bordeaux, Section 1, [Section 1, Bordeaux Birth Registrations], 1812, Birth #354, Jérome Émile Chiapella, digital image, *Archives municipales de Bordeaux,* État Civil en ligne," (https://archives.bordeaux-metropole.fr/: accessed 10/7/2019), Cote 1E 69, Image 63/155.

[228] Bordeaux, Gironde, France, Registres des actes de naissance de Bordeaux, Section 1, [Section 1, Bordeaux Birth Registrations], 1813, Birth #459, Michel Étienne Chiapella, digital image, *Archives municipales de Bordeaux,* État Civil en ligne," (https://archives.bordeaux-metropole.fr/: accessed 10/7/2019), Cote 1E73, Image 74/144.

[229] Bordeaux, Gironde, France, Registres des actes de mariage de Bordeaux, Section 1, [Section 1, Bordeaux Marriage Registrations], 1817, Marriage #63, Étienne Coudrin, surnommé Chiapella to Thérèze Roman, digital image, *Archives municipales de Bordeaux,* État Civil en ligne," (https://archives.bordeaux-metropole.fr/: acc. 10/17/2019), Cote 2E 95, Images 26 and 27/187. Note: The marriage record gave the wrong date of birth for Michel Étienne Coudrin-Chiapella. which was said to be 28 June 1813. His birth record, however, shows that he was born actually on 20 June 1813, with the civil registration taking place two days later.

Jerome on 22 April 1820.[230] Then again, two years later, and just months before his adopted father Jérome Chiapella died, Mr. and Mrs Chiapella and a child, along with Charles a mulatto man servant and native of New Orleans arrived at New Orleans on the ship *Factor* from Bordeaux on 2 February 1822.[231] We believe that arrival coincides with Étienne's decision to relocate his family back to New Orleans.

After Étienne received the bequest of 12,000 piastres subsequent to his adopted father's death in August 1822, he was able to purchase a brig which he named the *Amiable Matilda*. He registered the ship in New Orleans on 21 July 1825:

> 31. AMIABLE MATILDA, brig, of New Orleans. 'Built at Philadelphia, Pa., 1794. 236 11/95 tons; 85 ft. 6 in. x 25 ft. 8 in. x 12 ft. 10 in. Two decks, two masts, woman bust head. Previously registered, No. 64, December 24, at Charleston, SC, Registered, No. 59, July 21, 1825. Owner: Stephen Chiapella, mariner, New Orleans. Master: 'Stephen Chiapella.[232]

The advertisement for the thirty-one-year-old brig's first departure from New Orleans was published in French on page 3 of the *Louisiana State Gazette* dated Friday, August 19, 1825 and read [author's translation] "For France or England. The good solid brig *Aimable Matilde*[233], fine sailing ship, newly repaired, lined, nailed and pegged in copper, Captain Stephen Chiapella, will take charge of her for one of the above-mentioned ports, having room for a dozen passengers, comfortably accommodated. For price of freight and passage, see the Captain on board or Modeste Lefebvre at #17 St. Louis Street."[234]

We were able to trace three voyages of the *Amiable Matilda* which were memorialized in the Marine columns of old newspapers. On 21 May 1825 the *New York Evening Post* reported on the arrival the previous evening of a large number of ships that had come into port including the "*Amiable Matilda*, Chiapella, [for] New Orleans, 30th [May]." [235] On 7 March 1826, it was reported that the "Brig *Amiable Matilda*, Chiapella, from New Orleans for Bordeaux arrived at Boston on 4 March, headed for Bordeaux, leaky."[236] The *Marine Telegraphic Shipping List* reported on 22 July 1826 that "An American Brig, supposed to be the *Amiable Matilda*, Chiapella, from New Orleans, and last from Boston" had arrived at Bordeaux on 22 May 1826.[237]

While we have no further records for Étienne Chiapella's first-born son, Jérome Émile, and assumed that he died as a child, between 1817 and 1821 at Bordeaux, we know that his second son, one of the major players in the saga of the Aubry sisters, arrived in New Orleans from Bordeaux, Gironde, France, on 31 December 1829 on board the ship *Lélia*, accompanied by his father. Etienne was described as a fifty-two-year-old merchant born in the

[230] "New Orleans, Passenger List Quarterly Abstracts, 1820-1875," digital image, *Ancestry.com* (https://www.ancestry.com: accessed 10/9/2019), citing *Quarterly Abstracts of Passenger Lists of Vessels Arriving at New Orleans, Louisiana, 1820–1875*. M272, 17 rolls. Records of the U.S. Customs Service, Record Group 36. NARA, Arrival of É. Chiapella, 22 April 1820. Image 1/2
[231] "New Orleans, Passenger Lists, 1813-1963,"digital image, *Ancestry.com* (https://www.ancestry.com: accessed 10/9/2019), citing NARA, Work Projects Administration *Transcript of Passenger Lists of Vessels Arriving at New Orleans, Louisiana, 1813-1849*. Arrival of Chiapella family on 2 February 1822., Image 33/1024.
[232] Survey of Federal Archives, *Ships Registers and Enrollments of New Orleans, Louisiana/ prepared by the Survey of Federal Archives in Louisiana, Division of community services programs, Work projects administration*, Volume 2, 1821-1830, Baton Rouge, LA: Louisiana State University, 1941, 6. Available at https://catalog.hathitrust.org/Record/000968981, Image 38/254.
[233] Note: although registered as the *"Amiable Matilda,"* she appeared as the *"Aimable Matilde,"* in Chiapella's own advertisement, the French spelling for the name of his ship.
[234] "Pour France ou Angleterre," *Louisiana State Gazette*, 19 August 1825, digital image, *Newspapers.com* (https://www.newspapers.com: accessed 10/10/2019), p. 3, col. 6.
[235] Marine List, "Arrived Last Evening," *New York Evening Post*, 21 May 1825, digital image, *Genealogybank.com* (https://www.genealogybank.com: accessed 10/5/2019), p. 2, col. 5.
[236] "Port of Boston, March 4," *Eastern Argus* (Portland, ME), 10 March 1826, digital image, *Genealogybank.com* (https://www.genealogybank.com: accessed 4/4/2019) , p. 3, col. 4.
[237] "Shipping Memoranda," *Marine Telegraphic Shipping List* (Boston, MA), 22 July 1826, digital image, *Genealogybank.com* (http://www.genealogybank.com: accessed 4/4/2019), p.3, col. 2.

United States. His son, listed as "Achille" Chiapella was a sixteen-year-old boy born in France. This was the first instance we have found that his son, born Michel Étienne, ordinarily used the name "Achille."[238]

Étienne Coudrain Chiapella's wife, Thérèse Roman, died in New Orleans on 1 March 1832:

Archdiocese of New Orleans (Orleans Parish, LA), *St. Louis Cathedral Funerals 1832-1833*, p. 18, Act #97. (Courtesy of Emilie Leumas, Archivist – Kimberly Johnson and Katie Vest – Researching Archivists.)

Translated from French by the author, the document states: "#97. Mrs. Étienne Coudrain Chiapella, born Thérèse Aimée Roman, French woman. On 2 March 1832 was buried in the cemetery of the Cathedral and Parish Church of St. Louis, of the city of New Orleans, State of Louisiana, the body of the late Thérèse Aimée Roman, wife of Mr. Étienne Coudrain Chiapella, about 40 years old, born at Bordeaux, Gironde, France. Died the day before at noon. In faith of which I signed. Rev. J. Cavetta."

We could find no more records concerning any other voyages of the *Amiable Matilda*, although there may have been others that Étienne undertook after his brother Celestin and family moved back to France and began to develop their winery. Etienne did, however, remarry on 14 May 1836 to a widow whom he had probably met at Bordeaux after his first wife died. Marguerite Virginie Baqué was born on 1 August 1798 (15 thermidor, an VI) at Bordeaux to Bertrand Bacqué and his wife, Jeanne Castéra. She had contracted a brief marriage to Jean-Baptiste René Durand de Ramefort, an infantry officer, the son of Clément Joseph Durand de Ramefort and his wife Jeanne Marie Thérèze Ballodes, on 30 June 1821 at Bordeaux, Section 1, Gironde, France,[239] which ended with the death of her husband six months later on 3 January 1822 at Bordeaux, Section 2, Gironde, France.[240] The couple had no children. A copy of the original Baqué-Chiapella record reads (our translation):

Today, Saturday 14 May 1836, the 60th of the independence of the United States of America. By us, Louis Moni, undersigned priest of the church of St. Louis of New Orleans (Louisiana), the civil and canon formalities having been fulfilled without any legitimate opposition, were united in legitimate marriage by mutual consent given by word: Mr. Etienne Coudrain Chiapella born and domiciled in the above mentioned parish, adult son of the late Etienne Coudrain Chiapella and Pelagie Duvernay, deceased on one hand; and Miss Marguerite Virginia Baqué, married first to Jean Baptiste Durand de Ramefort deceased; born at Bordeaux, France, and living in this parish, legitimate daughter of the late Bertrand Baqué and the late

[238] "New Orleans Passenger Lists, 1813-1963," digital image, *Ancestry.com* (https://www.ancestry.com:accessed 9/28/2019) citing NARA, *Passenger Lists of Vessels Arriving at New Orleans, Louisiana, 1820-1902*; NARA Number: *2824927*; Record Group Title: *Records of the Immigration and Naturalization Service*; Record Group Number *85*. Arrival of Mr. Chapella [*sic*] and Mr. Achille Chapella [*sic*], Image 248/288, Lines 14,15.

[239] Bordeaux, Gironde, France, Registres des actes de mariage de Bordeaux, Section 1, [Section 1, Bordeaux Marriage Registrations], 1821, Marriage #220, Jean Baptiste René Durand de Ramefort with Virginie Baqué, digital image, *Archives municipales de Bordeaux*, "État Civil en ligne," (https://archives.bordeaux- metropole.fr/: accessed 8/8/2019), Cote 2E 111, Image 85/165. Note: The bride's date of birth was given in the marriage record.

[240] Bordeaux, Gironde, France, Registres des actes de décès de Bordeaux, Section 2, [Section 2, Bordeaux Death Registrations], 1822, Death #18, Jean Baptiste René Durand de Ramefort, digital image, *Archives municipales de Bordeaux*, "État Civil en ligne," (https://archives.bordeaux-metropole.fr/: accessed 8/8/2019), Cote 3E 117, Image 5/117.

Jeanne Castra, on the other hand. This marriage was celebrated in the presence of the following witnesses: James McFarlane, Peter Murphy and Alexis Leroy who signed the present act with us, as well as the contracting parties on the day month and year above. Signed) E. Coudrain Chiapella, Marguerite V. Baqué, Widow de Ramefort, James McFarlane, Peter Murphy, A. Leroy, L. Moni, priest[241]

The groom's father's name was given incorrectly as the "late Étienne Coudrain Chiapella" instead of the" late Pierre Coudrain." The bride's mother's surname was misspelled as "Castra" instead of "Castéra" which had appeared correctly in her daughter, Marguerite Virginie Baqué's, Bordeaux marriage record with her first husband: After his marriage to Virginie Baqué, Etienne Chiapella gave up his life as a ship's captain and was employed by the United States Treasury Department as a customs inspector at English Turn outside of New Orleans. A United States Civil Service Commission report for 1839 indicated that he was paid $1095 on 30 September 1839 for one year's employment.[242]

---

[241] Archdiocese of New Orleans (Orleans Parish, LA), *St. Louis Cathedral Marriages. Vol. 6 1834-1837*, Act #213. (Courtesy of Emilie Leumas, Archivist – Kimberly Johnson and Katie Vest – Researching Archivists.)

[242] U.S. Civil Service Commission, *Register of all Officers and Agents, Civil, Military, and Naval in the Service of the United States on the Thirtieth September 1839, with the Names, Force and Condition of all Ships and Vessels belonging to the United States and Where Built; Together with the Names and Compensation of All printers in Any Way Employed, by Congress or Any Department or Officer of Government*, (Washington D.C.: A.B. Claxton & Co., 1839), 62.

Chapter 11

ÉGLEE AUBRY AND ACHILLE CHIAPELLA

Michel Étienne, known as Achille Chiapella, probably met Eglée Aubry around the time of his father's remarriage. He was twenty-three years-old and Eglée was thirty-one with one surviving child, Marguerite Odalie Lorreins, from her relationship with Louis Hilaire Lorreins. Achille and Eglée's first child, most always identified as René Achille or R.A. Chiapella, was baptized as Michel Chapella (*sic*) on 8 January 1838 by the Rev. Felipe Asensio at St. Louis Cathedral. According to the record, he was born on 23 April 1837 to Michel Étienne "Chapella," a native of Bordeaux, Gironde, France, and Marie Eglée Aubry, a native of the parish. The child's godparents were Alphonse René David, and Louise (Virginie) Domingon, daughter of Eglé Aubry's sister, Félicité with Hilaire Julien Domingon. A copy of the record, written in French is included below:

Baptismal record for Michel Chapella et Aubry (*sic*). Archives of the Archdiocese of New Orleans, Saint Louis Cathedral Records Vol. 25, p. 269, #819. (Courtesy of Emilie Leumas, Archivist – Kimberly Johnson and Katie Vest – Researching Archivists.)

Achille and Eglée Aubry's second child, Joseph Émile Chiapella, was born ca. 1839. In 1877 Eglée swore in an affidavit that Joseph Emile's baptismal record from St. Vincent De Paul Church, 3051 Dauphine St. (now the Blessed Francis Xavier Seelos Catholic Church) was destroyed in a fire. At the time of Joseph Émile's birth, Achille Chiapella had just started his career as a notary, a position he held in New Orleans from 1 February 1839 through March 31, 1857. Forty-one volumes of records passed by him are housed at the Notarial Archives Research Center at 1340 Poydras Street, Suite 360, New Orleans, LA, 70112.

Achille and Eglée's last child together, Stephen Octave Chiapella, may have been baptized as well at St. Vincent de Paul Church whose records were destroyed, because we were unable to locate any birth certificate for him either. According to his burial information he was born on 15 September 1840 at New Orleans.

Achille's father, Etienne Coudrain Chiapella, died on 23 May 1842. Rufino Thomas Fernandez, born on 16 November 1799 at Galveztown, LA, keeper of the records for the Cathedral of St. Louis in New Orleans reported the death to the civil authorities. This is one of those rare death records which is replete with biographical information of the decedent. On 24 May 1842 Fernandez reported that "Etienne Coudrain Chiapella, born in this city on 12 November 1777, formerly a seaman and captain of vessels, and late Port Warden for the First Municipality, died last night at his domicile situated on Condé Street #165.[243] He was the legitimate son of Pierre Coudrain and Pelagie Duvernez, both deceased. Widower in a first marriage from Marie Thérèse Aimée Roman, a native of Bordeaux, France, who died in this city on 1 March 1832, and was secondly married in this city on 14 March 1836 to Mrs. Marguerite Virginie Baqué, widow of the late Mr. Jean-Baptiste René Durand de Ramefort, also a native of Bordeaux, his surviving consort, residing in this city."

Courtesy of State of Louisiana, Secretary of State, Division of Archives, Records Management, and History. *Vital Records Indices*. Baton Rouge, LA, USA citing *Orleans Death Indices 1804-1899*, Vol. 9, p. 296.

Unfortunately, Étienne Coudrain Chiapella left no will. There is only one record which may be that of his widow, Marguerite Virginie Baqué, in a *New Orleans City Directory* published in 1845 which reads "Chiapella, Mrs. Widow, 40 Condé Street."[244] We assume that she may have returned to France after this date because there seems to be no death record or succession for her here in Louisiana.

Étienne Chiapella's only surviving son, Michel Étienne, known as Achille Chiapella, continued to work as a notary. He learned his skills from Carlile Pollock who was a New Orleans notary from 30 April 1817 until his death on 8 April 1845. They shared an office on Exchange Alley near Conti Street from 1839 for about five years. The *New Orleans Annual and Commercial Register of 1846.* listed "Chiapella, Achille, notary public, Exchange Alley

---

[243] Condé Street was before 1865 a section of Chartres Street between Jackson Square and Esplanade Avenue. Source: John Chase, *Frenchmen, Desire, Good Children and Other Streets of New Orleans*, (Gretna, LA: Pelican Publishing Co., 2012), 22.

[244] E.A. Michel & Co., *New Orleans Annual and Commercial Register of 1846: Containing the Names, Residences and Professions of all the Heads of Families and Persons in Business of the City and Suburbs, Algiers and Lafayette, &C.,* (New Orleans, LA: E.A. Michel & Co., 1845, Reprinted by HardPress Publishing), 159.

n.c. Conti St., d.c. Good Children and Morales Sts."[245] The last address, Good Children/Bons Enfants (now St. Claude) and Morales (now Marais), was Achille's home address before he was married.

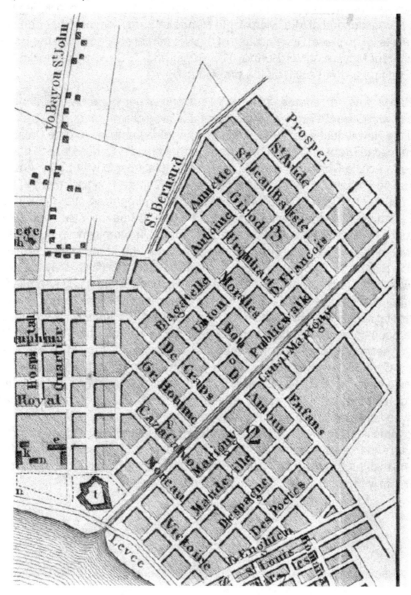

Map of Faubourg Marigny with original street names – Library of Congress Geography and Map Division.

It was not long after the death of Carlile Pollock that Achille Chiapella married the late notary's youngest daughter, Marie Louise Pollock, born on 8 February 1825. An excerpt from the St. Louis Cathedral sacramental records reads: "Pollock, Maria Luisa (Carlile Notary Public of this city, and Margarita Sarpy, both natives and residents of this city), b. 23 June 1826, born 8 Feb 1825, pgp: George Pollock and Catherine YET [Yates], mgp. Juan Bautista Lille Sarpy and Francisca Genoveva Amada Cavalier, s. Juan Bautista Sarpy and Maria Louisa Poree (SLC, B36, 183)." Achille and Marie Louise were married on 16 May 1846. The document reads in part:

> #301. Mr. Michel Étienne Achille Chiapella with Miss. Marie Louise Pollock. This day the sixteenth of May in the Year of Our Lord 1846 [...] by me Constantin Maenhaut, Curate of the Cathedral and Parochial Church of St. Louis of this city and Parish of Orleans Louisiana the license being granted by the Honorable Charles Maurian judge in and for the aforesaid Parish and after having received the mutual consent of the

---

[245] E.A. Michel & Co., *New Orleans Annual and Commercial Register of 1846*, 158. Note: Good Children (Bons Enfants) and Morales do not cross. They are parallel Streets. Between Rue d'Amour (Love), to the south and Urquhart, to the north, in the Faubourg Marigny. Michel's abbreviations: n = near; c. = corner; d = dwelling.

contracting parties in presence of the three witnesses required by law, I have united in the holy bonds of matrimony Mr. Michel Étienne Achille Chiapella, legitimate son and of age of Mr. Stephen Chiapella and of Mrs. Marie Thérèse Roman on the one hand. And Miss Marie Louise Pollock, legitimate daughter of Mr. Carlile Pollock deceased, and of Mrs. Marguerite Henriette Sarpy, on the other part. The publication of one ban of marriage has taken place. Dispensation of the two others obtained from the Ecclesiastical authorities, in testimony whereof Messrs. Victor Burthé, T.F. Pépin and Z. Cavelier witnesses who together with me and the contracting parties have signed the present act.[246]

The Pollock family was, of course, part of this story already. Jérome Chiapella, Achille's adopted grandfather, did business with Oliver Pollock, who was Marie Louise's great-granduncle. (See pp. 37-39). Moreover, Carlile Pollock handled the New Orleans business dealings of Agathe Lemelle, Jérome Chiapella's widow, after she and her husband had moved to France. We can also surmise that the late Carlile Pollock had had no qualms about his daughter's marriage to Achille Chiapella, despite the latter's relationship with Eglée Aubry, about which, given the size of New Orleans, he probably knew. Carlile's own father, George Pollock, after all, had had an illegitimate child, Marcella, born on 25 April 1818 (SLC, B31, 8), whom he had recognized at birth. with a woman identified as Maria Herrera. Marcella had been born long after his legitimate wife, Catherine Yates had died in New Orleans and was interred on 31 October 1805 (SLC F6,136). The extract of Marcella's baptismal record reads: "Pollock, Marcella (George, native of Newry in Ireland [County Down Northern Ireland] and Maria Dolores Errera, native of the town of Los Angeles, Provincia Interna [probably California], both residents of this city b. May 28, 1818, bn. April 25 1818, pgp John Pollock and Elizabeth Carlyle, mgp. Jose Errera and Raphaela Monteja, s. Thomas Pollock and Raphaela Monteja, infant's maternal grandmother (SLC, B31, 8)." To his credit, George Pollock, drew up a will in 1819 in which he recognized his illegitimate daughter, and wrote the following: "I earnestly recommend to the care of all my children my illegitimate daughter Marcella, now about a year and a half old, born of Maria Herrera an unmarried woman, but recommend her more strongly to the special and immediate protection of my said three daughters Catherine, Lorenza and Charlotte, that they may watch over her and bring her up in a decent manner."[247] We suspect that Carlile would have given Achille Chiapella similar advice concerning Eglée's children, who he would be leaving in the care of their mother at the tender ages of nine, seven and five years. While we have no specific evidence that Achille was intimately involved in their lives after his marriage to Marie Louise Pollock on 16 May 1846, we know that his three illegitimate sons of color were productive members of the community, one working as a merchant, another as a shoemaker and the third as a cigar maker, all professions where free men of color were regularly employed in the mid-1800s. We also have evidence that Achille continued to be involved with Eglée Aubry because she and other family members often used his notarial services.

---

[246] Archdiocese of New Orleans (Orleans Parish, LA), *St. Louis Cathedral Marriages. Vol. 9*, p. 310, Act #301. (Courtesy of Emilie Leumas, Archivist – Kimberly Johnson and Katie Vest – Researching Archivists.)

[247] *Louisiana, Wills and Probate Records, 1756-1984*, digital image, *Ancestry.com* (https://www.ancestry. com: accessed 18 October 2019), citing *Record of Wills, 1807-1901 Louisiana. Probate Court (Orleans Parish)*, Will of George Pollock dated 2 September 1819, Image 565/718.

CHAPTER 12

EGLÉE AUBRY IN ST. TAMMANY PARISH

On 12 June 1849, Eglée was the highest bidder for a piece of property at an auction of the possessions of the late Joseph Antoine Pueyo, who was the godfather of her son, Joseph Émile Chiapella. Eglée offered $70 and agreed to pay one-third in cash and the rest at intervals of six and twelve months with two promissory notes signed by her to the order of and endorsed by Odalie Lorreins, her daughter. If not paid at the appointed time, interest at 8% would accrue. The property Eglée purchased was located in the village of Mandeville, St. Tammany Parish, LA, and was described as Lot #10, Square 12, measuring 60 feet frontage on Marigny Walk by 190 feet deep between parallel lines. The act of sale was passed before Achille Chiapella on 3 October 1849 in New Orleans.[248] Joseph Antoine Pueyo had bought the property in Mandeville from Nelson Foucher, f.m.c, on 27 March 1838. Foucher had bought it on 1 April 1834 from Bernard de Marigny, who, during that year, had subdivided his land on which the city of Mandeville now sits into over 100 town lots. Although Eglée Aubry would purchase other pieces of property in St. Tammany Parish, her principal residence was still in New Orleans where she was raising her children.

On 13 January 1851, Eglée Aubry bought another piece of land, this time in Madisonville, St. Tammany Parish, a town across the Tchefuncte River from Mandeville where she had made her initial purchase two years previously. This time she paid cash in hand of $100 to Joseph Dias, f.m.c., for a plot of land "designated as Number "One," on a special plan made by General David Bannister Morgan dated 8 July 1836 and annexed to the act of sale from René Baham to Joseph Dias passed before Lyman Briggs then Parish Judge of this Parish on the 12th day of October 1836." The lot fronted 99 feet on Renez (now Rene) Street and ran back between parallel lines to the swamp of Bayou Dezert (now Bayou De Zaire). A copy of the 1836 Morgan map is below, followed by the act of sale from Dias to Aubry. The Covington Road, or "Old Covington Highway" is now Main Street. Aubry's lot, No.1 (at top of map) was on Main Street, running from René Street north to Bayou De Zaire.

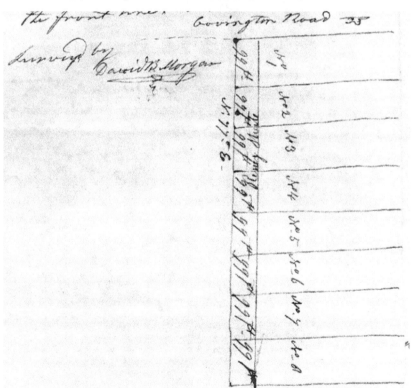

St. Tammany Parish Courthouse Records (Covington, St. Tammany Parish, LA), *Lyman Briggs Papers #2948* "Renez Baham to Joseph Dias f.m.c. sale of town lot," filed 12 October 1836. Note: Lot # 1 is at top of page.

---

[248] St. Tammany Parish Courthouse Records (Covington, St. Tammany Parish, LA), *Conveyance Office Book* B-2, p. 115, 116, "Estate of J.A. Pueyo to Eglée Aubry," filed 3 October, 1849.

STATE OF LOUISIANA.

Parish of St. Tammany. **BE IT KNOWN AND REMEMBERED,** That on this

Thirteenth day of *January* in the year of our Lord, one thousand eight hundred and

fifty *one*, and in the year of the Independence of the United States of America the seventy-*fifth* —

BEFORE ME, *John Jay Mortee* Recorder of the Parish of St.

Tammany, State of Louisiana, duly authorised by law to exercise the powers of NOTARY PUBLIC therein; personally came and

appeared *Mr Joseph Dias or Diaz a free man of color residing in the Parish of St Tammany State of Louisiana*

who did declare and say, that for the consideration hereinafter expressed, *he* do *es* by these presents grant, bargain, sell,

convey, transfer, assign and set over, with a full guarantee against all troubles, debts, mortgages, claims, evictions, donations,

alienations or other incumbrances whatsover, unto *Mrs Eglae Ossbry a free woman*

also residing in the Parish and State aforesaid.

here present accepting and purchasing for *himself & her* heirs and assigns, and acknowledging delivery

and possession thereof, *A certain Lot or parcel of Ground lying and being situate in the Town of Madisonville in this Parish designated as Number "One", on a special plan made by Gen. David B. Morgan dated 8th July 1836, & annexed to an act of Sale from René Paham to Joseph Dias passed before Lyman Briggs then Parish Judge of this Parish on the 12th day of October 1836. Said Lot, has a front of Ninety nine feet on Renez street and running back between parallel lines to the Swamp of Bayou Dezur being the Same property acquired by purchase by this vendor from Major Renez Paham per act passed before Lyman Briggs Parish Judge of this Parish on the 12th October 1836.*

[...]

John W. Merritt —   witnesses of lawful age, and domiciliated in this Parish, who have

hereunto signed their names, together with said appearers and me Recorder,

Joseph Dias —

Matthew Dicks

J. W. Merritt

Egle aubry

John I. Mentzo.
Recorder

The State of Louisiana
Parish of St Tammany ? I. Certify the foregoing to be
truly Recorded in my Office, Register of Conveyance C. pag
7. & 8. Witness my hand & impress of seal
of office this 13th Jany 1851,
John I. Mentz
Recorder

St. Tammany Parish Courthouse Records (Covington, St. Tammany Parish, LA), *Conveyance Office Book* C-2, p. 7 & 8, No. 180 Jos. Dias to Mrs Eglae Oubry [*sic*]" filed 13 January 1851.

Back of Eglée Aubry property at Madisonville as seen from Bayou Dezert (now Bayou De Zaire) taken on 5/5/2020 by the Author.

The bucolic nature of Eglée's property has changed little after the passage of 170 years except perhaps for the sound of traffic buzzing by on LA Highway 21, formerly Old Covington Highway, opposite the Madisonville, LA, Post Office. Although Eglée Aubry was a property owner in Mandeville and Madisonville, she maintained her home in District 1, Ward 1 in New Orleans where she and her four children were enumerated in the 1850 United States Federal Census. She was enumerated as "Eglee Aubry," a forty-year-old "mulatto" female born in Louisiana, living with "Odlie Loraince," age 27, a female mulatto, and her three sons by Achille Chiapella: Achille, age 13, Émile, age 11, and Octave, age 10.[249] The 1850 U.S. Federal Slave Census recorded that "Eglie" Aubry owned one female black, age 30 and one female black, age 13. The adult female she owned was probably the one she purchased on 17 July 1844 from the estate of Joseph Sauvinet, sold by Jean-Baptiste Sauvinet, the deceased man's brother and legal heir, before the notary Charles V. Foulon at New Orleans with the help of Achille Chiapella. The document, written in French, explains that she purchased Césaire, a "negress of about 24 years with her three children: Anna called Aimée, age 8, Caroline, age 6, and Catiche, age 3, all negresses." The price was $1100 piastres. Aubry paid $400 piastres in cash, with the balance due in two installments of $350 piastres plus eight percent interest, at six and twelve months from the date of purchase. The two notes were subscribed by the purchaser to the order of Achille Chiapella, who endorsed them each for the sum of $350 piastres. Until both payments were made, the slaves were mortgaged back to the seller, Jean-Baptiste Sauvinet with a promise not to sell or mortgage them. The purchase of the slaves which was facilitated by Chiapella was one of the ways in which a well-to-do white father would provide for the security of his free children of color through the acquisition of real estate in the name of their mother. Below is an excerpt from the purchase agreement describing the financial arrangement amongst the parties involved:

NARC, "Vente d'esclaves par M. Jean Bte. Sauvinet à Dlle. Eglé Aubry, f.c.l." dated 17 July 1844, passed by Notary Charles Foulon, Volume 15, Act #238. Courtesy Hon. Chelsey Richard Napoleon, Clerk of Civil District Court, Parish of Orleans.

Eglée Aubry continued to acquire land in St. Tammany Parish. On 15 November 1853 she purchased another tract in Madisonville from Mrs. Caroline Stein, who had originally acquired it from George Henry Penn, Esq.

[249] 1850 United States Federal Census, Orleans Parish, Louisiana, Municipality 1, Ward 1, Dwelling #219, Family #220, Eglée Aubry household, digital image, *Ancestry.com* (https://www.ancestry.com accessed 1/10/2019), citing NARA microfilm publication M432_235, p. 12B. Date of enumeration: 20 July 1850. Image 24/90.

on 6 August 1853. It consisted of a frontage of "132 feet on the military road leading from Madisonville to Covington" (present day Main Street or State Highway #21). The land had a frame dwelling house on it plus several "outhouses." (outbuildings). The purchase price was $725 of which $525 was paid in cash to the seller, Caroline Stein, "counted down in this office in the presence of the Recorder and witnesses undersigned." Aubry agreed to assume the original $200 mortgage that Caroline Stein had on the property when she bought it from Penn in August of that year and to pay it with 7% interest on 6 August 1854. The Steins were German immigrants and appeared in the United States Federal Census for St. Tammany Parish as William, a thirty-nine-year-old teamster, and Caroline "Stone" with their three children: Henry, Mary and Frederika. Of all the participants in this transaction only Caroline Stein was unable to sign her name:

St. Tammany Parish Courthouse Records (Covington, St. Tammany Parish, LA), *Conveyance Office Book* D-2, p. 28 & 29 "No. 428 Caroline Stein to Eglée Aubry, Sale of Land" filed 15 November 1853.

In the mid-1850s, Eglée Aubry and her Madisonville neighbor Numa Louis Chatellier commenced a feud that lasted several years. The two opponents faced one another in the 8th Judicial District Court on numerous occasions in both civil and criminal litigations. Numa Chatellier and his wife Marie Arsène St. Cyr had been residents of Madisonville since the late 1830s where their first child, Ellen Elizabeth Chatellier was born circa 1838. Numa was enumerated as N.L. Chatellier with his family in St. Tammany Parish in the 1840 United States Federal Census. The household included his wife, two children, a boy and girl as well as three male mulattos under the age of twenty-four years and one male mulatto under the age of ten years. His occupation was listed, unlike his neighbors who were farmers, as "manufacture and trade."[250] It is likely that he was engaged in boat building or in the tar pitch trade which was the major industry in the area at that time. Chatellier's wife, Marie Arsène had been born on 24 May 1817 in the newly formed parish of St. Michael the Archangel at Convent, St. James Parish, LA, to George St. Cyr and Marie Louise Eulalie Grégoire.[251] Numa Chatellier's birth record has not been found but most sources indicate he was born around 1803, some say in South Carolina, others say somewhere in Louisiana. We do know that his brother, Louis Henri Chatellier was born on 13 July 1812 in New Orleans and baptized at St. Louis Cathedral on 18 August 1812 (SLC, B25, 40). What is more significant is that this record shows that his father Louis/Luis Chatellier and mother Josephine Élizabeth Cay were both natives of Môle-Saint-Nicolas, a coastal town in north-west Saint-Domingue. His parents had been early immigrants to the United States who had left Saint-Domingue during the

---

[250] 1840 United States Federal Census, Saint Tammany Parish, LA, N.L. Chattellier (*sic*) household, *Ancestry.com* (https.www. ancestry.com: accessed 2/2/2019), citing NARA Microfilm Publication M704, Roll 129, p. 150, Image 7/32, line 11.

[251] Diocese of Baton Rouge, Department of Archives, *Diocese of Baton Rouge Catholic Church Records 1804-1819, Vol. 3* (Baton Rouge, LA: Catholic Diocese of Baton Rouge, 1982), 770.

slave uprisings and revolution. Many island refugees had fled to the east coast of the United States including to South Carolina, so Numa's birth in that state was a possibility.[252] The family's later arrival in New Orleans was not an uncommon occurrence either, as many refugees attempted to find a place which would replicate the climate, the social structure and the language which they had left behind on Saint-Domingue. Louisiana fit the bill perfectly for them. Numa's father, Louis Chatellier died at the age of thirty-eight years in New Orleans and was interred on 27 November 1812 (SLC, F7, 216).

The Madisonville issue of the *St. Tammany Historical Society Gazette* reported the following concerning the Chatellier family: "In an oath taken after the Civil War, Numa Chatellier stated that he had come to the state and the parish in 1844. Including Numa's father, six generations of Chatelliers have engaged in ship building, mainly in the Madisonville area. Numa Chatellier had a large family of thirteen children. [...] The Chatellier home was built on the Madisonville side of Bayou Dezert [now Bayou De Zaire] near the present-day Madisonville school."[253] Eglée Aubry was his neighbor.

The Chatellier and Aubry feud began when Eglée Aubry went to the Justice Court 6th Ward on 16 April 1855 to allege that N.L. Chatellier "did on Saturday 14th April 1855 in a wanton and malicious manner kill her dog by shooting him in her yard, on her premises contrary to law." The presiding Justice of the Peace, George M. Gilbert, issued an order that same day to have Chatellier brought in to answer the complaint.[254] Chatellier was arrested on 18 April 1855 and ushered into court by Constable E.B. Shahan. On that same day, Chatellier as principal, and George H. Penn as security, posted a bond of $100 to secure the former's appearance before the Grand Jury for the 8th Judicial District, Parish of St. Tammany which was to be convened on 4 June 1855:

Complaint signed by Eglée Aubry at the Justice Court, 6th Ward, against Numa Chatellier for killing her dog.

---

[252] One on-line genealogy indicates that Numa was born on 4 July 1803 at Charleston, Charleston Co., SC.

[253] Martha Lacy Hall, ed., *The St. Tammany Historical Society Gazette Madisonville Issue*, Vol. 4, March 1980 (Mandeville, LA: The St. Tammany Historical Society, Inc.), 40.

[254] St. Tammany Parish Courthouse Records (Covington, St. Tammany Parish, LA), Justice Court 6th Ward – Case #146, "The State vs. N.L. Chatellier," filed 16 April 1855.

In retaliation against the charge of killing her dog, Numa Chatellier accused Eglée Aubry of having inflicted cruel punishment on her slave, Eliza, on 1 November 1854. On 4 June 1855, at a session of the 8th Judicial District Court of Louisiana, Parish of St. Tammany, a Grand Jury was convened to hear the charges against Aubry as well as the testimony of two witnesses: Numa Chatellier and Lewis Brewer, a free man of color. A true bill was handed down by George W. Gilbert, foreman of the jury, on 7 June 1855, indicting Eglée Aubry for the crime of mistreating her slave:

THE STATE OF LOUISIANA :
Parish of St. Tammany.

At a Session of the EIGHTH JUDICIAL DISTRICT COURT of the State of Louisiana, begun and holden at the Court House, within and for the Parish of St. Tammany, on Monday the *fourth* day of ~~November~~ *June*, being the first Monday in said month, in the year of our Lord one thousand eight hundred and fifty *five*

The GRAND JURORS of the State of Louisiana, duly empanelled and sworn, in and for the Parish of St. Tammany, in the name and by the authority of the State of Louisiana, upon their oath present, THAT, *Eglé Aubrey. a f.w.c,* late of the Parish of St. Tammany, on the *first* day of *November* in the year of our Lord one thousand eight hundred and fifty-*four* with force and arms, at the Parish aforesaid, and within the jurisdiction of the Court aforesaid, *did wilfully inflict cruel punishment upon her slave Eliza, then and there in her possession; except flogging, striking with a whip, Leather thong, Switch, Small Stick, putting in Irons, or confining said Slave Eliza*

We the Grand Jury of P. St. Jf. do present Eglé Aubrey fw.C. with cruel treatment to her Slave Eliza in fall of ao. 1854

—witnesses—
N. L. Chatellier
Lewis Brewer fm.c

Geo W Gilbert foreman
7th June ao 1855

St. Tammany Parish Courthouse Records (Covington, St. Tammany Parish, LA), *Criminal Suit #109, 8th Judicial Court of Louisiana*, "The State of Louisiana vs. Eglé Aubry," filed 4 & 7 June 1855.

That same Grand Jury, on the same day heard testimony against Numa Chatellier for having killed Eglée Aubry's dog. The Grand Jury Foreman, George M. Gilbert announced a true bill and Numa Chatellier was indicted for the crime of killing a dog.

St. Tammany Parish Courthouse Records (Covington, St. Tammany Parish, LA), *Criminal Suit #80, 8th Judicial Court of Louisiana*, "The State of Louisiana vs. Numa L. Chatellier," filed 4 June 1855.

On 8 June 1855, Numa Chatellier as principal and George H. Penn as security, posted a bond of $100 guaranteeing the former's appearance in court to answer to the indictment against him for killing Eglée Aubry's dog. He also asked at that time for a jury trial. On that same date, witnesses against Chatellier were ordered to court to testify including Simon Rodriguez, Mrs. Boisseau and Eglée Aubry herself. The case was not heard again until 10 November 1856 when Simon Rodriguez was called to appear. The case was postponed again until in early June 1857 when more witnesses were called to testify including Casimir Baham, Simon Rodriguez, R.M. Cortes, T. Wappler, Michael Hass, Adolphe Gallatas, T.B. Harper, James Crattack, L.M. Carpenter, John Grayson, John Crosby and Drosin Burns. We could find no conclusion to the criminal case of the State vs. Numa Chatellier, however, on 12 June 1855, Eglée Aubry had also filed a civil suit against Numa L. Chatellier for having maliciously and illegally entered into the courtyard of her property and did much damage to it, and also killed a very valuable watch dog belonging to her. She asked for a judgment of $500. The complaint was drawn up in both English and French:

St. Tammany Parish Courthouse Records (Covington, St. Tammany Parish, LA), *Civil Suit #444, 8th Judicial Court of Louisiana*, "Aglaé Aubry vs. N.L. Chattellier," filed 12 June 1855.

The civil suit naming Chatellier as having killed her dog was apparently not heard until 1857 when a verdict was rendered on June 13th, wherein the defendant Numa Chatellier confessed and Eglée Aubry was awarded five cents in damages along with court costs. Since Eglée Aubry had asked that a witness, Simon Rodriguez, be produced to testify as to Chatellier's actions, the latter was not only liable for the five cents in damages, but also for Simon's thirty-three-day stint as her witness at $1 per day plus $2.80 in travel expenses, for a total of $35.80.

On 10 January 1856 an order was issued by the court for Eglée Aubry to be arrested for inflicting cruel punishment on her slave Eliza. Aubry was released after posting a bond of $500 to guarantee her appearance at trial on the indictment. The order was received on 16 January 1856 and executed on 20 February 1856. Upon her arrest, she gave the bond as principal with Simon Rodriguez as security as required by law, guaranteeing that she would appear to answer the charge against her. The document was signed by Lewis L. Morgan, the Sheriff at Covington, St. Tammany Parish, on 28 February 1856:

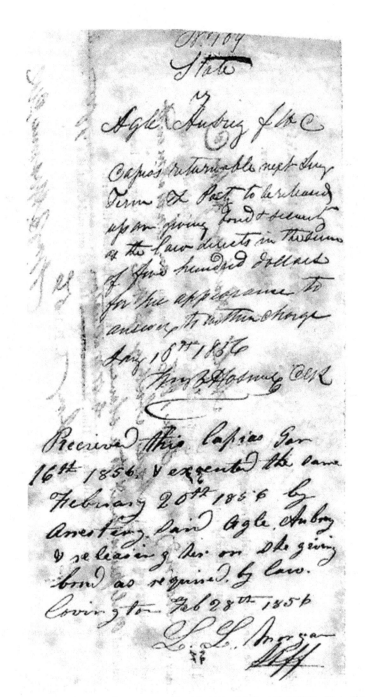

St. Tammany Parish Courthouse Records (Covington, St. Tammany Parish, LA), *Criminal Suit #109, 8th Judicial Court of Louisiana,* "The State of Louisiana vs. Aglé [*sic*] Aubry," filed 7 June 1855 and 28 Feb 1856.

The civil suit concerning the dog was not the only one settled on 13 June 1857. On 28 November 1856, Eglée Aubry had filed another charge against Numa Chatellier, this one for slander in the 8th Judicial District Court, Parish of St. Tammany. She alleged that in April 1855, Chatellier had accused her publicly of a capital crime, that of poisoning and killing his child. She asked for a judgment of $1,000 against him for slander as well as all court costs. Chatellier was served in person at Madisonville on the following day and through his lawyer, Penn Martin, denied the charges and demanded a trial by jury. Simon Rodriguez was, once again, a witness for the plaintiff, Eglée Aubry, and received one dollar per day for ten days as a witness in the case as well as seventy cents in mileage for travelling fourteen miles at six cents per mile for a total of $10.70. On 13 June 1857, before Judge Julius E. Wilson, the defendant confessed in open court to the slander. Eglée Aubry was awarded five cents in damages as well as court costs. Copies of the charges brought as well as the decision by the Judge may be seen on the next two pages.

Louisiana
8th Judicial District
Parish of St Tammany

To the Honble the Judge of the 8th Judicial District for the
Parish of St Tammany

The petition of Eglee Aubry, f.w.c. of the said
Parish, respectfully shews

That Numa Chatelain, of said Parish, on or about the ___ day of April 1855
in said Parish publicly defamed your petr. by declaring that your petr. had poisoned
& killed his child, — which accusation of a capital crime, is very malicious,
& untrue — to the damage of your petr. one thousand dollars —

Wherefore your petr. prays that said Numa Chatellier
may be cited & condemned to pay your petr. one thousand dollars in damages for his false & malicious
accusation aforesaid — with costs — General relief

Alfred Hennen
atty for petr.

Louisiane
8e Dist.
Paroisse St Tammany

A l'Honble Juge de la cour de District — 8me District, pour la
Paroisse St Tammany —

La petition d'Eglee Aubry, f.d.c.l. — de la dite
Paroisse — vous represente, avec respect —

Que Numa Chatellier de la dite Paroisse, a faussement & maliciausement
accusé votre petr. d'avoir empoisonné son enfant — au dommage de votre petr.
au montant de mille piastres —

C'est pourquoi votre petr. prie que le dit
Numa Chatellier soit cité & condemné de payer a votre petr. la dite somme de
$1000 — pour dommages — comme pour la dite fausse & malicieuse accusation —
avec frais — C'est justice

Alfred Hennen
avocat de petr.

[..]

This case having been called and the defendants appearing in open court, confessed judgement for the amount of five cents and as the written confession of the defendant and the plaintiff also being in open court and consenting. The law and confession of the defendant written and orally in open court. It is therefore adjudged and decreed that Egle Aubry do have and recover judgement of N L Chattelier for the sum of five cents damages and cost of suit.

June 13, 1857

Julius E Nilson
Judge of the Eighth Judicial
District of Louisiana

St. Tammany Parish Courthouse Records (Covington, St. Tammany Parish, LA), *Civil Suit #550, 8th Judicial Court of Louisiana*, "Aglae Aubry vs. Numa Chattelier," filed 28 November 1856, decided 13 June 1857.

It is a pity that there are no transcripts of all these legal proceedings which went on for over two years as they might have been quite instructive in being able to paint a more accurate portrait of the parties involved. We may conclude, however, that Eglée Aubry was not to be trifled with and was imminently capable of defending her honor and her property. In the nineteenth century, suits for slander were a very serious charge and much more common than they are today. As for the criminal case against Eglée Aubry for having inflicted cruel punishment on her slave Eliza, there seems to be no longer any records of a verdict in the case.

Perhaps all the conflicts with her neighbor were the impetus for Eglée Aubry to extend her land holdings in areas of St. Tammany Parish other than Madisonville. In the midst of all the legal turmoil on 17 September 1856 she purchased from Mr. Joseph Hartman forty acres with the buildings and improvements thereon as well as one sorrel horse about seven or eight years old for $360, being $300 for the land and $60 for the horse. She paid cash in hand to Hartman in the presence of the recorder, John J. Mortee, and witnesses Jesse Jones and John Crawford. Hartman's wife, Epsy Pendarvis, gave her permission for the sale. The legal description for the land was as follows: "the southwest corner of Section #31, Township #6 south of Range #12 East" [St. Tammany Parish, LA, St. Helena Meridian]. After converting this legal description to latitude and longitude (http://legallandconverter.com) we found that those forty acres were situated north of Main Street in Abita Springs, west of LA Highway 435 (Talisheek Hwy) and east of LA Highway 59. The area today is still farmland located on or near the Abita River:

St. Tammany Parish Courthouse Records (Covington, St. Tammany Parish, LA), *John J. Mortee Papers #653*, "Joseph Hartman to Eglé Aubry," filed 17 September 1856.

Although the sellers, Joseph and Epsy Hartman were unable to sign their names, "Mistress Eglé Aubry, a free woman of color" as she was characterized in the sale, as well as the recorder and witnesses all signed the document:

St. Tammany Parish Courthouse Records (Covington, St. Tammany Parish, LA), *John J. Mortee Papers #653*, "Joseph Hartman to Eglé Aubry," filed 17 September 1856.

Ten months later, on 1 September 1857 Eglé Aubry went to the St. Tammany Parish Courthouse to register her brand. The document was signed by John J. Mortee, the Parish Recorder:

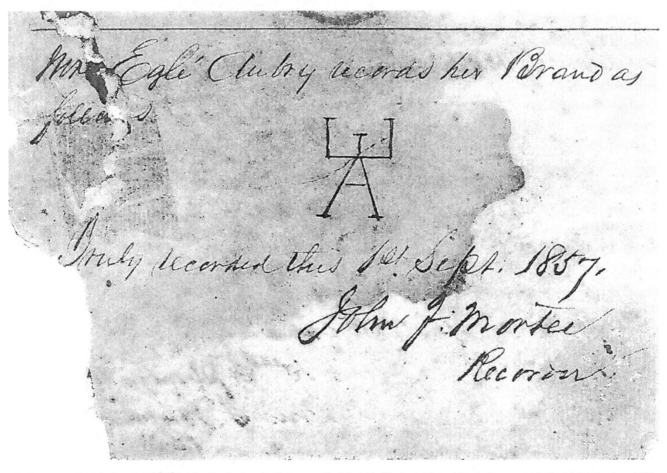

St. Tammany Parish Courthouse Records (Covington, St. Tammany Parish, LA), *Mark and Brand Book A*, page 215, filed 1 September 1857.

Eglée Aubry quadrupled her land holdings north of Abita Springs the following year when she purchased an 1812 Military Land Grant #43883, awarded originally to the widow of James B. Corkern on 16 March 1855. Corkern had served under Captains Thomas and William Bickham's Louisiana Militia from Washington Parish in 1814. The War of 1812 Roster from the National Park Service shows that Bickham's men were part of the 2nd Division, 12th and 13th Regiments Consolidated of Louisiana Militia, Florida Parishes, Section E of Amite River, 1814-1815. James Corkern was listed erroneously as "James Corker."[255] Phereba Magee had married James B. Corkern in Amite Co., MS Territory, on 12 May 1808. Corkern died on 11 April 1838. Once the Military Bounty Land Act of March 3, 1855 had passed, Phereba Magee Corkern had applied for and was granted 166.92 acres in St. Tammany Parish north of Abita Springs. She sold it to Eglée Aubry on 8 June 1858:

---

[255] Thomas Harrison, compiler, *National Park Service, War of 1812, Troop Roster, Second Division, 12th & 13th Consolidated Regiments*), 171, 172.

Military Bounty Land Act of March 3, 1855.

REGISTER'S OFFICE,

Greensburg La June 8th 1858.

MILITARY LAND WARRANT No. *43,833* in the name of *Phereba*

Corkern — — — — has this day been located by *Eglé Aubry*
upon the *South half and North West Quarter*
of *South East Quarter and South East Quarter of South West*
quarter of Section *Thirty one* in Township *Six South*
of Range *Twelve East* subject to any pre-emption
claim which may be filed for said land within forty days from this date.

Contents of tract located,
166 92/100 Acres.

W R

St. Tammany Parish Courthouse Records (Covington, St. Tammany Parish, LA), Papers attached to *Mortgage Office Book "B"*, page 562, and *John J. Mortee Papers #812*, "Mrs. Eglé Aubry to Mrs. Sarah E. Boyd, filed 27 August 1859.

There was an error in the accounting for the amount of land described in the Military Land Grant, originally said to be for 160 acres instead of 166.92 acres, which explains why Eglée Aubry had bought an additional 6.92 acres of land from Phereba Corkern for $8.65 two days later:

MILITARY BOUNTY LAND ACT OF MARCH 3, 1855.

No. *3057* Receiver's Office at *Greensburg La June 10th 1858*

RECEIVED from *Mr Eglé Aubry*
of *St Tammany Parish* County *Louisiana* the sum of
Eight dollars and *Sixty five* cents; being in full for
Six acres and *Ninety two* hundredths, of
the South half and North West Quarter of the South
East Quarter and the South East Quarter of the
South West Quarter of Section No. *Thirty one* Township
No. *Six S.*, of Range No. *Twelve E.*, being excess in said tract over the area located
in virtue of Military Land Warrant No. *43833* in favor of
Phereba Corkern widow of James B Corkern

J. B. McClendon Receiver.

$8.65

St. Tammany Parish Courthouse Records (Covington, St. Tammany Parish, LA), Papers attached to *Mortgage Office Book "B"*, page 562, and *John J. Mortee Papers #812*, "Mrs. Eglé Aubry to Mrs. Sarah E. Boyd, filed 27 August 1859.

The Military Land Grant document signed by President James Buchanan in 1860 showed that the grant was for 160 acres although below in the same document it stated the warrant was for 166.92 acres. A copy of the sale of the Military Warrant sold to Eglée Aubry from the United States Department of the Interior, Bureau of Land Management which includes a map of the location of the property showed that the grant was for 166.92 acres. The issue date for both documents was 10 May 1860. That is the date that the official sale document was signed by President James Buchanan although, by then, the widow Corkern had already sold her land to Eglée Aubry. Below are copies of both the official document signed by President James Buchanan in 1860 and the Bureau of Land Management record of the Military Warrant #43833:

THE UNITED STATES OF AMERICA,

To all to whom these Presents shall come, Greeting:

WHEREAS, In pursuance of the Act of Congress, approved March 3, 1855, entitled "An Act in addition to certain Acts granting Bounty Land to certain Officers and Soldiers who have been engaged in the military service of the United States," there has been deposited in the GENERAL LAND OFFICE, Warrant No. *43,833* for *160* acres, in favor of *Phereba Corkern, widow of James B. Corkern, Private, Captain Beckham's company, Louisiana, Militia, War 1812*

with evidence that the same has been duly located upon *the South half of the South East Quarter, and the North West Quarter of the South-East Quarter, and the South-East Quarter of the South-West Quarter, of Section Thirty-one, in Township Six, South, of Range Twelve, East; in the District of lands subject to sale at Greensburg, Louisiana, Containing One hundred and Sixty-six Acres, and Ninety-two hundredths of an acre,* according to the Official Plat of the Survey of said Lands returned to the GENERAL LAND OFFICE by the SURVEYOR GENERAL *The said Warrant having been assigned by the said Phereba Corkern to Egle Aubry, in whose favor said Tract has been located.*

NOW KNOW YE, That there is therefore granted by the UNITED STATES unto the said *Egle Aubry, as assignee as aforesaid, and to his heirs*

the tract of Land above described: TO HAVE AND TO HOLD the said tract of Land, with the appurtenances thereof, unto the said *Egle Aubry, as assignee as aforesaid, and to his*

heirs and assigns forever.

In testimony whereof, I, *James Buchanan* PRESIDENT OF THE UNITED STATES OF AMERICA, have caused these Letters to be made Patent, and the SEAL OF THE GENERAL LAND OFFICE to be hereunto affixed.

GIVEN under my hand, at the CITY OF WASHINGTON, the *Tenth* day of *May* in the year of our Lord one thousand eight hundred and *Sixty*, and of the INDEPENDENCE OF THE UNITED STATES the *Eighty-fourth.*

BY THE PRESIDENT: *James Buchanan*

By *J.M.B. Leonard* Sec'y.

J. M. Granger Recorder of the General Land Office.

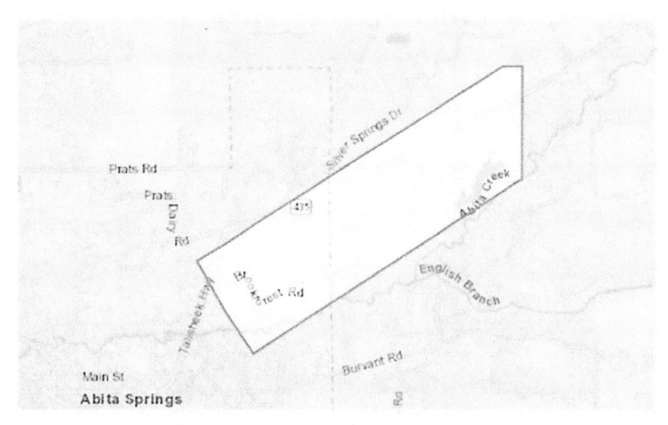

Location of 1812 Military Land Grant sold by Corkern to Eglée Aubry. U.S. Department of the Interior. Bureau of Land Management, *Military Warrant #43833*, available at https://glorecords.blm.gov/default.aspx.

The government paperwork was, however, late in coming, because by 1860 Eglée Aubry had already flipped the property. On 27 August 1859 she sold both the adjacent forty acres that she had bought from Joseph Hartman in 1856 as well as the 166.92 acre Military Land Grant that she had purchased from Phereba Corkern in 1858, to Mrs. Sarah E. Jones, wife separate in property of Mr. Jacob Boyd, her husband, for $1200, of which $400 was paid in cash and the rest mortgaged payable to the vendor in two installments of $400 plus 6% interest at one and two years after the date of purchase.[256]

Although Eglée Aubry had quickly liquidated her holdings in Abita Springs, she held on to her property in Madisonville and Mandeville. Perhaps she had originally thought that by purchasing property near Abita Springs that she would ensure her first-born son's future as a farmer in the area. Born Michel Chapella (*sic*), but always known as René Achille or R.A. Chiapella, at age twenty-two in 1859, he had determined to marry a young woman whose roots in eastern St. Tammany Parish went back several generations.

---

[256] St. Tammany Parish Courthouse Records (Covington, St. Tammany Parish, LA), Papers attached to *Mortgage Office Book "B"*, page 562, and *John J. Mortee Papers #812*, "Mrs. Eglé Aubry to Mrs. Sarah E. Boyd, filed 27 August 1859.

CHAPTER 13

THE AUBRY, CHIAPELLA, WATKINSON AND LEFLOT CONNECTIONS

On 24 November 1859, Michel Achille Chiapella, Jr. as principal and Charles Watkinson as security, both residents in the parish of St. Tammany signed a $100 marriage bond before J.H. Ruddock, clerk, at which time Chiapella was given a license to marry Watkinson's daughter, Marie Orelia:

The State of Louisiana, Parish of St. Tammany.

KNOW ALL MEN BY THESE PRESENTS, THAT WE *Michel Achille Chiapella Jr.* as principal, and *Charles Watkinson* as security, both of the Parish and State aforesaid, acknowledge ourselves held and firmly bound unto *Robert C Wickliffe* Governor of the State of Louisiana, and to his successors in office, in the just and full sum of *One hundred* dollars, for the payment of which well and truly to be made, we bind ourselves, our heirs, executors and administrators, jointly and severally, firmly by these presents, this *24th* day of *November* A. D. 185*9*.

The condition of the above obligation is such, that whereas the above bound *Michel Achille Chiapella Jr.* has this day applied for license to marry *Orelia Watkinson* Now, therefore, if there shall exist no legal impediment or objection to the consummation of said marriage, then and in that case the above obligation to be null and void, else to remain in full force and virtue in law.

Executed before me, this *24"* day of *November* A. D. 185*9*.

J. H Ruddock CLERK.

A. Chiapella Jr

C. F. Watkinson

St. Tammany Parish Courthouse Records (Covington, St. Tammany Parish, LA), Marriage Bond filed 24 November 1859.

Eglée Aubry, a fifty-five-year-old woman owning $3,000 in real estate and $1,000 in personal property, her daughter, "Odile Louner," (Odalie Lorreins), age 37, José Villas, Odalie's companion, age 44, a ship's carpenter from Spain, Eglée's sons, Achille, a clerk, age 23, Émile, age 21, an apprentice shoemaker, Octave, age 20, a cigar maker, and daughter-in-law "Orellia," age 23, Achille's wife, were enumerated in the 1860 United States Federal Census for New Orleans, Ward 5. All were said to be "mulatto."[257]

R.A. Chiapella's wife, Marie Orellia Watkinson was born ca. January 1837 in St. Tammany Parish to Charles Watkinson, a native of Great Britain who worked in the area as a sailor and Félicie Flot/LeFlot, a free woman of color, born in the parish to Étienne François LeFlot and Melanie Marie Simon, both free people of color, who had been married at St. Louis Cathedral on 7 December 1816 by the Reverend Antonio de Sedella. The groom's given names were listed in Spanish as Esteban Francisco, with his surname, LeFlot, omitted in the marriage record. He was said to be a "free mulatto" and native of New Orleans, the natural son of Félicité Lorence [*sic*, Lorreins], a free woman of color. Esteban Francisco, or Étienne François LeFlore/LeFlot was, however, according to other information, born in or near Pass Christian, Spanish Territory, West Florida (now Mississippi) in about 1792. The bride, Melania Simon was a "free mulata," a native of New Orleans, the daughter of Luis Simon and Marie/Maneta Leman. The couple also legitimized their first child, a son named Esteban/Étienne, who had been born on 12 December 1813:

---

[257] 1860 United States Federal Census, Ward 5, New Orleans, Orleans Parish, LA, Dwelling #1466, Family #1414, Eglie Aubry household, digital image, *Ancestry.com* (https://www.ancestry.com: accessed 2 October 2019), citing NARA microfilm publication M653_418, p. 780. Image 231/393 Date of enumeration: 1 July 1860.

Archdiocese of New Orleans, *St. Louis Cathedral, New Orleans Marriages of Slaves and Free People of Color Vol. 1, Part 1: 1777-1821*, page 52b, Act. #210.

Étienne LeFlot and Melanie Marie Simon were the parents of fourteen children born between 1813 and 1843. Felicité, the wife of Charles Watkinson, the couple's second child, was born Félicité Simon to Esteban Francisco (last name omitted) and Maria Simon, both natives and residents of New Orleans, on 8 September 1817 and baptized at St. Louis Cathedral on 19 February 1818. Her godfather was Louis Simon, her maternal grandfather. Her godmother was Margarita Francisca [last name omitted], (SLC, B29, 199) See also p. 155.

There is not much known about Charles Watkinson. Marie Orelia's father. He was born about 1800 in England and was first enumerated in Louisiana in the 1830 United States Federal Census for St. Tammany Parish, where he was living alone as a free white male between the ages of 23 and 29 years. Although the 1830 census did not indicate in which town he was living, his neighbors included Voltaire, Pierre, Lazare, Peter and Seymour Baham all of whom we know lived in or near Madisonville. Another relatively close neighbor of his was Félicité Lorreins, a free woman of color, Félicité Flot's grandmother, living with one free "colored" girl under ten years of age, and another free woman of color between the ages of 24 and 36. We have already seen, on p. 8, Note 14, that in the 1810 Federal Census for the Territory of Orleans, Félicité Lorreins had been enumerated living on Bourbon Street in New Orleans. Both Marguerite Cécile Aubry, Eglée Aubry's mother, and Eglée's sister, Félicité Aubry were also living on Bourbon Street and most certainly knew Félicité Lorreins, who was Orelia Watkinson's great-grandmother.

Félicité Lorreins left a very small footprint in St. Tammany Parish. The only other record we could find for her at the Parish Courthouse was the registration of her livestock brand which was done on 21 July 1827 a copy of which is below:

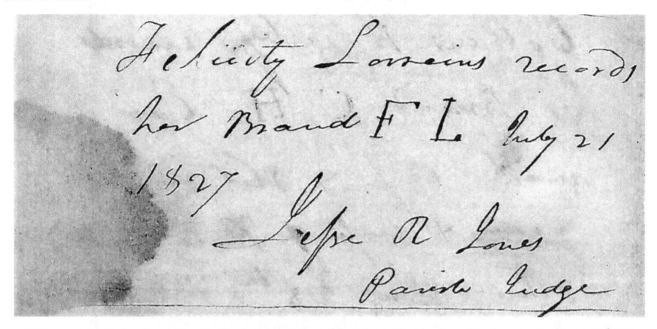

St. Tammany Parish Courthouse Records (Covington, St. Tammany Parish, LA), *Mark and Brand Book A*, page 37, filed 21 July 1827.

The Flot or LeFlot family of free persons of color who lived in St. Tammany Parish had settled in and around Abita Springs, St. Tammany Parish, east of the towns of Madisonville and Covington and north of Mandeville in the early nineteenth century. Their immigrant ancestor who came to Mobile, French Louisiana, was Jean-Baptiste LeFlot, who was said to have been born on 3 November 1710. In his 19 June 1735 marriage record to his first wife, Jeanne Boissinot, done at Mobile, Louisiana Territory (now Alabama), he indicated that his parents were Jacques LeFlot and Magdeleine Richet from Versailles, parish of Ste. Croix, Yvelines, France.[258] The only parish of Ste. Croix in the area was located in Mantes-la-Jolie, Yvelines, France, which is north and west of Versailles. There were no LeFlots listed in the parish registers from that commune. A thorough search of available records from Versailles, a town, southwest of Paris, the French Capital, did not uncover anyone with the surname LeFlot living there either. We did, however, locate his parents' marriage record in the commune of Rochefort-en-Yvelines, Yvelines, France, further south and west in the Yvelines Department, which uncovered some important details concerning their lives. First, it must be noted that, at that time, and in many places, their surname was spelled "LeFlocq." Records of that age are usually difficult to read, including the Rochefort marriage document dated 11 January 1698, for Jean-Baptiste LeFlot's parents, which is very faded. There exists, however, a certificate issued by Fr. Pierre Rober(t) Lambet, of the parish of St. Pierre, affirming that three bans had been read at Longvilliers, the groom's hometown, prior to the wedding, which took place in the bride's hometown, the neighboring commune of Rochefort-en-Yvelines. The groom, Jacques LeFlocq was the son of the late René LeFlocq, "receveur de la terre et seigneurie" (a well-to-do farmer who leased lands and the buildings thereupon back to the lord of the place in exchange for all the income with the exception of the amount of the lease) and his wife, Anne Garrochau/Garrochot, natives of Longvilliers. The bride, Magdeleine Richet/Richer, was the daughter of Michel Richet, a seller of hats, and his wife, Louise Boudin, both from Rochefort. Father Lambet found no opposition or impediment to the marriage and signed the certificate verifying the bans:

---

[258] Jacqueline Olivier Vidrine, *Love's Legacy*, 92, 93.

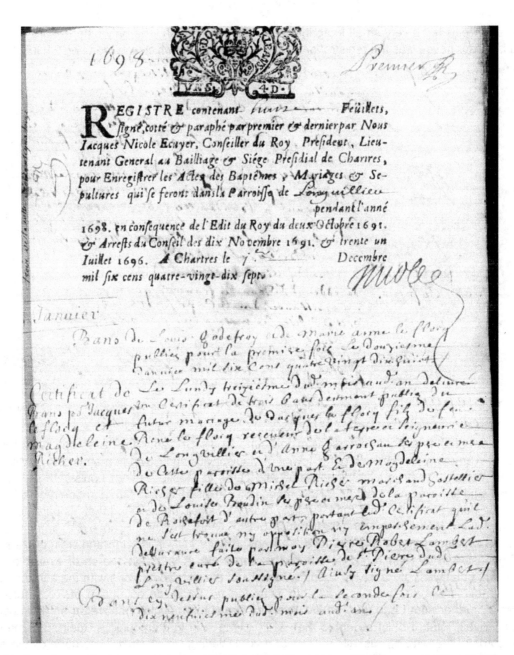

Longvilliers, Yvelines, France, Registres paroissiaux et d'état civil, B.M.S. [Parochial and Civil Records. Baptism, Marriages and Burials], 1696-1729, Bans January 1698, Jacques LeFlocq to Magdeleine Richet, digital image, *Archives départementales de Yvelines*, "État Civil en ligne," (http://archives.yvelines.fr/: accessed 4 November 2019), Cote 1133061 Image 20/231.

We could neither verify the date nor the location of Jean-Baptiste Leflocq's birth. We searched the Versailles, Yvelines, France, records between 1708-1712 and found no LeFlocq names there. While there were Leflocq records both at Longvilliers and at Rochefort-en-Yvelines, there was no record for any Jean-Baptiste between 1700 and 1715. We do know, however, that the couple was living in Longvilliers as late as 2 May 1708 where they buried their two-year-old son Jacques.[259]

The Mobile, AL, marriage document of Jean-Baptiste Leflot and Jeanne Boissinot had also revealed that the groom was a soldier in the Company commanded by Charles, Chevalier de Bombelles. Commissioned as a Captain in the French Army in Louisiana in 1732 after having served in Poland, the Chevalier de Bombelles appeared in Mobile ecclesiastical records at his marriage to Barbe Ursule de Bonnille on 26 January 1735 as

---

[259] Longvilliers, Yvelines, France, Registres paroissiaux et d'état civil, B.M.S. [Parochial and Civil Records. Baptism, Marriages and Deaths], 1696-1729, Baptisms, Marriages and Deaths, 1708, Jacques LeFlocq, digital image, *Archives départementales de Yvelines*, "État Civil en ligne," (http://archives.yvelines.fr/: accessed 11/4/2019), Cote 1133061 Image 96/231.

"captain of a detached company of the Marine, born at Marseilles, son of Messire Charles de Bombelles, deceased major general and inspector of the galleys [prison ships], and of Dame Renée de ---hambeau."[260] It may be concluded, therefore that Leflot had arrived in Mobile as a part of Bombelles Company. After the death of his first wife in 1752, Leflot had married Marie Jeanne Girard, daughter of Jean Girard and Marianne Dagneau ca. 1753. The parents of eight children, their third, Jean François Leflot, was baptized on 17 October 1756 at Mobile.

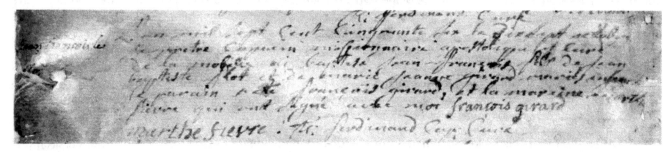

"In the year 1756, the 17th of October, I Capucin priest Curé of Mobile, have baptized Jean François, son of Jean Baptiste Flot and Marie Jeanne Girard, married. Godparents were François Girard and Marthe Fievre who signed with me. Fr. Ferdinand" Courtesy of the Archdiocese of Mobile Archives.

Forty-three-year-old Jean François died at Mobile on 6 April 1799:

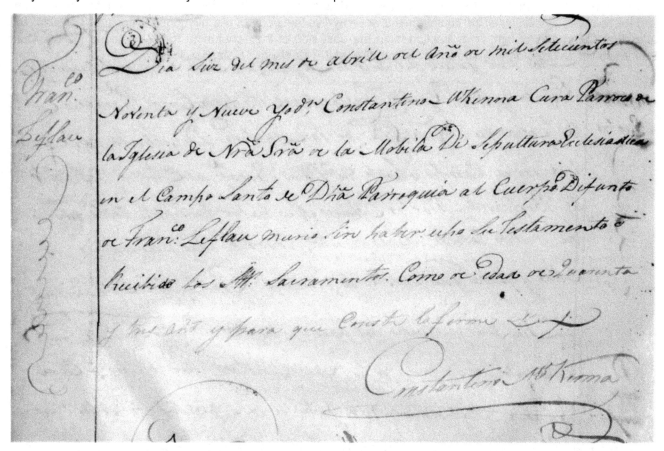

"On 6 April 1799, I, the undersigned pastor of Our Lady of Mobile, gave ecclesiastical burial in the parish cemetery to the body of the deceased Francisco Leflau, who died without making his will or receiving the sacraments at 43 years. In faith whereof I sign it. Father Constantine McKenna." Courtesy of the Archdiocese of Mobile Archives.

---

[260] Jacqueline Olivier Vidrine, *Love's Legacy*, 82893. Note: de Bombelles wife was Renée de Vimeur de Rochambeau according to their 5 January 1685 marriage at the Church of St. Eustache, Paris, France. (See: https://gw.geneanet.org/deret?n= de+bombelles&oc=&p=charles).

Although never married, Jean François Leflot had had two children with Félicité Lorreins, a free woman of color: Étienne François (Stephen) LeFlot born about 1792 and Adelaide LeFlot born two years later.

We have no direct evidence to prove which of the male members of the Lorreins family was Félicité's father, although we suspect that it may have been Jacques Lorreins dit Tarascon (b. 1734). Of the two sons of Jacques Lorreins dit Tarascon (b. 1700), and his wife Marie Avril de Tourigny, only Jacques had fathered any children. Pierre Charles, his elder brother, had had two wives and no issue. Three generations later, Orelia Watkinson, Félicité Lorreins' great-granddaughter, would marry Eglée Aubry's son, René Achille Chiapella. We know (See Chapter 2, p. 15) that before her relationship with Achille Chiapella, Eglée Aubry had had children with Louis Hilaire Lorreins, whose grandfather was Jacques Lorreins dit Tarascon, born in Mobile, French Louisiana ca. 1734, who had died in New Orleans in 1784. Without any concrete evidence so far, all we can say is that Jacques Lorreins dit Tarascon might have been Félicité Lorreins' father. It is clear, however, that the connection between the Lorreins and Aubry families had been ongoing for several generations.

After Jean François Leflot's death in 1799 at Mobile, we know that Félicité Lorreins and her children had moved from the Gulf Coast to New Orleans where she was enumerated in the 1810 Territorial Census living on Bourbon street near Felicité and Marguerite Cécile Aubry. After her son Etienne François Leflot's marriage to Melanie Marie Simon in 1816, the bride and groom moved to St. Tammany Parish to start a family and acquired property from Jacques Lorreins dit Tarascon's son, Jacques Baptiste Lorreins, (Louis Hilaire Lorreins's father) on 13 February 1817 for the sum of $150. It was described as bounded by the river "Chefoncte", containing a swamp and a small bayou including all the improvements seventy-five feet north of the "old house of Jacques Lorreins" with a total of 3.5 arpents of land. This location is on the east side of the Tchefuncte River located in the Del Oaks Subdivision in an area formerly known as Houltonville, at the Madisonville-Mandeville border.[261]

St. Tammany Parish Courthouse Records (Covington, St. Tammany Parish, LA), *Conveyance Office Book* A-1, p. 189-190, "Jacques Lorreins #329 Conveyance to Étienne Flou," dated 13 February 1817 and filed 15 February, 1817.

[261] St. Tammany Parish Courthouse Records (Covington, St. Tammany Parish, LA), *Conveyance Office Book* A-1, p. 189, "Jacques Lorreins to Etienne Flou," filed 15 October, 1817.

Given the business dealings between Etienne Flot and Jacques (Baptiste) Lorreins so soon after the former's arrival in St. Tammany Parish, it is not unreasonable to conclude that Lorreins may have been selling the property to a family member, his father's illegitimate daughter Félicité Lorreins' son.

After the birth of six of his fourteen children, Étienne Flot sold this property on 1 July 1825 to Eugene Marchand of New Orleans for the sum of $180. The conveyance document provides us with two interesting facts about Étienne Leflot and his family connections. First, Étienne was unable to write his name and signed with an "x." Moreover, one of the witnesses to the sale was (Pierre) Albert Lorreins, son of Jacques Baptiste Lorreins, the original owner of the property, who had died ca. 1818 in St. Tammany Parish.[262] Was Albert there to represent the interests of his probable half-aunt Félicité Lorreins' son Étienne?

Étienne Flot moved his family to Abita Springs, St. Tammany Parish, in the mid-1820s where many of the Flots and their descendants have been fixtures ever since. Félicie Flot, mother of Marie Orelia Watkinson was born on 8 September 1817. She was baptized on 19 February 1818 at St. Louis Cathedral as Félicité Simon, a legitimate "free mulata" born to Esteban Francisco (Étienne François) and Maria Simon both natives and residents of New Orleans:

Certificate of Baptism

ARCHDIOCESE OF NEW ORLEANS ARCHIVES

7887 Walmsley Ave.
New Orleans, Louisiana 70125

This is to Certify

That _FELICITÉ SIMON_ { legitimate free mulata
Child of _ESTEBAN FRANCISCO (omitted)_ } natives/residents
and _MARIA SIMON_ } of this city.
Born on the _8th of September 1817_
at _(not stated)_
Baptized on the _19th of February 1818_
at _the ST. LOUIS CATHEDRAL_
According to the Rite of the Roman Catholic Church
by the Rev. _ANTONIO de SEDELLA_
the Sponsors being _LUIS SIMON_
MARGARITA FRANCISCA (omitted)
A true and exact extract from the Baptismal Registers of
ST. LOUIS CATHEDRAL
which are now in the Archives of the Archdiocese of New Orleans
Vol. _Baptism Vol. 15_ Page _199_ Act No. _1045_
S/PC Part 2: 1817-1818
Certified by _Jack Belsom_
Date _22 March 2011_

Baptismal Certificate of Félicité Simon (aka Félicité Flot) courtesy of Fr. Philip Flott.

---

[262] St. Tammany Parish Courthouse Records (Covington, St. Tammany Parish, LA), *Conveyance Office Book* B-1, p. 64, "Etienne Flou to Eugene Marchand #1261," filed 21 July, 1825.

Félicité Flot and Charles Watkinson had a long life together. Charles Watkinson, listed as Charles Watkins, and Félicité Flot were enumerated in the 1840 United States Federal Census living in the same household with two free females of color under the age of ten years. We know that these were his daughters: Marie Orelia born about January 1837 and Ellen, born about 1839. Felicité Flot was only identified in this census as a free woman of color between the ages of 10 and 23.[263]

On 10 April 1842 Lyman Briggs recorded that Charles Watkinson purchased property from the Union Bank of Louisiana which had been seized from John and Mary Bickham the previous year. It was described as "being situated in the Division of St. John, Town of Covington, Parish of St. Tammany and State of Louisiana containing three and eleven hundredths acres, situated on the west bank of the Bogue Falia River with all the buildings and improvements thereon." Watkinson paid $600 in three installments furnishing three promissory notes for $200 each payable at six twelve and eighteen months from the date of purchase with 7% interest.[264] On 27 December 1844 Charles Watkinson sold the property to "Felicity LeFlour," the mother of his children for $200 cash in hand. In addition to the description in the previous sale between the Union Bank and Charles Watkinson, the property was further described as being "near the bridge on the Columbia Road." The document was signed by C. Watkinson, and witnesses Charles Smith and John D. White. The purchaser Felicity Le Flour marked the document with her "x."[265] Below is a map of the St. John Division Historic district of Covington. Félicité Flot's property was at the foot of Columbia Street on the Bogue Falaya River:

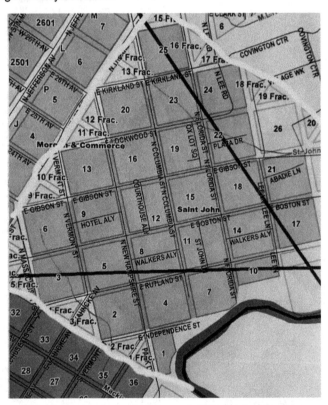

St. John Division, Covington, LA. Bogue Falaya River at Bottom of map. Watkinson property on river at the foot of Columbia Road (now North Columbia St.)
https://tammanyfamily.blogspot.com/2018/05/the-division-of-st-john-becomes.html.

---

[263] 1840 United States Federal Census, St. Tammany, LA, Charles Watkins household, digital image, *Ancestry.com* (https://www.ancestry.com accessed 10/10/2019), citing NARA microfilm publication M704, 580 rolls, p. 162. No date of enumeration. Image 31/32.

[264] St. Tammany Parish Courthouse Records (Covington, St. Tammany Parish, LA), *Conveyance Office Book* G-1, p. 701-702, #3905 Lyman Briggs Papers, "Union Bank of Louisiana to Charles Watkinson" filed 10 April 1842. The original sale of land and mortgage was passed before notary Adolphe Mazureau on 25 March 1842 at New Orleans, Vol. 25, p. 353.

[265] St. Tammany Parish Courthouse Records (Covington, St. Tammany Parish, LA), *Conveyance Office Book* H-1, p. 286, Not numbered. Lyman Briggs Papers, "Charles Watkinson to Felicity Le Flour" filed 30 December 1844.

Charles Watkinson and Félicité Flot were enumerated in the 1850 United States Federal Census as Charles Watkins, age fifty, white, born in England, a sailor with $500 in real estate, Felicity Watkins, age 32, a female "mulatto" from Louisiana who was unable to read or write. Orelia and Ellen Watkins, ages 14 and 11, both female "mulattos," born in Louisiana, and attending school, completed the family.[266] The 1850 Federal Slave Schedule showed that Charles Watkins was the owner of two slaves, probably household help, one female black, age 21 and her daughter, age 2 years.[267]

On 18 April 1855, Félicité "Le Flaut," a free woman of color filed a civil suit against Joseph Hartman in the 8th Judicial District Court, Parish of St. Tammany. She alleged that during the months of January and February 1855, Hartman, a resident of St. Tammany Parish, had illegally carried away large quantities of earth and sand from the street running by her property on which there was a "valuable dwelling house situated on the bank of the river Bogue "Falia" near the bridge which connects the town of Covington with the left bank of said stream." She also stated that because the stream often overflowed its banks near her house, she had made at considerable expense an embankment to protect her property. Hartman's digging and removal of earth and sand from her embankment had undermined it so that it no longer protected her property. She asked for $500 in damages with interest and court costs. Félicité also stated that she had asked Hartman to cease and desist but he continued to remove earth and sand and had also asked him to pay for damages to her property, but he refused. The defendant, Joseph Hartman, answered that he was the overseer of the Road District which terminated at the east end of the Bogue "Falia" Bridge and it was his job to make sure that the road was passible and safe. Since the road leading from the bridge into the Town of Covington had become almost impassable for carriages and other conveyances, he had used earth and sand only within the legal distance, to repair the road from the west end of the bridge into the town of Covington for the common good. Hartman asked that five witnesses on his behalf be called: John Davis, William Bagley, Isaac Bloom, Thomas Lacroix and J.W. Thompson to testify at the June term 1855, of the 8th Judicial District. On 15 November 1856, the attorney for Félicité Flot asked that the case be dismissed at the plaintiff's cost. Following is a copy of the jacket of the original suit along with the judgment written on the side by the order of Judge G.W. Washington:

---

[266] 1850 United States Federal Census, St. Tammany Parish, LA, Dwelling #465, Family #465, Charles Watkins household, digital image, *Ancestry.com* (https://www.ancestry.com accessed 1/11/2019), citing NARA microfilm publication M432_241, p. 275A. Date of enumeration: 21 August 1850. Image 53/98.

[267] 1850 United States Federal Census Slave Schedules, St. Tammany Parish, LA, Charles Watkins, owner, digital image, *Ancestry.com* (https://www.ancestry.com accessed 1/11/2019), citing NARA microfilm publication M432. Date of enumeration: 19 August 1850. Image 19/29.

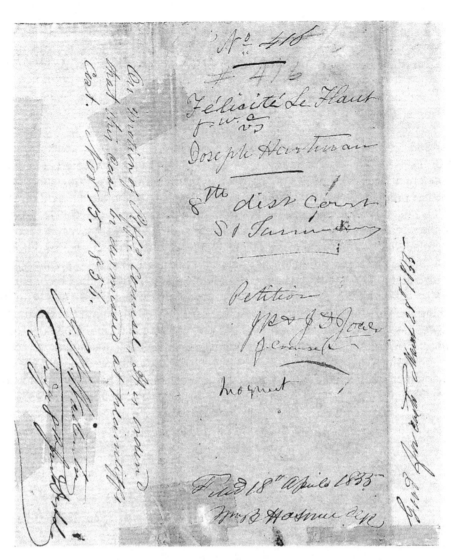

St. Tammany Parish Courthouse Records (Covington, St. Tammany Parish, LA), *Civil Suit #416, 8th Judicial Court of Louisiana*, "Félicité Le Flaut vs. Joseph Hartman" filed 18 April 1855.

Charles Watkinson, enumerated as C. Watkins, a sixty-one-year-old lake captain, and Félicité Flot, enumerated as forty-year-old F. Watkins, were enumerated living together in the 1860 United States Federal Census for St. Tammany Parish, Town of Covington.[268] The accompanying 1860 Federal Slave schedule indicated that C. Watkins was the owner of two slaves, a female African American, age 28, and an African American boy, age 5.[269] Their daughter, Orelia, had already left home to marry René Achille Chiapella, and we believe that Ellen/Elena Watkinson, the couple's other daughter was already deceased.

Félicité Flot bought more property in Covington in her own name on 26 November 1860 from Samuel B. Hall and his wife Theodosia for $200 cash in hand. The land on which there was an old dwelling house and some out buildings was located in Square #27, in the Division of Spring, having a front of 83 feet on each of Hospital and Temperance Streets with a depth of about 240 feet on Monroe Street. This was not far from the house that she

---

[268] 1860 United States Federal Census, St. Tammany Parish, LA, Dwelling #234, Family #234, C. Watkins household, digital image, *Ancestry.com* (https://www.ancestry.com accessed 9/11/2019), citing NARA microfilm publication M653_425, p. 30. Date of enumeration: 23 June 1860. Image 2/25.

[269] 1860 United States Federal Census Slave Schedules, St. Tammany Parish, LA, C. Watkins, owner, digital image, *Ancestry.com* (https://www.ancestry.com: accessed 9/11/2019), citing NARA microfilm publication M653. Date of enumeration: 22 June 1860. Image 19/29.

shared with Charles Watkinson at the foot of Columbia Street on the Bogue Falaya River.[270] That same year Charles "Watkins" appeared in the following record as "master" of the schooner *Martha Ann:*

> #823 MARTHA ANN schooner of Covington Built on Tchefuncta River 1889 Rebuilt upon the keel 1854. 41 50/ 95 tons, 56 ft 3 in. x 19 ft 6 in x 4 ft 6 1 /2 in. Flush deck, two masts, square stern, plain head. For earlier documentation see Vol III No 707 Enrolled No 72, Apr 7 1854 Owner Jesse R Jones St Tammany Parish. Master Charles Watkinson.[271]

According to an 1893 succession record, Charles Watkinson died in Saint Tammany Parish in August 1868, after which his widow returned to her father Étienne Flot's household in Abita Springs. She was enumerated there in the 1870 Federal Census as Felicia Flot, a fifty-one-year-old female "mulatto" with $300 in real estate and $100 in personal property, living with her ninety-year-old father, Étienne, her mother Mary (Melanie Simon), age 70, brothers Alexander, age 40, Antoine, age 28, Paul, age 26, and sister, Louisa, age 37. Her brothers, Simon and François Flot with their families were living on adjacent properties.

Félicité Flot, wife of Charles Watkinson. Photo courtesy of Father Philip .L. Flott.

---

[270] St. Tammany Parish Courthouse Records (Covington, St. Tammany Parish, LA), *Conveyance Office Book E-2*, p. 625-626, "Samuel B. Hall to Félicité Flaut," filed 14 February 1861.

[271] Survey of Federal Archives, *Ships Registers and Enrollments of New Orleans, Louisiana/ prepared by the Survey of Federal Archives in Louisiana, Division of community services programs, Work projects administration,* Volume 5, 1851-1860, Baton Rouge, LA: Louisiana State University, March 1942. Available at https://catalog.hathitrust.org/Record/000968981, Image 211/406.

Étienne Flot died in St. Tammany Parish on 10 April 1872, and was interred the following day as reported by Rev. P.A. Mandritta, pastor of St. Peter's Church in Covington, LA. Below is a copy of his Certificate of Burial followed by a photo of the family tomb where he was interred in the Flot Family Cemetery located on Oak Street, just north of Abita Springs. Étienne, his wife. Melanie Marie, and three children Flora, Paul and Antoine were all buried there.

Certificate of Burial

ARCHDIOCESE OF NEW ORLEANS
ARCHIVES
7887 Walmsley Ave.
New Orleans, Louisiana 70125

This is to Certify

That ETIENNE FLOT, in his 89th year, departed this life yesterday

and was buried on 11 APRIL 1872
                      date

in (not stated) — Cemetery

A true and exact extract from the Burial Registers of

ST. PETER CHURCH COVINGTON, LA.

REV. P. A. MANDRITTA

which are now in the Archives of the Archdiocese of New Orleans

Place of Birth (not stated) Age 89 yrs

Vol. Bap./Marr./Fun. Page 207 Act No. 1
1863~1922

Certified by Jack Belson

Date 12 October 2010

Courtesy of Father Philip L. Flott.

Photo of Etienne Flot family tomb, Flot Cemetery, Oak Street, Abita Springs, taken by author on 1 November 2019.

After Etienne's wife, Melanie Marie Simon died on 19 May 1885, his surviving children decided to sell a piece of property located north of Abita Springs, which had been bought by their father at a sale of public lands by the United States Government pursuant to an Act of Congress dated 24 April 1820. It consisted of 84.2 acres, divided into lots 3,4, and 5 of section #32 in township #6, south of range 12 east (St. Helena Meridian). The land, as can be seen on the following page, was just north of and adjacent to the present day Flot Cemetery:

Flot land bought from U.S. Government sale of public lands. Flot Cemetery is at the end of Oak Street. Flot land is just beyond that, and south of the Abita River.

The land patent, Certificate #1446, signed by President Ulysses S. Grant, on 20 March 1875 was issued after Étienne's death. On 27 January 1887 his children, including François Flot, Alexander Flot, Antoine Flot, Seymour Flot, Paul Flot, Louisa Flot, Mary Flot, Mary Josephine Flot, all of the parish of St. Tammany, as well as "Mrs. Aurelia Watkins, wife of R.A. Chiapella (daughter of the late Félicité Flot, who died in October 1880), and Mrs. Agnes Charbonnet, wife of Henry Angeletti, (daughter of the deceased Malvina Flot), both residents of New Orleans, all came together to sell the property to William H. Merkel of New Orleans, for the sum of $550, all cash in hand.[272]

Orelia Watkinson Chiapella and her husband did not make their home in St. Tammany Parish, although Achille had lived off and on there as a child with his mother Eglée Aubry. As newlyweds they had been enumerated in New Orleans in the 1860 United States Federal Census with Eglée Aubry, her daughter Odalie Lorreins, and sons Joseph Émile and Stephen Octave Chiapella. René Achille was working as a clerk. If they had ever thought to settle near other Flot family members in St. Tammany Parish, that idea was shelved after the end of the Civil War. On 19 June 1867, René Achille (aka Achille Chiapella, Jr.) transferred his livestock brand to his wife, Orelia Watkinson's uncle, Paul Flot.

This document, passed down through the Flot family, appears to have originally been a letter written in New Orleans by A. Chiapella, Jr., to the St. Tammany Parish Recorder, J.J. Mortee, transferring his brand to Paul Flot. It was returned to Flot with a note at the bottom written by J. J. Mortee affirming that he had transferred the brand from Chiapella to Paul Flot and indicating that he had made the change on page 216 of the St. Tammany Parish *Mark and Brand Book A*. This document led to a search by the St. Tammany Parish Director of Records Management, Robin L. Perkins, for the original Chiapella brand and the cancellation. What she found was that part of page 216, which is the reverse side of page 215 of the *Mark and Brand Book A* was missing. The brands on this page were from 1857, and the one located at the bottom of page 215 was the brand registered by Eglée Aubry a

[272] St. Tammany Parish Courthouse Records (Covington, St. Tammany Parish, LA), *Conveyance Office Book* M p. 39-44, " François Flot, et. al. to Wm. H. Merkel" filed 9 February 1887.

copy of which appears on page 144 of this book. It stands to reason that the brand at the top of the next page (216) would have been that of Aubry's then twenty-year-old son R.A. Chiapella's brand for the livestock kept on his mother's property in St. Tammany Parish. Whether the top of page 216 was lost over time or pilfered cannot now be ascertained. What we do know from the document pictured below, however, is that for a period of ten years from 1857 when the brand was recorded until 1867, Chiapella was the registered owner of a livestock brand in St. Tammany Parish:
:

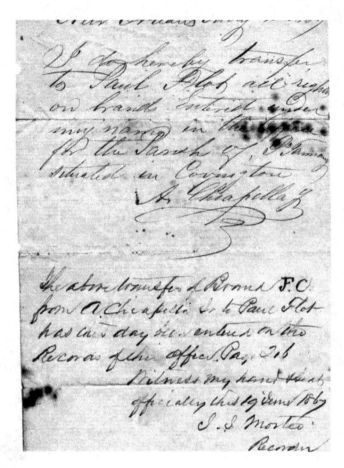

Document courtesy of Father Philip L. Flott, from the collection of the late Melba Flott (1918-2017) granddaughter of Paul Flot (1843-1898).

All of René Achille and Orelia's children were born in New Orleans, starting with their daughter, Félicité Aurelia born on 8 October 1860. Three other children were born during the Civil War: Henry Watkinson, on 10 August 1862, Bazile Charles Édouard, on 27 September 1863, and Marie Emilie, on 1 May 1865.[273] These four children all had the word "colored" written on their birth certificates.

After the Civil War, R.A. Chiapella continued working as a clerk until he had enough money to open his own dry goods store. Another daughter, Marie Emma, was born to them on 8 April 1867. Marie Amélie was born on 5 February 1873. Marie Alice was born on 2 March 1875. Their last-born child, Rita Chiapella, was born on 20 June 1877.[274] Of their eight children, only four, Aurelia, Henry, Marie Emma and Rita would live to be adults. Bazile Charles died on 30 January 1864; Marie Emilie on 11 March 1866; Marie Amélie on 13 June 1874 and Marie Alice

[273] "New Orleans, Louisiana, Birth Records Index, 1790-1915," [database on-line], *Ancestry.com* (https://www.ancestry.com: accessed 12/30/2019), citing *New Orleans, Louisiana Birth Records Index, 1790-1899*. Birth of Orelia Chiapella, Vol. 23, p. 369; Henry Chiapella, Vol. 30, p. 381; Bazile Charles Edouard Chiapella, Vol. 30, p. 381; Marie Emilie, Vol. 30, p. 646.
[274] "New Orleans, Louisiana, Birth Records Index, 1790-1915," [database on-line], *Ancestry.com* (https://www.ancestry.com: accessed 12/30/2019), citing *New Orleans, Louisiana Birth Records Index, 1790-1899*. Birth of Marie Emma Chiapella, Vol. 44, p. 524; Marie Amélie Chiapella, Vol. 61, p. 186; Marie Alice Chiapella, Vol. 63, p. 208; (Rita) Chiapella, Vol. 68, p. 784 Note: No first name given.

on 14 May 1876.[275] Their last four children, born during Reconstruction, had no racial identification marked on their birth records.

Michel (aka René Achille, or R.A.) Chiapella – Photo courtesy of Father Philip L. Flott.

In 1867 M.A. (using his birth name, Michel) Chiapella was listed in the *New Orleans City Directory* as a clerk working at #230 Royal Street. Two years later he was listed in the Directory as Achille Chiapella, Jr., a clerk working at #228 Royal Street, living at #332 Claiborne. The following year, the same directory listed "A.R. Chiapella" as a dry goods merchant at #230 Royal Street. The family of twenty-nine-year-old "Achel Chapella" appeared in the 1870 United States Federal Census for New Orleans, Ward 6. Achille was enumerated as a married, white, male working as a retail dry goods merchant with $1700 in personal property. His wife, Orelia, age 29, daughter, Orelia, age 9, son Henri, age 7, and youngest child, Emma, age 3 were enumerated as being white as well. A twenty-year-old female mulatto servant named Odelia Scott lived with the family.[276]

[275] "Orleans Death Indices,1929-1936" [database on-line], *Ancestry.com* (https://www.ancestry.com: accessed 12/30/ 2019), citing *New Orleans, Louisiana Death Records Index, 1804-1949.* Death of Charles Chiapella, Vol. 24, p. 784; Death of Emilie Chiapella, Vol. 32, p. 285; Death of Marie Amélie Chiapella, Vol. 61, p. 224; Death of Marie Alice Chiapella, Vol. 66, p. 175.
[276] 1870 United States Federal Census, New Orleans, Orleans Parish, LA, Ward 6, Dwelling #614, Family #825, Achel Chapella (*sic*) household, digital image, *Ancestry.com* (https://www.ancestry.com: accessed 2/22/2019), citing NARA microfilm publication M593_522. Date of enumeration: 21 June 1870, Image 202/307.

Henry Chiapella, son of R.A. Chiapella and Marie Orelia Watkinson. Courtesy of Father Philip L. Flott from collection of the late Marlene Flot.

Marie Emma Chiapella, daughter of R.A. Chiapella and Marie Orelia Watkinson. Courtesy of Father Philip L. Flott from collection of the late Marlene Flot.

Shortly before the 1870 Federal Census, on Wednesday, 30 March 1870 Chiapella began advertising his store in the Alexandria (Rapides Parish) *Louisiana Democrat.* That same year, on 1 June 1870 he took out a similar advertisement in the Franklin, (Attakapas Co.) LA, *Planters' Banner.* He hoped to attract new business from the farmers in surrounding parishes who made frequent trips to New Orleans to stock up on dry goods that they might not be able to acquire locally. Clippings from those two newspapers may be seen on the following page:

BARGAINS IN DRY GOODS AND FANCY
ARTICLES.

St. Philip Store
Near the French Market,
230 ROYAL ST., corner ST. PHILIP,
New Orleans.

R. A. CHIAPELLA,
DEALER IN
DRY GOODS,
Hats and Fancy Articles
at
Auction Prices!!
Feb 16–4m cu½

The (Alexandria) Louisiana Democrat, 30 March 1870, p. 1, col. 1, digital image, *Chroniclingamerica.loc.gov*
(http://chroniclingamerica.loc.gov/: accessed 11/15/2019).

MISCELLANEOUS CARDS.

BARGAINS!
IN DRY GOODS AND FANCY ARTICES.
ST. PHILIP STORE,
Near the French Market, 230 Royal street, corner St.
Philip, New Orleans.
R. A. CHIAPELLA,
Dealer in
DRY GOODS, HATS,
AND FANCY ARTICLES,
AT AUCTION PRICES.
feb9 4m

The (Franklin, LA) Planters' Banner, dated 1 June 1870, p. 4, col. 3, digital image, *Chroniclingamerica.loc.gov*
(http://chroniclingamerica.loc.gov/: accessed 11/15/2019).

R.A. Chiapella's foray into the dry goods business lasted off and on for several decades. The store began to lose money, and as was the case with many of these business ventures, Marie Orelia Chiapella sued her husband in order to protect her own assets in the marriage. On 7 April 1879 it was reported in the *Daily Picayune* that a default judgment had been confirmed and made final on 28 March 1879 in favor of "said plaintiff, Mrs. Marie Aurelia Watkinson, wife of René Achille Chiapella, her husband, and against defendant, René Achille Chiapella, her husband, decreeing a separation of property between her and her said husband, dissolving and putting an end to the community of acquets and gains heretofore existing between them."[277]

On 7 June 1880 the United States Federal Census taker paid a visit to the Chiapellas living at #184 Royal Street in New Orleans. He recorded that R.A. Chiapella, a male mulatto, age 43 worked as a shoe merchant. Living in the same household was his forty-three-year-old wife, Aurelia, his nineteen-year-old daughter Aurelia who was a school teacher, his seventeen-year-old son Henry, who was a clerk, as well as two minor children: Emma, age 12 who was in school, and Rita, age 2 years.[278]

The 1886 *New Orleans City Directory* listed René A. Chiapella as a dry goods merchant working at #230 Royal Street[279] with a residence at #219 Burgundy. His son, Henry W. Chiapella worked for his father as a clerk living at the same address along with Miss. Aurelia Chiapella, his daughter, a teacher at the St. Andrew School. Interspersed amongst the listings for R.A. Chiapella's family, were the names and addresses of his father Achille (aka Michel Étienne) Chiapella's "other" family. Louise Pollock Chiapella, Achille's widow lived at #81 Esplanade Avenue. Louise's son George Antoine was an agent for O. Beirne living at #169 Washington Ave. Her son (André) Henry, an attorney working at #162 Common, lived at Johnson, the southwest corner of Kerlerec Street.[280] R.A. Chiapella had managed to hold onto his dry goods business and spent the entire year of 1886 advertising in the *St. Tammany Farmer*, a weekly newspaper published in Covington. In addition to the accompanying advertisement pictured on the next page, the newspaper ran the following article:

> We call the attention of our readers to the advertisement of Mr. R.A. Chiapella in another column. His store is at 230 Royal Street, New Orleans, and the cars from the Pontchartrain depot will take you right to his door. He has a large stock of dry goods, fancy goods, etc., which he is selling at the lowest prices. Mr. Chiapella is well known to many of our readers, having formerly resided here. Be sure to call and examine his goods when you go to the city. He can suit you both in styles and prices, at 230 Royal Street.[281]

---

[277] The (New Orleans, LA) *Daily Picayune*, 7 April 1879, digital image, *Newspapers.com* (https://www.newspapers.com: accessed 11/23/2019), p. 3, col.3.

[278] 1880 United States Federal Census, New Orleans, Orleans Parish, LA, ED 33, Dwelling #135, Family #239, R.A. Chiapella household, digital image, *Ancestry.com* (https://www.ancestry.com: accessed 2/10/2019), citing NARA microfilm publication T9, roll 461. Image 24/50 Date of enumeration: 7 June 1880.

[279] #230 Royal Street (now #936-942 Royal corner of #636-640 St. Philip), was a three-story mixed-use building, that had belonged to New Orleans merchant Theodore Danziger since 1858. Danziger died in 1874. His heirs sold the building to Marie Madeleine Burthe in 1882 which was described as: "Two portions of ground, together with the buildings and improvements thereon... The improvements comprise the splendid three story brick buildings known as Danziger's Corner, divided into four tenements, viz: The first floor forming the corner of Royal and St. Philip streets as a dry goods store; the floor adjoining, fitted up and ready for occupation as a dry goods, boots and shoes, crockery or hardware store; the second floor on the corner as a residence and containing parlor, dining-room, and two bedrooms attached to main building, three story slated building with two rooms to each story; the upper story adjoining and fronting Royal Street contains parlor, dining-room, six bedrooms, hall vestibules; attached to main building three-story slated building with four rooms, cisterns, gas, etc. Part of the property now yields $95 per month. As a residence or store property, this corner is unsurpassed and should command the particular attention of those desirous of obtaining good homes in the center of the Second District, on one of the finest streets, and of those who wish to make safe and profitable investments in store property. To be sold in two separate pieces according to plan of Edgar Pilié, now at the Exchange." Source: The Collins C. Diboll Vieux Carré Digital Survey, Historic New Orleans Collection, (https://www.hnoc.org/vcs/property_info.php?lot=18553.

[280] "U.S. City Directories, 1822-1995," digital image, *Ancestry.com* (https://www.ancestry.com: accessed 11/1/2019), citing *Soard's 1886 Directory*, p. 222. Entries for Aurelia, George, Henry, Henry W., Louise and René A. Chiapella.

[281] "R.A. Chiapella," *The St. Tammany Farmer,* 19 June 1886, digital image, Library of Congress: *Chronicling America. Historic American Newspapers* (https://chroniclingamerica.loc.gov: accessed 2/11/2019), p. 3, col. 6.

Advertisement *St. Tammany Farmer* dated 19 June 1886 p. 3, col. 6.

Unable to continue his business, R.A. Chiapella had given up by 1890 and was working as a salesman in the Canal Street Store of Bernard Fellman. After Fellman's death on 2 September 1892, his widow, Anna Dreyfous, encouraged her brother Jules Simeon Dreyfous to take over management of the store which became Dreyfous & Co., Ltd. in 1893. Anna and Jules were the New Orleans-born children of Abel Abraham Dreyfous, born on 19 January 1815, at Belfort, Haut-Rhin, France, and his second wife Caroline Kaufman, a native of Ingenheim, Rheinpfalz, Germany. They had emigrated from their respective countries in the 1840s and had married in New Orleans on 26 June 1850. By the 1890s the Dreyfous and Fellman families were well-established merchants on Canal Street. A New Orleans *Daily Picayune* advertisement for the 11 November 1895 opening of Dreyfous Co., Ltd, Dry Goods, at 717-719 Canal Street, between Royal and Bourbon, with Jules S. Dreyfous, Manager, listed all of its employees termed as "Representative People in a Representative Store." Amongst the forty-four salesladies was Miss Emma Chiapella. Mr. R.A. Chiapella was listed as one of the twenty-nine salesmen. [282]

The year 1890 was also a year of sorrow because Chiapella and his wife, Aurelia Watkinson lost another child, Henry W. Chiapella who died on 25 October 1890 in New Orleans, as well as two grandchildren. Henry died at the age of 28 years from "laryingeal phthisis." (tuberculosis). He had been living at #28 Encampment Street near the Fairgrounds.[283] He worked as a store clerk for his father and had been married two years previously on 2 February 1888 to Louise Anne Cassan,[284] born on 25 August 1869 at Montpellier, Hérault, France, to Philippe Cassan and Antoinette Pauline Gros.[285] Henry and Louise's daughter, Alice, had been born on 11 November

[282] The (New Orleans, LA) *Daily Picayune*, 10 November 1895, digital image, *Newspapers.com* (https://www.newspapers.com: accessed 27 October 2017), p. 3, col.3.

[283] Courtesy of State of Louisiana, Secretary of State, Division of Archives, Records Management, and History. *Vital Records Indices*. Baton Rouge, LA, USA, citing *Orleans Death Indices 1877-1895*, Vol. 98, p. 111.

[284] Courtesy of State of Louisiana, Secretary of State, Division of Archives, Records Management, and History. *Vital Records Indices*. Baton Rouge, LA, USA, citing *New Orleans, Louisiana Marriage Records Index 1831-1964*; Vol. 12, p. 1004.

[285] Montpellier, Hérault, France, Naissances [Births], 1869, Birth of Louise Anne Cassan, digital image, *Archives départementales du Hérault*, "État Civil en ligne," (https://www.archives-pierresvives.herault.fr/: acc. 2/28/2020), Cote 5MI 1/89, Image 271/482.

1888.[286] Twins Louis and Philip Chiapella were born on 24 May 1890.[287] Philip died two weeks before his father on 11 October 1890 and Louis followed three weeks after his father's death on 15 November 1890.[288]

After Henry's death, Louise was married to Jean Louis Rotgé, a butcher, on 7 November 1891 in New Orleans.[289] Rotgé was born at Osmets, Hautes-Pyrénées, France, on 20 September 1852 to Bertrand Rotgé and his wife Marie Jeanne Dalier.[290] After the birth of their two children: Jeanne Léonie, on 31 July 1892 in New Orleans,[291] and Paul Maurice, on 2 November 1894 in France, Jean Louis Rotgé died in New Orleans on 4 September 1898.[292] Louise and her daughter, Alice Chiapella, followed her other daughter, Léonie Rotgé, and the latter's husband, John Almerico, out west in the early 1920s, where they settled in San Francisco, CA. Alice Chiapella died on 11 November 1924. She had never married. Léonie Rotgé, the wife of John Almerico (d. 4 March 1949), died in San Francisco on 15 March 1969. Louise Cassan Chiapella Rotgé died in San Francisco on 8 June 1955. Alice/Alyce, Louise, Léonie and her husband, John Almerico were all interred in Holy Cross Catholic Cemetery at Colma, San Mateo Co., CA.[293]

By 1890 the Democrat party in Louisiana had been able to pass laws instituting poll taxes and literacy tests in order to cripple the Republican Party by suppressing the African American vote whose constituents still adhered overwhelmingly to the party of Lincoln. This was also the year that the State Legislature had officially segregated the railroads operating within the state. On 12 September 1891, R.A. Chiapella registered to vote as a white lifelong resident of New Orleans, born in 1837. He listed his address as #53 Barracks St. in the 6th Ward and his occupation as clerk.[294] We do not know whether this was his way of protesting the racially charged atmosphere in the state, or simply the path of least resistance to facilitate his ability to vote. It was, however, a bold move on his part to sign up as "white" in a neighborhood where he must have been, at least in some quarters, known to be racially mixed.

Although Charles Watkinson had died in August 1868 and Félicité Flot had died in October 1880, their only heir at law, Aurelia Watkinson Chiapella, their surviving daughter did not file succession papers in St. Tammany Parish until 31 May 1893. In her affidavit she stated that with both parents deceased, and her only sibling,

---

[286] Courtesy of State of Louisiana, Secretary of State, Division of Archives, Records Management, and History. *Vital Records Indices*. Baton Rouge, LA, USA, citing *New Orleans, Louisiana Birth Records Index 1790-1899*, Birth of Alice Chiapella, Vol. 87, p.146.

[287] Courtesy of State of Louisiana, Secretary of State, Division of Archives, Records Management, and History. *Vital Records Indices*. Baton Rouge, LA, USA, citing *New Orleans, Louisiana Birth Records Index 1790-1899*, Birth of Philip and Louis Chiapella, Vol. 90, p.323.

[288] Courtesy of State of Louisiana, Secretary of State, Division of Archives, Records Management, and History. *Vital Records Indices*. Baton Rouge, LA, USA, citing *Orleans Death Indices, 1877-1895*, Death of Philip Chiapella, Vol. 98, p. 17; Death of Louis, Vol. 98, p. 283. Note: Both death records indicate that they were "colored." They both died of "enteritis."

[289] Courtesy of State of Louisiana, Secretary of State, Division of Archives, Records Management, and History. *Vital Records Indices*. Baton Rouge, LA, USA, citing *New Orleans, Louisiana Marriage Records Index 1831-1964*; Vol. 15, p. 565, Marriage of Mrs. Henry Chiapella to Jean Rotgé.

[290] Osmets, Hautes-Pyrénées, France, Naissances, Mariages, Décès [Births, Marriages and Deaths], 1852, Birth of Jean Louis Rotgé, digital image, *Archives départementales des Hautes-Pyrénées*, "État Civil en ligne," https://www.archives enligne65.fr/: accessed 5/20/2020), Cote 2E 3/1324, Act #7, Image 3/11.

[291] Courtesy of State of Louisiana, Secretary of State, Division of Archives, Records Management, and History. *Vital Records Indices*. Baton Rouge, LA, USA, citing *New Orleans, Louisiana Birth Records Index 1790-1899*, Birth of Jeanne Léonie Rotgé, Vol. 97, p.722.

[292] Courtesy of State of Louisiana, Secretary of State, Division of Archives, Records Management, and History. *Vital Records Indices*. Baton Rouge, LA, USA, citing *Orleans Death Indices, 1877-1895*, Death of Jean Rotgé, Vol. 117, p.339.

[293] *Findagrave.com*, database with images, (www.findagrave.com; accessed 9/30/2019) Memorial #105254433 – Alyce Chiapella; Memorial # 88671982 - Louise Cassan Rotgé; Memorial # 88677837 - Léonie Jeanne Rotgé Almerico; Memorial # 107918552-John Almerico.

[294] "Parish of Orleans, Register of Voters, Wards 6-7 1891-1896," in *Louisiana Orleans and St. Tammany Parish Voter Registration Records, 1867-1905*, digital image, *Familysearch.org* (https://www.familysearch.org, accessed 12/24/2019), R. A. Chiapella.

Elena/Ellen, having died unmarried and without issue before 1860, she asked to be put into possession of their estate which consisted of the property that her mother had bought from Samuel B. Hall and his wife Theodosia, on 26 November 1860. The property located in the town of Covington, Division of Spring, Square #27 with a front of 83 feet on each of Hospital and Temperance Streets by a depth and front of 240 feet on Monroe Street, was free of all debt. A Judge for the 16th Judicial District of Louisiana ruled in her favor on 27 May 1893. A copy of the last page of the petition to the 16th Judicial District as well as the affidavit signed by Marie Aurelia Watkinson Chiapella in New Orleans to launch her suit may be seen below:

St. Tammany Parish Courthouse Records (Covington, St. Tammany Parish, LA) Conveyance Office Book P, #307, 16th Judicial District Court, St. Tammany Parish, LA, "Succession of Charles Watkinson and Félicité Flot Watkinson, his wife," filed 27 May 1893.

R. A. Chiapella died in New Orleans on 18 April 1898 from cancer of the esophagus as diagnosed by Dr. Felix Formento, husband of his half-sister, Henriette Louise Chiapella. A brief obituary appeared in the New Orleans *Times Democrat* dated Tuesday, 19 April 1898 which read: "DIED. Chiapella – On Monday, April 18, 1898 at 8:30 o'clock p. m., R.A. Chiapella, aged sixty-one years, a native of this city. Friends and acquaintances are respectfully invited to attend his funeral from his late residence, No. 1662 Rousselin Street, at 4:30 o'clock p.m. Today (Tuesday).[295] A copy of his death certificate indicates that he was "colored," married, and a clerk living at #1662 Rousselin Street [Seventh Ward near the Fairgrounds]:

---

[295] "DIED. Chiapella," The New Orleans, Louisiana *Times Democrat*, 19 April 1898, digital image, *Newspapers.com* (https://www.newspapers.com: accessed 10/10/2019), p. 2, col. 7.

298

Be it Remembered, That on this day to-wit: the _Nineteen_ of _April_ in the year of our Lord one Thousand Eight Hundred and _Eighty Eight_ and the One Hundred and _12_ of the independence of the United States of America before me, ~~C. R. OLLIPHANT~~ _Edmd Souchon_ M. D., President Board of Health and Ex-Officio Recorder of Births, Deaths and Marriages. in and for the Parish of Orleans, personally appeared

Chs Medley an adult, native of _the city_

residing at _no 1311 N Rampart st_ who hereby declares, that

R. S. Chiapella (C.M.)

a native of _this city_, aged _6 years_

departed this life _Yesterday 18 April 1888_ at _no 1662_
Rousseau Street in the city

Cause of Death _Cancer of Oesophagus_

Certificate of Dr. _S Formento_

Deceased was Married a Colored

Thus done at New Orleans in the presence of the aforesaid _C Medley_ as also in that of Messrs _F Menargue, M S Allord_ both of this City witnesses, by me requested so to be, who have hereunto set their hands, together with me, after reading hereof, this day, month and year first above written

Cha Medley

President Board of Health and Ex-Officio Recorder

He was interred in the Chiapella Family Tomb in St. Louis Cemetery #2, SOC plat square 2, St. Patrick Aisle (3-R, M-20). Below is a photo of the top of the tomb which reads "Familles (Families) R.A. et (and) S.O. Chiapella." St. Louis Cemetery #2 in New Orleans has been the final resting place of many free people of color over the years.

Memorial for R.A. Chiapella. *Find A Grave.com, database with images,* (www.findagrave.com: accessed on 20 October 2019). Memorial # 148714790. Photographed by Donna Dinstel.

René Achille Chiapella's wife, Marie Aurelia died in New Orleans at her home on Castiglione Street at sixty-seven years of age on 11 November 1912 from "congestion of the lungs – asthma" according to Dr. L. C. Roudanez. She had lived in Los Angeles, Los Angeles Co., CA, with her widowed daughter Marie Emma Chiapella Edmunds, and had been enumerated there with her in the 1910 Federal Census. She was interred in St. Louis Cemetery #2 with her husband. Below is a copy of Orelia Watkinson Chiapella's New Orleans Death Certificate. With the rise of segregation ushered in by the Democrat party at the end of Reconstruction, it became mandatory for a person's race to be included with their vital records. Both Chiapella and his wife had "colored" written in parentheses after their names.

Be it Remembered, That on this day to-wit the ___Twelfth___ ___of Novem___
in the year of our Lord One Thousand Nine Hundred ___& Twelve___ *and the*
One Hundred and ___37___ *of the independence of the United States of America before me,*

W. T. O'REILLY, M. D., *Chairman Board of Health and Ex-Officio Recorder of Births, Deaths and Marriages*
in and for the Parish of Orleans, personally appeared

___P. J. McMahon_____ native of ___U.S_____
residing ___at No 1112 Baronne St_____ *who hereby declares that*
___Amelia Watterman, widow of Achille Chiapella___ (___Col.___)
a native of ___Louisiana_____, *aged* ___67 y_____,
departed this life ___Yest (11 Nov 1912)____ ___at No 205 Castiglione___
___Street_____
Cause of death ___Congestion of Lungs. Asthma_____
Certificate of Dr. ___L. C. Roudan_____

Thus done at New Orleans, in the presence of the aforesaid ___P. J. McMahon___
as also in that of ___J. N. Janvier___ *&* ___A. J. Keller_____ *both of this city*
witnesses by me requested so to be, who have hereunto set their hands together with me, after reading hereof this day, month and
year first above written.

W. S. O'Reilly M.D.
Chairman Board of Health and Ex-Officio Recorder.

Courtesy of State of Louisiana, Secretary of State, Division of Archives, Records Management, and History. *Vital Records Indices*. Baton Rouge, LA, USA citing *Orleans Death Indices 1908-1917*; Vol. 156 p. 252.

CHAPTER 14

JOSEPH ÉMILE CHIAPELLA

Eglée Aubry's middle son, Joseph Émile Chiapella, whose lack of a baptismal record was discussed on page 127 of this book, appeared with his mother and brothers by name in the 1850 and 1860 United States Federal Census records for New Orleans. In 1850 he was said to be eleven years old and attending school. In 1860, twenty-one-year old Émile Chiapella, a male "mulatto," was an apprentice shoemaker. He did not, however appear with his family in the 1870 United States Federal Census. That year, Eglée Aubry, a sixty-year-old female "mulatto," owning $3000 in real estate was living with her daughter "Odelle Lawrence," a forty-five-year-old female "mulatto" with no occupation, her son "Achille Aubry," age 32, a male, "mulatto," dry goods merchant with $1000 in personal property, and her youngest son, "Octave Aubry," age 30, a male mulatto working as a clerk in a store. Also living in the household was seventy-year-old Pauline Bossot, an unemployed female "mulatto," whom we could not identify.[296] Why did Eglée Aubry, whose children with Achille Chiapella had never been formally recognized by him, allow the census taker to enumerate her sons Octave and Achille as "Octave and Achille Aubry?" We cannot say. Perhaps it was not her choice. However, as noted previously (p. 164), Achille, his wife Orelia Watkinson, daughters Orelia and Emma, and son, Henry, were also enumerated living in the sixth ward as a white family whose head of household "Achel Chapella" (*sic)*, was a twenty-nine-year-old dry goods merchant with $1700 in personal property. Odelia Scott, a twenty-year-old, mulatto domestic servant, lived with them. [297] On 9 June 1870, Eglée Aubry was also enumerated in Mandeville, St. Tammany Parish, LA, as a sixty-year-old female mulatto with $400 in real estate. She was living with Cecilia Edwards a twenty-year-old female African American whose occupation was not given.[298] However, Joseph Émile was listed in neither household. It appears that he was not enumerated in the 1870 United States Federal Census.

He did, however, appear in the 1867 *New Orleans City Directory* as Émile Chiapella, a dealer in boots and shoes located at 47 Rampart Street, and again in 1869 as a shoe dealer at #51 Rampart Street with a residence on Main (Dumaine) Street near Robertson. He also appeared in the 1873, 1875 and 1877 *New Orleans City Directories* as a wholesale seller of boots and shoes working at #53 Rampart Street.

On 9 September 1874 Joseph Émile and his brother, Stephen Octave Chiapella bought from Emilie Gabrielle Poullantz (*sic)*[299], the widow of William Thomas Evershed two lots of ground in Faubourg Tremé, Second District, lots # 9 & 10 in Square #71 within Dumaine, Robertson, Claiborne and St. Philip measuring each 30 feet on Dumaine, between Robertson and Claiborne by 90 feet in depth together with all the buildings and improvements for $4,120. The brothers paid $2120 cash in hand and signed two promissory notes each for $1,000 payable in one and two years from the date of the purchase with 8% interest. They also agreed to keep fire insurance on the buildings and everything in good condition.[300] Octave and Émile's mother, Eglée Aubry would become the eventual owner of this parcel of land, which would appear in her succession records after her death in 1882.

---

[296] 1870 United States Federal Census, New Orleans, Orleans Parish, LA, Ward 5, Dwelling #876, Family #1225, Eglé Aubry household, digital image, *Ancestry.com* (https://www.ancestry.com: accessed 2/22/2019), citing NARA microfilm publication M593_521. Date of enumeration: 12 July 1870, Image 195/454.

[297] 1870 United States Federal Census, New Orleans, Orleans Parish, LA, Ward 5, Dwelling #614, Family #825, Achel Chapella household, digital image, *Ancestry.com* (https://www.ancestry.com: accessed 2/22/2019), citing NARA microfilm publication M593_522, p. 330A. Date of enumeration: 21 June 1870, Image 202/307.

[298] 1870 United States Federal Census, Mandeville, St. Tammany, LA, Dwelling #86, Family #79, Eagle Aubry household, digital image, *Ancestry.com* (https://www.ancestry.com: accessed 2/22/2019), citing NARA microfilm publication M593_532. Date of enumeration: 9 June 1870, Image 10/14.

[299] Emilie Gabrielle Poullant de Gelbois Evershed was born in Nantes, France in 1800. Abandoned by a first husband in New Orleans, she married Thomas Evershed. She was a poetess whose four collections of verse were published between 1843 and 1850 in France. She died in New Orleans in 1879.

[300] NARC, "Sale of Properties – Widow Thos. Evershed to Émile and Oct. Chiapella," dated 9 September 1874, passed by Notary Joseph Cuvillier, Act #116. Courtesy Hon. Chelsey Richard Napoleon, Clerk of Civil District Court, Parish of Orleans.

During the week ending Sunday April 15, 1877 the New Orleans Board of Health reported 129 deaths in the city. Forty-three of them were from smallpox, of which Joseph Émile Chiapella was one.[301] He died on 13 April 1877 at 9:00 a.m. on Columbus Street between Broad and Dorgenois. He was unmarried. The cause of death, variola (smallpox) was reported by Dr. Louis Roudanez, the same physician who had signed the death certificate for Charles Beauvilaire Pinta. Below is Joseph Émile Chiapella's death certificate:

Courtesy of State of Louisiana, Secretary of State, Division of Archives, Records Management and History. *Vital Records Indices*. Baton Rouge, LA, USA citing *Orleans Death Indices 1804-1876*; Vol. 68, p. 780.

A record held at the Archdiocese of New Orleans, Department of Archives, certified that "Emile Joseph Chiapella, born in Louisiana died of variola on Columbus Street near Broad at age 38 and was buried on 14 April 1877 in the St. Louis Cemeteries. Unfortunately, it did not give a location for his interment.[302]

On 9 May 1877, his mother and siblings filed his succession papers. Eglée Aubry 's affidavit requesting that she inherit his estate indicated that he had died intestate, had never been married, left no posterity, and had never been recognized by his natural father. His siblings, who would have been entitled to a share of his estate, his half-sister Odalie Lorrains (*sic*) and brothers René Achille and Stephen Octave Chiapella, annexed to her affidavit a statement that their mother should be recognized as his sole heir at law and be put in possession of all his property, moveable and immovable:

---

[301] "Mortuary Report," *The New Orleans Daily Democrat*, 17 April 1877, digital image, *Newspapers.com* (https://www.newspapers.com: accessed 10/10/2019), p. 8, col. 5.

[302] Archdiocese of New Orleans, Department of Archives, St. Louis Cemeteries Burial Records*, Vol. 1869-1880, Part III,* p. 306. (Courtesy of Emilie Leumas, Archivist – Kimberly Johnson and Katie Vest – Researching Archivists.)

Petition Paper from Succession Record of Joseph Émile Chiapella, signed by her children, recognizing her as the sole heir of their deceased brother Joseph Émile Chiapella, Image 548/1307 (See note #288).

Two witnesses, Dorson Louis Charbonnet and Henry Camps affirmed in writing that Eglée Aubry was, indeed, the mother who raised all four children. Eglée Aubry testified that she had her son baptized in 1842 at St. Vincent de Paul Church by Father Fauré, and that the child's godparents were Odalie Lorreins, her daughter, and J.A. Pueyo, a family friend. However, the church had since burned and the records were destroyed. A priest from St. Vincent de Paul Church was called to testify to this. Father Julies Étienne Fortier stated that St. Vincent de Paul's archives had been transferred to the German Church on St. Ferdinand Street, but that the church had burned down in 1851, destroying all the records.[303] The court ruled in Eglée Aubry's favor. There was, unfortunately no inventory attached to this succession record to describe the property which became hers after her son's death.

[303] "Louisiana, Wills and Probate Records, 1756-1984,"digital images, *Ancestry.com* (https://www.ancestry.com: accessed 3/4/2019), citing *Succession Records 1846-1880*; *Louisiana Probate Court (Orleans Parish)*. Succession of Joseph Émile Chiapella dated 9 May 1877, Images 545-554/1307.

CHAPTER 15

STEPHEN OCTAVE CHIAPELLA, EULALIE PINTA AND JOSEPH FERDINAND GRASS

Eulalie Pinta (See Chapter 9, pp 115,116), a native of Alabama, the daughter of Joseph Pinta and Julia Rabbi [*sic*], married Stephen Octave Chiapella, the son of Achille Chiapella and Marie Eglée Aubry in New Orleans on 19 March 1873:

Courtesy of State of Louisiana, Secretary of State, Division of Archives, Records Management, and History. *Vital Records Indices*. Baton Rouge, LA, USA from Orleans Parish Marriage Records Index 1831-1964; Vol. 3, p. 477.

The Pinta, Chiapella, and Raby families had been acquainted for generations, and given the ever-dwindling pool of free people of color within the greater New Orleans society, it was inevitable that a marriage amongst them would be facilitated. Eulalie's brother, Joseph Pinta, and Steven Chiapella's brother, René Achille Chiapella were witnesses to the issuance of the marriage license. No witnesses for the ceremony were listed.

Before his marriage to Eulalie Pinta, S. O. Chiapella, often called simply, Octave, had worked as a clerk with his eldest brother René Achille Chiapella in a store at #230 Royal Street according to the 1866 *New Orleans City Directory*. In 1869 a listing for the two brothers showed their place of employment as #230 Royal and their residence at #269 Main (Dumaine).

The Chiapellas, as well as their cousins in the Foy family, were not only concerned about their ability to make a living for themselves and their loved ones. They were frightened at the violence they saw that was occurring day after day after the cessation of hostilities between the North and the South. The struggle for equal rights for free people of color which had begun with Louisiana statehood in 1812 was only exacerbated after the Civil War which culminated in the New Orleans massacre of 30 July 1866. Similar riots had occurred in May 1866 in Memphis, TN. Louisiana Republicans, who had been angered that the post war legislature had enacted Black Codes and had refused suffrage to African American males, decided to reconvene a Constitutional Convention which Democrats called illegal and unconstitutional. After failing to get a quorum on 30 July 1866, the Republicans, mostly people of color, left the building and were confronted by an angry white mob in front of the Mechanics Institute. After the fighting subsided fifty people were dead, mostly African American. This unrest, coupled with the previous riots in Memphis, gave Republicans a huge victory in the national congressional elections of November 1866, enough to override a Presidential veto of the First Reconstruction Act which divided the South into five military districts. A subsequent Constitutional Convention in the Fifth Military District of Louisiana consisting of 98 delegates equally divided between whites and African Americans was convened in 1867. After voting in universal male suffrage, and withdrawing suffrage from many former confederates who were mostly all democrats, the state was set for an election. The Republican ticket with Henry Clay Warmoth for Governor carried the day. His tenure became a disappointment for African Americans who saw Warmoth as lukewarm to their demands. He appointed more whites than African Americans to important offices and had a constitutional amendment passed to rescind the article that had stripped former confederates from the right to vote. Moreover, he appointed some of them to public office. He also watered-down a bill which had granted equal access to public accommodations, by vetoing the part of the legislation which provided for a penalty for discrimination. The struggle between Republicans and Democrats led to years of political upheaval.

Warmoth's failure to support free and equal access to public accommodation which led to his finishing his term of office under the threat of impeachment in 1872 was the impetus for an appeal for the unification of the people of Louisiana under the leadership of free men of color such as physician, Dr. L.C. Roudanez, Aristide Mary and C.C. Antoine who organized a movement to press for equal rights for the "colored citizens" of Louisiana. The group's manifesto was published on 13 July 1873 in the *New Orleans Republican,* where all men of whatever race, color or religion were called to demand the right to frequent at will any place of public resort, and to travel at will on any public conveyance, including railroads, steamboats and steamships "upon terms of perfect equality." The group also asked that the schools be desegregated, that people be hired for jobs with no distinction of the races, that people of color as stockholders be allowed to serve on the boards of banks, insurance offices and other public corporations. In short, they asked for the "equal and impartial exercise by every citizen of Louisiana of every civil and political right guaranteed by the Constitution of the United States." A mass meeting was announced to take place at Exposition Hall on 15 July Amongst the organizers were Achille Chiapella (Jr.), his brother Stephen Octave, as well as their cousins, Léon Dupuy, son of their aunt Félicité Aubry, and Alcide St. Hubert, son of their cousin Julia Latrobe.[304]

This meeting had occurred shortly after Stephen Octave Chiapella's marriage to Eulalie Pinta in March 1873. Three of their four children were born in the turbulent 1870s. Joseph Octave Chiapella was born on 4 January 1874. At that time, towards the end of Reconstruction no racial designations were used on civil registrations of births, marriages or deaths. The birth certificate read in part that "Stephen O. Chiapella, a native of New Orleans, residing #231 Common Street in the city [...] declares that on the fourth day of January in the present year (January 4, 1874) at 6 o'clock A.M.at deponent's residence was born a male child named Joseph Octave Chiapella, Deponent's lawful issue with Eulalie Pinta, a native of Mobile" In very small handwriting, at the very bottom was written the following: "Altered to correct spelling by marriage of parents March 13, 1873, Book 62, Folio 82" Originally, both "Chiapella" and "Pinta" had been spelled incorrectly :

---

[304] "Grand Unification Mass Meeting," *New Orleans Republican*, 13 July 1873, digital image, *Newspapers.com* (https://www.newspapers.com: accessed 20 October 2019) p. 5, cols. 5-7.

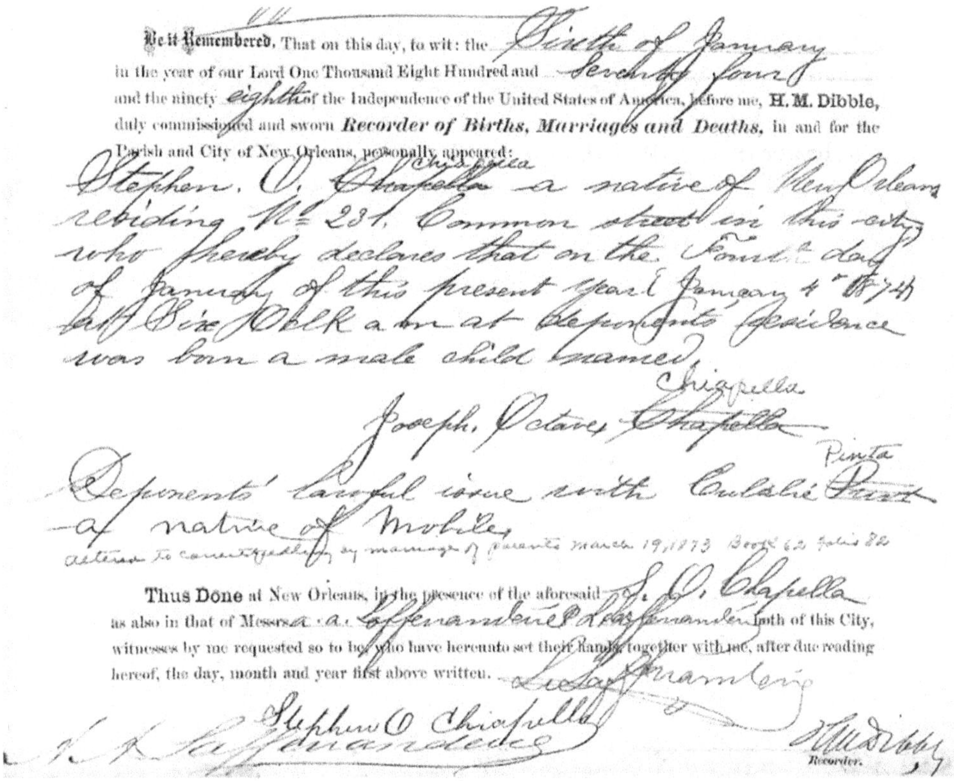

Courtesy of State of Louisiana, Secretary of State, Division of Archives, Records Management, and History. *Vital Records Indices*. Baton Rouge, LA, USA, from New Orleans, Louisiana Birth Records Index 1790-1899; Vol. 62, p. 82.

Maria Olivia was born on 12 March 1875 and died as a toddler on 30 August 1878. Although she was born in 1875 with no racial designation, she died two and one-half years later, on 30 August 1878, and was given a racial label. By this time local democrats had tightened their hold on local political appointments:

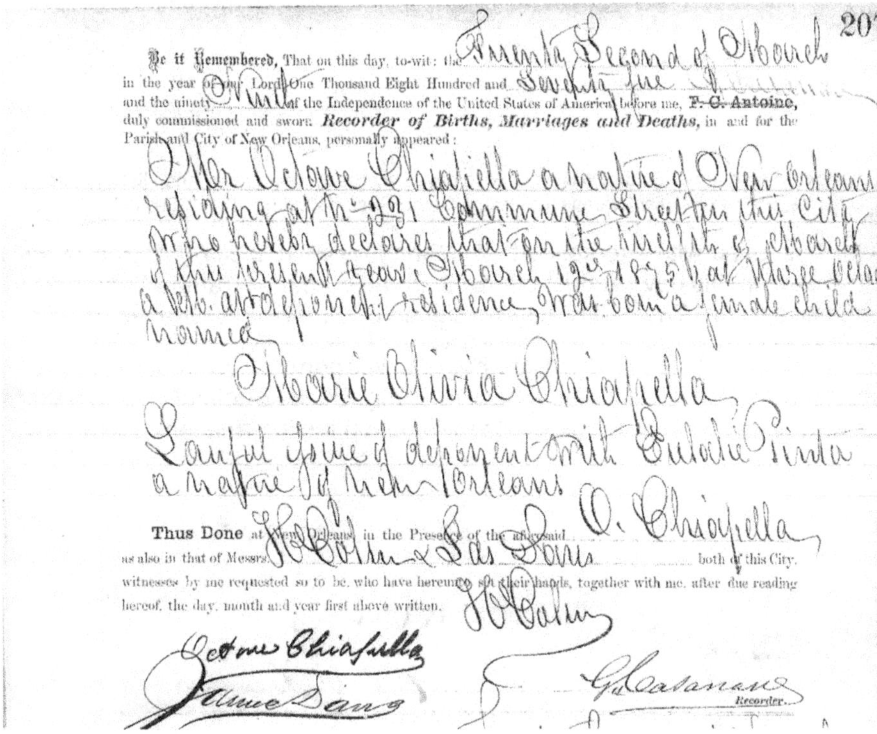

Courtesy of State of Louisiana, Secretary of State, Division of Archives, Records Management, and History. *Vital Records Indices*. Baton Rouge, LA, USA, from New Orleans, Louisiana Birth Records Index 1790-1899; Vol. 63, p. 207.

960

Be it Remembered, That on this day, to-wit: the *Thirtieth day of August* in the year of our Lord one Thousand Eight Hundred and Seventy *Eight* and the One Hundredth and *Third* of the Independence of the United States of America, before me, S. CHOPPIN, M.D. *President Board of Health and ex-officio Recorder of Births, Marriages and Deaths,* in and for the Parish and City of New Orleans, personally appeared :

James Toussin native of *Louisiana* residing *at the corner of Rampart & Common Sts* who hereby declares that *Marie Olivia Chiapella* (*Colored*), a native of *New Orleans* aged *2 years & 6 months* died on this *day of August 30, 1878, at the corner of Rampart & Common Sts in this city.*

cause of death *"Congestive fever"*

certificate of *L. L. Roudanez*

Thus Done at New Orleans, in the presence of the aforesaid *Jas. Toussin* as also in that of Messrs. *J. W. Duncan & L. Edwards* both of this City, witnesses by me requested so to be, who have hereunto set their hands, together with me, after due reading hereof, the day, month, and year first above written.

P. L. Edwards   J. W. Duncan

Jas Toussin

Sam Choppin

President Board of Health and ex-officio Recorder.

The above record, which is faded with age states that "Marie Olivia Chiapella (Colored) a native of New Orleans aged 2 years 6 months died on this day (August 30 1878) at the corner of Rampart and Common Sts. in this city. Cause of Death: Congestive fever." The certificate was signed by Dr. Louis Roudanez.

When the couple's third child, Edward Émile Chiapella was born on 17 August 1879, he was also designated as "colored." Although that word on the document had obviously faded, a helpful civil servant had written over the original word in black ink, for fear that someone would miss out on the information:

Be it Remembered, That on this day, to-wit: the _Eighteenth of August_
in the year of our Lord one Thousand Eight Hundred and Seventy _nine_ and the One Hundredth
and _fourth_ of the Independence of the United States of America, before me, S. CHOPPIN, M. D.
President Board of Health and ex-officio Recorder of Births, Marriages and Deaths, in and for the
Parish and City of New Orleans, personally appeared :

J. A. Bosseaux a native of _France_
residing _at No 234 Common Street_ who hereby declares that
on _the Seventeenth instant (17 August 1879)_ at _his_
aforesaid residence was born a _male_ child, named
Edwards Emile Chiapella (**Colored**),
lawful issue of _Steven O Chiapella_ a native of _this city_
aged _39_ years, occupation _Shoe Dealer_ and _Eulalie_
Onta a native of _Mobile Ala_ aged _26_ years

Thus Done at New Orleans, in the presence of the aforesaid _J. A. Bosseaux_
as also in that of Messrs _S C Hepburn & C H Lavarge_ both of this City,
witnesses by me requested so to be, who have hereunto set their hands, together with me, after due
reading hereof, the day, month, and year first above written.

C. H. Lavarge

Julian A. Bosseaux
Saml C Hepburn

Sten Choppin M.D.
President Board of Health and ex-officio Recorder.

Courtesy of State of Louisiana, Secretary of State, Division of Archives, Records Management, and History. *Vital Records Indices*. Baton Rouge, LA, USA, from New Orleans, Louisiana Birth Records Index 1790-1899; Vol. 74, p. 307.

The family was enumerated together for the only time in the 1880 United States Federal Census. Forty-year-old S.O. Chiapella, a male "mulatto," shoe dealer, his wife "Eulie" (*sic*), age 32, "mulatto," born in Alabama, and their two surviving children: Octave, age 6, and Émile, age two months, his "mulatto" sons completed the family unit living at #51 South Rampart Street.[305]

The couple's last child, Stephen Eugene Chiapella was born in New Orleans on 1 November 1881 and was also designated as "colored:"

---

[305] 1880 United States Federal Census, New Orleans, Orleans Parish, LA, ED 19, Dwelling #16, Family #20, S.O. Chiapella household, digital image, *Ancestry.com* (https://www.ancestry.com: accessed 4/4/2019), citing NARA microfilm publication T9, roll 459. Date of enumeration: June 1880. Stamped 24 July 1880, Image 1/55.

1056 **Be it Remembered,** That on this day, to-wit: the Fourth of November in the year of our Lord One Thousand Eight Hundred and Eighty one, and the One Hundred and Sixth of the Independence of the United States of America, before me, JOSEPH JONES, M. D., President Board of Health and Ex-Officio Recorder of Births, Deaths and Marriages, in and for the Parish and City of New Orleans, personally appeared:

Stephen Octave Chiapella, a native of this city residing at ___ Common Street, in this city who hereby declares, that on the first instant November 1 1881 at his aforesaid residence in this city was born a male child, named Stephen Eugene Chiapella. (Col.) Lawful issue of ___ a native of this city aged 41 years, occupation Shoe Dealer and Eulalie Pinta a native of Mobile Alabama, aged 33 years,

Thus done at New Orleans, in the presence of the aforesaid S. C. Chiapella as also in that of Messrs H. Peralta & P. H. Laranze both of this City, witnesses, by me requested so to be, who have hereunto set their hands, together with me, after due reading hereof, the day, month and year first above written. Js. Jones M.

President Board of Health and Ex-Officio Recorder.

Courtesy of State of Louisiana, Secretary of State, Division of Archives, Records Management, and History. *Vital Records Indices*. Baton Rouge, LA, USA, from New Orleans, Louisiana Death Records Index 1804-1939; Vol. 77, p. 1056.

Eight months later, on 17 June 1882, Stephen Octave Chiapella's life was cut short at the age of forty-one years and nine months. He died on that day from typhoid fever at his residence at the corner of Common and Rampart Streets. His death certificate was signed by an old comrade-in-arms from the equal rights movement, Dr. Louis Charles Roudanez. Reconstruction had been ended by the Compromise of 1877 on April 24th of that year when federal troops were withdrawn from Louisiana, the last federally-occupied southern state. From that time on the democrat party in control of the local governments began to reimpose laws segregating the races. The New Orleans Board of Health began singling out people of color by designating them as "(Col.)," or "colored" on official documents as was the case with Stephen Octave Chiapella and three of his children, Marie Olivia (in death), Edward Émile and Stephen Eugene. It had not been so for his brother Joseph Émile who had died eleven days before troops had been withdrawn from the state in 1877 or Stephen's first-born son, Joseph Octave born in 1874. Stephen Octave Chiapella's death certificate may be seen on the next page:

He was interred in St. Louis Cemetery #2 in the family tomb (SOC plat square 2, St. Patrick Aisle 3-R, M. 20).

On 24 and 25 July 1882 an inventory of his estate was done in order to settle his succession. The detailed record showed that the stock in the shoe store, including button boots for men women and children, balmorals, brogans, laced shoes, ladies button sandals, white button boots, white slippers, boys and men's gaiters, babies slippers, creole slippers, creole brogans, men's boots, children's button shoes, laces and blacking, etc. was worth $1827.34. The household furnishings on the second floor consisting of two bedrooms, a sitting room, and hall, included one mahogany bedstead with bedding, wash stand, armoire, chairs, looking glass, marble top table, curtains, shades, rugs, one bed and bedding, six chairs, a bureau, a book case, a sofa, two easy chairs, a corner stand, a marble top side board. On the third story there was a front room and room on the gallery where there was one small bed, one lounge, one toilet, one washtub. A hallway downstairs was furnished with one hat rack, two cane-bottom chairs and oil cloth. The kitchen had a stove, utensils, a table and chairs, crockery and glassware. All furniture and household items were appraised at $182.50. Cash on hand totaled $700 for an overall total of $2709.84. Real estate which was jointly owned by the couple included a plot of ground purchased on 18 March 1881 from Mr. and Mrs. Henry Ferguson, located in the First District in a square comprised within Palmyra, Common, Prieur and Roman Streets, fronting 34 feet 3 inches on Palmyra by 100 feet deep, valued at $2,000. Another piece of real estate consisting of two lots with all improvements had been bought jointly with his mother, Eglée Aubry, on 14 June and 14 October 1871 from Jacob Grosart and Alexander Stark located in the first district in the square bounded by Philippa (University Place), Common, Circus (now South Rampart) and Gravier Streets. At the time of Octave's death, his half and the portion he inherited from his deceased mother, Eglée Aubry, was worth $5000, for a total estate worth $7,354.92. Eulalie Pinta claimed that when she was married to her husband, the property he owned jointly with his mother was mortgaged for $4,000. During their marriage they had paid off that amount, so she was claiming one-half ($2,000) because it had been paid out of their community property.

Eulalie Pinta Chiapella was designated as natural tutrix of her minor children. Joseph Pinta, her elder brother was designated as their under-tutor. She was remarried on 20 October 1884 to Joseph Fernand Grass. The groom was barely twenty-two years old, while she was almost thirty-seven, although the marriage record indicated that she was twenty-four:

Courtesy of, State of Louisiana, Secretary of State, Division of Archives, Records Management and History. *Vital Records Indices*. Baton Rouge, LA, USA from Louisiana Marriage Records Index 1831-1964; Vol. 10, p. 845.

When she married Joseph Grass, she did so without calling a family meeting to continue the tutorship of her children by her deceased husband, so one was held later on 6 October 1886. Attending the meeting were: R.A. Chiapella, the children's uncle and three of their uncles by marriage: Joseph L. Montieu husband of Victoria Pinta, Charles Gaignard, husband of Ernestine Pinta, and Richard Joseph Gardiol, husband of Laura Luce Pinta. Several friends of the family were included as was Prosper Florville Foy, the children's second cousin, son of their deceased's aunt, Zélie Aubry, although he failed to attend any meetings. Eulalie Pinta Grass was reappointed tutrix to her children and the community property held between her and her deceased husband was adjudicated to her for the price at which it was appraised: $4,709.84. To pay for the expenses arising from her tutorship she proposed a special mortgage in favor of her minor children secured by four properties, the first being the property she had held in common with her late husband on Palmyra and the other three bought after her husband's death, to wit: a lot of ground and improvements on Rampart between Common and Gravier purchased on 5 November 1885, a lot of ground on the same square and front purchased by her on 13 April 1886, and a portion of ground located on Basin Street between Perdido and Gravier which she purchased from her brother-in-law and sister in-law, Achille Chiapella and Odalie Lorreins Vila, on 7 October 1882, all of which together were valued at $11,800 which would more than cover the indebtedness to her children for their portion of their late father's estate, which amounted to $5,948.60. Law required that special mortgages of this kind exceed the indebtedness by 25% to account for inflation. By 1901, after the last of her children with Chiapella had reached the age of emancipation and they received their inheritances, the special mortgages on her New Orleans properties were cancelled.[306]

Eulalie's second husband Joseph Fernand Grass's great-grandfather, Antonio Grass had immigrated from the island of Majorca located in the Mediterranean Sea off the Spanish Coast where he had been born ca. 1748. He had arrived in America probably in the mid-1770s. Grass was a pioneer settler in Spanish Louisiana who owned a large swath of what is today downtown Baton Rouge, East Baton Rouge Parish, LA. He was also a partner in a mercantile concern with fellow Majorcan, Francisco Bazo, at Natchez, Mississippi Territory. Grass married Geneviève Delatte/Dulat/Delattre on 15 January 1793 at Baton Rouge. The bride had been born on 9 December 1761 at the Pointe Coupée Post to Louis Delatre and his wife, Catherine Steigre.[307] A record from St. Joseph's

[306] "Louisiana, Wills and Probate Records, 1756-1984," digital images, *Ancestry.com* (https://www.ancestry.com: accessed 5/4/19), citing Louisiana District and Probate Courts, Civil District Court Case Papers, No. 6423-6492, S.O. Chiapella, Case #6448, Probate date 13 July 1882., Images 470-629.

[307] Diocese of Baton Rouge, Department of Archives, *Diocese of Baton Rouge Catholic Church Records, Pointe Coupée Records, 1722-1769, Vol. 1B* (Baton Rouge, LA: Catholic Diocese of Baton Rouge, 2002), 53.

Church reads: "GRASS, Antonio of Mayorca (Josef and Antonia Mulano) m. 15 Jan 1793, Genevieve Dulat (Luis and Catharina Stail of St. John the Baptist Parish) Wit. Antonio Estevan & Nicolas Balanger (SJO-3, 1)"[308]

Marriage of Antonio Grass and Genevieve Dulat [*sic*] dated 15 January 1793 (el dia 15 del mes de Enero de 1793). Courtesy of the Archdiocese of Baton Rouge Archives.

Grass and his wife donated two lots of ground on the corner of Main and Church Streets from his original Spanish land patent acquired on 12 June 1793, where St. Joseph's, a frame church, was erected at some time after 1804. When Grasse donated the land, he included the three other corners facing the proposed church so that, according to a 1929 newspaper article, no saloons could be built near it.[309] The wood frame church built on his property was eventually replaced by a larger building erected by Fr, Antoine Blanc in 1830.

Don Antonio Grass died at Baton Rouge: "Grass, Don Antonio, age 73[310] years of Mayorca, buried on 1 August 1811. (SJO-4, 55)."[311] He and his late wife, Geneviève, who had died at the age of forty-seven on 24 September 1809 (SJO-4, 49), were both interred in a vault under the altar inside the old St. Joseph's Church in Baton Rouge on the land that he had originally donated to the Church.

---

[308] Diocese of Baton Rouge, Department of Archives, *Diocese of Baton Rouge Catholic Church Records 1770-1803, Vol. 2* (Baton Rouge, LA: Catholic Diocese of Baton Rouge, 1980), 333.

[309] "Strange Street Names Rise Up from Realm of Forgotten Events," *The Advocate* (Baton Rouge, LA), 7 May 1929, digital image, *Genealogybank.com* (https://www.genealogybank.com: accessed 12/4/2019), p. 2, col. 3.

[310] Grass's age at death, seen on the next page, line 5, appears to be sesenta y tres (63) not setenta y tres (73), as abstracted in the SJO record, published in 1982.

[311] Diocese of Baton Rouge, Department of Archives, *Diocese of Baton Rouge Catholic Church Records 1804-1819, Vol. 3* (Baton Rouge, LA: Catholic Diocese of Baton Rouge, 1982), 375.

Antonio Grass buried on 1 August 1811 "in esta Santa Iglesia" (in this Holy Church) Courtesy of the Archdiocese of Baton Rouge Archives.

Death of Genoveva de Latto, legitimate wife of Don Antonio Grass who died the 24th of this month (September) and was buried in the Church. Courtesy of the Archdiocese of Baton Rouge Archives.

When that church was sold and torn down, a recently discovered letter by Father Lavay, S.J. to Archbishop Antoine Blanc dated 8 January 1856, asked where the remains of Grass, his wife and other benefactors interred in the church should be placed. Unfortunately, an answer to this question has not yet been found so their final resting place is unknown.[312]   Below is a copy of that portion of Fr. Lavay's letter seeking guidance as to where the remains of those buried under the altar in the old church should be transferred. Father Lavay had consulted Madame Sheppers (Alexandrine Olympia Grass, daughter of the deceased couple) who indicated that she would be guided by the decision of the Archbishop whether to inter them under the altar of the new Church or transfer them to the Cemetery:

---

[312] Frank M. Uter, *A History of the Catholic Church in Baton Rouge, 1792-1992*, (Baton Rouge, LA: St. Joseph Cathedral, 1992), 30.

Copy of a portion of the original letter from Father Joseph Lavay, S.J. to Archbishop Anthony Blanc dated 8 January 1856 courtesy of the University of Notre Dame Archives, Notre Dame, IN.

Antonio Grass and his wife left behind ten children of whom, Jean Louis Grass, their fourth-born child, was Joseph Fernand Grass's grandfather.

Baptized as "Juan Luis Gras" on 2 October 1797 at St. Louis Cathedral in New Orleans (SLC, B14, 43), Jean Louis Grass married Marie Victorine Espinosa on 25 November 1822: "Gras, Jean Luis (Antonio and Genoveba Delatte), native and resident of this city m. Maria Victoria Espinosa (Francisco, dec..former captain of fixed regiment of Mexico and Victoria Delatte), native and resident of this parish, married on Nov. 25, 1822 w. Godfredo Tisman, Martin Vizoso, Antonio Montan and Francisco Carrion (SLC, M7, 24)." Jean Louis and his new wife were first cousins, his wife's mother, Victoria/Victoire/Victorine Delattre/Deslattes, being his mother, Geneviève Delattre/Deslattes' sister.

Benjamin Franklin Grass was the last of Jean Louis and Victorine's seven children, born on 6 January 1840. Two of his siblings had died before his birth: Charles Pierre in 1829 at age 2 and Alphred Robert in 1838 at age 4. Benjamin Franklin Grass's civil birth record below reads in part: "Mr Louis Bernard a clerk residing on Love Street[Rampart now] between Trifle[313] and St. Anthony Streets in the Third Municipality, who by these presents declares that on the sixth day of January eighteen hundred and forty (6 January 1840) at six o'clock a.m. in a house situated on Bartholomew Street between Moreau and Casacalvo Streets, in the aforesaid municipality, was born a male child named Benjamin Franklin Grass, issue of the legitimate marriage of Mr. Jean L. Grass with Mrs. Victorine Espinosa:"

Courtesy of State of Louisiana, Secretary of State, Division of Archives, Records Management, and History. *Vital Records Indices*. Baton Rouge, LA, USA, from New Orleans, Louisiana Birth Records Index 1790-1899; Vol. 9, p. 335.

The child's father died on 10 March 1843, leaving Victorine as head of the household. Unfortunately, Jean Louis Grass's place of birth was not given. Although he had been baptized at St. Louis Cathedral, he may have actually been born at Natchez as had been three of his siblings. He died at the home of Louis Bernard on Love Street (Rampart) between Trifle (Pauger) and St. Anthony in the Faubourg Marigny. Bernard was a family friend who had reported the birth of Jean Louis' last child, Benjamin Franklin Grass in 1840. From several on-line directories we know that Louis Bernard was the cashier at the Improvement Bank. The death certificate for Jean Louis Gras(s) which was only recorded on 13 May 1843 may be seen on the following page:

---

[313] "Trifle" is an English attempt to translate "Bagatelle" Street, the name then in use. It is now Pauger Street.

Gras, Jean Louis.

461

BE IT REMEMBERED that this day, to wit the thirteenth of May in the year of our Lord one thousand eight hundred and forty three and the sixty seventh of the Independence of the United States of America, before me ⸻ duly commissioned and sworn **Recorder of Births and Deaths** in and for the Parish and City of Orleans, personally appeared, Isidore Antoine Luemper born in this Parish of Orleans on the thirtieth of July eighteen hundred and seventeen, employed as a Bookkeeper at the Office of the Records of the catholic cathedral church of St Louis of this city and Parish of New Orleans and residing on St Ann Street between Conde and Royale streets in the first Municipality, Who in the presence of the undersigned witnesses doth declare, that Mr Jean Louis Gras born at in the lawful marriage of the late Antoine Gras & the late Geneviève Delatte Died on the tenth of March this present year in the afternoon at the domicil of Mr Louis Bernard on Love Street between Crafts and St Anthony streets suburb Marigny in the third Municipality of Orleans — The said late Mr J Louis Gras was married to Marie Victoire Espinosa his surviving widow a native of this city and residing therein.

done at New Orleans in the presence of the ⸻ Mr Isidore Antoine Luempee and Antoine Dublec ⸻

Rudolph Reichhoffer

Ad Reichhoffer

Isidore Antoine Luempee

Courtesy of, State of Louisiana, Secretary of State, Division of Archives, Records Management and History. *Vital Records Indices*. Baton Rouge, LA, USA citing *Orleans Death Indices 1877-1895*; Vol. 9, p. 461.

Marie Victorine Espinosa was enumerated as "Louise Gras" in the 1850 Federal Census for New Orleans, Ward 1, with her surviving children: Elvina, age 26 years, William, age 17.5 years, a clerk, Henry, age 13 years, and Benjamin, age 11 years.[314] Ten years later, she was enumerated as V. S. Grass, a sixty-year-old female living with her unidentified daughter, age 20 (possibly Marie Louise, age 29) and two sons: Henry age 22 a clerk and Benjamin, age 20.[315] Victorine never remarried. She died on 21 February 1866 at #418 Love Street in the Third District, New Orleans. A neighbor Louis Brunet living on St. Ann Street reported her death to the authorities. She appears in the *Louisiana Death Indices* as "Victorine Espinosa Gras," using the alternative spelling "Gras," for "Grass," quite commonly used in French Louisiana.

Victorine's youngest son, Benjamin Franklin Grass, was married to Marie Ernestine Saucier on 23 May 1860 by the Rev. F. Berthaud at St. Augustine Catholic Church in the Tremé neighborhood just north of the French Quarter in New Orleans. St. Augustine was founded in 1841 by free people of color who bought pews for themselves as well as for slaves who lived in the area. The church also had many white parishioners at the outset and operated

---

[314] 1850 United States Federal Census, Orleans Parish, LA, Ward 1, Municipality 3, Dwelling #1028, Family #1174, Louise Gras household, digital image, *Ancestry.com* (https://www.ancestry.com accessed 11/2019), citing NARA microfilm publication M432_238, p. 58A. Date of enumeration: 31 July 1850. Image 115/204.

[315] 1860 United States Federal Census, Orleans Parish, LA, Ward 7, Dwelling #1262, Family #1456, V.S. Grass household, digital image, *Ancestry.com* (https://www.ancestry.com accessed 11/11/2019), citing NARA microfilm publication M653_419, p. 415. Date of enumeration: 18 June 1860. Image 175/332.

as a fully integrated place of worship for many years. Two of Benjamin Grass's brothers, Sheppers Henry (b. 5 October 1837) and Joseph William (b. 20 December 1832) were amongst the witnesses to the ceremony. Below is a copy of the marriage document recorded in French:

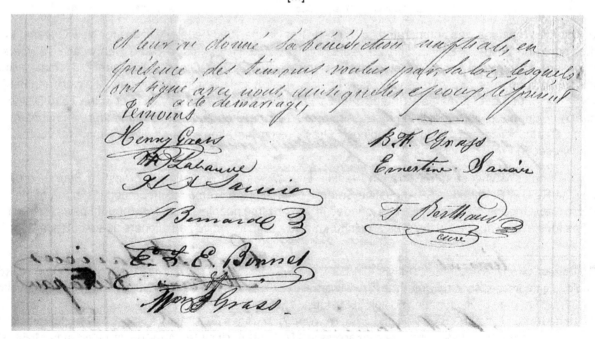

[...]

Archdiocese of New Orleans (Orleans Parish, LA), St, Augustine Church, New Orleans, Vol. 3 p. 117. (Courtesy of Emilie Leumas, Archivist – Kimberly Johnson and Katie Vest – Researching Archivists.) Marriage of Benjamin Franklin Grass and Ernestine Saucier.

The bride, Marie Ernestine, was born in New Orleans on 4 March 1841, to François Duverly Saucier, a third-generation Louisianian, and Marie Euphrosine Loup, the daughter of a Swiss immigrant, Emmanuel Loupe de Rougemont, born on 12 March 1783 at Orbe, Vaud, Switzerland,[316] and Marie Euphrosie Portale, a native of New Orleans. Marie Ernestine Saucier and Benjamin Franklin Grass were the parents of five children, only three of whom lived to be adults. Joseph Fernand Grass, their second child and the future husband of Eulalie Pinta was born on 6 September 1864 to Benjamin Franklin Grasse and Marie Ernestine (last name omitted) and baptized on 16 October 1864 at St. Mary's Assumption Church in New Orleans. The godparents were Alphonse D. Saucier and Euphrasie Sangier (*sic* perhaps Saucier?):

Archdiocese of New Orleans (Orleans Parish, LA), St, Mary Church, New Orleans, Vol. 4 p. 268, No. 124. (Courtesy of Emilie Leumas, Archivist – Kimberly Johnson and Katie Vest – Researching Archivists.)

After his 1884 marriage to Eulalie Pinta, Grass took over the management of the Chiapella shoe store. Joseph and Eulalie were the parents of five children all born in New Orleans. Eulalie Berthe Grass was born on 29 August 1885; Julia Blanche on 7 January 1887; Joseph Fernand, Jr. on 2 January 1890; Lillian Marie, on 21 September 1891 and Marie Eulalie on 17 February 1893. All the civil birth records for Joseph and Eulalie Grass's children specified that they were "white."[317]

The children's grandfather, Benjamin Franklin Grass, designated as "white," died on 17 September 1886 at #421 Bourbon Street. He was kicked by a mule in the "epigastrium" (upper central region of the abdomen) and died from his injuries at age forty-five. His death was reported to the authorities the following day:

---

[316] Several genealogies with fragmentary information on both *Geneanet.org* and *Myheritage.com* identify him as simply Emmanuel Loup, born in Orbe, Vaud Switzerland, to Rodolphe Frédéric Loup and Marie Marguerite Turin. His father, Rodolphe Frédéric was born in Rougemont, Vaud, Switzerland, which is why his son Emmanuel may have added the "de Rougemont" to his name. His 1819 New Orleans marriage to Milalie [*sic*] Euphrosine gives corroborating information of his parentage and place of birth: "Loupe de Rougemont, Manuel (Rodulpho Federico and Margarita Turin), native of [D']Orbe, Switzerland, resident of this city, m. Eufrosina Milalie Portale (Nicolas and Euffrosina Federico, native and resident of this parish), July 2, 1819, w. Jean Rondeau, Joseph Martin and Juan Luis Barre (SLC, M6, 232)."

[317] "New Orleans, Louisiana, Birth Records Index, 1790-1899," [database on-line], *Ancestry.com* (https://www.ancestry.com: accessed 3/3/2020), citing *New Orleans, Louisiana Birth Records Index, 1790-1915*. Birth of Eulalie Berthe Grass, Vol. 83, p. 118; Birth of Julia Blanche Grass, Vol. 85, p. 55; Birth of Joseph Fernand Grass, Jr., Vol. 89, p. 298; Birth of Lillian Marie Grass, Vol. 92, p. 798; Birth of Eulalie Marie Grass, Vol. 97, p. 3.

Courtesy of, State of Louisiana, Secretary of State, Division of Archives, Records Management and History. *Vital Records Indices*. Baton Rouge, LA, USA citing *Orleans Death Indices 1877-1895*; Vol. 89, p. 1111.

Mrs. Widow Frank Grass, née Ernestine Saucier (white), died on 13 February 1908 in New Orleans. She was sixty-eight years old. The cause of death was recorded as "endocarditis." She was interred in St. Louis Cemetery #1 in New Orleans in the Bernard/Bonnet tomb.

Courtesy of, State of Louisiana, Secretary of State, Division of Archives, Records Management and History. *Vital Records Indices*. Baton Rouge, LA, USA citing *Orleans Death Indices 1908-1917*; Vol. 143, p. 208.

Ultimately, Joseph Fernand Grass and Eulalie Pinta decided to take their blended racially-mixed family to a friendlier place. They moved to Los Angeles, CA, in 1895. We can only believe that with segregation having been reinstated by the democrats after the end of Reconstruction, and with Eulalie Pinta Chiapella's mixed-race heritage, that she and her husband sought to free her children once and for all from the racial discrimination that was on the rise in the South. While Mexico, Haiti or even France had been the preferred relocation destination for the early and mid-nineteenth century persons of color in Louisiana,[318] many of those seeking to flee the post-Reconstructionist onslaught saw California as the place with the most promise. It was a journey undertaken by many descendants of slaves and free people of color although in many cases it might have irrevocably split families apart. While Eulalie Pinta Chiapella Grass's children made lives for themselves in California, only two of René Achille Chiapella and Aurelia Watkinson's children, Marie Emma Chiapella Edmunds, (See Chapter 22), and Rita Chiapella, eventually followed their cousins out west. Rita, a seamstress who never married, lived primarily with her sister Aurelia Chiapella, the widow of Jean-Baptiste Olivier, and the latter's four children, Aline Aurelia (b. 1897), May (b. 1901), Rufus H. (b. 1904) and Ethel (b. 1906) in New Orleans. After her sister Aurelia died on 16 March 1938 in New Orleans,[319] Rita went west and died in Oregon on 19 August 1956. She was interred at Mount Calvary Cemetery, in Portland, Multnomah Co., Oregon.[320]

In the space of twenty-three years, Joseph Fernand Grass made quite a mark in California. It was said that he built the first home ever constructed on Hollywood Boulevard, arriving in the area where only twenty-five other families had already settled. He started out as a farmer, growing oranges and lemons on sixteen acres when the area was still undeveloped. He soon went into real estate, selling off land to newcomers. He developed the Lillian and Los Angeles View neighborhoods, amongst others. According to a biography of notable Los Angelinos he also "erected some thirty residences and business blocks from Cherokee Street to Las Palmas Boulevard."[321] At his death on 12 December 1918, he was living at 7102 Hollywood Boulevard. He left an estate worth over $60,000, with half going to his widow, Eulalie, $2,000 each to his Chiapella stepsons, and the residue equally divided amongst his son and four daughters.[322]

Stephen Octave Chiapella's eldest son with Eulalie Pinta, Joseph Octave Chiapella became a physician and surgeon in Chico, Butte Co. CA. He married Sarah Raetta Belle Colt on 2 August 1911 in Stockton, San Joaquin Co.[323] In 1931, Major J.W. Wooldridge published a three-volume work intitled *History of Sacramento Valley California*. In his second volume, he wrote a lengthy and partly fictional biography of Dr. Chiapella which started in this way:

---

[318] Mary Gehman writing in *The Free People of Color of New Orleans*, (New Orleans, LA: Margaret Media, Inc., 1994) points out that the population of free people of color had dropped from 19,000 in 1840 to 10,000 in 1850, due to a series of oppressive laws meant to curb the influx of free blacks into Louisiana, especially from the Caribbean Islands. The first law, promulgated, in 1830 was to discourage emancipation of slaves. Some 735 people of color owned 2,351 slaves who might even be family members whom they could easily manumit. By requiring the owner to post $1,000 bond and guarantee that the freed slave would leave Louisiana within 30 days, this requirement slowed emancipation down considerably. Those free blacks who had entered after statehood in 1812 were required to register with the state or leave within 60 days. All people of color were required to carry proof of their freedom at all times. (Gehman pp. 66-70) Manumission was outlawed in 1857 and the Louisiana General Assembly passed a law allowing any free black to choose a master and become a slave for life. (See H.E. Sterkx, The Free Negro in Ante-Bellum Louisiana, (Cranbury, NJ: Associated University Presses, 1972), pp. 118-177.

[319] "Deaths – Aurelia Chiapella Olivier," *The New Orleans States*, 18 March 1938, digital image, *Genealogybank.com* (https://www.genealogybank.com : accessed 3 April 2019), p. 4, col. 4. "Died on Wed. evening March 16, 1938 at 11:35 o'clock Aurelia Chiapella Olivier of 2838 Serantine St., wife of Jean B. Olivier. Funeral was held at 9:30 o'clock on Friday morning March 18, 1938, followed by mass at St. Leo the Great Church with interment in St. Louis Cemetery #2."

[320] *Findagrave.com*, database with images, (https://www.findagrave.com; accessed 9/30/2019), Memorial #135360147-Rita H. Chiapella.

[321] John Steven McGroarty, *Los Angeles from the Mountains to the Sea: With Selected Biography of Actors and Witnesses of the Period of Growth and Achievement, Volume 2* (Chicago, IL: The American Historical Society, 1921), 207, 208.

[322] "Large Estate Divided," *The Los Angeles* (California) *Times*, 18 December 1918, digital image, *Newspapers.com* (https://www.newspapers.com: accessed 12/24/2019) p. 21, col. 4. Note: A $60,000 legacy in 1918 would be worth one million dollars in 2019. (See: https://www.davemanuel.com/inflation-calculator.php).

[323] "Chiapella-Colt Wedding," *The Evening Mail* (Stockton, CA), 5 August 1911, digital image, *Newspapers.com* (https://www.newspapers.com: accessed 1/24/2020) p. 2, col. 3.

A native of California, Dr. J.O. Chiapella has always resided within the borders of the state and is well known in its professional circles as a distinguished representative of the medical fraternity of Chico. He was born in Los Angeles, January 1, 1880, and is a son of S.E. and Eulalie (Pinta) Chiapella. The father, who came to California in 1875, devoted his attention to the banking business and to mercantile affairs and his demise occurred during the childhood of Dr. Chiapella, who is the eldest in a family of three children. The others are: Edward E., a well-known artist, who lives in Los Angeles; and Stephen E., a mining engineer and metallurgist who has fully exploited old Mexico and who also makes his home in Los Angeles.[324]

We know, however, that Joseph Chiapella probably came to California in 1895, when he was twenty-one years old with his step father, two brothers, five half-siblings and mother, Eulalie Pinta, and that his father, Stephen Octave Chiapella, owner of a shoe store in New Orleans, had died there in 1882. What we do not know is who supplied his early fictional biography to the author of that book since federal census records routinely recorded the family's Louisiana roots. Chiapella studied medicine in California and became a well-known and prosperous eye, ear, nose, and throat specialist in Chico. He and his wife, Etta Colt were the parents of three sons. Their first, Karl Joseph Chiapella, was born on 15 August 1913 in Vienna, Austria, (SSDI) while his father was studying medicine abroad. Joseph Octave later owned a drugstore in Ripon, CA, and also dabbled in real estate, having forty lots of bungalows constructed in the town before leaving for Chico where his son, Clyde Parker Chiapella, was born on 14 March 1916 (SSDI), and William Colt Chiapella was born on 28 May 1919 (SSDI).

Karl Joseph married Ann Elizabeth Gorrill (b. 7 January 1919) on 5 September 1940 in Montreal, Canada. He had graduated from McGill University Medical School, and was interning at the Royal Victoria Hospital in Montreal. The couple had four daughters: Lynn Gorrill (b. 1941), Anne Page (b. 1942), Carla Diane (b. 1953), Michel Lee (b. 1956). He served with the Army Medical Corps in North Africa and Sicily during World War II and was awarded a Purple Heart, Bronze Star, Navy Silver Star and the French Legion of Honor. He returned to become a successful eye surgeon in Chico, Butte Co., CA. He was divorced from Ann in 1969, married Audrey Lachance in 1971 and was divorced from her in 1975. He died from a self-inflicted gunshot wound to the head on 15 November 1976. Ann Elizabeth Gorrill died on 15 June 2019 at the age of 100 + years at Redwood City, San Mateo Co., CA.

Clyde Parker Chiapella married Shirley L. Peterson (ca. 1967). They were divorced the following year. He had been a research librarian in San Luis Obispo, CA. He died on 15 October 1995.

William Colt Chiapella married Katherine Rhoda Markham on 27 March 1944, in San Francisco, CA. William was a physician educated at Stanford University School of Medicine in California. They had 3 children Joseph Alan (b. 1945), Ann Margaret (b. 1948), and Beth Meek (b. 1952). Chiapella and his wife were stabbed and beaten to death in their Chico, CA, home on 13 January 1987, allegedly by Steven Crittenden, a Chico State University student. The couple's son Joseph, also a physician, found their bodies. Crittenden was sentenced to death in 1989, but the verdict was overturned in 2013, alleging misconduct by the original prosecutor who excluded a prospective black juror from the pool. As of 18 January 2019, a new trial date had not been set due to a conflict of venue.

Stephen O. Chiapella and Eulalie Pinta's second son, Edward Émile Chiapella was a graduate of the Otis Art Institute, and established one of the first commercial art businesses, the American Sign Company, in Los Angeles, which he owned until his death. He was also a talented California artist.[325] He was married to Lillian Ceola Trapp on 21 June 1907 at the Grass family home on Hollywood Boulevard in Hollywood, California.[326] They were the parents of one son, Walter Eugene Chiapella born on 6 January 1909 in Los Angeles. Walter was a real estate agent in Laguna Beach, Orange Co., CA. He married Emma Louise Strother in Los Angeles, on 3 January 1942. They had two daughters: Ollie Jean (b. 1943) and Anita Louise (b. 1944). The family were members of the Church of Jesus Christ of Latter-Day Saints (Mormon). Walter and Emma moved to Grants Pass, Josephine Co., OR, in 1987. Edward Émile Chiapella, who died on 14 January 1951, and his wife, Lillian, who died on 24 December 1945 were both interred in Forest Lawn Memorial Park, in Glendale, CA. Their son, Walter passed away in Grants Pass,

---

[324] Major J.W. Wooldridge, *History of Sacramento Valley California*, Volume 2 (Chicago, IL: Pioneer Historical Publishing Co., 1931), 378-379.

[325] "E.E. Chiapella's Funeral Rites Set Thursday," *The Los Angeles* (California) *Times*, 16 January 1951, digital image, *Newspapers.com* (https://www.newspapers.com: accessed 1/24/2020) p. 34, col. 2.

[326] "Solemnize Pretty Wedding," *The Los Angeles* (California) *Daily Herald*, 2 July 1907, digital image, *Genealogybank.com* (https://www.genealogybank.com: accessed 1/29/2020) p. 6, col. 3.

Oregon, on 18 March 1991, and was interred at Pacific View Memorial Park in Corona del Mar, Orange Co., CA. Emma Strother Chiapella died on 7 June 2000 at Sandy, Salt Lake Co., UT, and was interred with her husband.[327]

Stephen Octave and Eulalie Pinta Chiapella's youngest child, Stephen Eugene Chiapella was a metallurgist and mining engineer who worked both in Mexico and in California. According to his son, he started college at USC but after one year transferred to the University of Arizona School of Mines. From a U.S. Consular Registration Certificate filed at Chihuahua, Mexico in 1912, we found that Stephen Eugene Chiapella, a native of Biloxi, MS (sic), left his residence in the United States in May 1905 and arrived in Parral, Chihuahua, Mexico, to work in the mining industry, where he was residing in March 1912, at Calle Mercaderes #8, with his new wife Dolores Martos. He listed his contact in the United States in case of his death or accident as Mrs. Eulalia Gress (sic), living at 795 Hollywood Boulevard (West), in Hollywood, L.A. California.[328] He had married Maria Dolores Martos at Indé, Durango, Mexico, on 30 January 1912, as Esteban Eugenio Chiapella, a thirty-year-old native of New Orleans, Louisiana, a Catholic, son of the late Esteban Octavio Chiapella and Eulalia Pinta de Grass. His mother was said to be a native of Pensacola, Florida, a resident of Los Angeles, California, and married for the second time. The groom indicated that he had been living at Cieneguilla, Durango, Mexico, for the past four years. The bride was 18 years of age, unmarried, a Catholic and a native of Indé, Durango, Mexico. She was the daughter of Mrs. Laura Martos, unmarried, native of the "Cofradia." (collective), a ranch which was a part of Santa Maria del Oro in the state of Durango, and a resident of Indé.[329] The couple moved back to California before the birth of their first child, Laura Eulalia Chiapella, who was born in Los Angeles on 12 September 1912.[330] Their second daughter, Eugenia Dolores was born on 9 February 1914 in Upland, San Bernardino Co., CA.[331] Chiapella worked his entire life in the mining industry. Information in his World War I Draft Registration Card (#3537) filled out on 9 September 1918, indicated that he was a chemist for the Liberty Manganese Mining Co. at the Erickson Mining District in Eureka, Utah, although he listed his address as a rented house at 323 West 30th Street in Los Angeles which he shared with his wife, children, mother-in-law, Laura Martos, and sister-in-law Josephine Martos.[332] The couple's third child, Marta Dolores Chiapella was born in Los Angeles on 13 February 1920.[333] Later on that year, Stephen Chiapella applied for a passport to travel to Guanajuato, Mexico, to accept a job as superintendent of the Guanajuato Mines and Reduction Company.[334] Stephen and Dolores's last child, Stephen Eugene Chiapella, Jr., was born on 19 January 1926 in Los Angeles.[335] The family lived in a series of rented houses until about 1937 when they moved to their own place at #503 North Arden Drive, off of Santa Monica Boulevard, in an area called the Hollywood Flats. The entire family was enumerated there in the 1940 Federal Census, along with Josephine Martos, Stephen's sister-in-law, a hat

---

[327] *Findagrave.com*, database with images (www.findagrave.com: accessed 3/4/2020), Memorial #85365375 for Edward Émile Chiapella; Memorial #85365376 for Lillian Ceola Trapp Chiapella; Memorial #95431400 for Walter Eugene Chiapella and Memorial #101173110 for Emma Louise Strother Chiapella.

[328] "Consular Registration Certificates, 1907-1918," digital image, *Ancestry.com* (https://www.ancestry.com: accessed 4/25/2020) citing *Consular Registration Certificates, compiled 1907–1918*. ARC ID: 1244186. General Records of the Department of State, 1763–2002, Record Group 59. NARA., Certificate # 33185 for Stephen Eugene Chiapella.

[329] "Durango, Mexico, Civil Registration Marriages, 1861-1951," digital image, *Ancestry.com* (https://www.ancestry.com: accessed 20 April 2020), citing "Mexico. State of Durango Civil Registration. Registro Civil del Estado de Durango, México." Courtesy of the Academia Mexicana de Genealogia y Heraldica., Image 1646/1927. Act # 12, Marriage of Esteban Eugenio Chiapella and Maria Dolores Martos.

[330] "California Birth Index, 1905-1995" [database on-line] *Ancestry.com* (https://www.ancestry.com:accessed 4/26/2020), citing *State of California. California Birth Index, 1905-1995*. Sacramento, CA, USA: State of California Department of Health Services, Center for Health Statistics. Note: Laura married Frank Edwin Blosdale on 2 October 1949. They had no children. Laura died in Los Angeles on 1 December 2001.

[331] Ibid., Birth of Dolores E. Chiapella 9 February 1914.

[332] "World War I Draft Registration Cards, 1917-1918," digital image, *Ancestry.com* (https://www.ancestry.com: accessed 4/25/2020) citing United States, Selective Service System. *World War I Selective Service System Draft Registration Cards, 1917-1918*. Washington, D.C.: NARA. M1509, Roll: *1530895*; Draft Board: 10, Los Angeles, CA., for Stephen Eugene Chiapella, #3537.

[333] "California Birth Index 1905-1995" [database on-line] *Ancestry.com* (https://www.ancestry.com:accessed 26 April 2020), Birth of Martha D. Chiapella, 13 February 1920.

[334] "U.S. Passport Applications, 1795-1925," digital images, *Ancestry.com* (https://www.ancestry.com: accessed 3/20/2019), citing *Selected Passports*. National Archives, Washington, D.C., Roll #1355, Certificate #89683, Images 628-632 of 786, Passport issued 11 September 1920.

[335] "California Birth Index 1905-1995" [database on-line] *Ancestry.com* (https://www.ancestry.com:accessed 26 April 2020), Birth of Stephen Eugene Chiapella, 19 January 1926.

designer, in a house worth $18,000. Stephen Chiapella was still working as a mining engineer.[336] Eighty-two-year-old Stephen Eugene Chiapella died on 1 December 1963 in Los Angeles. He was one of the oldest members of the American Institute of Mining Engineers. After a requiem mass, he was interred at Forest Lawn Memorial Park, Glendale (LA County, CA).[337] Dolores Martos Chiapella died on 19 September 1989. She was interred at Forest Lawn with her husband and her mother, Laura Martos who had died on 4 January 1932.[338]

A March 1946 edition of the *Los Angeles Times* published the announcement that Eugenia (Jeanne) Dolores Chiapella, daughter of Stephen Eugene Chiapella and Dolores Martos had married Dr. Gonzalo Puig, son of Mrs. Eva Puig (Eva Ladron de Guevara) of Beverly Hills and the late Dr. José Manuel Puig Casauranc of Mexico City, at the Blessed Sacrament Church.[339] Civil records indicate that the marriage took place on 18 February of that year. The Puigs were the parents of four children: Gonzalo Francisco (b. 17 September 1946 – d. 24 December 1997); Maria del Carmen (b. 16 November 1947); Luisa Victoria (b. 15 April 1952) and Juan Pablo (b. 26 June 1954).[340] Gonzalo was a physician like his father before him who died in Mexico in 1939. Gonzalo Puig died in Los Angeles on 21 October 1998 (SSDI). An obituary for Eugenia (Jeanne) Dolores Chiapella Puig which appeared on 26 October 2000, stated that she had been a self-employed artist working in water colors and oils, a fashion model for over sixty years, as well as a fashion designer for the "House of Adrian" in Los Angeles in the 1940s. Jeanne died on 13 October 2000 in Walnut Creek, Contra Costa Co., CA. She was survived by three children Maria del Carmen Puig-Casauranc, a Washington D.C. psychologist, Luisa Victoria Puig, the wife of Mark Alan Duchaineau of Livermore, Alameda Co., CA, and Juan Pablo Puig of Panorama City (Los Angeles, LA Co.), CA.[341]

Stephen Eugene Chiapella and Dolores Martos's daughter Marta Dolores had one child, a daughter, Maria Felice Heckman (b. 1958) with husband Alan Marion Heckman. She worked in advertising and raised her daughter in Santa Barbara, Santa Barbara Co., CA. Maria Felice married Donald P. Eastman, and later Dr. John Cunningham. Marta Dolores Chiapella Heckman died on 10 January 2016 at Novato, Marin Co., CA.[342]

Stephen and Dolores Martos Chiapella's only son, Stephen Eugene Chiapella, Jr., was born in Los Angeles on 19 January 1926. He served in the Philippines in World War II, and afterwards attended Stanford University to specialize in Hispanic American studies. Stephen married Jacqueline Ann Meyers on 20 January 1952 in San

[336] 1940 United States Federal Census, Beverly Hills, Los Angeles, CA, ED 19-40, Family #297, S.E. Chiapella household, digital image, *Ancestry.com* (https://www.ancestry.com accessed 3/3/2020), citing NARA Microfilm Publication Roll: m t0627-00221, p. 15B, Date of enumeration:11 May 1940. Image 30/38. Note: A May 2020 search on *Realtor.com* shows that 503 North Arden Drive, a six- bedroom five bath home built in 1937, is estimated to be worth 6.2 million dollars.

[337] "Obituaries – Stephen E. Chiapella," *The Los Angeles* (California) *Times*, 4 December 1963, digital image, *Newspapers.com* (https://www.newspapers.com: accessed 2/24/2020) p. 24, col. 8.

[338] There is a California death record for a Laura M. Benton, who died on the same day as Laura Martos, with the same record number (1180). This gives credence to genealogists who claim that Maria Dolores Martos and her sister Maria Josefina Martos (b. 7 May 1887) were the children of James Hay Benton, a Scottish immigrant who, with his brother, were miners, in the state of Durango, MX. (His brother, William Smith Benton, was later killed in 1914 allegedly for trying to assassinate Pancho Villa.) There is no father's name listed either on Maria Dolores Martos 's marriage record to Stephen Eugene Chiapella, or on her own birth record. Before his death, Stephen Eugene Chiapella, Jr., told stories about his family which he had heard from his mother, Dolores Martos, some of which seem quite fantastical. He said that his father was Scottish, Irish, French and English, and his mother was Spanish, French, and Austrian. If the Benton heritage is true, then, it was his mother Dolores Martos who had the Scottish, Irish and English heritage, while his grandmother, Eulalie Pinta, had the French heritage. Chiapella, Jr.'s interview is available on line here: http://www.livingstoriescollective.com/interviews/2017/11/2/a2yioeyuaqjoevrw 8cb1v vs1blhjqs.

[339] "Weddings – Puig-Chiapella," *The Los Angeles* (California) *Times*, 2 March 1946, p. 16, col. 8, digital image, *Newspapers.com* (https://www.newspapers.com: accessed 4/10/2020). Note: Between 1931 and 1933 Gonzalo's father, Dr. José Manuel Puig y Casauranc, was Mexico's Ambassador to the United States.

[340] All birth dates taken from: "California Birth Index, 1905-1995" [database on-line] *Ancestry.com* (https://www.ancestry.com:accessed 4/26/2020), citing *State of California. California Birth Index, 1905-1995*. Sacramento, CA, USA: State of California Department of Health Services, Center for Health Statistics.

[341] Obituaries/Funeral Announcements – Puig, Jeanne C. (aka Dolores Eugenia Puig,)" *The Los Angeles* (California) *Times*, 26 October 2000, digital image, *Newspapers.com* (https://www.newspapers.com: accessed 3/24/2020) p. 445, col. 5.

[342] "Obituaries– Dolores Chiapella Heckman," *The Sacramento* (California) *Bee*,17 January 2016, digital image, *Newspapers.com* (https://www.newspapers.com: accessed 3/24/2020) p. A19, col. 1. Dolores had three grandchildren: Lauran and Philip Eastman and Jacqueline Cunningham.

Francisco.[343] Jacqueline was born to Frederick Hartley Meyers and his wife Julia Catherine Bagley on 31 August 1927 in Brooklyn, New York.[344] Stephen and Jacqueline raised their seven children in Santa Ynez, Santa Barbara Co., CA: Julia Catherine (b. 9 January 1955), Stephen Eugene, III (b. 16 March 1956), Damian Gregory (b. 13 June 1958), Christopher John (b. 9 October 1959), Thomas Andrew (b. 26 September 1961), Marie Victoria (b. 24 April 1964), and Peter Anthony (b. 10 May 1968).[345] Stephen Eugene Chiapella, Jr., died on 24 June 2014. He was survived by his wife his seven children, ten grandchildren and one great-grandchild.[346]

Eulalie Pinta and her second husband Joseph Fernand Grass's five children also made their homes on the West Coast, continuing the Raby, Pinta and Grass lines in California. Their eldest daughter Eulalie Bertha married Chester Leland Hogan, a bank employee on 21 November 1908 in Hollywood, CA.[347] They were the parents of two children, Chester, Jr., born on 24 October 1910 and Virginia Lorraine, born on 17 February 1913. By 1940, Eulalie Bertha was living alone with her two grown children, and her daughter-in-law, Ella Marie, at 7869 Hillside Avenue in Los Angeles. Her son, Chester, was a studio technician. Her daughter, Virginia Mourant, was also part of the household.[348] Virginia's engagement had been announced on 7 May 1933 in the Los Angeles Times (p. 33, col 2), to Oleg Murat (or Mourat), occasionally referred to as "Prince Oleg Murat," a physical education instructor at the Black-Foxe Military Academy. However, we could find no record of any marriage.[349] Enumerated in her mother's 1940 household as Mrs. Virginia Mourat, she was working as an educator. Virginia was referred to in numerous newspaper articles as a "posture teacher" employed by the Los Angeles Board of Education. Eulalie Grass Hogan died on 21 November 1962. Her obituary indicated that she had been a member of the first graduating class at Hollywood Highschool.[350] Chester L. Hogan died at the age of 87 years, on 13 May 1972 at Studio City, Los Angeles, CA.(SSDI). Virginia Lorraine Hogan Mourat left no descendants. She died on 23 May 1994. (SSDI). Chester Leland Hogan, Jr. worked for the Technicolor Motion Picture Corporation in Los Angeles. He married Ella Marie White in Los Angeles on 2 August 1938.[351] They were the parents of three children born in Los Angeles: Judy Leigh Hogan (b. 1942), Michael Elliot Hogan (b. 1946) and Dana Leland Hogan (b. 1949).

Julia Blanche Grass, Joseph and Eulalie Pinta Grass's second child married Edward Nicholas Klarquist, a building contractor and native of Minnesota, at her parent's home in Hollywood on 21 April 1911.[352] They were the parents of two children: Berenice Klarquist, born on 2 September 1912 and Edward Fernand Klarquist, born on 17

---

[343] "Anniversaries – Births-Marriages - Deaths, CHIAPELLA-MEYERS" *The San Francisco* (California) *Examiner* , 22 January 1952, digital image, *Newspapers.com* (https://www.newspapers.com: accessed 3/24/2020) p. 15, col. 4.

[344] "New York, New York, Birth Index, 1910-1965," [database with images], *Ancestry.com* (https://www.ancestry.com: accessed 4/28/2020) citing, New York City Department of Health, courtesy of www.vitalsearch-worldwide.com.

[345] All birth dates for Stephen and Jacqueline's children taken from: "California Birth Index, 1905-1995" [database on-line] *Ancestry.com* (https://www.ancestry.com:accessed 26 April 2020), citing *State of California. California Birth Index, 1905-1995*. Sacramento, CA, USA: State of California Department of Health Services, Center for Health Statistics.

[346] "Obituaries – Stephen Eugene Chiapella, Jr.," *The Santa Ynez Valley News* (Solvang, CA), 17 July 2014, digital image, *Newspapers.com* (https://www.newspapers.com: accessed 3/24/2020) p. A6, col. 1. His wife died on 19 July 2020 at Santa Ynez. See: https://syvnews.com/jacqueline-ann-chiapella/article_6c4ec61f-4048-59f3-a500-6207f5e42bf2.html

[347] *California, County Birth, Marriage, and Death Records, 1849-1980* [database on-line], *Ancestry.com* (www.ancestry.com: accessed 3/2/2020), citing California County Birth, Marriage and Death records, 1849-1980, courtesy of www.vitalsearch-worldwide.com, Image 125/392, Line 19.

[348] 1940 United States Federal Census, Los Angeles, Los Angeles, CA, ED 60-115, Family #34, Eulalie B. Hogan household, digital image, *Ancestry.com* (https://www.ancestry.com accessed 3/3/2020), citing NARA Microfilm Publication Roll: m-t0627-00398, p. 61A, Date of enumeration: 3 April 1940. Image 27/36.

[349] We have found only one story about Murat, a shadowy figure. A 26 March 1930 article in the *Southern California Daily Trojan*, Vol. 21, #110,(p. 1, col. 5), which is part of the University of Southern California's Digital History Collection, reported information about a lecture that "Oleg Murat, former prince, and member of the imperial cavalry of Russia during the early days of the Soviet regime" was to give for members of the Cosmopolitan Club.(USC digital library: http://digitallibrary.usc.edu/cdm/ref/collection/p15799coll104/id/20588).

[350] "Obituaries – Mrs. Eulalie B. Hogan," *The Los Angeles* (California) *Times*, 21 November 1962, digital image, *Newspapers.com* (https://www.newspapers.com: accessed 3/24/2020) p. 16, col. 1.

[351] "California, County Birth, Marriage, and Death Records, 1849-1980," [database on-line] *Ancestry.com* (https://www.ancestry.com: accessed 3/2/2020), citing California County Birth, Marriage and Death records, 1849-1980, courtesy of www.vitalsearch-worldwide.com, Image 632/653, Line 38.

[352] "Events in Local Society," *The Los Angeles* (California) *Times* , 11 March 1911, digital image, *Newspapers.com* (https://www.newspapers.com: accessed 4/24/2020) p. 23 col. 1.

August 1918 in Hollywood. Klarquist died at the age of 41 years as the result of an automobile accident on 15 October 1927 in Los Angeles, CA. A small article in the *Ventura County Star* dated 19 0ctober 1927 identified him as Edward F. (*sic*) Klarquist, married to Mrs Blanche Klarquist. Three brothers were identified: John, Walter and Clarence, however, his two sisters, Olga Klarquist and Ebba Klarquist Leary, were misidentified as his children.[353] The "California Death Index for 1905-1939" recorded him as Edward "N." Klarquist, age 41, who died on 15 October 1927.[354] Julia Blanche appeared in the 1930 Federal Census for Los Angeles, CA, with her two children, Berenice and Edward. She married Norman W. McMillen later in life and died in Hollywood on 9 February 1952. She was interred in the Grass mausoleum at the Hollywood Forever Cemetery.[355]

Her daughter, Berenice Klarquist, married Lewis Seager Peck on 20 February 1935.[356] They had two children, Lewis Seager (Pete) Jr., born on 16 November 1936, and Patricia Berenice, born on 14 September 1941, both in Los Angeles.[357] Patricia B. Peck married Paul G. Nuhn on 25 January 1963 in Los Angeles.[358]Lewis Peck, Sr. died in Los Angeles on 1 November 1997.[359] His wife, Berenice Klarquist Peck, died on 4 May 2000 in Culver City, LA Co., CA (SSDI).

Edward Klarquist married Donna Marie Ohm in Los Angeles on 24 May 1959.[360] They had three children: Denise E. (b. 20 January 1960), Julie L. (b. 25 May 1962), and Edward Rex (b. 15 April 1964).[361] Edward Fernand Klarquist died on 13 March 1979 at Santa Ana, Orange Co., CA (SSDI). Donna died on 25 July 2006 (SSDI).

Joseph F. Grass and Eulalie Pinta's third child, Joseph Fernand Grass, Jr. married Helen Sprague Thomas on 24 May 1918 in Merced, Merced Co., CA. A *San Francisco Chronicle* announcement of their wedding indicated that Grass, Jr., formerly assistant farm adviser of Yolo County "was known through the Sacramento Valley as an expert on dairy subjects."[362] Two of their three children were born in Merced: Barbara Leigh, born on 30 November 1919 (d. 12 February 2008, Ashland, Buncombe Co., NC, SSDI) and Joseph Fernand Grass, III, born on 13 April 1922 (d. 28 January 2010 in Wayne, Delaware Co., PA, SSDI) Their last child, Richard Burton Grass, was born in West Kensington, London, England, on 8 March 1924 (d.30 November 2015, Seattle, King Co., WA, SSDI) while the family was enjoying a year-long stay in the United Kingdom.[363] Joseph Grass, Jr., died on 16 August 1967 in Alta Loma, San Bernardino Co., CA. (SSDI) His wife, Helen, followed on 31 May 1990 in Los Angeles. (SSDI).

---

[353] "Funeral Services for Edw, Klarquist," *The Ventura* (California) *County Star*, 19 October 1927, digital image, *Newspapers.com* (https://www.newspapers.com: accessed 4/24/2020) p. 8, col. 1.

[354] "California Death Index, 1905-1939" [database on-line] *Ancestry.com* (https://www.ancestry.com:accessed 26 April 2020), citing State of California Department of Health and Welfare, California Vital records – Vitalsearch (www.vitalsearch-Worldwide.com, Image 686/783.

[355] "Obituaries – Mrs. Blanche McMillen," *The Los Angeles* (California) *Times* , 11 March 1911, digital image, *Newspapers.com* (https://www.newspapers.com: accessed 4/24/2020) p. 60, col. 5.

[356] "California, County Birth, Marriage, and Death Records, 1849-1980," [database on-line], *Ancestry.com* (https://www.ancestry.com: accessed 3/2/2020), citing California County Birth, Marriage and Death records, 1830-1980, courtesy of www.vitalsearch-worldwide.com, Image 267/566, Line 27.

[357] "California Birth Index," [database on-line], *Ancestry.com* (https://www.ancestry.com: accessed 3/2/2020), citing California Department of health Services, Center for Health Statistics, Sacramento, CA. Entry for Patricia Berenice Peck.

[358] "California Marriage Index, 1960-1985," [database with Images], *Ancestry.com* (https://www.ancestry.com: accessed 5/2/ 2020), citing State of California. *California Marriage Index, 1960-1985*. Microfiche. Center for Health Statistics, California Department of Health Services, Sacramento, California. P. 19,624, line 17.

[359] "California Death Index, 1940-1997" [database on-line] *Ancestry.com* (https://www.ancestry.com:accessed 26 April 2020), citing State of California Department of Health Services, Center for Health Statistics. Image 686/783.

[360] *California, Marriage Index, 1949-1959* [database on-line], *Ancestry.com* (https://www.ancestry.com: accessed 3/2/2020), citing California Department of Health and Welfare, courtesy of www.vitalsearch-worldwide.com, Image 328/684, p. 664, line 23.

[361] All birth dates taken from: "California Birth Index, 1905-1995" [database on-line] *Ancestry.com* (https://www.ancestry.com:accessed 1 May 2020), citing *State of California. California Birth Index, 1905-1995*. Sacramento, CA, USA: State of California Department of Health Services, Center for Health Statistics.

[362] "Dairy Expert is Wedded in Merced", *San Francisco* (California) *Chronicle*, 25 May 1918, digital image, *Genealogybank.com* (https://www.genealogybank.com: accessed 4/3/2020), p. 7, col. 4.

[363] "U.S., Consular Reports of Births, 1910-1949," database with images, *Ancestry.com* (https://www.ancestry.com: accessed 3/31/2020), citing "Consular Reports of Birth, 1910–1949" Series ARC ID: 2555709 - A1, Entry 3001. General Records of the Department of State, Record Group 59. NARA at Washington D.C., File #131.

Lillian Marie Grass, Joseph and Eulalie Pinta Grass's fourth child, married Thomas Hart Nesbit in Los Angeles, on 28 June 1915.[364] Nesbit was a former citrus rancher and a real estate broker for many years. They were the parents of four daughters all born in Los Angeles: Patricia Estelle (b. 10 March 1916; d. 20 Sept 2002 as Patricia Nesbit Desoto, SSDI), Jeanne Renée Nesbit (b. 6 June 1918; d. 21 June 2008 in Dana Point, Orange Co., CA, SSDI), Nona Hartley Nesbit (b. 20 May 1920; d. 21 August 2019, Seattle, King Co., WA, as Nona Nesbit Voll, wife of George R. Voll, SSDI),[365] and Eulalie Nesbit (b. 26 June 1922; d. 24 August 2010, SSDI). Eulalie was married to Jack M. Boone on 23 June 1942 in Pomona, LA Co., CA.[366] They had one surviving daughter, Candace, born on 22 March 1945.[367] Eulalie Nesbit was later married to Lee A. Solomon.

Eulalie Pinta Grass's last child, Marie Eulalie Grass married Clinton William Evans on 26 April 1915 in Los Angeles, LA Co., CA. Evans was a college baseball coach at the University of California, Berkeley from 1930-1954, and a member of the University of California Hall of Fame. Their first child, Charlotte Jane Evans was born on 28 January 1920 in Twin Falls, Twin Falls Co., ID, where Clinton W. Evans was enumerated as a "farmer" living with his wife, Eulalie, and brother.[368] Their second child, John Hamilton Evans, was born in Pomona, LA Co., CA, on 8 June 1924. Evans returned to his Alma Mater, University of California, Berkeley (Class of 1912), in 1925 to become a football coach where their youngest, Clinton William Evans, Jr., was born on 2 October 1926, after the family moved back to Alameda Co., CA.[369] Evans, Sr., took over as a baseball coach at Berkeley in 1927, and became head coach three years later. He died at Orinda, Contra Costa Co., CA, on 10 March 1975.[370] His wife, Eulalie Marie Grass lived to be 102 years and died in Berkeley, Alameda Co., CA, on 24 August 1995 (SSDI).

Charlotte Jane Evans married Donald H. Thoms on 3 August 1946 in Oakland, Alameda Co., CA.[371] They had three children: Timothy (b. 1949), Lauralee Eulalia (b. 1952), and Jeffrey Evans (b. 1954). Jane Evans Thoms died on 7 December 2012 in Burbank, LA Co., CA (SSDI). John Hamilton Evans married Kathryn Lorraine Brazil on 23 April 1950 at San Luis Obispo, San Luis Obispo Co., CA.[372] They were the parents of two children: Nancy Lynn (b. 1952), and Carol Suzanne (b. 1955). Clinton William Evans, Jr., married Marilyn Merle Price on 3 September 1949 at Berkeley, Alameda Co., CA.[373] They were the parents of three children: Susan Marie (b. 1953), Sally Merle (b. 1955), and Clinton W. "Chip" (b. 1960). Clinton William Evans, Jr. died at Walnut Creek, Contra Costa Co., CA, on 16 April 2006 (SSDI) and his wife Marilyn followed on 25 August 2014 at Rossmoor, Orange Co., CA. (SSDI)

---

[364] "California, County Birth, Marriage, and Death Records, 1849-1980," database with images, *Ancestry.com* (https://www.ancestry.com: accessed 4/28/2020), citing "California, County Birth, Marriage, and Death Records, 1830-1980," California Department of Public Health, courtesy of www.vitalsearch-worldwide.com. Image 1482/3407.

[365] See also: https://www.seattlepi.com/local/obits/article/King-County-deaths-08-23-2019-14374779.php

[366] "Cathedral Nuptials Unite Miss Nesbit, Mr. Boone", *The Pomona* (California) *Progress Bulletin*, 24 June 1942, digital image, *Newspapers.com* (https://www.newspapers.com : accessed 4/3/2020), p. 6, cols. 2, 3.

[367] "California Birth Index, 1905-1995" [database on-line] *Ancestry.com* (https://www.ancestry.com:accessed 4/26/2020), citing *State of California. California Birth Index, 1905-1995.* Sacramento, CA, USA: State of California Department of Health Services, Center for Health Statistics.

[368] 1920 United States Federal Census, Twin Falls, Twin Falls, ID, Dwelling #289, Family #294, Clinton W. Evans household, digital image, *Ancestry.com* (https://www.ancestry.com accessed 5/1/2020), citing NARA microfilm publication T625_295, page 14b, Date of enumeration: 29, 30, 31 January 1920. Image 28/32.

[369] "California Birth Index, 1905-1995" [database on-line] *Ancestry.com* (https://www.ancestry.com:accessed 5/3/2020), citing *State of California. California Birth Index, 1905-1995.* Sacramento, CA, USA: State of California Department of Health Services, Center for Health Statistics. Note: John listed as John H. Evans, and his younger brother as Clinton William Evans

[370] "Ex-Cal Coach Clint Evans Dead at 85," *The San Francisco* (California) *Examiner*, 11 March 1975, digital image, *Newspapers.com* (https://www.newspapers.com : accessed 5/3/2020), p. 47, col. 3.

[371] "Evans-Thoms Wedding Set," *The Oakland* (California) *Tribune*, 30 July 1946, digital image, *Newspapers.com* (https://www.newspapers.com : accessed 5/3/2020), p. 8, col. 1.

[372] "Bridal Couple Go on Coronado Honeymoon," *The Oakland* (California) *Tribune*, 29 April 1950, digital image, *Newspapers.com* (https://www.newspapers.com : accessed 5/3/2020), p. 6, cols. 4, 5.

[373] "Price-Evans Wedding Has 'Grad' Guests," *The Oakland* (California) *Tribune*, 5 September 1949, digital image, *Newspapers.com* (https://www.newspapers.com : accessed 5/3/2020), p. 8, col. 5.

The descendants of the Chiapella, Pinta and Grass family who moved to California just before the turn of the twentieth century never looked back. Louisiana, with all its problems, was brushed aside as Joseph Ferdinand Grass and Eulalie Pinta carved out a whole new identity and life for their blended family. Their children, grandchildren and great-grandchildren prospered as their families grew. Opportunities that they might have been denied in the South were theirs for the taking in California where they were amongst the pioneer families of the West Coast.

CHAPTER 16

EGLÉE AUBRY'S FINAL YEARS

Eglée Aubry and her family led a "bi-coastal" life, living and owning property in both New Orleans and in St. Tammany Parish. We surmised that she had been guided in her choices by the father of her children, Achille Chiapella. However, her residence in, and familiarity with, property in St. Tammany Paris had probably taken root during her previous relationship with Louis Hilaire Lorreins, father of her daughter, Marguerite Odalie. She had bought property in Madisonville and would later exploit opportunities in Abita Springs. She had also invested in a lot of ground (Lot 10, square 12) in Mandeville which she had purchased from the estate of Joseph Pueyo in October 1849. An intriguing legal document found in the papers of John J. Mortee, the Recorder for St. Tammany Parish revealed that the notary Achille Chiapella secretly owned a huge amount of real estate in Mandeville beginning in 1853. Had Eglée turned Chiapella on to the prospects at Mandeville, or vice versa?

During the early 1830s, Bernard de Marigny, had been buying up land between the plantation of Judge Joshua Lewis (now Lewisburg) and Bayou Castine, fronting on Lake Pontchartrain, for which he paid a total of $11,620 for some 5000 arpents. In January 1834 he decided to subdivide the land and auction off the lots. After the three-day sale, Marigny had gotten almost $80,000 for 426 lots.[374] However, the panic of 1837 caused the real estate bubble to explode and people with a bit of ready cash could pick up property easily. Many of those who had initially invested in Bernard de Marigny's auction of Mandeville real estate in 1834 had lost their land to the Citizen's Bank of Louisiana. Lot 10, square 12 had passed from Marigny to Nelson Foucher to Joseph Pueyo and finally to Eglée Aubry in 1849. In December 1853, while still working as a New Orleans notary, Achille Chiapella made a huge purchase in the same area. The details of this transaction copied into the Mortee document are both unusual and puzzling.

Achille Chiapella had given up his notarial practice in the spring of 1857, just before he was made President of the Union Insurance Company of New Orleans. In February 1865, as the Civil War was winding down, he was elected as a Director of the Citizen's Bank of Louisiana, later becoming its Vice-President. On 25 May 1866, Achille Chiapella appeared before the New Orleans notary Edward G. Gottschalk and produced for him a notarized document written in French, and in the words of Gottschalk "required of me to transcribe the same in my current records." This document was also recorded in St. Tammany Parish court records in the same year. It concerned the declaration by Athalie Drouillard, a free woman of color, and resident of New Orleans that she had purchased from the Citizens' Bank of Louisiana on 23 December 1853 before the notary Adolph Boudousquié, a certain number of lots in Mandeville under her name, which legitimately belonged to Achille Chiapella, who had furnished the 850 piastre purchase price.[375] She explained that "la vente n'a été fait en mon nom que pour les motifs de convenance mutuelle." (the sale was only made in my name for motives of mutual convenience). The original document filed in the office of Adolph Boudousquié in December 1853 listed each individual lot, of which there were 67, as well as 35 full squares each having four lots which Drouillard had agreed to purchase from the Citizens' Bank. These lots had been put up for auction on 15 February 1849 and were the ones which did not sell at the time. The total included nine lots which had been bought at the auction, but whose owners did not follow through with the purchase. Lots in this sale were located in Old Town Mandeville, as well as on the north side of Florida Street (now Highway 190, but then called "Florides,"), both east and west of Louisiana Highway 59 (the extension of Gerard Street, now Girod Street). At the act of sale Drouillard had given over 283.33 piastres to James D. Denegre of the Citizens' Bank and a note countersigned by Achille Chiapella for 566.66 piastres payable in one year with 8% interest from the date of

---

[374] Anita R. Campeau & Donald J. Sharp, *The History of Mandeville From the American Revolution to Bernard de Marigny de Mandeville,* (New Orleans, LA: Cornerstone Book Publishers, 2014), 329-332.

[375] Included in the sale were the following squares containing all the lots: 36, 42, 55, 63, 64, 75, 77, 80, 152, 144, 113, 155, 186, 197, 224, 231, 163, 178, 205, 216, 243, 256, 278, 295, 309, 327, 341, 360, 120, 134, 165, 176, 207, 214, 245, 254, 280, 293, 311, 325, 343, 358, 370. In addition, the following partial squares were sold: Lots 12, 13, sq.11; lots 8, 9, sq. 13; lot 2, sq. 40; lot 1, sq. 44, lots 3, 4, sq. 47; lot 4, sq. 54, lot 2, sq. 59, lot 1, sq. 67; lots 1-3, sq. 70; lots 1,2,4, sq. 72; lots 2 & 3, sq. 73; lots 1,3,4, sq.74; lot 1 sq. 75; lots 1,2, sq. 78; lots 2,3, sq. 79, lot 1, sq. 85; lots 1,4, sq. 89; lots 2,3, sq. 90.

the sale on 19 December 1853, due on 19 December 1854.[376] Her agreement with Chiapella was memorialized in a document dated 26 December 1854, in which Drouillard also stated that in case of her death, her heirs should know that the property in question had always belonged to Chiapella, with the exception of ten or so lots she had sold with his approval. Chiapella stated that because of the assistance she had given him, that any profits realized from the sale of said lots, after all costs, would be divided equally between them. The St. Tammany Parish document was entered into the record on 23 August 1866.[377]

As a notary, Achille Chiapella came to know many free people of color who had used his services to buy and sell real property, including slaves. Perhaps the two most prominent free women of color who owned real estate were Eulalie de Mandeville Macarty (aka CeCe Macarty) and Athalie Drouillard. Free women of color owned an astonishing amount of property, much more than their male counterparts. Jennifer Spear provided the following analysis:

> According to the 1850 federal census, there were more than 10,000 free adult women of color living in the lower south (from Georgia to Texas); just over one-third of them resided in the city of New Orleans. Of the 561 throughout the region who were noted as heads of households and owners of real property, almost one-half lived in New Orleans, with another quarter living elsewhere in Louisiana. The property holdings of Louisiana's free women of color averaged $3,602, 20% more than the regional average for this group. Their combined total wealth was more than 1.5 million dollars, a staggering 92% of the total property held by free women of color in the lower South. New Orleans' 257 free women of color property holders were, however, just a tiny minority of the city's gens de couleur libre, comprising just under 3%.[378]

Athalie Drouillard and Chiapella had had more than just a formal notary and client relationship. They had combined their interests and their assets to acquire land on both sides of the lake. Eglée Aubry, the mother of Chiapella's three eldest sons, was also part of this equation. She would continue, up until her death, to acquire wealth through small investments both in New Orleans and in St. Tammany Parish.

Athalie Drouillard had made her home with Pierre Passebon, an immigrant from La Rochelle, Charente-Maritime, France, who arrived in New Orleans in 1832. He was naturalized in 1840 and worked as a builder and real estate developer. He was listed in the *New Orleans Annual and Commercial Register of 1846* as "Pierre Passebon, Builder, St. Peter between Claiborne and Derbigny Streets."[379] Pierre and Athalie had had four daughters together: Philomène born in 1840, Odile, born in 1842, Eugénie born in 1845 and Marie Caroline born on 13 October 1848. Odile and Eugénie had died four days apart in 1849, and Philomène had died the previous year. Only Marie Caroline lived to be an adult and to have descendants. Athalie Drouillard had been enumerated in the 1850 United States Federal Census living with Passebon, her daughter, Marie Caroline, and an elderly woman from Saint-Domingue[380], Marie Noël Cordier, age 75, who may have been her mother. Everyone in the household, with the exception of Pierre Passebon was listed as "mulatto." Athalie had also declared $10,000 in real estate, while Passebon had listed no income of his own.[381] Eglée Aubry had been enumerated in New Orleans in the same

---

[376] NARC, "Vente de propriété à Mandeville par La Banque des Citoyens à Athalie Drouillard, dated 19 December 1853, passed by Notary Adolph Boudousquié, Act #229. Courtesy Hon. Chelsey Richard Napoleon, Clerk of Civil District Court, Parish of Orleans.

[377] St. Tammany Parish Courthouse Records (Covington, St. Tammany Parish, LA), *John J. Mortee Papers, p. 480-481*, "Record of a French Document by Achille Chiapella," filed 23 August 1866.

[378] Spear, *Race, Sex and Social Order*, 213.

[379] E.A. Michel & Co., *New Orleans Annual and Commercial Register of 1846*, 458.

[380] That Athalie or her mother, or both were immigrants from Saint Domingue is further bolstered by a 5 January 1789 marriage document from Port-au-Prince, Saint Domingue, between Joseph Nicolas Rasteau, a quadroon, son of Louise Desbrosses, and Marie Sophie, also a quadroon, where Charles Drouillard, a free mulatto, acted as a witness. Louise Desbrosses was also the mother of Modeste Rateau, who was the mother of Luce Henriette Grandmaison, the latter who had 8 children with Jean Baptiste Pinta.

[381] 1850 United States Federal Census, Orleans Parish, LA, Ward 7, Municipality #1, Dwelling #2034, Family #2771, Athalie Drouillard household, digital image, *Ancestry.com* (https://www.ancestry.com accessed 12/2019), citing NARA microfilm publication M432_236, p. 385B. Date of enumeration: 27 September 1850. Image 62/94.

census with her children, but no real estate holdings had been shown. However, ten years later, she declared $3,000 in real estate and $1,000 in personal estate.

Once Nathalie Drouillard died on 24 August 1865, Achille Chiapella was forced to press his ownership of the land publicly so that he would not be caught up in litigation over her estate. He had also perhaps found it wise to reveal his interests in an effort to be transparent about his previous dealings with a bank of which he was now one of the directors. Her death also presented a problem for Pierre Passebon and his only surviving child, Marie Caroline. We believe that Passebon, and perhaps his son-in-law Théodule Matherne, had created an elaborate fiction to spare his daughter the stigma of illegitimacy. Pierre Passebon had himself reported Nathalie's death to the civil authorities, and although not stating that she was his wife, gave her name as Nathalie Passebon (born Drouillard) who had died at 3:00 A.M. on 24 August 1865 at the age of forty-six at his residence. When he died three years later on 6 March 1868 at the age of fifty-eight, his marital status was not mentioned. In his succession record, his executor, Théodule Matherne, Marie Caroline's first husband, had indicated that his wife was Passebon's "natural child duly recognized by him." None of the births of Passebon's children with Nathalie Drouillard had been registered with the civil authorities, although the deaths of Odile, Eugénie and Philomene had been recorded with the information that they were the "natural" children of Passebon and Nathalie. Yet, three weeks after Passebon's death, on 31 March 1868, Mrs. Élise Beaumé reported to the civil authorities that on 13 October 1848 Marie Caroline Passebon, the legal issue of the late Pierre Passebon, a native of La Rochelle, France, and Miss Athalie Drouillard, a native of New Orleans, had been born. The document was signed by the recorder, Severin Latorre and two witnesses Joseph Numa Liautaud and Azénor Sindos, all three men of color who would perform a similar service for Edgard Ambroise Edmunds several months later (See pp. 329, 330):

Courtesy of State of Louisiana, Secretary of State, Division of Archives, Records Management, and History. *Vital Records Indices.* Baton Rouge, LA, USA, from New Orleans, Louisiana Birth Records Index 1790-1899; Vol. 47, p. 282.

Unfortunately, only the cover page and Matherne's petition papers to be appointed administrator of his father-in-law's estate remain in the succession files, the rest of which, including the inventory, is missing.

Eglée Aubry had been enumerated both in New Orleans as well as in Mandeville, St. Tammany Parish, LA, in the 1870 United States Federal Census. By the 1870s, she had expanded her real estate holdings in

Mandeville, the third town to be developed in St. Tammany Parish, after Madisonville and Covington. She had purchased her first plot of ground, Lot 10 in Square 12, in 1849 from the estate of Joseph Pueyo, her son Joseph Émile's godfather. Always eager for a bargain, Eglée Aubry, bought Lots 15 and 16 next to one another in Square 13, each sixty feet fronting on Marigny Street by 190 feet deep, from Marie Sophie Foy, her niece, on 23 May 1874 for $80 cash in hand. [382] Marie Sophie Foy, wife of Louis Rigaud, had purchased the two lots on 18 September 1849 from Augustin Ovide Dauphin, who had acquired them from Bernard de Marigny. Augustin Ovide Dauphin, whose wife, Julie Allain, had to agree to the sale uncovered an interesting connecting point between the Aubry, Allain and Chiapella families. Julie Allain's father, Valefroy Allain, was the son of Amaranthe Lassize. Amaranthe had also had a child with Charles LaChiapella, brother of Jérome Chiapella. The latter was the adopted grandfather of Achille Chiapella who had three sons with Marie Eglée Aubry, Marie Sophie Foy's aunt. So, this sale was not made between strangers, but between three allied families of color. The two Mandeville lots were purchased for $60 cash in hand. Two other lots (four and five in square 18) were purchased from Dauphin by Madeleine Deynaud, alias Philis at the same time and on the same document, also for $60 cash in hand.[383]

A year later, Eglée Aubry bought Lot 11 in Square 12 in the town of Mandeville, next to one she already owned, for the price of $20.35 from the St. Tammany Parish Office of the State Tax Collector. The lot fronted 60 feet on Marigny Street, by a depth of 190 feet on Madison Street.[384] At all tax sales of this sort there was a stipulation that should the original owner wish to redeem the property, he had only to pay the current owner the amount paid plus 50% along with all costs associated with the purchase.[385] That same day Eglée purchased from the same St. Tammany Parish tax auction Lot 9 in Square 12 which measured 60 feet by 190 feet deep for $20 in back taxes and fees with the same stipulation that the unknown original owner had 6 months to redeem it from her.[386]

On 21 April 1877, Mrs. Marie E. Aubry sold property in New Orleans in the Third District in the square bounded by Broad, Columbus, Dorgenois and Laharpe streets forming part of the property known as Gueno's Brickyard, designated as Lots #7, 8, 9, and 10, and measuring each one, 31 feet 4 inches front on Columbus Street by 158 feet in depth, to Enrique Belleau d'Hamel for $3500. Eglée Aubry received $500 from Belleau d'Hamel cash in hand and three promissory notes: one payable for $500 on 1 January 1878 and two others, each for $1250, due on 1 January 1879 and 1 January 1880 respectively, with interest of 8% per annum until maturity. The purchaser also agreed to keep $3000 in fire insurance coverage to be paid to the vendor until final payment. He further agreed that all city and state taxes had been paid, except for the state tax for 1876 and the city tax for 1877 which he promised to pay immediately.[387]

On 17 August 1878, Mrs. E. Aubry sold her three Lots 9,10, and 11 in Square 12 in the town of Mandeville to Oliver C. Williamson of McComb, Pike Co., Mississippi. She had had Lot 10 in Square 12 since 1849, but had purchased the other two lots at tax sales only 3 years before. Williamson agreed to pay $390 in cash and $110 with

---

[382] St. Tammany Parish Courthouse Records (Covington, St. Tammany Parish, LA), *Conveyance Office Book* H-2, p. 350, 351, Not numbered. "Mme. Marie Sophie Foy to Mme. Marie Eglée. Aubry" dated 30 March 1874 by Joseph Cuvillier, Notary at New Orleans. Copied and recorded in St. Tammany Parish on 23 May 1874 by A. Bosqué, Recorder.

[383] St. Tammany Parish Courthouse Records (Covington, St. Tammany Parish, LA), *Conveyance Office Book* B-2, pp. 198-200, Not numbered, "Augustin Ovide Dauphin to Marie Sophie Foy and Madeline Deynaud, alias Philis " dated 18 September 1849, recorded 21 January 1850.

[384] This lot is four blocks from Lake Pontchartrain in the same square as the famous Dew Drop Jazz and Social Hall, formerly Dew Drop Social and Benevolent #2 of Mandeville, the oldest surviving rural jazz dance hall which fronts on Lamarque Street.

[385] St. Tammany Parish Courthouse Records (Covington, St. Tammany Parish, LA), *Conveyance Office Book* H-2, pp. 561, 562, Not numbered. "Mr. L. C. Leblanc, Tax Collector to Mrs. E. Aubry" dated 6 May 1875, recorded 23 September 1875.

[386] St. Tammany Parish Courthouse Records (Covington, St. Tammany Parish, LA), *Conveyance Office Book* H-2, pp. 611, 612, Not numbered. "State of Louisiana to Egle Aubry" dated 6 May 1875, recorded 4 January 1876.

[387] NARC, "Sale of Property – Marie E. Aubry to E. Belleau d'Hamel," dated 21 April 1877, passed by Notary Alexander E. Bienvenu, Vol. 36, Act #54. Courtesy Hon. Chelsey Richard Napoleon, Clerk of Civil District Court, Parish of Orleans.

8% interest within six months. She had made a nice profit, having bought Lot #10 for $70, and Lots 9 and 11 for $43.35.[388]

On 11 November 1878, Mr. Jean Paul Bergé sold to Miss. Eglée Aubry a plot of ground, being a portion of Lot #22 in Square #298 with all the buildings and improvements in the First District, bounded by St. John (now Basin), Circus (now South Rampart), Perdido and Gravier Streets, with a frontage of about 32 feet on St. John by 90 feet in depth for $1500. Aubry paid $500 cash in hand, and gave her promissory note for $1,000 payable in four months after the date of the sale at the Union National Bank in New Orleans with 8% interest. Bergé had purchased the property from Washington Henry McLean on 15 February 1865, before Notary Abel Dreyfous (COB 90, folio 326). Below is a copy of the survey of her property marked "A" on the diagram, by the City Surveyor J.A. d'Hémécourt:

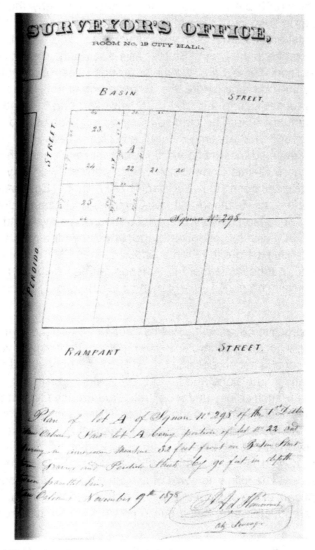

NARC, "Sale of Property – J.A. Bergé to Miss Eglée Aubry" dated 11 November 1878, passed by Notary James Fahey, Act #318, Vol. 16A. Courtesy Hon. Chelsey Richard Napoleon, Clerk of Civil District Court, Parish of Orleans.

In June 1880 Eglée Aubry was enumerated in that year's United States Federal Census as Mary Aubry, a seventy-five-year-old mulatto, female, widowed and living with her daughter, O. Vilar (*sic*, O. Vila), a fifty-year-old mulatto widow at # 229 Common Street in New Orleans. It is noteworthy that she and her daughter lived next door

---

[388] St. Tammany Parish Courthouse Records (Covington, St. Tammany Parish, LA), *Mortgage Book D*, pp. 233,234, Not numbered. "O.C. Williamson to Mrs. E. Aubry [incorrect marginal note, should be vice versa]" dated 17 August 1878, recorded 8 October 1878.

to Rodolphe Lucien Desdunes, the prominent poet, historian, civil rights activist and customs inspector, and his wife Mathilde Cheval and their four children.[389]

On 25 June 1880, around the same time that Eglée Aubry and her daughter were enumerated as residents of New Orleans in the 1880 census, the French and American Claims Commission, was formed jointly by the United States and France to investigate claims filed by French citizens against the United States for acts committed against them and/or their property by United States troops between 13 April 1861 and 20 August 1866. Eglée Aubry was the twenty-fifth person to file a claim before the Commission.

Eglée Aubry claimed that she was a French citizen, having been born in the Territory of Orleans on 3 January 1803. There is no doubt that the territory had become French first by the treaty of San Ildefonso, a secret agreement signed on 1 October 1800 between Spain and France, whereby the former agreed in principle to exchange Louisiana for territories in Tuscany. The terms were later confirmed by the March 1801 Treaty of Aranjuez. Eglée Aubry, however, was mistaken about her birth year, which was 1805, which had occurred after the transfer of the Louisiana Territory from France to the United States. This discrepancy, most likely unknown to them, did not influence the Commission's decision. There were two major ground rules, or perhaps better termed as stumbling blocks, to becoming a successful claimant before the Commission. First, it was necessary to prove French citizenship at the time of one's losses during the Civil War. However, one still had to be a French citizen at the arbitrarily assigned date of 15 January 1880. This caused many claims to be denied because a large number of the claimants who were "French" in 1865, had become naturalized citizens between 1865 and 1880. This quirk in the Commission's regulation also prevented those who were French citizens during the Civil War from being able to claim damages before the Southern Claims Commission whose purpose was only to adjudicate claims made by people who were United States citizens during the Civil War. These rules put Eglée Aubry at a double disadvantage. She could not press a claim before the Southern Claims Commission because she had not been an American Citizen during the Civil War, not because she was French, but because slaves and free people of color were not granted citizenship until 9 July 1868 with the adoption of the 14th Amendment to the United States Constitution. Nor could she claim French citizenship before the French and American Claims Commission, not because she was not "French" during the Civil War, but because the 14th Amendment had made her an American citizen on 9 July 1868, and therefore ineligible to claim damages as a French citizen. In effect the date of her birth was irrelevant to the claim which was denied.

Still, her memorial is instructive because it gives us another small window into the life of a person who left little written legacy other than legal documents chronicling her real estate dealings, various church, civil and census records, her last will and testament and her succession records. Eglée Aubry stated that she was a woman of color, a resident of the Parish of Orleans in Louisiana and the original and sole claimant, born on 3 January 1803 in the Territory of Orleans which was a French colony under control of the French Government. "that from the 13th day of April 1861, to about February 1864, she resided in the summer in St. Tammany Parish and in New Orleans in the winter, after which until August 20 1865 she resided in New Orleans, LA." Her losses occurred in February 1864, and although they do not specify where, other than St. Tammany Parish, we believe that she referred to her place in Madisonville which she had owned since the early 1850s and where as late as 1856 she and Numa Louis Chatellier had had their differences. The following items of her property which composed the claimant's homestead were taken possession of by officers of the army of the United States under General Cuvier Grover and used at first for the Provost Marshal's office and later, after being pulled down, used for constructing quarters for soldiers and

---

[389] 1880 United States Federal Census, Orleans Parish, LA, ED #19, Dwelling #422, Family #915, Mary Aubry household, digital image, *Ancestry.com* (https://www.ancestry.com accessed 12/11/2019), citing NARA microfilm publication T9, roll 459, p. 400A. Date of enumeration: 24 July 1880, Image 53/55. Note: Desdunes was the author of *Nos Hommes et Notre Histoire*, published in Montreal, Canada, in 1911 which told the history of free people of color in New Orleans. He was also one of the members of the Comité des Citoyens, who organized the challenge of the 1890 Separate Car Act. His son Daniel boarded a white-only car for Mobile Alabama but was arrested before the train left New Orleans. The case was thrown out of court because the 1890 Separate Car Act only regulated interstate travel not intra-state travel, and Daniel had been arrested in Louisiana. Comité member Homer Plessy challenged the same law soon after and was arrested out of state. The Supreme Court case *Plessy vs. Ferguson*, which was heard in 1896 found that Plessy's rights had not been violated, thereby sanctioning segregation.

for fuel in February 1864: one dwelling house worth $2,000, one kitchen worth $800, stables worth $300, three out houses worth $700, fences surrounding the above buildings worth $250, furniture in the above buildings worth $800, library (books) worth $150, and fruit trees and rare plants worth $200. The total claim was for $5200. She signed along with two witnesses, her son, R.A. Chiapella, and J. F. Coffey. The document was notarized by John L. Laresche, a New Orleans notary, under the date 24 December 1880. There never seemed to be a question about the validity of her claim, only if she was eligible to make it. There had been federal forces in Madisonville in 1864 although the Union Army was not very active across the lake after their occupation of New Orleans in May 1862. There had only been a limited number of forays over to enemy territory, north of the lake, since the area was more sparsely settled than parishes south and west of New Orleans.

Soon after New Orleans fell, trade with St. Tammany Parish, still in Confederate hands ceased. Citizens living north of the lake petitioned their government to be able to continue to do business with New Orleans. An answer from General Daniel Ruggles, CSA, through the District Provost Marshal, James O. Fuqua, made it clear that all intercourse with the enemy in New Orleans would be considered as treason and punishable by death. This answer, however did not deter St. Tammany residents from starting a flourishing illicit trade to smuggle goods into and out of New Orleans. This trade caught the eye of the Federals who were determined to stop it. In February 1863, St. Tammany Parish had been under particular Union surveillance because it was then that several thousand New Orleans residents, who had refused to sign loyalty oaths to the United States, had been loaded on boats with their meager belongings and deported to Madisonville. While most did not stay in the area but made their way east into Mississippi, Madisonville was once again in the crosshairs. Known for shipbuilding, its fledgling logging industry with the production of timber, tar and turpentine, all products necessary for the Union Army's ability to house and maintain its large occupation force, the little town held an irresistible attraction to Federal forces. The invasion of Madisonville was launched on 28 December 1863. St. Tammany Parish historian Frederick S. Ellis wrote:

> On Dec 28, 1863 the U.S.S. *Commodore* was ordered to report to Colonel W.K. Kimball of the 12th Maine Volunteers, to accompany him across the lake and assist him in any military enterprises in which he might engage. The enterprise proved to be the occupation of Madisonville by a substantial federal force. The objectives of the occupation were to obtain timber, lumber, tar, turpentine, bricks and wood, and to attempt to break up the smuggling and the running of Confederate mail across the lake.[390]

Kimball and 1000 troops left New Orleans on 3 January 1864 and took over Madisonville the same day without a shot being fired. They stayed there over a month, using the town as a base camp to conduct operations as far north as Franklinton and as far west as Ponchatoula, in Tangipahoa Parish. They sent out scouting parties to chase the few Confederate patrols who took an occasional shot at them, confining their operations between the Tchefuncte and Tangipahoa Rivers:

> They arrived back in Madisonville on February 3rd, bringing in 12 mules, 3 yoke of oxen, 15 horses, 157 cattle, 76 sheep, 9 shotguns, and 1000 rounds of ammunition all of which they had confiscated during their patrol. The cattle were in such poor condition that they turned most of them loose outside of Madisonville. They reported "no enemy within our reach except small roving parties." [...] The occupation of Madisonville was a hard time for its citizens, since the Union soldiers foraged for much of their food and took whatever they could lay their hands on.[391]

In October 1864, after Lieutenant Commander J.C.P. de Krafft. USN, who commanded the gunboats *Elk* and *Fort Gaines* returned with a detachment of troops to the north shore of Lake Pontchartrain, he reported the following:

> Madisonville appears to be nearly deserted, and the inhabitants of this whole region painfully destitute and needy, with scarcely clothing. The appearance of the whole country is that of a silent wilderness, in which no laborers could be found to build launches for offensive purposes if any such project had ever been entertained.[392]

Hundreds of the over seven hundred French and American Claims Commission claims had been for the systematic dismantling of Confederate houses, stables, outbuildings and fencing in order to construct accommodations for

---

[390] Frederick S. Ellis, *St. Tammany Parish L'Autre Côté du Lac*, (Gretna, LA : Pelican Publishing Co., 1998), 141, 142.

[391] Ellis, *St. Tammany Parish L'Autre Côté du Lac*, 142,143.

[392] Ellis, *St. Tammany Parish L'Autre Côté du Lac*, 148.

Union soldiers. There is no doubt that Federal troops took what they needed out of Madisonville and dismantled fences and buildings to construct shelters for the thousand men who occupied the town for over a month. It seems clear from Eglée Aubry's memorial, however, that she had not been in Madisonville during the winter of 1864, as, in her own words, she only spent her summers there. Neighbors had apparently reported her losses to her. A copy of her original three-page memorial (#25) now housed in the National Archives has been reproduced on the following three pages:[393]

---

[393] The memorials, depositions, and correspondence for all 727 claims are available from the National Archives and Records Administration (NARA) filed in *RG76, Records of Boundary and Claims Commission and Arbitrations. Docketed French Claims against the United States, 1880-1884.*

To the Honorable Commissioners on French and American Claims, under the Treaty of January 15th, 1880.

The Memorial of _Egle Aubry a woman of Color and resident of the Parish of Orleans in the State of Louisiana_

respectfully represents:

1st. That this claim is presented by your memorialist as _original Claimant in her own Sole and Exclusive right_

2d. That _She Egle Aubry_ was born _in the Territory of Orleans on the third day of January AD 1803 whilst it was a French Colony and under the Control of the French Government_ and that _she_ resided from the 13th day of April, 1861, to the 20th day of August, 1866, _that from the 13th day of April 1861, to about February AD 1864 she resided in the Summer in St Tammany Parish and in New Orleans in the winter, after that to August 20. 1866 she resided in New Orleans La_ and that the present post office address of your memorialist _is Parish and City of New Orleans in the State of Louisiana_

3d. That _she was a native born subject as aforesaid_ ~~native born citizen~~ of France when this claim accrued, and _has_ never been naturalized, or taken any steps to become naturalized, in any other country

4th. That _She Egle Aubry was_ never at any time in the service of the enemies of the United States, and never voluntarily gave aid and comfort to the same.

5th. That this claim accrued as follows, to wit: The said _Egle Aubry being_ the owner of and in possession of the property hereinafter itemized, with dates prefixed, and the value of each item annexed, to wit:

1st. About February 1864 Dwelling House $2.000
2° About February 1864 Kitchen " 800
3° About February 1864 Stables " 300
4th About February 1864 Wood Out House 700
5th About February 1864 Fences surrounding the above buildings 250
6th About February 1864 Furniture in the above buildings 800

7th About February 1864 Library $ 150

8th About February 1864 fruit trees and

rare plants } $ 200

$ 5 200

The above items of property composing claimants Homestead and situated in the Parish of St Tammany in the State of Louisiana was taken possession of by officers of the army of the United States and used at first for the Provost marshalls office and afterward who pulled down the Houses and used them for Constructing quarters for Soldiers and for fuels &c &c

and that while your memorialist was _____, the owner and in possession of said property at the dates aforesaid, the same was taken possession of by mili= tary authorities of the United States, and appropriated or converted to the use and benefit of the United States, to wit: Items Nos 1 to 8 inclusive were taken by the Army of the United States at that time under the Command of Genl Sherman as claimant has been informed and believes

That said property, at the respective dates above given, was fully and fairly worth the sum affixed to each item thereof, aggregating the sum of Five thousand two hundred ($5.200) dollars

And your memorialist further charges that _____ (_____ suffered personally from the injuries and wrongful acts committed by the military authorities of the United States, as follows, to wit: _____

6th. That this claim has never been presented for consideration to, nor disposed of by any tribunal, or any diplomatic, judicial or other authority,

7th. That no vouchers or writings were made or delivered on account of said property.

3

to memorialist or to any person for his other knowledge.

And that no money was received on account of said claim,

8th. That no transfer of this claim or any part thereof has been made, *by claimant to any person or party.*

9th. That there is justly due from the United States to your memorialist, in consideration of the premises, the principal sum of *Five Thousand Two hundred dollars,* in the standard money of the United States, with interest, at the rate of six per centum per annum, from the respective dates when the said property was taken and converted as aforesaid, to-wit: *at the dates as before stated in respect of the several items.*

which said sum your memorialist respectfully prays your Honorable Commission to award to him.

And for the purpose of prosecuting this claim before your Honorable Commission, your memorialist hereby nominates and appoints *John Ray of New Orleans La* and GEORGE TAYLOR, of Washington City, *her* attorneys in fact, giving *her* said attorneys, or either of them, full power and authority to prosecute said claim, and to receive and receipt for any and all drafts issued in payment thereof, and in consideration of expenses already incurred by the said attorneys, and services performed by them, this power is made irrevocable.

Egle Aubry

Signed in presence of

J. H. Offre

R. L. Chapella

State of Louisiana }
Parish of Orleans } ss:

Personally appeared before me, the undersigned *John L Lavesche, a Notary Public* in and for *Said Parish and State Egle Aubry of New Orleans La* personally known to me to be the party who subscribed the foregoing memorial and power of attorney; and being duly sworn, deposes and says: That *she is* the party *?* therein named; that *she has* read said memorial, and knows the facts therein stated to be true of *her* own knowledge, except those which are stated on information and belief, and that *she* believes them to be true. And after having had the above power of attorney read and fully explained to *her* acknowledges the same to be *her* act and deed for the purposes therein named.

Sworn to and subscribed before me, this *Twenty fourth* day of *December*, 1880.

J. H. Lavesche Notary

Egle Aubry

The decision not to honor Aubry's claim was summarized in two handwritten pages submitted by the French Commissioner, Louis de Geofroy, and his American counterpart, Asa Owen Aldis. The findings hinged on an interpretation of Article III of the treaty transferring the Louisiana territory to the United States which stated: "The inhabitants of the ceded territory shall be incorporated in the union of the United States, and admitted as soon as possible, according to the principles of the Federal Constitution, to the enjoyment of all the rights, advantages and immunities of the citizens of the United States; and in the meantime they shall be maintained and protected in the free enjoyment of their liberty, property, and the religion which they profess." The two commissioners concluded that there was nothing in the treaty to indicate that it was the intention of either France or the United States that the inhabitants, or any of them, were to remain citizens of France. The argument proposed by Eglée Aubry's counsel that because she was a person of color she had remained French until the ratification of the 14th Amendment, and if she had wished then to become a United States citizen, she would have had to formally apply for citizenship as would any alien, was rejected. Since the inhabitants of Louisiana had automatically become citizens in what is known as "collective naturalization," in 1803, she would have automatically become a United States citizen with the passage of the 14th Amendment which, in her case had been "as soon as possible, according to the principles of the Federal Constitution." Accordingly, her claim was dismissed for want of jurisdiction on 28 June 1881 because she had automatically become a United States citizen in 1868.

Not long after she filed her claim with the French and American Claims Commission, she made some final land acquisitions. She purchased three parcels of ground in New Orleans on 27 October 1880, from her son, Stephen Octave Chiapella for $5200 cash in hand before the notary James Fahey. The first parcel, for which she paid her son $1200, was located in the Faubourg Tremé and included one undivided half of Lots 9 and 10 in Square 71 between Dumaine, Robertson, Claiborne and St. Philip with 30 feet fronting on Dumaine by 90 feet in depth. Eglée Aubry had already inherited the other half of this property from her deceased son, Joseph Émile Chiapella in 1877, from the lots that the two brothers had bought from Mrs. Emilie Evershed in 1874. The second parcel included the one undivided half of two lots (#2, and #3) in the First District bounded by Philippa (now Dryades), Common, Circus (now South Rampart), and Gravier. Lot #2 measured just over 22 feet fronting on Common by almost 64 feet deep. Lot # 3 measured almost 22 feet fronting on Circus by about 62 feet deep. Stephen Octave Chiapella had bought the parcel from his mother on 15 March 1879, and she bought it back for $1500. The third parcel she bought was also in the First District, Square #6 between Canal, Philippa (now Dryades), Common, and Circus (now South Rampart) with 50 feet fronting on Common by 95 feet deep, which Stephen Octave had bought from his mother on 15 March 1879, and which she bought back for $2,500.[394]

Eglée Aubry died in New Orleans at her residence, #219 Burgundy Street, on 22 April 1882 at the age of seventy-seven years. The cause of death was listed as "apoplexy" as certified by Dr. E. A. Murphy. Her certificate of burial from the Archdiocese of New Orleans, Office of Archives and Records indicates that she was interred in St. Louis Cemetery #2 at "Square 3, Tomb #6, facing Customhouse Street between Grand Alley and Claiborne."

A copy of her New Orleans death certificate as well as the St. Louis Cathedral Cemetery burial record may be seen on the following page. It is interesting to note that while there is a parenthesis after her name on the death certificate, her ethnicity was never included:

---

[394] NARC, "Sale of Property – Octave Chiapella to Mrs. Eglé Aubry," dated 27 October 1880, passed by Notary James Fahey, Act #281, Vol. 20A. Courtesy Hon. Chelsey Richard Napoleon, Clerk of Civil District Court, Parish of Orleans.

Courtesy of, State of Louisiana, Secretary of State, Division of Archives, Records Management and History. *Vital Records Indices*. Baton Rouge, LA, USA citing *Orleans Death Indices 1877-1895*; Vol. 80, p. 691.

"Mme Marie Aubry 77 ans 23 avril 1882, Tombe #6, face à la rue Douane entre la grande allée à Claiborne, 3ème islet)"
(Mrs Marie Aubry 77 years, 23 April 1882. Tomb #6, facing Customhouse Street between the Main Alley and Claiborne, Square 3). Courtesy of the Archdiocese of New Orleans, Office of Archives and Records, Vol 1880-1888, p. 146, # 3. (Courtesy of Emilie Leumas, Archivist – Kimberly Johnson and Katie Vest – Researching Archivists.)

Marie Eglée Aubry had written her last will and testament on 10 January 1881 before the New Orleans Notary James Fahey. Below is the author's English translation of the original French document:

My name is Marie Eglé Aubry. I was born in New Orleans on 3 January 1805 where I live. I have 3 children named Rene Achille Chiapella, Stephen Octave Chiapella and Marguerite Odile Lorrains, the widow of

Joseph Villa, whom I recognize as my own children. I give to my son Stephen Octave Chiapella one half of the grounds and stores which are situated in this town at #53 and #55 Rampart Street between Common and Gravier. I give to my son Rene Achille Chiapella and my daughter Marguerite Odile Villa to be equally divided all the other properties that I possess at the day of my death and name my children Steven Octave Chiapella, René Achille Chiapella and Marguerite Odile Villa as my only heirs and universal legatees. I name my son Stephen Octave Chiapella my testamentary executor, without his having to furnish any security for his administration of the estate. I give to my son Stephen Octave Chiapella $1000 piastres represented by a note and guaranteed by a mortgage on my property facing on Basin Street with the numbers 105 and 107 on this street, according to an act made before notary James Fahey dated 11 November 1878. I declare that I owe to Stephen Octave Chiapella besides the aforementioned note, a sum of $580 piastres which he lent me and which I used to repair my house on Common Street and for these two obligations I would like to reimburse him without interest as soon as possible after my death. I declare that I have advanced my son René Achille Chiapella $1200 piastres on my future succession recognized by the act before James Fahey on this date. I revoke all other wills I have made.

/s/ Eglé Aubry. Witnesses who signed: Michel V. Dejean, Henry B. Elfer, Paul Maspero, and James Fahey, Notary[395]

Her succession was filed in New Orleans on 13 July 1882 (Civil District Court, Division E, # 6447), at which time an inventory of her estate was made. Michael V. Dejean and Henry Forcelle were appointed by the court as appraisers with Richard Marquez and Edward Hernandez as witnesses. The following is a summary of the inventory recorded in English:

REAL ESTATE OR LANDED PROPERTY

(1) 2 lots of ground in 2nd District #9 and #10 in Square #71 bounded by Robertson, Dumaine, Claiborne and St. Philip, 30 feet fronting on Dumaine Street and 90 feet in depth together with all the buildings and improvements acquired by Mrs. Aubry; to wit one undivided half by purchase from Octave Chiapella by act passed in this office on 27 October 1880: Conveyance book 115, folio 39, the other one undivided half thereof by inheritance from Emile Chiapella recognized as his sole and only heir and put into possession of his property by judgement rendered in 9 May 1877 by the late Second District Court in the matter of his succession #39,446. Said Emile Chiapella had purchased same from Emilie G. Evershed on 9 September 1874 (Conv. Book 105, folio 490). Value: #267 Dumaine = $600 and #269 and 269 ½ valued at $1500. Totaling $2100.

(2) One undivided half of the described property along with buildings and improvements: two lots of ground situated in First district in square bounded by Philippa, Common, Circus and Gravier, designated as #2 and #3, #2 measuring American 22 feet one inch and 4 lines front on Circus Street by 63 feet 11 inches and two lines in depth, #3 measuring American 21 feet 2 inches and 2/8 front on Circus Street by 61 ft 11 inches and 2/8 in depth, including an alley way common to said lot and others opening on Common Street and being in the rear of said lot 2, acquired by Mrs. Aubry from Octave Chiapella on 27 October 1880 valued at $2500.

(3) A lot of ground with buildings and improvements in First District in Square #6 bounded by Common, Dryades, Canal and Rampart designated as Lot #76, measuring 50 feet front on Common Street by a depth of 95 feet on the line dividing it from Lot #75, of 104 feet on the line dividing it from Lot #77, and 51 feet in width in the rear French measure (one French foot = 12.79 inches) acquired by Mrs. Aubry, by purchase from Octave Chiapella on 27 October 1880, valued at $2500.

---

[395]"Louisiana, Orleans Parish Will Books, 1805-1920," digital images, *FamilySearch.org* (https://familysearch.org/ark:/61903/3:1:3QS7-L99C-WBT6?cc=2019728 &wc=SJ76-HZ9%3A341296001 : accessed 12/10/2018) citing *Will book 1880-1883*, Vol 21, image 486 of 835; City Archives & Special Collections, New Orleans Public Library, New Orleans. Will of Mrs. Marie Eglé Aubry filed July 13, 1882.

(4) A lot of ground with buildings and improvements First District: Sq. 298 bounded by St. John, Circus, Perdido and Gravier measuring 32 feet front on Basin by 90 feet, purchased by Mrs. Aubry from Jean P. Bergé on 11 Nov 1878. Valued at $900.

(5) 5 lots of ground with improvements situated in Third District in a square bounded by St. John the Baptist, St. Avid, Port and St. Ferdinand designated as lots 1,2,3,4, and 14 in square #22, lots 1,2,3,4 being contiguous measuring in English 29 ft 6 inches on Port Street by a depth of 131 feet 6 inches and two lines. Lot 14 corner of St. Avid and St. Ferdinand 105 feet deep and front on St. Ferdinand by a front of 31 feet 7 inches on St. Avid. Acquired by Mrs. Marie Eglé Aubry by inheritance from Emile Chiapella who had purchased same from Achille Chiapella, by act passed before Joseph Cuvillier, notary on 29 Jan 1874 (CO Book 103, folio 219), valued at $20 per lot = $100.[396]

Total Value of property $8,100.............

Indebtedness: Rene Achille Chiapella to his mother by act passed in this office on 10 Jan 1881, $1200 which he received in April 1877 on account of his rights to her future succession. Total amount of inventory $9,300.

Property also owned which was part of the estate:

Two lots of ground with buildings and improvements situated in Mandeville, St. Tammany Lots 15 and 16 of square 13 contiguous to each other measuring 60 feet front on Marigny's Avenue by 190 feet which she purchased from Marie Sophie Foy on 30 March 1874. St. Tammany Conveyance Book H page 350, which had to be inventoried in St. Tammany Parish.

Included with the inventory was a statement of unpaid taxes in Orleans Parish for $28.58 levied against the estate. There was also an accounting of the expense of Marie Eglé Aubry's funeral. The undertaker. G. Casanave, 88 Bourbon Street, presented a bill for $103.50 which included a wooden casket with silvered handles, a hearse with window for $60, 5 cars at $20, 106 printed notices for $5. Opening and closing of the tomb $5.00, scarf for the cross $1.50, 3 candles 75 cents, crepe for the door 75 cents, death certificate 50 cents and payment to St. Louis Cemetery in the amount of $10. Excluding the St. Tammany Parish properties, and after subtracting the debts owed by the estate, her succession was worth approximately $220,000 in 2019 dollars.

On 31 July 1883 Joseph A. Reid purchased the two St. Tammany Parish lots #15 and 16 in square 13 belonging to the estate of Marie Eglé Aubry, at a tax sale made by William B. Cook, Sheriff and Tax Collector for the parish account of unpaid state and parish taxes for the year of 1882. On 13 September 1883 Eglée's children, R.A. Chiapella, and the widow Joseph Vila (Odalie Lorreins) redeemed the two lots from him for a payment of $17.80 which included the taxes, costs and interest. Witnesses to the transaction included Hardy H. Smith, François Flot (R.A. Chiapella's wife, Orelia Watkinson's uncle), and W. Kennedy, Deputy Clerk, St. Tammany Parish. A copy of the signatures of all the parties may be seen on the following page:

---

[396] The notarial record indicates that Achille Chiapella sold the property to his brother, Joseph Émile, on 29 January 1874 for $100 which property his half-sister, "Odile Lorreins," had sold to him on 11 June 1856. Source: NARC, "Sale of 5 Lots of Ground - Achille Chiapella to Émile Chiapella" dated 29 January 1874, passed by Notary Joseph Cuvillier, Act #53. Registered in COB 103, Folio 219 on 2 February 1874. Courtesy Hon. Chelsey Richard Napoleon, Clerk of Civil District Court, Parish of Orleans.

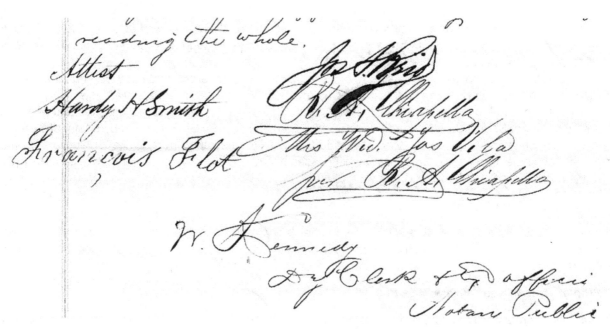

St. Tammany Parish Courthouse Records (Covington, St. Tammany Parish, LA), *Conveyance Office Book* L, pp. 50-51, " Joseph A. Reid to R.A. Chiapella and Widow Jos. Vila, heirs of Eglé Aubry."

Chiapella and his half-sister, Odalie Lorreins Vila held on to lots 15 and 16 in square 13 in Mandeville, St. Tammany Parish, until 10 August 1889 when they sold the property to Raymond Gaillard, a resident of St. Tammany Parish for $60 cash in hand.[397]

Eglée Aubry had left her children and grandchildren a substantial amount of wealth, all in real property when she died in 1882. Real estate had always been at the core of her success as a business woman. Even after the difficult years during the Civil War and Reconstruction she had been able to keep her family together thanks to her wise investments. Her two surviving sons had had a profitable dry goods and shoe business, but their mother had taught them the value of acquiring property as well. Eglée Aubry's association with the Lorreins family, had early on shown her the benefits of purchasing real property in St. Tammany Parish, where she had bought and sold parcels of land. Achille Chiapella, the father of her three sons, also invested heavily in the North Shore as did another of his business partners, Athalie Drouillard, who with her white consort, Pierre Passebon scooped up large portions of Mandeville before the Civil War.

Unlike her older sisters, Félicité, who had a lasting relationship with Hilaire Julien Domingon, and Zélie who had an equally long but rocky relationship with René Prosper Foy, Eglé Aubry had not been able to share a home with Achille Chiapella, who married in 1846. Their business relationship, however, carried on for many years at a time when the lives of many free women of color and their white consorts moved freely in the pre-Civil War society and supported one another in both their intimate lives and their business dealings. From Jérome Chiapella and his wife Agathe Lemelle to Samuel P. Moore and Dorothée Lassize, to Jean-Baptiste Pinta and Luce Henriette Grandmaison, to Joseph Antoine Raby and his companion Maria Louisa Croiset, these early stable relationships helped to expand a productive, and affluent class of free people of color in Louisiana.

---

[397] St. Tammany Parish Courthouse Records (Covington, St. Tammany Parish, LA), *Conveyance Office Book* N, p. 264, "Mrs. J. Vila and A. Chiapella to R. Gaillard," filed 17 August, 1889.

Chapter 17

ACHILLE CHIAPELLA'S OTHER FAMILY

When Achille Chiapella died on 9 July 1881 in New Orleans, a short, but telling obituary appeared in the *Daily Picayune*:

Yesterday occurred the death of Mr. Achille Chiapella, one of the most honored and highly esteemed citizens of New Orleans. Mr. Chiapella was born sixty-eight years ago in Bordeaux, France, but has resided in this city for forty years. He was for a long time a leading notary, Vice President of the Citizen's Bank and President of the Union Insurance Company from the date of its organization up to 1880. *The deceased leaves a large and interesting family* [italics ours], and a host of friends. He was the father of Mr. Henry Chiapella, a well-known lawyer, and Mr. Geo. Chiapella, who was the confidential secretary of the late John Burnside. He was also connected with the Barthe, Formento, Pollock and Labarre families.

New Orleanians who occupied the same social stratum as the deceased certainly knew how to read between the lines. Chiapella's history was not unlike many of theirs – two families separated by race and social class sharing a common surname. Unlike other affluent white men of his time however, Michel Étienne "Achille" Chiapella neither made a permanent home and commitment to a free woman of color, nor did he remain with his companion after he had established himself with a "suitable" white wife and children. Although only occasional business partners, it is difficult to say if he had any real personal relationship with his sons by Eglée Aubry after his 1846 marriage to Louise Pollock, the daughter of his deceased partner in the notarial business they had shared. It was, however, inevitable considering the size of the city that the paths of the Chiapella half-siblings had crossed more than once, and, that they may have been casually acquainted with one another later on when they became adults.

Achille had been working as a notary with his future father-in-law, Carlile Pollock since 1839 at Exchange Alley near Conti. The *1846 New Orleans Annual and Commercial Register* listed Chiapella still as a notary at the same location, with his home address as Good Children (now St. Claude) and Morales (now Marais). It is presumably this address where he took his bride, Marie Louise Pollock after their marriage on 16 May 1846 (See pp. 129,130). Their first child, André Henri Chiapella, was born in New Orleans on 5 April 1847.[398] Henri was a little less than seven years younger than his half-sibling Stephen Octave Chiapella. André Henri was educated in Louisiana and later sent to France to attend school. Upon his return he was enrolled at Harvard University where he graduated in 1867. He returned to Louisiana where he worked as a lawyer, and was later appointed to the Bench. He married Angèle Toutant Beauregard, the widow of Frederick Hall, on 10 November 1880.[399] Angèle was a first cousin once removed to General Pierre Gustave Toutant Beauregard, a graduate of West Point, engineer during the Mexican Wars, and the first Brigadier General of the Confederate States of America. She was raised on a plantation in St. Bernard Parish by her parents Gabriel Toutant Beauregard and Marie Lucie Ducros.

Gabriel's great-grandfather Jacques Toutant Beauregard had been born on 12 July 1726 at Saint-Martin-de Villeneuve (now La Grève-sur-Mignon), Charente Maritime, France. He had come to Louisiana in the early 1750s with his wife Marie Magdeleine Cartier. In France his surname "Toutant" was often spelled "Toutans." In Jacques' father Simon Toutant Beauregard's marriage record to Marie Landriau which took place on 18 November 1711 at Sainte-Soulle, Charente Maritime, France, he signed "Simon Toutant," just above his bride's signature. Others in the wedding party signed "Toutant de Beauregard."

---

[398] "New Orleans, Louisiana, Birth Records Index, 1790-1899," [database on-line], *Ancestry.com* (https://www.ancestry.com: accessed 12/30/2019), citing *New Orleans, Louisiana Birth Records Index, 1790-1915*. Birth of André Henri Chiapella, Vol. 9, p. 732.

[399] State of Louisiana, Secretary of State, Division of Archives, Records Management, and History. *Vital Records Indices.* Baton Rouge, LA, USA, *Ancestry.com* (https://www.ancestry.com: accessed 6/21/19) citing *New Orleans, Louisiana Marriage Records Index 1831-1964*; Vol. 8, p. 308. Marriage of Henry Chiapella to Angele Hall.

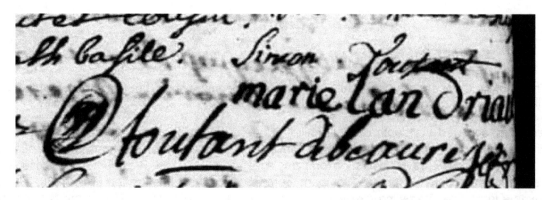

Signatures of Simon Toutant and Marie Landriau at their marriage on 18 November 1711 at Sainte-Soulle, Charente Maritime, France. No call number-Collection Communale-Paroissial-Baptêmes Mariages Sépultures 1710-1715, *Archives Départementales de la Charente Maritime.* (http://www.archinoe.net/v2/ad17/registre.html), Image 29/83.

The marriage record itself indicates that Simon's parents were Jean Toutans "Sieur de Beauregard" and Anne Chaillot.[400] Thus, "Beauregard" was the name of Jean Toutans's estate and as part of the landed gentry, he ordinarily used "de Beauregard" as part of his surname. Eventually the family, after using a hyphenated form "Toutant-Beauregard," dropped the hyphen and used "Toutant" as a given name. Louis Toutant Beauregard, Angèle's great-grandfather, had been the chief provincial mayor of New Orleans under the Spanish régime in Louisiana, as had her great-great-grandfather, Jacques Toutant Beauregard.

Before her marriage to Henry Chiapella, Angèle had wed Frederick Hall and was the mother of two children, Lucie (b. 1869) and Berthe (b. 1872). She had two daughters with Chiapella, Marguerite Amélie born on 19 August 1882[401] (later Mrs. Pierre Jorda Kahle) and Henriette Laure born on 12 August 1884[402] (later Mrs. August J. Tête).

Henry Chiapella was appointed the United States Commissioner for the Eastern District of Louisiana in 1906 and served until his death on 9 March 1911 at his home on 1713 Burgundy Street. He had also served for years on the New Orleans School Board. Two months after his death, the family home, described as a two-story frame residence with double parlors, a hall, library, dining room, pantries, kitchen, four bedrooms, a bathroom, two gallery rooms, with gas and water works and a frame building in the rear yard studded with shade and other trees, was put up for auction.[403] Angèle Toutant Beauregard Chiapella died at # 1271 Octavia Street in New Orleans on 5 June 1926 and was interred in St. Louis Cemetery #2.[404]

Achille and Louise Pollock Chiapella's second child, Henriette Louise was born in New Orleans on 24 June 1848.[405] Still working as a notary, Achille Chiapella was employed on a regular basis in that capacity for the Louisiana State Bank. The family was enumerated in the 1850 Federal Census living in the third municipality in a house they shared with Achille's mother-in-law, Marguerite Henriette Sarpy Pollock, Carlile's widow. While three-year-old Henry Chiapella was enumerated with his family, the baby, Henriette Louise did not appear in the census. Achille, age 32, born in France, was the owner of $3,000 in real estate.[406]

---

[400] Jean Toutans, Sieur de Beauregard and Anne Chaillot were Angèle Toutant Beauregard's 5th great grandparents.

[401] "New Orleans, Louisiana, Birth Records Index, 1790-1899," [database on-line], *Ancestry.com* (https://www.ancestry.com: accessed 8/30/2019), citing *New Orleans, Louisiana Birth Records Index, 1790-1915*. Birth of Amélie Chiapella, Vol. 79.

[402] Ibid., Birth of Henriette Laure Chiapella, Vol. 81, p. 919.

[403] "Judicial "Advertisement," The New Orleans *Daily Picayune*, 7 May 1911, digital image, *Genealogybank.com* (https://www.genealogybank.com : accessed 4/3/2019), p. 26, col. 5.

[404] "Died," The (New Orleans) *Times Picayune*, 27 June 1926, digital image, *Genealogybank.com* (https://www.genealogybank.com: accessed 9/14/2019), p. 74, col. 7.

[405] "New Orleans, Louisiana, Birth Records Index, 1790-1915," [database on-line], Ancestry.com (https://www.ancestry.com: accessed 12/30/2019), citing *New Orleans, Louisiana Birth Records Index, 1790-1899*. Birth of Henriette Louise Chiapella, Vol. 9, p. 1340.

[406] 1850 United States Federal Census, Orleans Parish, Louisiana, Ward 1, Municipality #3, Dwelling #725, Family #849, Achilles (sic) Chiapella household, digital image, *Ancestry.com* (https://www.ancestry.com accessed 12/4/2019), citing NARA microfilm publication M432_238, p. 40B. Date of enumeration: 27 July 1850. Image 80/204.

Henriette Louise became the second wife of George Édouard François Félix Formento, a prominent New Orleans physician. Formento was the son of Félix Barthelemy Marie Formento, who came to New Orleans as a Napoleonic war refugee from Turin, Italy. The elder Dr. Formento, who graduated in medicine from the University of Turin in 1813, was a physician in the last campaign of the Emperor Napoleon I. After the fall of the Empire in 1815, he fled to America and undertook to help found a settlement on the Trinity River in Texas, known as "Champ d'Asile." After its failure in 1818, he came to New Orleans. Whether true or legend, Formento was supposed to have saved one of the privateer Jean Lafitte's daughters from death, possibly from typhoid fever, and was rewarded with the means to live comfortably in the city where he married Palmyre Henriette Lauvé in 1836. George Édouard François Félix Formento, their first child was born on 17 March 1837. Three other children followed. Ruined by the panic of 1837, Dr. Formento struggled to make ends meet, but finally took his family back to Italy in 1851, only to return to New Orleans in 1860 where his wife died on 3 May 1860. After the fall of the city to Union troops in 1862 he returned to Italy and died there on 6 January 1888 at Pinerolo, a suburb of Turin, in Piedmont, Italy. [407] His son, Dr. Felix Formento, Jr. was educated at the University of Turin and graduated at age 20 as a physician. He subsequently travelled to Paris where he attended the École Practique to study dissections and surgery. When war broke out in 1859 between Austria and France and its ally Piedmont, he joined the Franco-Sardinian Army under Napoleon III, and was assigned as a surgeon, serving during the battles of Magenta and Solferino. He and his father had just returned to New Orleans when Louisiana seceded from the Union. At the age of twenty-four, Dr. Felix Formento, Jr., served during the Civil War as chief surgeon for the Confederacy at the Louisiana hospital in Richmond, VA. [408] He married Celestine Voorhies on 12 June 1861.[409] She was the daughter of Bennet Pemberton Voorhies, a wealthy New Orleans commission merchant born in Kentucky[410] and his wife, Augustine Azélie Gradenigo, the granddaughter of Giovanni/Jean Gradenigo, a Venetian immigrant to Central Louisiana. Dr. Formento, Jr. and Celestine Voorhies had four children, of whom only their last, William Joseph Formento, born on 26 February 1869, lived to adulthood. William became a prominent lawyer in the city. Celestine Voorhies died at Nice, Alpes-Maritimes, France, on 6 March 1875 at the age of thirty-four.[411]

Dr. Félix Formento, Jr. married Henriette Louise Chiapella on 27 February 1878 at New Orleans.[412] The couple had one child, Nita Marie Thérèse Formento born on 13 March 1886, who died the same year on 5 September. Dr. Formento was associated with the Baronne Street, and later the Circus Street Infirmaries with Dr. James Trudeau. In 1880 he was appointed to the State Board of Health. He was a noted authority on yellow fever, and pioneered some of the first skin grafting while on duty at Richmond during the Civil War. Formento and his wife, Louise were enumerated in the 1900 Federal Census for New Orleans, Seventh Ward. Also living with the couple were his son, William J. Formento, his mother-in-law, Louise Pollock Chiapella, and an unmarried sister-in-law,

[407] "Death of Dr. Felix Formento, Sr.," The (New Orleans) Daily Picayune, 7 January 1888, digital image, Genealogybank.com (https://www.genealogybank.com: accessed 9/14/2019), p. 4, cols. 2, 3.
[408] "Dr. Felix Formento Dies Suddenly While at Dinner. Was famous on Two Continents for Achievements.," The (New Orleans) Daily Picayune, 5 June 1907, digital image, Genealogybank.com (https://www.genealogybank.com: accessed 9/14/2019), p. 11, cols. 4, 5, 6.
[409] "New Orleans Justice of the Peace Marriage Records Index, 1846.1880," [database on-line], New Orleans Public Library (https://www.nutrias.org: accessed 1/2/2020), Call Number: VEE 678, p. 266 (Formento, Felix to Voorhies, Celestine).
[410] The Voorhies, or "Van Voorhies" family can be traced back to Cornelius Van Voorhies and his wife, Altie Gerretse Couwenhoven, Dutch settlers living in Nieuw Amersfoort (Flatlands), Brooklyn, New York, as early as 1687. The Voorhies family spread out across the United States. The Daniel Van Voorhies branch of the family moved to New Jersey, then to Kentucky, and finally to Louisiana where they had descendants in Avoyelles, Rapides, and St. Landry parishes. Celestine Voorhies was born at Washington, St. Landry Parish, LA on 18 May 1841.
[411] "Décédée," Le Courrier des Opelousas (Opelousas (Louisiana) Courrier), 3 April 1875, digital image, Library of Congress: Chronicling America. Historic American Newspapers (https://chroniclingamerica.loc.gov: accessed 11/2/2019), p. 1, col. 4. Original record at: Archives départementales des Alpes-Maritimes: http://www.basesdocumentaires-cg06.fr/ archives/ index EC.php (She was staying at the Promenade des Anglais, Hôtel de Rome at Nice as Celestine Voorhies, the wife of Félix Formento, born at Washington, LA, to B.P. Voorhies, deceased and Azélie Gradenigo. (Image 119/524 at Nice – Décès [Deaths], 1875).
[412] "New Orleans Justice of the Peace Marriage Records Index, 1846.1880," [database on-line], New Orleans Public Library (https://www.nutrias.org: accessed 12/31/2019), Call Number: VEC 678, p. 58 (Formente (sic), Felix to Bella Margaret Louise Chica (sic).

Marguerite Chiapella.[413]   Dr. Formento died on 4 June 1907 in New Orleans. He was interred in the Chiapella-Formento family tomb in St. Louis Cemetery #1 along with his wife Henriette Louise Chiapella Formento, his baby girl, Marie Thérèse Formento, his son, William J. Formento, his sisters-in-law Françoise Amélie and Marguerite Chiapella, his mother-in-law, Louise Pollock Chiapella, and father-in-law Achille (aka Michel Étienne) Chiapella.[414] Henriette Louise Chiapella died on 5 May 1928 at the family home on 735 Esplanade Avenue. outliving her husband by almost 20 years. Her obituary indicated that she was known as a fine pianist and was also noted for her literary achievements.[415]

Achille and Marie Louise Pollock's third child, Françoise Amélie Chiapella was born on 26 November 1849.[416] She died as a child on 4 April 1858[417] and was interred in the Chiapella-Formento family tomb in St. Louis Cemetery #1.

George Antoine Chiapella, the couple's fourth child was born on 23 October 1852 in New Orleans. He attended the Mississippi Institute where he graduated in 1870. He was employed by Webster and Co., a wholesale grocery where he rose to the position of head bookkeeper. He was a member of the Louisiana Grays and held a commission as a Captain in the Louisiana Field Artillery.

Between 1872 and 1874 Louisiana was in a state of turmoil. William Pitt Kellogg, the federal custom's collector at New Orleans who had been appointed by President Lincoln, ran for Governor of Louisiana on the Republican ticket. He won a disputed election against the democrat John McEnerny in 1872. Both men held inaugurations and certified or appointed local candidate slates. This unrest led to white democrat members of state militias outside of New Orleans to take up arms to oust black Republicans from office by any means necessary. The Colfax (Grant Parish) massacre in 1873 and the subsequent Coushatta (Red River Parish) massacre in early 1874 saw the assassination of black republican voters and the ousting and subsequent execution of Republican officeholders. These paramilitary units, often called the "White League" in the local newspapers made their appearance in 1874. Everything came to a head in New Orleans when Kellogg had the New Orleans Metropolitan Police Force attempt to confiscate a shipment of arms to the "White League," which sought to take over the state government by force. In a three-day battle known as the Battle of Liberty Place, five thousand white democrats routed the police and laid siege to the State House, the City Hall and the Arsenal until federal troops sent by President Ulysses S. Grant restored order. While few if any names of the organizers of the White League in New Orleans appeared in print, it is significant that George Chiapella's association with the movement as one of the "organizers of the white league" should have appeared in his 1902 obituary.[418] One wonders if he faced any of his three half-siblings during the Battle of Liberty Place. Just as brother may have fought against brother during the Civil War, hundreds of free people of color probably faced relatives on the other side of the barricades in New Orleans during that September three-day period.

1874 was also the year that Webster and Co. folded and George Chiapella was hired by the enigmatic Irishman John Burnside to assist in the management of his vast estates in St. James and Ascension Parishes, LA. Burnside, who had emigrated from Northern Ireland to West Virginia in the early 1820s became the partner of Andrew Beirne a wealthy local merchant. Beirne sent Burnside with his own son, Oliver, to New Orleans where they opened a large mercantile establishment on Canal Street. Very successful over the course of the years, Burnside

---

[413] 1900 United States Federal Census, Orleans Parish, Louisiana, Ward 7, Dwelling #298, Family #415, Felix Formento household, digital image, *Ancestry.com* (https://www.ancestry.com accessed 12/2/2019), citing Family History Library microfilm # 1240572. Date of enumeration: 12 June 1900. Image 39/40.

[414] "Famille Chiapella," *Findagrave.com*, database with images (https://www.findagrave.com; accessed 12/30/2019), Memorial #100091884 for Dr. Felix Formento.

[415] "Mrs. Formento Claimed by Death," The (New Orleans) *Times Picayune,* May 6, 1928, digital image, *Genealogybank.com* (https://www.genealogybank.com: accessed 1/4/2020), p. 2, col. 2.

[416] "New Orleans, Louisiana, Birth Records Index, 1790-1915," [database on-line], *Ancestry.com* (https://www.ancestry.com: accessed 2/2/2019), citing *New Orleans, Louisiana Birth Records Index, 1790-1899*. Birth of Françoise Amélie Chiapella, Vol. 11, p. 599.

[417] "Orleans Death Indices, 1804-1876" [database on-line], *Ancestry.com* (https://www.ancestry.com: accessed 2/2/2019), citing *New Orleans, Louisiana Death Records Index, 1804-1949*. Death of Amélie Henriette Chiapella, Vol. 18, p. 755.

[418] "Captain Chiapella's Death. Sketch of the Deceased Officer's Career," The (New Orleans) *Daily Item,* 19 February 1902, digital image, *Genealogybank.com* (https://www.genealogybank.com: accessed 1/4/2020), p. 2, cols. 1, 2.

invested his profits in the acquisition of plantations in St. James Parish along the Mississippi River. He saved his fortune in sugar and land during the Civil War by convincing Union General Benjamin Franklin Butler that he was a British subject. George Antoine Chiapella was his accountant for seven years until Burnside's death on 29 June 1881 at White Sulphur Springs, West Virginia. Burnside was interred with the Beirne family in Green Hill Cemetery, Union County WVA.[419] He died a bachelor and left a will dated 28 April 1857 which gave over the majority of his estate to his partner Oliver Beirne. Burnside's total wealth, according to newspaper reports of the contents of the inventory of his estate, came to $363,445.23.[420] George Chiapella remained with Beirne as the agent for the deceased millionaire's plantation interests which included the Armant, Valcour Aimé and Ferry Plantations in St. James Parish and the Narcisse, Allen, Thomas, Colomb, Marchant, Riverton, Orange Grove and Houmas Plantations in Ascension Parish.

After having secured his job with the Burnside plantation interests as the owner's confidential clerk, George wed Marie Alice White on 26 January 1878 at St. Louis Cathedral in New Orleans.[421] Alice was the daughter of George Aaron White, a native of Jamaica, British West Indies, and commission merchant in the city, and Armantine Catherine Sanchez, born in New Orleans. George and Marie Alice were the parents of two children. George Antoine Michel Chiapella was born on 29 September 1882.[422] A daughter, Marie Eda Chiapella was born on 6 March 1887.[423] In addition to his managerial duties with the Burnside organization George was, towards the end of his life, a Director of the New Orleans Sugar and Rice Exchange.[424] After a brief illness, Chiapella died on 18 February 1902 at New Orleans.[425] His wife, Marie Alice White Chiapella followed on 16 March 1918.[426]

Achille and Louise Pollock's last child, Marguerite Chiapella was born in New Orleans on 7 December 1857.[427] Marguerite never married. As an adult she lived with her sister Henriette Louise Chiapella Formento. After Louise was widowed, Marguerite became her constant companion. The duo travelled extensively and spent time at the Formento country home in Covington, St. Tammany Parish, LA. After Louise's death in 1928 Marguerite continued to live with her sister's stepson William J. Formento in the Chiapella-Formento family home at 735 Esplanade Avenue. She also worked as a teacher of music for many years. Marguerite Chiapella died on 29 December 1940 and was interred the following day in the Chiapella-Formento family tomb in St. Louis Cemetery #1.[428]

Marguerite Chiapella had been born the same year that Achille Chiapella became the President of the newly-formed Union Insurance Company of New Orleans. This was also the year that the family was able to move into their palatial townhouse located at #735 Esplanade Avenue between Royal and Bourbon Streets (originally #81 Esplanade Street). Mrs. Louise Chiapella, separated in property from her husband (see line 6,7 on the next page -

[419] *Findagrave.com*, database with images (www.findagrave.com; accessed 2/9/2019.), Memorial #6252966 for John Burnside.

[420] "The Burnside Estate," The (New Orleans) *Daily Picayune,* 4 August 1881, digital image, *Genealogybank.com* (https://www.genealogybank.com: accessed 1/4/2020), p. 2, cols. 2, 3. Note: This amount of money in 1881 had the same buying power as $8,864,512 in 2019 dollars.

[421] "Our friend Mr. George A. Chapella", The (New Orleans) *Daily Picayune,* 27 January 1878, digital image, *Genealogybank.com* (https://www.genealogybank.com : accessed 6/3/2019), p.6, col. 1.

[422] "New Orleans, Louisiana, Birth Records Index, 1790-1899," [database on-line], *Ancestry.com* (https://www.ancestry.com: accessed 12/30/2019), citing *New Orleans, Louisiana Birth Records Index, 1790-1915.* Birth of George Antoine Michel Chiapella, Vol. 79, p. 254.

[423] Ibid., Birth of Marie Eda Chiapella, Vol. 85, p. 364.

[424] "George A. Chiapella. Death Claims a Leader in Many Branches of Civic Activity," The (New Orleans) *Daily Picayune,* 19 February 1902, digital image, *Genealogybank.com* (https://www.genealogybank.com: accessed 1/1/2020), p. 10, cols. 4, 5.

[425] Orleans Death Indices,1894-1907" [database on-line], *Ancestry.com* (https://www.ancestry.com: accessed 12/30/2019), citing *New Orleans, Louisiana Death Records Index, 1804-1949.* Death of George Antoine Chiapella, Vol. 126, p. 916.

[426] Orleans Death Indices,1918-1928" [database on-line], *Ancestry.com* (https://www.ancestry.com: accessed 12/30/2019), citing *New Orleans, Louisiana Death Records Index, 1804-1949.* Death of Alice White Chiapella, Vol. 171, p. 825.

[427] New Orleans, Louisiana, Birth Records Index, 1790-1899," [database on-line], *Ancestry.com* (https://www.ancestry.com: accessed 12/30/2019), citing *New Orleans, Louisiana Birth Records Index, 1790-1915.* Birth of Marguerite Chiapella, Vol. 48, p. 545.

[428] "Famille Chiapella," *Findagrave.com*, database with images, (https://www.findagrave.com; accessed 12/30/2019)., Memorial #100091403 for Marguerite Chiapella.

"séparée de biens de Achille Chiapella") had signed a contract to pay the architect, Nicolas Duru, $13,500. to build the two-story structure on 23 October 1856 on land that had belonged to her family for decades. Carlile Pollock, Achille Chiapella's deceased partner and father-in-law, had begun purchasing lots in the 700 block of Esplanade in the 1820s. Louise Chiapella acquired the lot on which #735 was to be built from Charlotte Pollock, her aunt.[429] Many married women in Louisiana, with the consent of their husbands took legal measures to protect any assets which they had brought into their marriage, including their dowries, in case their spouses fell into financial difficulty or even bankruptcy. For this reason, Louisiana courts routinely issued orders separating spouses from financial entanglement with each other. It was a prudent step on the part of the Chiapellas because it allowed their family home to be secured from creditors, or from others who might engage Achille Chiapella in legal proceedings in the future. The contract with Duru was twenty pages in length and written in French. It outlined every detail of the house, the size and number of its rooms, the finishes on the walls, the material to be used etc. Initially in the negotiations with Duru, the Chiapellas had opted for a frame house. By the time the contract was signed, however, they had decided on a brick structure, probably out of fear of the many fires that plagued the city. This caused the last two pages of the contract to be one long "change order." All of the initial measurements of the rooms were altered slightly due to the new thickness of brick walls as opposed to a frame structure. As a tribute to its construction and with many of its original details intact, the house still stands on Esplanade Avenue over 160 years after the contract below was signed.:

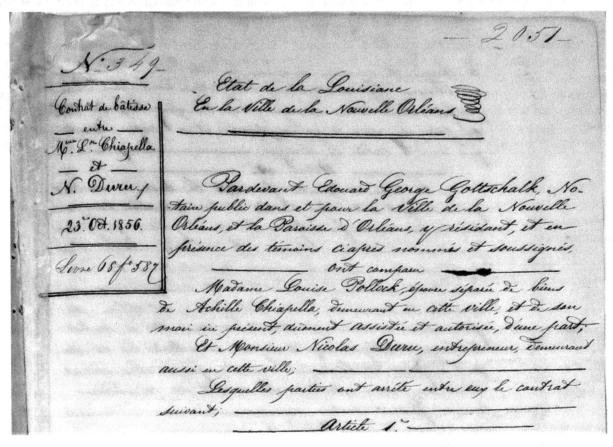

[…]

---

[429] For further information on the house please see: Mary Louise Christovich, Sally K. Evans, Roulhac Toledano, *New Orleans Architecture, Volume IV: The Creole Faubourgs* (Gretna, LA: The Pelican Publishing Co., 2006) 141-142.

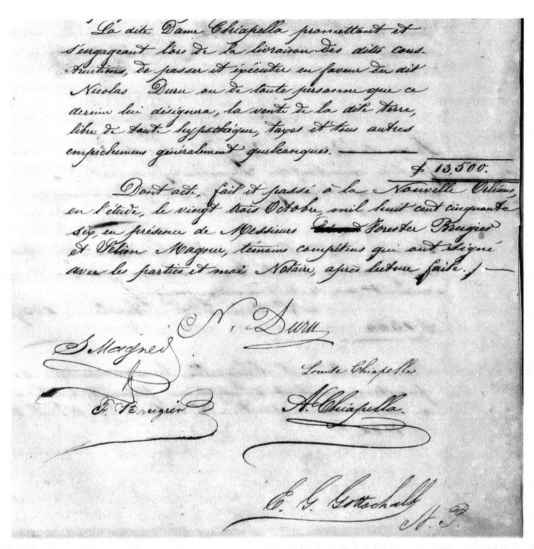

NARC, "Contrat de bâtisse entre Mme. Louise Chiapella et N. Duru" dated 23 October 1856, passed by Notary E.G. Gottschalk, Volume 2, Act #349, 20 pages. (Page 1 top and p. 19 bottom reproduced here) Courtesy Hon. Chelsey Richard Napoleon, Clerk of Civil District Court, Parish of Orleans.

The family was enumerated in the 1860 Federal Census for the 7th Ward in New Orleans at their new home. Forty-six-year-old "H. Chiappela (*sic*), his wife Louisa, and children: H. Chiappella, age 12 (Henry), Louise, age 11, George, age 8 and Maria (Marguerite), age 2, lived in the new house along with sixty-four-year-old L. Polloque (sic), whom we suppose might have been Carlile Pollock's sister, Lorenza who died a year later. Achille, as head of the household declared his worth as $25,000 in real estate and $1,000 in personal property. His place of birth was listed in error as New Orleans and his occupation was given as "Pres. U.I. Comp'y" or President of Union Insurance Company.[430]

Achille Chiapella was almost fifty years of age when the Civil War began. He did not serve, and afterwards he was always known as a loyal citizen of the United States, a position which garnered him many appointments after the War. He was however, connected with an event which was advertised on 22 August 1861, before the fall of the city to federal authorities. A comedy, intitled *London Assurance* was performed at the New Opera House, located at the corner of Bourbon and Toulouse, for the purpose of providing winter clothing for the New Orleans Volunteers who were fighting for the Confederacy. He, along with ninety or so other fellow New Orleanians, including

---

[430] 1860 United States Federal Census Orleans Parish, LA, Ward 7, Dwelling 117, Family # 116, A. Chiapella household, digital image, *Ancestry.com* (https://www. ancestry.com accessed 11/1/2019), citing NARA microfilm publication M653_419. Date of enumeration: 4 June 1860. Image 16/332.

members of the Trudeau, Pollock, Forstall, Urquhart, Boudousquié, Toledano, and other notable families were members of the reception committee for the event.[431]

On 16 April 1863 Achille Chiapella purchased a lot at #1037 North Rampart Street with a three-bay creole cottage on it from Eugénie Berquier. When Berquier had had the house built in 1849, Achille Chiapella had been the notary who had drawn up the contract between her and the builder, John Gastel. Chiapella bought the property from her in 1863 with the understanding that she would keep the usufruct of the house. On 27 September 1867 he sold the house back to her for $2,000.[432]

Chiapella, President of the Union Insurance Company, had always been a personal supporter of the New Orleans Opera Company and had served as one of its directors until 1871. During the final years of the Civil War the owners of the new Opera House building had gone into bankruptcy. The Union Insurance Company was amongst the principal bond holders. On 1 October 1864, it was reported in the New Orleans Era that "Sheriff Shaw yesterday sold at the Merchants' and Auctioneers' Exchange, the new Opera House under a write of seizure and sale. Mr. A. Chiapella, President of the Union Insurance Company, and acting on its behalf, was the highest and last bidder, and obtained the property for $80,000."[433] A further explanation of the sale was reported in the Daily Picayune which indicated that: "The new Opera House at the corner of Bourbon and Toulouse Streets was sold yesterday for $80,000, which we are informed is just about the amount of claims against the property. The law requires that property sold at Sheriff's sale shall bring two-thirds of the appraisement which, in this case, was $120,000. The Union Insurance Company, upon whose suit the theatre was sold, was the purchaser. The cost of the establishment, as it stands, was about $250,000."[434]

After the end of the Civil War, with his home and reputation still intact, Chiapella was elected to the Board of Directors of the Citizens' Bank of Louisiana. He was also appointed to the New Orleans School Board by Mayor Hugh Kennedy.[435] Just a few weeks previously, on 27 July 1865 he had been elected one of the directors of the New Orleans, Opelousas, and Great Western Railroad, which had been under the control of the Union army for three years, as a condition precedent to the return of the railroad into civilian hands.[436] Only male citizens who had been loyal to the Union, and who had not served with the Confederacy were eligible for the appointments.

In April 1867, Achille Chiapella was one amongst twenty-five male residents of the 7th Ward, Third District in New Orleans to call for the organization of a political club. All men, who were not ineligible to vote due to their proscription by law, were asked to assemble on 25 April 1867, at "the Spanish Cock-pit on Columbus Street between Love and Good Children streets." This action on their part was just one of many efforts to begin to organize to combat the effects of Federal Reconstruction and to enable the Democrat party to seize the State government back from Republican control.[437]

The Chiapella family was, once again, enumerated at their Esplanade Avenue home in the 1870 United States Federal Census for New Orleans. Achille, the President of an insurance company, with $18,000 in real estate and $1500 in personal property was living with his wife Louise, and children Louise, Henry, George and Maggie.

[431] "New Opera House," The (New Orleans) Daily Picayune, 22 August 1861, digital image, Newspapers.com (https://www.newspapers.com: accessed 12/24/2019) p. 2, col. 5.
[432] Roulhac Toledano and Mary Louise Christovich, New Orleans Architecture, Volume VI: Faubourg Tremé and the Bayou Road (Gretna, LA: The Pelican Publishing Co., 2003) 178-179.
[433] "Sale of the New Opera House," The (New Orleans) Era, 1 October 1864, digital image, Genealogybank.com (https://www.genealogybank.com: accessed 1/2/2020) p. 2, col. 5.
[434] "Sale of the Opera House," The (New Orleans) Daily Picayune, 1 October 1864, digital image, Genealogybank.com (https://www.genealogybank.com: accessed 12/14/2019) p. 2, col. 1.
[435] "The Board of School Directors," The New Orleans Times, 27 August 1865, digital image, Genealogybank.com (https://www.genealogybank.com: accessed 12/24/2019) p. 5, cols. 1, 2.
[436] " Directors of the New Orleans, Opelousas and Great Western Railroad" The (New Orleans) Daily Picayune, 27 July 1865, digital image, Genealogybank.com (https://www.genealogybank.com: accessed 12/24/2019) p. 4, col. 1.
[437] "To the Voters of the 7th Ward, Third District," The New Orleans Tribune, 25 April 1867, digital image, Genealogybank.com (https://www.genealogybank.com: accessed 1/2/2020) p. 4, col. 6.

Also included in the household were three servants: Maggie Brown, age 22, from England, Anna Reiner, age 18, from Ireland, and Antoinette Green, age 50, born in Louisiana.[438]

Achille Chiapella was enumerated for the last time on 1 June 1880 in that year's United States Federal Census at his Esplanade Avenue townhouse as a sixty-five-year-old notary. Included in the household were his wife, Louise, his son Henry, who would marry later on in the year, his daughter Marguerite, his wife's sister Emma Pollock, and his daughter Louise with her new husband, Felix Formento, a physician, and Formento's eleven-year-old son, William. Four servants, Antoinette Clark, Martha Taylor, Hanna Patterson, and the cook, Antoinette Gastien lived with the family.[439]

Achille Chiapella died at his home on 9 July 1881. The cause of death was listed as "softening of the brain," the diagnosis given by Dr. Felix Formento, his son-in-law, who signed the death certificate:

Courtesy of, State of Louisiana, Secretary of State, Division of Archives, Records Management and History. *Vital Records Indices*. Baton Rouge, LA, USA citing *Orleans Death Indices 1877-1895*; Vol. 79, p. 126.

He was interred in the Chiapella-Formento family mausoleum is St. Louis Cemetery #1. His last will and testament, written in 1869, left his estate to his legitimate wife and four children. If he had helped his other children by Marie

---

[438] 1870 United States Federal Census Orleans Parish, LA, Ward 7, Dwelling 940, Family #1135, A. Chiapella household, digital image, *Ancestry.com* (https://www. ancestry.com accessed 11/22//2019), citing NARA microfilm publication M593_522. Date of enumeration: 7 July 1870. Image 466/470.

[439] 1880 United States Federal Census, New Orleans, Orleans Parish, LA, ED 48, Dwelling #25, Family #37, Achille Chiapella household, digital image, *Ancestry.com* (https://www.ancestry.com: accessed 12/29/2019), citing NARA microfilm publication T9, roll 461. Date of enumeration: 1 June 1880, Image 5/25.

Eglée Aubry, who outlived him by just over nine months, throughout the course of his life, there was no mention of any other provisions in his will. He appointed his wife and son Henry as co-executors testamentary of his estate.

Louise Pollock Chiapella lived the rest of her life in the family home at 735 Esplanade Avenue. She died on 11 May 1902 and was interred the next day in the Chiapella-Formento family tomb in St. Louis Cemetery #1. The New Orleans Daily Picayune published a brief obituary notice on 12 May 1902 which read: "Chiapella – On Sunday, May 11, 1902 at 12:30 o'clock A.M., Mrs. Louise Pollock, widow of Achille Chiapella, a native of this city. Relatives, friends and acquaintances of the Chiapella and Formento families are respectfully invited to attend the funeral which will take place this (Monday) Morning, May 12, at 10:00 o'clock from her late residence, No. 735 Esplanade avenue. Please omit flowers."[440]

---

[440] "Died, Chiapella, Mrs. Louise Pollock," *The (New Orleans) Daily Picayune* , May 12, 1902, digital image, *Genealogybank.com* (https://www.genealogybank.com: accessed 1/4/2020) p. 4, col. 5.

CHAPTER 18

FÉLICITÉ AUBRY, LOUIS ALEXANDRE DUPUY AND HILAIRE JULIEN DOMINGON

We have examined Eglée Aubry's elder sister Félicité Aubry's early life previously in this book (See p. 7,8). The father of her first five children, Louis Alexandre Dupuy, an attorney, ended their relationship about 1816 and died thirteen years later. Like many men of his rank, he chose to take a white wife later on in his life. His 4 June 1829 marriage document to Victorine Constance Leblanc was recorded at St. Louis Cathedral: "Dupuy [@ Dupuy de Gurad, Dupuy de Gurard], Louis Alexander (Jean Étienne Dupuy de Gurad and ? Jourdain), Écuyer [Esq.], Sieur de Gurad, native of Braye, dept. of Seine-et-Oise in France, resident of this parish, m. Victorine Constance Leblanc, June 4, 1829, w. Joseph August Martin, Carlos Vallefoze [@ Vallefos], Manuel Eugenio Torrens (SLC M7, 156)."

Information from this record led us to a book reproduced on the internet at *www.geneanet.org* intitled *Dictionnaire biographique sur les pensionnaires de l'académie royale de Juilly (1651-1828), Tome II (1746-1795)* where we found the following information : "Né à Bray-et-Lû le 9 août 1769, Louis Alexandre Dupuy fut baptisé le 17 août suivant. Il était fils de messire Jean Étienne Dupuy, sieur de Gurard, ancien officier d'infanterie et de demoiselle Marie-Catherine Jourdain, filleul de messire Louis François Dupuy, écuyer, sieur de Gerville, demeurant à Paris, […]"[441] Below is a copy of Louis Alexandre Dupuy's baptismal record done at Bray on 17 August 1769, which we translated as follows: "Louis Alexandre Dupuy was born on 9 August 1769 at Bray-et-Lû, Val-d'Oise, France, and baptized on 17 August. He was the son of Jean-Étienne Dupuy, Sieur of Gurard, former infantry officer, and of Marie-Catherine Jourdain. His godparents were his uncle, Louis François, Sieur de Gerville, living at Paris, who was represented by proxy at the baptism by Louis Jouvenne, and by Charlotte Alexandrine Dupuy, widow of Annibal Lhuilier, represented by proxy by Geneviève Lhuilier, wife of Louis Jouvenne." The document's extended length is unusual because most baptismal records did not exceed four lines or so. However, because Louis Alexandre Dupuy was descended from landed gentry, from men who had served king and country, and upon whom had been bestowed several titles of nobility, the length of his baptism record was befitting his station in life:

---

[441] Étienne Broglin, *Dictionnaire biographique sur les pensionnaires de l'académie royale de Juilly (1651-1828), Tome II (1746-1795)*, Centre Roland Mousnier, 2017 (http://www.centrerolandmousnier.fr/). The title of the work is *Biographical Dictionary of the Pensioners of the Royal Academy at Juilly (1658-1828) Volume II (1746-1795)*. The translated excerpt reads: "Born at Bray-et-Lû on 9 August 1769, Louis Alexandre Dupuy was baptized the following August 17th 1769. He was the son of Mr. Jean Étienne Dupuy, sire of Gurard, former infantry officer, and of Miss. Marie-Catherine Jourdain, godson of Mr. Louis François Dupuy, squire, sire of Gerville, living at Paris." From other sources we learned that his paternal grandparents were Antoine Dupuy and Anne de Crèvecoeur.

Bray-et-Lû, Val d'Oise, France, Baptêmes, mariages, sépultures 1717-1722, 1724-1775. [Baptisms, Marriages and Burials], Baptism of Louis Alexandre Dupuy dated 17 August 1769, digital image, *Archives départementales du Val d'Oise*, "État Civil en ligne," (http://archives.valdoise.fr/: accessed 11/4/ 2019), Cote E-Depot 19 E3, Image 122/138. Note: The proxy papers for both godparents may be seen on previous Images 119-121.

The first clue we have to Louis Alexandre Dupuy's life in New Orleans was discovered in Roulhac Toledano and Mary Louise Christovich's book intitled *New Orleans Architecture, Volume VI, Faubourg Tremé and the Bayou Road.* Before Claude Tremé and his wife decided to sell their New Orleans plantation in 1810 to the City of New Orleans, they had disposed of some of their land to Louis Alexandre Dupuy. On 5 October 1803 they sold him sixty feet fronting on Bayou Road, having a depth of 145 feet in an act passed before the notary Pierre Pedesclaux. Below is a copy of a portion of the signature page:

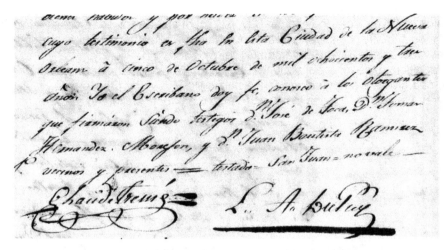

NARC, "Claude Tremé to Louis Alexandre Dupuy Sale of property with mortgage" dated 5 October 1803, passed by Notary P. Pedesclaux, Volume 45, p. 803. Courtesy Hon. Chelsey Richard Napoleon, Clerk of Civil District Court, Parish of Orleans.

On 10 October 1803 the Tremés entered into a privately signed contract (un sous-seing privé) with Dupuy to donate to him a thirty ft. by 145 ft. lot at the corner of Bayou Road and North Rampart Street which was adjacent to the property he had bought five days previously. The donation was made by them under the condition that he improve the property. When the Tremés sold their plantation before the notary Michel de Armas on 17 March 1810, they indicated that since Dupuy had abandoned the land and left the city, their agreement was void and they wanted the small lot back. The adjoining 60 feet on Bayou Road had been sold by Dupuy to Sieur Godefroy before 1810 and there was no challenge to his title.[442] Below is a copy of the map which was made part of the Tremé sale of their property to the City of New Orleans. The Dupuy lots were numbered 27 and 27 bis, on the left side of Bayou Road (Chemin du Bayou) at the bottom left of the map:

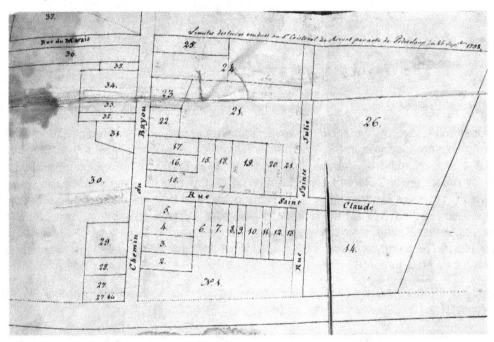

NARC, Map of 37 lots sold by Claude Tremé before 1810, passed by Notary Michel de Armas, Volume 3, Act #54 (page 13 of the act). Courtesy Hon. Chelsey Richard Napoleon, Clerk of Civil District Court, Parish of Orleans. (Note: The street below lot 27 bis at bottom is Rampart. Rue Sainte Julie is now Esplanade. Eleven lots were sold to free women of color and six to free men of color.)

Below is a copy in French of the description of the Dupuy lots as appears in the 17 March 1810 sale of land from Mr. and Mrs. Claude Tremé to the City of New Orleans, which reads in part in our translation:

---

[442] Toledano and Christovich, *New Orleans Architecture, Volume VI*, 17-19.

On the left side of Bayou Road leaving the City. #27 lot of sixty feet more or less facing Bayou Road by 145 feet in depth, sold to Mr. Louis Alexandre Dupuy before Pedesclaux, Notary, under the date of 5 October 1803, and now occupied by the Gentleman Godefroy.

#27 bis. An addition to the lot of about 30 feet on Bayou Road with the same depth of 145 feet that Mr. and Mrs. Tremé had given and abandoned to the same Mr. Dupuy by private sale of 10 October 1803 which the sellers are pursuing by litigation to be returned to them for his failure to execute the terms of agreement.

NARC, "Vente d'habitation par Sieur et Dame Tremé à la Corporation de la Nouvelle Orleans," dated 17 March 1810, passed by Michel de Armas, Volume 3, Act #54, (page 9 of the act). Courtesy Hon. Chelsey Richard Napoleon, Clerk of Civil District Court, Parish of Orleans.

From subsequent records, we know, however, that Dupuy had not left the city. The next clue we have to his residence in Louisiana appeared in the *Télégraphe* (*Commercial Advertiser and New Orleans Price Current*) dated 21 July 1804, (1st Volume, also dated 4 Thermidor, An XII in the French Revolutionary Calendar), published in New Orleans by Beleurgey and Renard, Rue Bourbon #199. It was a bilingual newspaper, with advertisements of all types in which Louis Alexandre Dupuy alerted the public that he had changed his address in a short item which when translated read that "he has the honor of alerting the Public, and especially the persons with whom he is conducting business that he keeps his office on Customhouse Street, in the house of Mrs. Fuselier, opposite Mr. Garland's place. He can be found regularly in his office from 8 AM until noon, and in the evening from 3 PM until 6 PM." The notice was dated 9 June (1804)[443]

Although an attorney-at-law, Dupuy also continued buying and selling property. In March 1805 he advertised lots for sale in *The Orleans Gazette*:

LOTS FOR SALE. The subscriber offers for sale a few LOTS, within two or three miles of this city, and on the same side of the river. They are situated immediately on the margin of the river, and are calculated to secure to a family all the advantages of country life, being sufficiently large for a garden, poultry yards, etc. Besides the advantages common to lots in general, those immediately on the banks of the Mississippi have one peculiar to themselves – namely, that firewood may be obtained without price, the river conveying it to the very door. In point of situation, health and salubrity of air, these lots are excelled by none in the territory,

---

[443] "Changement de domicile," (Change of Address) *Télégraphe et le Commercial Advertiser*, July 21, 1804, digital image, *Genealogybank.com* (https://www.genealogybank.com: accessed 8 January 2020), p. 2, col. 2.

and will afford a convenient and agreeable summer retreat from the yellow fever – and it is well known that flight is the only security against that dreadful calamity. The terms will be made easy to purchasers. For further particulars, apply to the subscriber, at his office in the principal. L. A. Dupuy, Attorney at Law, February 25.[444]

Dupuy had moved his office and residence again, as early as 29 October 1807, to #10 Bourbon Street. Although there are no records for this move, he had probably been there at least a year or so earlier, as he had fathered his first child, Edmond Dupuy born on 29 August 1806, with Félicité Aubry, who was enumerated living next to him in an the 1810 United States Federal Census for the Territory of Orleans (See p. 8). Shortly after the birth of Edmond, Dupuy was busy representing "Mrs. Widow Panis," owner of a place called Rousseau's Plantation "only three or four acres from the Suburb Robin." The widow had decided to subdivide the plantation into lots which had been named the "Quartier de Bel-Air." Dupuy advertised in the *Orleans Gazette and Commercial Advertiser*, just as he had when he sold lots outside the city two years previously, that they were a welcome and healthy refuge from the city, with plenty of room to grow vegetables, and at high enough ground not to fear that the levee would break. As an added inducement to buy, the widow was forever relinquishing her rights to the land lying between the first lots and the river, where the purchasers would find an abundance of timber for building and fencing as well as pasture for their cattle.[445]

Louis Alexandre and Félicité's second child, Léon Dupuy was born about January 1808, and his predicament later on in life, when his baptismal record could not be produced, has already been previously discussed (See pp. 9, 10). Alexander Edouardo Dupuy was born on 26 June 1810 and baptized by Fr. Jean Pierre Koüne: "Dupuis, Alexander Edouardo (Luis Alexandro, native of Paris, resident of this city and Felicitas Obry, native and resident of this city) b. March 17, 1811, bn. June 26, 1810, s. Pablo Mon (camp?) and Anna Fazende (SLC, B24, 17)." Their next child, baptized simply as Alexandre Dupuy, was born three years later: "Dupuy, Alexandre (Louis Alexandre, native of Paris, a lawyer and Felicité Aubry, native of this parish) b. 4 Nov 1813, bn. Mar. 15, 1813, s. Joseph Demahy and Henriette Macarty, all residents of this parish (SLC B26, 153)." He died sixteen months later as Alexandro "Auvry" (*sic*): "Auvry, Alexandro (Félicité) 16 mo. i. July 31, 1814 (SLC, F9, 203)." While Alexandre Eduardo Dupuy's baptismal record is mostly illegible now due to bleeding through of the ink on the other side of the page, Alexandre Dupuy's record, written by Fr. Claude Thoma, is quite clear:

Baptismal record for Alexandre Dupuy, mestive libre. Archives of the Archdiocese of New Orleans, Saint Louis Cathedral Records Vol. 13, p. 153, #64. (Courtesy of Emilie Leumas, Archivist – Kimberly Johnson and Katie Vest – Researching Archivists.)

---

[444] "Lots for Sale," *The Orleans Gazette*, March 30, 1805, digital image, *Genealogybank.com* (https://www.genealogybank.com: accessed 1/8/2020), p. 3, col. 4.
[445] " Notice," *The Orleans Gazette and Commercial Advertiser*, November 16, 1807, digital image, *Genealogybank.com* (https://www.genealogybank.com: accessed 1/8/2020), p. 4, col. 4.

The couple's last child Victoria Dupuy was born in 1815, and is of major significance to this story: "Dupuy, Victoria (Luis Alexander, native of Abeville in Normandy resident of this parish and Felicitas Obry, native and resident of this parish) b. 13 April 1817, bn May 19, 1815, s. Hilario Juliano Domingon and Margarita Obry, child's aunt (SLC, B29, 120)." Below is a copy of the baptismal record in Spanish written by Abbé Jean Pierre Koüne. Margarita Obry was Mercelite Aubry, several times seen in records as "Marguerite," Félicité's sister:

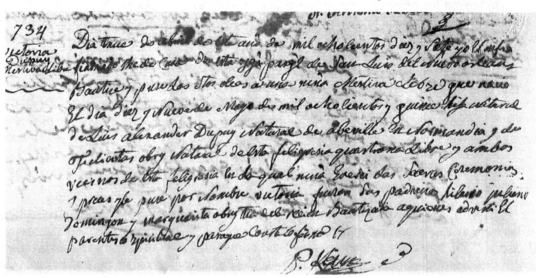

Baptismal record for Victoria Dupuy, mestiva libre. Archives of the Archdiocese of New Orleans, Saint Louis Cathedral Records Vol. 15, p. 120, #734. (Courtesy of Emilie Leumas, Archivist – Kimberly Johnson and Katie Vest – Researching Archivists.)

One wonders if Louis Alexander Dupuy was at the baptism, or if his friend, Hilaire Julien Domingon, the godfather, made an educated but incorrect guess about the father's place of birth. Perhaps Félicité had already broken with Dupuy? On 2 August 1818, Estelle Obry [sic], aged about twenty months, the child of Félicité Aubry was interred in the St. Louis Church Cemetery (SLC F10, 158). No father's name was given.

After that loss, Félicité began an almost twenty-year relationship with Hilaire Julien Domingon, the godfather of Victoria her last child with Dupuy. Domingon was several decades younger than his rival, Dupuy, who died on 14 October 1829, four months after his marriage to Victoire Constance Leblanc. As was customary, he was interred the following day: "Dupuy, Louis Alexandre de Gurard (Jean Etienne, dec, and [o] Jourdain, dec. native of Bray, dept. of Seine-et-Oise [Bray, dept. of Val d'Oise] in France, lawyer, m. in this city to Victoire Constance Leblanc, bn. Aug. 9, 1769, i. Oct. 15, 1829, d. Oct. 14, 1829 (SLC, F15, 85)." A note at the bottom left of the document stated that he was born on 9 August 1769, correcting his age of 80 years (crossed out) according to the baptismal record:

Burial record for Louis Alexandre Dupuy de Gurard, French, Archives of the Archdiocese of New Orleans, Saint Louis Cathedral Records Vol. 1829-1831, p. 85, #561. (Courtesy of Emilie Leumas, Archivist – Kimberly Johnson and Katie Vest – Researching Archivists.)

Hilaire Julien Domingon's early life was difficult to trace. From information he gave us, he was born ca. August 1789 at Cap Français (aka Le Cap, now Cap Haïtien), Saint-Domingue. Unfortunately, the only vital records that exist for Le Cap end in 1788. Everything else was destroyed during the 1791 slave revolt, and the 1793 battles between rebel forces and French revolutionaries which resulted in the destruction of practically the entire town by fire. However, there are a few clues to pursue. Jean Antoine Olympe Domingon de Brettes born on 18 April 1760 at Montech, Tarn-et-Garonne, France, to Jean François Honoré Domingon and Jeanne Antoinette Victoire Herpailler Duchesneau, was stationed at Le Cap between 1783-1792, first as Sergeant then Sub-Lieutenant in the French Army. Granted 8 months leave to return to France in 1786 on account of a six-month long persistent fever, he returned to St. Domingue via Bordeaux in 1787. On 27 April 1788 Mariette Labatut's father wrote to Domingon's superiors that the officer has absconded with his only daughter, taking her from his home in Toulouse. Mariette wrote to her parents that Domingon had married her but later confessed that she had not left with Domingon but with someone else who abandoned her after she became pregnant. She fled to Bordeaux where she met Domingon who facilitated her getting passage to Saint Domingue. Domingon de Brettes was acquitted of the charge of seduction and kidnapping.[446] One record at Le Cap does bear his name. He was a witness to the 22 December 1788 funeral of Jean Geraud de la Faussière.[447] This signature and the dossier containing the accusation of Mariette Labattut's father are the only two bits of evidence that a Domingon lived at Le Cap at the time Hilaire Julien claimed he was born. While these facts are far from proof that Jean Antoine Olympe was Hilaire Julien's father, it is, at least, a place to start. Domingon stated that he arrived in New Orleans in 1803. If this is so, he was fourteen, and probably came with a younger brother, Joseph Gusman Domingon, born ca, 1797 in Saint-Domingue. Hilaire Julien established himself as an auctioneer in the city and worked at that profession until just before his death.

Hilaire and Félicité's first child, Louise Virginie Domingon was baptized at St. Louis Cathedral on 8 June 1819 at the age of about five months. Her godparents were Diego Grioles and Eglée Aubry, [her aunt] all residents of the parish. (SLC, B30, 117) Domingon first appeared in a local New Orleans paper in 1821 to offer a $20 reward for two runaway slaves, Venus and Honey, the former from Kentucky, tall, pleasant looking and very "dark." Honey, aged about 18 or 19, was "ugly with missing front teeth, and badly shaped." Both, however spoke good French.[448] This ad appeared for several days with any outcome unknown to us. The couple's first son, Charles Victor Domingan (*sic*) was born the same year: "Domingan, Charles Victor (Julien, native of Cap Français on Santo Domingo, resident landowner in this city, and Felicite Auby, native of this parish) b. Aug 26 1821, bn 25 May 1821 s. Jean Charles Rebel and Pauline Debergue (SLC, B. 32, 85)." A second daughter was born just a year later: "Domingon, Josephine[449] (Julien, native of Santo Domingo, resident of this parish and Felicite Aubry, native of this city) b. Dec 25, 1826, bn. Feb 1, 1822 in New Orleans. s. Joseph Domingon and Virginie Domingon (SLC, B 37, 55)." Hilaire's brother and his first-born daughter were the godparents.

We believe that Domingon started his career as an auctioneer working for Isaac L. McCoy. This latter advised the public that he had gone back into business again in 1824, selling at auction, houses, lots, furniture, and goods, either on the levee, or in the owners' stores. He advised that Mr. J.H. Domingon would be conducting the auctions.[450]

A second son, Auguste Julien Domingon, was born to Hilaire and Félicité on 7 March 1824: "Dommingon [*sic*], Auguste Julien (Julien, native of Santo Domingo, resident of this parish and Félicité Aubry, native of this city), b. Dec 25, 1826, bn. Mar. 7, 1824 in New Orleans, s. Auguste Pujaud and Lydie Latrabe [*sic*] (SLC, B37, 55)."[451]

---

[446] Base nominative Personnes et Familles, Domingon de Brettes, Jean Antoine Olympe, sous-lieutenant au régiment du Cap, à Saint-Domingue, faussement accusé de l'enlèvement d'une jeune fille de Toulouse. digital image, *Archives nationales d'outre-mer*, "État civil en ligne," (http://anom.archivesnationales.culture. gouv.fr/nominatif/ : accessed 6/24/2020, COL E 135, Images 431-493. Note : Jean Antoine Olympe had one brother : Jean Joseph François Hilaire Domingon born in 1763.

[447] Le Cap, Saint-Domingue, Registres de l'état civil [Civil registrations], Tous actes [All records] 1788, not numbered, Funeral of Jean Geraud de la Faussière., digital image, *Archives nationales d'outre-mer*, "État civil en ligne," (http://anom.archivesnationales.culture. gouv.fr/caomec2/: accessed 6/24/2020), Image 82/ 91.

[448] "Twenty Dollars Reward," *Courrier de la Louisiane*, April 2, 1821, digital image, *Genealogybank.com* (https://www.genealogybank.com: accessed 8/3/2019), p. 2, col. 2.

[449] She was also known as Josephine Laure Domingon.

[450] "Avis," *Courrier de la Louisiane*, January 5,1824, digital image, *Genealogybank.com* (https://www.genealogybank.com: accessed 8/3/2019), p. 2, col. 4.

[451] Lydie "Latrabe" is most likely Lydia Sellon Boneval Latrobe, Henry Sellon Boneval Latrobe's sister, one of two children of Benjamin Henry Latrobe, the famous architect, and his first wife, Lydia Sellon. Their son, Henry Sellon, and his connection to

We also know that as of March 1825, Domingon had joined in a short-lived partnership to conduct auctions with Joseph Ducayet, a native of Port-au-Prince, Saint Domingue, who had lived outside the capitol at Croix-des-Bouquets. One of their first clients was the estate of Julien Poydras. The partners conducted the first half of the auction on 19 April 1825 at the decedent's late home located in the Faubourg St. Mary at the corner of Tchoupitoulas and Poydras streets. At that time all the movables including silver and furniture were sold. On 22 April 1825 Poydras's real estate, which included thirteen lots of prime New Orleans properties, was put up for sale at the Elkins' Coffee House at the corner of St. Louis and Chartres Streets.[452] The firm enjoyed a brief success. By October, they advertised that they had moved to more spacious and fireproof quarters at the corner of St. Louis and Royal where they would hold public auctions every Monday, Thursday and Saturday.[453]

Domingon's partner, Jean Marie Joseph Ducayet died in New Orleans on 27 February 1828 (SLC, F14, 253), after having contracted a deathbed Catholic marriage to his wife, Flore Catherine Rittier, a native of Léogâne, Saint Domingue, on 16 February 1828 to which Hilaire Domingon, was a witness. A marginal entry indicated that the couple had previously been married civilly. (SLC, M7, 113).

Domingon immediately replaced Ducayet as his partner with Joseph Théodore Bauduc, a native of Les Cayes, Saint-Domingue. On 4 March 1828 he advertised an auction at the same address, St. Louis corner of Royal, by "Bauduc & Domingon," which included items such as English thread, shoes, hats, chewing tobacco, olive oil, sperm candles and chocolate.[454]

By 24 April 1828, the partnership seemed to be on firm grounds when the two men signed a contract to build a house on St. Louis Street between Chartres and Levée on a lot measuring 24 feet by 64 feet for $4,500. to be leased to them.[455] However, a purchase of property in 1827 by Félicité Aubry, which was paid for by Domingon, became the centerpiece for a bitter legal dispute between Domingon and Bauduc. On 3 February 1827 in an act passed before the New Orleans notary William Boswell, Félicité Aubry "a free woman of colour of this city" purchased from Joachim Viosco and his wife, lot #116 along with its buildings in the Faubourg Marigny, measuring 60 feet in front on Craps (now Burgundy) Street by 120 feet on History (now Kerlerec) Street, of which it formed the corner for $1410. Félicité paid with three promissory notes endorsed by Hilaire Julien Domingon, each for $470. payable at six, twelve and eighteen months. A marginal note to this document indicated that the mortgage was paid in full on 6 August 1828. Below is a portion of the signatory page of this five-page act of sale, endorsed by the sellers Joachim Viosco and his wife Carmélite Elliot, the buyer, Félicité Aubry, two witnesses, Jean. M. Castarede and William Lake, as well as the notary, William Boswell:

---

free people of color in New Orleans will be explained in Chapter 19 which treats his relationship with Mercelite Aubry, Félicité's sister. Lydia Latrobe Roosevelt must have been in New Orleans in 1826, since there was no proxy named in the record. She had been there twice before: in 1809 when she accompanied her husband, Nicolas Roosevelt on a flatboat down the Mississippi to New Orleans, and again in 1812 when the couple made the first steamboat trip down the Mississippi in the *New Orleans*, leaving Pittsburgh on 11 October 1811, and arriving in New Orleans on 10 January 1812. See: Mary Helen Dohan, *Mr. Roosevelt's Steamboat: The First Steamboat to Travel the Mississippi*, (Gretna, LA: The Pelican Publishing Co., 2004.)

[452] "By Ducayat and Domingon," *The Courier*, March 18, 1825, digital image, *Genealogybank.com* (https://www.genealogybank.com: accessed 10 August 2019), p. 3, col. 4.

[453] "Removal," *The Louisiana Advertiser*, October 6, 1826, digital image, *Genealogybank.com* (https://www.genealogybank.com: accessed 8/10/2019), p. 2, col. 1.

[454] "By Bauduc and Domingon," *The Argus*, March 4, 1828, digital image, *Genealogybank.com* (https://www.genealogybank.com: accessed 8/10/2019), p. 2, col. 2.

[455] The Historic New Orleans Collection, *The Collins C. Diboll Vieux Carré Digital Survey* (https://www.hnoc.org/vcs/property_info.php?lot=18453: accessed 1/10/2020), "511 St. Louis Street."

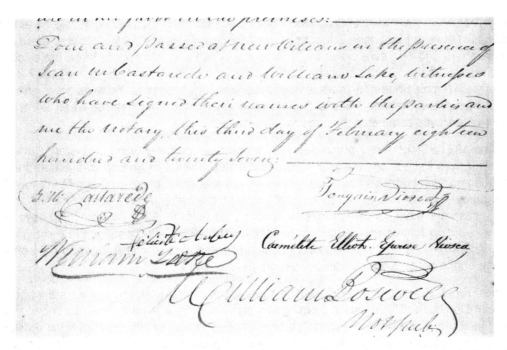

NARC, "Sale and Renunciation Joachim Viosco and wife, to Félicité Aubry, f.w. c.," dated 3 February 1827, passed by Notary William Boswell, Volume 3, pp. 67-71. Courtesy Hon. Chelsey Richard Napoleon, Clerk of Civil District Court, Parish of Orleans.

In early 1829 Bauduc brought an action against Hilaire Julien Domingon for monies owed to him. Bauduc had paid off some debts left by the late firm of Ducayet and Domingon for which he had not been reimbursed, as well as for the "deficit in the affairs of a partnership which had existed between the plaintiff and the defendant, under the style of Bauduc and Domingon." During the course of the trial, Bauduc, the plaintiff, had discovered information which he desired to include in the suit by amendment, however, a lower court had overruled his lawyer's motion. Taken to the Louisiana Supreme Court, Eastern District for appeal, a decision was handed down in January 1830, overturning the lower court's decision. Bauduc had asked in his amendment to add Félicité Aubry to the suit because he had discovered that "monies due by the defendant had been invested by him in the purchase of a house and lot, and three slaves which "he conceals under the name of Félicité Aubry, his concubine; and as the monies belonged to the two firms of Ducayet & Domingon, and Bauduc & Domingon, the deficit in whose affairs had been made up by the petitioner, he had a lien on the property." Bauduc was afraid that Félicité would sell, mortgage or otherwise dispose of the property during the pendency of the lawsuit. By the decision of the higher court she became a party to the suit and was enjoined from disposing of the property.[456]

After that acrimonious parting of ways, Domingon would not take another partner for many years. By March 1830 he was on his own, appearing in an advertisement for the auction of the stock of a retail general store located on the Levée between Jefferson and St. Peter Streets. There was to be a private sale of groceries and liquors until the 31st of March, after which Domingon would auction off the rest.[457] He appeared again in the New Orleans *Bee* later on in the year when he auctioned off two lots in the new Faubourg Marigny on Frenchmen Street. On 18 June 1830 Domingon auctioned off two "American negro slaves:" James, a 24-year-old coachman, and good peddler, and Mary, a 24-year-old washer, cook and seamstress at the Exchange Coffee House. On that same day at Hewlett's Coffee House he put nine lots of ground adjoining one another situated in the square between Elysian Fields (Champs Élysées) or Canal Marigny, Love (N. Rampart), Marigny and Craps (Burgundy) streets on the auction block. Finally, on the same day, he put another lot up for sale on Bourbon Street between Hospital (Governor Nicholls) and Convent (Ursulines).[458]

[456] François-Xavier Martin, *Martin's Reports of Cases Argued and Determined in the Supreme Court of the State of Louisiana, Comprising Louisiana Term Reports, Vol. VIII, N.S.*, Vol. X, (New Orleans, LA: J.B. Steel, 60 Camp Street, 1852), 226-228.
[457] "For Sale," *La Abeja* (The New Orleans *Bee*), March 23, 1830, digital image, *Genealogybank.com* (https://www.genealogybank.com: accessed 8/10/2019), p. 2, col. 2.
[458] "By H.G. Domingon," *The Courier* (*Courrier de la Louisiane*), June17, 1830, digital image, *Genealogybank.com* (https://www.genealogybank.com: accessed 8/10/2019), p. 1, col. 6.

Domingon and his family were enumerated in the 1830 Federal Census living in "the lower suburbs of New Orleans, specifically between Esplanade Street and Canal Marigny [Elysian Fields]." He was listed as the only free white male between 40 and 49 years old at that residence. Also living there were three male "colored" children under 10 years of age (Victor, Auguste Julien, and another son, Alfred, newly born, ca. 1829 but with no birth record), one "colored" female under ten years of age (Josephine), two "colored" females between 10 and 23 years of age (Louise Virginie and perhaps Victoria Dupuy), and one "colored" female between 24 and 35 years old (Félicité). Two female slaves completed the large family picture.[459]

On 1 June 1831 Félicité Aubry purchased another piece of property using the notary Carlile Pollock, from Alexander William Lewis Palmer and his wife, Theresa Zimsler. The lot of ground was situated in the Faubourg Marigny, measuring sixty feet front on Champs Élysées by 120 feet deep, between Great Men (now Dauphine) and Craps (now Burgundy) Streets, designated as Lot #172, with all the buildings and improvements for $2600. Félicité put down $300 in cash and gave her own promissory note to the seller for $300 payable in 90 days. The rest of the money, $2000, was put up in three promissory notes each for $666.66 2/3 by Domingon to be paid at one, two, and three year intervals.[460] A note on the original act of sale indicated that Félicité Aubry had paid off her four notes and the mortgage on the property which was cleared on 15 April 1840.

After the French Revolution of 1789, whose repercussions were felt throughout the world, and nowhere more than in Saint Domingue, Hilaire Julien Domingon's place of birth, it is no wonder that new unrest in Europe, beginning with the Revolution of 1830, also called the July Revolution which installed Louis-Philippe as King of France, followed by unrest and political revolts in Belgium, Portugal, and Italy, caused waves in New Orleans, whose preponderance of French and Creole residents followed the events in Europe with a close eye. A surge of patriotism swept the city as men dusted off their uniforms and began drilling in the public square. A November 1831 issue of the New Orleans *Bee* devoted a whole column to announcements from the "Dragons d'Orléans, the Chasseurs-à-Cheval d'Orléans, the Lancers d'Orléans, La Bataillon d'Artillerie, the Grenadiers d'Orléans, the Voltigeurs d'Orléans, the Casadores d'Orléans, the Tirailleurs Louisianais and the Chasseurs d'Orléans" to take up arms and to report for duty the following day. The Captain of the Chasseurs d'Orléans, forty-two-year old H.J. Domingon, ordered his men to report on 27 November in full uniform including blue trousers.[461]

On 30 April 1834 Domingon, acting on his own behalf, purchased two large lots of ground from the estate of the late Judge Joshua Lewis and his late wife, America Lawson, at Lewisburg, St. Tammany Parish, LA. The acts of sale were recorded by William Christy in New Orleans, and one was copied into the St. Tammany Parish Conveyance Book by Lyman Briggs, the Parish Judge, on 14 March 1835. The heirs of Joshua Lewis had offered their deceased parents' plantation at an auction which was held on 22 March 1834 by Messrs. Hewlett and Bright, public auctioneers, at the New Exchange Coffee House. Although mortgages on both the land and slaves were accepted for the sales, Domingon chose to pay $300 in ready money for a lot of ground marked #18 fronting on Lake Pontchartrain measuring one-half arpent on Lake Avenue by seven arpents 26 feet and one inch in depth running through to Copal Avenue with the same frontage.[462] Domingon also purchased lot #17 with the same dimensions as #18 for $320. This lot was financed by three promissory notes of $106.66 due one, two and three years from the date of purchase drawn to the order of and endorsed by his brother, Joseph Gusman Domingon, who himself had bought lots #11 &12.[463] There were six lots totaling three arpents between Hickory and Magnolia numbered 15 through 20. Domingon's two lots measuring together one arpent in width. Both extended as far back as Copal Avenue. Part of the original survey map of Lewisburg showing the lower portion from Lake Pontchartrain to Copal Avenue done by Jean-Antoine Bourgerol, submitted in 1834 at the time of the subdivision of Judge Lewis's

[459] 1830 United States Federal Census, Orleans Parish, Louisiana, Lower Suburbs, H.G. Domingon household, digital image, *Ancestry.com* (https://www.ancestry.com accessed 10/1/2019), citing NARA microfilm publication M19 Roll 45, No date, p. 33. Image 19/42.

[460] NARC, "Sale of Property from A.W. L. Palmer to Félicité Aubry" dated 1 June 1831, passed by Notary Carlile Pollock, Volume 38, p. 157. Courtesy Hon. Chelsey Richard Napoleon, Clerk of Civil District Court, Parish of Orleans.

[461] "Chasseurs d'Orléans," *L'Abeille* (The New Orleans *Bee*), 26 November 1831, digital image, *Genealogybank.com* (https://www.genealogybank.com: accessed 5/10/2019), p.4, col. 5.

[462] St. Tammany Parish Courthouse Records (Covington, St. Tammany Parish, LA), *Conveyance Office Book F-1*, pp. 19-21, Lyman Briggs Papers, #2597 "Heirs of Jos. Lewis to Hilaire Domingon" filed 14 March 1835.

[463] NARC, "Sale of property J. Domingon from Heirs of Lewis," dated 30 April 1834, passed by Notary William Christy, Vol. 18, pp 173-176. Courtesy Hon. Chelsey Richard Napoleon, Clerk of Civil District Court, Parish of Orleans.

plantation, is reproduced below. The street at the top of the portion of the map we have had reproduced is Copal Avenue. Only the word "Avenue" can be read. The streets intersecting Copal are from left to right: Mulberry, Hickory, Magnolia, and Fountain. Lot #17 is visible. #18 is to the left of it, between Hickory and Magnolia. The lake is at the bottom:

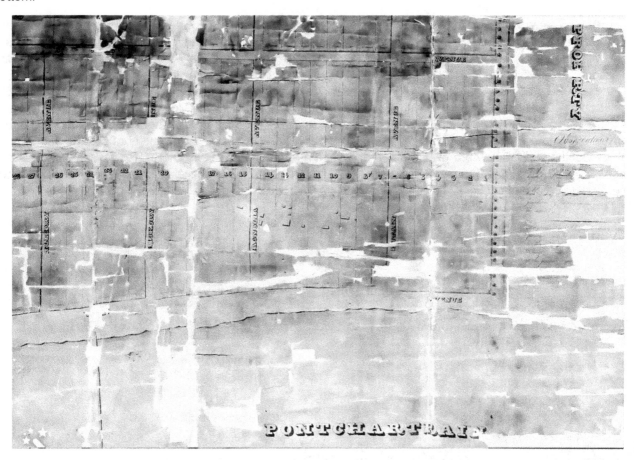

NARC, Portion of Map of Lewisburg drawn by Jean-Antoine Bourgerol dated 14 March 1834 Plan Book #92, Plan #14. Courtesy Hon. Chelsey Richard Napoleon, Clerk of Civil District Court, Parish of Orleans.

As the 1830s wore on Domingon continued to auction properties and slaves at Hewlett's Exchange. It was reported in the *Courrier de la Louisiane* on 14 January 1835 that Domingon would be auctioning off possessions of John Fleming on 16 February 1835 to satisfy his debts. One slave family, Warner and Gussie, both "mulattoes," and their child, William, were to be sold together. A 960 arpent sugar plantation in Iberville Parish on the right bank of the river, with a steam engine and some buildings, some cattle, fodder, a quantity of cane as well as four male slaves was also for sale. The previous day, Domingon had teamed up with auctioneers Tricou and Canonge to sell eight lots of ground in the Faubourg St. Mary at the corner of Poydras and St. Peter.[464]

Félicité and Hilaire's last child, a daughter, Alexandrine Aline Domingon was born ca. 1837 in New Orleans. The couple and their children were enumerated in the 1840 United States Federal Census for both New Orleans and St. Tammany Parish. We cannot be sure that they were living, at least, on a part of the acreage that Domingon had bought in 1834 in Lewisburg because the St. Tammany Parish 1840 Census did not designate any towns or post offices when enumerating its residents. We can assume that Domingon must have been cultivating the land as he was indicated as the owner of 9 slaves, four of them children, under the care of three adult males and two adult females. He was enumerated there with six mixed-race children all under ten years of age. Could he have misrepresented the ages of his children, who, with the exception of Alexandrine, were now adults? Félicité was not

---

[464] "Sales at Auction," *Courrier de la Louisiane*, January 14, 1835, digital image, *Genealogybank.com* (https://www.genealogybank.com: accessed 5/1/2019), p.3, col. 7.

enumerated with him.[465] The 1840 United States Federal Census taken at New Orleans for the Domingon family was even more puzzling. There was one free white person (himself) in the family, along with 10 free colored persons and twenty-one slaves. It would appear that Félicité may have been included in this count being the one free "colored" female between 36-54.[466]

We do know, however, that Félicité and Hilaire came to the office of the St. Tammany Parish Judge, Lyman Briggs, on 24 July 1840, so that Félicité could register a mortgage on two properties she owned in New Orleans to cover two debts that Domingon owed: the first, a loan to him by Alexander Philips of New Orleans for $1500, and the second, an additional loan to him of $1500 by Achille Rivarde also of New Orleans. The properties thus mortgaged were her 1827 purchase from Viosco at Craps (Burgundy) and History (Kerlerec), and her 1831 purchase from Alexander Palmer at Elysian Fields between Craps and Great Men (Dauphine). Félicité declared that there were no other liens or mortgages on the property except the one granted by her before Theodore Seghers, notary, on 23 June 1840 in favor of the Citizen's Bank of Louisiana to secure the payment of $6,000. due the said bank by Domingon.[467] Below are excerpts of a copy of that mortgage in favor of the Citizens Bank of Louisiana, whose President, William Charles Cole Claiborne, signed along with Félicité Aubry, Hilaire Domingon, two witnesses: J.F. Gaudin and Louis Quimper, and the Notary Théodore Seghers:

[...]

---

[465] 1840 United States Federal Census, St. Tammany Parish, Louisiana, H.G. Domingon household, digital image, *Ancestry.com* (https://www.ancestry.com accessed 11/9/2019), citing NARA microfilm publication M704_129, p. 151, Image 9/32.

[466] 1840 United States Federal Census, New Orleans, LA, Ward 3, H.G. Domingon household, digital image, *Ancestry.com* (https://www.ancestry.com accessed 11/9/2019), citing NARA microfilm publication M704_134, p. 159, Image 143/245.

[467] St. Tammany Parish Courthouse Records (Covington, St. Tammany Parish, LA), *Mortgage Book* 1838-1847, pp. 174-175, Lyman Briggs Papers, "Felicité Aubry to A. Philips and A. Rivarde," filed 3 August 1840.

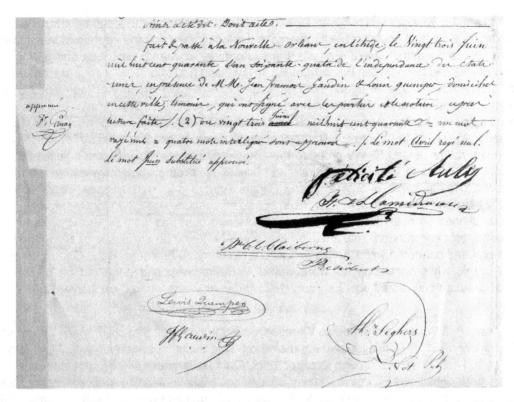

NARC, "Hypothèque par Félicité Aubry pour Domingon en faveur de la Banque des Cit.," (Mortgage by Félicité Aubry for Domingon in favor of the Citizens' Bank), dated 23 June 1840, passed by Notary Théodore Seghers, Volume 34, Act #280. Courtesy Hon. Chelsey Richard Napoleon, Clerk of Civil District Court, Parish of Orleans.

The family's financial crunch lasted apparently through 18 February 1841 when Domingon sold the two lots (# 17 & 18) that he had bought in Lewisburg, St. Tammany Parish, on 30 April 1834 from the estate of the late Judge Joshua Lewis. Included in the sale were two houses each having three apartments, with fireplaces, cisterns, servants' rooms and any other appurtenances and improvements belonging to each lot of ground. The purchaser, Lewis Adolph Gunst agreed to a price of $3,000 for the property using three promissory notes of $1,000 each due at six, twelve and eighteen months from the date of sale.[468] The notes were made out to and endorsed by Edward Barnett, a notary, by virtue of an adjudication by Maurice Barnett, a New Orleans auctioneer in settlement of a lawsuit against the seller.

Bleak financial reversals as well as simply the passage of time finally drove Félicité and Hilaire apart. An inspection of the *New Orleans Annual and Commercial Register for 1846* revealed that Félicité Aubry was living at #36 Moreau Street with J.A. Bonneval, an auctioneer who had just had his first child with Félicité's eldest daughter Louise Virginie Domingon. Included in the same household were Félicité's three sons, Victor, Jules and Alfred Domingon. Hilaire Julien Domingon was living on St. Ann, between Claiborne and Derbigny.[469]

Joseph Alexander Bonneval, Virginie Domingon's partner, was the second child of Charles Alexander Bonneval, a native of Paris, and his wife, Marie Elizabeth Durand de St. Romes. His parents had been married at New Orleans on 6 October 1811: "Bonneval, Alexandro (Francisco and Ana Rachel Finau), native of Paris, resident of this city, m. Maria Isavel St. Rome (Carlos Durand De St. Rome and Theresia Chevalier), native of Port-au-Prince on the island of Santo Domingo, resident of this city, Oct. 6, 1811, with Juan Bautista Guicquel, Hipolito Prospero, Santiago Giloon, Juan Bautista Demoruel (SLC, M6, 102)." J.A. Bonneval was born on 23 February 1814: "Bonneval, Joseph (Alexandre, native of Paris, parish of St. Eustache, and Marie Elizabeth Durand de St. Romes, native of Port-au-Prince on Santo Domingo) b. Feb 11, 1815, bn, Feb 23, 1814 s. Joseph Sauvinet, merchant and Genevieve Demoruelle, widow Malecheaux, all residents of this city (SLC, B25, 149)."

---

[468] St. Tammany Parish Courthouse Records (Covington, St. Tammany Parish, LA), *Conveyance Office Book G-1*, pp. 435-437, Lyman Briggs Papers, #3684 "H.J. Domingon to L.A. Gunst," filed 12 April 1841.
[469] E.A. Michel & Co., *New Orleans Annual and Commercial Register of 1846*, 45, 104, 214, 215.

Bonneval and his younger brother Jean Alexandre had started out in the steamboat business. Throughout 1841 Jean Alexander Bonneval posted advertisements in the local papers as the captain of the steamboat *Walker* which made regular trips across Lake Pontchartrain, stopping at Mandeville, Lewisburg, Madisonville and Covington. The *Walker* had been built in Pittsburgh, PA in 1839 and had one deck, a square stern, and a plain bow with an upper cabin. Advertisements under the Bonneval name and ownership had continued until April 1842. Joseph Alexander Bonneval and James Brown mortgaged her on 4 March 1841 in favor of James W. Breedlove for $2,000, and registered her the following day as co-owners, showing James A. Bonneval as Master. The boat was remortgaged in May of 1842, and re-registered that same month to another owner after which advertisements under the Bonneval name ceased.[470] We propose that the Domingon family, who had a residence at Lewisburg until forced to sell in 1841, and Captain Bonneval and possibly his brother may have first met on this steamboat which serviced the coastal towns of St. Tammany Parish. After a gap in newspaper reports, J. A. Bonneval reappeared in a 21 March 1844 newspaper advertisement as an auctioneer working for Beard and Richardson. The firm, like most, auctioned off everything, from slaves to lots of ground, as well as furniture, imported wines and spirits from Europe, produce, tobacco, oil, anything that could be found on the docks of New Orleans. By May of that year, Bonneval had partnered with Charles A. Labuzan to carry on business at the Camp Street Auction Mart three days per week, while continuing his work with J.A. Beard, who had gone out on his own. Bonneval's partnership with Labuzan only lasted until February 1845, after which he worked exclusively for J.A. Beard & Co. as their auctioneer.

On 17 May 1845 Bonneval and Louise Virginie Domingon had their first child, Marie Laure, who died as a child on 10 December 1851.[471] Bonneval tried another short-lived auction partnership with J.O. Pierson beginning in the summer of 1847 which lasted through October 1848. On 1 December 1848 Bonneval announced a new co-partnership, this time with Louise Virginie Domingon's father Hilaire. "Auction Notice. The undersigned have associated themselves in the Auction Business for the Sale and Purchase of Real Estate, Negroes, Merchandise, Succession, and will act as Brokers and attend to all business appertaining thereto under the firm of Bonneval and Domingon. Office: No. 54 Toulouse street – J.A. Bonneval & H.J. Domingon."[472] This partnership could not have lasted but a few years at most, the last record for which appeared in the 1850 *New Orleans City Directory* for Domingon and Bonneval, auctioneers and commission merchants still located on Toulouse Street opposite the Citizens' Bank.

We have not yet been able to find when Félicité Aubry died. We know that she appeared in the 1846 *New Orleans Annual and Commercial Register.* We know for certain that she was deceased when Eglée and Zélie Aubry helped Félicité's son, Léon Dupuy to procure a birth certificate from the Archdiocese of New Orleans in December 1864. During that eighteen-year period there are no more records for her. Hilaire Julien Domingon was enumerated in the 1850 Federal Census living in the First Municipality, Ward Five with Carolina Domingon, age 42, an immigrant from France, whom he would marry twelve years later.[473] But Félicité was nowhere to be found in the 1850 United States Federal Census or anywhere else later. While she had been living with her daughter Louise Virginie Domingon and Joseph Alexander Bonneval according to the *New Orleans Annual and Commercial Registry* for 1846, she was not enumerated in the Bonneval household in 1850 either. J.A. Bonneval, age 37, a white auctioneer was enumerated with Virginia Domingon, age 30, a mulatto, and their three children: Marie Laure (b. 1845), Félicité

---

[470] Survey of Federal Archives. *Ships Registers and Enrollments of New Orleans, Louisiana/ prepared by the Survey of Federal Archives in Louisiana, Division of community services programs, Work projects administration.* Volume 4, 1841-1850, Baton Rouge, LA: Louisiana State University, 1941, 293. Available at https://catalog.hathitrust.org/Record/000968981, Image 337/436 (#1478, Steamboat *Walker*).

[471] "New Orleans, Louisiana, Birth Records Index, 1790-1899," [database on-line], *Ancestry.com* (https://www.ancestry.com: accessed 12/30/2019). Birth of Marie Laure Bonneval, Vol. 6, p. 214; and Orleans Death Indices 1804-1876, Vol. 14, p. 16, Death of Marie Laure Bonneval, age 6.

[472] "Auction Notice," *The* (New Orleans) *Daily Crescent*, December 4, 1848, digital image, *Genealogybank.com* (https://www.genealogybank.com: accessed 12/1/2019), p.4, col. 5.

[473] 1850 United States Federal Census, Orleans Parish, Louisiana, Ward 5, Municipality #1, Dwelling #1379, Family #1980, J.H. Domingon household, digital image, *Ancestry.com* (https://www.ancestry.com accessed 1/4/2020), citing NARA microfilm publication M432_236, p. 224A. Date of enumeration: 3 September 1850. Image 107/140.

Aline (b. abt. 1847) and Lise (b. Louise Mathilde on 1 December 1851[474]). Also included in the household, were Virginia's two sisters twenty-year-old (Josephine) Laure and eighteen-year-old Aline.[475] Perhaps Félicité Aline had been named after Virginie's deceased mother, Félicité Aubry.

In the fall of 1857, Domingon was hired by the auction house of Devergès and St.-Romes (J.A. Bonneval's mother was a St.-Romes from Saint-Domingue). They announced his arrival as "H.J. Domingon, so favorably known in this community, as one of the most experienced auctioneers. Mr. Domingon has been doing this sort of business for twenty years."[476] Domingon, a seventy-one-year-old auctioneer from Saint Domingue, owning $1000 in real estate was enumerated with Caroline Domingon, a forty-five-year-old French woman in the 1860 United States Federal Census. Also living in the household was fourteen-year-old Victorine Domingon, born in New Orleans, whom we could not identify.[477]

Hilaire Julien Domingon finally took out a license to marry Caroline Haussman on 22 January 1862. Joseph Castanedo and Edward Robert were his witnesses. The bride's surname was spelled "Housemene" and "Widow Matassy" was added after her name.[478] It must have been a civil union because there is no record of a religious marriage with the Archdiocese of New Orleans. Moreover, the license was directed to a Judge and not a clergyman. Domingon's last will and testament was dated the same day as the issuance of the marriage license. The notary who took down the document in French, Antoine Doriocourt, travelled to Domingon's house on Orleans Street between Claiborne and Derbigny where he found him "sick in body but clear of mind." One of the three witnesses attending was Joseph Castanedo, who had just been a witness to the marriage license. Domingon declared that his mother and father were deceased and that he had neither legitimate ascendants or descendants. He left his entire estate to his wife, Caroline Husman (*sic*) and indicated that everything he possessed he earned in concert with his wife.[479] Domingon died on 10 July 1862 at his residence on Orleans Street. His death was reported six months later, on 12 January 1863, by Alphonse Cuyala, in order to commence the probate of his small estate:

---

[474] "New Orleans, Louisiana, Birth Records Index, 1790-1899," [database on-line], *Ancestry.com* (https://www.ancestry.com: accessed 12/30/2019). Birth of Mathilde Bonneval, Vol. 10, p. 471. Note: Mathilde and Marie Laure were the only Bonneval children with a civil birth record, and both were identified as "colored."

[475] 1850 United States Federal Census, Orleans Parish, Louisiana, Ward 6, Municipality #1, Dwelling #1379, Family #1980, J.A. Bonneval household, digital image, *Ancestry.com* (https://www.ancestry.com accessed 1/4/2020), citing NARA microfilm publication M432_236, p. 272B. Date of enumeration: 29 October 1850. Image 64/227.

[476] "Devergès et St.-Rome, Encanteurs," (Devergès and St. Rome, Auctioneers), *The* (New Orleans) *Semi-Weekly Courier,* October 7, 1857, digital image, *Genealogybank.com* (https://www.genealogybank.com: accessed 12/20/ 2019), p.5, col. 5. (My translation of this announcement).

[477] 1860 United States Federal Census, Orleans Parish, Louisiana, Ward 5, Dwelling #2143, Family #2084, H.J. Domingon household, digital image, *Ancestry.com* (https://www.ancestry.com accessed 1/4/2020), citing NARA microfilm publication M653_418, p. 873. Date of enumeration: 15 July 1860. Image 328/393.

[478] "Orleans Parish, Louisiana Marriage Licenses and certificates, 4th Justice of the Peace 1859-1864," digital image, *Familysearch.org* (https://www.familysearch.org/: accessed 1/21/2020), License #396 for Hilaire Julien Domingon and Caroline Housemene (*sic*), Image 555/872.

[479] "Orleans Parish Will Books, Vol. 12, 1860-1863," digital images, *Ancestry.com* (https://www.ancestry.com: accessed 1/15/2020), citing *Louisiana, Wills and Probate Records, 1756-1984*, J.H. Domingon, Will #19321, filed Jan. 15, 1863, Images 583, 584/669.

327 **324**

BE IT REMEMBERED, that on this day to wit the *Twelfth of January*
in the year of our Lord one thousand eight hundred and sixty *three* and the eighty *eight*
of the Independence of the United States of America, before me, PIERRE L. WOOSTE, duly commissionned and sworn
RECORDER OF BIRTHS AND DEATHS, in and for the Parish and City of Orleans, personally appeared

Mr. Alphonse Cuyala, a native of "France" residing on Orleans Street between Derbigny & Claiborn who hereby declares that

St. Hilaire julien Domingon a native of St. Domingo aged about seventy three years. Departed this life on the tenth of july eighteen hundred & sixty five (10th july 1865) at at his domicile on Orleans Street between Claiborn & Derbigny

Courtesy of State of Louisiana, Secretary of State, Division of Archives, Records Management, and History. *Vital Records Indices.* Baton Rouge, LA, USA citing "Orleans Death Indices 1804-1876." Vol. 23, p. 324.

An inventory of his estate was taken on 15 January 1863 that showed his assets amounted to approximately $972 which included some money owed to him, his furniture and possessions, a slave named Lina, and his house and property on Dumaine Street between Rocheblave and Dorgenois. After the appraisal nothing seems to have been done, except, that at some point the house and lot were sold to cover some of the debts of the estate.[480] Caroline lived in poverty until her death on 17 August 1866. At that time, she was living with a friend (or relative) Julia Gazelle, a native of Le Havre, Seine-Maritime, France, at 141 Burgundy Street. Julia reported her death on the same day, stating that Caroline Domingon, a native of "Havre, France," aged sixty years died on 17 August 1866 at four o'clock A.M. at # 141 Burgundy Street. No cause of death was listed on the certificate seen on the following page:

---

[480] "Louisiana, Wills and Probate Records, 1756-1984," digital images, *Ancestry.com* (https://www.ancestry.com: accessed 1/20/2020), citing *Succession Records 1846-1880*; *Louisiana Probate Court (Orleans Parish).* Succession of Hilaire Domingon, no date, Case # 19321, Images 476-524/1241, and Succession of (Widow) F.H. Domingon case # 27228 dated 28 August 1866, Images 599-619/1267.

A succession record for the Widow F.H. Domingon, shows that the estate had been reduced to $77.08 which included the widow's furniture and personal effects. The real estate had been sold, and the slave, Lina, freed at the end of the Civil War.

Félicité Aubry, whose death we could not pinpoint, had eight children that survived her, but by the time of the Widow Domingon's death in 1866, only two remained alive: Léon Dupuy and Auguste Julien Domingon. No heirs had ever come forth to claim the 1866 succession which had dwindled to less than $100. On 23 May 1913, a half-century after Hilaire Domingon's death, P. J. Flanagan, a public administrator opened the dormant succession one more time, after discovering another piece of property belonging to the decedent in the 3rd District, Square #1208 bounded by Frenchmen, Virtue (now Rocheblave), Force (now Tonti), and Union (now Touro), Lot #2 (formerly Lot #16), fronting thirty feet on Union and 120 feet deep which he acquired on 3 August 1839. Due to the absence of legitimate heirs the lot was sold to pay off debts owed by the estate. The rest was turned over to the Louisiana State Treasury Department.

Félicité Aubry's first-born, Edmond, with French attorney Louis Alexander Dupuy left a very small footprint in New Orleans. He appeared in only one census record listed as an individual and head of household. He was enumerated in the 1850 United States Federal Census for the 1st Municipality, 6th Ward as Edmond Dupuy, age 40, a male fisherman born in Louisiana. The household also included Marguerite (no last name given, but perhaps "Dupuy" implied), age twenty-two, a "mulatto" born in Louisiana, Elizabeth Labaux, also age twenty-two and "mulatto," and Alita Morbuk, a seventeen-year-old black female. On this page of the census, the majority of heads of household were said to be fishermen, with a large number of them whose last name was Labeau an alternate spelling for Labaux, which also appears in other places as Labeaud.[481] From other records we learn that Edmond Dupuy and Marguerite Labeaud, both free persons of color, had a daughter, Marie, who was born at their house on Bayou St. John in New Orleans on 12 January 1853. It was reported by Louis Dupuy, a free man of color. Louis signed with an "X" not knowing how to write:

Courtesy of State of Louisiana, Secretary of State, Division of Archives, Records Management, and History. *Vital Records Indices*. Baton Rouge, LA, USA, citing "Orleans, Louisiana Birth Records Index 1790-1899," Vol. 10, p. 615.

Marguerite Labeau died in New Orleans on 17 January 1854 at the age of thirty years. The document is too faded to reproduce but reads in part that "Louis Dupuy, a free man of color, residing at the Bayou St. John, Second District of this city, by these presents declares that his step-mother Marguerite Labeau, a native of this city, a free woman of color, aged thirty years, departed this life on the seventeenth instant (January 17, 1854) at three o'clock P.M. at the deponents aforementioned residence. Deponent being unable to write, has made his ordinary mark"[482] Louis Dupuy, for whom we have no concrete information, was, according to this record, another of Edmond Dupuy's children by a different mother.

---

[481] 1850 United States Federal Census, Orleans Parish, Louisiana, Ward 6, Dwelling #3107, Family #4626, Edmond Dupuy (indexed as "Dutney") household, digital image, *Ancestry.com* (https://www.ancestry.com accessed 1/11/2020), citing NARA microfilm publication M432_236, p. 312A. Date of enumeration: 8 November 1850. Image 143/227.

[482] Courtesy of State of Louisiana, Secretary of State, Division of Archives, Records Management, and History. *Vital Records Indices*. Baton Rouge, LA, USA, citing New Orleans, Louisiana Death Records Index 1804-1939; Vol. 14, p. 245.

After Marguerite Labeau's death, Edmond had two daughters with Elizabeth Labeaud.[483] Félicité Dupuy, named for her grandmother, was born on 10 July 1860.[484] She died on 16 June 1874 in New Orleans from dysentery:

Courtesy of State of Louisiana, Secretary of State, Division of Archives, Records Management, and History, citing "New Orleans, Louisiana Death Records Index 1804-1949," Vol. 61, p. 250.

Félicité's sister Eulalie Dupuy was born on 21 March 1863. Her birth record, which is too faded to reproduce for this book, reads that:

> Mr. Louis Rochelle, a native of New Orleans residing on Dorgenois Street between Maine [Dumaine] and St. Ann streets, 2nd District in this city who by these presents declare that on the 21st day of March of this present year (21 March 1863) at one o'clock P.M. in a house situated at the Bayou St. John was born a female child named Eulalie Dupui issue of the lawful marriage of Mr. Edmond Dupui, f.m.c. with Miss Elizaberth Labod, f.w.c., both natives of New Orleans.[485]

---

[483] We have not been able to confirm the relationship between Marguerite and Elizabeth Labeau.

[484] "New Orleans, Louisiana, Birth Records Index, 1790-1899," [database on-line], *Ancestry.com* (https://www.ancestry.com: accessed 12/30/2019. Birth of Félicité Dupui (Colored) daughter of Edmond Dupui and Elizabeth Labeaud, Vol. 30, p. 317.

[485] Courtesy of State of Louisiana, Secretary of State, Division of Archives, Records Management, and History. *Vital Records Indices*. Baton Rouge, LA, USA, from New Orleans, Louisiana Birth Records Index 1790-1899; Vol. 30, p. 318.

According to his death record filed by his brother, Léon Dupuy, Edmond Dupuy, a native of New Orleans, aged fifty-seven years, died on 7 July 1863 at eight A.M. in a house situated in Bayou St. John in the third district:

Courtesy of State of Louisiana, Secretary of State, Division of Archives, Records Management, and History. *Vital Records Indices*. Baton Rouge, LA, USA, citing "New Orleans, Louisiana Death Records Index 1804-1939," Vol. 22, p. 233.

Edmond left no will and no succession records. His wife, Elizabeth Labeaud, died on 16 October 1866. The death was reported by a relative, Médard Labeaud who stated that Elizabeth, a Louisiana native, aged about forty-two years, the lawful wife of Edmond Dupuy, died at his residence on Bayou St. John.[486]

Edmond Dupuy's daughter, Marie Dupuy, married André Dominguez, a Mexican immigrant to New Orleans on 20 May 1876. Although very difficult to read, the record on the following page states that the Rev. François C. Mittelbronn married André Dominguez, a native of Mexico, son of Alcide Dominguez and Adelaide Petit to Miss Marie Dupuis, daughter of Edouard Dupuis and Margaret Labouy (*sic*). The marriage license was obtained on 10 May 1876. The Rev. Mittelbronn was pastor of St. Rose of Lima Catholic Church in the Third District:

---

[486] Courtesy of State of Louisiana, Secretary of State, Division of Archives, Records Management, and History. *Vital Records Indices*. Baton Rouge, LA, USA, citing *Orleans Death Indices 1804-1876*; Vol. 36, p. 22.

Courtesy of State of Louisiana, Secretary of State, Division of Archives, Records Management, and History. *Vital Records Indices*. Baton Rouge, LA, USA, citing "New Orleans, Louisiana Marriage Records Index 1831-1964," Vol. 5, p. 654.

André and his wife Mary were enumerated together in the 1880 Federal Census living on Maurepas Street. André was a thirty-seven-year-old shoemaker from Mexico. His wife Mary, age twenty-three, a "mulatto", and their two mulatto children, Manuela, age three and Rita (b. 1878; d. 19 January 1894), age two, were enumerated with them. Also included in the family was a one-year-old child said to be adopted, Émile Anglado, as well as André's sister-in-law, seventeen-year-old "mulatto" Eulalie Dupuy. André and the baby Émile were enumerated as "white."

Edmond's other daughter who lived to be an adult, Eulalie Dupuy, had seven children with Myrtil Boutté, who worked as a carpenter in New Orleans. Although we could find no marriage record for them, their first child, Lucia, was born on 16 May 1883 in New Orleans. Six other children followed: Lucien on 2 December 1885, Anthony on 16 October 1887, Marie on 6 November 1891, François on 14 July 1894, Fernand on 9 July 1897 and George on 12 September 1899.[487] The family was enumerated in both the 1900 and 1910 Federal censuses living at their home on 2129 St. Ann Street.

Myrtil Boutté a native of New Orleans died at the age of 53 years in New Orleans on 30 June 1917. The cause of death on the death certificate was illegible, but the physician who attended the deceased was Dr. G.A. Roudanez. Myrtil's parents were identified as Lucien Boutté and Celimire Robert.[488] Eulalie Dupuy Boutté spent the last years of her life living with her youngest son, George Boutté, also a carpenter, his wife Lillian Grace Christophe, and their two children Lydia (b. 1920) and George (b. 1922). Eulalie died on 13 March 1947 in New Orleans from heart failure.[489]

Félicité Aubry's son, Léon, was never wed. He worked in New Orleans as a plasterer and bricklayer. Léon saved his money and invested in real estate. On 22 June 1844, Dupuy had finalized the purchase of a piece of property that he had bought at an auction held by Abat & Domingon (Hilaire Julien), from Manuel Elliot. The real

---

[487] "New Orleans, Louisiana Birth Records Index, 1790-1899," [database on-line] *Ancestry.com*. (https://www.ancestry.com: accessed 1/27/2020), Births of: Lucia, Vol 96, p.313; Lucien, Vol. 96, p. 312; Anthony, Vol.96, p. 312; Marie, Vol. 96, p. 311; François, Vol. 115, p.1139; Fernand, Vol 115, p. 1140; There is no birth record for George, but the SSDI gives 12 September 1899.

[488] Courtesy of State of Louisiana, Secretary of State, Division of Archives, Records Management, and History. *Vital Records Indices*. Baton Rouge, LA, USA, citing "Orleans Death Indices 1908-1917," Vol. 169, p. 677.

[489] Courtesy of State of Louisiana, Secretary of State, Division of Archives, Records Management, and History. *Vital Records Indices*. Baton Rouge, LA, USA, citing "Orleans Death Indices 1937-1948," Certificate # 1502 for Eullia Boutté.

estate was located in the square bounded by Robertson, Columbus, Claiborne and La Harpe Sts, fronting 33 feet 2 inches and one line on Columbus by 157 feet 1 inches and 7 lines in depth. Dupuy paid 100 piastres with one-half up front and the additional amount of 50 piastres in six months.[490] On 1 June 1846, Dupuy invested in another piece of property, this time purchasing from Charles Gaudion Lot #81 in the square bounded by Columbus, Robertson, LaHarpe and Claiborne in the Faubourg Tremé, a triangular shaped lot at the corner of Columbus and Robertson. The lot fronted on Columbus measuring 35 feet 3 inches and 11 lines, by 134 feet in depth fronting on Robertson, by 138 feet 11 inches in depth on the third side. Dupuy paid 115 piastres cash in hand.[491] On 19 April 1849, Dupuy bought another plot of ground, this time from Michel Joseph Lombard located in the Faubourg Marigny in Square #46, Lot #460, measuring 60 feet on Girod Street by 120 feet in depth for which he paid 300 piastres in cash. Below is the signature page for the act passed before Joseph Cuvillier, with the signatures of Léon Dupuy, the seller Joseph Lombard with permission from his wife Amelia, and two witnesses, John Hahn, and the famous New Orleans Notary, Abel Dreyfous:

NARC, "Vente de terre – Jh. Lombard à Léon Dupuy," dated 19 April 1849, passed by Notary Joseph Cuvillier, Volume 52, Act 80. Courtesy Hon. Chelsey Richard Napoleon, Clerk of Civil District Court, Parish of Orleans.

Léon Dupuy was enumerated in the 1870 United States Federal Census for Ward 7, New Orleans, as a sixty-two-year-old "mulatto", working as a brick mason with $3000 in real estate and $200 in personal property.[492] He dictated his last will and testament on 5 June 1873 at which time he stated that he had never been married, and was residing at # 265 Robertson Street. He left a list of bequests to be distributed to a nephew and some cousins.

---

[490]NARC, "Vente de lot de terre par M. Manuel Elliot à Léon Dupuy," dated 22 June 1844, passed by Notary Charles Foulon, Vol. 15, Act #202. Courtesy Hon. Chelsey Richard Napoleon, Clerk of Civil District Court, Parish of Orleans.

[491] NARC, "Vente de terre, Ch. Gaudion à L. Dupuy," dated 1 June 1846, passed by Notary Joseph Cuvillier, Vol. 44, Act #135. Courtesy Hon. Chelsey Richard Napoleon, Clerk of Civil District Court, Parish of Orleans.

[492] 1870 United States Federal Census, New Orleans, Orleans Parish, LA, Ward 7, Dwelling #705, Family #1038, Leon Dupuy household, digital image, Ancestry.com (https://www.ancestry.com: accessed 10/22/2019), citing NARA microfilm publication M593_522. Date of enumeration: 9 July 1870. Image 298/470.

Each of the following family members was to receive $500 piastres: Alexandre Dupuy, his nephew, (possibly a son of his brother Alexander Edward Dupuy); René Achille Chiapella, his cousin, son of Eglée Aubry; Marie Josephe Sophie Foy, and Elina Marguerite Félicité Foy, his cousins, daughters of Zélie Aubry (See Chapter 20), Julia Latrobe, widow Joseph St. Hubert, his cousin, daughter of Mercelite Aubry (See next chapter).[493] The fact that Léon did not list any of his Dupuy siblings in his will indicates to us that they had all predeceased him. While we are sure of the dates of death of Edmond, and Alexandre, who died as an infant, we have not been able to trace any more information about Alexander Eduardo, born in 1810 or Victoria, born in 1815.

Léon Dupuy's death was reported by an undertaker, Raoul Bonnet, who stated that "Léonce Dupuy (white)" a New Orleans native about seventy-one years old died on 17 December 1880, at his residence, at the corner of Columbus and Robertson Streets. The cause of death was listed as "softening of the brain" (dementia?):

Courtesy of State of Louisiana, Secretary of State, Division of Archives, Records Management, and History. *Vital Records Indices*. Baton Rouge, LA, USA, citing "New Orleans, Louisiana Death Records Index 1804-1939," Vol. 77, p. 995.

His succession was opened on 22 December 1880 with his cousin, Prosper Florville Foy, acting as his testamentary executor. An inventory of the estate commenced a week later. Between cash and possessions, including real estate, Léon's assets were valued at $5,158.23 (or about $125,810 in 2019 dollars).

Four of Félicité Aubry's six children with Hilaire Julien Domingon, predeceased their father in 1862. Louis Alfred Domingon had been living with his mother at #36 Moreau Street according to the *New Orleans Annual and*

---

[493] It was this bequest to Julia Latrobe, along with Julia's being named godmother to Eglée Aubry's son Gustave Joseph Lorreins as well as Mercelite Aubry's appearance as the godmother of Félicité Aubry's son Edmond Dupuy, that led us to conclude that Mercelite Aubry was Eglée, Félicité, Martin and Zélie Aubry's sister.

Commercial Register of 1846.[494] He was working as a cigar maker by 1850 and was enumerated as a twenty-two year old "mulatto" male living with several other men employed in the same industry in the First Municipality, Ward 5.[495] On 15 December 1856, *L'Abeille de la Nouvelle Orleans* (*The New Orleans Bee*) published an obituary for twenty-seven-year-old Alfred Domingon which indicated that he had died the night before and that his funeral cortege would leave from a house on Rue Bagatelle (now Pauger), between Craps (now Burgundy) and Amour (now North Rampart).[496] We could find no civil death record for him.

Alexandrine Aline Domingon died unmarried on 4 March 1861. Her death was reported by her sister Virginie's partner, Joseph A. Bonneval:

Courtesy of State of Louisiana, Secretary of State, Division of Archives, Records Management, and History. *Vital Records Indices*. Baton Rouge, LA, USA, citing "New Orleans, Louisiana Death Records Index 1804-1939," Vol. 22, p.80.

Thanks to Alexandrine Aline's last will and testament written on 7 February 1861, we know that her sister Josephine Laure Domingon had passed away before that date, leaving two children: Marie Virginie and Marguerite, to whom she left all her possessions.[497] We were unable to trace either of her children any further or obtain an exact date of death for Josephine Laure.

Charles Victor Bernard Domingon, known simply as Victor died on 11 September 1861 in New Orleans. His death record indicates that he was married to Marie Coralie Hébrard, however we could not find a record of that

---

[494] E.A. Michel & Co., *New Orleans Annual and Commercial Register of 1846*, 215.
[495] 1850 United States Federal Census, Orleans Parish, Louisiana, Ward 5, Municipality #1, Dwelling #1135, Family #11646, François Hardy household, digital image, *Ancestry.com* (https://www.ancestry.com accessed 1/12/2020), citing NARA microfilm publication M432_236, p. 206B. Date of enumeration: 22 August 1850. Image 72/140.
[496] "Décédé hier soir." *L'Abeille de la Nouvelle Orleans* (*New Orleans Bee*) dated 15 December 1856, Vol. 46 June-Dec, 1856, digital image, Jefferson Parish Library (https://nobee.jplibrary.net/: accessed 1/2/2020), 1856_12_0051.pdf (Col. 6).
[497] "Louisiana, Wills and Probate Records, 1756-1984," digital images, *Ancestry.com* (https://www.ancestry.com: accessed 1/29/2020), citing *Record of Wills, 1807-1901*; *Louisiana Probate Court (Orleans Parish)*. Will of Alexandrine Aline Domingon dated 7 February 1861, Case # 17965, Image 150/708.

marriage. Marie Coralie also went by the name of Marie Coralie Neel, which we will see later on, may have been her maiden name:

Courtesy of State of Louisiana, Secretary of State, Division of Archives, Records Management, and History. *Vital Records Indices*. Baton Rouge, LA, USA, citing "New Orleans, Louisiana Death Records Index 1804-1939," Vol. 22, p.117.

Victor and Coralie had two children. Marie Leticia Domingon born on 15 November 1852[498] and Josephine Louise Aline Domingon who was born on 23 September 1858, but died on 10 November 1858 in New Orleans. Josephine's death was reported by her father, Victor Domingon, who stated that "Josephine Aline Domingon, a native of this city, aged one month and a half died in this city on the tenth instant (Nov. 10, 1858) at deponent's residence (Girod Street between St. Bernard and Annette streets). The deceased was the daughter of deponent with Coralie Hebrard."[499] Both birth records for Coralie's children, as well as the death record of baby Josephine give her name as Marie Coralie Hebrard. Victor and Coralie Domingon were enumerated in the 1860 United States Federal Census for New Orleans. Thirty-year-old Victor, twenty-eight-year-old Coralie and six-year-old "Luticia" Domingon were living with a fifty-four-year-old immigrant from the West Indies named Berenice Bienaimé, and two young women, Philomène and Marie Bienaimé. Victor worked as a grocer and reported $2000 in real estate. All the members of the household were designated as "mulatto."[500]

---

[498] "New Orleans, Louisiana Birth Records Index, 1790-1899," [database on-line] *Ancestry.com.* (https://www.ancestry.com: accessed 1/27/2020), Birth of Marie Leticia Domingon, Vol. 10, p. 527.

[499] Courtesy of State of Louisiana, Secretary of State, Division of Archives, Records Management, and History. *Vital Records Indices*. Baton Rouge, LA, USA, citing *Orleans Death Indices*; Vol. 15, p. 552.

[500] 1860 United States Federal Census, New Orleans, Orleans Parish, LA, Ward 7, Dwelling #2128, Family #2687, Victor Domingon household, digital image, *Ancestry.com* (https://www.ancestry.com: accessed 10/22/2019), citing NARA microfilm publication M653_419, Date of enumeration: 6 July 1860. Image 308/332.

After her husband's death, Marie Coralie was enumerated in the 1870 United States Federal Census for New Orleans as Vve. (Widow) Victor Domingo (*sic*), age 38, with $1500 in real estate and $150 in personal property, living with her daughter Leticia, age nineteen. Both women were said to be "white."[501] When nineteen-year-old Marie Leticia married José Fernando Bonaventura, a native of the "Canary Islands," on 23 October 1871 in New Orleans her parents' names were given as Victor Domingon and, in one case, "Maria C. Neel," and in another of the records, "Mary Cora Neel." The groom's parents were Francisco F. Bonaventura (spelled numerous ways on the record including "Bunabentura.") and Francisca B. Gonzalez, or simply Betia Gonzalez.[502]

Thereafter Marie Coralie Hebrard would style herself either as the Widow Victor Domingon or Marie Coralie Neel. Marie Leticia Domingon died on 17 January 1876 in New Orleans. Her husband reported the death which stated that "José Buenaventura, a native of Cuba, residing at the corner of Craps and Spain Streets in this city who hereby declares that his wife Mrs. Letitia Buenaventura (born Domingo) a native of New Orleans aged twenty-three years died on the 17th instant (January 17, 1876) at deponents residence in the City." The cause of death was "scarlatina." [503] Letitia had given birth to two children before her death at age twenty-three: Valentine Fernando Bonaventure on 14 April 1873 and Victor Fernando Bonaventure on about 21 January 1875.[504] Both children used the surname "Fernando." Only one record exists for the children, that of Valentine Bonaventura whose birth was registered by her mother on 29 October 1873. In the record Letitia Domingon, residing on Frenchmen Street declared that on 14 April 1873 at 3 o'clock P.M. a female child was born at her residence named Valentine Bonabentura (*sic*), the lawful issue of deponent with Joseph Bonabentura, a native of the West Indies."[505]

Letitia Domingon's two children were raised by Marie Aurore Francisque, also known as Marie Francise Barbe, a native of Cuba, born about 1805, who lived with Pierre Louis Neel, a white French immigrant to New Orleans, born ca. 1799, with whom she had had at least four children, including: Jean Arman Neel, b. 8 February 1838, François Hortaire Neel, b. 11 December 1841, Édouard Louis Neel, b. 27 Feb 1843, and Marie Félicie Neel born on 10 August 1847.[506] There was, however, no birth record for Marie Coralie Neel. During the occupation of New Orleans by Union troops, some couples had prevailed upon Union officers to perform the marriage ceremony. After the Civil War when interracial marriages were legalized by the Reconstruction government, many couples took advantage of the period between 1868 until 1894 to wed. Marie Francise Barbe and Pierre Louis Neel were married in New Orleans on 16 April 1868 just two months before his death on 16 June 1868.[507]

Aurore Bache (*sic*), a seventy-five-year-old widow from Cuba was enumerated in the 1880 United States Federal Census living at 3444 Ursulines Street, with a forty-six-year-old daughter Marie Neil (*sic*), a seamstress, a twenty-six-year-old granddaughter, Felicia Neil (*sic*), also a seamstress and both of Leticia Domingon's children,

[501] 1870 United States Federal Census, New Orleans, Orleans Parish, LA, Ward 7, Dwelling #159, Family #205, Vve. Victor Domingon household, digital image, *Ancestry.com* (https://www.ancestry.com: accessed 10/22/2019), citing NARA microfilm publication M593_522. Date of enumeration: 7 June 1870. Image 210/470.

[502] "Louisiana Parish Marriages, 1837-1957," database with images, *FamilySearch.org* (https://familysearch.org/ark:/61903/1:1:QKJH-3HK5 : accessed 3/12/2019), Mary Cora Neel in entry for Jose Fernando Beunabontora and Marie Leticia Domingon, 23 Oct 1871; citing Orleans, Louisiana, U.S.A., various parish courthouses, FHL microfilm 911,640.

[503] Courtesy of State of Louisiana, Secretary of State, Division of Archives, Records Management, and History. *Vital Records Indices*. Baton Rouge, LA, USA citing *Orleans Death Indices 1804-1876*; Vol 65, p. 348.

[504] Victor Bonaventura was known as Victor Frank Fernando. He worked as a head waiter in Atlantic City, Atlantic Co., NJ, for many years. He was married to Amy Louise Wingrove in London, England, on 28 August 1907. They had no children. Victor died on 28 September 1937 in Manhattan, NY.

[505] Courtesy of State of Louisiana, Secretary of State, Division of Archives, Records Management, and History. *Vital Records Indices*. Baton Rouge, LA, USA from New Orleans, Louisiana Birth Records Index 1790-1915; Vol 64, p. 127. Note: Valentine Bonaventura Reader died in Los Angeles, LA Co., CA, on 13 November 1948 (SSDI). She was married to Dennis Jacob Reader, a dining car steward working for a railroad. They had no children.

[506] Courtesy of State of Louisiana, Secretary of State, Division of Archives, Records Management, and History. *Vital Records Indices*. Baton Rouge, LA, USA citing *New Orleans Birth Records Index 1790-1915,* Births of Jean Armand Neel, Vol. 5, p. 540; François Hortaire Neel, Vol. 6, p. 541; Édouard Louis Neel, Vol. 6, p. 541; Marie Felicie Neel, Vol 10, p. 75, all children of Pierre Louis Neel and Marie Aurore Francisque.

[507] "Louisiana Parish Marriages, 1837-1957," database with images, *FamilySearch.org* (https://familysearch.org/ark:/61903/1:1:QKJC-9G96 : accessed 3/12/2019), Pierre Louis Nell and Marie Francise Barbe, 16 Apr 1868; citing Orleans, Louisiana, U.S.A., various parish courthouses, FHL microfilm 903,915.

whom she had indicated were her grandchildren: Valentine Fernando, aged about 7 years, and Victor Fernando, aged about 5 years.[508]

Mrs. Marie Coralie Neel, widow of Victor Domingon, living at 2112 Ursulines Street in New Orleans dictated her last will and testament on 14 March 1895. The document was written in French. We have translated a portion of it here in English:

My name is Marie Coralie Neel, I am the widow of Victor Domingon. My mother and father are both dead. I have no children. I only had one daughter named Letitia Domingon who was married to Joseph Pepe Bonaventure. She died leaving two children named Victor and Valentine Bonaventure. They are known by the names of Victor and Valentine Fernando. I also have a sister named Felicie Neel. I name my two grandchildren and my sister, all three of them as my universal legatees. I name my sister Felicie Neel my testamentary executrix. [509]

The Widow Victor Domingon (white) died in New Orleans on 12 May 1895 at #2112 Ursulines St. We have yet to completely unravel the disparity in her use of a surname. Was Félicie Neel her sister, or a half-sister? Had she wed a Hébrard before marrying Victor Domingon? There is not enough evidence yet to reach a conclusion:

Courtesy of State of Louisiana, Secretary of State, Division of Archives, Records Management, and History. *Vital Records Indices.* Baton Rouge, LA, USA, from New Orleans, Louisiana Death Records Index 1804-1939; Vol. 108, p.720.

---

[508] 1880 United States Federal Census, New Orleans, Orleans Parish, LA, Ward 7, Dwelling #104, Family #146, Aurore Bache household, digital image, *Ancestry.com* (https://www.ancestry.com: accessed 1/22/2019), citing NARA microfilm publication T9 Roll 461., Date of enumeration: 7 June 1880, Image 28/114.

[509] "Orleans Parish Will Books, Vol. 26, 1893-1895," digital image, *Ancestry.com* (https://www.ancestry.com: accessed 1/25/2020) Case #45960, Testament of Mme. Marie Coralie Neel, widow Victor Domingo, Images 788,789/838.

Félicité Aubry's eldest child, Louise Virginie Domingon died in New Orleans in 1866. Joseph A. Bonneval, the father of her children, who resided with her on Marais Street between Ursulines and Bayou Road reported the death of Virginie Domingon, aged 48 years at ten o'clock P.M. on 30 July 1866. No cause of death was given. Was it a coincidence that she died on the date of the New Orleans Massacre of 1866?

Courtesy of State of Louisiana, Secretary of State, Division of Archives, Records Management, and History. *Vital Records Indices*. Baton Rouge, LA, USA, from New Orleans, Louisiana Death Records Index 1804-1939; Vol. 32, p.505.

Louise Virginie Domingon was survived by five of her seven children with Joseph Alexander Bonneval. After the birth of Marie Laure Bonneval in 1845, who died as a child in 1851(See p. 242), another daughter, Félicité Aline was born ca, 1847, for whom we have no birth record. Félicité married Charles Schnabel on 28 April 1877 in New Orleans,[510] but died twelve days later on 10 May 1877.[511]

---

[510] "Louisiana Parish Marriages, 1837-1957," database with images, *FamilySearch.org* (https://familysearch.org/ark:/61903/1:1:QKJW-VYGV : accessed 4/8/2019), Charles Schnabel and Felicité Aline Bonneval, 28 Apr 1877; citing Orleans, Louisiana, U. S. A., various parish courthouses, Louisiana; FHL microfilm 907,693.
[511] "New Orleans, Louisiana Death Records Index, 1804-1949," [database on-line] *Ancestry.com*. (https://www.ancestry.com: accessed 1/27/2020), Death of Félicité Aline Schnabel,. Vol 68, p. 983.

Louise Matilde Bonneval was born in New Orleans on 1 December 1851,[512] but died as a child on 19 March 1853.[513]

Élise (Lize) Josephine Bonneval was born ,ca. May 1852. She contracted a marriage with Jean/John Beppouey, the son of John Beppouey and Jeanne Momus, a native of New Orleans, on 18 March 1880.[514] The couple had no children. They were enumerated together in the 1900 federal census living at #921 Dumaine Street, New Orleans, Ward 5, in a rented house. Jean, both of whose parents had been born in France, indicated that he was forty-eight-years old, white, born in February 1852, and married for twenty years. He worked as a conductor on an electric railway. Elizabeth Beppouey, also aged about 48, having been born in May 1852, was a white unemployed female with no children.[515] John Beppouey died in New Orleans on 18 February 1903.[516] Thereafter, his wife, Elise Josephine lived in a series of rented apartments in the French Quarter and worked as a dressmaker. She died on 10 May 1931 in New Orleans.[517]

Joseph M. Bonneval born ca. 1853 and Daniel Lewis Bonneval born ca. 1856 to Virginie Domingon and Joseph Bonneval both died just a year apart, the former on 3 November 1875 and the latter on 12 November 1876 in New Orleans.[518] Other than their appearance in the 1860 federal census with their parents, there is no other information regarding their short lives, or any evidence that they had descendants. The couple's last child, Benjamin Peter Bonneval was their only male child to live to be an adult.

When Benjamin Peter Bonneval, (aka Pierre B. Bonneval) and Georgette Brown were enumerated in the 1880 federal census for New Orleans living on Orleans Street, they indicated that they had been wed that year. There is, however, no civil record, for that marriage. Benjamin Bonneval, a white male, aged about twenty-one, worked as an ice dealer. His twenty-year-old bride, Georgette, a white female, was keeping house.[519] They were the parents of three children: Benjamin Joseph, born on 4 October 1880, Georgette Lucille, born on 29 August 1882, and Montigue Louis, born on 27 February 1888.[520]

According to the 1900 federal census, Benjamin (erroneously enumerated as "Franklin,"), born in July 1858 was working as a butcher alongside his son, twenty-year-old Benjamin Joseph. His wife, Georgette, born about September 1860, and he had been married twenty-one years and were the parents of three children. Their daughter

[512] "New Orleans, Louisiana Birth Records Index, 1804-1849," [database on-line] *Ancestry.com*. (https://www.ancestry.com: accessed 27 January 2020), Birth of Mathilde Bonneval, child of Joseph Alexander Bonneval and Virginie Domingon, Vol. 10, p. 471.

[513] "New Orleans, Louisiana Death Records Index, 1804-1876," [database on-line] *Ancestry.com*. (https://www.ancestry.com: accessed 1/27/2020), Death of Louise Mathilde Bonneval. Vol 14, p. 165.

[514] "Louisiana Parish Marriages, 1837-1957," database with images, *FamilySearch.org* (https://familysearch.org/ ark:/61903/1:1:QKJW-2N7L : accessed 4/8/2020), John Beppouey to Lize Josephine Bonneval, 18 Mar 1880; citing Orleans, Louisiana, United States, various parish courthouses, Louisiana; FHL microfilm 907,694.

[515] 1900 United States Federal Census, New Orleans, Orleans Parish, LA, Ward 5, Dwelling #86, Family #115, John Beppouey household, digital image, *Ancestry.com* (https://www.ancestry.com: accessed 12/22/2019), citing NARA microfilm publication T623, FHL Film 1240571. Date of enumeration: 4 & 5 June 1900, Image 9/42.

[516] "Orleans Death Indices,1894-1907" [database on-line], *Ancestry.com* (https://www.ancestry.com: accessed 12/30/ 2019), citing *New Orleans, Louisiana Death Records Index, 1804-1949.* Death of John Beppouey, Vol. 129, p. 350.

[517] "Orleans Death Indices,1929-1936" [database on-line], *Ancestry.com* (https://www.ancestry.com: accessed 12/30/ 2019), citing *New Orleans, Louisiana Death Records Index, 1804-1949.* Death of Elise Bonneval, Vol. 202, p. 917.

[518] "New Orleans, Louisiana Death Records Index, 1804-1949," [database on-line] *Ancestry.com*. (https://www.ancestry.com: accessed 1/27/2020), Death of Joseph M. Bonneval, aged 23, Vol 64, p. 887; Death of Daniel Lewis Bonneval, aged 20, Vol. 67, p. 530.

[519] 1880 United States Federal Census, New Orleans, Orleans Parish, LA, E.D. 34, #30 Orleans St., Dwelling #229, Family #612, Benj. Bonneval household, digital image, *Ancestry.com* (https://ancestry.com: accessed 12/22/2019), citing NARA microfilm publication T9_461. Date of enumeration: 11 June 1880, Image 39/52.

[520] "New Orleans, Louisiana Birth Records Index, 1790-1915," [database on-line] *Ancestry.com*. (https://www.ancestry.com: accessed 27 January 2020), Birth of Joseph Benjamin Bonneval , Vol. 76, p. 383; Birth of Georgette Bonneval, Vol. 79, p. 45; Birth of Louis Bonneval, Vol. 86, p. 231.

Georgette, age 17, and son, Montigue, age 12, were in school.[521] Soon after that census, Benjamin Bonneval gave up butchering and began working on a steamboat. Shortly before his death on 20 February 1920,[522] he was enumerated with his wife, Georgette, his daughter Georgette, and her husband, Blaise Lannes, as an officer on a ferry boat. The family lived together at #736 Josephine Street. Georgette and her husband Blaise Lannes, a sugar sampler for the United States government, never had children. Montigue Louis Bonneval married Edna Gertrude Wunsch. They lived in Plaquemines Parish where Montigue managed a dairy. They had three children: Montigue E. (b. 1914), Robert L. (b. 1915), and Ralph Trique (b. 1921).[523] Benjamin Peter Bonneval and Georgette's eldest son, Benjamin Joseph, married Edna Leitz. They were the parents of four children: Elmore Benjamin (b. 1908), Elmo James (b. 1909), Elaine Violet (b. 1910) and Georgette Edna (b. 1913).[524] The Bonneval descendants continued to live in or near New Orleans where there was never any indication of their racial diversity.

Félicité Aubry's son, Auguste Julien Domingon (See other information p 235 & 237), with Hilaire Julien Domingon, obtained a license to marry Marie Henriette Rey(es) in New Orleans on 31 May 1848.[525] Henriette was the daughter of Joseph Reyes, a Spanish immigrant to New Orleans, and his wife, Artine Declouet. Her New Orleans birth record reads: "Reyes, Maria Antonia (José, native of Reyes in Catalonia and Antonia Decluet, native of this city) b. Jun 2, 1828, bn. Feb 7, 1828 s. Mariano Pelegrin and Brigida Rodriguez (SLC, B39, 118)." They were the parents of three children: Joseph Raymond, born on 31 August 1849; Arnold Charles, born on 7 August 1853; and Marie Louise Rita, born on 30 July 1855.[526] Jules and Henriette were enumerated in the 1850 United States Federal Census for New Orleans, Ward 2. Recently married, Jules, a twenty-five-year-old "mulatto" male was working as a cigar maker, an occupation that many men of color followed. His twenty-one-year-old wife was at home with their baby Joseph, aged about 1 year. Another cigar maker, Charles Gallatin, shared their house.[527] The couple's first-born child, Joseph Raymond probably died as a child as there are no subsequent civil records for him. Jules Domingon, a "mulatto male," aged about 37 years, a "cigar man" with $200 in personal estate was enumerated with his wife, Henriette, and their two surviving children, Rita and Arnold, all identified as "mulatto," in the 1860 Federal Census for the 7th Ward, New Orleans. Jules's mother-in-law, the widow A(rtine) Declouet who owned $2000 in real estate and $300 in personal property was living with them.[528]

Auguste Jules Domingon died at the family home on 113 Mandeville Street on 11 October 1874 from "Paludienne fever," a type of intermittent malarial fever:

[521] 1900 United States Federal Census, New Orleans, Orleans Parish, LA, Ward 10, 2048 Rousseau St., Dwelling #221, Family #233, Franklin Bonneval household, digital image, *Ancestry.com* (https://www.ancestry.com: accessed 12/22/ 2019), citing NARA microfilm publication T623 FHL Film 1240574, Date of enumeration: 7 June 1900, Image 32/46.

[522] "New Orleans, Louisiana Death Records Index, 1918-1928," [database on-line] *Ancestry.com*. (https://www.ancestry.com: accessed 2/2/2020), Death of Benjamin Peter Bonneval, age 59, Vol 178, p. 506.

[523] *Findagrave.com*, database with images, (www.findagrave.com; accessed 2/9/2020.), Memorial #39801486 – Montigue Louis Bonneval; Edna Wunsch Bonneval, Memorial # 39801524; Ralph Trique Bonneval, Memorial #5822782; Robert L. Bonneval, Memorial # 39801619; Montigue E. Bonneval, Memorial # 114152206.

[524] *Findagrave.com*, database with images, (www.findagrave.com; accessed 2/9/2020.), Memorial #39801393 – Benjamin J. Bonneval; Edna Leitz Bonneval, Memorial #34931623; Elmo James Bonneval, Memorial # 157131042.

[525] "Louisiana Parish Marriages, 1837-1957," database with images, *FamilySearch.org* (https://familysearch.org/ ark:/61903/1:1:QKJC-S76H : accessed 13 March 2018), Jules Domingon and Marie Henriette Rey, 31 May 1848; citing Orleans, Louisiana, United States, various parish courthouses, Louisiana; FHL microfilm 903,929.

[526] "New Orleans, Louisiana Birth Records Index, 1790-1899," [database on-line] *Ancestry.com*. (https://www.ancestry.com: accessed 1/27/2020), Birth of Joseph Raymond Domingon (Colored) , Vol. 10, p. 238; Birth of Arnold Charles Domingon (Colored), Vol. 10, p. 585; Birth of Marie Louise Rita Domingon (white), Vol. 15, p. 206.

[527] 1850 United States Federal Census, Orleans Parish, Louisiana, Municipality 3, Ward 2, Dwelling #2214, Family #2636, Jules Domingon household, digital image, *Ancestry.com* (https://www.ancestry.com accessed 12/11/2019), citing NARA microfilm publication M432_238, p. 131B. Date of enumeration: 16 August 1850. Image 58/92.

[528] 1860 United States Federal Census, Orleans Parish, Louisiana, Ward 72, Dwelling #1617, Family #1950, Jules Domaigen (*sic*) household, digital image, *Ancestry.com* (https://www.ancestry.com accessed 12/11/2019), citing NARA microfilm publication M653_419, p. 465. Date of enumeration: 23 June 1860. Image 225/332.

Be it Remembered, That on this day, to-wit: the *Twelfth of October* in the year of our Lord One Thousand Eight Hundred and *Seventy four* and the ninety *Ninth* of the Independence of the United States of America, before me, F. C. Antoine, duly commissioned and sworn *Recorder of Births, Marriages and Deaths*, in and for the Parish and City of New Orleans, personally appeared:

Alexander Slater, a native of Maryland, residing at N°. 88 Bourbon Street in this City who hereby declares that

Jules Domingon

a native of New Orleans, aged Fifty years, Died, October the Eleventh instant in this present year (October 11th 1874) at Nine o'clock P.M. at N°. 113 Mandeville Street in this City.

Cause of death "Paludium Fever" Certificate of D°. A Dupaquier

Thus Done at New Orleans, in the Presence of the aforesaid *A. Slater* and in that of Messrs. *A Cole & A° Cauis* both of this City witnesses by me requested so to be, who have hereunto set their hands, together with me, after due reading hereof, the day, month and year first above written.

F. C. Antoine
Recorder.

Courtesy of State of Louisiana, Secretary of State, Division of Archives, Records Management, and History. *Vital Records Indices*. Baton Rouge, LA, USA citing *Orleans Death Indices 1804-1876*; Vol. 62, p. 100.

Domingon's widow, Henriette Reyes, died in New Orleans on 21 July 1902 from apoplexy, at her residence on 2333 Burgundy Street. She left her small estate to her surviving daughter Rita, the wife of William John Daunoy, employed as an inspector on a street railway, and to her grandchildren born to her late son, Arnold Charles Domingon and his wife Sarah Josephine Lyons who had married on 16 April 1879,[529] leaving three children: Henriette Josephine Domingon, born on 31 March 1881 and Julia Marie Domingon, born on 20 March 1884, and Rita Domingon, born ca. 1888.[530] Arnold Charles Domingon had died in New Orleans on 22 February 1890.[531]

[529] "Louisiana Parish Marriages, 1837-1957," database with images, *FamilySearch.org* (https://family search.org/ark:/ 61903/1:1:QKJW-KY1W : accessed 2/4/2020), Arnold Charles Domingon and Sarah Josephine Lyon, 16 Apr 1879; citing Orleans, Louisiana, United States, various parish courthouses, Louisiana; FHL microfilm 907,694.

[530] "New Orleans, Louisiana Birth Records Index, 1790-1899," [database on-line] *Ancestry.com*. (https://www.ancestry.com: accessed 1/27/2020), Birth of Henrietta Josephine Domingon (white) , Vol. 77, p. 93; Birth of Julia Marie Domingon (white), Vol. 81, p. 315. Note: There is no birth record for Rita. Henriette Josephine married Edwin Faust Long on 9 June 1909. They had two sons, Clifton and Alvin Edwin. Neither Rita nor Julia ever married.

[531] "New Orleans, Louisiana Death Records Index, 1804-1949," [database on-line] *Ancestry.com*. (https://www.ancestry.com: accessed 1/29/2020), Death of Henriette Reyes, widow Jules Domingon (white), aged 75, Vol. 127, p. 1137; Death of Arnold C. Domingon, aged 35 (*sic*), Vol. 96, p. 766.

Félicité Aubry's granddaughter Rita Marie Domingon married William John Daunoy, the son of Charles Joseph Daunoy and Marie Benoite Moore, in New Orleans on 26 October 1876.[532] Marie Benoite Moore was enumerated in both the 1850 and 1860 Federal Census records as a "mulatto." Her husband, Charles Daunoy, was enumerated with her in the 1860 federal census also as a "mulatto" who worked as a grocery clerk. When Benoite Moore Daunoy died in New Orleans on 21 August 1864 at her home on 199 Love Street, there was no indication of her race.[533] When her husband, seventy-nine-year-old Charles Daunoy, died years later on 23 August 1904 at the asylum of the Little Sisters of the Poor in New Orleans his race was shown as "white."[534]

Nine children were born to William John Daunoy and Rita Domingon all registered as "white": William John, on 11 November 1877; Charles Henry Waldo, on 11 October 1880; Marie Rita, on 10 August 1882; Robert Sidney, on 12 October 1884; Stella Josephine, on 7 April 1887; Harry Louis, on 12 April 1889; Aline Benoite, on 13 March 1891; Henrietta Marie, on 11 September 1892; and Inez Hilda Louise on 26 August 1897.[535] The family appeared in subsequent federal census records as being white as well. William John Daunoy died in New Orleans on 6 December 1922, and his wife followed on 18 December 1924.[536] Although they had nine children, they only had three grandchildren, and two great-grandchildren.

Five of the Daunoy children never married: William John, Jr. who died on 19 April 1930[537], Charles Henry Waldo, who died on 15 December 1949 (SSDI), Marie Rita, who died on 24 March 1976, Henrietta Marie, who died on 8 May 1983[538] and Inez Hilda Louise, who died on 15 May 1974 (SSDI), all in New Orleans. Harry Louis Daunoy married Marie Henrietta Lochridge, a Texas native, in 1913. They had no children. He died on 11 February 1958 in Metairie, Jefferson Parish, LA (SSDI). His wife died on 10 January 1980 in Marble Falls, Burnet Co., TX.[539] Aline Benoite Daunoy married Milton R. Fetterly, a native of Michigan, where the couple lived most of their lives. They had no children. Returning to New Orleans in 1954, Milton died there on 7 January 1958, and Aline died on 4 September 1968.[540]

Robert Sidney Daunoy married Evelyn Margaret Fleischer on 15 June 1910 in New Orleans. They had two children: Myrle Henrietta, on 6 March 1911, and Elden Leo, on 2 January 1913, both born in New Orleans. The family lived in Houston, Harris Co., TX. Myrle married Howard Ellis Tyson in Texas. They had two sons: Kenneth (b. 1937), and Howard M. (b. 1939). Elden married Catherine Russell Munger, but they had no children.

Stella Josephine Daunoy married Ernest Reinhardt Burkhardt in New Orleans on 25 April 1912. They had one daughter, Muriel Ann, born on 5 March 1913, who married Joseph George Vollenweider on 15 June 1939. The Vollenweiders had no children.

---

[532] "Louisiana Parish Marriages, 1837-1957," database with images, *FamilySearch.org* (https://family search.org/ark:/61903/1:1:QKJH-89YX : 12 March 2018), William John Daunoy and Rita Marie Domingon, 26 Oct 1876; citing Orleans, Louisiana, United States, various parish courthouses, Louisiana; FHL microfilm 911,647.

[533] Courtesy of State of Louisiana, Secretary of State, Division of Archives, Records Management, and History. *Vital Records Indices*. Baton Rouge, LA, USA, citing *Orleans Death Indices 1804-1876*; Vol. 26, p. 540.

[534] Courtesy of State of Louisiana, Secretary of State, Division of Archives, Records Management, and History. *Vital Records Indices*. Baton Rouge, LA, USA, citing *Orleans Death Indices 1894-1907*; Vol. 133, p.423.

[535] "New Orleans, Louisiana Birth Records Index, 1790-1899," [database on-line] *Ancestry.com*. (https://www.ancestry.com: accessed 1/27/2020), Births of: William Joseph, Vol 71, p.202; Charles Henry Waldo, Vol. 76, p. 440; Marie Rita, Vol.78, p. 1186; Robert Sidney, Vol. 81, p. 1166; Stella Josephine, Vol. 85, p. 243; Harry Louis, Vol 87, p. 727; Alice Benoit, Vol. 91, p. 649; Henrietta Marie, Vol. 95, p. 174; Inez Hilda Louise, Vol. 111, p. 525.

[536] "New Orleans, Louisiana Death Records Index, 1804-1949," [database on-line] *Ancestry.com*. (https://www.ancestry.com: accessed 1/29/2020), Death of William John Daunoy, age 68, Vol. 186, p. 15; Death of Rita Domingon Daunoy, age 68, Vol. 189, p. 1459.

[537] "Deaths," The (New Orleans) *Times-Picayune*, 20 April 1930, digital image, *Genealogybank.com* (https://www.genealogybank.com: accessed 13 February 2020) death of William John Daunoy, p. 2, col. 4.

[538] "Deaths," The (New Orleans) *Times-Picayune*, , digital images, *Genealogybank.com* (https://www.genealogybank.com: accessed 13 February 2020) death of Rita Marie Daunoy, reported on 26 March 1976, p. 16, col. 2; Death of Henrietta Marie Daunoy, reported on 10 May 1983, p. 13, col. 4.

[539] "Deaths," The (New Orleans) *Times-Picayune*, 13 January 1980, digital image, *Genealogybank.com* (https://www.genealogybank.com: accessed 13 February 2020) death of Marie Lochridge Daunoy, p. 20, col. 4.

[540] "Deaths," The (New Orleans) *Times-Picayune*, digital images, *Genealogybank.com* (https://www.genealogybank.com: accessed 13 February 2020), death of Milton R. Fetterly, issue dated 8 January 1958, p.2, col. 5; and death of Aline Daunoy Fetterly, issue dated 5 September 1968, p. 26, col. 7.

CHAPTER 19

MERCELITE AUBRY, HENRY SELLON BONEVAL LATROBE AND LOUIS PAUL BRINGIER

Mercelite Aubry, Marguerite Cécile Aubry's second youngest daughter, was perhaps sixteen-years-old when she met Henry Sellon Boneval Latrobe, who had been sent in 1811 by his father, the famous architect of the Capitol in Washington, D.C., Henry Benjamin Latrobe, to complete a contract to build a water works for New Orleans, using steam power technology. Latrobe, Sr., had completed a similar project for the city of Philadelphia in 1801. Although yellow fever was generally associated with tropical regions, the year 1793 had brought an epidemic to Philadelphia that killed off about one-tenth of the population. Subsequent epidemics in 1797 and 1798 convinced the city fathers that a system to bring clean water into the town was worth the expense. Benjamin Henry Latrobe designed and supervised the construction of a series of steam driven pumps to bring water from the Schuylkill River into the city center. After it was launched successfully, other locations clamored for this improvement. No place was more in need than New Orleans with its semi-tropical climate and almost yearly epidemics of cholera, yellow fever, and dysentery. Latrobe, busy with projects in Washington D.C., was confident that his eldest son, Henry Sellon Boneval Latrobe, the first child of he and his wife Lydia Sellon, could complete the job.

The young man, born in London, England, on 19 July 1792, and baptized at Camden, Percy Chapel, St. Pancras on 25 August 1792,[541] was fluent in French, and already, at the age of nineteen, a budding architect and engineer in his own right. Benjamin Latrobe secured the New Orleans franchise in April 1811. His son intended to have the plant built on a lot adjacent to the United States Customhouse that his father had designed in 1807, which had been constructed by a contractor whose execution was so bad that it had to be torn down a decade later. However, the lot next to the Customhouse was owned by the Federal Government which refused to relinquish it.

While waiting for a location to begin construction of the water works, Latrobe sold a steam pump, which had lately arrived on the Brig *Thaddeus* from New York, to the New Orleans merchant Laurent Millaudon on 6 September 1811, by virtue of a power of attorney given to him by his father, Benjamin Henry Latrobe. Millaudon paid Latrobe 1,000 piastres in cash and agreed to pay an additional 2,993 piastres and ten cents on two notes that Latrobe had signed and were endorsed by Mr. (Edward) Hollander to be turned over to the firm of Talcott and Bowers in payment for the pump as well as for its transport down to New Orleans.[542] Interest would soon be shown by sugar planters around New Orleans to secure these pumps for their sugar mills. By the end of November 1812, Henry Latrobe had negotiated contracts for two more engines to be sent down to New Orleans.[543]

In February 1812 Latrobe finally secured a piece of property from the city of New Orleans on the opposite end of town between St. Philip and Ursulines, south of the Levee Road, for which the City took twelve shares. The following month Latrobe took bids for construction of the building that would house the steam engines to pump water from the Mississippi River into six elevated wooden casks for purification and desalination. The building was completed in 1813. A system of pipes was also to be installed to bring the fresh water into the city.[544] In July 1812 the City Council agreed to pay $3,000 towards the project, with another $3,000 when it was completed. Even with this infusion of money, financial problems beset the undertaking. An indefinite delay caused by the onset of the War of 1812 doomed it to failure. Out of an abundance of caution, Latrobe's father would not allow the steam pumps to be loaded onto a ship to be transported down to New Orleans for fear that they would be seized by enemy British ships patrolling the waters up and down the east coast of the United States. While the construction of the water

---

[541] "Church of England Parish Registers, 1538-1812," digital image, *Ancestry.com* (https.www.ancestry.com: accessed 2/2/2020), Baptism of Henry Sellon Latrobe, Image 117/122.

[542] NARC, "Sale, Boneval Latrobe to Laurent Millaudon," dated 6 September 1811, passed by Notary Pierre Pedesclaux, Vol. 73, folio 520, 2 pages. Courtesy Hon. Chelsey Richard Napoleon, Clerk of Civil District Court, Parish of Orleans. (Notary Philippe Pedesclaux, Pierre's son, wrote and signed this document.)

[543] John C. Van Horne, ed., *The Correspondence and Miscellaneous Papers of Benjamin Henry Latrobe, Volume 3, 1811-1820* (New Haven, CT & London: Yale University Press, 1988), 385.

[544] Morris A. Pierce, *Documentary History of American Water-works*, http://www.waterworkshistory.us/LA /New Orleans/ (accessed 2/4/2020).

purification system on the Mississippi River progressed at a snail's pace, minds were more focused on the war with Great Britain.

Near the end of 1812, Henry Latrobe signed contracts with the city to construct a barracks to house some 2000 Tennessee volunteers at Fort St. Leon located at English Turn in Plaquemines Parish on the Mississippi River, for which he hoped to be paid in excess of $100,000 piastres.[545] Tennessee and Kentucky volunteers would be instrumental in staving off the English at the Battle of New Orleans just two years later. In the spring of 1813, Latrobe petitioned the City Council for another water works extension until 1 May 1815. The war had caused a delay in the manufacture of the steam pumps at Washington D.C. causing the elder Latrobe to have to move his factory to a safer place in Pittsburgh, PA. The barracks project at English Turn kept his son busy through the spring of 1813, where, after spending fifty-thousand or so piastres in construction and labor costs, he hoped to clear six or seven thousand for himself.[546]

During the summer of 1813, young Henry Latrobe, with more time on his hands than money, had forged a bond with the Aubry sisters, through a friendship with René Prosper Foy/Foix, a French immigrant from Orléans, Loiret, France. Foy was a rich plantation owner, a man of letters, intensely interested in the arts and theater, as well as the companion of Zélie Aubry, a free woman of color, the sister of Mercelite, Félicité, Eglée and Martin Aubry, with whom he would have ten children over the course of the years. He was one of the few white men who did not abandon his mistress for marriage to a woman "of his own class," although the couple's relationship was somewhat rocky over the years. (See the following chapter for the story of Foy and Zélie Aubry).

At the age of about sixteen years, Mercelite Aubry gave birth to twenty-one-year-old Henry Sellon Boneval Latrobe's only son, Henry Belmont Latrobe on 25 March 1814. The original record reads: "On 29 May 1828 was baptized by me the undersigned [Fr. Louis Moni], Henry Belmont born in New Orleans on 25 March 1814, an illegitimate son of the late Henry Latrobe, a native of Baltimore and Marguerite Aubry, native of this parish. Godfather: Pierre Colin Blanque. Godmother Madame Lalaurie, widow Blanque, born MacCarty."

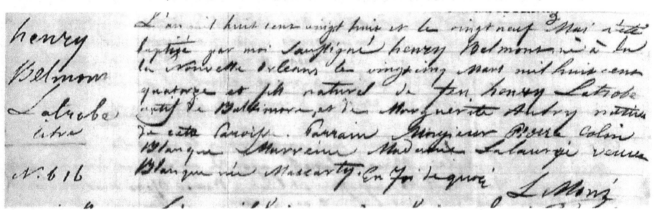

Courtesy of the Archives of the Archdiocese of New Orleans, Saint Louis Cathedral Records, Sacramental Register of St. Louis Cathedral, Baptisms – Vol. 1827-1828, p. 114, #615. Baptism of Henry Belmont Latrobe, libre (free). (Courtesy of Emilie Leumas, Archivist – Kimberly Johnson and Katie Vest – Researching Archivists.)

The large gap between the boy's birth and his baptism is puzzling. Henry, while a British citizen, was raised in the Moravian Church, where his grandfather was a Minister, but he had been educated at St. Mary's Academy in Baltimore, MD. Perhaps Mercelite needed the baptism for identification purposes. A surprising aside to this record is the presence of the godmother, "Madame Lalaurie, the widow Blanque, born MacCarty." Six years later in 1834, Madame Lalaurie would be run out of town by enraged citizens of New Orleans, after a fire at her house uncovered slaves bound in her attic that had been cruelly abused for long periods of time. She died in Paris in 1849.[547]

There is additional proof that René Prosper Foy and Henry Latrobe were close because Foy convinced Latrobe to stand as the godfather in 1815 to Foy and Zélie Aubry's second child, a daughter, Elizabeth Pauline Foy:

[545] John C. Van Horne, ed. *The Correspondence of Benjamin Henry Latrobe, Volume 3*, 428, Note 1.
[546] Ibid, 457.
[547] For a thorough treatment of the infamous Madame Lalaurie, please see Carolyn Morrow Long's book *Madame Lalaurie, Mistress of the Haunted House* (Gainesville, FL: University Press of Florida, 2012).

"Foiy (@Foy), Elizabeth Pauline (Prosper, native of Orleans in France [dept. of Loiret] and Eloisa Aubry, native of this parish) b. Sept 2, 1815, bn. Mar. 17, 1813, s. Henrico Bonneval LATROPE [sic] and Juana Paulin Des (P?)erque (SLC, B27,143)."

In the meantime, Henry Latrobe busied himself with other projects. He was befriended by Arsène Lacarrière Latour and Hyacinthe Laclotte, two Frenchmen who were, as was Latrobe, both architects and engineers. (See pp. 63-68). In 1814 Latour and Latrobe teamed up to design a house at #721 Gov. Nicholls Street for Jean-Baptiste Thierry, the editor of a local newspaper, *Le Courrier de la Louisiane*. The house, unusual because it was constructed in the Greek revival style, was L-shaped, a floor plan made possible by the owner's purchase of a portion of the rear lot which faced onto Bourbon Street. It had a large back courtyard and a detached kitchen which was common to the architecture of the day.[548] Latrobe was hoping that his private architectural commissions would bring in enough money to keep the waterworks project afloat.

On 1 December 1814, as the second war with Britain drew closer to Louisiana, General Andrew Jackson arrived in New Orleans to make preparations for the imminent attack on the city. Arsène Lacarrière Latour and Henry Sellon Latrobe were engaged to work as engineers to design and build the fortifications to protect the city from invasion. While Latour was given the title of "Chief Engineer," and could be found most often at Jackson's side, Lieutenant Latrobe spent much of his time in the field. Latrobe was not the only member of his mixed-race family circle on the battlefield during late December 1814 through early January 1815. Martin Aubry, Mercelite's brother, was a First Lieutenant in Alexander Lemelle's Company of Free men of Color (also called Col. Baker's Regiment). René Prosper Foy/Foix, Zélie Aubry's partner, was the First Lieutenant and Adjutant in the Uniformed Battalion of Orleans Volunteers, serving under Major Jean-Baptiste Plauché. Celestin Chiapella, great-uncle of Eglée Aubry's sons with Achille Chiapella, had enlisted as a private in De la Ronde's 3rd Regiment, Louisiana Militia and Jean-Baptiste Pinta, Eulalie Pinta Chiapella's grandfather, was a captain in Cavelier's 2nd Regiment Louisiana Militia.

Latrobe served admirably in what was termed by Arsène Lacarrière Latour in his 1816 book *Historical Memoire of the War in West Florida and Louisiana in 1814-1815*, as "the affair of the 28th December 1814." The British had been moving northward through the various plantations in St. Bernard Parish. Their advance was temporarily stopped at Chalmette's Plantation by the efforts of the ship *Louisiana*, who from the Mississippi River, fired upon the British forces. In a tip of his hat to Latrobe, Latour wrote:

> The *Louisiana* suffered the enemy's columns to advance a considerable space; and as soon as they had got as near to her as her commander wished, she opened on them a tremendous and well-directed fire. This was at first briskly answered by the enemy's artillery, which was soon silenced by the guns of the ship, and those of our lines. That very morning the engineer, H.S. Bonneval Latrobe, had established, under the fire of the enemy's artillery and a cloud of rockets, a twenty-four pounder on the left of the battery No. 1, on the line. This gun dismounted one of the field pieces which the enemy had placed in battery on the road.[549]

When Latrobe's father visited the battlefield in February 1819, he drew a sketch of the field of battle including the battery "erected on the 26 by Henry Latrobe." Underneath the sketch he wrote in his own hand:

> Latour in his history of Louisiana. General Jackson in many conversations with me and Mr. Nolte who was on the spot also, have stated that my son exhibited in the erection of this battery in the open field almost a degree of cool courage and presence of mind which would have done honor to any soldier. He was 21 only and it is equally worthy of remark that the ground around him and his men was torn up by balls and rockets. And one wounded.[550]

After Lieutenant Latrobe secured the emplacement of the gun on 28 December 1815, according to *Major Howell Tatum's Journal while Acting Topographical Engineer (1814) to General Jackson commanding the Seventh Military District*, he began to secure one of the lines of defense that General Jackson had planned, to thwart any

---

[548] The Collins C. Diboll Vieux Carré Digital Survey, Historic New Orleans Collection (https://www.hnoc.org/vcs/property_info.php?lot=22850), 721 Governor Nicholls Street, Square #54, Lot #22850.

[549] Arsène Lacarrière Latour, *Historical Memoir of The War in West Florida and Louisiana in 1814-15*, 120.

[550] Benjamin Henry Boneval Latrobe, *Impressions Respecting New Orleans: Diary and Sketches 1818-1820*, edited by Samuel Wilson, Jr., (New York: Columbia University Press, 1951), 44. Note: See more about Vincent Nolte, pp.272, 273.

British surprises to his rear. To the north of Line Jackson, Line Dupre was constructed to transect the land between the cypress swamp and the river. Tatum described Latrobe's participation at length:

> A number of negroe [sic] men were now procured from the citizens to ease the labour of the soldiery and preserve their health and activity for more important service. The negroes were divided and allotted to the different corps on the lines. And another large party was collected, and placed under the direction of a Monsr. Latrobe, an Engineer, engaged as an assistant by the Commanding General for the purpose of constructing and errecting [sic] a line of defense in reserve, at Madame Dupree's Mill and Canal about one mile to the rear of the principal line. This line was immediately commenced and progressed with great rapidity & strength. A Demi Bastion on the right (at the Levey) raked the Canal in front of the Breast Works and played obliquely over the plane from those in its face. Another Battery was erected at the commencement of the swamp at the distance of about 600 paces, which formed a cross fire with that on the Levy. A strong bridge was thrown over the canal a few paces below the Demi Bastion by which it was protected, as also by another Battery erected on the lower works of the Mill, about forty paces below the Bridge. The waters on this canal were from 5 to 6 feet deep with a strong line of defense on its upper side.[551]

Line Dupré, which was described as having been built with a banquette parapet fitted with planks, was defended by General Villeré's First Division Louisiana Militia using heavy artillery, and protected, as well, by a wet ditch. After 4 January 1815, Kentucky troops led by Brigadier-General John Adair occupied the area between Line Dupré and the Piernas Canal. Should Lines Jackson and Dupré be breached by the British, the Line Montreuil was the last defense for the city of New Orleans.

Lieutenant Latrobe remained at Line Dupré, at least through, January 7, 1815, when he dispatched a letter to Major-General Villeré asking for more men to carry out an order from General Jackson in order to shore up the line.[552] The following day, 8 January 1815 was the decisive battle of New Orleans, which would put an end to the British Army's plan to take the city. The map on the next page is a partial scan of Plate #5 from the Atlas which Arsène Lacarrière Latour published as an addendum to his account of the War of 1812, titled "Map Shewing (sic) the Landing of the British Army, its several Encampments and Fortifications on the Mississippi and the Works they erected on their Retreat, also the different posts Encampments and Fortification made by the several Corps of the American Army during the whole Campaign:"

---

[551] Howell Tatum "Major Howell Tatum's Journal while Acting Topographical Engineer (1814) to General Jackson commanding the Seventh Military District," ed. By John Spencer Bassett, Smith College Studies in History VII (October 1921-April 1922), Reprint, Franklin Classics, United States, 2018, p. 119.

[552] The Historic New Orleans Collection, "MSS 14. Villeré (Jacques Philippe) Papers, 1813-1815, " 106 items. Hnoc.org (https://www.hnoc.org/BNO/pdf/ mss014.pdf: accessed 4/11/2020), Folder 31, 1815, Jan.7.

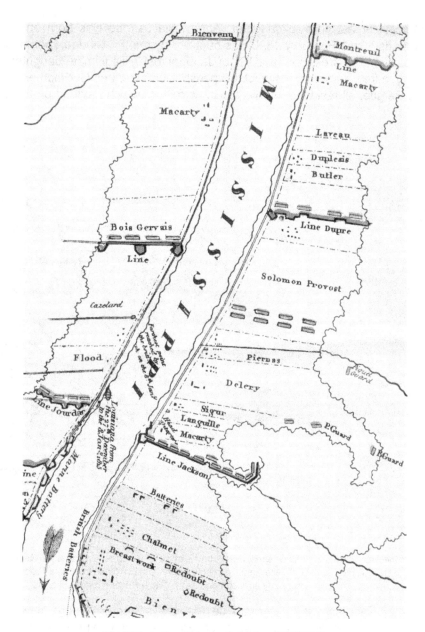

The Historic New Orleans Collection 1979.238.7.

The above map shows the top portion of Latour's Plate #5 indicating the position of Lines Jackson, Dupré and Montreuil, from south to north, in relationship to the plantations in St. Bernard Parish. The shaded portion at the bottom is indicative of the portion of the parish which had been temporarily occupied by the British. The city of New Orleans lay just above Line Montreuil.[553]

The spring of 1815 brought a relative peace back to the city of New Orleans. Latrobe struggled to keep his father's project going. In May he appeared before the City Council to ask for an extension of the contract that the City had granted his father to install the machinery and piping necessary to furnish clean water to the city and suburbs. He explained that he had been unable to finish due to the recent war, but that the project was well advanced. He was given until August 1816 to finish the installations, but was required to put up a bond to guarantee that he would be done by that date.

---

[553] Arsène Lacarrière Latour, *Historical Memoir of The War in West Florida and Louisiana in 1814-15, With an Atlas.* (Gainesville, FL: University of Florida Press, 1964), Plate #5, Courtesy of The Historic New Orleans Collection 1979.238.7.

Henry and Mercelite's last child, a daughter, Anne Julia Latrobe was born on 18 January 1816. The document, in French reads:" On 6 February 1820 was baptized by me, Fr. Claude Thoma, pastor in the St. Louis parish, Julie Anne, racially mixed, free, born the 18th of January 1816, illegitimate daughter of Mr. Henry Latrobe and of Marguerite Aubry, a free quadroon, native of this parish. Godfather and Godmother were Mr. Norbert Soulié and Anne Pauline De Bergue, all residents of this parish, in faith of which I signed on the day. Month, and year stated above."

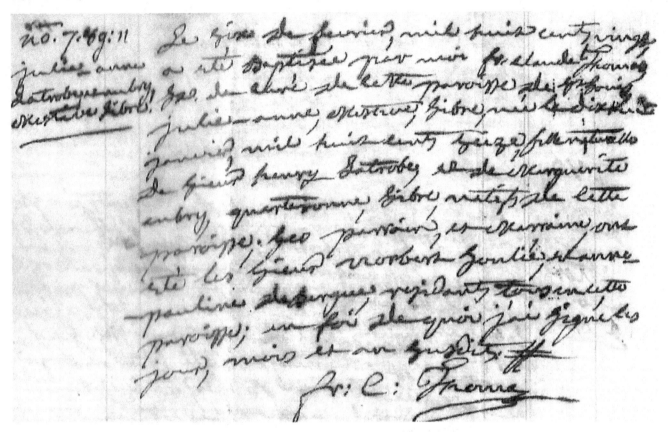

Courtesy of the Archives of the Archdiocese of New Orleans, Saint Louis Cathedral Records, Sacramental Register of St. Louis Cathedral Baptisms – Vol. 1820-1823, p. 170, #789. Baptism of Julie Anne Latrobe y Aubry, mestiva libre (free mixed-race person) (Courtesy of Emilie Leumas, Archivist – Kimberly Johnson and Katie Vest – Researching Archivists.)

Meanwhile, on 27 February 1816, Bernard de Marigny appeared before New Orleans notary Pierre Pedesclaux to formalize a contract for the construction of two houses on Chartres Street to be designed and built by Henry S. Boneval Latrobe, which had been agreed to under private contract dated 16 December 1815. At that time Marigny had paid Latrobe 11,500 piastres towards the project. It is not known how much of that money might have been used to breathe life into the stalled waterworks project. The building contract with Marigny was expected to cost a total of 22,000 piastres. Latrobe agreed to finish and hand over the keys to him within six months. The description of the building materials was so detailed that the thickness of bricks used for the external construction, the thickness of the wooden planks for the floors, the size of windows and doors, the size of each room, was agreed to in writing. Moreover, only cypress wood was to be used in the construction of the windows, doors and floors. The courtyard was to be paved with a slight pitch to allow for drainage. Marigny agreed to pay Latrobe the additional 10,500 piastres in three installments. The first, when the walls of the first floor were completed, the second when the roof was completed, and the third when the keys were handed over to him. An addendum to the contract indicated that a wrought iron balcony running the length of the house on Chartres would be identical to the balcony on Mr. Girod's house which was opposite the Exchange on Chartres Street. A scan of the final page of that contract with the signatures of Latrobe, Marigny, and two witnesses, may be seen on the following page:

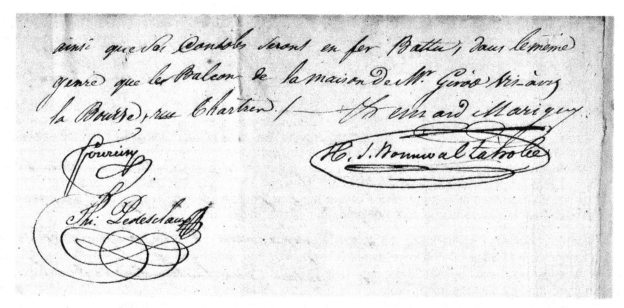

NARC, "Contract to Design and Build between Bernard Marigny and H.S. Boneval Latrobe," (No title in margin) dated 27 February 1816, passed by Notary Pierre Pedesclaux, Volume 72, folio 367, 5 pages. Courtesy Hon. Chelsey Richard Napoleon, Clerk of Civil District Court, Parish of Orleans.

On 6 May 1816 the Mississippi River breached a levee about five miles above New Orleans at the Macarty Plantation. The City Council tasked Henry Latrobe and Jacques Tanesse to gather 200 workers to repair the levee, but the following day the Governor overruled the Council and sent in his own men under a Mr. Joublanc to fix the breach. Joublanc had the ship *Louisiana* sunk in the crevasse, which failed to stop the water. As a consequence, the city was partially inundated, remaining so until early June.[554] Naturally the chaos which followed the flood caused, yet again, delays to the waterworks project.

On 25 May 1816, in an effort to raise money, Henry Latrobe came before Pierre Pedesclaux, notary to finalize a sale of property to Jean Marie Vinot, a resident of Plaquemines Parish. The land and buildings in question were situated at English Turn ("au detour des anglais") in Plaquemines Parish, on the left bank of the river, approximately seventeen miles from New Orleans. The plot of ground measured ninety feet by one hundred eighty feet deep bounded on one side by the land of Mr. "Nelhender" and on the other side by Mr. "Watey." Latrobe had bought the land from Francis Wood on 22 May 1815 by an act of sale passed before Plaquemines Parish Judge Arnould DuBourg. Vinot paid Latrobe 300 piastres for the real estate.[555]

Benjamin Henry Latrobe wrote to his sister Anna Louisa Elenora Latrobe Foster in May 1816, concerning his family and said this about his eldest son: "Henry is at New Orleans where he greatly distinguished himself by his bravery and good conduct as Engineer, during the campaign of 1815, under General Jackson. He is there making his fortune as an Architect and Civil Engineer, and altho' only 21, has been employed by the government in the most important works, and entrusted with the expenditure of large sums of money."[556]

On 11 June 1816, Marigny and Henry Latrobe went again before the notary Pierre Pedesclaux to finalize Latrobe's purchase of a plot of land in Square # 59 between St. Ann, Bourbon, Orleans and Royal Streets. on the corner of St. Ann and Bourbon. Latrobe paid Marigny 3,000 piastres before Pedesclaux and two witnesses. The seller had purchased the property originally on 6 June 1800 before the notary Marc Lafitte from François Dusuau de la Croix and Joseph Rofiniaco creditors of the late Joseph Montegut. The property had a frontage of 60 feet on

[554] John C. Van Horne, ed. *The Correspondence of Benjamin Henry Latrobe, Volume 3*, 788 and Note #1.

[555] NARC, "Sale of Property. Henry S. Bonneval Latrobe to Jean Marie Vinot," (No title in margin) dated 25 May 1816, passed by Notary Pierre Pedesclaux, Volume 72, folio 294, 2 pages. Courtesy Hon. Chelsey Richard Napoleon, Clerk of Civil District Court, Parish of Orleans.

[556] John C. Van Horne, ed. *The Correspondence of Benjamin Henry Latrobe, Volume 3*, 775.

St. Ann street, adjacent to the Théâtre d'Orléans, by 80 feet six inches on Bourbon Street.[557] The Théâtre d'Orléans had only been recently opened, but three months after Latrobe's purchase, the theater was completely destroyed.

On Monday 30 September 1816 it was reported in the *Louisiana Gazette and Mercantile Advertiser* that on Saturday about noon:

> A new building adjoining the theatre in Orleans Street was discovered to be on fire, and in less than two hours, the whole of the square from the theatre to Bourbon street, the one above from Orleans to St. Peter Streets (except the fireproof building of C. Moulon) and two-thirds of the buildings on the southwest side of St. Peter Street were on fire. Among the houses destroyed, were the one in which the fire commenced and the Orleans Theatre, several dwelling houses and a number of retail shops, the old theatre in St. Peter street, a large storehouse in the same street full of red and white wine. The damage occasioned by the fire cannot be estimated at less than three or four hundred thousand dollars. The buildings destroyed were, probably about sixty, and from many of them not a single article was saved.[558]

It is not clear whether the lot on the corner of Burgundy and St. Ann that Latrobe had purchased from Bernard Marigny on 11 June 1816 had yet been developed by him. What was worse for the younger Latrobe, however, was the destruction by that 28 September 1816 fire of the original Orleans/Davis's Ballroom which had just been completed by him. His father wrote to one of his own financiers in New York, Jacob Mark, that his son had lost $12,000 by the catastrophe, but that his creditors had given him three years to pay off his debts.[559] Never one to give up, three days after the fire, on 1 October 1816, Henry Latrobe met Edward Hollander in the office of the notary Pierre Pedesclaux, where Henry recorded an act of sale transferring the corner lot on St. Ann and Burgundy measuring approximately 60 feet facing St. Ann by 81 feet facing Bourbon, to Edward Hollander for the sum of 3,300 piastres cash in hand. The top portion of the act may be seen below:

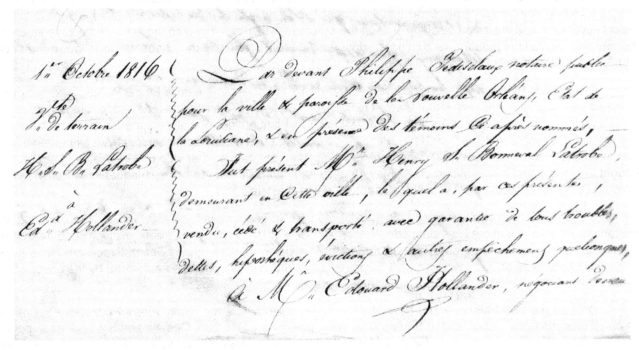

NARC, "Vente de terrain, H.S.B. Latrobe à Ed'd Hollander," [Sale of Land H.S.B. Latrobe to Ed'd Hollander) dated 1 October 1816, passed by Notary Philippe Pedesclaux in his father Pierre Pedesclaux's office, Volume 72, folio 566, 3 pages. Courtesy Hon. Chelsey Richard Napoleon, Clerk of Civil District Court, Parish of Orleans.

---

[557] NARC, "Sale of Property Bernard Marigny to H.S. Boneval Latrobe," (No title in margin) dated 11 June 1816, passed by Notary Pierre Pedesclaux, Volume 72, folio 347, 2 pages. Courtesy Hon. Chelsey Richard Napoleon, Clerk of Civil District Court, Parish of Orleans.

[558] "Dreadful Fire," *Louisiana Gazette and Mercantile Advertiser*, 30 September 1816, digital image, *Newspapers.com* (https://www.newspapers.com: accessed 2/10/2020), p. 2, col. 1.

[559] John C. Van Horne, ed. *The Correspondence of Benjamin Henry Latrobe, Volume 3*, 842, Note 1.

On 7 November 1816, Henry S. Latrobe completed the design for a lighthouse to be built at the mouth of the Mississippi River opposite the Balize on Frank's Island at the North East Pass, a project that he never completed, although he and Commodore Patterson chose this spot because of its maritime position and for the ability to be able to do the work safely. A contract for its erection was dated 20 January 1818. In April 1819, Latrobe's father Benjamin visited the island to find that the foundation had been finally laid.[560]

On 2 April 1817, Latrobe signed a contract with Charity Hospital to construct a new building adjoining the original building he had designed and had built in 1814-1815 on Canal Street between Baronne and Philippa (later University Place) Streets. Work on this addition was still in progress at the time of his death.[561] Latrobe accepted his last commission to design and build a house for a New Orleans resident on 24 April 1817 when he signed a contract with Margaret Clark, the widow of Claude Chabot. Margaret had been enumerated in the 1805 Matthew Flannery census of New Orleans as "Madame Shabot" living in a double house on #15 Conti Street with her daughter, two other unidentified people, and ten slaves.[562] In 1810 she was enumerated living on Bourbon Street as Vve. (Widow) Chabot with 14 slaves.[563] On 23 December 1817, she and Margaret Kennedy, a minor, went before the notary Philippe Pedesclaux to formalize the sale of a property on Bourbon Street between Bienville and Customhouse Streets (221-225 Bourbon, Square 68) next door to Mrs. Chabot's family dwelling. Margaret Kennedy, with the approval of her then tutor and later husband, William Carr Withers, gave the lot of ground and buildings to Margaret Clark Chabot in exchange for a portion of Mrs. Chabot's estate to be collected after the settlement of her succession. Margaret Chabot had had only one child, Marie Marguerite Céleste Chabot, then the widow of Pierre Le Barbier Duplessis. Her daughter was the mother of seven children with whom Margaret Kennedy was to receive, in parity with the seven Duplessis grandchildren, one-eighth of four-fifths of Margaret Clark Chabot's estate. Margaret Chabot had formalized this agreement in her last will and testament, written on 9 September 1818.[564] According to her wishes, the house to be built would be 37 French feet[565] wide by 59 feet in depth, with a raised foundation. The exterior would be brick with stucco and all wood used would be cypress except for pine flooring on the second level. The whole of the interior of the house was to be plastered with "a handsome cornice in the dining room and parlour." The terrace was to be tiled or bricked, the roof guaranteed to be leak free for two years, the doors and window frames of solid cypress at least four inches thick. Mrs. Chabot sought to cover every detail of the house, often using examples of things she liked from other homes in the neighborhood: chimneys similar to the ones found at Mr. Kennedy's house in Bourbon Street, interior doors and shutters like Mr. Carraby's at the corner of St. Louis and Bourbon, the sash doors in front of the house like Mr. Nicholson's, etc. The kitchen was in a separate "outhouse" which included two servants' rooms, each 14x15 feet with the kitchen the same size. The oven would be "exactly similar to those in the kitchen of the Louisiana Hotel." An open-worked fence atop a brick wall about a foot and a half high would extend from the kitchen out to the "privies," with a wooden fence extending from the street to the adjoining lot (about 63 feet in length). Latrobe agreed to provide all the bricks, glass, tin, paint, plaster, lime and timber and any other items necessary to complete the house, in consideration for which she would pay $6,000 with $2,000 given over at the time of contract. The house was to be completed in eight months, with the following provision. For every month's delay to the project, Latrobe agreed to deduct $80.from the price of the house. If he should finish the house before the end of the contract, he would receive a bonus of $80 per month.[566]

The only hint that Benjamin Latrobe knew of Henry's children with Mercelite, at least in letters which have come down through the family, was written to his son on 4 June 1817:

---

[560] Benjamin Henry Boneval Latrobe, *Impressions Respecting New Orleans*, edited by Samuel Wilson, Jr., 124, Note 8. See also Appendix A, 170-175.

[561] Ibid., 41, Note 2.

[562] Access the Flannery census here: http://louisianadigitallibrary.org/islandora/ object/fpoc-p16313coll51%3A35436 . Image #9 of 46.

[563] 1810 United States Federal Census, New Orleans, Orleans Parish, Louisiana, Bourbon Street, Line 11 (left column), Vve. (Widow) Chabot household, digital image, *Ancestry.com* (https://www.ancestry.com accessed 1/2/2020), citing NARA microfilm publication M252, Roll 10. Date of enumeration: None given. Image 29/65.

[564] "Orleans Parish Will Books, Vol. 3, 1817-1824," digital image, *Ancestry.com* (https://www.ancestry.com: accessed 2/2/2020) Images 144,145/475. Margaret Clark, widow Chabot (Probate date; 16 November 1819).

[565] One French foot = 12.79 inches.

[566] NARC, "Chabot to Latrobe, agreement to build," dated 24 April 1817, passed by Notary Michel de Armas, Vol. 12A. Act #212. Courtesy Hon. Chelsey Richard Napoleon, Clerk of Civil District Court, Parish of Orleans.

You[r] character, I can tell You, stands as high as you could wish it. I am gratified by every word that is said of You. Coll. Kemper, the Floridian, has been often at my house; he sincerely esteems You, and does everybody else, I believe, but Benj. Morgan. This is some comfort amidst your vexations; to us it is and certainly must be so to you. [Virtue dep]ends, like all we do, very much upon habit. You are now 23, and will not easily change, But beware of *liaisons dangereux* [Latrobe's emphasis]. I still hope you will visit Europe, better guarded against its elegant temptations, and of course, not less susceptible of enjoyment but better qualified to "*try all things and hold fast that which is best.*" Nor do I look forward to you constantly and for life, residing at N. Orleans. Your profession is daily rising in public estimation, and I hope to see you yet the Phidias of a healthier climate.[567]

Unfortunately, Henry S.B. Latrobe was a victim of that year's yellow fever epidemic. He died on 3 September 1817. He had not finished Marguerite Clark Chabot's house, and he left the partially-finished waterworks project in a state of financial ruin, which his father would later try to rectify. He also left Mercelite with two children to raise: three-year-old Henry Belmont, and one-and-a-half-year-old Ann Julia. It is said that he was interred in the Protestant section of St. Louis Cemetery #1, although there is no burial record for him. A bronze plaque was dedicated to Henry S.B. Latrobe and his father Benjamin Henry Latrobe in 1904, by descendants of the Latrobe family, indicating that the two men had been buried in the Protestant section of the cemetery.

On the day he died, the Justice of the Peace, Mathias Peychaud accompanied by two witnesses went to the pump house by the river to place a seal on the belongings of Henry Latrobe. The rooms were filled with parts for the steam pumps, tools, a small library of books, and an area used as a laboratory. Marcellin Aubry, the building's watchman, greeted the men and indicated that he would continue to stay there to keep the contents of the building safe. Could this man have been Martin Aubry, Mercelite's brother? Although he ordinarily lived in St. Martinville, Attakapas Territory, he frequently travelled to New Orleans because his mother, Marguerite Cécile, and sisters still lived there. We searched records to see if another "Marcellin Aubry" could be found in census, birth or other miscellaneous records between 1805 and 1845, but could find no other person using that name. Why "Marcellin" and not "Martin." We had seen Martin's signature, and had never found him to use the name Marcellin, although many in his family used different names at different times. A comparison of the two signatures of Martin and of Marcellin Aubry showed that they bore a striking resemblance to one another. Martin's signature was taken from his 19 November 1811 marriage record to Lucille Ozenne. Marcellin Aubry's signature was taken from the Orleans Parish Estate File of Henry Sellon Boneval Latrobe, dated in late 1817. One is struck by the similarities of the two letters "M," the hook on the left side of the letter, the formation of the "a" in Martin and Marcellin. The capital letter "A" for Aubry with its characteristic hook, and the "y" written with a similar flourish at the bottom, as well as a similar slant of the signature on the paper, while not conclusive, give one pause to wonder if Martin, who had fought at the Battle of New Orleans in Captain Alexandre Lemelle's Company of Free Men of Color as a First Lieutenant on the same field as Latrobe and who was Latrobe's children's uncle, might have been an occasional employee during the construction of the New Orleans waterworks:

---

[567] John C. Van Horne, ed. *The Correspondence of Benjamin Henry Latrobe, Volume 3*, 890,891.

Signature on previous page taken from marriage record of Martin Aubry and Lucille Ozenne 19 November 1811 (Original record courtesy of Candy Brunet, Associate Archivist, Diocese of Lafayette, Lafayette, LA.) Signature of Marcellin Aubry on this page taken from "Louisiana, Orleans Parish Estate Files, 1804-1846," database with images, *FamilySearch.org* (https://familysearch.org/ark:/61903/3:1:S3HY-DYC8-JT?cc=1388197&wc=MG4Y-K6D%3A13750001%2C15665701 : accessed 1/4/ 2020), Estate of Latrobe, Henry Bonneval (1817), Image 3 of 45; New Orleans City Archives.

While it is tempting to draw this conclusion, we could find no other information on Marcellin Aubry in the estate files other than that he had been paid $165 for his guardianship of the premises until the estate, such as it was, could be liquidated. Overwhelmed with debt, the estate's assets, after an auction to dispose of Latrobe's personal property, tools, and some building materials, amounted to $969.82, while his outstanding debts reached $23,934.01. Listed as unfinished were private contracts that Latrobe had made for the design and construction of buildings for William Kenner & Co., Honoré Landreaux, Toussaint Mossy, Marguerite Clark Chabot, and the Administration of the Charity Hospital.

Henry's father, Benjamin Henry Latrobe, wrote to the Mayor and City Council of New Orleans a letter dated 13 October 1817, indicating that he had only heard of Henry's death ten days previously, and being stricken with grief, could only hope that he be allowed to complete the project that his son had started.[568] We have only found a few newspaper articles concerning his son's death. The Providence *Rhode Island American,* dated 10 October 1817, reported deaths in the United States and elsewhere: "DIED, In New Orleans [...] Mr. Henry S. B. Latrobe, son of B. Henry Latrobe, Esq. of Washington city, aged 24 years. He was a young gentleman of distinguished talents and science."[569] *The Correspondence and Miscellaneous Papers of Benjamin Henry Latrobe, Volume 3, 1811-1820*, edited by John C. Van Horne, included an article published in the *National Intelligencer* (Washington D.C.) dated 1 October 1817, unsigned, but attributed to Benjamin Henry Latrobe, where several columns were devoted to the life story of Henry S.B. Latrobe and started with this obituary "DIED, At New Orleans, of the prevailing fever, after an illness of only five days, Mr. HENRY SELLON BONEVAL LATROBE, eldest son of B. Henry Latrobe, Esq. of this city." [570]

While he poured out his grief in several heart-felt letters in early October 1817, less than two years later, in March of 1819, when Benjamin Latrobe wrote five pages of notes on New Orleans cemeteries, he did not mention his son. When he came to the Protestant section where his son had been interred, he only gave a cursory description of the tombs which he stated were located parallel to the sides of the enclosure. He never mentioned Henry's resting place, although he had written to an acquaintance on October 7, 1817 that his son had been befriended by Norbert Soulié who had told him that his "Sons Workmen united and in an hour erected a tomb over

---

[568] Latrobe, *Impressions Respecting New Orleans*, xviii-x-xix.

[569] "DIED," *The* (Providence) *Rhode-Island American*, 10 October 1817, digital image, *Genealogybank.com* (https://www.genealogybank.com: accessed 13 February 2020), p.3, col. 2.

[570] John C. Van Horne, ed., *The Correspondence and Miscellaneous Papers of Benjamin Henry Latrobe, Volume 3, 1811-1820*, 945-948. Note: According to a 30 September 1817 memorandum in his letter book the elder Latrobe wrote: "heard the afflicting news of the death of my son Henry at New Orleans." (p. 948)

his grave, which he (Soulié) directed."[571] Latrobe described in detail only the monument to the wife, child and brother-in-law of William C.C. Claiborne, which had been sculpted by Giuseppe Franzioni, under the elder Latrobe's own direction in Washington D.C. in 1811. Continuing his impressions of the city, Latrobe then launched into observations of the high water table in New Orleans, the number of crawfish in the streets, and the wisdom of cremation as opposed to burial in order to maintain the health of overcrowded cities.[572] Latrobe's seven journals, each a copybook with from 40 to 65 pages remained in the hands of his great-grandson, Ferdinand Claiborne Latrobe's family for many years. An eighth copybook is missing. Latrobe wrote of his son, for the most part, in conjunction with the young man's work for him in New Orleans. There was nothing, unless it might be in the "lost" journal, that was of a distinctly personal nature. Whether Latrobe, his wife, or other family members, ever met his son's children by Mercelite Aubry during their sojourn in New Orleans is a question we cannot answer. We may be, however, fairly sure that Norbert Soulié, whom the elder Latrobe met in New Orleans after his son's death, had filled him in on Henry's children, because Soulié was the godfather of Julia Anne Latrobe. We do know however, that someone made arrangements for a modicum of security for Mercelite, Henry Belmont and Anne Julia, by documents which still exist in the New Orleans Notarial Archives Research Center. We have found a few. More still may be out there.

Of particular note to us, also, are two friends of both Benjamin and Henry Latrobe: Vincent Nolte and Edward Hollander. It may only be coincidental but was certainly fortuitous that after Benjamin Latrobe sent his nineteen-year-old son down to New Orleans to secure financing and to oversee his waterworks project in the last months of 1810, that Nolte, born in Livorno, Tuscany on 21 November 1779, and Hollander born at Riga, Empire of Russia (now Latvia) on 2 December 1786 would soon follow. Both men applied to be naturalized in the District Court of Philadelphia, PA, on 14 November 1811.[573] Nolte had met Hollander in London, where they agreed to become partners in a venture in New Orleans. He and Hollander arrived in New York on 7 October 1811 after an arduous forty-eight-day voyage.[574] Had they met either Benjamin or Henry Latrobe in the northeast or only later in New Orleans? We know that Nolte had been back and forth to New Orleans, arriving there for the first time in 1806. In his *Impressions*, the elder Latrobe had called Nolte his friend. He roomed in a house Nolte had rented for his "foreign friends" in New Orleans and took breakfast with him every morning.[575] It was Nolte who took him out to the battlefield at Chalmette, and had shown Latrobe the remnants of Line Dupré that his son had built. Both Nolte and Hollander had been comrades-in-arms with the younger Latrobe.[576] The two naturalized immigrants had been members of the Uniformed Battalion of Orleans Volunteers under the leadership of Major Jean Baptiste Plauché, and were listed as soldiers in Captain Pierre Roche's Company of Carabiniers seeing action between 16 December 1814 and 15 March 1815.[577] Moreover Nolte, who was a local merchant and cotton factor in New Orleans, had given over 250 bales of cotton to shore up the defenses of Line Dupré constructed by Lieutenant Henry Latrobe as well as other nearby defensive barricades. His cotton, badly waterlogged and torn up by shells during the Battle of New Orleans, Nolte was offered a pittance for compensation for its loss and blamed General Jackson for his financial woes.

We can surmise that Benjamin Latrobe was informed, not only by Soulié, but also, no doubt, by Hollander and also probably by Nolte, if not by Mercelite herself, that his son had left two racially-mixed children behind when he reached New Orleans in February 1819. However, there is no mention of the children in Latrobe's collected writings, although he made numerous observations about slaves and slavery, about which he seemed both

---

[571] Ibid, 948, Note 1. Norbert Soulié, was an architect, real estate developer and free man of color, son of Jean Soulié, a white French immigrant to New Orleans, and Eulalie Mazange, born into slavery but freed in 1784.

[572] Latrobe, *Impressions Respecting New Orleans*, 83-86.

[573] "Pennsylvania Federal Naturalization Records, 1795-1931," digital images, *Ancestry.com* (https://www.ancestry.com: accessed 2/4/2020), citing NARA Record Group Title: M1522. Edward Hollander, Image 164/516 and Vincent Nolte, Image 165/516.

[574] Vincent Nolte, *The Memoirs of Vincent Nolte: Reminiscences in the Period of Anthony Adverse or Fifty Years in Both Hemispheres* (New York: G. Howard Watt, Publisher, 1934), 174-176.

[575] Wilson, ed., *Impressions*, 106.

[576] Wilson, ed., *Impressions*, 42-46.

[577] Thomas Harrison, compiler, National Park Service, *Troop Roster, Tennessee Volunteers & Militia, Kentucky Volunteers & Militia, Battalion of Free Men of Color, Louisiana Volunteers & Militia,* 190.

ambivalent and curious. He rarely wrote about free people of color in New Orleans, whom he termed as "yellow" unlike the slaves who were "black."

Upon arriving from the Balize at the mouth of the Mississippi to the levee protecting New Orleans he described the crowd of people he saw: "White men and women, & of all hues of brown, & of all classes of faces, from round Yankees, to grisly & lean Spaniards, black negroes & negresses, filthy Indians half-naked, mulattoes, curly & straight-haired, quarteroons of all shades, long-haired and frizzled, the women dressed in the most flaring yellow & scarlet gowns, the men capped & hatted."[578] Further along, Latrobe remarked that free colored persons were required to carry a certificate with them at all times to prove that they were free, but made no judgement about that law which affected his own grandchildren. He did point out that he found Section 40 so curious that he had to transcribe it because it was enacted "to regulate moral feeling!!" [Emphasis his]: "Free people of color ought never to insult or strike white people nor presume to think themselves equal to the white, but on the contrary they ought to yield to them on every occasion, & never speak to, or answer them but with respect, under penalty of imprisonment according to the nature of the offense." He ended his musings by finding that the criminal part of the code was much more just and humane than he had imagined.[579]

In late 1819 Latrobe returned to Philadelphia by sea to close out his business and bring his family and furnishings by wagon and then steamboat down the Ohio and Mississippi Rivers to New Orleans where he hoped to settle down permanently. Benjamin Henry Latrobe, his second wife, Mary Elizabeth Hazelhurst, his daughter Juliana Elizabeth, and son Benjamin, Henry, Jr., arrived in New Orleans on 4 April 1820. Five months later, Benjamin Henry Latrobe succumbed to yellow fever on 3 September 1820, on the third anniversary of his son's death. The *Louisiana Courier* dated 4 September 1820 reported that "Mr. H.B.H. Latrobe died yesterday at 4:00 o'clock P.M., leaving a numerous family to deplore the irreparable loss they have sustained."[580]

Any aid that Mercelite Aubry had perhaps hoped from her children's grandfather was not immediately forthcoming. Both the son's as well as the father's estates were burdened by debt. Any money that either of them had earned from outside construction projects had been reinvested in the New Orleans waterworks. It was only through the charity of friends, including $100 given to her by Vincent Nolte, that Latrobe's widow Elizabeth was able to depart New Orleans for Philadelphia, where she hoped to settle.[581] Leaving her husband's debts behind, she had her furniture shipped out as soon as possible so it could not be seized and sold. She informed the court that she would make no claims on the estate, and headed north.

Twelve years after the death of Henry Latrobe, Mercelite had a child with Louis Paul (Don Louis) Bringier on 16 August 1829, who was named John Gustave McDonogh Bringier. His baptismal record reads as follows: "Bringier, John Gustave McDonogh (Louis and Marcelite Oubry, [both] residents of this parish), b. Dec 12, 1829, bn. Aug. 16, 1829 in New Orleans s. John McDonogh[582] and Marie [*] CO[R/U]R[E/C]A (SLC, B41, 83)." It is understandable that John McDonogh, who was one of the largest land owners in the New Orleans area, would agree to be the godfather to the racially-mixed child of his longtime friend and colleague, Louis Bringier, the Surveyor General of Louisiana. McDonogh supported the American Colonization Society which organized transportation for freed blacks to Liberia, and arranged the self-purchase of many of his own slaves. Shortly before the birth of his son, Louis Paul Bringier had accepted the position of curator ad litem to Elina Marguerite Félicité Foy, Prosper and Zélie Aubry's daughter, in order to further a court petition by her mother to be able to sell the child's slave.[583]

Louis Paul Bringier, born on 22 October 1784 to Emmanuel Pons Marius Bringier owner of Whitehall Plantation in St. James Parish, LA, and his wife Marie Françoise Durand, had become the Surveyor General of the State of Louisiana, after having spent the best part of his life as the irresponsible son in the family, who charged with at least two important financial missions in New Orleans on behalf of his father, had failed in his duties. A boy raised in St. James Parish, away from the noise and excitement of the city, he had been seduced by the glitz and

---

[578] Wilson, ed., *Impressions*, 22.

[579] Wilson, ed., *Impressions*, 56.

[580] Wilson, ed., *Impressions*, 166, Note 16.

[581] Wilson, ed., *Impressions*, Appendix D, 184.

[582] John McDonogh (1779-1850) was a merchant, plantation owner, and real estate speculator, who never married. He left his immense fortune to the cities of Baltimore and New Orleans to further the education of poor whites and free blacks.

[583] See p. 300.

glamour of New Orleans and frequented the gambling houses and other "dens of iniquity." After his 1807 visit to New Orleans at which time he lost all the proceeds of the cotton and indigo from the family plantation that he had brought to market, he disappeared from Louisiana, only to reappear just before the Battle of New Orleans in late 1814. Don Louis and his brother Michel Doradou Bringier served in Captain Jean Chauveau's Company of Cavalry from 18 December 1814 until 14 March 1815.[584] This may be when Bringier became acquainted with Henry Sellon Boneval Latrobe and René Prosper Foy, who both served in New Orleans regiments, and, by extension, may have become acquainted with Mercelite and Zélie Aubry. After the war, Bringier had one more adventure. He had long sought to enrich the family by discovering a cache of precious metals. Rumors of gold and silver deposits had fueled the thoughts of many early nineteenth century Americans. Off to Mexico and lucky at first, he came back to Louisiana with a large amount of silver, but upon his return to Mexico, he incurred the enmity of the Mexican government, was arrested, and nearly executed. Only the intervention of New Orleans Bishop Louis William Valentine Dubourg and the promise that the family would pay a handsome ransom allowed him to escape back to New Orleans. Two years after the birth of his son, John Gustave with Mercelite, forty-seven-year-old Louis Paul Bringier, married Marie Josephine Hermione Guignaud on 22 October 1831 in New Orleans (SLC, M8, 63) and had three legitimate children: Letitia, Louise, and Charles Pendleton Bringier.[585]

Before the birth of Gustave Bringier, the Latrobe family had apparently sought to give some security to Mercelite's children with Henry Latrobe with the cooperation of their late son's friend Edward Hollander. This arrangement only came to light in a legal document formalized ten years later in 1836. Central to this project was the lot of ground on St. Ann and Burgundy Streets that Latrobe had sold to Hollander for 3,300 piastres in 1816 after fire had devastated the block. (See p. 268). On 30 December 1836 Mercelite Aubry and Edward Hollander appeared before the notary Carlile Pollock and his assistant Achille Chiapella to draw up a contract. It is no coincidence that Pollock was chosen for this task. Achille Chiapella was in a relationship with Mercelite's sister, Eglée Aubry, who four months later would bear his son René Achille Chiapella. The contract was for the transfer of a portion of the property on St. Ann and Bourbon Street from Edward Hollander to Mercelite Aubry, upon his declaration that the said property "has been in the possession of the said Mercelite Aubry for upwards of twenty years past." After this sentence the word "Null" was written, although what came before it was not crossed out. Pollock started over, giving a description of the property once more: "a lot of ground situated in this city on the islet comprised between Royal, Orleans, St. Ann and Bourbon streets, forming the corner of the two latter streets, and having French measure more or less, thirty-one feet eight inches in front on St. Ann Street , by fifty-four feet in front on Bourbon Street, and thirty-one feet eight inches width in the rear together with the buildings and improvements." It was also indicated that this was only part of the property that Latrobe had sold to Hollander in 1816. This transfer was, according to Hollander, made in consideration of a payment of $3,000 that Hollander had received from Mercelite Aubry "sometime in the year 1825." Since that time, Aubry, according to Hollander "had been in full possession of said premises and had exercised all rights of ownership therein, by paying taxes and receiving rents and paving the streets, and keeping the buildings in repair." Had $3,000 really changed hands ten years before? We do know that Lydia Latrobe, Henry Sellon Boneval Latrobe's sister and the wife of Nicholas Roosevelt,[586] was in New Orleans on 25 December 1826 when she stood as godmother to Hilaire Julien Domingon and Félicité Aubry's racially-mixed son Auguste Julien Domingon (See p. 235). How long had Lydia been in New Orleans? Had she brought the funds to secure the purchase of this lot on behalf of Mercelite and her brother's children?

A diagram of the original lot may be seen on the next page, with the two portions sold off by Hollander: the first on 19 May 1817 to Honoré Landreaux 25 feet on Bourbon by 60 feet and the use of the partition wall belonging to the kitchen next to the theater; the second on 23 June 1826 sold to Alex Barron with 28 ft. 4. Inches fronting on St. Ann by 56 ft. 6 inches behind the Orleans theater. The map is significant because the remaining portion of the

---

[584] The roster of members of Chauveau's Cavalry company shows their names as "Donradon Brangier" and "Louis Brangier." (See National Park Service Troop Rosters, p. 123/198).

[585] For an in-depth study of the Bringier family please see Craig A. Bauer, *Creole Genesis: The Bringier Family and Antebellum Plantation Life in Louisiana* (Lafayette, LA: University of Louisiana at Lafayette Press, 2011).

[586] The unconventional Lydia Latrobe married Roosevelt, an inventor and partner of Robert Fulton, when she was 17 and he was 41 years old in 1808. She made two trips down the Ohio and Mississippi Rivers to New Orleans, one in 1809 by flatboat, and one in 1811-1812 on her husband's steamboat, the *New Orleans*. She was pregnant both times and delivered while travelling. For further details see the website of Kathy Warnes, *History Because It's Here*: https://historybecauseitshere.weebly.com/lydia-latrobe-roosevelt-and-the-first-mississippi-river-steamboat.html.

original lot belonging to Hollander since 1816 was not labeled as the lot belonging to Hollander but "the lot and dwelling belonging to the heirs of Latrobe."

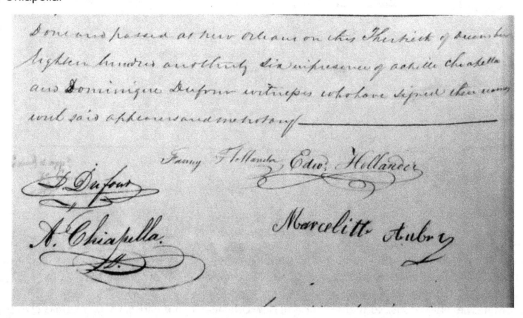

NARC, "Edward Hollander to Mercelite Aubry Sale of property," dated 30 December 1836, passed by Notary Carlile Pollock, Volume 55, p. 396. Courtesy Hon. Chelsey Richard Napoleon, Clerk of Civil District Court, Parish of Orleans.

Below is a copy of a portion of the signature page showing the vendor Edward Hollander, with the acquiescence of his wife, Fanny (Sauvé) Hollander, the purchaser, "Marcelitte" Aubry, and the two witnesses, Dominique Dufour and Achille Chiapella:

NARC, "Edward Hollander to Marcelite Aubry Sale of property," dated 30 December 1836, passed by Notary Carlile Pollock, Volume 55, p. 399. Courtesy Hon. Chelsey Richard Napoleon, Clerk of Civil District Court, Parish of Orleans.

It is clear from this that Mercelite Aubry had been the de facto owner of this piece of property between 1816 and 1836. While she may not have always lived there with her children, she collected the rents, which she used as income for herself and for her children.

While early census records are bereft of most helpful information, the 1820 Federal Census for the City of New Orleans was divided by streets. In looking for Mercelite Aubry we found one strong possibility for her inclusion in that record. Enumerated as a free woman of color, the household for "Marceline" living on Bourbon Street included one free colored boy under 14, two male free colored men between 14 and 26, two female colored girls under 14, and one fee colored woman between 14 and 26. This is most likely Mercelite (between 14 and 26), her son Henry Belmont and daughter Anne Julia, both under 14 years of age living at the Bourbon Street property sold to Hollander by Henry Latrobe in 1816. The two men between 14 and 26 cannot be identified, nor can one of the females under 14 years of age.[587] They could be relatives or even boarders. Much more clear cut is her enumeration ten years later as "Marcilitte Aubry" living between Bayou Road and L'Amour (Love) Streets in Faubourg Marigny with one free colored male under 10 years (Gustave Bringier), one free colored male between 10-23 (Henry Belmont), one free colored female between 10-23 (Anne Julia), and one free colored female between 36-54 (Mercelite)[588] At this point she was clearly renting out the entire Bourbon Street property for income to support her family.

Mercelite Aubry's eldest son Henry Belmont Latrobe forged a relationship with Marie Casimir. Two sons were born to them, Jean-Baptiste Belmont Latrobe, born, according to his mother on 24 June 1834 and Henry Latrobe, born on 19 August 1836. His original record, in French reads: "In the year of Our Lord 10 June 1839, I the undersigned, Paul Armand, priest and vicar of the Cathedral of St. Louis of this city and parish in New Orleans, in the state of Louisiana, United States of America: baptized solemnly, Henry Latrobe, born in this same parish on 19 August 1836; illegitimate child of Henry Latrobe and of Marie Casimir. Godfather and Godmother: Edward Lavigne and Louise Biera. In faith of which I signed with the father of the child:"

[...]

[587] 1820 United States Federal Census, New Orleans, New Orleans City, LA, Marceline f.w.c household, digital image, *Ancestry.com* (https://www.ancestry.com accessed 2/2/2020), citing NARA microfilm publication M33_32, Date of Enumeration: 7 August 1820, Image 10/82.

[588] 1830 United States Federal Census, Northern Suburbs of New Orleans, Orleans Parish, LA, Maralitte (*sic*) Aubry household, digital image, *Ancestry.com* (https://www.ancestry.com accessed 2/2/2020), citing NARA microfilm publication M19, Roll 45, Date of Enumeration: Not given, Image 33/42.

Courtesy of the Archives of the Archdiocese of New Orleans, Saint Louis Cathedral Records, Sacramental Register of St. Louis Cathedral Baptisms – Vol. 1839-1840, p. 71, #183. Baptism of Henry Latrobe et Casimir (Courtesy of Emilie Leumas, Archivist – Kimberly Johnson and Katie Vest – Researching Archivists.)

The identity of Marie Casimir Is problematic. It is possible that she may have been a descendant of Modeste Rasteau, whose daughter Luce Henriette Grandmaison, born in Port-au-Prince, Saint-Domingue, had a half-brother, Jean-Baptiste Casimir Menial born about 1800 in the same place. (See p 111, note 196). He followed Luce Henriette and her French husband, Jean-Baptiste Pinta to America and settled in St. Martinville, Attakapas Territory, LA, where he raised a large family with Marie Pomelar Olivier. Jean-Baptiste Casimir, used both Casimir and Pinta as surnames in Louisiana records. After the death of Martin Aubry in 1844, Casimir Pinta was appointed tutor to three of the decedent's children who had not yet reached their majority: Marguerite, Émile, and Tréville Aubry, but he refused to serve.[589] So the Aubry and Casimir (Pinta) families were certainly close. Moreover, the Grandmaison, Pinta and Chiapella families were all related by marriage. Given a diminishing population of free people of color in the 1830s, the chance that Marie Casimir was part of that larger family circle while possible, is as yet, impossible now to prove conclusively.

Henry Belmont Latrobe's son Henry Latrobe died as a child of about three years old, at half past four o'clock in the morning, on 13 June 1839, just three days after his belated baptism. His death was reported by Rufino Thomas Fernandez, then the "Keeper of the Records of the Catholic and Cathedral Church of St. Louis," who wrote in part that " Henry Latrobe, a child born in this parish of New Orleans, aged about three years, departed this life yesterday, the thirteenth instant at half past four o'clock A.M. at the domicile of his mother situated at the corner of Ursulines and Marais streets Suburb Tremé in this first municipality. He was the natural son of Belmon (*sic*) Latrobe and of Marie Casimire (*sic*)" A copy of the original record filed on the following day may be seen on the next page:

[589] Louisiana, Wills and Probate Records, 1756-1984," digital images, Ancestry.com (https://www. ancestry.com: accessed 3/20/2019), citing "Estate Files From Attakapas County and Parish, LA and St. Martin Parish, LA," Louisiana. Parish Court (St. Martin Parish); Probate Place: St. Martin, Louisiana," Case #1020, Succession of Martin Aubry, Image 241 & 243/627.

Latrobe Henry

BE it remembered that on this day to wit: the *fourteenth of June* the year of our Lord thousand eight hundred and thirty- *nine* and the *Sixty third* of the Independence of the United States of America, before me *Vincent Ramos* duly commissioned and sworn RECORDER OF BIRTHS AND DEATHS in and for the Parish and City of Orleans, personally appeared *Mr Rufino Thomas Fernandez born at Galveston in this State of Louisiana on the Sixteenth day of November in the year Seventeen hundred and Ninety nine, keeper of the Records of the Catholic and Cathedral Church of St Louis of this Parish of New Orleans, residing on St Ann Street between Conde and Royal Streets, Who by these presents Doth Declare that Henry Latrobe, a child born in this Parish of New Orleans, aged about three years, Departed this life yesterday the thirteenth instant at half past four o'clock A. M. at the domicil of his mother Situated at the corner of Ursulines and Marais Streets Suburb Treme in this first Municipality. He was the natural Son of Belmon Latrobe and of Marie Casimire* THUS done at New-Orleans in the presence of the aforesaid *Mr Rufino Thomas Fernandez* as also in that of Messrs. *Amadeo Morel and Andre D. Doricourt* both of this city witnesses by me requested so to be, who have hereunto set their hands together with me after due reading hereof, the day month and year first above written.

Vincent Ramos
Recorder

Courtesy of State of Louisiana, Secretary of State, Division of Archives, Records Management, and History. *Vital Records Indices*. Baton Rouge, LA, USA citing *Orleans Death Indices 1804-1876*; Vol. 6, p. 289.

Anne Julia Latrobe, Henry Sellon Boneval Latrobe's only daughter, married Joseph St. Hubert, a free man of color said to be born about 1811 in New Orleans,[590] who was employed as a carpenter, at St. Louis Cathedral on 8 July 1833 in New Orleans. Written in French, it reads in part: (Our translation):

> On July 8, 1833, I the undersigned vicar (De L'hoste) of the Cathedral and parish of St. Louis, in New Orleans, after three publications of banns, and no impediment found, and a license being issued by the parish judge, have united in marriage Joseph St. Hubert, son of Joseph St. Hubert and Marie Victoire Leboull, and Julia Latrobe, daughter of Henry Bonneval Latrobe and Marcelite Aubry, and blessed their

[590] It was only when we read Joseph and Julia's daughter Lise St. Hubert's succession record that we discovered that Joseph St. Hubert's mother, Marie Victoire Leboull was married a second time to Simon M. Cohen. They had a daughter, Augustine Lise Cohen, Joseph St. Hubert's half-sister, who was born ca. 1819 in Santiago de Cuba. Augustine Lise married Charles Bacarisse on 19 October 1840 in Mobile, Mobile Co., AL. Charles and Augustine had two children, Victorine, who never wed, and Charles Jr. who had seven children with Antoinette Berallier. Victorine and Charles Bacarisse's children became Lise St. Hubert's heirs. (Source: "Louisiana, Wills and Probate Records, 1756-1984,"digital images, *Ancestry.com* (https://www.ancestry.com: accessed 7/22/2020), citing *Case Papers, 1880-1929*; Louisiana Civil District Court (Orleans Parish). Succession of Elise St. Hubert dated 6 May 1924, Case #152099, Images 1137-1167/1723); Note: Members of the Bacarisse family including Simon M. Cohen, Marie Victoire Leboull, Lise Cohen Bacarisse, Charles and Victorine Bacarisse are all interred in the Bacarisse mausoleum in St. Louis Cemetery #3.

marriage in the presence of the following undersigned witnesses: Armand Lanusse, Chrétien Mongruin, Villarson Montcartier (*sic*, Macarty), Manuel Silva, L. Boisdoré, who signed with me in faith of which......

Below is a copy of their original marriage record.

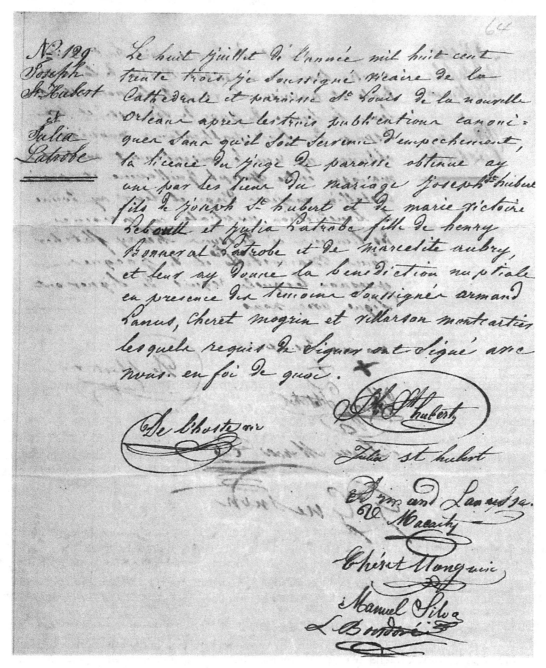

Marriage record of Joseph St. Hubert and Julia Latrobe, Archdiocese of New Orleans (Orleans Parish, LA), Vol. #2, p. 64, Act #129. (Courtesy of Emilie Leumas, Archivist – Kimberly Johnson and Katie Vest – Researching Archivists.)

Their first child, Lydia St. Hubert, obviously named after Lydia Latrobe Roosevelt, Julia Latrobe St. Hubert's aunt. was born ca. 1835, followed by Ernest in 1837. Léda St. Hubert was born, according to her death record, on 10 December 1838. Laure Marie was born in 1840, Lise in 1843 and Victoire Léda on 5 November 1848. A son, Louis Belmont St. Hubert, was born on 20 August 1845. A copy of his birth record below which reads in part that Belmont St. Hubert was the legitimate issue of Joseph St. Hubert, aged 35, living at the corner of Main (Dumaine) and Robertson Streets in the First Municipality, and his wife Julia Latrobe, a native of the city, age 28 years:

St. Hubert, Belmont

BE it remembered that on this day to wit, the *Seventh of October* the year of our Lord one thousand eight hundred and ~~thirty~~ *forty seven*, and the ~~thirty~~ *seventieth* of the Independence of the United States of America, before me ~~VICTOR WILTZ~~ *me delegate*, duly commissioned and sworn **RECORDER OF BIRTHS AND DEATHS** in and for the Parish and City of Orleans, personally appeared, *Mr. Joseph St. Hubert, a free man of color, native of this city, aged thirty five years, y residing on the corner of Robertson y Dumaine Streets in the first Municipality who by these presents declare that on the twentieth day of August of this present year 1845 at four o'clock P.m. was born at his aforesaid residence a male child named Belmont St. Hubert, issue of the legitimate marriage of appearer and Julie Latrobe a native of this city, aged 23 years.*

THUS done at New-Orleans, in the presence of the aforesaid *Mr. Joseph St. Hubert* as also in that of Messrs. *Theodule Lucian au y Antoine Dubois* both of this city, witnesses by me requested so to be, who have hereunto set their hands together with me after due reading hereof, the day month and year first above written.

Courtesy of State of Louisiana, Secretary of State, Division of Archives, Records Management, and History. *Vital Records Indices*. Baton Rouge, LA, USA citing *Orleans Death Indices 1804-1876*; Vol. 6, p. 289.

Joseph St. Hubert reported that his legitimate son Belmont St. Hubert died on 1 June 1847.[591] The couple's daughter, Léda, aged 9 years, died the following year on 23 October 1848.[592] Joseph and Julia St. Hubert and their five surviving children, all identified as "mulatto," were enumerated together in the 1850 United States Federal Census living in the Fifth Ward, First Municipality, where St. Hubert worked with another carpenter, Louis Thomas. St. Hubert declared real estate holdings of $1500.[593] We know that Ernest St. Hubert died before 1860, but probably earlier than that.

Henry Sellon Boneval Latrobe's only son, Henry Belmont Latrobe died in New Orleans on 25 July 1845, leaving Marie Casimir to raise Jean-Baptiste Belmont on her own. Henry Belmont's death record which was filed on 7 August 1845 read in part: "Henry Belmont Latrobe, a free man of color, native of this city aged thirty-two years (32 years) departed this life on the 25th day of July last past 1845 at eleven o'clock P.M. in a house situated on the corner of Maine [Dumaine] and Robertson Streets in the First Municipality of the City of New Orleans."[594]

The late Henry Belmont Latrobe's partner Marie Casemille (*sic*), a forty-three-year-old female mulatto with $800 in real estate was enumerated with three young mulatto males in the 1850 United States Federal Census for Ward 1, Third Municipality, New Orleans: twenty-three-year-old Aristide Dorville, a mason, fourteen-year-old Numa

---

[591] Courtesy of State of Louisiana, Secretary of State, Division of Archives, Records Management, and History. *Vital Records Indices*. Baton Rouge, LA, USA, from New Orleans, Louisiana Death Records Index 1804-1939; Vol. 10, p. 473.

[592] Courtesy of State of Louisiana, Secretary of State, Division of Archives, Records Management, and History. *Vital Records Indices*. Baton Rouge, LA, USA, citing *Orleans Death Indices 1804-1876*; Vol. 10, p. 574.

[593] 1850 United States Federal Census, Orleans Parish, Louisiana, Municipality 1, Ward 5, Dwelling #1047, Family #1537, Louis Thomas household, digital image, *Ancestry.com* (https://www.ancestry.com accessed 1/15/2020), citing NARA microfilm publication M432_236, p. 200B. Date of enumeration:21 August 1850. Image 60/140.

[594] Courtesy of State of Louisiana, Secretary of State, Division of Archives, Records Management, and History. *Vital Records Indices*. Baton Rouge, LA, USA citing *Orleans Death Indices 1804-1876*; Vol. 10, p. 342. Note: The document in our possession was too faded to be able to be reproduced.

Dorville, and thirteen-year-old, M. (sic, Jean-Baptiste Belmont) Latrobe.[595] Also in 1850, the late Henry Belmont Latrobe's mother Mercelite was enumerated living in the Fifth Ward with her son, twenty-one-year-old Gustave Bringier, who worked as a clerk, and Philippe Fernand a fifty-five-year-old market worker from Spain.[596]

There is no baptismal record for Henry Belmont and Marie Casimir's only surviving son, Jean-Baptiste Belmont Latrobe, only his mother's word for his 1834 birth in a document which was filed to gain tutorship of the boy after his grandmother, Mercelite Aubry's death, on 28 October 1852. Joseph St. Hubert, Julia Latrobe's husband, reported Mercelite's passing on 8 November 1852. While the record is too faded to duplicate here it reads in part that: "Joseph St. Hubert residing on Maine (Dumaine) Street between Robertson and Claiborne [...] declares that Mercelite Aubry, a native of this city, aged fifty-five years died on the twenty-eighth day of October of this present year (28 October 1852) in Orleans Street between Robertson and Villeré Streets, Second District of this city."[597]

Anne Julia Latrobe's husband, Joseph St. Hubert was the administrator of Mercelite Aubry's estate, which consisted of the property that she had acquired from Edward Hollander on 30 December 1836 before the notary Carlile Pollock, the property on Dumaine Street which she had bought on 23 December 1836 from Joseph and Émile Laurant before the notary William Young Lewis, as well as Mercelite's household furniture and effects, and a negress slave for life named Sarah, aged about 27 years, a cook, washer and ironer. Her 23 December 1836 purchase of a lot of ground fronting 30 feet on Dumaine Street by 80 feet deep, French measure, with all the improvements for $1250, at which time she had given $150 down, had been financed by Joseph St. Hubert who accepted her three promissory notes for $366.66 2/3 at intervals of six twelve and eighteen months.[598] In order to settle all claims which St. Hubert stated had amounted to almost $1900 dollars, the property located in the square bounded by Royal, Orleans, Bourbon and St. Ann, forming the corner of Bourbon and St. Ann, measuring 31 feet 8 inches front on St. Ann by 54 feet in depth on Bourbon Street, with all the buildings and improvements, her household furniture and the slave Sarah were ordered to be sold on 30 December 1852. The auctioneer Joseph A. Bonneval (Félicité Aubry's daughter Virginie Domingon's children's father) was in charge of the sale, which resulted in the purchase of the real estate by Jean Crusius for $5150, and the purchase of the slave, Sarah, by Julia Latrobe St. Hubert for $910. The terms and conditions of the sale were as follows: Crusius was to pay off a mortgage that Mercelite had taken out for $1050 at 8% per annum dated 12 August 1852 payable at twelve months from that date. For the balance, Crusius gave ¼ in cash and the balance at six, twelve and eighteen months bearing a mortgage at 8% per annum on the property. It was also noted that the property had been rented for $600 per year to Francisco Roque, payable monthly on a lease of five years from 13 September 1852 by an act passed before the notary Achille Chiapella on 13 September 1852. Sarah was sold to Julia St. Hubert for one-third in cash, with the balance due the estate in six and 12 months from the date of sale with interest at 8% per annum. The sales of the property and slave belonging to the estate of Mercelite Aubry were formalized on 7 February 1853 before the notary, Achille Chiapella, father of Mercelite Aubry's sister Eglée's last three children.[599]

Julia Latrobe and her half-brother Gustave Bringier inherited the Dumaine Street property which was to be equally divided between the two of them. However, on 4 January 1853, Gustave Bringier and Julia went before the notary Achille Chiapella to transfer Gustave's share of the property back to Julia for $400 cash in hand. The property which was located in Faubourg Tremé had a 30-foot frontage on Dumaine by 80 feet in depth and was designated

[595] 1850 United States Federal Census, Orleans Parish, Louisiana, Municipality 3, Ward 1, Dwelling #1559, Family #1770, M. Casemille (sic) household, digital image, Ancestry.com (https://www.ancestry.com accessed 1/14/2020), citing NARA microfilm publication M432_236, p. 90A. Date of enumeration:6 August 1850. Image 178, 179/204.

[596] 1850 United States Federal Census, Orleans Parish, Louisiana, Municipality 1, Ward 5, Dwelling #716, Family #1346, Marcelite Aubry household, digital image, Ancestry.com (https://www.ancestry.com accessed 1/14/2020), citing NARA microfilm publication M432_236, p. 90A. Date of enumeration:10 August 1850. Image 41/140.

[597] Courtesy of State of Louisiana, Secretary of State, Division of Archives, Records Management, and History. Vital Records Indices. Baton Rouge, LA, USA citing Orleans Death Indices 1804-1876, Vol. 14, p. 117.

[598] NARC, "Sale of Property – J. & E. Laurant to Mte. Aubry," dated 1 February 1837, passed by Notary William Y. Lewis, Conveyance Office Book, Vol 22, fol. 298. Courtesy Hon. Chelsey Richard Napoleon, Clerk of Civil District Court, Parish of Orleans.

[599] NARC, "Sale of Property – Estate of Mercelite Aubry to J. Crusius," dated 7 February 1853, passed by Notary Achille Chiapella, Act #86 (20 pages), Vol. 30. Courtesy Hon. Chelsey Richard Napoleon, Clerk of Civil District Court, Parish of Orleans.

as part of Lots 11 and 12 in Square 71. In the act of sale Gustave indicated that he had inherited half of the property from his mother, Mercelite Aubry at her death and that Julia had inherited the other half. He also stated that the buildings on his part of the property had been paid for by Julia. Below is a portion of the signature page from that act of sale with the signatures of Gustave Bringier, Julia St. Hubert, her husband, Joseph St. Hubert, the notary Achille Chiapella, and two witnesses, Selim Magner, and Edward George Gottschalk:

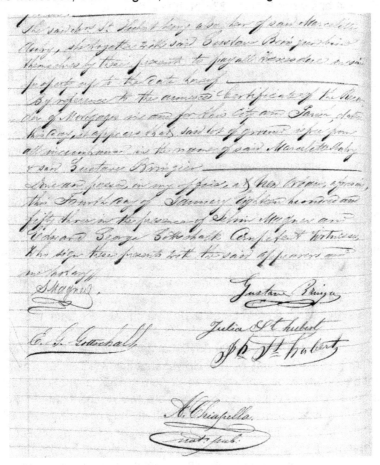

NARC, "Sale of Property, Bringier to Julia St. Hubert," dated 4 January 1853, passed by Notary Achille Chiapella, Volume 30, act 7. Courtesy Hon. Chelsey Richard Napoleon, Clerk of Civil District Court, Parish of Orleans.

Another of Mercelite's heirs, Jean-Baptiste Belmont Latrobe, her late son Henry Belmont Latrobe's only child, was still a minor at her passing. For this reason, Marie Casimir f.w.c. applied for the tutorship of her son, Jean-Baptiste Belmont, by opening a succession for his late father, Henry Belmont Latrobe, which was filed on 10 March 1853. In her petition, it was written in part that:

> She is the mother of Jean-Baptiste Latrobe, a minor, born on the 24th June 1834, of her co-habitation with Henry Belmont Latrobe f.m.c., that said Belmont Latrobe f.m.c. the natural father of said minor Jean-Baptiste Latrobe, departed this life on the 25th day of July 1845, as appears by the certificate hereto annexed. That said minor has an interest in the settlement of the Estate of Marcelite Aubry f.w.c., his grandmother, and that your petitioner is entitled to the natural tutorship of her said minor child, in order to represent him in said Estate.

The tutorship was granted to Marie Casimir with Armand François Duberalde appointed as under-tutor to Jean-Baptiste Belmont Latrobe.[600]

---

[600] "Louisiana, Wills and Probate Records, 1756-1984," digital images, *Ancestry.com* (https://www.ancestry.com: accessed 1/22/2020), citing *Succession Records 1846-1880*; *Louisiana Probate Court (Orleans Parish)*. Succession of Henry Belmont Latrobe dated 10 March 1853, Case #6140, Images 222-226/1333.

Although we were unable to find Marie Casimir, Numa Dorville, or J.B. Belmont Latrobe in the 1860 United States Federal Census for New Orleans, they reappeared in both the 1870 and 1880 federal census records for the city as a family unit. Numa Dorville worked as a carpenter, while Belmont Latrobe was a shoemaker. In the 1870 United States Federal Census for New Orleans, Marie Casimir was enumerated as the Widow Marie Boidoret (*sic*), aged 65, a female "mulatto" keeping house with $1000 in real estate and $100 in personal estate. Living with her was thirty-nine-year-old Numa Dorville and thirty-six-year-old Belmont Latraube (*sic*), both "mulatto" males. Belmont was the only one in the household who could read and write.[601] Belmont appeared regularly in New Orleans City Directories as a shoemaker living variously on Robertson, Kerlerec, and Villeré Streets. Ten years later, the family was still together. They were enumerated in the 1880 United States Federal Census for New Orleans living in the 7th Ward at #358 Derbigny Street. Seventy-six-year-old Marie Boisdoré, a white female, was keeping house for her two sons: Numa Boisdoré, a white, male, aged 50, working as a carpenter who suffered from gastritis, and Belmont Boisdoré, a white, male, aged 47, who was employed as a shoemaker. Both men were unmarried. Whether the surname "Boisdoré" used for Marie's sons was offered by her or assumed by the census taker is a question we cannot answer.[602]

Jean-Baptiste Belmont Latrobe died on 14 October 1884 at #285 Marais Street in New Orleans. The cause of his death was said to be "aneamia" (*sic*). Although his age was given as 55 years and 2 months, all other records including his mother's testimony point to his having been only fifty years of age.[603] He was unmarried at death, the only child of Henry Belmont Latrobe and Marie Casimir to have reached maturity.

Anne Julia Latrobe and her husband Joseph St. Hubert had one more child before her husband's death. Alcide Joseph St. Hubert was born on 6 April 1851 in New Orleans.[604] Joseph St. Hubert died in New Orleans on 2 February 1854.[605] Less than two months after her husband's death, Julia Latrobe St. Hubert appeared before the notary Achille Chiapella to buy a piece of property from Celestin Morel de Guiramond adjacent to hers on Dumaine Street. The parcel was located on the square bounded by Dumaine, Robertson, Claiborne and St. Philippe, forming the corner of Dumaine and Robertson with a 30-foot frontage on Dumaine and a 40-foot frontage on Robertson along with the buildings and improvements. She agreed to a price of $1800, giving $450 in cash and the rest in 3 promissory notes each for $450 with 8% interest, payable at six, twelve and eighteen months at the Louisiana State Bank.[606] Julia Latrobe St. Hubert was enumerated in the 1860 United States Federal Census as the "Widow St. Hubert" a forty-one-year-old "mulatto" living in the Fifth Ward with her five surviving children. She valued her real estate holdings at $3,000 and her personal estate at $100. Living with her daughters "Lidia," age 24, "Laure", age 18, "Lize," age 17, "Eleda," age 11, and her son, "Alcide," aged 9, was Gustave Bringier, a 29-year-old "mulatto" peddler, Julia Latrobe's half-brother.[607] Laure Marie St. Hubert died on 19 October 1876 without issue. Her death record indicates that she died from "Phthisis pulmonalis" (tuberculosis) at #196 Robertson Street and was the

[601] 1870 United States Federal Census, New Orleans, Orleans Parish, Ward 7, Dwelling #896, Family #1278, Widow Marie Boidoret household, digital image, *Ancestry.com* (https://www.ancestry.com: accessed 1/20/2020), citing NARA microfilm publication M593_522, p. 548B. Date of enumeration: 15 July 1870, Image 328/470.

[602] 1880 United States Federal Census, New Orleans, Orleans Parish, Ward 7, Dwelling #60, Family #63, Marie Boisdoré household, digital image, *Ancestry.com* (https://www.ancestry.com: accessed 1/20/2020), citing NARA microfilm publication T9 roll 462, p. 609D. Date of enumeration: 2 June 1880, Image 8/56.

[603] Courtesy of State of Louisiana, Secretary of State, Division of Archives, Records Management, and History. *Vital Records Indices.* Baton Rouge, LA, USA, citing *Orleans Death Indices 1877-1895*; Vol. 85, p. 1178.

[604] Courtesy of State of Louisiana, Secretary of State, Division of Archives, Records Management, and History. *Vital Records Indices.* Baton Rouge, LA, USA, citing *New Orleans, Louisiana Birth Records Index 1790-1899*, Birth of Joseph St. Hubert, Vol. 10, p. 367.

[605] "Orleans Death Indices,1804-1876" [database on-line], *Ancestry.com* (https://www.ancestry.com: accessed 3/20/ 2020), citing *Orleans, Death Indices, 1804-1876.* Death of Louis Belmont St. Hubert, Vol. 14, p. 254.

[606] NARC, "Sale of Property – C. Morel de Guiramond to Mrs. Jos. St. Hubert," dated 23 March 1854, passed by Notary Achille Chiapella, Act #210, Vol. 35. Courtesy Hon. Chelsey Richard Napoleon, Clerk of Civil District Court, Parish of Orleans.

[607] 1860 United States Federal Census, New Orleans, Orleans Parish, Ward 5, Dwelling #1460, Family #1409, Widow St. Hubert household, digital image, *Ancestry.com* (https://www.ancestry.com: accessed 1/2/2020), citing NARA microfilm publication M593_522, p. 548B. Date of enumeration: 1 July 1860, Image 231/393. Note: Eglée Aubry and her children were living just six houses down (Dwelling #1466, Family # 1414).

legitimate wife of Henry Balland, her surviving spouse, who worked as a cotton weigher.[608] "Anna" St. Hubert, a 61-year-old widowed "mulatto" was enumerated in the 1880 United States Federal Census living at #251 St. Ann Street with her daughters "Idia" (*sic*), age 32, "Lise," age 27, and "Laida" (*sic*), age 25, and her 23-year-old son, Alcide, a merchant. All of her children were still unmarried.[609]

Alcide finally married on 9 May 1882. The bride was Maria Dora Sheyward, a native of Texas, the twenty-two-year-old daughter of William Sheyward and Lina Smith.[610] Alcide Joseph St. Hubert died a year and a half later on 8 December 1883 at #73 Conti Street. The attending physician stated that he died from phthisis pulmonalis (tuberculosis).[611] The couple had no children.

Anna Julia Latrobe died in New Orleans at her home on the corner of Robertson and Dumaine on 23 December 1890 at the age of seventy-one. The cause of death was listed as "bronchitis and cardiac hypertrophy."[612] She was survived by her three daughters, Lydia, Lise and Léda St. Hubert, none of whom ever married. According to the 1900 United States Federal Census for New Orleans, Ward 5, the three women identified as "white" lived together at #1601 Dumaine Street in a house that they owned. Lydia gave her date of birth as December 1845, Lise (Élise) as June 1851, and Léda as November 1855.[613] Ten years later they were still living together on Dumaine Street, all said to be white, none employed. Lydia and Lise were both younger than they had been in 1900!

Léda, daughter of Joseph St. Hubert and Julia"Lathrop" died on 29 April 1914 in New Orleans. She was waked from her late residence #1601 Dumaine Street, between North Robertson and Claiborne and interred in St. Louis Cemetery #3.[614] Lydia St. Hubert died on 25 June 1920, from heart failure, at 1601 Dumaine Street where she had been living with her sister Lise.[615] Lise St. Hubert died four years later on 8 April 1924 at #1601 Dumaine Street from "valve heart disease."[616] Her death ended the Henry Sellon Boneval Latrobe line in New Orleans. Neither Henry Belmont Latrobe nor his sister Anne Julia Latrobe had any grandchildren. Gustave Bringier, Julia's half-brother, did not appear in any records past the 1860 federal census. When and where he died could not be ascertained.

---

[608] Courtesy of State of Louisiana, Secretary of State, Division of Archives, Records Management, and History. *Vital Records Indices*. Baton Rouge, LA, USA, citing *New Orleans, Louisiana Death Records Index 1804-1939*, Vol. 67, p. 387. Note: Henri Balland remarried in 1883 to Helene Lydia Smith. His 1903 last will and testament indicates that there was no issue from either marriage.
[609] 1880 United States Federal Census, New Orleans, Orleans Parish, ED 38, Dwelling #427, Family #427, Anna St. Hubert household, digital image, *Ancestry.com* (https://www.ancestry.com: accessed 1/2/2020), citing NARA microfilm publication T9 Roll 461, p. 288C. Date of enumeration: 12 June 1880, Image 43/50.
[610] "Louisiana Parish Marriages, 1837-1957," database with images, *FamilySearch.org* (https://familysearch.org/ark:/61903/1:1:QKJW-LB2P : accessed 2/6/2020), Alcide St Hubert and Marie Dora Sheyward, 09 May 1882; citing Orleans, Louisiana, United States, various parish courthouses, Louisiana; FHL microfilm 907,696.
[611] Courtesy of State of Louisiana, Secretary of State, Division of Archives, Records Management, and History. *Vital Records Indices*. Baton Rouge, LA, USA, citing *Orleans Death Indices 1877-1895*; Vol. 84, p. 61. Note: Unlike Louis Belmont and Laura Marie, the record indicated that he was "colored."
[612] Courtesy of State of Louisiana, Secretary of State, Division of Archives, Records Management, and History. *Vital Records Indices*. Baton Rouge, LA, USA, citing *Orleans Death Indices 1877-1895*; Vol. 98, p. 652. Note: The record indicated that she was "colored."
[613] 1900 United States Federal Census, Orleans Parish, Louisiana, Ward 5, Dwelling #202, Family #217, Lydia St. Hubert household, digital image, *Ancestry.com* (http://www.ancestry.com accessed 1/15/2020), citing Family History Library microfilm # 1240572. Date of enumeration: 11 June 1900. Image 24/36.
[614] "Died", *The Times Democrat and The Daily Picayune*, Thursday April 30, 1914, digital image, *Genealogybank.com* (www.genealogybank.com: accessed 3/3/2020), p. 10, col. 6. Note: The cause of her death on the death certificate was illegible. She was also said to be "colored."
[615] Courtesy of State of Louisiana, Secretary of State, Division of Archives, Records Management, and History. *Vital Records Indices*. Baton Rouge, LA, USA, citing *Orleans Death Indices 1918-1928*; Vol. 179, p. 539. Note: She was said to be "colored."
[616] Courtesy of State of Louisiana, Secretary of State, Division of Archives, Records Management, and History. *Vital Records Indices*. Baton Rouge, LA, USA, citing *Orleans Death Indices 1918-1928*; Vol. 168, p. 1031. Note: She also was designated as "colored." See also p. 278 of this book.

CHAPTER 20

ZÉLIE AUBRY and RENÉ PROSPER FOY

Zélie Aubry, also familiarly called "Azélie," "Héloïse," "Louise," and "Eloisa," Marguerite Cécile Aubry's third oldest child, had a relationship with René Prosper Foy, a white French immigrant plantation owner, marble cutter and literary bon vivant, for over a quarter of a century. Foy was born on 3 July 1787 at Orléans, Parish of Saint Paul, Loiret, France, and baptized the same day. The record, signed by "Bourdon, Vicaire," reads: "Le même jour (3 juillet) audit an a été Batisé René Prosper né du même jour du légitime mariage de Jacques Foy et de Marie Jeanne Maisonneuve, le parrain René Pitrou la maraine Marie Sophie Maisonneuve tante dudit enfant qui n'ont pas signer " (On the same day [3 July] of the aforesaid year, was baptized René Prosper, born on the same day of the legitimate marriage of Jacques Foy and Marie Jeanne Maisonneuve, the godfather René Pitrou, the godmother Marie Sophie Maisonneuve his aunt, who did not sign).[617] René Prosper's, younger brother, Jacques, who came to New Orleans ca. 1816, and appears in later French records as a "paver" or stone mason, was born on 10 September 1790 at Orléans.[618] The elder Jacques Foy was a café owner (cabaretier) at Orleans.

According to many sources Foy had been one of Napoleon's soldiers and had come to Louisiana from Bordeaux, with a stop in Saint-Domingue. Had he fought with Leclerc's French troops on the Island he would have been fifteen or sixteen years old. Had he come later, after the defeat of the French in 1804 he would have found an island in chaos, an extremely dangerous place for whites, who if not killed during the war, had fled for their lives to Cuba or to the United States. Of Napoleon's soldiers, who numbered about 31,000 at the beginning of 1802, fewer than 7,000 survived the slaughters and the yellow fever. It seems difficult to reconcile that such a young man could not only have been one of Napoleon's soldiers as well as a professional marble cutter and New Orleans land owner at the age of nineteen. However, we know from the previous chapter that Henry Sellon Boneval Latrobe was a professional architect, builder and property owner in New Orleans at that same age.

That being said, the first Louisiana record for the young Prosper Foy that we found was from the first decade of the nineteenth century. It is a restaurant receipt dated 7 July 1806 from the Marine Hotel where the young Foy had dined with some friends. He paid for five dinners at $2.00 apiece and four bottles of Chateau Leffitte (*sic*) which cost $1.00 per bottle for a total of $14.00.

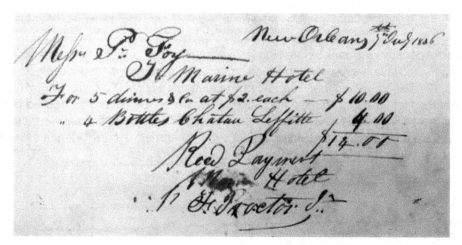

Prosper Foy Restaurant receipt, dated 7 July 1806, Prosper Foy Papers, LaRC-443, Tulane University Special Collections, Howard-Tilton Memorial Library, Tulane University, (Courtesy of Lori Schexnayder,, Assistant University Archivist.)

---

[617] Orléans, (Saint Paul) Loiret, France, Baptêmes, Mariages, Décès [Baptisms, Marriages, Deaths], 1787, Baptism, not numbered, René Prosper Foy, digital image, *Archives départementales du Loiret*, "État Civil en ligne," (https://www.archives-loiret.fr/: accessed 2/28/2020), Cote 3NUM 234/1527, Image 39/78.

[618] Orléans, (Saint Paul) Loiret, France, Baptêmes, Mariages, Décès [Baptisms, Marriages, Deaths], 1790, Baptism, not numbered, Jacques Foy, digital image, *Archives départementales du Loiret*, "État Civil en ligne," (https://www.archives-loiret.fr/: accessed 2/28/2020), Cote 3NUM 234/1530, Image 55/81.

Prosper's usual occupation was marble cutter. Soon, however, he would be a major land and slave owner. In 1807 Prosper had just turned twenty-years-old and already seemed well-fixed in the community. On 27 June 1807, Henry Dukeilus sold a nineteen-year-old mulatto slave named Harisse to Prosper Foy for 660 piastres. Foy had paid cash for the slave who was guaranteed to be free of any illnesses or defects. The notary Narcissus Broutin signed the contract along with Dukeilus, Foy, and two witnesses, François Munhall and Pierre François Simon Godefroy:

NARC, "Vente d'esclave par Sieur Henry Dukeilus au Sieur Prosper Foy," dated 27 June 1807, passed by Notary Narcissus Broutin, Volume 16, fol. 154. Courtesy Hon. Chelsey Richard Napoleon, Clerk of Civil District Court, Parish of Orleans.

Three weeks later Prosper Foy was back before Narcissus Broutin to demand his money back from Henry Dukeilus claiming that, although the slave had been guaranteed against all illnesses and "capital defects (défauts capitaux)," he had run away, and having been caught, was now lodged in the city jail. Foy was told by the authorities at the jail that this was not the first time that Harisse had been incarcerated. Dukeilus was notified of this protest on 20 July 1807, but we do not know the outcome. In this document, part of which is seen below, we see the first indication that Prosper Foy was exercising his profession of marble cutter (marbrier) in New Orleans as early as 1807:

NARC, "Protestation par Sieur Prosper Foy contre Sieur Henry Dukeilus," dated 18 July 1807, passed by Notary Narcissus Broutin, Volume 17, fol. 9, verso. Courtesy Hon. Chelsey Richard Napoleon, Clerk of Civil District Court, Parish of Orleans. Note: Second line – "Est comparu le sieur Prosper Foy marbrier demeurant en cette ville." (Appeared Mr. Prosper Foy marble cutter living in this city.)

On 6 February 1809 Prosper Foy obtained marble from José Fernandez in consideration of the latter's lending him 2,930 piastres without interest. Foy received 40 slices of marble "ready wrought," 2 blocks of white marble, 6 marble tables set in mahogany frames, 34 marble tables, 1200 pieces of square marble, 4 large tombs, 3 chimney ornaments, several marble ink stands, two chimney mantels, 12 marble sun dials, 3000 pounds of Plaster of Paris, 4 stoves, 4 coffee cups in green marble, and 6 small bathing tubs in red marble, set upon granite. According to this arrangement Fernandez agreed to leave all the marble with Foy so that he could prepare and sell the finished products. After repayment of the amount lent to Foy, Fernandez agreed to pay him 14 piastres per month for his work. Fernandez also agreed that in consideration for lending Foy the 2,930 piastres he would be satisfied with whatever amount the finished marble could be sold for.[619]

Prosper probably met Zélie Aubry ca. 1809-1810 when she was 15 or 16 years old. Their relationship was cemented at the birth of their first child, whom Prosper recognized as his own at the 1811 baptism: "Foy, Marguaritta Felecitas (Prosper, native of Orleans [France], and Eloisa Obry, native of this parish), b. December 24, 1811, bn. Dec. 22, 1810, s. Antonio Obet [sic] and Marguarita Cecelia (o) (SCL, B24, 117). The godfather was Dr. Antonio Abat. The child's godmother was her grandmother, Marguerite Cécile Aubry. While a copy of the child's birth record is available on-line from the Archdiocese of New Orleans, it is barely legible.[620] Fortunately, a copy that Zélie Aubry had gotten later was attached to Prosper Foy's 1854 succession record. Abbé Jean-Pierre Koüne, who performed many sacraments for the city's free people of color, and who had baptized the child in 1811, also made the copy seen on the following page for Zélie Aubry in 1816. The significant part of the document, written in Spanish, reads:

On the 24th of December in the year 1811, I the undersigned priest in the parish church of St. Louis of New Orleans, baptized with holy oil, a free racially mixed baby girl who was born on the 22nd of December of the last year 1810, illegitimate child of Prosper Foy, a native of Orleans in France and of Eloise Obry, a native of this parish, both parents residents of this city, in which the child after the sacred ceremony, was named Marguarita Felicitas. Her godparents Dr. Antonio Abat and Marguarita Cecilia.

The document was signed by J.P. Koüne as well as the natural father, Prosper Foy, who obviously also had been in attendance:

---

[619]NARC, "Articles of Agreement between José Fernandez and R. Prosper Foy," dated 6 February 1809, passed by Notary Michel de Armas, Volume 48, fol. 668 verso. Courtesy Hon. Chelsey Richard Napoleon, Clerk of Civil District Court, Parish of Orleans. Note: Although found among the Michel de Armas records, the notary was Peter Francis Simon Godefroy, and the agreement was written in English.

[620] Archdiocese of New Orleans (Orleans Parish, LA), *St. Louis Cathedral, New Orleans, Baptism Slaves and Free People of Color, 1811-1812,* digital images, Baptism of Marguaritta Felecitas, mestiva libra, (https://nolacatholic.org/church-records), Image 30/126, #534.

Louisiana, Wills and Probate Records, 1756-1984 [database and images on-line], citing *Record of Wills, 1846-1880 Louisiana. Probate Court (Orleans Parish). Will of Joseph [sic] Foy, dated 7 February 1854, Ancestry.com* (http://www.ancestry.com: accessed 2/18/2020), Image 621/1365.

It can be seen that Abbé Koüne affirmed that Prosper Foy, a native of Orléans in France, was the father, and that he had signed the original baptismal record along with him in the presence of the godparents, Antoine Abat, Foy's friend, a French immigrant from the Department of Ariège, in France, and Marguerite Cécile, whom we know was Zélie (Eloisa) Aubry's mother.

Earlier that year, Foy had been involved in a land dispute with Mathieu Bernard over a piece of property Foy owned on St. Ann Street. At issue was a small strip of land measured not in feet but in inches that ran the length of his property. In lieu of going to court, Foy accepted 125 piastres from Bernard as payment for ceding the land to him.[621]

Prosper Foy and Zélie Aubry's second child, Elizabeth Pauline Foy was born on 17 March 1813, but not baptized until after the conclusion of the War of 1812 on 2 September 1815. A transcription of the baptismal record revealed that Henry Sellon Boneval Latrobe, Prosper Foy's comrade-in-arms during the War of 1812 was the child's godfather:

> "Foiy (@Foy), Elizabeth Pauline (Prosper, native of Orleans in France [dept. of Loiret] and Eloisa Aubry, native of this parish) b. Sept 2, 1815, bn. Mar. 17, 1813, s. Henrico Bonneval LATROPE [sic] and Juana Paulin Des (P?)erque. SLC, B27,143)."

On 27 July 1814 Bernard Marigny sold to Prosper Foy, who was living in Faubourg Tremé, a large narrow plot of ground, in an area of the city known as the "Nouveau" (New) Marigny. The plot was 1009 feet facing St. Bernard Street by 176 feet facing Good Children (Rue des Bons Enfants now St. Claude Avenue), with a depth of 189 feet. This is the location where Foy would develop his tile, brick and marble works. Along with this sale, Foy acquired four other plots from Marigny in the adjacent Faubourg Marigny with all buildings and improvements: (1) Sixty feet facing Love (North Rampart) street by 120 feet deep (Lot #107) (2) Thirty-one feet facing Love Street by 120 feet deep (part of Lot #108), (3) Sixty feet facing History (Kerlerec) street by 31 feet deep (part of Lot #109), (4) Lot # 123 on Love Street, an irregular plot adjacent to Lots 122, 124, 125 and 126. A portion of the Jacques Tanesse map done in 1815 showing parts of the area of the Faubourg Marigny and Faubourg Nouveau Marigny where Foy made his purchase may be seen on the following page.

Rue St. Bernard, in the Nouveau Marigny, is at the top. St. Bernard Avenue meets Rue des Bons Enfants (Good Children) at a 50-degree angle about one-third down the page and was the location of Foy's tile, brick and marble works. The four lots on Love (Rue d'Amour) Street, in the Marigny, were located on the west end of Rue d'Amour (Love Street), one block south of Rue des Bons Enfants,[622] near Foy's tile and brick yard.[623] The property was bought by Foy for 2000 piastres cash in hand:

---

[621] NARC, "Vente de terre [Sale of land] par Prosper Foy à Mathieu Bernard," dated 19 May 1811, passed by Notary Narcissus Broutin, Volume 24, fol. 119 recto. Courtesy Hon. Chelsey Richard Napoleon, Clerk of Civil District Court, Parish of Orleans.

[622] The east-west streets in the Nouveau Marigny were from the top: St. Bernard, Annette, St. Antoine, Bagatelle, Union, Frenchmen (Rue des Français), and Elysian Fields (Champs Élysées). The streets running more or less north to south were: Prosper, St Avide, St. Jean, Girod, Urquhart, Morales, Good Children (Rue des Bons Enfants), and Love (Rue d'Amour)

[623] NARC, No marginal title – (Marigny to Foy) dated 27 July 1814, passed by Notary Pierre Pedesclaux, Volume 69, fol. 307 verso. Courtesy Hon. Chelsey Richard Napoleon, Clerk of Civil District Court, Parish of Orleans.

Library of Congress, Geography and Map Division, Louisiana: European Explorations and the Louisiana Purchase, showing Tanesse, J., William Rollinson, Charles Del Vecchio, and P Maspero. *Plan of the city and suburbs of New Orleans: from an actual survey made in.* New York: Charles Del Vecchio; New Orleans: P. Maspero, 1815. Map. https://www.loc.gov/item/90684205/.

A few months later, on 6 December 1814 Foy bought Bob, a thirty-five-year-old slave, from New Yorker Hermann Skaats through Fort, Clement & Co., for $300, using as collateral one of his properties on Love Street that he had bought from Bernard Marigny in 1814. In the next several years he would purchase more slaves to help develop his property.[624]

In December 1814, New Orleans was preparing for a battle to stave off the British attempt to capture New Orleans. Interrupting the development of his property, Prosper Foy volunteered to defend the city joining the Uniformed Battalion of Orleans Volunteers from 16 December 1814 until 15 March 1815. The roster shows him as "R. Prosper Foix," a first Lieutenant and Adjutant, serving as a staff officer to Major Jean-Baptiste Plauché who commanded five regiments consisting of Louisiana natives, and one company of Irishmen, the Louisiana Blues.[625] While we do not know the details of Foy's service, we know that Major General Andrew Jackson presented Foy with a dagger for his exemplary service during the Battle of New Orleans, an artifact which was said to be in

[624] NARC, "Sale and Mortgage," dated 6 December 1814, passed by Notary John Lynd, Volume 11, folio 479. Courtesy Hon. Chelsey Richard Napoleon, Clerk of Civil District Court, Parish of Orleans.
[625] Thomas Harrison, compiler, National Park Service, *Troop Roster, (War of 1812),* 190.

possession of the Louisiana State Museum. Amongst his comrades in arms were four other members of the extended family bound together by the four Aubry sisters, including Martin Aubry, their brother, as well as Henry Sellon Boneval Latrobe, Louis Paul Bringier, Celestin Chiapella, and Jean-Baptiste Pinta.

Back to work on his own place after the American victory, Prosper, who, despite living with a racially mixed family of his own, was a frequent buyer and seller of slaves, purchased three more in May 1815 before the notary Pierre Pedesclaux: Hercule, a male black, aged thirty-five years from Jean-Baptiste Patrice Chapdu for 210 piastres, and a mother and son, Mélite, a black female aged thirty-four years and her son, Télémaque aged five years from Louis Habine, all for 1244 piastres.[626]

On 10 January 1816, Zélie Aubry gave birth to their third child, a girl, Zélia Foy, who died on 16 June 1816.[627] The first record we found concerning Foy's brother Jacques Foy's residence in New Orleans, was dated 13 July 1816. At that time, Prosper Foy had purchased two slaves from the estate of Ignace Delino: a forty-year-old black male named Noel and a thirty-year-old black female named Marianette for 770 piastres. Prosper presented a note endorsed by Jacques Foy dated 13 July 1816, payable within one year, with the said slaves being mortgaged back to the estate until payment was received.[628] On 20 December 1816 Foy sold to Antoine Bayon, a resident of Donaldsonville, the nineteen-year-old female slave Aimée for 575 piastres. Bayon gave Foy 310 piastres in cash and the rest in a note he said he would pay in April 1817.[629] The following year, on 10 January 1817 Foy bought Marie, a nineteen-year-old female black slave from Baltimore, MD, from Jean Garnier, for 660 piastres, probably to help with his growing family with Zélie Aubry.[630] A second record for Prosper's brother Jacques was dated 25 March 1817, at which time Prosper sold to Jacques a twenty-two-year-old male black slave named Georges, said to be a good plantation worker and wagon driver for 900 piastres cash. A copy of part of the signature page from that sale, showing both signatures of the Foy brothers as well as those of the notary, Narcissus Broutin and two witnesses may be seen on the following page:

---

[626] Midlo Hall, editor, *Databases,* Hercule: Doc. #613; Mélite & Télémaque, Doc. #624.

[627] Births and deaths of four of Prosper Foy's children, undated, Prosper Foy Papers, LaRC-443, Tulane University Special Collections, Howard Tilton Memorial Library, Tulane University (Courtesy of Lori Schexnayder, Assistant University Archivist). Note: See the image on page 295.

[628] NARC, "Delino Heirs to Prosper Foy. Sale of Slaves with mortgage" dated 13 July 1816, passed by Notary Pierre Pedesclaux, Volume 73, folio 422 verso. Courtesy Hon. Chelsey Richard Napoleon, Clerk of Civil District Court, Parish of Orleans.

[629] NARC, "Foy, Prosper to Antoine Bayon. Sale of Slave" dated 13 July 1816, passed by Notary Pierre Pedesclaux, Volume 73, folio 718 verso. Courtesy Hon. Chelsey Richard Napoleon, Clerk of Civil District Court, Parish of Orleans.

[630] "Gwendolyn Midlo Hall, compiler, "Louisiana, Slave Records, 1719-1820" [database on-line], *Ancestry.com* (https://www.ancestry.com: accessed 3/3/2020) citing Midlo Hall's database intitled *Afro-Louisiana History and Genealogy 1719-1820* , Document # 20 – Jean Garnier to Prosper Foy. Note: This document may also be found gratis at the following website: http://www.ibiblio.org/laslave/.

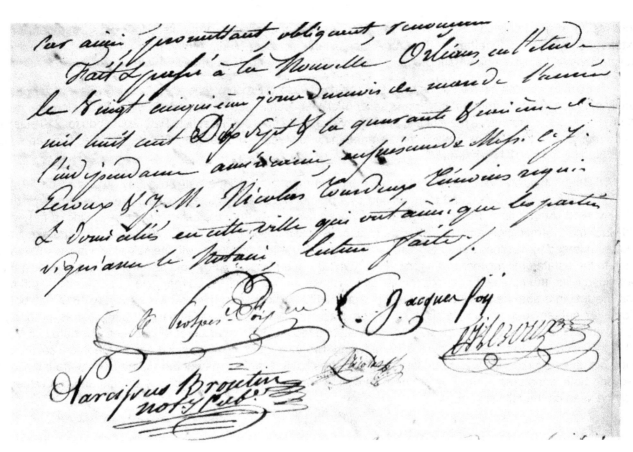

NARC, "Vente d'esclave [Sale of slave], Prosper Foy to Jacques Foy dated 25 March 1817, passed by Notary Narcissus Broutin, Volume 36. Courtesy Hon. Chelsey Richard Napoleon, Clerk of Civil District Court, Parish of Orleans.

On 24 September 1816, Prosper Foy went before the notary Narcissus Broutin to finalize the transfer of one slave and some property to his two surviving daughters with Zélie Aubry: Marguerite Félicité and Elizabeth Pauline. We have included the first and third pages of this important document written in French which Prosper Foy and Zélie Aubry used to insure a certain measure of financial security for her children should Foy die. The document reads in part (my translation)

Before Narcissus Broutin, duly commissioned public notary for the city and parish of New Orleans, second senatorial district of the State of Louisiana, and in the presence of witnesses, hereinafter named who signed: Mr. Prosper Foy, a property owner living in this city [...] makes an inter-vivos and irrevocable donation to Marguerite Félicité and Pauline Elizabeth, his two daughters born out of wedlock, the first born in this parish on 22 December 1810 and the second on 17 March 1813 also in this parish, and both baptized under his name, which donation is accepted for the said minors by Héloïse Aubry their mother living in this parish: (1) a negress named Philotine, aged 16 years (2) a lot of ground situated on Love Street, Faubourg Marigny, designated under #107 and part of #108 having together 92 feet six inches facing Love Street by 120 feet in depth, bounded on one side by land (p. 2 not photographed for this book) belonging to the City, on the other by the rest of lot #108, and in the back by lot #111 [...]

The document continued, stating that during the children's minority the property was to be administered by their mother and father, or by one of them. Foy had purchased Philotine on 7 October 1813 from Louis Lecesne, along with her mother Marie Jeanne for 600 piastres, and the land from Bernard Marigny on 27 July 1815. Together they were valued at 1200 piastres and were declared free of any mortgages or other debts:

24 9bre 1816.
Donation
par

Prosper Foy
à
Ses Enfans naturels

f. C.

Pardevant Ariste Broutin dument
Commissionné & autorisé notaire public
pour la ville & paroisse de la nouvelle
orléans, second district sénatorial de
L'état de la Louisiane & en presence des
temoins ci-après nommés & soussignés.

Est present Mr. prosper foy propriétaire
demeurant en Cette ville.

Lequel a, par Ces presentes, fait Donation
entre-vifs & irrévocable à Marguerite
felicité & praulim Elizabeth, Ses deux
filles naturelles, la première née en Cette
paroisse le Vingt deux Decembre mil huit
Cent Dix et la Seconde le Dix sept mars
mil huit Cent treize aussi en Cette paroisse
& l'une & l'autre Baptisées Sous son nom
Ce qui est accepté pour les Dites mineures
par heloise Aubrey leur mère, Demeurant
en Cette paroisse & à ce presente 1°. d'une
Negresse nommée philotene agée de
Seize ans. 2° D'un emplacement De terre
Situé rue D'amour faubourg marigny
désigné sous le N°. 107 & partie duN°
108. ayant ensemble quatre-vingt douze
pieds Six pouces De face à La Dite
rue D'amour, sur Cent Vingt pieds de
profondeur. Borné Du Coté de la ville

[...]

NARC, "Donation par Prosper Foy à Ses Enfants Naturels" dated 24 September 1816, passed by Notary Narcissus Broutin, Volume 35, Pages 1 & 3. Courtesy Hon. Chelsey Richard Napoleon, Clerk of Civil District Court, Parish of Orleans.

The gift of a slave and land was made by Foy "pour donner à sesdites filles des preuves de son amitié parce que telle est au surplus sa volonté " (to give to his daughters proof of his friendship because that is moreover his wish), a boiler plate phrase found in many of these donations which were made by a white father transferring property to his racially-mixed children born out of wedlock while the father was still living, because they would be legally prohibited from inheriting from him after his death.

NARC, "Donation par Prosper Foy à Ses Énfants Naturels" dated 24 September 1816, passed by Notary Narcissus Broutin, Volume 35. Courtesy Hon. Chelsey Richard Napoleon, Clerk of Civil District Court, Parish of Orleans. Note: The above sentence is the key phrase from page 2 of the document used to justify this type of inter-vivos donation to children born out of wedlock.

Just before the birth of their fourth child on 13 March 1817, Prosper Foy bought property with a house in the Faubourg Tremé from Émile Sainet. The lot, located on St. Claude Street, measured sixty feet by 280 feet in depth and backed up onto property already owned by Foy who gave his note to the seller for 410 piastres. He used as collateral, his forty-six-year-old slave Nero.[631]

Zélie and Prosper's first son, Hippolyte Foy was born on 29 June 1817, but died on 22 September 1819, the day of his baptism (SLC, B30, 141). He was interred the next day in the Church cemetery (SLC F12, 25). A small scrap of paper contained in the Prosper Foy Papers at the Howard -Tilton Memorial Library, Tulane University, New Orleans, gave the birth and death dates of Hippolyte, Zelia, and Émile Foy, none of whom appeared in St. Louis Cathedral records. Joseph's birth and deaths were, however, found in Church records:

Birth and death dates of four of Prosper Foy's children, undated, Prosper Foy Papers, LaRC-443, Tulane University Special Collections, Howard-Tilton Memorial Library, Tulane University (Courtesy of Lori Schexnayder, Assistant University Archivist.)

In the fall of 1817, Prosper Foy had determined to return to France for an indefinite period. To that end, he sold his marble works to his superior officer who commanded the Uniformed Battalion of Orleans Volunteers during the War of 1812, Jean-Baptiste Balthazar Plauché, on 3 October 1817, before notary Cristoval de Armas. The act of sale included an inventory of his stock: 18 large white marble tombs (900 piastres), four tomb decorations with pilasters (100 piastres), six large stair treads (54 piastres), five headstones (tombes à l'anglaise) large and small

---

[631] NARC, "Vente de terre et maison [Sale of land and house], by E. Sainet to Prosper Foy dated 13 March 1817, passed by Notary Narcissus Broutin, Volume 36, folio 112 verso. Courtesy Hon. Chelsey Richard Napoleon, Clerk of Civil District Court, Parish of Orleans.

(45 piastres), 5 tomb doors of different colored marble (40 piastres), two large mantels of veined marble (29 piastres), one white sculpted marble fireplace surround (20 piastres), 20 pieces of marble used for stair treads or as small tombstones (80 piastres), 900 marble squares @ 18 cents each (160 piastres). Foy stipulated in the sale that he would forever renounce the profession of marble cutter in the state of Louisiana (except for items for his personal use) under the threat of a 2000 piastre fine paid to the buyer (Plauché) or to his heirs. Jean-Baptiste Plauché paid Foy 1430 piastres cash in hand, at which time Foy reserved the right to sell any other marble items not included in the sale for his own profit for a period of two months. Below is a copy of Foy's marble inventory:

NARC, "Vente d'un fond de marbrier Par Prosper Foy au M. Jean-Bte. Balthazar Plauché" dated 3 October 1817, passed by Notary Cristoval de Armas, Volume 1, Folio 178. Courtesy Hon. Chelsey Richard Napoleon, Clerk of Civil District Court, Parish of Orleans.

Although Foy had made this agreement with Plauché, he never entirely gave up his work as a marble cutter. Examples of his work may be found in the St. James Cemetery in Vacherie, LA, near his St. James Parish plantation, where he carved headstones for some of his neighbors. He also advertised as a sculptor and marble cutter in the 1832 New Orleans City Directory, working at #56 Basin Street, a venue his son Florville would take over in the late 1830s.

On 3 December 1817, Foy paid off the mortgage on the two slaves, Noel and Marianette that he purchased from the estate of Ignaze Delino, transferring 770 piastres over to the heirs.[632] Later that month, on 30 December 1817, Foy sold to Jean-Baptiste Royer a plot of ground shaped like an irregular pentagon situated in the Faubourg Marigny (lot #123) with its buildings, facing Rue d'Amour (Love Street, now North Rampart), bounded by lots #119, #122, #124, #125 and #126. This was one of the same lots that he had bought on 27 July 1814 from Bernard Marigny. Royer promised to pay the entire amount of 1200 piastres one year from the date of sale, with the land mortgaged back to the seller until final payment.[633]

On 19 February 1818, Foy advertised his brick and tile works for sale in the *Louisiana State Gazette*. He described it as situated in the Faubourg's Tremé and Marigny, near the College, having 500 feet facing St. Claude Street and 1020 feet facing St. Bernard Street on which were a large number of buildings, including a main house with a tile roof and porches on all sides, raised on brick pillars, a flower garden with pathways paved in brick, an orchard and vegetable garden, kitchens, servants quarters and a store all in brick, a stable, chicken coop, a tiled double oven surrounded by covered porches for drying materials, a large octagonal mill with porches all around for drying manufactured products, two large dry sheds with many shelves for storing materials, along with all the tools necessary in the manufacture of tiles, bricks and paving stones. Eighteen slaves were also for sale, fourteen being men, all accustomed to the work as laborers, barrel makers, cart men, cattle drivers, grinders, gardeners and wood choppers. The women were washers, ironers and vegetable sellers. Finally, six mules and horses with their harnesses, carts, tumbrels were also for sale. The brick kiln and its dependencies could be had at one, two, and three years credit, the slaves at one, and two years credit all with endorsed notes and mortgages on the property. The mules and horses were available at 90 days credit. The advertisement ended by saying that the proprietor was selling out because of his impending departure.[634] Everything that did not sell privately was to be put up for auction on 23 March 1818 by the firm of Dutillet & Sagory.[635]

On 21 May 1818 Prosper Foy sold to Manuel Andry and his two sons, Michel and Hortaire Andry, nine slaves, all male blacks: Lindor (30), Anthony (24), Sunday (38) Isaac (20), Horace (15), Boucaud (36), Tom (35), Noel (40), and Jean Baptiste (26) for 10,500 piastres.[636] The Andrys were in the City Court by August of the same year. They looked to get their 10,500 piastres returned by Foy because the first six slaves listed above, had fled, and the Andrys claimed that Foy knew them to be notoriously bad characters. The case went all the way to the Louisiana State Supreme Court on appeal. A June 1919 decision only allowed the Andrys 6500 piastres in recompense for the six slaves that had actually run away.[637] Foy was forced to mortgage his brick and tile works to Manuel Andry on 19 August 1819 in order to try to satisfy his debt to him.

On 10 June 1818, Prosper Foy acknowledged a debt to the merchant tailor, James Hopkins for 1460 piastres. We assume that it was for clothing that he purchased for his trip to France. In lieu of payment he mortgaged to Hopkins until 15 September 1818 a lot of ground (#517) in the Faubourg Marigny with 60 feet facing St. Bernard Street by 180 feet deep, along with the two slaves, Nero, aged thirty years and Josephine, aged 35 years.[638] Foy paid off the note on 18 September 1818.[639]

---

[632] NARC, "Prosper Foy to the heirs of Delino" dated 3 December 1817, passed by Notary Philippe Pedesclaux, Volume 3, Folio 826 verso. Courtesy Hon. Chelsey Richard Napoleon, Clerk of Civil District Court, Parish of Orleans.

[633] NARC, "Prosper Foy to Jean-Baptiste Royer – Sale of land" dated 30 December 1817, passed by Notary Philippe Pedesclaux, Volume 3, Folio 886 verso. Courtesy Hon. Chelsey Richard Napoleon, Clerk of Civil District Court, Parish of Orleans.

[634] "À Vendre (For Sale)", *Louisiana State Gazette*, 19 February 1818, digital image, *Genealogybank.com* (https://www.genealogybank.com: accessed 5/3/2020), p. 3, col. 4.

[635] "By Dutillet & Sagory," *New Orleans Argus*, 18 March 1818, digital image, *Genealogybank.com* (https://www.genealogybank.com: accessed 5/3/2020), p. 3, col. 5.

[636] . NARC, "Sale of slaves, Prosper Foy to M. & M. Andry" dated 21 May 1818, passed by Notary Philippe Pedesclaux, Volume 4, Act. #439. Courtesy Hon. Chelsey Richard Napoleon, Clerk of Civil District Court, Parish of Orleans.

[637] "Andry v. Foy, 5 Mart (o.s.)," *Case Law Access Project*, Harvard Law School, https://cite.case.law/mart-os/5/33/.

[638] NARC, "Mortgage by Foy to Hopkins" dated 10 June 1818, passed by Notary John Lynd, Volume 11, Folio 47 recto. Courtesy Hon. Chelsey Richard Napoleon, Clerk of Civil District Court, Parish of Orleans.

[639] NARC, "Foy, Prosper, to Hopkins paid mortgage" dated 18 September 1818, passed by Notary John Lynd, Volume 14, Folio 80. Courtesy Hon. Chelsey Richard Napoleon, Clerk of Civil District Court, Parish of Orleans.

It was during this time in late 1818 that Prosper Florville Foy, Zélie's fourth child, was conceived. He was born on 29 June 1819 and baptized on 6 February 1820, with Norbert Soulié, dear friend of the late Henry Sellon Boneval Latrobe, and Marguerite Aubry, either the boy's grandmother or Zélie's sister Marguerite/Mercelite as godparents. (SLC B30, 170). Florville, the most famous of all the Foy children, would live a long life and become one of the premier marble cutters and tomb makers in New Orleans.

Although other sources indicate that Prosper Foy spent five years in Europe around this time, neither the births of his various children, nor notarial records bear this out. We can deduce that he may have left New Orleans after November 1818, but had returned before 15 June 1819, because he attended an auction held by Dutillet & Sagory at the Bourse Maspero where he was the highest bidder for a plot of land sold by the city of New Orleans (The "Corporation") designated as #32, with 94 feet facing Rue Bourgogne (Burgundy St.) by 60 feet facing the Rue du Quartier (now Barracks St.) for which he paid 980 piastres. He signed a notarized document before Michel de Armas on 30 June 1819, promising to pay one-third of the sale price in the first year, one-third in the second year, and the final third in the third year.[640] Foy lost this real estate purchase to Manuel Andry under a First Judicial District Court order in September 1822. The sheriff auctioned off the property and it was sold to Andry for 800 piastres.[641]

Prosper Foy finally sold the property on St. Bernard Street on 30 March 1820 along with eight slaves and all the materials to be able to run a brickyard manufactory to Marguerite Melanie Plauché, the wife of Jean Vital Michel for 35,000 piastres before the notary Hugues Lavergne. The transaction was not without its complications. Marguerite Plauché agreed to pay in six installments. She ceded to Foy a lot of ground between Bourbon and Royal Streets with a 30-foot frontage on Dumaine Street worth 5000 piastres for immediate occupancy. This was to be followed by five equal payments of 6000 piastres each in January of 1821, 1822, 1823, 1824 and 1825. Manuel Andry, who had been awarded 6,500 by the State Supreme Court for the six slaves that he had bought from Foy in 1818 who had fled, intervened in the sale as the mortgage holder on the property. He agreed to accept Marguerite Plauché's first 6000 piastre payment in January 1821. Foy issued Andry an additional mortgage on other property for the remaining 500 piastres, plus 850 piastres for Andry's "trouble."[642] Foy and his family were enumerated in the Faubourg Marigny, on Esplanade Street, in New Orleans, in the 1820 United States Federal Census. "Prosper Foix," white, aged between 26 and 45 years, was living with three slaves, one male and two females, and four free people of color: one male under 14 (his son, Florville), two females under 14 (his daughters, Marguerite Félicité and Elizabeth Pauline), and one female between 26 and 45 years (his companion, Zélie).[643]

On 1 February 1821 Foy sold to Jean Rodriguez the lot of ground, the house and its dependencies on Dumaine Street that he had accepted as partial payment for his tile and brick works from Marguerite Plauché, for 4000 piastres. He received 2000 piastres in cash. Rodriguez agreed to pay Foy the additional 2000 piastres on the day that he received the keys to the house on Dumaine Street. Until that time, Foy agreed to pay Rodriguez 30 piastres per month rent.[644]

On 23 March 1821, Foy bought a property from Julien J. Renoy that the latter had acquired from the city of New Orleans in 1819: to wit, Lot #34 which had a 63 feet frontage on Rue du Quartier (Barracks St.) by 74 feet deep. Foy paid 325 piastres to the seller and assumed the remaining portion of the mortgage that Renoy had with

[640] NARC, "Vente de Terre – LA Corporation à Prosper Foix" dated 30 June 1819, passed by Notary Michel de Armas, Volume 17a, Act 390a. Courtesy Hon. Chelsey Richard Napoleon, Clerk of Civil District Court, Parish of Orleans.
[641] The Collins C. Diboll Vieux Carré Digital Survey, Historic New Orleans Collection, (https://www.hnoc.org/vcs/property_info.php?lot=23180).
[642] NARC, "Vente de terre, edifices, esclaves par M. Prosper Foy" (Sale of land buildings and slaves by Prosper Foy), dated 30 March 1820, passed by notary Hugues Lavergne, Vol. 3, act 369. Courtesy Hon. Chelsey Richard Napoleon, Clerk of Civil District Court, Parish of Orleans.
[643] 1820 United States Federal Census, New Orleans City, Prosper Foix household, digital image, Ancestry.com (https://www.ancestry.com accessed 10/10/2019), citing NARA microfilm publication M33_32, Image 103. Date of enumeration: Not given, but due by 7 August 1820. Image 65/82.
[644] NARC, "Vente de propriété par le Sieur Prosper Foy au Sieur Jn. Rodriguez, avocat (Sale of property by Prosper Foy to Jean Rodriguez, lawyer)" dated 1 February 1821, passed by Notary Carlile Pollock, Volume 2, Folio 392. Courtesy Hon. Chelsey Richard Napoleon, Clerk of Civil District Court, Parish of Orleans.

the city.[645] Less than two months later Prosper and Zélie (identified as "Louise Obry,") welcomed another girl into the family. Marie Josephe Sophie Foy was born on 2 July 1821 and baptized on 24 October 1824. (SLC, B34, 165) On 3 April 1821 Prosper Foy advertised in the *Louisiana State Gazette* for the return of three runaway slaves. Anthony, aged 26 and Lindor, aged 32, whom he had briefly sold to Manuel Andry who had been missing for over two years. In addition, L'Éveillé, a forty-five-year-old male black from Guinea, Africa, had been gone from his place for eight months. He offered a 100 piastre reward for their return.[646] Prosper and Zélie's second son, Joseph was born on 16 January 1823 in New Orleans: "Foy, Joseph (Prosper, native of Orleans [Dept. of Loiret] in France, and Eloise Aubry) b. 2 Feb 1823, bn. 16 Jan 1823, s. Joseph Haicard and Marie Josephine Duplessis (SLC, B 32, 194)." He was interred just over a month later as "Aubry, Joseph (Zélie) 1. mo. buried 27 Feb 1823 d. [o] (SLC, F12, 115)."

The wrangling over Foy's brick and tile works sale lasted until the beginning of the 1830s. The property had passed from Marguerite Melanie Plauché, to the firm of Manuel Perez and Jean B. Juette on 27 September 1820. This latter firm went bankrupt the following year, at which time Manuel Andry bought the property from their creditors on 4 September 1821 before the notary Hugues Lavergne. Andry transferred it to Louis H. Guerlain in an exchange of property before the notary Felix de Armas on 8 February 1823. Shortly before the death of Guerlain, who was interred in New Orleans on 3 September 1825 (SLC, F14, 76), some of the lots previously belonging to Foy were put up for sale as part of a lottery. The *Louisiana State Gazette* dated 30 May 1825 published Foy's warning and protest:

> CAUTION – Having seen announced in the *Louisiana Advertiser* of the 12th instant; a lottery of certain lots of ground situated in St. Claude and St. Bernard streets, Faubourg Tremé, I make this formal protestation that, all the lots a part of a plantation on which I have just and legal claim, for although I had sold the same, I have not been paid the purchase money; I have been grievously deceived & the bad faith of the purchasers has had a ruinous effect in unjustly depriving me of my property acquired by fifteen years of active professional labour, and with the sweat of my brow [...] I forewarn all such persons who intend to take tickets in said Lottery or those who have the intention to purchase the whole or part of said property; that I reserve my right to the same against all possessors, and that I shall not desist therefrom, until I am paid for my property or received a just and reasonable compensation therefor.[647]

Foy's protest was followed by a notice in the same newspaper, signed by Lewis H. Guerlain who stated that Foy had no reason to object to the sale, because he had bought the property from Andry with a warrantee deed which was deposited in the notarial office of Carlile Pollock. Foy's former plantation was still in dispute when the property was to be sold in the spring of 1831, at which time Prosper published another series of protests in the local newspapers.

The first cracks in the relationship between Prosper and Zélie showed up during the 1820s, brought about by his precarious financial standing after the fight for and loss of most of the money allegedly due to him from the sale of the St. Bernard Avenue property, and perhaps also by an embarrassing brush with the law which was reported in the 8 July 1822 edition of the *Courrier de la Louisiane* which reads:

> Prosper Foy, charged with being an accomplice in the forgery which we have mentioned in our number of Monday last, has been arrested by J. Roffignac, our worthy Mayor. [...] Since Saturday he has never ceased to be on the track of Prosper Foy, and after several expeditions which he headed in person, he last night succeeded in arresting him in a house on Bayou Road, where it was known he had taken refuge.[648]

Unfortunately, we could find no previous or subsequent articles concerning this accusation against Foy, probably because, when all was said and done, nothing came of it.

---

[645] NARC, "Vente de Terre – J.J. Renoy to Prosper Foy" dated 23 March 1821, passed by Notary Michel de Armas, Volume 20, Act #97. Courtesy Hon. Chelsey Richard Napoleon, Clerk of Civil District Court, Parish of Orleans.

[646] "100 Piastres de Récompense," *Louisiana State Gazette*, 3 April 1821, digital image, *Newspapers.com* (https://www.newspapers.com: accessed 3/10/2020), p.4, col. 2.

[647] "Caution," *Louisiana State Gazette*, 30 May 1825, *Newspapers.com* (https://www.newspapers.com: accessed 3/10/2020), p. 1, col. 2.

[648] "Friday, July 5, 1822," *Courrier de la Louisiane*, July 3, 1822, digital image, *Genealogybank.com* (https://www.genealogybank.com: accessed 8/20/2019), p. 1, col. 4.

In April 1825 Foy had petitioned the court to become the curator ad bona of his two natural daughters Marguerite Félicité and Elizabeth Pauline, with François Langlois as the curator ad litem. In the petition his two daughters stated that their natural father had given them property in the Faubourg Marigny and slaves during their infancy and with the donation had reserved to himself the administration of said property, and that now above the age of twelve they wish to have him appointed curator until their majority. Zélie's answer was brief and to the point in an effort to protect her children's property from their father and his creditors. She stated that Foy had recently seduced her daughters from their right and proper home with her, and had convinced them to sign the petition presented to the court, answering through her attorney that:

> your petitioner avers that no such appointment can be lawfully made and that your petitioner until the majority of her aforesaid children is entitled to the right of keeping them and administering on their property, that they could be provided with curator ad bona and curator ad litem only in the event of the death of your petitioner and that the said Prosper Foy would be bound to give security for his good administration, because legitimate fathers alone are dispensed by law from giving security & your petitioner avers, if any further averment be necessary, that the said Prosper Foy is unworthy of the trust of curator by his character, morals, and conduct and ought by law to be excluded from such functions.

Judge James Pitot ordered that the decision appointing Foy and Langlois as curator ad bona and ad litem to the minors, Marguerite Félicité and Elizabeth Pauline be annulled, and that the children be restored to the domicile and to the keeping of the petitioner, Zélie (called Héloise in this document) Aubry.[649]

On 2 April 1828, Zélie Aubry as mother and natural tutrix of her two daughters, appeared before Judge James Pitot to petition for a family meeting on behalf of the girls to decide if she would be allowed to sell the slave Philotine that Prosper Foy had donated to his two daughters, Marguerite and Elizabeth Pauline. She asked that a family meeting been held by Hyacinthe Simon, Louis Dolliole, and Bazile Crocker, all free men of color and friends, as well as James Esnard and Charles Belot, in order to deliberate "if it is not necessary for the interest of said minors, that said slave called Philotine should not be sold as bearing prejudice to said minors by her frequent absences and the privation of her services which are the sole support of said minors and of your petitioner." For this meeting to take place, the Judge appointed Marguérite Cécile, Zélie's mother as curatrix ad bona of Marguerite (called Aubry, and not Foy in this petition), and Louis Bringier, lately the companion of Zélie's sister, Mercelite, as the child's curator ad litem. At the meeting it was decided to sell the slave for the benefit of the children.[650]

We believe that Prosper and Zélie's last daughter, Rose Euphémie Foy, was born ca. July 1829, although we found no baptism record for her. Another son, Émile Foy, was born on 21 September 1831, but died on 4 May 1833. We found no other records for him, other than the previously cited notation from the Prosper Foy Papers at Tulane University (See p. 295) which also gave the birth and death dates of Hippolyte, and Zelia Foy, who did not appear in St. Louis Cathedral records either, and Joseph Foy, for whom there is a baptismal and an interment record.

On 28 February 1833, Prosper Foy appeared before the notary Carlile Pollock with Hyacinthe Raphael, and Molière Duvernay, both free people of color,[651] to accept a mortgage on some property in St. Charles Parish owned by Raphael. She had put up as collateral two lots of ground in St. Charles Parish and several slaves inherited from her mother, Marie Rose Fatime, a free negress, at her death in 1824, for a payment by Foy of 1895 piastres. Molière Duvernay had held a mortgage on the same property since 4 January 1832 after he had lent Hyacinthe 1200.63 piastres. He travelled to New Orleans to acknowledge before Pollock that he had been repaid. The land in question was situated about 27 miles from New Orleans in St. Charles Parish on the left bank of the Mississippi River, having a frontage of one arpent on the river by the ordinary depth (usually 120 arpents), bounded on one side by the

[649] "Louisiana, Orleans Parish Estate Files, 1804-1846," database with images, *FamilySearch.org* (https://familysearch.org/ark:/61903/3:1:S3HY-6X9Q-D4M?cc=1388197&wc=MGH3-2NB%3A13749401%2C15916001 : accessed 5/20/2019), Foy, Unknown (1825) > images 1-11; New Orleans City Archives.

[650] "Louisiana, Orleans Parish Estate Files, 1804-1846," database with images, *FamilySearch.org* (https://familysearch.org/ark:/61903/3:1:S3HT-DHP7-G5V?cc=1388197&wc=MG4X-2J4%3A13748701%2C16477801 : accessed 5/20/2019), Aubry, Zelie, (1828), images 1-24; New Orleans City Archives.

[651] Molière's white father, Joseph Duvernay, was the first cousin of Marie Pelagie Duvernay, mother of Etienne and Celestin Coudrain Chiapella. Therefore, Molière Duvernay and Étienne and Celestin Coudrain Chiapella were second cousins.

property of Octave Alcée and Drausin Labranche, and on the other by Joseph Duvernay, The second portion, also inherited from her mother, was a one-third interest in a piece of property also consisting of one arpent facing the river adjacent to the first piece, as well as the following slaves: Marianne, Manon and Eugenie, all negresses, aged 37, 45, and 35 respectively as well as Eugenie's three children: ten-year-old Fortune, eight-year-old, Michael, and three-year-old Rosette. Hyacinthe Raphael's payment was due on 19 February 1834. It was also stipulated that there would be no extensions, and if not paid on the date due, the mortgage would have the "full force and effect of a judgment rendered in a court of competent jurisdiction in this state."[652] Foy sued in the District Court one year later to have the property seized because of Hyacinthe Raphael's inability to pay him back. One of the witnesses to the document was Achille Chiapella, future father to Eglée Aubry's sons, who was, at twenty years of age, an apprentice in Pollock's notarial office, having arrived from France in 1829 with his father Étienne Coudrain Chiapella.

Foy and Azélie had lost their toddler Émile on 4 May 1833. Just two days later, their twenty-year-old daughter Elizabeth Pauline Foy was taken from them. Unfortunately, her civil death record does not list the cause, but diseases such as cholera, dysentery and even tuberculosis were prevalent in the city and could have hastened her early demise. Although very faint, her death certificate, dated 4 March 1847, states that "Pauline Elizabeth Foy, a native of this city, born on the 17th of March 1813, the natural daughter of Prosper Foy and of Azélie Aubry departed this life on the sixth of May 1833 in a house on Love Street between Esplanade and History (now Kerlerec) Streets in the Third Municipality of this city." Mrs Lalanne, Eualie Urquhart, f.w.c., reported the death.

Courtesy of State of Louisiana, Secretary of State, Division of Archives, Records Management, and History. *Vital Records Indices*. Baton Rouge, LA, USA citing *Orleans Death Indices 1804-1876*; Vol. 10, p. 444.

---

[652] NARC, "Mortgage Prosper Foy from Hyacinthe Raphael" dated 28 February 1833, passed by Notary Carlile Pollock, Volume 43, Folio #93. Courtesy Hon. Chelsey Richard Napoleon, Clerk of Civil District Court, Parish of Orleans.

Prosper was so moved by his daughter's death that he wrote the following epitaph:

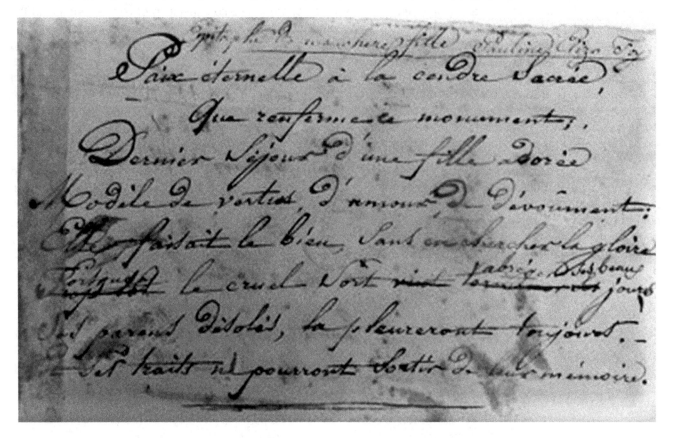

Paix éternelle à la cendre sacrée (Eternal peace to the sacred ashes)// Que referme ce monument (That this monument holds)// Dernier séjour d'une fille adorée (Last resting place of an adored daughter)// Modèle de vertu, d"amour , de dévouement (Model of virtue, love and devotion)// Elle faisait le bien sans en chercher la gloire (She did good works without seeking out glory)// Lorque le cruel sort abrège ses beaux jours (When cruel fate cut her days short)// Ses parents désolés la pleureront toujours (Her devastated parents will mourn her forever)// Et ses traits ne pourront sortir de leur mémoire (And her likeness will not fade from their memory) Epitaph to his deceased daughter, undated, but after 6 May 1833, Prosper Foy Papers, LaRC-443, Tulane University Special Collections, Howard-Tilton Memorial Library, Tulane University. (Courtesy of Lori Schexnayder, Assistant University Archivist.)

Perhaps the closest relationship he had with his children was with his son, Florville, whom he sent to France as a young boy to be educated. Returning ca. 1836, Florville apprenticed with his father, and soon took over his marble cutting business and his workshop on Basin Street. After 1840, Prosper stayed mainly at his St. James Parish plantation much to the disappointment of his children, and of Zélie Aubry, his longtime companion. According to Prosper's 1854 succession record, the St. James Parish property was described as being on the right bank of the Mississippi River, about 67 miles from New Orleans, measuring 2 arpents 25 toises (Note that there are 30 toises in an arpent) facing the river by 80 arpents deep and having a main house as well as other buildings and improvements worth about 4,500 piastres.[653] Foy was enumerated there in the 1840 United States Federal Census, living with another white male between the ages of 30 and 39 and 14 slaves.[654] The unidentified "white male" may have been his brother, Jacques, despite a slight disparity in age, who after leaving New Orleans to return to France, had returned. Jacques had applied for a passport at Bordeaux, Gironde, France, on 23 February 1838, at which time he affirmed that he had been born at Orléans (Loiret), was currently living at Bordeaux, and was headed for New Orleans. He was described as forty-seven years old, 5 ft. 2 in. (1m 68) in height, with dark brown hair, a high forehead, brown eyes, a round chin, a brown beard, an oval face with a florid complexion. He gave his occupation

[653] "Louisiana Wills and Probate Records, 1756-1984," digital images, *Ancestry.com* (https://www.ancestry.com: accessed 3/5/2020) citing *Louisiana, Orleans Parish Estate Files*, Inventories of Estates, F – Surnames Faurie, 1854-Foressier, 1855, Inventory of the estate of Prosper Foy dated 13 March 1854, Images 147-161/250.

[654] 1840 United States Federal Census, Orleans Parish, Louisiana, Prosper Foy household, digital image, *Ancestry.com* (https://www.ancestry.com accessed 11/2/2019), citing NARA microfilm publication M704, Roll 135 p. 265. No date given, Image 3/12.

as "paveur," paver or stone mason.[655] Foy left Bordeaux in March 1838 aboard the *Talma*, arriving in New Orleans on 11 May 1838. He was identified as a forty-seven-year-old stone cutter from France.[656] According to information in Prosper Foy's succession records, his brother, Jacques, died in America before 1854, although we could find no date for it, or any other records for him.

Although Zélie did not appear in the 1840 United States Federal Census, we believe that she may have been enumerated in the household of her mother, Marguerite Aubry where 13 other free people of color, 7 males and 6 females, including 3 children under 10 years of age, and 5 young people between the ages of 10 and 23, were living in the First District, Third Municipality.[657] Judging by a letter that Florville Foy wrote to his father in September 1840 there was much turmoil in Zélie's life. Florville apologized for his previous angry letter to his father, which has not been preserved, but in which we may presume that he had chastised his father for leaving Zélie alone with a dying child, when even strangers had rushed to give final aid which was owed to the pour unfortunate little one. (des étrangers, qui accouraient tous en foule, pour rendre les derniers services qui était (*sic*) dus à ce (*sic*) malheureuse.) He also reminded his father that Zélie was still inconsolable because of the premature loss of the child, and he feared that she might become ill from it. It appears that a woman named Julie had been working for Zelie and had brought her own child into the household. The noise that the toddler made was so unbearable to Zélie that Julie was sent away "back to her own mistress." For that reason she asked Florville to prevail upon Prosper to send Rosa's little maid back to New Orleans to replace her, although she did not ask for Rosa to return as well.[658] In a letter written a week later, Florville acknowledged the receipt of his "little sister's letter," not named, but obviously ten-year-old Rosa, and was happy that she was having such a good time in the country with her father. In the same letter he announced to his father that another tragedy had befallen the family, the loss of their good friend Mr. de Perdroville (*sic* Perdreauville), the elder, an event which had caused Zélie much pain. While Florville Foy's letters illustrate the often warm and affectionate feelings he had towards his father, they also show a distance between them that could never be breached. Florville always used the formal French "vous, votre, vos," instead of the familiar "tu, ton, tes," when addressing his father in writing. This formal use of the language appears not only in letters Florville wrote to his father, but also in a letter preserved from fourteen-year-old Rosa's correspondence to him. She wrote (Our translation):

New Orleans, 29 November 1844. My Dear Father, What has caused your delay which worries me so. Has some misfortune befallen you or are you sick? You said you would be in town by the 7th, and here it is the 16th, and I have received no news. Please tell us the reason which has delayed you from coming. We would be infinitely grateful. Everyone is well and sends you their regards. P.S. Mr. Lovinsquy came to visit and asks of news of you. Your very obedient daughter, Rosa Foy.

A copy of the letter in Rosa's beautiful hand may be seen on the next page.

---

[655] Bordeaux, Gironde, France, *Passeports pour l'étranger 1800-1889* (*Passports for Travel Abroad 1800-1889*), 1838, Registre #97, Passeport #90, Jacques Foy, digital image, *Archives départementales de la Gironde*," (https://archives.gironde.fr/archive/recherche/passe ports//n:245: accessed 8/15/2019), Cote 4M718/90, Image 1/1.

[656] "New Orleans Passenger Lists, 1813-1963," digital image, *Ancestry.com* (https://www.ancestry.com:accessed 9/28/2019) citing NARA, *Passenger Lists of Vessels Arriving at New Orleans, Louisiana, 1820-1902*; NARA Number: *2824927*; Record Group Title: *Records of the Immigration and Naturalization Service*; Record Group Number *85*. Arrival of Jacques Foy, Image 245, Line 13.

[657] 1840 United States Federal Census, Orleans Parish, Louisiana, Marguerite Aubri household, digital image, *Ancestry.com* (https://www.ancestry.com accessed 4/11/2019), citing NARA microfilm publication M704, Roll 134 p. 188. No date of enumeration. Image 201/245.

[658] Letter from Florville Foy to his father dated 9 September 1840, Prosper Foy Papers, LaRC- 443, Tulane University Special Collections, Howard-Tilton Memorial Library, Tulane University. (Courtesy of Lori Schexnayder, Assistant University Archivist.)

Letter from Rosa Foy to Prosper Foy dated 29 November 1844, Prosper Foy Papers, LaRC-443, Tulane University Special Collections, Howard-Tilton Memorial Library, Tulane University. (Courtesy of Lori Schexnayder, Assistant University Archivist.)

While we know that Prosper had paid to educate his son, Florville, before he sent him off to France to complete his studies, it is also clear from the above letter that he and Zélie had tended to the education of their surviving daughters as well.

There was another problem causing turmoil in the household in 1840. Zélie may have suspected that Prosper had had another child with a woman named Julia Moore. Two letters from Julia seeking his continued attention and patronage dated 9 June 1840 and 14 September 1840 have been preserved in the Prosper Foy Papers. The first, in very formal English, and not in the same hand as the second letter cited below, reads in small part:

> Well sir, if you have the leist [sic] sparks of that attractive flame which seemed to glow for your now disponding Julia, I am truly grieved, sir at your treatment. [...] for a person who has made such ardent professions of love would have take [sic] the privileges of wounding a heart[...] excuse me for expressing myself in such manner, but I hope you consider me worthy of coming and explain [sic] me the cause of your absence.[659]

---

[659] Letter from Julia Moore to Prosper Foy dated 9 June 1840, Prosper Foy Papers, LaRC-443, Tulane University Special Collections, Howard-Tilton Memorial Library, Tulane University. (Courtesy of Lori Schexnayder, Assistant University Archivist.)

The second letter, dated only 14 September, with no year, but perhaps 1840 implied, which seems to be in the hand of Julia herself (She signs "Julli Moere") is in very badly spelled French. In it she turns down an invitation that Prosper extended to her to join him at his plantation because the "saison des maladies," that is, the yellow fever season, was very advanced. If she were alone, she would be happy to come but not with her numerous family members. She hopes that autumn will bring him back to her. She ends by writing: "Veuillez me donné [*sic*] de vos aimables nouvelles. Elles me sont toujours agréable [*sic*]. Agréez mes amitiés bien sincere (*sic*)." (Please give me news of you. It is always agreeable to me. Please be assured of my sincere friendship.)[660] Efforts to find a trace of Julia Moore other than the two above-mentioned letters came to very little. There is no conclusive evidence that the "Julie" who was working for Zélie, and who was sent away with her child, mentioned in Florville's letter to his father sent in September 1840 is the same "Julia Moore who was corresponding with Prosper. There was, however, a certain "Julie Maure, f.c.l." who was enumerated in the 1840 Federal Census for the Third Municipality, First District, New Orleans, living with four free colored children under ten years of age, three free colored people between ten and twenty-four years, and seven other free colored adults, a numerous family indeed, if this be the same person.[661]

Although Florville Foy was on his own at the marble works, he did, occasionally correspond with his father for help and advice. In a 5 July 1841 letter to Prosper, who was at his plantation in St. James Parish, he wrote:

Comme voilà les approches de la Toussaint je me prépare d'avance à finir mes ouvrages qui sont déjà commandés pour ne pas être ahuri au dernier moment. Il m'a été donné aujourd'hui une inscription par un jeune homme pour le marbre sepulchral (*sic*) de son père, Monsieur Jean Joseph Sondé, et comme il me paie bien pour la lui graver sur un beau marbre noir, je vous l'envoie dans cette lettre pour que vous me la corigiez (*sic*), afin que je puisse la graver dans les règles de l'orthographe, n'oubliez pas les lettres capitales surtout. Je serais bien aise si vous pouviez me la renvoyer le plus vite possible, par la poste.

Nous nous portons toujours très bien. Maman et Rosa vous disent bien des choses. Moi, je vous souhaite une bonne santé et du courage pour pouvoir surmonter les revers que Mr. Joseph Aguillard vous a fait éprouver.

(Now that All Saints approaches, I am preparing in advance to finish my commissions that have already been ordered, so as not to be swamped at the last minute. I just received another order today from a young man for the funerary marble of his father, Mr. Jean Joseph Sondé, and as he is paying me well to engrave a fine black marble slab, I am sending it [the inscription] to you in this letter so that you may correct it before I inscribe it using the correct spelling, do not forget the capital letters, especially. I would be very glad if you could send it back to me as quickly as possible through the mail.

We are all fine. Mama and Rosa send you their best. I wish you good health and the courage to overcome the business woes that Mr. Joseph Aguillard has made you endure.)

A copy of the letter may be seen on the next page. It was penned in French in Florville's firm hand, showing his lovely ornate signature similar to his fathers since it was probably Prosper who had taught him how to write in furtherance of a career in marble sculpting that the elder Foy hoped he would follow:

---

[660] Letter from Julia Moore to Prosper Foy dated 14 September 1840? (le 14 7bre), Prosper Foy Papers, LaRC-443, Tulane University Special Collections, Howard-Tilton Memorial Library, Tulane University. (Courtesy of Lori Schexnayder, Assistant University Archivist.)

[661] 1840 United States Federal Census, Orleans Parish, Louisiana, Julie "Maure" household, digital image, *Ancestry.com* (https://www.ancestry.com accessed 11/14/2019), citing NARA microfilm publication M704, Roll 134 p. 194. No date of enumeration. Image 213/245.

Letter from Florville Foy to Prosper Foy dated 5 July 1841, Prosper Foy Papers, LaRC-443, Tulane University Special Collections, Howard-Tilton Memorial Library, Tulane University. (Courtesy of Lori Schexnayder, Assistant University Archivist.)

Like his father, Florville Foy took an active interest in the real estate market in New Orleans. As his marble carving business grew, he sought an appropriate property in New Orleans to expand. On 10 January 1848 he went before the notary Achille Chiapella, the father of his aunt Eglée Aubry's three sons, to purchase from Henry Raphael Denis a plot of ground in the square bounded by Rampart, Conti, Basin and St. Louis Streets designated as number 3 of Islet #12. The lot of ground had a French measure of 34 feet front on Rampart Street, with the same front on Basin Street by 120 feet deep bounded on one side by the property of François Goubault, and on the other side by the Obituary Chapel,[662] together with all the buildings and improvements for $3000 cash in hand.[663] That Florville would have that much ready money is a tribute to his business acumen. Besides his commission work for individuals, he had been employed between 1836 until May 1837 by the St. Louis Cathedral church wardens to construct eighty-four wall vaults in St. Louis Cemeteries #1 and #2 at $35 per vault.[664] He also manufactured many other items. A 3 November 1848 advertisement in the New Orleans *Daily Picayune* read:

> ITALIAN MARBLES. FLORVILLE FOY. MARBLE CUTTER, CARVER and GILDER. Rampart Street, near the Obituary Church,[665] Respectfully informs his friends and the public in general that he has just received from Genoa, per the Sardinian bark *Silenzio*, a full cargo of superior ITALIAN MARBLE, of the first quality and different colors and dimensions – such as large Blocks of every size, superb pieces, long and wide, of one, two and three inches thick, fit for tables, chimneys, mantels, etc. Also, Marble Squares for engraving in mosaic style, and an assortment of beautiful Statuary Marble; finally, 50 elegant and well-made Funeral Vases, adapted for the Mausoleums. Moreover, 50 barrels of light POMICE STONES, of Mount Vesuvius, the best of the kind, etc.[666]

The *New Orleans Annual and Commercial Register of 1846* had listings for three of the Aubry sisters. Miss Azélie Aubry was living at #16 Love Street, Félicité Aubry was at 36 Moreau Street, and Mercelite Aubry at #143 Rampart St. Florville Foy's address was 105 Rampart Street. His occupation was given as "marble sculptor."[667]

Florville Foy met Louisa Frances Whitaker, said to have been born in Natchez, Adams Co., MS, ca. 1825, sometime before 1850. They lived together in New Orleans for most of their lives. According to the 1850 Federal Census, Florville Foy, a twenty-five-year-old "mulatto" marble cutter with $5,000 in real estate was living with Louisa Whitaker, a twenty-five-year-old white female in Ward #2, First Municipality, New Orleans.[668] They had two male black slaves: one aged twenty years, and the other aged five years,

Florville's father was enumerated at his St. James Parish plantation in 1850, living with his thirty-three-year-old overseer, Drauzin Clouâtre and eleven slaves, including six males and five females, of whom two were under ten years of age.[669] Florville's sister, Marie Josephe Sophie Foy was living with Jean Louis Rigaud, and their racially-mixed children: Octave Joseph, born about 1840, Marie Laure, born about 1841 and Marie Althée, born on 19 August 1846.[670] Louis Rigaud was enumerated in the 1850 United States Federal census as a forty-five-year-old white male tax collector with $2500 in real estate, living with M.J. Foy, a twenty-seven-year-old "mulatto" female with $500 in real estate. Only two children were recorded with couple in that year: Octave, age 10 years and Laura,

---

[662] The mortuary chapel of St. Anthony, at the corner of North Rampart and Conti was dedicated in 1827.

[663] NARC, "Plot of Ground. H.R. Denis to Florville Foy," dated 10 January 1848, passed by Notary Achille Chiapella, Volume 14, Act #10, Courtesy Hon. Chelsey Richard Napoleon, Clerk of Civil District Court, Parish of Orleans.

[664] Patricia Brady, "Free Men of Color as Tomb Builders," in Glen R. Conrad, ed., *Cross, Crozier and Crucible: A Volume Celebrating the Bicentennial of a Catholic Diocese in Louisiana.* (New Orleans, LA: The Roman Catholic Church of the Archdiocese of New Orleans, 1993), 483.

[665] The mortuary chapel of St. Anthony.

[666] "ITALIAN MARBLES," The New Orleans *Daily Picayune*, 3 November 1848, digital image, *Newspapers.com* (https://www.newspapers.com: accessed 3/32020), p. 3, col. 4.

[667] E.A. Michel & Co., *New Orleans Annual and Commercial Register*, 45, 261.

[668] 1850 United States Federal Census, Orleans Parish, Louisiana, Municipality 1, Ward 2, Dwelling #1456, Family #1466, Florville Foy household, digital image, *Ancestry.com* (https://www.ancestry.com accessed 10/14/2019), citing NARA microfilm publication M432_235, p. 81B. Date of enumeration: 3 September 1850. Image 73/79.

[669] 1850 United States Federal Census, St. James Parish, Eastern District, Louisiana, Dwelling #4, Family #4, Prosper Foy household, digital image, *Ancestry.com* (https://www.ancestry.com accessed 10/14/2019), citing NARA microfilm publication M432_239, p. 206A. Date of enumeration: 29 July 1850. Image 1/81.

[670] "New Orleans, Louisiana, Birth Records Index, 1790-1899," [database on-line], *Ancestry.com* (https://www.ancestry.com: accessed 1/15/2020), citing *New Orleans, Louisiana Birth Records Index, 1790-1899.* Birth of Marie Althé Rigaud (Colored), Vol. 6, p. 692. Note: She died on 12 November 1869, presumably without issue. See: "New Orleans, Louisiana Death Records Index, 1804-1876," [database on-line] *Ancestry.com.* (https://www.ancestry.com: accessed January 2020), Death of Marie Alté Rigaud, Vol 46, p. 297.

age 9 years.[671] According to this census and the subsequent one taken in 1860, Louis Rigaud was said to have been born in Cuba. We believe he was the elder brother of Louis Honoré Rigaud baptized at St. Louis Cathedral: "Rigaud, Honoré Louis (Louis Pierre, native of Jérémie on Santo Domingo, and Marie Louise Destouches, native of L'Artibonite, dependency of St. Marc, also on Santo Domingo), b. Feb. 25 1819, bn. July 7, 1817 s. Honoré Deblieur and Marie Charlotte Jaunay, Widow De Santo, all residents of this parish (SLC, B31, 54)." His parents, like many of the residents of Saint-Domingue, had fled to Cuba, where they stayed for several years, having at least two children while there, until, being expelled from the island in 1809 as a result of the Peninsular War between France and Spain, came to New Orleans. The first Louisiana record for Louis Pierre Rigaud and Marie Louise Destouches appeared in a baptismal entry for their daughter Marie Victoire Françoise born on 4 October 1811 and baptized on 17 November 1811 at St. Louis Cathedral. (SLC, B22, 162). A marriage record for their daughter Marie Caroline Rigaud to Ursin Bruno Jaquet on 26 August 1826 indicated that the bride had been born at Santiago de Cuba as well. (SLC, M7, 88) When Louis Pierre Rigaud's last child, Émile was born on 11 May 1827, and baptized on 26 February 1828, the godfather was the child's brother, Jean Louis Émile Rigaud (SLC B38, 116). Finally, when Marie Françoise Victoire Rigaud married Aimé Willoz in New Orleans on 5 January 1830, her full name "Marie Françoise Victoire Althée Rigaud" was used (SLC, M7, 181). Althée was the unusual name given by Louis Rigaud and Sophie Foy to their daughter born in 1846. Jean Louis Rigaud's father Pierre Louis Rigaud died on 29 October 1831, and was interred the next day (SLC F15, 275). It was Louis Rigaud, Sophie Foy's companion, who reported the 1854 death of Prosper Foy to the Civil Recorder. The record reads in part:

> Be it remembered, that on this day, to wit: the seventh of February in the year of our Lord one thousand eight hundred and fifty four and the seventy-eighth of the Independence of the United States of America, before me, N. Trépagnier duly commissioned, and sworn RECORDER OF BIRTHS AND DEATHS, in and for the parish and City of Orleans, personally appeared Mr. Louis Rigaud residing in Love Street between Union and Frenchmen Streets, Third District of this city, who by these presents declares that Prosper Foy, a native of France, aged about sixty-five years, departed this life on the morning of February 7, 1854 at eight o'clock in a house situated on Love Street, between Esplanade and Mysterious[672] Streets in the aforementioned District of the city. Deponent further declares that the deceased was not married:

---

[671] 1850 United States Federal Census, Orleans Parish, Louisiana, Municipality 3, Ward 1, Dwelling #1020, Family #1166, Louis Rigaud household, digital image, *Ancestry.com* (https://www.ancestry.com accessed 10/14/2019), citing NARA microfilm publication M432_238, p. 57B. Date of enumeration: 31 July 1850. Image 73/79.

[672] While there is a "Mystery" Street in New Orleans near the Fairgrounds, there never was a "Mysterious" Street. We believe that the recorder misunderstood Louis Rigaud, who probably said, or meant to say "History" Street. The correct address, between Esplanade and History Street, was given in Foy's succession record.

On the day of Prosper's death, Dominique François Boulin petitioned the court to become administrator of his estate, alleging that Foy had died intestate, had no forced heirs, and if any other heirs did exist that they lived in a foreign country. Elina Foy filed a notice on 18 February 1854 claiming that she was the only one of Foy's children to have been recognized legally by him both on her baptismal certificate as well as in a notarial act before Narcisse Broutin dated 24 September 1816 at which time he had made a donation of property to his two natural daughters.(See pp.292-295) She concluded that, therefore, the succession was not vacant, that she was the only legitimate heir and should be appointed the administrator of her father's estate. Elina soon withdrew her objection. On 21 February 1854, Florville Foy and Dominique François Boulin went before the notary Achille Chiapella to ask to be appointed administrators of the estate of Prosper Foy and to have an inventory made of his property. The three men went to the house of Marguerite Elina Felicité Foy, Prosper's daughter, on Love Street, between Esplanade and History[673] Streets where Prosper had died. They were accompanied by Pierre M. Bertin, who represented the "absent heirs" in France. Foy's personal belongings were valued at 61 piastres including clothing, some silverware, a gold watch, and one lot of old books, as well as cash in the amount of $1100. in the Bank of Louisiana. Foy's personal papers consisted of records of slave sales, titles to the plantations in St. Charles and St. James parishes, unpaid notes, protested notes, and various contracts, acts and mortgages in favor of the deceased, as well as his commission papers as adjutant, with the rank of First Lieutenant in the Orleans Battalion. Inventory was also taken at the St. James Parish plantation which consisted of personal effect, many books, horses, mares, cattle, bulls, creole horses, mules and sows, a rice mill, marble squares, chickens, several carriages and the following slaves : Abraham (60), Sam (65), Peter (70), Louis (65), Pierre (80), George (65), Grace (65), Mathilde (45) and her children Marie (9), and Millie (7), and Josephine (15). The plantation was worth $4,500, with the totality

[673] History Street is now Kerlerec St.

of movables and immovables at St. James, being worth 7,322.50 piastres. Prosper's overseer, Drauzin Clouâtre claimed 900 piastres in salary for three years work.[674] An auction of the decedent's personal possessions, animals and slaves was held at his St. James plantation on 15 May 1854 which netted 3483.54 piastres. Louisa Whittaker attended in order to bid for the things that Florville wanted from his father's estate. She was awarded: 42 lots of books (82.35)[675], one miniature boat (0.35), one bureau (1.00), 99 prints (2.25) 4 oil paintings (0.50), one lot of paper (4.75), one lot of marble fruit (1.50), one cotton hat (0.25), one world globe (.50), 2 chickens (0.25), one young cow (18.50), one cow and calf (41.00), one sow (1.25), one lot of atlases (6.00), and the slave Abraham, aged 60 years (450.) The entire succession was valued at 9,134.65 piastres (1100 cash on hand, 51.50 for furniture sold at New Orleans, 3483.15 proceeds from St. James Parish auction, 4500 for St. James Parish plantation). Expenses to settle the estate were 2348.10 piastres, leaving 6,786.55 piastres. As one of the two administrators of the estate, Florville was entitled to one half of 2.5% of 8487.50, or one-half of 212.09. He was also reimbursed 150 piastres for the tomb, 5 piastres to open the tomb, 5 piastres for refreshments provided the day of the inventory at New Orleans, 60 piastres for three trips to St. James Parish, and 25 piastres to buy clothes for the slaves.

After the news of Foy's demise was sent abroad, Foy's relatives provided over 150 pages of genealogical information concerning their worthiness to divide up his estate, which was filed with the 2nd District Court in December 1854. Given that Foy's parents had both died in 1841, and that all his siblings had predeceased him,[676] the spoils were left to nine French relatives of the deceased, a decision which was only finalized on 12 February 1856. Zélie Aubry made one last claim on the estate which did not show up in the final tableau. She wrote that for many years the decedent had occupied a room furnished by her in her house which he used for eight months out of the year, after which he would return to his estate in the country. He also took his board at her table, and she did his washing and ironing. He had promised to pay her but never did. For that reason, she presented the estate with a bill for 1020 piastres which included four years of food and laundry for eight months each year at 15 piastres per month (480) plus four years rent for the furnished room at 15 piastres per month, made available to Foy during the entire year (540). This bill to the estate was signed with no objection by Florville Foy on 3 July 1854.[677] After a lifetime of work in Louisiana, and with four living natural children left behind, the proceeds of Prosper Foy's estate were shipped off to France to be enjoyed by relatives he had probably never met. Moreover, after a lifetime of loyalty to Prosper, we wonder if Zélie ever saw the money she had asked for in room and board from her former companion, at least there is no record of it. And yet, until the end of her life she referred to herself as "the widow Prosper Foy."

---

[674] "Inventories of Estates, F Surnames, Faurie, 1854 - Foressier, 1855," *Louisiana Wills and Probate Records,1756-1984*, database with images, *Ancestry.com* (www.ancestry.com: accessed 3/15/2020), Inventory of the estate of Prosper Foy dated 13 March 1854, Images 147-161/250.

[675] All prices were quoted in "piastres." One piastre = one dollar.

[676] Foy's brother Jacques died before 1854 in America. Foy's sister Marie Rosalie died on 22 July 1833 at Bordeaux, Gironde France, as did another brother Jean-Baptiste Pascal Foy on 21 July 1826. Foy's father Jacques Adrien had died on 27 December 1841 at Orleans, Loiret, France, and his mother Marie Jeanne Maisonneuve died on 10 January 1841 at Bordeaux.

[677] "Louisiana Wills and Probate Records,1756-1984," database with images, *Ancestry.com* (https://www.ancestry.com: accessed 3/16/2020), Probate of the estate of Joseph (*sic*, Prosper) Foy dated 7 February 1854, Case # 7355, Images 485-668/1365.

CHAPTER 21

PROSPER FLORVILLE FOY

In order to expand his business, Florville Foy went before the notary Adolphe Boudousquié on 31 May 1856 to purchase property from Gabriel Jacques Goubeau, a resident of Paris, who had inherited it from François Goubeau. The latter had worked as an investment broker in New Orleans until his death on 27 September 1855. The property was located in the Second District in a square bounded by Rampart, St. Louis, Basin and Conti Streets, designated as Lot #4 in Square #12 measuring 34 ft on each of Rampart and Basin Streets by 120 feet deep together with the buildings and improvements. He also acquired twenty-nine shares at $100 each of the capital stock of the Citizens Bank of Louisiana, which said shares were secured by the land he had just purchased. Foy paid $3150 cash in hand for the land and stock.[678]

Towards the end of the 1850s, with his reputation as a tomb builder and sculptor growing, Florville Foy indebted himself to buy two more pieces of property in March 1859, both to enlarge his marble works, and to indulge his love for animal husbandry. On 3 March 1859 before the notary Eusèbe Bouny (recorded on 24 March 1859) he purchased 28 lots of ground from the City of New Orleans deriving from the estate of the late John McDonogh in the Second District, bounded by Broad, St. Philippe, Dumaine and White Streets, for $5400. He paid one-fifth, or $1080 in cash, and presented twenty promissory notes at 6% interest, endorsed by himself, payable to the Citizen's Bank at intervals of one, two, three, and four years. It was at this property on White and Dumaine that he established his farm where he bred horses, cows, goats, and hogs that he imported from far and wide.[679] As late as 1892, he was advertising for sale "Berkshire and Poland China Pigs and Angora Goats. Florville Foy, 83 North Rampart Street."[680]

On 7 April 1859 Florville Foy went before the notary Selim Magner to legalize a purchase of land he had made at an auction held by Charles E. Forstall in the city of New Orleans on the same day for $9,100. The real estate was situated in the Second District in the square bounded by Conti, Rampart, St. Louis and Burgundy Streets. Said lot formed the corner of Conti and Rampart, with 63 ft. 11 in. 5 lines on Conti by 127 ft. 10 in. 5 lines deep and front on Rampart Street. The buildings sold included a large house built of brick between posts, a frame building in the yard with three rooms, a gallery and closets, another building of three rooms, and water works. It was stipulated that all the other improvements belonged to the lessee or tenant of said premises and were not included in the sale. The property Foy bought had been owned by Constance Virginia Fleitas, the widow of Louis Aimée Pigneguy, who had since remarried to Louis Auguste Alfred Bourdeley and was currently living in Paris. Foy gave $2275 in ready money and the balance in two promissory notes for $3412.50 each with 6% interest, payable in one and two years at the Louisiana State Bank.[681]

On 13 May 1859 Florville Foy was granted permission by the City of New Orleans to construct a railroad from property he owned in the Third District to the wharf fronting the same in order to transport marble:

---

[678] NARC, "Sale of Property and stock by G.J. Goubeau to Florville Foy," dated 31 May 1856, passed by Notary Adolphe Boudousquie, Vol. 10a, Act #157, Folio 310 r. Courtesy Hon. Chelsey Richard Napoleon, Clerk of Civil District Court, Parish of Orleans.

[679] NARC, "Sale of Property – City of New Orleans (Jno. McDonogh's est.) to F. Foy," dated 24 March 1859, passed by Notary Eusèbe Bouny, Conveyance Office Book #76, Folio 567. Courtesy Hon. Chelsey Richard Napoleon, Clerk of Civil District Court, Parish of Orleans.

[680] "For Sale," The (New Orleans Louisiana) *Daily Picayune,* 15 June 1892, digital image, *Genealogybank.com* (https://www.genealogybank.com: accessed 2 April 2020) p. 5, col. 6.

[681] NARC, "Sale of Property – Mrs. Bourdeley to F. Foy," dated 7 April 1859, passed by Notary Selim Magner, Vol. 6, Act #91. Courtesy Hon. Chelsey Richard Napoleon, Clerk of Civil District Court, Parish of Orleans.

[No. 4572.]

Resolved, That permission be and the same is hereby given to Florville Foy to make a railroad, at his own expense and under the supervision of the City Surveyor, from four lots owned by him in the Third District, situate at the corner of Bartholomew and Levee streets to the wharf fronting the same, in order to land marble, provided the lessees of said section of the wharves give consent thereto per notarial act. Said railroad to remain during the pleasure of the Common Council.

[Signed] CHAS. H. WALDO,
President Board of Assistant Aldermen.
[Signed] J. O. NIXON,
President Board of Aldermen.

Approved May 13, 1859.
my14   [Signed]   GERARD STITH, Mayor.

The above notice was attached to a notarial record passed before Eusèbe Bouny, official notary of the city of New Orleans, on 31 May 1859, at which time Henry Hope Stanley, assignee of Thomas A. Stone, deceased, lessee of the sixth section of the wharves of New Orleans, granted Foy permission to build his railroad from the wharf to his lots situated at the corner of Barthélemy and Levee Streets. Permission was granted on the condition that if Foy's operation caused any damage to either the levee or the wharf that he would have it repaired at his own expense.[682]

Although neither Florville Foy nor Louisa Whitaker appeared in the 1860 Federal Census, Florville did take out a full-page ad in the 1861 *Gardner's New Orleans Directory* just as the Civil War was breaking out. "Florville Foy, Marble Cutter and Sculptor. No. 81 (Late 83) Rampart Street, New Orleans. Tombs. Monuments. Tomb Slabs. Grave Stones and Marble Work of all descriptions executed and made to order. Grave Yard Work of All Kinds Done."[683] Burial services, especially in times of war, never lacked for business. We did not find any record of military service for Florville, either in Confederate or in Union files.

On 5 November 1864, Florville Foy attended another auction where he acquired more real estate on Conti Street. The plot of ground in question was sold pursuant to a judgment of the Second District Court in October of the same year directing the sale at auction of the land in order to settle a family dispute between Jean Alexandre Wale vs. Marie Angèle Wale, wife of Honoré Couvertier. The property in question was on the northeast side of Conti Street consisting of a frontage of 30 feet facing Conti by 120 feet deep with all the buildings and improvements. Foy was the highest bidder at 3750 piastres. He and Marie Angèle Wale appeared before the notary Onesiphore Drouet on 12 November 1864 to consummate the deal at which time Foy made the all-cash purchase.[684]

As New Orleans grew in population after the Civil War, so did Foy's clientele. The New Orleans *Times Democrat* published a long article praising the opening of "Zimmerman's elegant stores" on #94 and #96 Canal Street, in time for the Christmas season of 1865, which praised their beautifully appointed main floor. The solid white Carrera marble countertops had been supplied by Florville Foy for this high-end jewelry emporium.[685]

Beginning in the late 1860s Foy employed as many as nine workers, including some former slaves who worked for him for the next four decades at his large marble yard, showroom and dwelling house which stretched from Conti to Basin Street, located near Saint Louis Cemetery #1. The number of people who appeared in his household at the time of the 1870 Federal Census is a vivid illustration of the wealth of his marble establishment with its workshops and dwellings. Florville and Louisa Foy, ages 50 and 45 respectively employed the Jean-Baptiste Oscar family, all mulattos, as servants: Jean-Baptiste (48), Rosalie (35), Jules (17), Julia (15) and John (7). In

[682] NARC, "Consent by H.H. Stanley in fav. of F. Foy," dated 31 May 1859, passed by Notary Eusèbe Bouny, Volume 4, Act #125. Courtesy Hon. Chelsey Richard Napoleon, Clerk of Civil District Court, Parish of Orleans.

[683] "U.S. City Directories, 1822-1995," digital image, *Ancestry.com* (https://www.ancestry.com: accessed 11/24/ 2019), citing *1861 Gardner's New Orleans Directory*, p. 8., Entry for Florville Foy, sculptor, Image 320/340.

[684] NARC, "Vente de Propriété par M.A. Wale, femme de H. Couvertier à F. Foy," dated 12 November 1864, passed by Notary Onesiphore Drouet, Volume 22, Act #233. Courtesy Hon. Chelsey Richard Napoleon, Clerk of Civil District Court, Parish of Orleans.

[685] "How in the Name of Thrift Does He Rake This Together," The New Orleans, Louisiana *Times Democrat*, 3 December 1865, digital image, *Newspapers.com* (https://www.newspapers.com: accessed 10 March 2020), p. 7, col. 4.

addition, the following white artisans and other workers lived on the property and were counted in the household: J.F. Johnson (34), marble cutter; E. Ferare (45), midwife from France; Artes Silvain (50) servant; Edouard Degase (30) laborer from France; Jennie Forrest (35) housekeeper from Ireland; Jack Black (40) no occupation; H. Hart (75) from Hamburg; and L. Flory (22), hats and caps dealer from France. Both Florville and Louisia were also enumerated as white in this census.[686] On the other hand, Florville's mother, Zélie Aubry who appeared in the 1870 *New Orleans City Directory* as "Zelia Foy, widow, Prosper, living at 333 Villere St.," was enumerated shortly before her death on 13 July 1870 as '"Vve, Zélie Foy (the widow Zélie Foy), aged about 70 years, a "mulatto," born in Louisiana.[687] A month later, she was gone. Her death was reported by L. P. Quézergue who stated that: "Zélie Aubry, widow of P. Foy, a native of New Orleans aged 78 years died on the 24th instant (August 24, 1870) at the corner of Villeré and Kerlerec streets in this city. Cause of Death: Marasmes[688]. Cert. Dr Roudanez."

Courtesy of State of Louisiana, Secretary of State, Division of Archives, Records Management, and History. *Vital Records Indices*. Baton Rouge, LA, USA citing *Orleans Death Indices 1804-1876*; Vol. 48, p. 381.

After Zélie's death, Marie Eglée was the only one of Marguerite Cécile Aubry's children left alive.

---

[686] 1870 United States Federal Census, New Orleans, Orleans Parish, LA, Ward 4, Dwelling #94, Family #94, Floville (*sic*) Foy household, digital image, *Ancestry.com* (https://www.ancestry.com: accessed 10/2/2019), citing NARA microfilm publication M593_521, p. 830A. Date of enumeration: 5 June 1870, Image 201/342. Note: The first three people listed at this "dwelling" were John Angelo, a fruit dealer from Austria, his wife, Domenica, and their servant, Mary Slavich who were probably renting one of the number of dwellings on Foy's property.

[687] 1870 United States Federal Census, New Orleans, Orleans Parish, LA, Ward 7, Dwelling #815, Family #1183, Vve. Zélie Foy household, digital image, *Ancestry.com* (https://www.ancestry.com: accessed 3/2/2020), citing NARA microfilm publication M593_522, p. 541B. Date of enumeration: 13 July 1870, Image 314/470.

[688] Malnutrition, weight loss due to dehydration, chronic diarrhea.

The 1870s was a tumultuous time for the residents of Louisiana who had endured a fifteen-year Union military occupation until 24 April 1877 when President Rutherford B. Hayes, finally withdrew federal troops from the state as a part of the Compromise of 1877. Divisions between the races had only gotten worse with the 30 July 1866 New Orleans Massacre where over fifty mostly African Americans were bludgeoned to death on the corner of Common and Dryades Street opposite the Mechanics Institute, as well as the subsequent ratification of the 14th and 15th Amendments to the Constitution in 1868 and 1870 respectively. Every election in Louisiana beginning in 1868 through the 1872 Governor's race between John McEnery (D) and William P. Kellogg (R) was rife with violence and corruption as former male slaves and free people of color attempted to exercise their right to vote. One of the worst episodes of violence in Louisiana was the Colfax (Grant Parish) massacre which took place on Easter Sunday 13 April 1873 where over 150 black men were murdered by white Militia members. The first trial of those responsible for the deaths resulted in a hung jury. The second trial of J.W. Cruikshank, William Irwin and John P. Hadnot, and others who were charged with conspiracy and murder, began in May 1874. The *New Orleans Republican* published the news on 19 May 1874 that eight jurymen had been secured: "Their names are as follows, all white: John Mulvey, Alexander McKee, Thomas Kelley, Joseph Dastingue, J.C. Ganns (*sic*, Gantz) , George D. Wright, Charles Barnard, Florville Foy."[689] It is difficult to imagine how Florville Foy, a man of color, designated in both the 1870 Federal Census, as "white" as well as being publicly named as one of the "white" jurors on a panel tasked with a judgment in such a racially charged case might have navigated the deliberations and the subsequent fallout of the jury's verdict. On 17 June 1874, Cruikshank, Irwin and Hadnot were found guilty of conspiracy and murder while five others were acquitted. When the jury was polled, each man declared it was a unanimous decision. It was reported that two jurors had held out until the last minute, but had finally capitulated late in the evening of the 17th when the verdict was finally read.[690] However, the presiding Judge, Joseph Bradley, dismissed the convictions on his own authority, ruling that the prosecution failed to prove a racial component to the massacre, and that the men had acted on their own accord and were not acting as part of a governmental body, thereby making their convictions void under the Enforcement Act of 1870. The men were released on bail, with other charges pending for the murder of William Williams, another African American killed in the massacre. The defendants promptly disappeared, and no one was ultimately punished.

Life, however, went on as usual. Reconstruction and the financial crises of the 1870s took its toll on Foy's business. However, he had bought so much property, the majority of which he rented out that he was never in any real financial danger. Florville and Louisa Whitaker bought, sold and traded real estate as independent investors, using as little or as much capital as they had to expand one another's enterprises. Occasional transfers between the two parties were made in order to pay off or extend existing mortgages. In August 1877, Florville transferred four lots to Louisa: the first two in the square bounded by Customhouse, Prieur, Roman and Bienville, the third lot in the square bounded by Customhouse, Bienville, Marais and Villeré, and the last lot bounded by Bartholomew, Levee and Moreau Streets, in consideration for $6,000.[691] Three years later it was reported in the *New Orleans Item* that Mrs. Louisa Whitaker had sold back to Florville Foy two lots and buildings on Customhouse, between Roman and Prieur, and one portion of ground and buildings, forming the corner of Levee and Bartholomew for $4,900.[692]

Florville Foy was a member of a sixteen-man grand jury which served during the first half of 1878. In addition to trying 273 cases, they were tasked with visiting all the hospitals, police stations, jails, city and court archives, orphanages, and homes for the elderly in the city in order to make a written report of their condition. The document was published in the New Orleans *Daily Picayune* in July. The jurors had high praise for many of the Catholic, Protestant and Jewish-run orphanages and homes for the aged. They were less enthusiastic about the conditions in the various police stations, the city "insane asylum" which warranted a special report, and the conditions at the

---

[689] "The Grant Parish Prisoners," *The New Orleans Republican,* 19 May 1874, digital image, *Genealogybank.com* (https://www.genealogybank.com: accessed 2 April 2020) p. 2, col. 5. Note: Subsequently four other jurors were added: Jacob Wolf, E.S. Carey, Sidney Bruny, and John R. Shields.

[690] "The Verdict," *The* (Alexandria Louisiana) *Caucasian,* 20 June 1874, digital image, *Genealogybank.com* (https://www.genealogybank.com: accessed 2 April 2020) p. 1, cols. 4, 5.

[691] "Transfers of Property," *The New Orleans Item,* 18 August 1877, digital image, *Genealogybank.com* (https://www.genealogybank.com: accessed 2 April 2020) p. 4, col. 1.

[692] "Transfers of Real Estate," *The New Orleans Item,* 20 October 1880, digital image, *Genealogybank.com* (https://www.genealogybank.com: accessed 2 April 2020) p. 4, col. 4.

Superior Criminal Court where they noted that jurors were forced to leave the building and use outdoor facilities on Royal street in view of the public, due to the lack of water closets and washrooms inside the building.[693]

On 18 October 1880 Florville Foy purchased from James F. Johnson, who worked for him for years as a marble cutter, two lots of ground with the buildings, improvements, with all the rights, ways, and servitudes for $2800. It was situated in the Third District in the square bounded by Villeré, Robertson Kerlerec and Columbus Streets designated by # 1 and #2, fronting thirty feet on Villeré Street with a depth and front on Kerlerec Street of 117 feet, 10 inches and 5 lines, forming the corner of Villeré and Kerlerec Streets where Zélie Aubry had died in 1870. It was the same property that Johnson had bought from Florville Foy on 22 March 1878.[694] Johnson was not the only longtime employee that worked for Florville. His former slave, Jules, who was probably the same person as Jules "Oscar," enumerated as one of his servants in the 1870 Federal Census, worked for him until his death, acting as his caretaker and running his business.

Florville, as a well-to-do business man and real estate owner in the city, was never spoken of in anything but respectful terms. His racially-mixed ancestry was all but ignored, even during the difficult times of Reconstruction, and afterwards, during the racial unrest of the late nineteenth century. Moreover, before the Civil War, when free people of color were supposed to use the letters f.m.c. or f.w.c, (free man of color or free woman of color) after their names in all legal documents, these letters never appeared after his name. Several newspaper articles which appeared in the 1880s illustrate his standing in the community. On 16 January 1882 he was elected with seven other men as one of the directors of the Carondelet Canal and Navigation Company.[695] On another note, a short article which appeared in the 10 October 1883 edition of the *Daily Picayune* read in part: "Mr. Florville Foy and several friends were on a bird hunt last winter having with them two red Irish setters. The setters scented some game and started in pursuit. [...]When the hunters came in sight of the setters again, they were guarding a tree. [...] At the top was a fox. [...] Mr. Foy shot the animal, and was quite proud of the exploits of his canines."[696]

After having lived together for over thirty-five years, Florville married Louisa Whittaker on 5 March 1885 before the Honorable J.R. Rozier, Judge of the First City Court. Florville's parents were listed as Prosper Foy and "Zellie Aubry," while Louisa's were given as Francis Whittaker and Federica Bruning. The marriage was performed in front of the notary James Fahey, who had drawn up their marriage contract, Michel V. Ryan, J. F. Johnson, the manager of Foy's marble works, and J. T. Fitzgerald.[697] The couple's marriage contract had specified that they were "separate in property" in order to protect one another's assets, and to facilitate any transfers of property from one to the other.

Florville did not content himself with just carving monuments. He also purchased cemetery plots and built brick tombs on speculation in the local cemeteries, some in conjunction with the renowned New Orleans architect Jacques Nicolas Bussière de Pouilly. He also expanded his business to the Gulf Coast, doing work for the old Biloxi Cemetery, and for St. Michael's Catholic Cemetery in Pensacola, FL. He was especially known for his floral bouquets as well as ivy carved in stone which decorate many local tombs. Of course, tombs and funerary objects were only a portion of Foy's repertoire. He carved marble mantels, table tops, stair treads, and retail store counters. One of his most ambitions works, however, was commissioned by the Association of Louisiana Veterans in 1887. The organization financed the importation and execution of a large monument to the Louisiana Confederate soldiers

---

[693] "Among the Institutions. An Exhaustive Report of the Grand Jury," *The* (New Orleans LA) *Daily Picayune,* 31 July 1878, digital image, *Genealogybank.com* (https://www.genealogybank.com: accessed 4/2/2020) p. 2, cols. 1-5.

[694] NARC, "Sale of Property James F. Johnson to Florville Foy," dated 18 October 1880, passed by Notary James Fahey, Volume 20a, Act #275. Courtesy Hon. Chelsey Richard Napoleon, Clerk of Civil District Court, Parish of Orleans.

[695] "Special Notices," (The New Orleans*) Times-Democrat*, 9 February 1882, digital image, *Newspapers.com* (https://www.newspapers.com: accessed 6/5/2019), p. 9, col. 2. Note: Foy was one of the major users of the Carondelet Canal through which he received his shipments of marble from Italy.

[696] "Fox Hunting," *New Orleans Daily Picayune*, 10 October 1883, digital image, *Newspapers.com* (https://www.newspapers.com: accessed 6/5/2019), p. 4, col. 4.

[697] "Louisiana Parish Marriages, 1837-1957," database with images, *FamilySearch.org* (https://familysearch.org/ark:/61903/1:1:QKJW-PGB1 : accessed 4/4/2020), Florville Foy and Louisa Whittaker, 05 Mar 1885; citing "Orleans, Louisiana, United States, various parish courthouses, Louisiana," FHL microfilm 907,698.

who died in the Civil War during the Battle of Vicksburg, which was to be erected in that Mississippi city. Florville Foy was selected to do the work. The *Vicksburg Evening Post* dated 1 June 1887 ran the following item:

> A reporter of the *States* yesterday visited the workshops of Mr. Florville Foy, on Rampart street between Conti and St. Louis Streets to see the monument that is to be unveiled in Vicksburg, Miss., on the 11th of next month and which is being erected to the memory of the Louisiana soldiers who died while defending that now historic city.
>
> The Monument when up will be twenty feet high; the base is a solid granite block eighteen inches in depth and cut octagonal in shape, being five feet in diameter. On this granite block will stand the rest of the monument, which is of the finest Italian marble. The first section of it is a solid block of marble two and a half feet in diameter and four feet high, cut in pyramidal form with the corners rounded and a shield elegantly carved on each of the four faces. On these shields are being engraved the inscriptions formulated by the committee, and which have already been published in the *States*.
>
> On top of this marble block will stand another of beautiful shape and purity and on it an urn about three feet high and eighteen inches in diameter, and from the top of which clouds of incense are represented as rising.[698]

From the Photo Collection of the Old Courthouse Museum, Vicksburg, MS.

---

[698] "The Vicksburg Monument," *The Vicksburg Evening Post*, 1 June 1887, digital image, *Newspapers.com* (https://www.newspapers.com: accessed March 2020), p. 2, col. 2.

The photographer, J. Mack Moore, who took the shot of the monument shown on the previous page, had a studio in Vicksburg from the late 1800s into the early 1940s. According to Jordan Rushing, Historian with the Vicksburg and Warren County Historical Society, the photo would have had to be taken in the very early 1900s based on the street still being unpaved. Below is a detail from the monument showing one of the four shields that Florville carved with the Louisiana pelican mother feeding her young with her blood, along with the state motto "Union, Justice and Confidence."

From the Photo Collection of the Old Courthouse Museum, Vicksburg, MS.

The various news items which were published following the ceremony to dedicate the monument did not mention Florville Foy, nor did he seem to have been on the guest list of those who attended the ceremony. There was one participant, however, from the extended Aubry family, George Antoine Chiapella, the son of Achille Chiapella and Louise Pollock.

On 9 July 1892 Elina Marguerite Félicité Foy called the notary Michel Victorin Dejan to her residence at #334 North Rampart Street, between Kerlerec and Esplanade Streets, to dictate her last will and testament. She had no "forced" heirs, but left $800 piastres to several acquaintances, and $250 piastres apiece to her surviving sisters, Sophie Foy Rigaud and Rosa Foy Edmunds. The rest of her estate she left to her two grandchildren, Josephine and Gilbert Léonard, the surviving children of her deceased daughter Marie Anais Bouligny. She appointed Prosper Florville Foy to be her executor to serve without furnishing any monetary guarantees. Elina Foy died on 2 August 1892 at her home on North Rampart Street at the age of eighty-two years. The cause of death was said to be gastroenteritis:

Although we were unable to discover the identity of Marie Anaïs Bouligny's father, we know from census records that she was born ca. 1842. She and Patrice V. Léonard (born ca. 1822 in Louisiana), had four children: Mary, born on 1 April 1858, Patrice, born on 29 June 1861, Josephine Victoire, born on 3 March 1862, and John Gilbert born on 17 June 1863.[699] The family was enumerated in the 1870 Federal Census for Plaquemines Parish, where Patrice, aged 48 years, a "mulatto," was employed as the Sheriff with $3000 in real estate and $1000 in personal estate. Anais, a "mulatto" aged 38 years, was keeping house. Three children were living with them: Patrice, Jr., age 9 years, Josephine, age 8 years, and Gilbert, age 6 years.[700] The family moved to New Orleans in the 1880s, residing on Ursulines Street, where Patrice Leonard served as a United States Commissioner in 1887. Marie Anaïs Bouligny, his wife, died on 8 May 1888, at 334 North Rampart Street in New Orleans. The cause of death was "hypertrophy

---

[699] "New Orleans, Louisiana, Birth Records Index, 1790-1915," [database on-line], *Ancestry.com* (https://www.ancestry.com: accessed 5/29/2019), citing *New Orleans, Louisiana Birth Records Index, 1790-1899*. Birth of Mary Leonard, Vol. 48, p. 501; Birth of Patrick Leonard, Vol. 30, p. 384; Birth of Victoire Leonard, Vol. 30 p. 385; Birth of John Leonard, Vol. 30, p. 385.

[700] 1870 United States Federal Census, Plaquemines, Louisiana, LA, Dwelling #1533, Family #1586, Patrice V. Léonard household, digital image, *Ancestry.com* (https://www.ancestry.com: accessed 3/22/2020), citing NARA microfilm publication M593_526, p. 244A. Date of enumeration: 20 July 1870, Image 181/265.

of heart.[701] Patrice Leonard followed soon after on 8 November of the same year from meningitis. Both Patrice and his wife were said to have been "colored."[702]

An auction of the two properties belonging to Elina Marguerite Félicité Foy was advertised in the New Orleans *Daily Picayune* dated 12 October 1892. The first was #338 North Rampart Street between Esplanade and Kerlerec occupied by George D. Geddes, Funeral Director on a five-year lease from 1 April 1892. The lot measured 33 feet 3 inches 3.5 lines facing on North Rampart by 127 feet 10 inches and four lines in depth on which there were large buildings with stables. The second property was #334 North Rampart Street between Kerlerec and Esplanade Streets, measuring 32 feet front on North Rampart by 127 feet 10 inches and four lines in depth and included a raised cottage, brick between posts, with side hall, three rooms, a one-story kitchen with two rooms, a garden with peach and fig trees, a cistern and closets.[703]

Detail on the tombstone of the Cahier Family. The carving of the lamb was executed ca. 1895 by Florville Foy, Covington Cemetery #1, Covington, St. Tammany Parish, LA. Author's photograph taken 5/5/2020.

---

[701] "Orleans Death Indices,1877-1895" [database on-line], *Ancestry.com* (https://www.ancestry.com: accessed 3/3/ 2019), citing *New Orleans, Louisiana Death Records Index, 1804-1949.* Death of Mrs. Patrice Leonard, Vol. 93, p. 101.

[702] "Orleans Death Indices,1877-1895" [database on-line], *Ancestry.com* (http://www.ancestry.com: accessed 30 December 2019), citing *New Orleans, Louisiana Death Records Index, 1804-1949.* Death of Patrice Leonard, Vol. 94, p. 125.

[703] "By Spear and Escoffier," The New Orleans *Daily Picayune*, 12 October 1892, digital image, *Newspapers.com* (http://www.newspapers.com: accessed 30 October 2019), p. 10, col. 3.

Florville continued his business, with the assistance of Jules, and the other artisans in his workshop, until just before his death in March 1903. Apparently, no job was either too large or too small, for the marble works which was always a beehive of activity. In one of the final documents we have found bearing his signature, Florville signed off on a $7.00 inscription to add the name and dates of birth and death for Marie Henriette Reyes, the wife of Auguste Julien Domingon to the marble slab belonging to the family. Domingon was his first cousin, the son of his aunt, Félicité Aubry. (See also pp. 258, 259):

CHAPTER 22

ROSE EUPHÉMIE FOY and EDGARD AMBROISE EDMUNDS

Florville's last living sibling, his little sister, Rose Euphémie Foy died on 21 October 1897 in New Orleans. She was described as "Mrs. Widow Edgar Edmunds, born Rose E. Foy (colored), a native of this city, aged 68 years and 3 months departed this life yesterday (21 October 1897) at 1480 North Claiborne Street. Cause of death: chronic gastro enteritis, certified by Dr. J. M. Elliot"[704] Her husband, Edgard Ambroise Edmunds had died just six months previously. According to his death certificate, "Edgar Edmunds (colored), a native of New Orleans, aged 72 years died on 14 April 1897 at the corner of Claiborne and Columbus Streets from cardiac hypertrophy and chronic nephritis."[705]

Edmunds had left his wife a sizeable estate worth $33,761.62, and what is more remarkable, no debts to pay other than a few physicians' bills during his last illness, as well as his funeral expenses. He left about $5000 in real estate, as well as shares in various insurance companies worth almost $10,000, cash on deposit with his employer the Joseph Bowling Company, Ltd. worth $15,696.98, and about $900 deposited in the New Orleans National Bank[706]. His total estate in today's dollars was worth just over $1,023,000.

The couple had been enumerated for the first time in the 1850 Federal Census as Edgard Edmonds, a twenty-six-year-old white male working as a clerk, and Rosa Edmonds, a nineteen-year-old white female. Edmunds worked as a clerk and then a salesman for a series of wholesale dry goods importers. On 16 April 1856 he applied for a passport to go abroad for business. In an accompanying affidavit he declared that he had been born in New Orleans, that he was thirty-two-years old, 5ft. 11 in. (English), with a high forehead, aquiline nose, dark brown eyes, an ordinary mouth and chin, an oval face, a dark complexion, and dark brown hair (bald). He was seeking the passport to travel to Europe for business. Attesting to the veracity of the affidavit was Richard H. Yale. The passport was to be sent to Cyrus Yale, Jr. in care of Cameron & Edwards, a wholesale dry goods firm located at #161 Broadway in New York City. On the back of the passport (#12367), which was issued by the Department of State on 25 April 1856, were stamps in both 1856 and 1857 attesting to Edgard Edmonds's travels between New York, London and Paris. The last stamp was issued on 11 August 1857 at Le Havre, France, for passage on the *North Star* to New York.[707] A check of that ship's manifest confirmed that E. Edmunds, age 31 from U.S.A. was a passenger on that ship which docked in New York on 25 August 1857.[708] Over the course of his career Edmunds worked for a number of New Orleans Importing firms including Frank & Haas, and Yale & Bowling.

Two of the couple's children, Edgar Joseph Edmunds and Arnold Joseph Edmunds were born before his European travels. Edgar Joseph was born on 26 January 1851 in New Orleans. However, his civil birth record is dated 20 May 1868. By registering his son after the Civil War, Edmunds was able to give him a birth record devoid of any mention of a racial component. Severin Latorre, the recorder of births and deaths for the city of New Orleans, and two witnesses Joseph Numa Liautaud and Azénor Sindos, all three men of color would be instrumental in issuing many of these certificates where any mention of race was omitted (See also p. 205):

---

[704] Courtesy of State of Louisiana, Secretary of State, Division of Archives, Records Management, and History. *Vital Records Indices*. Baton Rouge, LA, USA, citing *Orleans Death Indices 1894-1907*; Death of Mrs. Widow Edgar Edmunds, Vol. 114, p. 1109.

[705] "Orleans Death Indices,1894-1907" [database on-line], *Ancestry.com* (https://www.ancestry.com: accessed 3/11/ 2019), citing *New Orleans, Louisiana Death Records Index, 1804-1949*. Death of Edgar Edmunds, Vol. 113, p. 605.

[706] Louisiana, Wills and Probate Records, 1756-1984," digital images, *Ancestry.com* (https://www.ancestry.com: accessed 5/1/2020), citing Louisiana District and Probate Courts, Civil District Court Case Papers, No. 53348, Edgar Edmunds, Probate date 4 May 1897., Images 1632-1665/1924.

[707] "U.S. Passport Applications, 1795-1925," digital images, *Ancestry.com* (https://www.ancestry.com: accessed 3/20/ 2019) citing *Selected Passports*. National Archives, Washington, D.C., Roll 054, 1 March 1856-28 April 1856, Images 1136-9 of 1223. See also original passport Roll #070 dated 3 May 1858-22 May 1858, Images 803-4/965.

[708] "New York, Passenger and Crew Lists (including Castle Garden and Ellis Island), 1820-1957," digital images, *Ancestry.com* (https://www.ancestry.com: accessed 3/23/2020) citing *New York, New York*; Microfilm Serial: *M237, 1820-1897*; Microfilm Roll 178; Line: 1; List Number: *1018.* (Image 25/567).

Be it Remembered, That on this day to wit: the Twentieth of May in the year of our Lord One Thousand Eight Hundred and Sixty Eight and the ninety Second of the Independence of the United States of America, before me, S. LATORRE, duly commissioned and sworn RECORDER OF BIRTHS AND DEATHS, in and for the Parish and City of Orleans, personally appeared: Edgar Edmunds, a native of New Orleans, residing at No. 353 Claiborne Street (Third District in this City) who hereby declares that on the twenty-Sixth of January Eighteen Hundred and Fifty-One (26th of January 1851) at Seven o'clock A. M. on Orleans Street, between Claiborne & Robertson Streets in this city, was born a male child named — Edgar Joseph Edmunds — Issue of his legitimate marriage with Miss Rose Euphémie Foy, a native of N. Orleans.

Thus done at New Orleans, in the presence of the aforesaid Edgar Edmunds, as also in that of Messrs. A. Sindos & F. A. Cautain both of this City, witnesses by me requested so to be, who have hereunto set their hands together with me, after due reading hereof, the day, month and year first above written.

E. Edmunds

A. Sindos

Recorder.

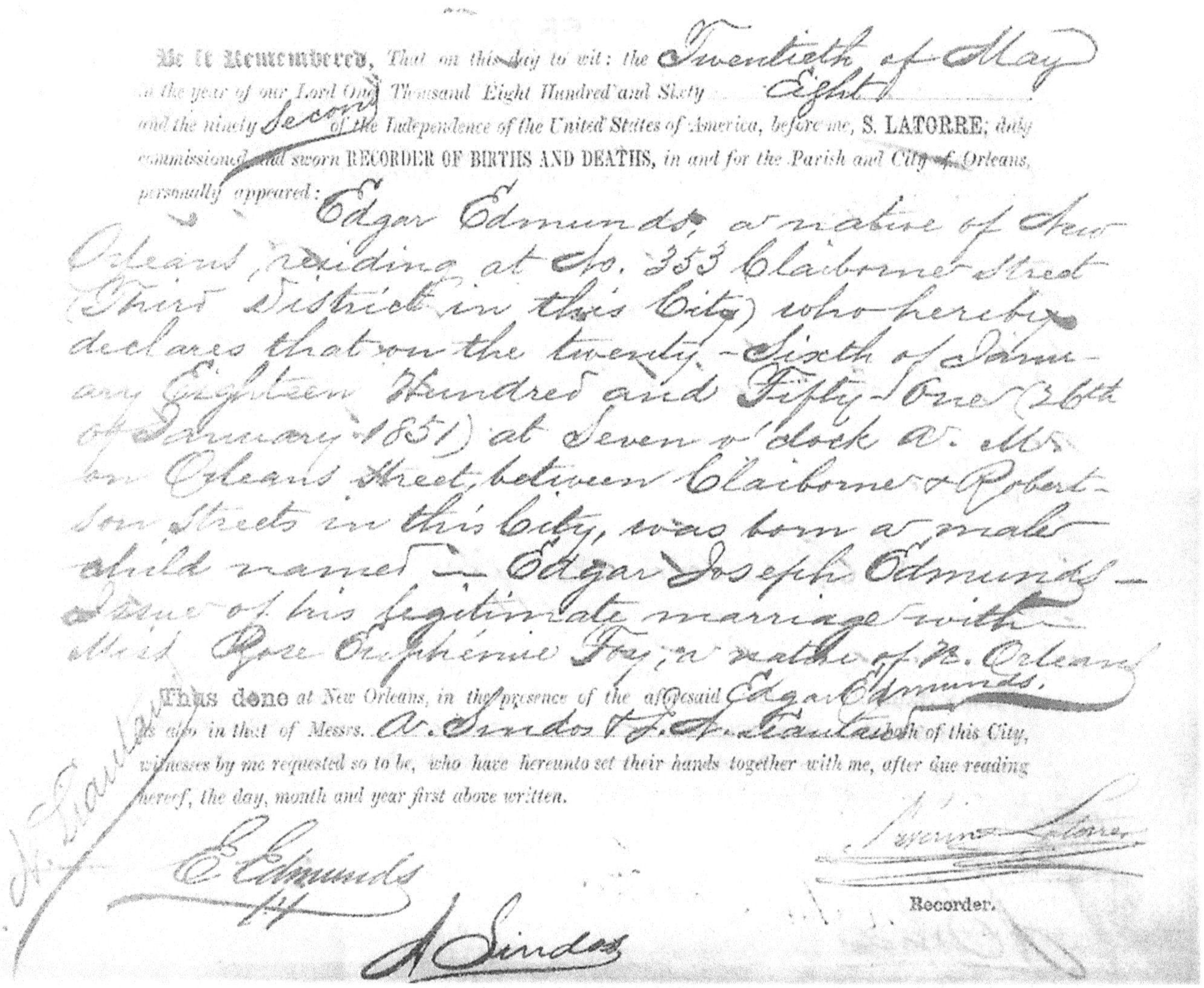

Courtesy of State of Louisiana, Secretary of State, Division of Archives, Records Management, and History. *Vital Records Indices*. Baton Rouge, LA, USA, from New Orleans, Louisiana Birth Records Index 1790-1899; Vol. 47, p. 433.

Edgar Edmunds was a mathematical prodigy whose father probably had found tutors who were capable of teaching the mathematical theory which was not widely available in Louisiana schools of the time.[709] As a free person of color, before, during and even after the Civil War, he would not have been allowed to attend schools for white children, a struggle his sister Olivia would endure in 1868. However, his birth record, seen above, did not give a hint of his mixed-race heritage. We know from newspaper accounts in 1870 and 1871 that he attended the Fillmore School, a boy's public school on Bagatelle (now Pauger) Street between Morales(now Marais) and Good Children (St. Claude) Streets.[710] He was sent to France at the conclusion of the Franco-Prussian War by his parents, took the entrance examination to prestigious École Polytechnique, and was admitted as a student in September 1871. The exam consisted of questions on analytic geometry, logarithms, French composition, Latin, German, and architectural drawing, as well as oral exams in physics and chemistry. He placed 135 out of 140, at the bottom of the entrance class.

---

[709] For further information please see an exhaustive work on Edgar Joseph Edmonds, his life and struggles as a light-skinned Afro-Creole professor of mathematics in 19th Century New Orleans, by Sian Zelbo, published in the *History of Education Quarterly*, Volume 59, Issue 3 (pp 379-406). Zelbo's doctoral dissertation intitled "Edgar Joseph Edmunds (1851-1887), Mathematics Teacher at the Center of New Orleans' Post-Civil War Fight Over School Integration" (PhD diss., Columbia University, 2020), is available here: https://academiccommons.columbia.edu/doi/10.7916/d8-v5c8-e409.

[710] "Our Public Schools," *The* (New Orleans) *Daily Picayune*, 23 June 1870 and 23 June 1871, digital images, *Genealogybank.com* (https://www.genealogybank.com: accessed 4/4/2020), p. 2, cols. 2, 3. in 1870, and p. 2, cols.2-4 in 1871.

Matriculation card. École Polytechnique - Left column: Student number 10447. Examined at Paris. Score 135, Registered on 4 November (4 9bre). Signature. Received uniform and some equipment. To the right, below his name, place of birth and parents' names, his physical description was given: hair and eyebrows - dark brown, high forehead, large nose, brown eyes, large mouth, dimpled chin, long face, height: 1m 79 (about 5ft. 9 in.). His father was a merchant in New Orleans. He passed from the 1st Division in 1872 as #125 out of 144 students. He was admitted to the Artillery service in 1873 as #37 out of 52 students.

Edgard Joseph Edmunds at the École Polytechnique. Close-up cropped from a class photo 1871-72. Courtesy ©Collections École polytechnique (Palaiseau, France).

Inquiries made via email at the Center for Historical Resources of the École Polytechnique turned up interesting information concerning his stay in France. In an answer to our questions, it was explained that Americans were not admitted to matriculate at the school, but, infrequently, had been allowed to audit classes. At the time, however, Edgar was considered to be French because one parent, his mother, Rosa Foy, was French. Her father, Prosper Foy, a French citizen, was never naturalized, and his daughter, although born in Louisiana, was French as well because as a free woman of color, her American citizenship came only with the passage of the 14th amendment in 1868, well after the birth of her first child. We were also told that he was not the first person of color to have been admitted to the school. François August Perinon, a native of the island of Guadeloupe, had been admitted in 1832.[711] Further information revealed that after the first semester he was ranked 119 out of 146, and in the second 134 out of 145. As he went into his second year, ranking 125 out of 144, he was chosen with fifty-two other students, amongst them, Ferdinand Foch, to join the Artillery School (l'école d'application de l'artillerie et du génie) which had just been moved from Fontainebleau to Metz because of the Franco-Prussian War. He entered there in January 1873 and received a four-month crash course in the second-year curriculum of the École Polytechnique. Yearbooks indicate that from there, he went to Paris where he stayed with the Lazarists, a religious order, before returning to the United States. He gave the address of Georges Alcès, a Creole cigar manufacturer in New Orleans, as his contact for the Polytechnic Institute's Alumni Association.[712]

After his return to Louisiana he taught mathematics at the Sumner Boys' School for African American children and was appointed as its principal for a few months until the close of the Spring term in 1875, before being asked to join the all-white Boys' Central Highschool in September of the same year. This appointment, backed by African American members of the School Board including P.B.S. Pinchback, caused a firestorm of protests which were reported in all the New Orleans newspapers. Some of the boys staged a walk-out the first day of classes. As polemics in the press became more heated, someone stepped forth to state that Edmunds had to be lying about his diploma from the École Polytechnique, because only French citizens could attend the school. Edmunds invited him to his house to see the diploma. His enemies claimed that it had to be fraudulent. Despite constant attacks in the newspapers Edmunds stuck it out at Central Boys Highschool for several years until Reconstruction ended in 1877 and the democrats took back control of the Louisiana legislature.

It was during this mounting controversy that Edgar Edmonds was married to Charlotte Rosa Morant on 15 November 1876 by the Rev. Joseph Subileau of St. Augustine's Roman Catholic Church. The bride's parents were Charles Morant, who attended the wedding and Catherine Rosa Callico.[713] Edgar's siblings, Olivia and Arnold Edmunds, were also in attendance.[714] Four children were born to the couple. We could find no civil birth records for their first two children, Marguerite Marie born ca. July 1877, and Rose Marie, born ca. Aug. 1878. Their third child, Blanche Marie Edmunds was born on 16 September 1879 and their only son Francis Edgar (Frank) Edmunds was born on 12 February 1881. Both records for the children indicated that they were "colored," although they were never enumerated in any subsequent federal census as being anything but "white." Both Blanche and Frank's births were registered by their mother, Rosa Morant Edmunds on 29 April 1893, six years after her husband's death.[715]

Once segregation began to take hold, Edgar Edmonds was moved in the fall of 1877 to Academy #4, also known as the Colored Highschool, where he was appointed principal in November. That same year he also became assistant-principal and professor of mathematics at the newly formed Colored Normal Institute which was organized to train African American teachers to work in the newly segregated schools. His ill health and funding cuts for these schools were instrumental in his leaving both endeavors. In March 1880 Edmunds announced that he would be starting to teach from his home:

---

[711] Email dated 17 January 2019 from Olivier Azzola, Archivist, Centre des Ressources Historiques, École Polytechnique, Palaiseau, France, to Daniel Vernhettes, fowarded to the author.

[712] Bibliothèque centrale–École Polytechnique (See http://bibli-aleph.polytechnique.fr/F/?func=find-b&request= EDMUNDS+ Edgard+Joseph+1871& find_code=WPE&adjacent=N&local_base=BCXC2).

[713] Although Charles Morant, a sugar broker, and his wife, Catherine Rosa Callico, were enumerated as white in the 1860, 1870 and 1880 Federal Census records for New Orleans, Charles was listed as "white" on his 21 September 1889 death record, yet Catherine Rosa Callico was listed as "colored" on her 2 November 1893 death certificate.

[714] "Louisiana Parish Marriages, 1837-1957," digital images, *FamilySearch.org* (https://familysearch.org/ark:/61903/1:1:QKJW-VKNY : accessed 4/4/2020), Edgard J Edmunds and Charlotte Rosa Morant, 15 Nov 1876; citing Orleans, Louisiana, United States, various parish courthouses, Louisiana; FHL microfilm 907,693.

[715] "New Orleans, Louisiana, Birth Records Index, 1790-1915," [database on-line], *Ancestry.com* (https://www.ancestry.com: accessed 30 March 2020), citing *New Orleans, Louisiana Birth Records Index, 1790-1899*. Birth of Blanche Edmunds, Vol. 97, p. 629; Birth of Frank Edmunds, Vol. 97, p. 629.

Prof. E.J. Edmonds informs his friends and the public that on the first day of March (Monday next) he will open at his residence 347 ½ North Villeré street, 7th ward, 3rd district, an evening school where all grades will be taught. French and Mathematics a specialty. He can be seen every day at his residence from 5 p.m. to 9 p.m. Terms moderate. Classes from 7 p.m. to 9.p.m. Only a limited number taken.[716]

From a mathematical problem that Professor Edmunds submitted to *The Analyst – A Journal of Pure and Applied Mathematics*, Volume 8 (p. 199) which was published in September 1880, it appears that he had temporarily relocated to Paris, France, probably to seek medical attention amongst other things.[717] The apartment was just two blocks off the Boulevard Saint-Michel near the renowned Sorbonne University. "Problem #329. By E.J. Edmunds, Professeur de Français, d'Anglais et de Mathématiques, 11, rue Toullier, Paris. – Three points A, B, C, being given, to find a point M, whose distance from A, B, and C, shall be a minimum." Since he had been enumerated with his family living on North Villeré Street in New Orleans on 23 June 1880, and had advertised his private school at that address in March of the same year, it would seem that his sojourn in Europe, had probably occurred at some time in late 1880.

A newspaper article dated 21 October 1880, recorded the deliberations concerning the opening of an institution of higher learning for African American students to be housed in a building on Calliope Street between St. Charles and Camp that had been built as a "Hebrew" Girls' School. Called the Southern University, Professor E.J. Edmunds was proposed as its first president, but lost the vote to Dr. Alfred Richard. Gourrier. Edmunds was unanimously elected as the chair of the mathematics department, but was recorded as "absent in France" during the deliberations.[718] The first classes were held in March 1881. A newspaper from that year indicated that Professor Edmunds was paid $400 on 24 September 1881 "under four orders" as professor of mathematics at Southern University.[719]

During the intervening years between 1881 and Edmunds's death in 1887, there were few mentions of him in the local papers. An embarrassing personal incident, however, was described in an article dated 8 April 1881. Edmunds's wife, Charlotte had left him several months before and had moved back with her parents taking the children with her. On 5 April 1881 Edmunds had attempted to see his wife, but her parents had prevented him from entering their Robertson Street home. A physical altercation had erupted in the street and the professor was accused of striking her parents. Arrested for disturbing the peace, he spent the night in jail. Going before Judge Miltenberger, presiding over the Second Recorder's Court the next morning, he was released because the Judge felt that a husband seeking to see his wife could not be considered a disturbance of the peace. On 7 April his in-laws, the Morants, pressed charges against him for assault and battery and insult and abuse. He was rearrested but made bond.[720] Like many of these incidents we could not find any disposition of this case in the press. We did find that his wife, Charlotte Rose Morant, had sat for a competitive examination to become a teacher in the public schools and was awarded a position in September 1881.[721] It is likely that he and his wife had never reconciled. When he died on 2 July 1887, an obituary which appeared in the *Daily Picayune* the next day made no mention of his wife and children:

> EDMUNDS – On Saturday, July 2, 1887 at 1:30 o'clock a.m., Prof. E.J. Edmunds, aged 38 years, a native of New Orleans. Friends and acquaintances of the family are invited to his funeral, which will take place This (Sunday) Morning at 10: o'clock, from his father's residence, 354 Claiborne street, corner Columbus. New York and Paris, France, papers please copy.[722]

---

[716] *The Weekly Louisianian*, 3 April 1880, digital image, *Newspapers.com* (https://www.newspapers.com: accessed 3/20/2020), p. 3, col. 2.

[717] The Analyst is available on-line at www.google.com/books.

[718] "The Colored State University," The (New Orleans, LA) *Daily Picayune*, 21 October 1880, digital image, *Newspapers.com* (https://www.newspapers.com: accessed 4/10/2020), p.27, col. 3.

[719] "Official Journal of the First General Assembly of the State of Louisiana – Extra Session," The (New Orleans, LA) *Times-Democrat*, 13 December 1881, digital image, *Newspapers.com* (https://www.newspapers.com: accessed 4/10/ 2020), p. 7, col. 1.

[720] "A Warlike Schoolmaster. How Prof. Edmunds Found His Way into the Calaboose," The (New Orleans, LA) *Daily Picayune*, 1 October 1881, digital image, *Genealogybank.com* (https://www.genealogybank.com: accessed 4/10/2020), p.2, col. 1.

[721] "Competitive Examination. List of the Fortunate Candidates," The (New Orleans, LA) *Daily Picayune*, 1 October 1881, digital image, *Genealogybank.com* (https://www.genealogybank.com: accessed 4/10/2020), p. 2, col. 1.

[722] "Died" The (New Orleans, LA) *Daily Picayune*, 3 July 1887, digital image, *Genealogybank.com* (https://www.genealogybank.com : accessed 4/10/2020), p. 4, col. 4.

Another article in the same day's *Daily Picayune* intitled "Death of a Colored Teacher (p. 11, col.6) ended this way: "Some years ago his mind became deranged, and his latter days were passed in the Louisiana Retreat."[723] Charlotte Rose Edmunds's separation from her husband followed by the 1881 episode of violence against her parents was probably the culmination of her ability to deal with his erratic behavior. His death certificate, seen below, reads in part: "E.J. Edmunds (Colored) a native of Louisiana, aged 36 years, departed this life, this day (2 July 1887) at the Louisiana Retreat, in this city. Cause of death: General paralysis. [...] Deceased was married and a teacher by occupation."

Be it Remembered, That on this day, to wit: the Second of July in the year of our Lord One Thousand Eight Hundred and Eighty Seven and the One Hundred and Eleventh of the Independence of the United States of America before me, JOSEPH HOLT, M. D., President Board of Health and Ex-Officio Recorder of Births, Deaths, and Marriages in and for the Parish of Orleans, personally appeared

C. H. Boucherau, an Undertaker native of this city residing at No 45 St Ann Street who hereby declares, that

E. J. Edmunds (Colored)

a native of Louisiana aged 36 years departed this life, this day (2 July 1887) at the La Retreat, in this city.

Cause of Death General Paralysis

Certificate of Dr. C. T. Shepard

Deceased was Married & a Teacher by occupation

Thus done at New Orleans, in the presence of the aforesaid C. H. Boucherau as also in that of Messrs [illegible] both of this City witnesses, by me requested so to be, who have hereunto set their hands, together with me, after reading hereof, the day, month and year first above written.

President Board of Health and Ex-Officio Recorder.

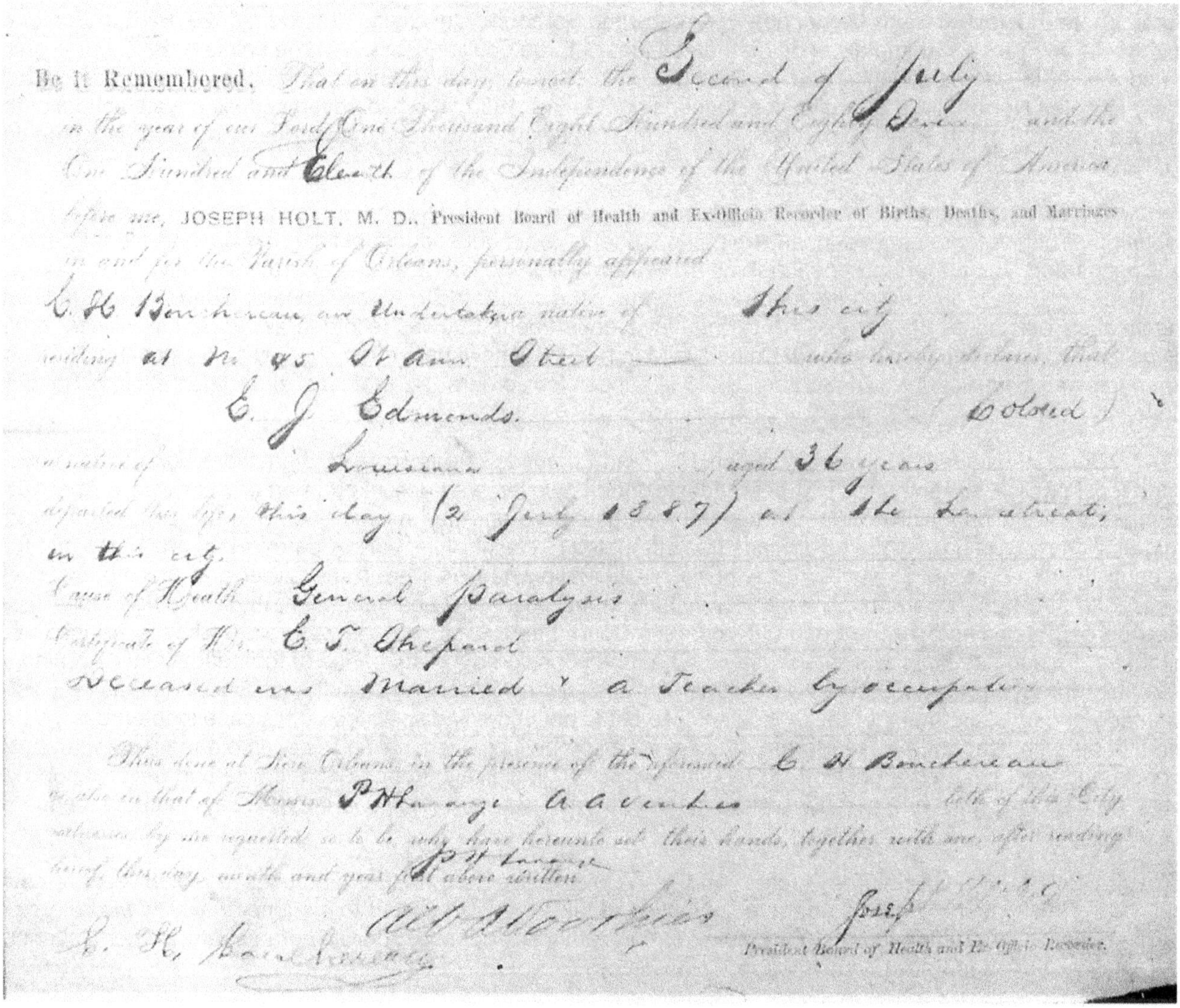

Courtesy of State of Louisiana, Secretary of State, Division of Archives, Records Management, and History. *Vital Records Indices*. Baton Rouge, LA, USA, citing Orleans Death Indices 1877-1895; Vol. 91, p. 509.

None of Edmunds's three daughters ever married. They lived together with their mother, Rose Charlotte Morant, at their Tricou Street home until she died on 27 July 1943. Her son, Frank, reported her death at #535 Tricou Street, from "cardiac valvular disease:" A copy of her death certificate may be seen on the following page.

[723] The Louisiana Retreat Insane Asylum on Nashville Avenue, corner of Magazine Street in New Orleans, which opened in 1864, was run by the Sisters of Charity.

Courtesy of State of Louisiana, Secretary of State, Division of Archives, Records Management, and History. *Vital Records Indices*. Baton Rouge, LA, USA, citing *Orleans Death Indices 1937-1945*; Vol. 219, p. 4565.

Blanche Marie Edmunds died on 26 December 1924. Rose Marie died on 31 March 1958.[724] Edmunds's son Francis Edgar (Frank) married late in life (between 1920-1930) to Bertha Marie Merlin. They had no children. He died on 22 January 1963 at their Tricou Street address, leaving only his wife and sister Marguerite to mourn him. We were not able to find a date of death for Marguerite.[725]

Arnold Joseph Edmunds was born on 11 November 1854 to Edgard Ambroise Edmunds and Rose Euphémie Foy. However, his civil birth record wasn't submitted until 15 February 1873, thereby avoiding the issue of race. He followed in his father's footsteps, working as a clerk and salesman, and later as an accountant for local dry goods firms. He was married to Maria Hermann on 23 August 1881 by the Rev. Joseph Subileau at St. Augustine's Church with his father, and the bride's father Edmond Samuel Hermann, in attendance. The bride's

---

[724]Courtesy of State of Louisiana, Secretary of State, Division of Archives, Records Management, and History. *Vital Records Indices*. Baton Rouge, LA, USA, citing *Louisiana Statewide Death Index, 1819-1964*, Death of Blanche Edmunds, Vol. 189, p. 1573; Death of Rose Mary Edmunds, Vol. 0, p. 2594.

[725]Courtesy of State of Louisiana, Secretary of State, Division of Archives, Records Management, and History. *Vital Records Indices*. Baton Rouge, LA, USA, citing *Louisiana Statewide Death Index, 1819-1964*, Death of Frank Edmunds, Vol. 0, p. 556.

mother was Clemence Evelina Chessé.[726] The bride, Maria Hermann, born on 5 December 1856[727] was the only one of her three other sisters to have a birth record that was not marked "colored." Samuel Hermann, a retail grocer, and his family were, with the exception of the 1870 Federal census, always enumerated as being "white."

Arnold and Marie Hermann Edmunds had three daughters: Marie Lucie, born on 21 June 1882, Marie Berthe, born on 23 August 1884, and Marie Alice, born on 30 July 1887.[728] Each of the girls had their birth records marked "colored." However, neither they nor their parents were ever enumerated as anything but "white" in Federal Census records. Arnold and Marie's daughters never married. They lived together at the family home on 2825 LePage Street. Marie Hermann Edmunds died on 16 January 1904, and Arnold followed on 3 May 1925.[729] According to census records, only Marie Alice ever worked outside the home. She was a stenographer, and later a book keeper for a cotton broker in New Orleans. Alice died on 15 May 1959, followed by Berthe who died the same year on 19 September. Lucie died in New Orleans on 24 February 1962.[730]

Olivia Marie Edmunds, Edgard and Rosa Foy's third child was born just before the Civil War on 6 April 1859. Her first civil birth record was filed on 19 April 1864, wherein it was stated that:

> Be it remembered, that on this day, to wit the nineteenth day of April, in the year of our Lord one thousand eight hundred and sixty-four, and the eighty-eighth of the Independence of the United States of America, before me F. M. Crozat duly commissioned and sworn RECORDER OF BIRTHS AND DEATHS, in and for the Parish and City of Orleans personally appeared: Edgar Edmunds a native of New Orleans, a free man of color residing at the corner of Columbus and Claiborne Streets in this city who by these presents declares that on the sixth day of April eighteen hundred and fifty-nine (April 6, 1859) in this city was born a female child named Olivia Edmunds issue of the lawful marriage of deponent with Euphémie Edmunds a free woman of color a native of New Orleans:

---

[726] "Louisiana Parish Marriages, 1837-1957," digital images, *FamilySearch.org* (https://familysearch.org/ark:/61903/1:1:QKJW-LFPS : accessed 4/3/2020), Arnold Joseph Edmunds and Marie Hermann, 31 Aug 1881; citing Orleans, Louisiana, United States, various parish courthouses, Louisiana; FHL microfilm 907,695.

[727] "New Orleans, Louisiana, Birth Records Index, 1790-1915," [database on-line], *Ancestry.com* (https://www.ancestry.com: accessed 12/30/2019), citing *New Orleans, Louisiana Birth Records Index, 1790-1899*. Birth of Maria Hermann, Vol. 18, p. 678.

[728] "New Orleans, Louisiana, Birth Records Index, 1790-1915," [database on-line], *Ancestry.com* (https://www.ancestry.com: accessed 4/12/2020), citing *New Orleans, Louisiana Birth Records Index, 1790-1899*. Birth of Marie Lucie Edmunds, Vol. 78, p. 946; Birth of Marie Berthe Edmunds, Vol. 81, p. 952; Birth of Marie Alice Edmunds, Vol. 85, p. 557.

[729] Courtesy of State of Louisiana, Secretary of State, Division of Archives, Records Management, and History. *Vital Records Indices*. Baton Rouge, LA, USA, citing *Louisiana Statewide Death Index, 1819-1964*, Death of Marie Hermann, Vol. 131, p. 824; Death of Arnold Joseph Edmunds, Vol. 190, p. 1026.

[730] Courtesy of State of Louisiana, Secretary of State, Division of Archives, Records Management, and History. *Vital Records Indices*. Baton Rouge, LA, USA, citing *Louisiana Statewide Death Index, 1819-1964*, Death of Marie Alice Edmunds, Vol. 0, p. 3337; Death of Marie Berthe Edmunds, Vol. 0, p. 6218; Death of Marie Lucie Edmunds, Vol. 0, p. 1486.

Be it Remembered, THAT on this day to wit: the _____ in the year of our Lord one thousand eight hundred and sixty _____ and the eighty _____ of the Independence of the United States of America, before me, PIERRE LACOSTE, duly commissioned and sworn Recorder of Births and Deaths, in and for the Parish and City of Orleans personally appeared:

THUS DONE at New Orleans in the presence of the aforesaid _____ as also in that of Messrs. _____ both of this city, witnesses by me requested so to be, who have hereunto set their hands together with me after due reading hereof, the day, month and year first above written.

Courtesy of State of Louisiana, Secretary of State, Division of Archives, Records Management, and History. *Vital Records Indices*. Baton Rouge, LA, USA, from New Orleans, Louisiana Birth Records Index 1790-1899; Vol. 30, p. 403.

In April 1868, Olivia Edmunds, then nine-years-old, was attending the Bayou Road Girl's School in Tremé, which was a "white" school. Acting upon a rumor that some "colored" children had been admitted, the Superintendent of Schools, William O. Rogers, asked the Principal, Mrs. S. Bigot to investigate. She reported that at least twenty-eight girls might not be white. Olivia Edmunds was amongst those singled out as being colored, although according to Mrs. Bigot she was admitted upon a certificate of white birth.[731] In the midst of this controversy, Edgard Edmonds had filed another birth record for Olivia dated 26 May 1868, wherein the first sentence removed the designation free man of color from Edgar Edmunds's description and indicated that "Olivia Edmunds [was the] issue of the lawful marriage of deponent with Miss. Rose Euphémie Foy of Louisiana:" There was no longer any mention of her father and mother having been persons of color. This reissuance of a birth certificate, simply marked "second" would not have been possible without the complicity of the recorder, Severin Latorre, and witnesses Azénor Sindos, and Joseph Numa Liautaud, all men of color. These are the same three men who, on 31 March 1868, had issued a birth certificate for Marie Caroline Passebon who had been born twenty years earlier to Pierre Passebon (See p. 205), a French immigrant to New Orleans and his companion Athalie Drouillard, a woman of color. They had also issued the birth certificate for Edgar Joseph Edmunds, born in 1851, with a birth record dated 20 May 1868, where there was no mention of the race of the child or parents (See p. 322):

[731]Mishio Yamanaka, *Erasing The Color Line: The Racial Formation Of Creoles Of Color And The Public School Integration Movement In New Orleans*, 1867-1880 (Thesis submitted to the faculty of the University of North Carolina at Chapel Hill in partial fulfillment of the requirements for the master's degree of History in the Department of History, 2013), 22-24. (Available on-line at: https://cdr.lib.unc.edu/indexablecontent/uuid:b65de853-a74e-4224-9581-45632bb5f922).

Courtesy of State of Louisiana, Secretary of State, Division of Archives, Records Management, and History. *Vital Records Indices*. Baton Rouge, LA, USA, from New Orleans, Louisiana Birth Records Index 1790-1899; Vol. 47, p. 452.

It was later reported in the *New Orleans Republican* that twelve pupils had left the school, nine had furnished satisfactory evidence of being white, six had neglected to furnish any evidence and two had refused to furnish any evidence.[732] Olivia was one of those who had furnished "proof of being white" and had stayed. She was listed amongst those girls to give recitations to the Superintendent of Schools and visiting dignitaries on 22 June 1870. Her presentation was intitled, "Washington's Name."[733] Olivia was included in a list of teachers qualified to instruct in Louisiana Public Schools in May 1874. She was certified to teach the second grade.[734] She never married and lived all her adult life with her brother Arnold and his family. In a will she made in 1919, she appointed Arnold her testamentary executor. After she died on 21 May 1922, she left an estate of just over $8,000 after expenses, including money from the sale of a rental property she had purchased in 1912 at 1729-1731 Terpsichore Street, cash in several banks, the collection of one outstanding mortgage and the liquidation of stock in the New Orleans Brewing Company. The money was left to her two surviving brothers: Arnold and Raoul/Ralph Edmunds, and the six children of her two deceased brothers: Edgar Joseph and Ernest Joseph Edmunds.[735]

---

[732] "Board of School Directors," *New Orleans Republican*, 28 May 1868, digital image, *Genealogybank.com* (https://www.genealogybank.com: accessed 4/2/2020), p. 2, cols. 5-6.

[733] "The School Examination," *New Orleans Republican*, 23 June 1870, digital image, *Genealogybank.com* (https://www.genealogybank.com: accessed 4/2/2020), p. 2, col. 4.

[734] "Teachers," *New Orleans Republican*, 8 May 1874, digital image, *Genealogybank.com* (https://www.genealogybank.com: accessed 4/2/2020), p. 1, col. 5.

[735] "Louisiana, Wills and Probate Records, 1756-1984," digital images, *Ancestry.com* (https://www.ancestry.com: accessed 3/11/2020), citing *Louisiana Civil District Court (Orleans Parish) Case Papers, No 142226-142414, 1922.* Case #142397, Will of Olivia Edmunds, (Images 1482-1578 of 1684). An $8,000 legacy in 1922 would be worth just under $120,000 today.

There is no civil birth record for Edgar and Rosa's fourth child, Ernest Joseph Edmunds, although we know he was born ca. October 1860 in New Orleans. He worked as a clerk in various mercantile concerns and did not marry until he was forty years of age. On 5 March 1900 he took Marie Emma Chiapella, his second cousin, the thirty-three-year old daughter of René Achille Chiapella and Orelia Watkinson, as his wife. They were married by the Rev. Joseph Subileau of St. Augustine's Roman Catholic Church with his sister, Olivia Edmunds, and two acquaintances as witnesses.[736] The newlyweds were enumerated together in the 1900 United States Federal census living in New Orleans on #121 Hennessey Street in the Fourth Ward.[737] They had one son, born prematurely, who lived one hour on 19 October 1900.[738] Ernest and Emma moved almost immediately afterwards to Los Angeles, LA County, CA, to live near her Chiapella cousins, children of her uncle Steven Octave Chiapella and Eulalie Pinta. Ernest and Emma's two children were both born in Los Angeles: Ralph Edgar Edmunds on 18 August 1901[739] and Lucile Marie Edmunds on 16 February 1903,[740] before Ernest died on 22 September 1903. His California death record indicates that he was a forty-four-year-old, white, married male, working as a liquor salesman, who died from pneumonia.[741] Thereafter Marie Emma supported her children by working as a clerk at the Ville de Paris dry goods store in Los Angeles. Marie Emma also took in washing to make ends meet, and by 1920 she was enumerated as a practical nurse working as a midwife's assistant. Her mother-in-law, Aurelia Watkinson, the widow of René Achille Chiapella, came west to help her after Ernest's death, and was enumerated with Emma and her grandchildren, Ralph and Lucille, in the 1910 United States Federal Census, living at # 1036 East 56th Street in Los Angeles.[742]

Ernest and Marie Emma's son Ralph Edgar Edmunds had a brief marriage with Gerda Julina Tranberg, an immigrant from Sweden. They were married in Los Angeles on 30 September 1930[743] and had two daughters: Beatrix Ann (b. 3 July 1931)[744] and Adele Marie (b. 13 May 1935).[745] They were divorced before 1940. Ralph married

[736] "Louisiana Parish Marriages, 1837-1957," digital images, *FamilySearch.org* (https://familysearch.org/ark:/61903/1:1:QKJ4-3FN5 : accessed 4/14/2020), Ernest Edmunds and Emma Chiapella, 05 Mar 1900; citing Orleans, Louisiana, United States, various parish courthouses, Louisiana; FHL microfilm 907,708.

[737] 1900 United States Federal Census, Orleans Parish, Louisiana, Ward 4, Dwelling #83, Family #92, Ernest Edmunds household, digital image, *Ancestry.com* (https://www.ancestry.com accessed 2/2/2020), citing Family History Library microfilm # 1240571. Date of enumeration: 6/7 June 1900. Image 9/18.

[738] "Louisiana, Orleans Parish Death Records and Certificates, 1835-1954", database, *FamilySearch* (https://familysearch.org/ark:/61903/1:1:C183-99N2 : 16 April 2020), Edmunds, 1900.

[739] "U.S. WWII Draft Cards Young Men, 1940-1947," digital image, *Ancestry.com* (https://www.ancestry.com: accessed 4/4/2020), citing, The National Archives in St. Louis, MO, *Records of the Selective Service System, 147, Box 509*, Ralph Edgar Edmunds, Order # T, 11,854.

[740] "California County Birth, Marriage and Death Records, 1849-1980," digital image, *Ancestry.com* (https:www.ancestry.com: accessed 4/5/2020) citing, *California Department of Public Health*, courtesy of www.vitalsearch-worldwide.com., Birth of Edmunds (Female), child of E.J. Edmunds (white) and Mary E. Chiapella (white)

[741] "California, County Birth, Marriage, and Death Records, 1849-1980," [database on-line], *Ancestry.com* (https:www.ancestry.com: accessed 3/2/2020), citing *California County Birth, Marriage and Death records, 1849-1980*, courtesy of www.vitalsearch-worldwide.com, Digital images, *Los Angeles deaths 1903-1905*. Image 44/182, Line 5. Note: The 1903 Los Angeles City Directory listed him as a member of the firm of Edmunds and Redman, owning a saloon at the corner of East 2nd & S. Los Angeles.

[742] 1910 United States Federal Census, Los Angeles, Assembly Dist. 70, Dwelling #418, Family #441, Emma Edmunds (*sic*) household, digital image, *Ancestry.com* (https://www.ancestry.com accessed 2/2/2020), citing NARA microfilm publication T624 -81, page 14b, Family History Library microfilm # 1374094. Date of enumeration: 25 April 1910. Image 28/37.

[743] "California County Birth, Marriage and Death Records, 1849-1980," digital image, *Ancestry.com* (https:www.ancestry.com: accessed 4/5/2020) citing, *California Department of Public Health*, courtesy of www.vitalsearch-worldwide.com., Marriage of Ralph E. Edmunds and Gerda J. Tranberg, Image 473/522.

[744] "California Birth Index, 1905-1995," database, *Ancestry.com* (https://www.ancestry.com: accessed 4/4/2020), citing State of California. California Birth Index, 1905-1995. Sacramento, CA, USA: State of California Department of Health Services, Center for Health Statistics, Birth of Beatrix Ann Edmunds. Note: Beatrix married Robert B. Brownfield ca. 1951, with three children: John (b. 1955), Jack S. (b. 1958) and Adele K. (b. 1961). Beatrix died on 6 Sept 2017 in Solana Beach, San Diego Co., CA (See: http://www.legacy.com/obituaries/ranchosantafereview/obituary.aspx?n=beatrix-edmunds-brownfield&pid=187592688).

[745] Ibid, Birth of Adele Marie Edmunds. Note: Adele Edmunds married Conrad Wade Tambor (b. 1932) in 1955 in Los Angeles with three children: Leann M. (b. 1956), Eric D. (b. 1958) and Patrick W. (b. 1965).

twice more, to Phyllis V. Jones and Margaret Beverly Brandenburg, but had no more children. He died in Fresno, Fresno Co., CA, on 5 September 1983 (SSDI).

Ernest and Emma's daughter, Lucile Marie married Harold D. Thomas in Los Angeles on 7 December 1923.[746] Harold died on 2 July 1924 in Van Nuys, CA, from a burst appendix.[747] Their only child, Millicent Thomas was born on 14 February 1925. Lucile supported her daughter by working as a stenographer. She had a late marriage to Werner Julius Hunziker, an Iowa native. They were wed on 7 June 1941. Lucile Hunziker died on 10 March 1998 and was interred in Forest Lawn Cemetery in Glendale, LA County, CA.[748] Her husband, Werrner Hunziker followed on 9 June 2007 and was interred with her.

Millicent Thomas met Robert Oliver Scow in San Francisco, where she was studying nursing, and he was training to be a physician. They married in September 1948, lived in New York, then in Maryland, where Dr. Scow worked at the National Institutes of Health until retirement. They were the parents of four children, John (b. 1949), Kate (b. 1951), James (b. 1953) and Ann (b. 1957).

Raoul (Ralph) Joseph Edmunds was born at #352 Claiborne Street in New Orleans on 4 September 1869 to Edgard Edmunds and Rose Euphémie Foy. Rosa Foy Edmunds reported the birth to the civil authorities on 16 October 1871. Efforts to trace his life have been without result. We do know that he was mentioned in his mother's 1897 succession as residing in New York, and was one of the beneficiaries of his sister Olivia's estate in 1922.

Edgar and Rosa Foy's last child, René Joseph Edmonds was born on 28 July 1871 also at the Claiborne Street address.[749] His birth was reported to the authorities by his mother on 16 October 1871, the same day that she had reported the birth of his brother Raoul. There was no indication of race on either certificate. René lived only eleven months. He died on 20 June 1872 in New Orleans.[750]

The Edgard Edmonds and Rose Euphémie Foy's line of descendants dwindled in the twentieth century. Three of their sons carried on the Edmunds name to give them nine grandchildren, seven girls and two boys. However, six of the seven granddaughters never married. Only their son, Ernest Joseph Edmunds and his wife Marie Emma Chiapella who moved to California in the early twentieth century had children who had posterity. Arnold and Olivia Edmunds were the recipients of the largest portion of their uncle Prosper Florville Foy's estate when he passed away in 1903.

---

[746] "California County Birth, Marriage and Death Records, 1849-1980," digital image, *Ancestry.com* (https:www.ancestry.com: accessed 4/5/2020) citing, *California Department of Public Health*, courtesy of www.vitalsearch-worldwide.com., Marriage of Lucile M. Edmunds to Harold D. T.Hanse (*sic* Thomas,) Image 126/490, Line 29.

[747] "Obituaries," The *Los Angeles* (CA) *Times*, 4 July 1924, digital image, *Newspapers.com* (https://www.newspapers.com: accessed 10 March 2020), p. 14, col. 8. Note: Cause of death courtesy of Kate Scow.

[748] *Findagrave.com*, database with images (www.findagrave.com; accessed 5/30/ 2020), Memorial # 55982863 for Lucile M. Hunziker.

[749] "New Orleans, Louisiana, Birth Records Index, 1790-1915," [database on-line], *Ancestry.com* (https://www.ancestry.com: accessed 3/30/2020), citing *New Orleans, Louisiana Birth Records Index, 1790-1899*. Birth of René Edmonds (*sic*), Vol. 58 1/2, p. 1224.

[750] "New Orleans, Louisiana Death Records Index, 1804-1949," [database on-line], *Ancestry.com* (http://www.ancestry.com: accessed 3/30/2020), citing *Orleans Death Indices 1804-1876*, Death of René Joseph Edmunds, Vol. 55, p. 21.

CHAPTER 23

PROSPER FLORVILLE FOY AND JULES FOY

During the last years of Florville Foy's life, he relied more and more on his former slave turned employee, Jules, whom he had taught the art of marble carving. We believe that Jules may have been the same person as "Jules Oscar," who was enumerated with Florville and Louisa Whitaker, along with Jean-Baptiste and Rosalie Oscar, his parents and two siblings, John and Julia Oscar. Unfortunately, we were unable to find either Jules Oscar or Jules Foy or any member of his family in the 1880 Federal Census, although Florville, a marble cutter, and Louisa Whitaker had been enumerated that year as Mr. and Mrs. F. Foy, both white, with one eight-year-old male servant in the household named Henry Black.[751]

On 4 November 1897 Florville Foy went before Judge Fred D. King to make out his last will and testament. He left to his wife, Louisa Whittaker, separated from him in property by their marriage contract dated 5 April 1885, $750 on the condition that she not contest his will. He left his estate to his surviving sister Sophie, her children, to Arnold and Olivia Edmunds, and to his trusted assistant, Jules.[752]

As if in retaliation. on 6 December 1898, Mrs. Louisa Foy went to the office of the notary Michel Victorin Dejan to make out her last will and testament. She gave her name, her date and place of birth as Natchez, MS, in 1825, and that she was married to Florville Foy, but was separate in property as per the terms of her marriage contract. She set aside from her estate $1000 in order to buy a plot in Metairie Cemetery, and to have erected a tomb where she should be buried. She left her furniture, clothes, diamonds, and cash to her nieces and nephews, as well as real estate located at #367 Customhouse Street, between Roman and Prieur Streets to her brother Louis F. Whittaker. She left $50 apiece to John, Jules, and Baptiste, three of her husband's employees, as well as $100 to James F. Johnson, manager of the marble works, and $50 to his wife. She appointed her husband, to whom she left nothing, the executor of her estate to serve without bond. After all debts and legacies were paid, she left the residue of her estate to be equally divided between her brother Louis F. Whittaker, and to the children of her deceased brothers Charles and William Whittaker.[753]

Although in 1898 Louisa Foy had named Florville Foy as her husband, she was apparently living separately from him in 1900. In that year's United States Federal Census, she was enumerated as Louisa Foy, born in August 1825 in "Kentucky," divorced, living at 1919 Customhouse Street with her sixteen-year-old nephew Frederick Whittaker in a house she owned.[754] Similarly, Florville who was enumerated in the same census, indicated he was divorced, a white, male, living at #415 North Rampart, age 79 years, born in 1821 (*sic*), the proprietor of a marble works. Living in his household was Jules Foy, his "brother," a black male, born May 1860, age 40 years, married 8 years, his sister-in-law, Clotilde Foy, a black female, born in 1877, married to Jules for 8 years with five children: Viola, Florville's niece, born July 1893, Manuel, his nephew, born May 1894, Antony, his nephew, born April 1895, Pauline, his niece, born in February 1897, and Hilda, his niece, born in 1899. We must point out that the designations of "brother, sister-in-law," etc. were written over something else which had been erased and is now illegible. It is clear that Jules was not Florville's brother. In his last will and testament, Florville had recognized Jules as "his faithful servant, living with me, son of my former servant Charlotte called Rosalie." Information in the 1870 census had identified a "Rosalie Oscar" and son "Jules" living in Florville's household. While we must take him at his word, it is also clear that he apparently allowed Jules to adopt his surname. Moreover, to complicate matters further, when Jules Foy married Clotilde Journée on 17 November 1897 the groom gave his parents' names as Florville Foy and Rosalie Foy. We know with certainty that his mother was "Charlotte called Rosalie," probably the same Rosalie that

---

[751] 1880 United States Federal Census, New Orleans, Orleans Parish, ED. 29, Dwelling #186, Family #248, F. Foy household, digital image, *Ancestry.com* (https://www.ancestry.com: accessed 3/2/2020), citing NARA microfilm publication T9 roll 460, p. 48C, Date of enumeration: 4 June 1880, Image 22/30.

[752] "Orleans Parish Will Books, Vol. 10, 1901-1903," digital image, *Ancestry.com* (https://www.ancestry.com: accessed 2/2/2020), Case #70093, Images 323/705. (Probate date; 19 March 1903).

[753] "Orleans Parish Will Books, Vol. 30, 1901-1903," digital image, *Ancestry.com* (https://www.ancestry.com: accessed 2/2/2020), Case #66503, Images 96,97/832. (Probate date; 18 December 1901).

[754] 1900 United States Federal Census, Orleans Parish, Louisiana, Ward 4, Dwelling #230, Family #279, Louise Foy household, digital image, *Ancestry.com* (https://www.ancestry.com accessed 3/2/2020), citing Family History Library microfilm # 1240571. Date of enumeration: 7 June 1900. Image 25/32.

appeared in the 1870 Federal Census with Florville Foy. Was Florville his birth father, perhaps, or his adopted father? Only DNA testing of his descendants might give us some clarity:

Courtesy of State of Louisiana, Secretary of State, Division of Archives, Records Management, and History, *Vital Records Indices*, Baton Rouge, LA, USA, citing *New Orleans, Louisiana Marriage Records Index 1831-1964*, Vol. 20, p. 214. Marriage of Jules Foy and Clotilde Journée.

In 1897, Florville had just one remaining sibling still alive, his sister Sophie Foy Rigaud. He was already separated from Louisa and in his late seventies, growing more infirm and less able to do the arduous job of marble sculptor. Jules had taken up the challenge of becoming his caretaker and was living in Florville's household with Clotilde and their many children.

Louisa Whittaker Foy died alone at her home at 1919 Customhouse Street on 16 December 1901, the victim of a horrible accident. Old and infirm, she was seated by her fireplace when her clothes caught fire. Neighbors finally heard her screams, but the door was locked, and by the time the door was broken down, she was already dead. The *Times-Democrat* spared no detail, reporting that "Several men made their way to the second room and found the body of the poor old woman. Her clothing had been burned off, her body was almost coal black and her lower limbs had been consumed by the flames." [755] He body was taken to the coroner's office where the cause of death was "burns of entire body." Her death certificate identified her as "Louise Frances Whittaker (white), lawful wife of Florville Foy, a native of Natchez, MS, aged 78 years who died at #1919 Customhouse Street on 16 December 1901:

[755] "Burned to Death," The New Orleans, Louisiana *Times Democrat*, 17 December 1901, digital image, *Newspapers.com* (https://www.newspapers.com: accessed 10 March 2020), p. 8, col. 5.

Be it Remembered, That on this day to-wit: the _Seventeenth_ of _December_ in the year of our Lord One Thousand Nine Hundred and _one_ and the One Hundred and _26_ of the independence of the United States of America, before me, QUITMAN KOHNKE, M. D., Chairman Board of Health and Ex-Officio Recorder of Births, Deaths and Marriages, in and for the Parish of Orleans, personally appeared

Wm Dillon Jr. an Undertaker, native of U. S. residing at no 1112 Dryades St — who hereby declares, that

Louise Frances Whittaker lawful wife of Florville Foy (White) a native of Natchez Miss , aged 78 years

departed this life, yesterday (16 Dec 1901) at no 1919 Constance Street, in the city

Cause of Death Burns of Entire Body.

Certificate of Dr. S. F. Morton Asst. Coroner

Deceased was a resident of this city for 50 years

Thus done at New Orleans, in the presence of the aforesaid W. Dillon Jr. as also in that of P. Haranne & J. Toumand both of this City witnesses by me requested so to be who have hereunto set their hands, together with me, after reading hereof, this day, month and year first above written.

Wm Dillon Jr.
P. Haranne
Jno. Toumand
Quitman Kohnke M.D.
Chairman Board of Health and Ex-Officio Recorder

Florville Foy died on 16 March 1903 at the age of 83 years and 9 months. His death certificate indicated that he was "colored," although in all other records, including notarial documents as well as United States Federal Census, he had been enumerated as "white." The deceased, a widower and a marble cutter, died at #415 Rampart Street from apoplexy as reported by a local undertaker, Raoul Bonnot, and certified by Dr. G.W. Lewis:

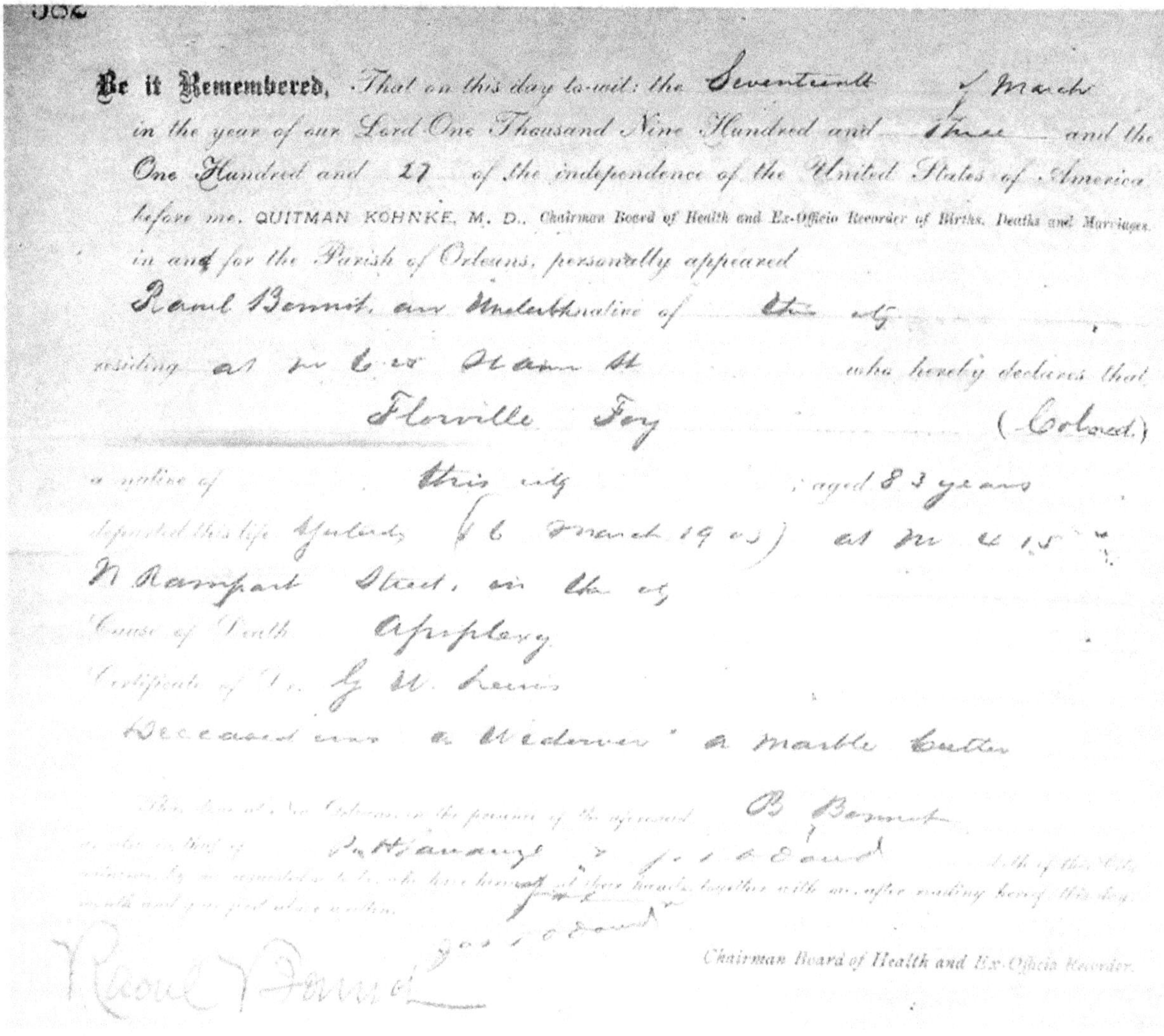

Be it Remembered, That on this day to-wit: the Seventeenth of March in the year of our Lord One Thousand Nine Hundred and three and the One Hundred and 27 of the independence of the United States of America before me, QUITMAN KOHNKE, M. D., Chairman Board of Health and Ex-Officio Recorder of Births, Deaths and Marriages in and for the Parish of Orleans, personally appeared

Raoul Bonnet, an Undertaker of the city residing at No 625 Main St who hereby declares that

Florville Foy (Colored)

a native of this city aged 83 years departed this life yesterday (16 March 1903) at No 415 N Rampart Street, in the city

Cause of Death Apoplexy

Certificate of Dr. G M Lewis

Deceased was a Widower a marble cutter

[handwritten witness lines, partly illegible] R Bonnet

[illegible] Jos. I. O'Dowd

Chairman Board of Health and Ex-Officio Recorder.

Raoul Bonnet

Courtesy of State of Louisiana, Secretary of State, Division of Archives, Records Management, and History. *Vital Records Indices*. Baton Rouge, LA, USA citing *Orleans Death Indices 1894-1907*; Vol. 129, p. 582.

The New Orleans *Daily Picayune* published a lengthy article memorializing Florville's life in their 17 March 1903 edition. It is not known who gave the *Picayune* the information contained in this story especially concerning Jules, although it may have been someone in the Edmunds family. Moreover, there was no mention of Florville's mixed-race origins:

Florville Foy, the oldest marble cutter in the city of New Orleans, whose wealth of architectural design in building fine tombs had made him famous, died at his home, No. 415 Rampart Street, yesterday morning, in his 84th year. The end came at 9 o'clock. His faithful old servant, Jules, went to Mr. Foy's room at that hour, to call him for breakfast, to find him in the last stage. He died in a few minutes. Apoplexy is believed to have been the immediate cause, although old age had undermined the once rugged system and had given ample warning of the end.

"Florville" was his signature. Mr. Foy never used his last name in designating his work. He possessed the true instinct of the artist, and in his time, he had known many of the most famous the South had produced. Perelli, a well-known sculptorer [*sic*] of this city, was an intimate friend of the marble cutter, and in the year 1855 he carved a bust of him that today occupies a favorite spot in the old man's apartments. The house, at 415 North Rampart Street, is known all through the city and in real estate [illegible] as the "Florville" residence. It was built under his personal direction. The whole lower portion is devoted to his work. The marbles still stand in their places and tell of Death's grim visage, while the hand that had given them shape lies cold as clay in the room just overhead.

The handiwork of Florville Foy is to be found in most every cemetery of the city. In the old St. Louis burial ground, rows of his tombs are to be seen, and it is not unusual to note clusters of them together. At one time he had slight competition, and everyone came to him. His stone cutting shops were busy beehives of industry. He was devoted to the art and originated many of the designs which brought him the greatest favor.

"Jules," the devoted servant of the aged man, was once owned by him as a slave. Mr. Foy purchased Jules and his mother in 1858 and the mother died only a few years ago. [...]

The life of Florville Foy was devoted solely to his art. Had he lived until June 29 he would have been 84 years of age. He was born in this city, being the son of Prosper Foy, who was a descendant of the celebrated General Foy, of France. The father was a marble cutter before the son, the latter taking up the chisel when the parent dropped it. Both had lived and worked in the same shop and at the same spot on Rampart Street when New Orleans was only a village compared with its present size. [...] He [Florville] has monuments to his art and memory all over the State of Louisiana. His card can be found in the old City Directory of 1845. [...]

The funeral will take place from the late residence, No. 415 North Rampart street, this afternoon, at 8:30 o'clock, and the religious services will be held at the St. Louis Cathedral. Interment will take place at the New St. Louis Cemetery.[756]

Michel Victor Déjan, his executor, opened Florville's succession on 17 March 1903. Florville left to his sister Sophie, and her daughter Laure Rigaud, share and share alike, the usufruct during their lives of his two properties: at the corner of Villeré and Kerlerec under the old numbers of 333, 333 1/2, 335, 335 1/2 Rue Villeré, and the two properties themselves to his niece and nephew Arnold and Olivia Edmunds. He left $100 each to his nephew Octave Rigaud's three children: Amélie, Marie Louise and Charles Rigaud. To Jules, his faithful domestic, he left $6,000 (the equivalent of $176,471 in 2019 dollars). He left $200 to his godson Florville Louis Whittaker. He gave other small legacies to some faithful workers: M. Sowerly $100; Baptiste $200; M. André his gardener $200; M. Augustin, marble polisher $100. After all the bequests, outstanding bills and costs of settling the estate, he left its residue to Olivia and Arnold Edmunds. Jules, "a reputable person living in the house" was guardian of the seals after Florville's death.

The best idea one could have of just how Florville lived can be seen in the minutiae of the inventory of his estate taken over several days after his death in his several houses. Two appraisers, along with Michel Déjan, and Arnold and Olivia Edmunds, made a list of all of his possessions. In the iron safe: in his shop there was jewelry, including gold chains, diamonds, pins, one English watch and chain, one ladies gold watch and chatelaine, 1 ruby and rose scarf pin, diamond shirt studs, cuff buttons set with pearls and amethysts, etc., silverware; less than $5 in Mexican money, and money from other countries. Also within the iron safe was a copy of his marriage contract, a title for two plots in Metairie Cemetery, lots 17 & 18 in section 86 (The executor of Foy's estate asked that he be able to continue the work on Louisa Whittaker Foy's tomb there with the money she had left for its construction), a certificate in name of deceased as Honorary member of Orleans Artillery Battery A, dated August 8, 1877. In the armoire was found more jewelry including a watch chain, diamond pin, scarf pin with horse head, a gold heart, sundries, padlocks, coins, compass, ties, handkerchiefs, eyeglasses. The contents of Florville's desk included a Meerschaum pipe with silver cover, compass, ruler, plans and loose designs, books, including *Histoire des Croisades*, by Michaud, one pair of glasses, one prayer book, several lots of books. In Florville's workshop, store, and marble yard there were several lots of marble, 1 marble bust (Marie Louise), several marble tombstones, tools, marble crosses, one marble angel, one marble Madonna, one marble obelisk, marble mantles black marble, granite, etc. In the back yard of his residence there were pigeons, geese, ducks, other poultry, a kettle, bird cage, forge, anvils, coal tools. In his carriage room they found a dray for hauling marble, a sulky, a leather top buggy, an open buggy, harness, saddle, bridle, 1 lot of old books, and 1 lamp. In the loft above the carriage room there were harnesses, a mill, an armoire with ammunition, a game bag and other hunting implements, more books, blinds, and doors, more books and engravings, one red buggy pole. In the deceased's home on Rampart St. they found: a broom, cigar stand, gents necessary, wearing apparel and underwear, 30 volumes of Buffon's works, 2 vols. *Discours du Général Foy*; some bound and unbound books, sheets, towels, an old mosquito bar in drawers of book case, one lot of books on his night stand, one marble top mahogany wash stand, one mahogany desk and bookcase combination, one white marble top bureau, 6 cane chairs, 4 rugs, a spittoon 2 pictures on wall, curtains and iron

---

[756] "Florville Foy," The New Orleans *Daily Picayune*, March 17, 1903, digital image, *Genealogybank.com* (https://www.genealogybank.com: accessed 3 March 2020), p. 10, col. 4.

rods, 2 family portraits, 179 engravings, 1 French atlas, 1 Moore and Harris London percussion cap hunting gun with case, 1 Belgian laminated steel breach loader gun, 1 cypress chest, 1 mahogany armoire, 1 deer skin on top of iron bed, 1 shoe stretcher, one bed, looking glass, secretary, wash stand, large leather trunk, and 1 cane seat invalid chair. In the second floor parlor there were several lots of vases, 1 black cover opera glass, 1 cane seat, sofa with pillows, 2 walnut arm chairs, 76 volumes medical and miscellaneous books, one bronze bust of General Foy, one china rooster, one wax hand and forearm, napkins, 1 stuffed doe, one frame picture under glass intitled "Schoolmaster," 2 engravings: "Eucharis and Telemachus," and "Calypso and Telemachus," 1 engraving intitled "Horse Fair in Paris," 1 painting Flemish scene (Herman Vidal); six-light center glass chandelier, a liquor stand containing four decanters and 16 glasses, 12 cane seat chairs, one crayon portrait of deceased on wall, 5 swords, one tomahawk, one painting by Perelli called "Papabote," one metal dog, metal statuette of Liberty, one clock and statuette on mantle, one deer head with horns; 2 paintings "Snipe," and "Partridges," glassware, decanters, one painting on wall intitled "Two dogs," one cigar cutter, several mahogany tables, one oak wood sideboard, one carpet sweeper, step ladder, blankets, rattan rocker, one pair gold mounted eyeglasses, two spittoons. In the back gallery they found 1 ice box, oak hat rack, globe, wooden safe and contents, coffee dripping apparatus, plate warmer, and some table linens. Finally, in his cottage on #2731 Dumaine Street, including the storeroom, stable and yard there were items appraised at only $41.00.

At death, his real estate holdings included: (1) Second District, Sq. 121 between Rampart, Conti, Basin and St. Louis - 34 by 120 deep facing Rampart, bought 10 January 1848, valued at $5,000. (2) A second lot same place adjacent to #1, bought on 31 May 1856, valued at $3,000. (3) Corner lot on Conti and Rampart 66 ft by 96 feet front on Conti, bought on 19 Jan 1895, valued at $6,000. (4) Second District, northeast side of Conti, between Burgundy and Rampart, Sq. 98, bounded by streets aforementioned and St. Louis St., 32 feet fronting on Conti by 96 ft deep, bought 12 November 1864, valued at $2400. (5) Third District - two lots bounded by Villeré, Robertson, Kerlerec and Columbus bought on 22 March 1878. Lot #1 fronts on Kerlerec; lot #2 fronts on Villeré, bought on 18 Oct 1880, both lots together valued at $3,300. (6) Second District - 14 lots of ground - Sq. #355 bounded by Broad, Dumaine, St. Philip and White (lots # 3,4,12,13,14,15,16,17, 30, 31, 32, 33, 34, and 35), bought on 3 March 1859, valued at $6,200. His total real estate holdings were worth $25,900. He also had $1,128 cash in the bank. The entire estate was valued at $29,140.88, with the buying power of over $857,088 in 2019.[757]

Jules bought six lots from the Florville Foy farm in the square between Broad. St. Philip, Dumaine and White for $2650, and about $100 in personal property from the estate out of his $6,000 bequest from Florville. Jules Foy continued on as the successor to Florville's store and marble works until his death in 1929. We know that Jules had, at least nine children. His first child, Adèle Foy was born on 29 April 1885 to him and to Eulalie Cappoursouette. Unusual, even for a French name, we hypothesize that it may simply be a phonetic spelling for the Dutch name Cowperthwait.[758] There are civil birth records for three more children born to them: Jules born on 8 February 1887, George, born on 13 February 1888, and Prosper, born on 24 May 1890.[759] Eulalie Cappoursouette died as Eulalie Foy on 26 September 1893 at the age of thirty-three years at #443 North Claiborne Street in the city. The cause of death was "shock during confinement."[760] Jules's children with Eulalie appeared in the 1900 Federal Census residing at 1403 St. Anthony Street in the household of Jean Sabatier, an elderly African American carpenter, and his wife Lamartine. They were enumerated as Sabatier's nieces and nephews. Along with Adele, Jules, George

---

[757] "Louisiana, Wills and Probate Records, 1756-1984," digital images, *Ancestry.com* (https://www.ancestry.com: accessed 4/1/2020), citing *Civil District Court Case Papers, Louisiana, Orleans Parish, 1903*. Succession of Florville Foy, Case #70093, Images 1642-1755/2052.

[758] We know that Jacob Cowperthwait, a Quaker, came to New Orleans from Philadelphia in 1785, where he settled down to become a slave trader. He abandoned his religion and married Charlotte O'Brien on 10 April 1787 at St. Louis Cathedral (SLC, M5, 52). Although records show that they were the parents of four daughters, we cannot be sure that Jacob did not father any children out of wedlock, or that one of his slaves did not adopt his surname.

[759] Courtesy of State of Louisiana, Secretary of State, Division of Archives, Records Management, and History. *Vital Records Indices*. Baton Rouge, LA, USA, citing New Orleans, Louisiana Birth Records Index 1790-1899; Birth of Adele Foy, Vol. 98, p. 344; Birth of Jules Foy, Vol. 98, p. 344; Birth of George Foy, Vol. 98, p. 345; Birth of Prosper Foy, Vol. 98, p. 345.

[760] Courtesy of State of Louisiana, Secretary of State, Division of Archives, Records Management, and History. *Vital Records Indices*. Baton Rouge, LA, USA, citing *Orleans Death Indices 1877-1895*; Death of Eulalie Foy, Vol. 104, p. 1061.

and Prosper, Jeanne Foy, born in May 1891 and for whom there is no birth record, was included in the group.[761] Jules's children with Clotilde Journée were: Viola, born on 11 July 1890, Manuel, born on 18 January 1892, Antoine, born on 1 April 1894, and Victoria, born on 1 July 1896. After the couple was legally wed their daughter Hilda was born on 29 August 1898. They had three more children together: Rosa, born on 30 September 1902, Nellie, born ca. 1905, for whom there is no civil birth record, and Raymond, born on 15 February 1907.[762]

Seventy-two-year-old Jules F. Foy (colored) died on 12 December 1929 at #2008 St. Philip Street from "Gastritis." A notation read: "Deceased was married to Clotilde Journée; a marble cutter, and the son of Florville Foy and Rosalie Foy, both natives of Louisiana:"

Courtesy of State of Louisiana, Secretary of State, Division of Archives, Records Management, and History. *Vital Records Indices.* Baton Rouge, LA, USA citing *Orleans Death Indices 1894-1907*; Vol. 199, p. 1191.

---

[761] 1900 United States Federal Census, Orleans Parish, Louisiana, Ward 7, Dwelling #349, Family #408, Jean Sabatier household, digital image, *Ancestry.com* (https://www.ancestry.com accessed 2/3/2020), citing Family History Library microfilm # 1240572. Date of enumeration: 12 June 1900. Image 36/57.

[762] Courtesy of State of Louisiana, Secretary of State, Division of Archives, Records Management, and History. *Vital Records Indices.* Baton Rouge, LA, USA, citing New Orleans, Louisiana Birth Records Index 1790-1915; Birth of Viola Foy, Vol. 107, p. 291; Birth of Manuel Foy, Vol. 107, p. 291; Birth of Antoine Foy, Vol. 107, p. 292; Birth of Victoria Foy, Vol. 107, p. 292; Birth of Hilda Foy, Vol. 114, p. 82; Birth of Rosa Foy, Vol. 124, p. 661; Birth of Raymond Foy, Vol. 134, p. 745.

CHAPTER 24

MARIE JOSEPHE SOPHIE FOY AND LOUIS RIGAUD

Prosper Foy and Zélie Aubry's last living child, Marie Josephe Sophie Foy died in New Orleans on 2 May 1907. She was eighty-five years old, the widow of Louis Rigaud, and died from "senile debility."

Courtesy of State of Louisiana, Secretary of State, Division of Archives, Records Management, and History. *Vital Records Indices.* Baton Rouge, LA, USA citing *Orleans Death Indices 1894-1907*; Vol. 140, p. 1046.

Sophie Foy's husband, Jean Louis Rigaud, had died in New Orleans on 19 August 1867, leaving her to raise her three children by herself: Octave Joseph, Marie Laure, and Marie Althéé,(See also p. 307). Jean Louis Rigaud's New Orleans death certificate indicated that he was a native of St. Yago (*sic*), Cuba, aged 64 years and that he died on 19 August 1867 at 5:00 p.m. at #428 Morales (Marais) Street between St. Anthony and Bagatelle (now Pauger) in the Third District. There was no mention of his marital status. It is interesting that his other given name, "Émile" was crossed out on this record. It had been used when he stood as the godfather to a younger brother, Émile Rigaud baptized on 26 February 1828 (see p. 308):

Courtesy of State of Louisiana, Secretary of State, Division of Archives, Records Management, and History. *Vital Records Indices*. Baton Rouge, LA, USA, from New Orleans, Louisiana Death Records Index 1804-1939; Vol. 37, p. 345.

Sophie Foy's son, Octave Joseph Rigaud, had married Louise Amelia St. Fort d'Aubry also in 1867, according to the latter's 1892 succession record. Two years later, Sophie's daughter, twenty-three-year-old Marie Althée died on 12 November 1869,[763] leaving Sophie and her daughter Laure who were enumerated together in the 1870 United States Federal Census as "Vve [Widow]. Sophie Rigot," age 48, a white female born in Louisiana with $1200 in real estate and $100 in personal estate, and "L'Or (unusual phonetic spelling of Laure) Rigot," age 25, white female, born in Louisiana.[764] Mother and daughter were enumerated together in the 1880 United States Federal Census as "Sophie Rigau," age 58, "mulatto" female, widow, keeping house, born in New Orleans, living at 428 Marais Street, and her daughter 'Laure Rigau," age 25, a female "mulatto", also born in New Orleans.[765] They were living at # 428 Morales Street in the same house where Jean Louis Rigaud had died in 1867. It was also in that year that a city ordinance had changed the names of Morales and Plauché Streets to Marais Street.

Mother and daughter were enumerated together for the last time in the 1900 Federal Census as "Louise Rigaud," a black, female, living at 1820 Marais Street, born in July 1821, to a father born in France and a mother born in Louisiana, aged 79 years, a widow, who owned her own home, and who could not read, write, or speak English. Laura was enumerated as her daughter, a black, female, born in September 1841, age 59, unmarried, a seamstress able to read, write and speak English.[766] In subsequent census records, after her mother's death in

[763] "Orleans Death Indices,1804-1876" [database on-line], *Ancestry.com* (https://www.ancestry.com: accessed 12/30/ 2019), citing *New Orleans, Louisiana Death Records Index, 1804-1949.* Death of Marie Alte Rigaud, Vol. 46, p. 297.

[764] 1870 United States Federal Census, New Orleans, Orleans Parish, LA, Ward 7, Dwelling #339, Family #487, Vve. Sophie Rigot (*sic*) household, digital image, *Ancestry.com* (https://www.ancestry.com: accessed 4/1/2020), citing NARA microfilm publication M593_522, p. 503A. Date of enumeration: 24 June 1870, Image 237/470.

[765] 1880 United States Federal Census, New Orleans, Orleans Parish, LA, ED 30, Dwelling #247, Family #322, Sophie Rigau household, digital image,, *Ancestry.com* (https://www.ancestry.com: accessed 4/1/2020), citing NARA microfilm publication T9, roll 462. Date of enumeration: 7 June 1880, Image 34/51.

[766] 1900 United States Federal Census, Orleans Parish, Louisiana, Ward 7, Dwelling #89, Family #100, Louise Rigaud household, digital image, *Ancestry.com* (https://www.ancestry.com accessed 4/1/2020), citing Family History Library microfilm # 1240572. Date of enumeration: 5 June 1900. Image 9/50.

1907, Laura was enumerated living alone on her own income, either as a "mulatto," or as "white." She last appeared in the 1930 United States Federal Census as Laura Rigaud, an 87-year-old white female, living at 1449 Villeré Street, in a house that she owned worth $2500.[767] She died in New Orleans on 12 December 1932.[768]

Octave Joseph Rigaud was the only one of Sophie Foy's children to have descendants. He and Amelina St. Fort d'Aubry, a native of Cuba, born ca. 1842, were the parents of three children: Amélie Marie born on 5 January 1870, Louise, born on 1 October 1871, and Charles Joseph, born on 5 October 1873.[769] O.J. Rigant (*sic*), a forty-year-old white, broker, residing at #3337 St. Ann Street in New Orleans, was enumerated in the 1880 United States Federal Census living with his wife Amelina "Rigant," a black thirty-five-year-old female, and his three "mulatto" children Amélie, age 10, Louise, age 8, and Charles, age 6.

Octave Joseph Rigaud died on 28 October 1892, leaving a small legacy to his wife, Amelina, and his three children, including a few hundred dollars in cash and the ownership of a plot of ground situated in the Third District, designated as #312 in the square bounded by Marais, St. Anthony, St. Claude and Bourbon Streets, measuring 50 feet front on Marais Street by 150 feet in depth, acquired jointly with Marie Laure Rigaud, and Marie (Althée) Rigaud, by purchase from Marie Sophie Foy on 14 April 1863 (Notary J. Cuvillier, Conveyance Office Book #78, folio 648). After the death of his sister, Marie Althée, in 1869, Octave Joseph Rigaud had acquired one-half of her interest in the property.[770]

Like many of her relatives, Amelina St. Fort Rigaud was enumerated with her children in the 1900 United States Federal Census as "white", but in the 1910 United States Federal Census she and her two daughters were said to be "mulatto." That year Amelia Rigaud, a 60-year-old widow was living on 1817 St. Ann Street in New Orleans, with her 24-year-old daughter, Louise Rigaud, a milliner and her 27-year-old daughter, Amelia Rigaud.[771] While the 1900 census had indicated that Amelina Rigaud had immigrated from Spain to Louisiana in 1851, in the 1910 United States Federal Census she was said to be Cuban born as had been her parents. Her daughters, Amelia and Louise had both been born in Louisiana to two Cuban parents.[772]

Amelina Rigaud died in New Orleans on 24 July 1912 at the age of seventy.[773] After the will was probated in New Orleans on 5 September 1913 she left to her three surviving children Amelia, Louise and Charles, "a certain portion of ground with buildings and improvements in the Second District in the square comprised within St. Ann, Dumaine, Roman and Derbigny Streets by an act of sale before Paul E. Laresche, notary, on March 13, 1861. The lot measured 19 feet 5 inches on St. Ann by 117 feet 2 inches 7 lines deep. Being the same which Marie Elina Dabdeuil, widow of St. Fort Guillaume Aubry purchased from Théophile Macarty before Charles T. Soniat, notary, on May 6, 1873 (COB 101, Folio 748)." After her mother, Elina Dabdeuil St. Fort, died, Amelina had inherited it as the sole heir.[774]

[767] 1930 United States Federal Census, Orleans Parish, Louisiana, Ward 7, Dwelling #176, Family #186, Laura Rigaud household, digital image, *Ancestry.com* (https://www.ancestry.com accessed 3/2020), citing Family History Library microfilm # 2340540. Date of enumeration:10 April 1930. Image 23/55.

[768] *New Orleans, Louisiana Death Records Index, 1804-1949*, [database on-line], *Ancestry.com* (https://www.ancestry.com: accessed 3/30/2020), citing *Orleans Death Indices 1929-1936*, Death of Laure Rigaud, Vol. 204, p. 708.

[769] "New Orleans, Louisiana, Birth Records Index, 1790-1899," [database on-line], *Ancestry.com* (https://www.ancestry.com: accessed 3/30/2020), citing *New Orleans, Louisiana Birth Records Index, 1790-1915*. Birth of Amelie Marie Rigaud, Vol. 53, p. 291; Birth of Louise Rigaud, Vol. 59, p. 635; Birth of Charles Joseph Rigaud, Vol. 62, p. 86.

[770] "Louisiana, Wills and Probate Records, 1756-1984," digital images, *Ancestry.com* (https://www.ancestry.com: accessed 3/3/2020), citing *Civil District Court Case Papers, Louisiana, Orleans Parish, 1892*. Succession of Joseph Octave Rigaud, Case #37229, Images 1080-1104/1667.

[771] While no occupation was shown for Amelia, the daughter, she had appeared in the 1901 *New Orleans City Directory* as a milliner living at 1817 St. Ann Street. Her sister, Louise, was listed in the same directory as a dressmaker living at the same address.

[772] 1910 United States Federal Census, New Orleans, Ward 5, ED 0077, Dwelling #168, Family #190, Louise Rigaud household, digital image, *Ancestry.com* (https://www.ancestry.com accessed 2/2/2020), citing NARA microfilm publication T624 -521, page 9b, Family History Library microfilm # 1374534. Date of enumeration: 20 April 1910. Image 18/32.

[773] "Orleans Death Indices,1908-1917" [database on-line], *Ancestry.com* (https://www.ancestry.com: accessed 3/3/ 2020), citing *New Orleans, Louisiana Death Records Index, 1804-1949*. Death of Amelina L. St. Fort D'Aubry Rigaud.

[774] "Louisiana, Wills and Probate Records, 1756-1984," digital images, *Ancestry.com* (https://www.ancestry.com: accessed 3/5/2020), citing *Civil District Court Case Papers, Louisiana, Orleans Parish, 1913*. Succession of Octave J. Rigaud (Mrs.), Case #105590, Images 1491-1498/1976. Note: Amelina inherited from her mother on 27 December 1884. For that reason, we

The only one of Marie Josephe Sophie Foy's grandchildren to have descendants was Charles Joseph Rigaud, Amelina and Octave's only son. Charles married Marie Blanche Toca in New Orleans on 12 December 1897.[775] The groom's parents were Joseph Alonzo Toca and Georgiana Coriel. Joseph Toca was a shoemaker and a native of New Orleans. During the Civil War he had served as a Colonel with the Louisiana Native Guards (Union), Company A, (91st Regiment, United States Colored Infantry) and was, in March 1863, on detached service from Fort Macomb (Chef Menteur, Orleans Parish) at Tower Dupre which guarded the entrance to Bayou Dupre from Lake Borgne in St. Bernard Parish.[776] Charles, who first worked as a cigar maker and later worked as a liquor distiller in New Orleans, and Blanche Toca Rigaud had one child, Charles Joseph Rigaud, Jr., born on 17 September 1897 in New Orleans.[777] Charles, Blanche and their son lived, at least through 1919 in New Orleans, where they were routinely enumerated as being "black" or "mulatto." On 16 April 1910 they were living on 2716 St. Philip Street. Charles was still working as a distiller.[778] The couple had been married for 12 years and Charles, Jr. was an only child. The family moved to New York, where they were enumerated in the 1920 Federal Census, living at #2134 Amsterdam Avenue in Manhattan, New York. Charles Rigaud, a white male, 48-years-old, was working as a machinist for an Electrical company. This is the first time we see that the family claimed that they had all been born in Texas and that Blanche's parents were French. Charles, Jr., aged about 21 years, was also working as a machinist.[779]

According to the 2 April 1930 United States Federal Census, Charles, Jr. was heading the household now located at 423 Calhoun Avenue in the Throgs Neck neighborhood of the Bronx, New York. A white, male, aged about 31 years, he had been married three years to Ethel Reynolds, aged about 28 years. She was a native of England. Charles worked as a model maker for a Telegraph Company. Also living in the Rigaud household was his mother, Blanche, aged about 49 (*sic*) years, a widow, and her granddaughter, Ethel, born on 14 Sept 1929 (SSDI), who was 9 months old.[780] Another child, Blanche Marguerite was born to them on 5 January 1931 at Throgs Neck, Bronx, NY (SSDI). Although we could not find the family in the 1940 United States Federal Census, we know that Charles filled out a World War II Selective Service Card from 139-16 109th Road in Jamaica, Queens, New York, where he was living with his wife, Ethel. He worked for the American District Telephone Company in Manhattan. He gave his date of birth erroneously as 19 September 1897 in El Paso, TX.[781] He died on 15 April 1953 in Queens, New York. His wife died on 29 March 1955 at Massapequa, Nassau Co., NY.[782]

Footnote believe that her mother died as "Elina Sainfort," born in 1809, who died in New Orleans on 1 December 1884 (*Orleans Death Indices*, 1877-1895; Volume 86, p. 294, which reads in part that "Mrs. Widow Elina Sainfort, a native of Santiago de Cuba, aged 75 years departed this life this day (Dec. 1, 1884) at #331 ½ St. Ann Street in this city. Cause of death: Heart disease." Moreover, it was Octave J. Rigaud, who reported Elina Sainfort's death and signed the death certificate.

[775] "Louisiana Parish Marriages, 1837-1957," digital images, *FamilySearch.org* (https://familysearch.org/ark:/61903/1:1:QKJ4-S24X : accessed 4/8/ 2020), Charles Joseph Rigaud and Marie Blanche Toca, 12 Dec 1896; citing Orleans, Louisiana, United States, various parish courthouses, Louisiana; FHL microfilm 907,706.

[776] "U.S., Returns from Military Posts, 1806-1916," [database on-line], *Ancestry.com* (https://www.ancestry.com: accessed 4/8/2020), citing *Returns From U.S. Military Posts, 1800-1916*; (National Archives Microfilm Publication M617, 1,550 rolls); Records of the Adjutant General's Office, 1780's-1917, Record Group 94; National Archives, Washington, D.C, Louisiana, Macomb Fort, January 1828-August 1866, Image 315/448.

[777] "New Orleans, Louisiana, Birth Records Index, 1790-1915," [database on-line], *Ancestry.com* (https://www.ancestry.com: accessed 3/4/2020), citing *New Orleans, Louisiana Birth Records Index, 1790-1899*. Birth of Charles Joseph Rigaud, Jr., Vol. 111, p.1038.

[778] 1910 United States Federal Census, New Orleans, Ward 5, ED 0077, Dwelling #168, Family #190, Charles Rigo (*sic*) household, digital image, *Ancestry.com* (https://www.ancestry.com accessed 2/2/2020), citing NARA microfilm publication T624 -521, page 3b, Family History Library microfilm # 1374534. Date of enumeration: 16 April 1910. Image 6/29.

[779] 1920 United States Federal Census, New York, Manhattan Assembly District 23, Dwelling #10, Family #176, Charles Rigaud household, digital image, *Ancestry.com* (https://www.ancestry.com accessed 2/4/2020), citing NARA microfilm publication T625_1226, page 5b, Date of enumeration: 5 January 1920. Image 10/25.

[780] 1930 United States Federal Census, Bronx, Bronx, New York, ED 0790, Dwelling #20, Family #22, Charles Rigaud household, digital image, *Ancestry.com* (https://www.ancestry.com accessed 2/4/2020), citing Family History Library Microfilm 2341210, Date of enumeration: 2 April 1930. Image 4/15.

[781] "U.S. WWII Draft Cards Young Men, 1940-1947," digital image, *Ancestry.com* (https://www.ancestry.com accessed 2/5/2020), citing *Draft Registration Cards for New York City, 10/16/1940 - 03/31/1947*. 1376 boxes. NAI: 7644743. Records of the Selective Service System, 1926–1975, Record Group 147. NARA, St Louis, Missouri.

[782] "New York, New York, Death Index, 1949-1965," [database on-line], *Ancestry.com* (https://www.ancestry.com: accessed 2/9/2020), citing New York City Department of Health,(www.vitalsearch-worldwide.com.)

****

In conclusion, it is important to remember that like-minded white men who took free women of color as the mothers of their children supported one another's choices, often standing as godfathers to one another's "natural" children, or being witnesses to one another's nuptials. They facilitated one another in the purchase and/or exchange of real estate including slaves. They frequented certain notaries such as Carlile Pollock, or one of their own, Achille Chiapella, and called upon certain priests such as Fr. Jean Pierre Koüne, of Fr. Claude Thoma, who would dutifully record baptisms and marriages with no fuss or judgement. They were obliged to form a tight-knit and cohesive society within the larger New Orleans community because their actions to secure a modicum of support for their children were often in contravention of existing laws and customs. While they often lived full or part-time in the Faubourgs Marigny or Tremé with their companions and children, they were never judged by their peers, when, by choice, they abandoned their responsibilities in order to secure a more suitable circumstance for themselves. It is also important to remember that free women of color, who could have been completely crushed by the relentless oppression of racial and sexual discrimination in early New Orleans, had many weapons in their arsenal, not the least of which was the legal authority to protect their own children and their common assets in local courts. Not bound by marriage, they were freer than their white female married counterparts who lived under a legal system that stripped them of the right to make contracts, to buy and sell property, and even to protect their children, without the permission of a spouse, father or other legal guardian. These women managed their own affairs, grew their own wealth, and were able to bequeath it to their descendants without any legal interference. While it would take several generations before all women would be granted equal rights under the law, and several more generations before women and men of color would enjoy those same rights, many descendants of the Aubry sisters, unwilling to wait, left the south, taking their children out west or up north to be able to flourish in a new, healthier, and relatively freer society.

Although Marguerite Cécile Aubry's four daughters all had children, and all survived their child-bearing years, many of their children did not survive to be adults due to the numerous contagious diseases that ran rampant in nineteenth century New Orleans. Childhood diseases, especially diphtheria, was one of the major killers. Poor nutrition and deplorable hygiene took the lives of many infants and toddlers. Yellow fever, cholera, dysentery, tuberculosis, typhoid fever and other maladies struck down many who survived to be young adults, but before they could marry.

Félicité Aubry, whose death has eluded us, although we are sure she did not survive the Civil War, had five children with Louis Alexandre Dupuy. One died as a child, two disappeared from records shortly after their birth, and two lived to be adults. However, Léon Dupuy never married, and only one, Edmond Dupuy, married and had children leaving the Myrtil (Martin) Boutté and the André Dominguez lines which produced descendants well into the twentieth century in New Orleans. Félicité had six children with Hilaire Julien Domingon. While two lived into their twenties, they never married. Her daughter, Louise Virginia Domingon, had five children with Joseph Alexander Bonneval. Three of them lived to be married, but only one, Benjamin Peter Bonneval, had descendants. Félicité's son, Charles Victor Bernard Domingon, had two children, but only one lived to marry: Marie Letitia Domingon, who had two children with José Fernando Bonaventura, both of whom used the surname Fernando. Both of Marie Letitia's children married, but neither had children. Félicité's daughter, Josephine Laure Domingon, had two children out of wedlock, both of whom used the Domingon name, but could not be traced. Félicité's son, August Julien had the most posterity. Although Arnold Charles had three daughters, only Henrietta married. Julia and Rita died without issue. Arnold's sister, Marie Louise Rita, had nine children with William John Daunoy, but only three grandchildren and two great-grandchildren. Most of Félicité's descendants remained in Louisiana.

Zélie Aubry had nine children with René Prosper Foy, of which four did not live to marry. Their eldest, Elina Marguerite Félicité's only child, Marie Anais Bouligny had four children with Patrice V. Léonard. Unable to trace three of them, one son, John Gilbert Léonard, a jeweler and watchmaker in New Orleans, had two daughters with his wife, Louisa Gertrude Remmers: Anna (b. 1888) and Gertrude (b. 1889). We know that Zélie"s first son, Prosper Florville Foy, never had children, unless Jules Foy was his "natural" child, which he never affirmed. Zélie's daughter, Marie Joseph Sophie Foy had three children with Jean Louis Rigaud, of which, only their son Octave Joseph, married. Of his three children, only one son, Charles Joseph, married and had children of his own. He and his family moved to New York in the 1920s. Finally, Rose Euphémie Foy had six children with Edgard Edmunds, of which, only three married. Their eldest, Edgar Joseph, had four children, but no grandchildren. Arnold Joseph had three daughters, but none ever married. Ernest Joseph had two children, born in California, with his second cousin, Marie Emma Chiapella, who produced three grandchildren and ten great-grandchildren.

Mercelite Aubry had a son and a daughter with Henry Sellon Boneval Latrobe. Henry Belmont lived to have two children, but there were no grandchildren. Mercelite's daughter Julia, had eight children with Joseph St. Hubert, but only two of them had ever married, Alcide Joseph and Marie Laure. Both died young, with no issue. Mercelite's son with Louis Paul Bringier, John Gustave McDonogh Bringier, last appeared in records living with his half-sister, Julia Latrobe St. Hubert in the 1860 United States Federal Census. He was still unmarried and there were no subsequent records for him. The New Orleans Latrobe line died out where it had begun.

Marie Eglée Aubry's child with Louis Hilaire Lorreins, Marguerite Odalie, married, but had no children. Of Marie Eglée's three sons with Achille Chiapella, only two lived to have children. Her eldest child, René Achille Chiapella had eight children with Marie Orelia Watkinson, but four died as infants, and one, Rita, never married. Their daughter Marie Félicité Aurelia had four children with Jean-Baptiste Olivier. The Oliviers had four children. Only their son, Rufus Henry had one son, Jean René Olivier, ca. 1934, with his wife, Tennie Hickman. He left New Orleans, lived in Shreveport, Caddo Parish, LA, and later Lake Charles, Calcasieu Parish, where he worked as a mechanic. He died in Lake Charles in1982. The three Olivier sisters, Aline Aurelia, May Ann and Ethel Mary were all enumerated in the 1940 United States Federal Census for New Orleans, living with their Aunt Rita Chiapella. They were all unmarried. Aline and Ethel followed their Aunt Rita Chiapella, to Portland, Oregon, where they finished their days. Aline, Ethel Olivier, and Rita Chiapella were all interred in Calvary Cemetery in Portland, Multnomah Co., OR. We believe that May Ann remained behind and died ca. 1997 in New Orleans. René Achille Chiapella's son Henry, had three children with Louise Anne Cassan before his premature death. Only one, Alice, survived infancy. She never married, and followed her mother, step-father and Chiapella cousins out west to California. René Achille Chiapella's daughter Marie Emma, married her second cousin, Ernest Joseph Edmunds. Their son and daughter were born in Los Angeles, California. There were three grandchildren, two born to Ralph Edmunds and one born to Lucille Marie Edmunds Thomas, as well as ten great-grandchildren.

Although Marie Eglée's son Stephen Eugene Chiapella never lived to see the three surviving of his four children grow up, his widow, Eulalie Pinta used the family resources, and with the help of her second husband, Joseph Fernand Grass, they moved their blended family to California, where Grass turned their hard-earned money into a small fortune. Eulalie's three children with Chiapella and her five children with Grass all lived to be adults, all had children, and then grandchildren and beyond. Several of the Chiapella descendants were physicians. One was a graphic artist, several were real estate developers, and one was a mining engineer. They probably would not have had the same opportunities had Eulalie and Joseph Fernand Grass stayed in New Orleans to manage the family shoe store. While they left other extended family members behind, they also escaped the relentless diseases that had felled may of their ancestors. They abandoned Louisiana, where the hope of universal suffrage and equal rights for all ushered in by the defeat of the Confederacy, had been crushed by the return of democrat party rule after the compromise of 1877. Theirs was a choice, either to stay and fight, or leave and thrive. Their Chiapella cousins, children of Celestin and Amada Lachaise, had found permanent homes in France well before the Civil War. However, towards the end of the nineteenth century, many New Orleans people of color, no longer so attached to their French culture and language as had been previous generations, made the decision to head west to a new frontier who hoped that a brighter future awaited them in a new American community. This was an individual choice made by a number of the Aubry descendants, some of whom made the move as young adults, and others who left near the end of their days.

While the Aubry sisters' lives were filled probably with more tragedies than triumphs, we must savor the latter. Remember Zélie Aubry, who challenged Rene Prosper Foy in court, when, in need of money, he threatened the assets of two of her children by trying to usurp her legal rights as their mother. Not only did she win her case, but she called out the father of her children as morally bankrupt and an unfit parent, the record of which remains to this day in New Orleans legal records. Remember also, Eglée Aubry's criminal complaints against her troublesome St. Tammany Parish neighbor, Numa Chatellier, and her subsequent civil action against him for slander, a bold move, which cost him time and money in court, as well as an admission of his guilt. All four sisters, including Félicité, who mortgaged her own property to prop up Hilaire Julien Domingon during one of his many periods of financial difficulty, and Mercelite, who found a way to secure assets due her from the Latrobe family, were property owners, and sometimes landlords, who managed their own affairs, grew their own assets, and provided for their own children in a society which was engineered to make their lives as difficult as possible.

BIBLIOGRAPHY

Abernathy, Thomas Perkins. *The South in the New Nation, 1789-1819: A History of the South.* Baton Rouge, LA: Louisiana State University Press, 1961.

Bauer, Craig A. *Creole Genesis: The Bringier Family and Antebellum Plantation Life in Louisiana.* Lafayette, LA: University of Louisiana at Lafayette Press, 2011.

Boagni, Ethel Haas. *Madisonville, Louisiana.* Mandeville, LA: St. Tammany Parish Historical Society, 1980.

Boelhower, William, ed. *New Orleans in the Atlantic World.* London and New York: Routledge, 2010.

Brasseaux, Carl A. & Glenn R. Conrad, eds. *The Road to Louisiana: The Saint-Domingue refugees, 1792-1809.* Lafayette, LA: University of Louisiana at Lafayette Press, 1992.

Brasseaux, Carl A, Keith P. Fontenot, and Claude F. Oubre. *Creoles of Color in the Bayou Country.* Jackson. MS: University Press of Mississippi, 1994.

Cable, George Washington. *The Creoles of Louisiana.* Gretna, LA: Pelican Publishing Co., 2000. (First published in 1884 by Charles Scribner's Sons.)

Calagaz, Ann, ed. *Sacramental Records of the Roman Catholic Church of the Archdiocese of Mobile, Vol. 1, Section 1, 1704-1739.* Mobile, AL: Archdiocese of Mobile, 2001.

Campeau, Anita R. and Donald J. Sharp. *The History of Mandeville From the American Revolution to Bernard de Marigny de Mandeville.* New Orleans, LA: Cornerstone Book Publishers, 2014.

Carter, Clarence Edwin, ed. *The Territorial Papers of the United States, Vol. IX, The Territory of Orleans 1803-1812.* Washington D.C.: United States Government Printing Office, 1940.

Chase, John. *Frenchmen, Desire, Good Children and Other Streets of New Orleans.* Gretna, LA: Pelican Publishing Co., 2012.

Chiapella, Celestin. *Manuel de L'Oiseleur et de L'Oiselier contenant La manière de conserver et de faire produire tous les petits Oiseaux de Cage et de Volière.* Bordeaux, France: Féret et Fils and Paris, France: G. Masson, 1873-1874. (Author's Collection)

Clark, Emily. *The Strange History of the American Quadroon Free Women of Color in the Revolutionary Atlantic World.* Chapel Hill, NC: The University of North Carolina Press, 2013.

Conrad, Glenn R, ed. *Cross, Crozier and Crucible: A Volume Celebrating the Bicentennial of a Catholic Diocese in Louisiana.* New Orleans, LA: The Roman Catholic Church of the Archdiocese of New Orleans, 1993.

Cotton de Bennetot, Arlette. *Histoire et Généalogie de la Famille Cotton de Bennetot.* Bordeaux, France: 150 copies printed by subscription, 1981. (Author's Collection)

Deggs, Sister Mary Bernard. *No Cross, No Crown: Black Nuns in Nineteenth Century New Orleans.* Edited by Virginia Meecham Gould and Charles E. Nolan. Bloomington and Indianapolis, IN: Indiana University Press, 2001.

DeVille, Winston, *Mississippi Mélange*, Volume 1. Baton Rouge, LA: The Provincial Press, 1995.

De Ville, Winston. *Pointe Coupée Documents 1762-1803: A Calendar of Civil records for the Province of Louisiana.* Ville Platte, LA: The Provincial Press, 1997.

De Ville, Winston. *Slaves and Masters of Pointe Coupée. Louisiana: A Calendar of Civil records, 1762-1823.* Ville Platte, LA: The Provincial Press, 1988.

Devron, Gustavus M.D. "Two Original and Newly Founded Documents of the Departure, Shipwreck and Death of Mr. Aubry, the last French Governor in Louisiana." *Louisiana Historical Society*, Vol.2, Part 1, (1897): 28-34.

Din, Gilbert C. *Spaniards, Planters, and Slaves: The Spanish Regulation of Slavery in Louisiana*, 1763-1803. College Station, TX: Texas A&M University Press, 1999.

Diocese of Baton Rouge. *Diocese of Baton Rouge Catholic Church Records, Pointe Coupée Records, 1722-1769* Vol 1B. Baton Rouge, LA: Diocese of Baton Rouge, Department of Archives, 2002.

Diocese of Baton Rouge. *Diocese of Baton Rouge Catholic Church Records, Vol 2, 1770-1803*. Baton Rouge, LA: Diocese of Baton Rouge, Department of Archives, 2009.

Diocese of Baton Rouge. *Diocese of Baton Rouge Catholic Church Records, Vol 3, 1804-1819*. Baton Rouge, LA: Diocese of Baton Rouge, Department of Archives, 1982.

Dohan, Mary Helen. *Mr. Roosevelt's Steamboat: The First Steamboat to Travel the Mississippi*. Gretna, LA: The Pelican Publishing Co., 2004.

Ellis, Frederick S. *St. Tammany Parish L'Autre Côté du Lac*. Gretna, LA: Pelican Publishing Co., 1998.

Garrigoux, Jean, trans. Gordon S. Brown. *A Visionary Adventurer: Arsène Lacarrière Latour 1778-1837 The Unusual Travels of a Frenchman in the Americas*. Lafayette, LA: University of Louisiana at Lafayette Press, 2017.

Gayarré, Charles. *History of Louisiana The French Domination*, Vols. 1, 2. New York, NY: Redfield, 1854; reissued by Book Renaissance www.ren-books.com.

Gayarré, Charles. *History of Louisiana. The Spanish Domination*, Vol. 3. Gretna, LA: Pelican Publishing Co., 1974.

Gayarré, Charles. *History of Louisiana. The American Domination*, Vol. 4. Gretna, LA: Pelican Publishing Co., 1974.

Gehman, Mary. *The Free People of Color of New Orleans*. New Orleans LA: Margaret Media, Inc., 1994.

Giraud, Marcel, trans. Brian Pearce. *A History of French Louisiana Volume 5, The Company of the Indies, 1723-1731*. Baton Rouge, LA: Louisiana State University Press, 1991.

Hall, Gwendolyn Midlo. *Africans in Colonial Louisiana: The Development of Afro-Creole Culture in the Eighteenth Century*. Baton Rouge, LA and London: The Louisiana State University Press, 1995.

Hall, Gwendolyn Midlo, ed. *Databases for the Study of Afro-Louisiana History and Genealogy*. Baton Rouge, LA: Louisiana State University Press, 2000, CD-ROM.

Hall, Martha Lacy, ed. *The St. Tammany Historical Society Gazette Madisonville Issue*, Vol. 4, March 1980. Mandeville, LA: The St. Tammany Historical Society, Inc.

Hanger, Kimberly S. *Bounded Lives, Bounded Places: Free Black Society in Colonial New Orleans, 1769-1803*. Durham, NC & London: Duke University Press, 1997.

Harrison, Thomas, compiler, National Park Service, *Troop Roster, Tennessee Volunteers & Militia, Kentucky Volunteers & Militia, Battalion of Free Men of Color, Louisiana Volunteers & Militia,* Military Reference Library dated 28 May 1954, available at: https://www.nps.gov/jela/learn/historyculture/upload/CHALTroopRoster.pdf.

Historic New Orleans Collection, The Collins C. Diboll Vieux Carré Digital Survey. https://www.hnoc.org/vcs/.

Holmes, Jack D. L. "The Abortive Slave Revolt at Pointe Coupée, Louisiana 1795." *Louisiana History: The Journal of the Louisiana Historical Association*, Vol. 11, No. 4 (Autumn 1970): 341-362.

King, Grace. *Creole Families of New Orleans*. New Orleans, LA: Cornerstone Book Publishers, 2010. (First published in 1921).

Kolb, Frances Bailey. "Contesting Borderlands: Policy and Practice in Spanish Louisiana, 1765-1803." PhD diss. Vanderbilt University, 2014.

Korn, Bertrand Wallace. *The Early Jews of New Orleans*. Waltham, MA: American Jewish Historical Society, 1969.

Landau, Emily Epstein. *Spectacular Wickedness: Sex, Race and Memory in Storyville, New Orleans.* Baton Rouge, LA: Louisiana State University Press, 2013.

Landers, Jane G., ed. *Against the Odds: Free Blacks in the Slave Societies of the Americas.* London & Portland, OR: Frank Cass & Co., Ltd., 1996.

Latour, Arsène Lacarrière. *Historical Memoir of The War in West Florida and Louisiana in 1814- 15, With an Atlas.* New Orleans, LA: The Historic New Orleans Collection and The University Press of Florida, 1999. Note: The maps have been moved to the Web site of the Historic New Orleans Collection and may be accessed here: http://www.hnoc.org/latour/latour.php.

Latour, Arsène Lacarrière. *Historical Memoir of The War in West Florida and Louisiana in 1814-15, With an Atlas.* Gainesville, FL: University of Florida Press, 1964, (Facsimile reproduction of the 1816 Edition with maps).

Latrobe, Benjamin Henry Boneval. *Impressions Respecting New Orleans: Diary and Sketches 1818-1820*, edited by Samuel Wilson, Jr. New York, NY: Columbia University Press, 1951.

Latrobe, Benjamin Henry. *The Journal of Latrobe. Being the Notes and Sketches of an Architect, Naturalist and Traveler in the United States from 1796 to 1820.* New York: D. Appleton & Co., 1905. Reprinted by FB & C. Ltd., London, 2015, (Forgotten Books).

Leumas, Emilie G & Roland Gravois, eds. *Diocese of Baton Rouge Catholic Church Records Pointe Coupée Records 1770-1900: Individuals without Surnames.* Baton Rouge, LA: Department of Archives, Catholic Diocese of Baton Rouge, 2007.

Long, Carolyn Morrow. *Madame Lalaurie, Mistress of the Haunted House.* Gainesville, FL: University Press of Florida, 2012.

Maduell, Charles R., Jr. *The Census Tables for the French Colony of Louisiana from 1699 through 1732.* Baltimore, MD: Genealogical Publishing Co., Inc., 1972.

McBee, May Wilson, compiler. *The Natchez Court Records 1767-1805: Abstracts of Early Records.* Baltimore, MD: Clearfield Co., Inc., by Genealogical Publishing Co., Inc., 1994, 2003.

McGroarty, John Steven. *Los Angeles from the Mountains to the Sea: With Selected Biography of Actors and Witnesses of the Period of Growth and Achievement, Volume 2.* Chicago, IL: The American Historical Society, 1921. (Available at www.googlebooks.com).

Michel & Co., E. A. *New Orleans Annual and Commercial Register of 1846: Containing the Names, Residences and Professions of all the Heads of Families and Persons in Business of the City and Suburbs, Algiers and Lafayette, &C.* New Orleans, LA. E.A. Michel & Co., 1845, Reprinted by HardPress Publishing, Miami, FL., 2013.

Moser, Harold D., David R. Hoth, Sharon Macpherson, & John H. Reinbold, eds. *The Papers of Andrew Jackson Volume III, 1814-1815.* Knoxville, TN: The University of Tennessee Press, 1991.

Nasatir, A. P., ed. "Government Employees and Salaries in Spanish Louisiana." *The Louisiana Historical Quarterly,* Volume 29, #4 (October 1946), 885-1040.

Nolte, Vincent. *The Memoirs of Vincent Nolte: Reminiscences in the Period of Anthony Adverse or Fifty Years in Both Hemispheres.* New York: G. Howard Watt Publisher, 1934.

Powell, Lawrence N., ed. *The New Orleans of George Washington Cable The 1887 Census Office Report.* Baton Rouge, LA: The Louisiana State University Press, 2008.

Reinders, Robert C. "The Free Negro in the New Orleans Economy, 1850-1860." *Louisiana History: The Journal of the Louisiana Historical Association,* Vol. 6, no.3 (Summer 1965): 273-285.

Riffel, Judy, compiler and editor. *New Orleans Register of Free People of Color 1840-1864.* Baton Rouge, LA: Le Comité des Archives de la Louisiane, Inc., 2008.

Schweninger, Loren. "Antebellum Free Persons of Color in Postbellum Louisiana." *Louisiana History: The Journal of the Louisiana Historical Association,* Vol. 30, No. 4 (Autumn, 1989): 345-364.

Shaw, Lacy, Jr., ed. *Not a Slave! Free People of Color in Antebellum America, 1790-1860.* New York, NY: Custom Publishing Group (Forbes Inc.), 1995.

Spear, Jennifer M. *Race Sex and Social Order in Early New Orleans.* Baltimore, MD: Johns Hopkins University Press, 2009.

Sterkx, H. E. *The Free Negro in Ante-Bellum Louisiana.* Cranbury, NJ: Associated University Presses, Inc., 1972.

Survey of Federal Archives. *Ships Registers and Enrollments of New Orleans, Louisiana/ prepared by the Survey of Federal Archives in Louisiana, Division of community services programs, Work Projects Administration.* 5 Volumes, 1804-1860. (Baton Rouge, LA: Louisiana State University, 1941-1942). Available on line here: https://catalog.hathitrust.org/Record/000968981.

Thorp, John T. *French Prisoners' Lodges: A Brief Account of Twenty-Six Lodges and Chapters of Freemasons Established and Conducted by French Prisoners of War in England and Elsewhere between 1756 and 1814.* London, England: Brother George Gibbons, King Street, 1900. (Available at www.googlebooks.com).

Toledano, Roulhac, Sally K. Evans and Mary Louise Christovich. *New Orleans Architecture Volume IV: The Creole Faubourgs.* Gretna, LA: Pelican Publishing Co., 2006.

Toledano, Roulhac, and Mary Louise Christovich. *New Orleans Architecture Volume VI: Faubourg Tremé and the Bayou Road.* Gretna, LA: Pelican Publishing Co., 2003.

Uter, Frank M. A. *History of the Catholic Church in Baton Rouge, 1792-1992.* Baton Rouge, LA: St. Joseph Cathedral, 1992.

Van Horne, John C., ed. *The Correspondence and Miscellaneous Papers of Benjamin Henry Latrobe, Volume 3, 1811-1820.* New Haven, CT & London: Yale University Press, 1988.

Vidrine, Jacqueline Olivier. *Love's Legacy: The Mobile Marriages Recorded in French, Transcribed with Annotated Abstracts in English*, 1724-1786. Lafayette, LA: University of Southwestern Louisiana, 1985.

Wilson, Samuel, Jr. *The Pitot House on Bayou St. John.* Gretna, LA: Pelican Publishing Co., 1992.

Woods, Rev. Earl C., and Dr. Charles E. Nolan, eds. *Sacramental Records of the Roman Catholic Church of the Archdiocese of New Orleans, Volumes 1-19, 1718-1831.* New Orleans, LA: Archdiocese of New Orleans, 1989-2004.

Zelbo, Sian. "E. J. Edmunds, School Integration, and White Supremacist Backlash in Reconstruction New Orleans." *History of Education Quarterly,* Vol. 59, Issue 3, pp. 379-406. Published online by Cambridge University Press: 07 August 2019.

Zelbo, Sian. "Edgar Joseph Edmunds (1851 – 1887), Mathematics Teacher at The Center of New Orleans' Post-Civil War Fight over School Integration." PhD Diss., Columbia University, 2020.

INDEX

CPSIA information can be obtained
at www.ICGtesting.com
Printed in the USA
JSHW050245060521
14295JS00003B/66